THE GENDERED SOCIETY READER

edited by

MICHAEL S. KIMMEL
State University of New York, Stony Brook

with Amy Aronson

New York Oxford
OXFORD UNIVERSITY PRESS
2000

Oxford University Press

Oxford New York
Athens Auckland Bangkok Bogotá Buenos Aires Calcutta
Cape Town Chennai Dar es Salaam Delhi Florence Hong Kong Istanbul
Karachi Kuala Lumpur Madrid Melbourne Mexico City Mumbai
Nairobi Paris São Paulo Singapore Taipei Tokyo Toronto Warsaw

and associated companies in
Berlin Ibadan

Published by Oxford University Press, Inc.,
198 Madison Avenue, New York, New York, 10016
http://www.oup-usa.org
1-800-334-4249

Library of Congress Cataloging-in-Publication Data

The gendered society reader / edited by Michael S. Kimmel with
contributing editor Amy Aronson.
p. cm.
Includes bibliographical references.
ISBN 0-19-512586-X (pbk. : alk. paper)
ISBN 0-19-512585-1 (cloth : alk. paper)
1. Sex role. 2. Sex differences (Psychology) 3. Gender identity.
4. Sex discrimination. I. Kimmel, Michael S. II. Aronson, Amy.
HQ1075 .G4672 1999
305.3—dc21 99-31078
CIP
Rev.

Printing (last digit): 10 9 8 7 6 5 4 3
Printed in the United States of America on acid-free paper

The GENDERED SOCIETY READER

For

Zachary Aaron Kimmel

Kate Morris

H. Perry Tunick-Hatchfield

and the transformation of gender relations
of which they will be a part.

CONTENTS

INTRODUCTION

Michael S. Kimmel

Every day there's another story about how women and men are different. They say we come from different planets—women from Venus, men from Mars. They say we have different brain chemistries, different brain organization, different hormones. Different bodies, different selves. They say we have different ways of knowing, listen to different moral voices, have different ways of speaking and hearing each other.

You'd think we were different species. In his best-selling book, pop psychologist John Gray informs us that not only do women and men communicate differently, "but they think, feel, perceive, react, respond, love, need, and appreciate differently" (Gray, 1995, p. 5). It's a miracle of cosmic proportions that we ever understand one another!

Yet here we all are, together, in the same classes, eating in the same dining halls, walking on the same campus, reading the same books, being subject to the same criteria for grading. We live in the same houses, eat the same meals, read the same newspapers, and watch the same TV shows. What gives?

One thing that seems to be happening is that we are increasingly aware of the centrality of gender in our lives. In the past three decades, the pioneering work of feminist scholars, both in traditional disciplines and in women's studies, has made us increasingly aware of the centrality of gender in shaping social life. We now known that gender is one of the central organizing principles around which social life revolves.

This wasn't always the case. Three decades ago, social scientists would have listed only social class and race as the master statuses that defined and proscribed social life. If you wanted to study gender in the 1960s in social science, for example, you would have found one course to meet your needs—"Marriage and the Family"—which was sort of the "Ladies Auxiliary" of the Social Sciences. There were no courses on gender. But today, gender has joined race and class in our understanding of the foundations of an individual's identity. Gender, we now know, is one of the axes around which social life is organized, and through which we understand our own experiences.

While much of our cultural preoccupation seems to be about the differences between women and men, there are two near-universal phenomena that define the experiences of women and men. First: *Why is it that virtually every society differentiates people on the basis of gender?* Why are women and men perceived as different in every known society? What are the differences that are perceived? Why is gender at least one of—if not the central—basis for the division of labor? And, second: *Why is it that virtually every known society is based on male domination?* Why does virtually every society divide social, political, and economic resources unequally between women and men? Why is a gendered division of labor also an unequal division of labor? Why are women's tasks and men's tasks valued differently?

Of course, there are dramatic differences among societies regarding the type of gender differences, the levels of gender inequality, and the amount of violence (implied or real) that is necessary to maintain systems of difference and domination. But the basic facts remain: *virtually every society is founded on assumptions of gender difference and the politics of gender inequality.*

Most of the arguments about gender difference begin, as will this book, with biology. Women and men *are* biologically different, after all. Our reproductive anatomies are different, as are our reproductive destinies. Our brain structures differ, our brain chemistries differ. Our musculature is different. We have different levels of different hormones circulating through our different bodies. Surely, these add up to fundamental, intractable, and universal differences, and these differences provide the foundation for male domination, don't they?

In these models, biological "sex"—by which we mean the chromosomal, chemical, anatomical apparatuses that make us either male or female—leads inevitably to "gender," by which we mean the cultural and social meanings, experiences, and institutional structures that are defined as appropriate for males and females. "Sex" is male and female; "gender" refers to cultural definitions of masculinity and femininity—the meanings of maleness and femaleness.

Biological models of sex difference occupy the "nature" side of the age-old question about whether it is nature or nurture that determines our personalities. Of course, most sensible people recognize that both nature *and* nurture are necessary for gender development. Our biological sex provides the raw material for our development—and all that evolution and those different chromosomes and different hormones have to have some effect on who we are and who we become.

But biological sex varies very little, and yet the cultural definitions of gender vary enormously. And it has been the task of the social and behavioral sciences to explore these variations in definitions. Launched originally as critiques of biological universalism, the social and behavioral sciences—anthropology, history, psychology, sociology—have all had an important role to play in our understanding of gender.

What they suggest is that what it means to be a man or a woman will vary in four significant ways. First, the meanings of gender vary from one society to another. What it means to be a man or a woman among aboriginal peoples in the Australian outback or in the Yukon territories is probably very different from what it means to be a man or a woman in Norway or Ireland. It has been the task of anthropologists to specify some of those differences, to explore the different meanings that gender has in different cultures. Some cultures, like our own, encourage men to be stoic and to prove their masculinity, and men in some of these cultures seem even more preoccupied with demonstrating sexual prowess than American men seem to be. Other cultures prescribe a more relaxed definition of masculinity, based on civic participation, emotional responsiveness, and the collective provision for the community's needs. Some cultures encourage women to be decisive and competitive; others insist that women are naturally passive, helpless, and dependent.

Second, the meanings of masculinity and femininity vary within any one culture over time. What it meant to be a man or a woman in seventeenth-century France was probably very different from what it means today. My own research has suggested that the meanings of manhood have changed dramatically from the founding of America in 1776 to the present (see Kimmel, 1996). (For reasons of space I do not include any historical material in this volume. However, inquiries into the changing definitions of gender have become an area of increasing visibility.)

Third, the meanings of masculinity and femininity change as a person grows. Following Freudian ideas that individuals face different developmental tasks as they develop, psychologists have examined the ways in which the meanings of masculinity and femininity change over the course of a person's life. The issues confronting a man about proving himself and feeling successful, and the social institutions in which he will attempt to enact those experiences, will change, as will the meaning of femininity for prepubescent women, women in child-bearing years, and postmenopausal women, or for women entering the labor market or those retiring from it.

Finally, the meanings of gender vary *among* different groups of women and men within any particular culture at any particular time. Simply put, not all American men and women are the same. Our experiences are structured by class, race, ethnicity, age, sexuality, region of the country. Each of these axes modifies the others. Just because we make gender visible doesn't mean that we make these other organizing principles of social life invisible. Imagine, for example, an older black gay man in Chicago and a young white heterosexual farm boy in Iowa. Wouldn't they have different definitions of masculinity? Or imagine a 22-year-old heterosexual poor Asian-American woman in San Francisco and a wealthy white Irish Catholic lesbian in Boston. Wouldn't their ideas about what it means to be a woman be somewhat different? The interplanetary theory of gender differences collapses all such differences, and focuses *only* on gender. One of the important elements of a sociological approach is to explore the differences *among* men and *among* women, since, as it turns out, these are often more decisive than the differences between women and men.

If gender varies across cultures, over historical time, among men and women within any one culture, and over the life course, that means we really cannot speak of masculinity or femininity as though they were constant, universal essences, common to all women and to all men. Rather, gender is an ever-changing fluid assemblage of meanings and behaviors. In that sense, we must speak of *masculinities* and *femininities*, in recognition of the different definitions of masculinity and femininity that we construct. By pluralizing the terms, we acknowledge that masculinity and femininity mean different things to different groups of people at different times.

At the same time, we can't forget that all masculinities and femininities are not created equal. American men and women must also contend with a dominant definition, a culturally preferred version that is held up as the model against which we are expected to measure ourselves. We thus come to know what it means to be a man or a woman in our culture by setting our definitions in opposition to a set of "others"—racial minorities, sexual minorities. For men, the classic "other" is of course, women. It often feels imperative that men make it clear—eternally, compulsively, decidedly—that they are not "like" women.

For both women and men, this is the "hegemonic" definition—the one that is held up as the model for all of us. The hegemonic definition of masculinity is "constructed in relation to various subordinated masculinities as well as in relation to women," writes sociologist R. W. Connell (1987, p. 183). The sociologist Erving Goffman once described this hegemonic definition of masculinity like this:

> In an important sense there is only one complete unblushing male in America: a young, married, white, urban, northern, heterosexual, Protestant, father, of college education, fully employed, of good complexion, weight, and height, and a recent record in sports. . . . Any male who fails to qualify in any one of these ways is likely to view himself—during moments at least—as unworthy, incomplete, and inferior. (Goffman, 1963, p. 128)

Women also must contend with such an exaggerated ideal of femininity. Connell calls it "emphasized femininity." Emphasized femininity is organized around compliance with gender inequality, and is "oriented to accommodating the interests and desires of men." One sees emphasized femininity in "the display of sociability rather than technical competence, fragility in mating scenes, compliance with men's desire for titillation and ego-stroking in office relationships, acceptance of marriage and child care as a response to labor-market discrimination against women" (Connell, 1987, pp. 183, 188, 187). Emphasized femininity exaggerates gender difference as a strategy of "adaptation to men's power," stressing empathy and nurturance; "real" womanhood is described as "fascinating" and women are advised that they can wrap men around their fingers by knowing and playing by "the rules."

The articles in the first four sections of this book recapitulate these disciplinary concerns and also present the development of the sociological argument chronologically. Following Darwin and others, people employed biological evidence in the nineteenth century to assert the primacy of sex differences. Part 1, on biological differences, presents some evidence of distinct and categorical biological differences, and two critiques of that research from a neurobiologist and a psychologist. Cross-cultural research by anthropologists, among them Margaret Mead, perhaps the nation's most historically celebrated cultural anthropologist, offered a way to critique the claims of biological inevitability and universality lodged in those biological arguments. The selections in Part 2 demonstrate how anthropologists have observed the cross-cultural differences and have used such specific cultural rituals as initiation ceremonies or the prevalence of rape in a culture to assess different definitions of gender.

Psychological research also challenged biological inevitability, locating the process of *acquiring* gender within the tasks of the child in his or her family. Achieving successful gender identity was a perilous process, fraught with danger of gender "inversion" (homosexuality), as the early and renowned social psychologist Lewis Terman saw it in his treatise on *Sex and Personality* in 1936. Subsequent psychological research has refined our understanding of how individuals acquire the "sex roles" that society has mapped out for them, as discussed in Part 3.

It falls to the sociologist to explore the variations *among* different groups of women and men, and also to specify the ways in which some versions of masculinity or femininity are held up as the hegemonic models against which all others are arrayed and measured (Part 4). Sociologists are concerned less with the specification of sex roles, and more with the understanding of *gender relations*—the social and political dynamics that shape our conceptions of "appropriate" sex roles. Thus sociologists are interested not only in gendered individuals—the ways in which we acquire our gendered identities—but also in gendered institutions—the ways in which those gendered individuals interact with one another in the institutions of our lives that shape, reproduce, and reconstitute gender.

In that sense, sociologists return us to the original framing questions—the near-universality of assumptions about gender difference and of male domination over women. Sociologists argue that male domination is reproduced not only by socializing women and men differently, but also by placing them in organizations and institutions in which specifically gendered norms and values predominate and by which both women and men are then evaluated and judged. Gendered individuals do not inhabit gender-neutral social situations; both individual and institution bear the mark of gender.

The three central, institutional sections of this book (Parts 5–7) explore how the fundamental institutions of family, education, and the workplace express and normalize gender difference, and, in so doing, reproduce relations of inequality between women and men. In each of these arenas, the debates about gender difference and inequality have been intense, covering questions about the division of household labor, divorce, day care, coeducation or single-sex schooling, comparable worth, sexual harassment, and workplace discrimination and a variety of other critical policy debates. The articles in these sections will enable the reader to make better sense of these debates and understand the ways in which gender is performed and elaborated within social institutions.

Finally, we turn to our intimate lives, our experiences of friendship, love, and sex (Part 8). Here differences between women and men do emerge. Men and women have different ways of loving, of caring, and of having sex. And it turns out that this is true whether the women and men are heterosexual or homosexual—that is, gay men and heterosexual men are more similar to each other than they are different; and equally, lesbians and heterosexual women have more in common than either have with men. On the other hand, the differences between women and men seem to have as much to do with the shifting definitions of love and intimacy, and the social arenas in which we express (or suppress) our emotions as they do with the differences in our personalities. And there is significant evidence that the gender gap in love and sex and friendship is shrinking as women claim greater degrees of sexual agency and men find their emotional lives (with lovers, children, and friends) impoverished by adherence to hegemonic definitions of masculinity. Men and women do express some differences in their intimate lives, but these differences are hardly of interplanetary cosmic significance. It appears that women and men are not from different planets—not opposite sexes, but neighboring sexes. And we are moving closer and closer to each other.

This may be the most startling finding that runs through many of these articles. What we find consistently is that the differences between women and men do not account for very much of the different experiences that men and women have. Differences *between* women and men are not nearly as great as the differences *among* women or *among* men—differences based on class, race, ethnicity, sexuality, age, and other variables. Women and men enter the work place for similar reasons, though what they find there often reproduces the differences that "predicted" they would have different motivations. Boys and girls are far more similar to each other in the classroom, from elementary school through college, although everything in the school—their textbooks, their teachers, their experiences on the playground, the social expectations of their aptitudes and abilities—pushes them to move further and further apart.

On the other hand, violence remains the most significant and intractable difference between women and men. As we see in Part 9, it is overwhelmingly men who commit murder and assault, who plan and prosecute war, who utilize violence in both institutional and interpersonal arenas. That masculinity should be so tied to violence is among the more pressing political, as well as sociological, questions of our era.

And yet, with that lone exception, the evidence remains pretty conclusive that women and men are not from different planets at all. In the end, we're all Earthlings!

References

Connell, R. W. *Gender and Power.* Stanford: Stanford University Press, 1987.

Goffman, Erving. *Stigma.* Englewood Cliffs, NJ: Prentice-Hall, 1963.

Gray, John. *Men Are from Mars, Women Are from Venus: A Practical Guide for Improving Communication and Getting What You Want in Your Relationships.* New York: Harper Collins, 1992.

Kimmel, Michael. *Manhood in America: A Cultural History.* New York: The Free Press, 1996.

PART 1

ANATOMY AND DESTINY

Biological Arguments About Gender Difference

Anatomy, many of us believe, is destiny; the constitution of our bodies determines our social and psychological disposition. Biological sex decides our gendered experiences. Sex is temperament. Biological explanations offer perhaps the tidiest and most coherent explanations for both gender difference and gender inequality. The observable differences between males and females derive from different anatomical organization, which makes us different as men and women; thus anatomical differences are the origin of gender inequality. We believe that these differences are innate, immutable, and resistant to cultural change.

Biologists rely on three different sets of evidence. Evolutionists, such as sociobiologists and evolutionary psychologists, argue that sex differences derive from the differences in our reproductive anatomies—which compel different reproductive "strategies." Because the woman must invest much energy and time in ensuring the survival of one baby, her "natural" evolutionary instinct is toward high sexual selectivity and monogamy; women are naturally modest and monogamous. Men, by contrast, are naturally promiscuous, since their reproductive success depends upon fertilizing as many eggs as possible without emotional constraint. Men who are reproductively unsuccessful by seduction, biologists tell us, may resort to rape as a way to ensure their reproductive material is successfully transmitted to their offspring.

A second source of evidence of biological difference comes from differences in brain function and brain chemistry. In the late nineteenth century, studies showed definitively that men's brains were heavier or more complex than women's, and thus that women ought not to seek higher education or vote. (Similar studies also "proved" that the brains of white people were heavier and more complex than those of black people.) Today, such studies are largely discredited, but we still may read about how males and females use different halves of their brains, or that they use them differently, or that the two halves are differently connected.

Finally, some biologists rely on the ways the hormonal differences that produce secondary sex characteristics determine the dramatically divergent paths that males and females take from puberty onward. Testosterone causes aggression, and since males have far more testosterone than females, male aggression—and social, political, and economic dominance—is explained.

To the social scientist, though, this evidence obscures as much as it reveals, telling us more about our own cultural needs to find these differences than the differences themselves. Biological explanations collapse all other sources of difference—race, ethnicity, age—into one single dichotomous variable that exaggerates the differences between women and men, and also minimizes the similarities between them. "Believing is seeing," notes sociologist Judith Lorber, and seeing these differences as decisive is often used as a justification for gender inequality.

The readings in this section offer a cross section of those biological arguments. David Buss summarizes the evidence from evolutionary psychology that different reproductive strategies determine different psychological dispositions. Neurobiologist Robert Sapolsky suggests that the research on hormonal differences does not make a convincing case, while social psychologist Carol Tavris takes on the assumptions of biological research, arguing that biology's inherent conservatism—justifying existing inequalities by reference to observed differences and ignoring observed similarities—is more than bad politics: it's also bad science.

DAVID M. BUSS

Psychological Sex Differences: Origins Through Sexual Selection

Evolutionary psychology predicts that males and females will be the same or similar in all those domains in which the sexes have faced the same or similar adaptive problems. Both sexes have sweat glands because both sexes have faced the adaptive problem of thermal regulation. Both sexes have similar (although not identical) taste preferences for fat, sugar, salt, and particular amino acids because both sexes have faced similar (although not identical) food consumption problems. Both sexes grow callouses when they experience repeated rubbing on their skin because both sexes have faced the adaptive problem of physical damage from environmental friction.

In other domains, men and women have faced substantially different adaptive problems throughout human evolutionary history. In the physical realm, for example, women have faced the problem of childbirth; men have not. Women, therefore, have evolved particular adaptations that are absent in men, such as a cervix that dilates to 10 centimeters just prior to giving birth, mechanisms for producing labor contractions, and the release of oxytocin in the blood-stream during childbirth.

Men and women have also faced different information-processing problems in some adaptive domains. Because fertilization occurs internally within the woman, for example, men have faced the adaptive problem of uncertainty of paternity in putative offspring. Men who failed to solve this problem risked investing re-

Reprinted by permission of David M. Buss, Dept. of Psychology, University of Michigan, Ann Arbor, MI 48109-1109. References have been edited.

sources in children who were not their own. All people descend from a long line of ancestral men whose adaptations (i.e., psychological mechanisms) led them to behave in ways that increased their likelihood of paternity and decreased the odds of investing in children who were putatively theirs but whose genetic fathers were other men. This does not imply, of course, that men were or are consciously aware of the adaptive problem of compromised paternity.

Women faced the problem of securing a reliable or replenishable supply of resources to carry them through pregnancy and lactation, especially when food resources were scarce (e.g., during droughts or harsh winters). All people are descendants of a long and unbroken line of women who successfully solved this adaptive challenge—for example, by preferring mates who showed the ability to accrue resources and the willingness to provide them for particular women. Those women who failed to solve this problem failed to survive, imperiled the survival chances of their children, and hence failed to continue their lineage.

Evolutionary psychologists predict that the sexes will differ in precisely those domains in which women and men have faced different sorts of adaptive problems. To an evolutionary psychologist, the likelihood that the sexes are psychologically identical in domains in which they have recurrently confronted different adaptive problems over the long expanse of human evolutionary history is essentially zero. The key question, therefore, is not whether men and women differ psychologically. Rather, the key questions about sex differences, from an evolutionary psychological perspective, are (a) In what domains have women and men faced different adaptive problems? (b) What are the sex-differentiated psychological mechanisms of women and men that have evolved in response to these sex-differentiated adaptive problems? (c) Which social, cultural, and contextual inputs moderate the magnitude of expressed sex differences?

SEXUAL SELECTION DEFINES THE PRIMARY DOMAINS IN WHICH THE SEXES HAVE FACED DIFFERENT ADAPTIVE CHALLENGES

Although many who are not biologists equate evolution with natural selection or survival selection, Darwin (1871) sculpted what he believed to be a second theory of evolution—the theory of sexual selection. Sexual selection is the causal process of the evolution of characteristics on the basis of reproductive advantage, as opposed to survival advantage. Sexual selection occurs in two forms. First, members of one sex can successfully outcompete members of their own sex in a process of intrasexual competition. Whatever characteristics lead to success in these same-sex competitions—be they greater size, strength, cunning, or social skills—can evolve or increase in frequency by virtue of the reproductive advantage accrued by the winners through increased access to more numerous or more desirable mates.

Second, members of one sex can evolve preferences for desirable qualities in potential mates through the process of intersexual selection. If members of one sex exhibit some consensus about which qualities are desirable in the other sex, then members of the other sex who possess the desirable qualities will gain a preferential mating advantage. Hence, the desirable qualities—be they morphological features such as antlers or plumage or psychological features such as a lower threshold for risk taking to acquire resources—can evolve by virtue of the reproductive advantage attained by those who are preferentially chosen for possessing the desirable qualities. Among humans, both causal processes—preferential mate choice and same-sex competition for access to mates—are prevalent among both sexes, and probably have been throughout human evolutionary history.

HYPOTHESES ABOUT PSYCHOLOGICAL SEX DIFFERENCES FOLLOW FROM SEXUAL ASYMMETRIES IN MATE SELECTION AND INTRASEXUAL COMPETITION

Although a detailed analysis of psychological sex differences is well beyond the scope of this article, a few of the most obvious differences in adaptive problems include the following.

Paternity Uncertainty. Because fertilization occurs internally within women, men are always less than 100% certain (again, no conscious awareness implied) that their putative children are genetically their own. Some cultures have phrases to describe this, such as "Mama's baby, papa's maybe." Women are always 100% certain that the children they bear are their own.

Identifying Reproductively Valuable Women. Because women's ovulation is concealed and there is no evidence that men can detect when women ovulate, ancestral men had the difficult adaptive challenge of identifying which women were more fertile. Although ancestral women would also have faced the problem of identifying fertile men, the problem is considerably less severe (a) because most men remain fertile throughout their life span, whereas fertility is steeply age graded among women, and (b) because women invest more heavily in offspring, making them the more "valuable" sex, competed for more intensely by men seeking sexual access. Thus, there is rarely a shortage of men willing to contribute the sperm necessary for fertilization, whereas from a man's perspective, there is a pervasive shortage of fertile women.

Gaining Sexual Access to Women. Because of the large asymmetry between men and women in their minimum obligatory parental investment—nine months gestation for women versus an act of sex for men—the direct reproductive benefits of gaining sexual access to a variety of mates would have been much higher for men than for women throughout human evolutionary history. Therefore, in social contexts in which some short-term mating or polygynous mating were possible, men who succeeded in gaining sexual access to a variety of women, other things being equal, would have experienced greater reproductive success than men who failed to gain such access.

Identifying Men Who Are Able to Invest. Because of the tremendous burdens of a nine-month pregnancy and subsequent lactation, women who selected men who were able to invest resources in them and their offspring would have been at a tremendous advantage in survival and reproductive currencies compared with women who were indifferent to the investment capabilities of the men with whom they chose to mate.

Identifying Men Who Are Willing to Invest. Having resources is not enough. Copulating with a man who had resources but who displayed a hasty postcopulatory departure would have been detrimental to the woman, particularly if she became pregnant and faced raising a child without the aid and protection of an investing father. A man with excellent resource-accruing capacities might channel resources to another woman or pursue short-term sexual opportunities with a variety of women. A woman who had the ability to detect a man's willingness to invest in her and her children would have an adaptive advantage compared with women who were oblivious to a man's willingness or unwillingness to invest.

These are just a few of the adaptive problems that women and men have confronted differently or to differing degrees. Other examples of sex-linked adaptive problems include those of coalitional warfare, coalitional defense, hunting, gathering, combating sex-linked forms of reputational damage, embodying sex-linked prestige criteria, and attracting mates by fulfilling the differing desires of the other sex—domains that all have consequences for mating but are sufficiently wide-ranging to span a great deal of social psychology. It is in these domains that evolutionary psychologists anticipate the most pronounced sex differences—differences in solutions to sex-linked adaptive problems in the form of evolved psychological mechanisms.

PSYCHOLOGICAL SEX DIFFERENCES ARE WELL DOCUMENTED EMPIRICALLY IN THE DOMAINS PREDICTED BY THEORIES ANCHORED IN SEXUAL SELECTION

When Maccoby and Jacklin (1974) published their classic book on the psychology of sex differences, knowledge was spotty and methods for summarizing the literature were largely subjective and interpretive. Since that time, there has been a veritable explosion of empirical findings, along with quantitative meta-analytic procedures for evaluating them. Although new domains of sex differences continue to surface, such as the recently documented female advantage in spatial location memory, the outlines of where researchers find large, medium, small, and no sex differences are starting to emerge more clearly.

A few selected findings illustrate the heuristic power of evolutionary psychology. Cohen (1977) used the widely adopted *d* statistic as the index of magnitude of effect to propose a rule of thumb for evaluating effect sizes: 0.20 = "small," 0.50 = "medium," and 0.80 = "large." As Hyde has pointed out in a chapter titled

"Where Are the Gender Differences? Where Are the Gender Similarities?," sex differences in the intellectual and cognitive ability domains tend to be small. Women's verbal skills tend to be slightly higher than men's (*d* = –0.11). Sex differences in math also tend to be small (*d* = 0.15). Most tests of general cognitive ability, in short, reveal small sex differences.

The primary exception to the general trend of small sex differences in the cognitive abilities domain occurs with spatial rotation. This ability is essential for successful hunting, in which the trajectory and velocity of a spear must anticipate correctly the trajectory of an animal as each moves with different speeds through space and time. For spatial rotation ability, *d* = 0.73. Other sorts of skills involved in hunting also show large magnitudes of sex differences, such as throwing velocity (*d* = 2.18), throwing distance (*d* = 1.98), and throwing accuracy (*d* = 0.96; Ashmore, 1990). Skilled hunters, as good providers, are known to be sexually attractive to women in current and traditional tribal societies.

Large sex differences appear reliably for precisely the aspects of sexuality and mating predicted by evolutionary theories of sexual strategies. Oliver and Hyde (1993), for example, documented a large sex difference in attitudes toward casual sex (*d* = 0.81). Similar sex differences have been found with other measures of men's desire for casual sex partners, a psychological solution to the problem of seeking sexual access to a variety of partners. For example, men state that they would ideally like to have more than 18 sex partners in their lifetimes, whereas women state that they would desire only 4 or 5. In another study that has been replicated twice, 75% of the men but 0% of the women approached by an attractive stranger of the opposite sex consented to a request for sex.

Women tend to be more exacting than men, as predicted, in their standards for a short-term mate (*d* = 0.79). Women tend to place greater value on good financial prospects in a mate—a finding confirmed in a study of 10,047 individuals residing in 37 cultures located on six continents and five islands from around the world (Buss, 1989). More so than men, women especially disdain qualities in a potential mate that signal inability to accrue resources, such as lack of ambition (*d* = 1.38) and lack of education (*d* = 1.06). Women desire physical protection abilities more than men, both in short-term mating (*d* = 0.94) and in long-term mating (*d* = 0.66).

Men and women also differ in the weighting given to cues that trigger sexual jealousy. Buss, Larsen, Westen, and Semmelroth (1992) presented men and women with the following dilemma: "What would upset or distress you more: (a) imagining your partner forming a deep emotional attachment to someone else or (b) imagining your partner enjoying passionate sexual intercourse with that other person" (p. 252). Men expressed greater distress about sexual than emotional infidelity, whereas women showed the opposite pattern. The difference between the sexes in which scenario was more distressing was 43% (*d* = 0.98). These sex differences have been replicated by different investigators with physiological recording devices and have been replicated in other cultures.

These sex differences are precisely those predicted by evolutionary psychological theories based on sexual selection. They represent only a sampling from a larger body of supporting evidence. The sexes also differ substantially in a wide variety of other ways that are predicted by sexual selection theory, such as in thresholds for physical risk taking, in frequency of perpetrating homicides, in thresholds for inferring sexual intent in others, in perceptions of the magnitude of upset people experience as the victims of sexual aggression, and in the frequency of committing violent crimes of all sorts. As noted by Donald Brown (1991), "it will be irresponsible to continue shunting these [findings] aside, fraud to deny that they exist" (p. 156). Evolutionary psychology sheds light on why these differences exist.

CONCLUSIONS

Strong sex differences occur reliably in domains closely linked with sex and mating, precisely as predicted by psychological theories based on sexual selection. Within these domains, the psychological sex differences are patterned in a manner that maps precisely onto the adaptive problems men and women have faced over human evolutionary history. Indeed, in most cases, the evolutionary hypotheses about sex differences were generated a decade or more before the empirical tests of them were conducted and the sex differences discovered. These models thus have heuristic and predictive power.

The evolutionary psychology perspective also offers several insights into the broader discourse on sex differences. First, neither women nor men can be considered "superior" or "inferior" to the other, any more than a bird's wings can be considered superior or inferior to a fish's fins or a kangaroo's legs. Each sex possesses mechanisms designed to deal with its own adaptive challenges—some similar and some different—and so notions of superiority or inferiority are logically incoherent from the vantage point of evolutionary psychology. The metatheory of evolutionary psychology is descriptive, not prescriptive—it carries no values in its teeth.

Second, contrary to common misconceptions about evolutionary psychology, finding that sex differences originated through a causal process of sexual selection does not imply that the differences are unchangeable or intractable. On the contrary, understanding their origins provides a powerful heuristic to the contexts in which the sex differences are most likely to be manifested (e.g., in the context of mate competition) and hence provides a guide to effective loci for intervention if change is judged to be desirable.

Third, although some worry that inquiries into the existence and evolutionary origins of sex differences will lead to justification for the status quo, it is hard to believe that attempts to change the status quo can be very effective if they are undertaken in ignorance of sex differences that actually exist. Knowledge is power, and attempts to intervene in the absence of knowledge may resemble a surgeon operating blindfolded—there may be more bloodshed than healing.

The perspective of evolutionary psychology jettisons the outmoded dualistic thinking inherent in much current discourse by getting rid of the false dichotomy between biological and social. It offers a truly interactionist position that specifies the particular features of social context that are especially critical for processing by our evolved psychological mechanisms. No other theory of sex differences has been capable of predicting and explaining the large number of precise, detailed, patterned sex differences discovered by research guided by evolutionary psychology. Evolutionary psychology possesses the heuristic power to guide investigators to the particular domains in which the most pronounced sex differences, as well as similarities, will be found. People grappling with the existence and implications of psychological sex differences cannot afford to ignore their most likely evolutionary origins through sexual selection.

References

Brown, D. (1991). *Human universals.* Philadelphia: Temple University Press.

Buss, D. M. (1989). Sex differences in human mate preferences: Evolutionary hypotheses tested in 37 cultures. *Behavioral and Brain Sciences, 12,* 1–49.

Buss, D. M., Larsen, R., Westen, D., & Semmelroth, J. (1992). Sex differences in jealousy: Evolution, physiology, and psychology. *Psychological Science, 3,* 251–255.

Cohen, J. (1977). Statistical power analysis for the behavioral sciences. San Diego, CA: Academic Press.

Darwin, C. (1871). *The descent of man and selection in relation to sex.* London: Murray.

Hyde, J. S. (1996). Where are the gender differences? Where are the gender similarities? In D. M. Buss & N. Malamuth (Eds.), *Sex, power, conflict: Feminist and evolutionary perspectives.* New York: Oxford University Press.

Maccoby, E. E., & Jacklin, C. N. (1974). *The psychology of sex differences.* Stanford, CA: Stanford University Press.

Oliver, M. B. & Hyde, J. S. (1993). Gender differences in sexuality: A meta-analysis. *Psychological Bulletin,* 114, 29–51.

ROBERT M. SAPOLSKY

The Trouble With Testosterone: Will Boys Just Be Boys?

Face it, we all do it. We all believe in certain stereotypes about certain minorities. The stereotypes are typically pejorative and usually false. But every now and then, they are true. I write apologetically as a member of a minority about which the stereotypes are indeed true. I am male. We males account for less than 50 percent of the population, yet we generate an incredibly disproportionate percentage of the violence. Whether it is something as primal as having an ax fight in an Amazonian clearing or as detached as using computer-guided aircraft to strafe a village, something as condemned as assaulting a cripple or as glorified as killing someone wearing the wrong uniform, if it is violent, males excel at it.

Why should that be? We all think we know the answer. A dozen millennia ago or so, an adventurous soul managed to lop off a surly bull's testicles and thus invented behavioral endocrinology. It is unclear from the historical records whether this individual received either a grant or tenure as a result of this experiment, but it certainly generated an influential finding—something or other comes out of the testes that helps to make males such aggressive pains in the ass.

That something or other is testosterone.[1] The hormone binds to specialized receptors in muscles and causes those cells to enlarge. It binds to similar receptors in laryngeal cells and gives rise to operatic basses. It causes other secondary sexual characteristics, makes for relatively unhealthy blood vessels, alters biochemical events in the liver too dizzying to even contemplate, has a profound impact, no doubt, on the workings of cells in big toes. And it seeps into the brain, where it binds to those same "androgen" receptors and influences behavior in a way highly relevant to understanding aggression.

What evidence links testosterone with aggression? Some pretty obvious stuff. Males tend to have higher testosterone levels in their circulation than do females (one wild exception to that will be discussed below) and to be more aggressive. Times of life when males are swimming in testosterone (for example, after reaching puberty) correspond to when aggression peaks. Among numerous species, testes are mothballed most of the year, kicking into action and pouring out testosterone only during a very circumscribed mating season—precisely the time when male–male aggression soars.

Impressive, but these are only correlative data, testosterone repeatedly being on the scene with no alibi when some aggression has occurred. The proof comes with the knife, the performance of what is euphemistically known as a "subtraction" experiment. Remove the source of testosterone in species after species and levels of aggression typically plummet. Reinstate normal testosterone levels afterward with injections of synthetic testosterone, and aggression returns.

To an endocrinologist, the subtraction and replacement paradigm represents pretty damning proof: this hormone is involved. "Normal testosterone levels appear to be a prerequisite for normative levels of aggressive behavior" is the sort of catchy, hummable phrase that the textbooks would use. That probably explains why you shouldn't mess with a bull moose during rutting season. But that's not why a lot of people want to understand this sliver of science. Does the action of this hormone tell us anything about *individual* differences in levels of aggression, anything about why some males, some human males, are exceptionally violent? Among an array of males—human or otherwise—are the highest testosterone levels found in the most aggressive individuals?

Generate some extreme differences and that is precisely what you see. Castrate some of the well-paid study subjects, inject others with enough testosterone to quadruple the normal human levels, and the high-testosterone males are overwhelmingly likely to be the more aggressive ones. However, that doesn't tell us much about the real world. Now do something more subtle by studying the normative variability in testosterone—in other words, don't manipulate anything, just see what everyone's natural levels are like—and high levels of testosterone and high levels of aggression still tend to go together. This would seem to seal the case—interindividual differences in levels of aggression among normal individuals are probably driven by differences in levels of testosterone. But this turns out to be wrong.

Okay, suppose you note a correlation between levels of aggression and levels of testosterone among these normal males. This could be because *(a)* testosterone elevates aggression; *(b)* aggression elevates testosterone secretion; *(c)* neither causes the other. There's a huge bias to assume option *a,* while *b* is the answer. Study after study has shown that when you examine testosterone levels when males are first placed together in the social group, testosterone levels predict nothing about who is going to be aggressive. The subsequent behavioral differences drive the hormonal changes, rather than the other way around.

Because of a strong bias among certain scientists, it has taken forever to convince them of this point. Behavioral endocrinologists study what behavior and hormones have to do with each other. How do you study behavior? You get yourself a notebook and a stopwatch and a pair of binoculars. How do you measure the hormones? You need a gazillion-dollar machine, you muck around with radiation and chemicals, wear a lab coat, maybe even goggles—the whole nine yards. Which toys would you rather get for Christmas? Which facet of science are you going to believe in more? Because the endocrine aspects of the business are more high-tech, more reductive, there is the bias to think that it is somehow more scientific, more powerful. This is a classic case of what is often called physics envy, the disease among scientists where the behavioral biologists fear their discipline lacks the rigor of physiology, the physiologists wish for the techniques of the biochemists, the biochemists covet the clarity of the answers revealed by the molecular biologists, all the way down until you get to the physicists who confer only with God.[2] Hormones seem to many to be more real, more substantive, than the ephemera of behavior, so when a correlation occurs, it must be because hormones regulate behavior, not the other way around.

As I said, it takes a lot of work to cure people of that physics-envy, and to see that interindividual differences in testosterone levels don't predict subsequent differences in aggressive behavior among individuals. Similarly, fluctuations in testosterone levels within one individual over time do not predict subsequent changes in the levels of aggression in that one individual—get a hiccup in testosterone secretion one afternoon and that's not when the guy goes postal.

Look at our confusing state: normal levels of testosterone are a prerequisite for normal levels of aggression, yet changing the amount of testosterone in someone's bloodstream within the normal range doesn't alter his subsequent levels of aggressive behavior. This is where, like clockwork, the students suddenly start coming to office hours in a panic, asking whether they missed something in their lecture notes.

Yes, it's going to be on the final, and it's one of the more subtle points in endocrinology—what is referred to as a hormone having a "permissive effect." Remove someone's testes and, as noted, the frequency of aggressive behavior is likely to plummet. Reinstate precastration levels of testosterone by injecting that hormone, and precastration levels of aggression typically return. Fair enough. Now this time, castrate an individual and restore testosterone levels to only 20 percent of normal and . . . amazingly, normal precastration levels of aggression come back. Castrate and now generate twice the testosterone levels from before castration—and the same level of aggressive behavior returns. You need some testosterone around for normal aggressive behavior—zero levels after castration, and down it usually goes; quadruple it (the sort of range generated in weight lifters abusing anabolic steroids), and aggression typically increases. But anywhere from roughly 20 percent of normal to twice normal and it's all the same; the brain can't distinguish among this wide range of basically normal values.

We seem to have figured out a couple of things by now. First, knowing the differences in the levels of testosterone in the circulation of a bunch of males will not help you much in figuring out who is going to be aggressive. Second, the subtraction and reinstatement data seem to indicate that, nevertheless, in a broad sort of way, testosterone causes aggressive behavior. But that turns out not to be true either, and the implications of this are lost on most people the first thirty times you tell them about it. Which is why you'd better tell them about it thirty-one times, because it is the most important point of this piece.

Round up some male monkeys. Put them in a group together, and give them plenty of time to sort out where they stand with each other—affiliative friendships, grudges and dislikes. Give them enough time to form a dominance hierarchy, a linear ranking system of numbers 1 through 5. This is the hierarchical sort of system where number 3, for example, can pass his day throwing around his weight with numbers 4 and 5, ripping off their monkey chow, forcing them to relinquish the best spots to sit in, but, at the same time, remembering to deal with numbers 1 and 2 with shit-eating obsequiousness.

Hierarchy in place, it's time to do your experiment. Take that third-ranking monkey and give him some testosterone. None of this within-the-normal-range stuff. Inject a ton of it into him, way higher than what you normally see in a rhesus monkey; give him enough testosterone to grow antlers and a beard on every neuron in his brain. And, no surprise, when you then check the behavioral data, it turns out that he will probably be participating in more aggressive interactions than before.

So even though small fluctuations in the levels of the hormone don't seem to matter much, testosterone still causes aggression. But that would be wrong. Check out number 3 more closely. Is he now raining aggressive terror on any and all in the group, frothing in an androgenic glaze of indiscriminate violence? Not at all. He's still judiciously kowtowing to numbers 1 and 2, but has simply become a total bastard to numbers 4 and 5. This is critical: testosterone isn't *causing* aggression, it's *exaggerating* the aggression that's already there.

Another example just to show we're serious. There's a part of your brain that probably has lots to do with aggression, a region called the amygdala.[3] Sitting right near it is the Grand Central Station of emotion-related activity in your brain, the hypothalamus. The amygdala communicates with the hypothalamus by way of a cable of neuronal connections called the stria terminalis. No more jargon, I promise. The amygdala has its influence on aggression via that pathway, with bursts of electrical excitation called action potentials that ripple down the stria terminalis, putting the hypothalamus in a pissy mood.

Once again, do your hormonal intervention; flood the area with testosterone. You can do that by injecting the hormone into the bloodstream, where it eventually makes its way to this part of the brain. Or you can be elegant and surgically microinject the stuff directly into this brain region. Six of one, half a dozen of the other. The key thing is what doesn't happen next. Does testosterone cause there to now be action potentials surging down the stria terminalis? Does it turn on that pathway? Not at all. If and only if the amygdala is *already* sending an aggression-provoking volley of action potentials down the stria terminalis, testosterone increases the rate of such action potentials by shortening the resting time between them. It's not turning on the pathway, it's increasing the volume of signaling if it is already turned on. It's not causing aggression, it's exaggerating the preexisting pattern of it, exaggerating the response to environmental triggers of aggression.

This transcends issues of testosterone and aggression. In every generation, it is the duty of behavioral biologists to try to teach this critical point, one that seems a maddening cliché once you get it. You take that hoary old dichotomy between nature and nurture, between biological influences and environmental influences, between intrinsic factors and extrinsic ones, and, the vast majority of the time, regardless of which behavior you are thinking about and what underlying biology you are studying, the dichotomy is a sham. No biology. No environment. Just the interaction between the two.

Do you want to know how important environment and experience are in understanding testosterone and aggression? Look back at how the effects of castration were discussed earlier. There were statements like "Remove the source of testosterone in species after species and levels of aggression typically plummet." Not "Remove the source . . . and aggression always goes to zero." On the average it declines, but rarely to zero, and not at all in some individuals. And the more social experience an individual had being aggressive prior to castration, the more likely that behavior persists sans *cojones.* Social conditioning can more than make up for the hormone.

Another example, one from one of the stranger corners of the animal kingdom: If you want your assumptions about the nature of boy beasts and girl beasts challenged, check out the spotted hyena. These animals are fast becoming the darlings of endocrinologists, sociobiologists, gynecologists, and tabloid writers. Why? Because they have a wild sex-reversal system—females are more muscular and more aggressive than males and are socially dominant to them, rare traits in the mammalian world. And get this: females secrete more of certain testosterone-related hormones than the males do, producing the muscles, the aggression (and, as a reason for much of the gawking interest in these animals, wildly masculinized private parts that make it supremely difficult to tell the sex of a hyena). So this appears to be a strong vote for the causative powers of high androgen levels in aggression and social dominance. But that's not the whole answer. High up in the hills above the University of California at Berkeley is the world's largest colony of spotted hyenas, massive bone-crunching beasts who fight with each other for the chance to have their ears scratched by Laurence Frank, the zoologist who brought them over as infants from Kenya. Various scientists are studying their sex-reversal system. The female hyenas are bigger and more muscular than the males and have the same weirdo genitals and elevated androgen levels that their female cousins do back in the savannah. Everything is in place except . . . the social system is completely different from that in the wild. Despite being stoked on androgens, there is a very significant delay in the time it takes for the females to begin socially dominating the males—they're growing up without the established social system to learn from.

When people first grasp the extent to which biology has something to do with behavior, even subtle, complex, human behavior, there is often an initial evangelical enthusiasm of the convert, a massive placing of faith in the biological components of the story. And this enthusiasm is typically of a fairly reductive type—because of physics envy, because reductionism is so impressive, because it would be so nice if there were a single gene or hormone or neurotransmitter or part of the brain that was *it,* the cause, the explanation of everything. And this way the trouble with testosterone is that people tend to think in an arena that really matters.

This is no mere academic concern. We are a fine species with some potential. Yet, we are racked by sickening amounts of violence. Unless we are hermits, we feel the threat of it, often as a daily shadow. And regardless of where we hide, should our leaders push the button, we will all be lost in a final global violence. But as we try to understand and wrestle with this feature of our sociality, it is critical to remember the limits of the biology. Testosterone is never going to tell us much about the suburban teenager who, in his after-school chess club, has developed a particularly aggressive style with his bishops. And it certainly isn't going to tell us much about the teenager in some inner-city hellhole who has taken to mugging people. "Testosterone equals aggression" is inadequate for those who would offer a simple solution to the violent male—just decrease levels of those pesky steroids. And "testosterone equals aggression" is certainly inadequate for those who would offer a simple excuse: boys will be boys and certain things in nature are inevitable. Violence is more complex than a single hormone. This is endocrinology for the bleeding heart liberal—our behavioral biology is usually meaningless outside the context of the social factors and environment in which it occurs.

Notes

1. Testosterone is one of a family of related hormones, collectively known as "androgens" or "anabolic steroids." They all are secreted from the testes or are the result of a modification of testosterone, they all have a similar chemical structure, and they all do roughly similar things. Nonetheless, androgen mavens spend entire careers studying the important differences in the actions of different androgens. I am going to throw that subtlety to the wind and, for the sake of simplification that will horrify many, will refer throughout to all of these related hormones as "testosterone."

2. An example of physics envy in action. Recently, a zoologist friend had obtained blood samples from the carnivores that he studies and wanted some hormones in the sample assays in my lab. Although inexperienced with the technique, he offered to help in any way possible. I felt hesitant asking him to do anything tedious but, so long as he had offered, tentatively said, "Well, if you don't mind some unspeakable drudgery, you could number about a thousand assay vials." And this scientist, whose superb work has graced the most

prestigious science journals in the world, cheerfully answered, "That's okay, how often do I get to do *real* science, working with test tubes?"

3. And no one has shown that differences in the size or shape of the amygdala, or differences in the numbers of neurons in it, can begin to predict differences in normal levels of aggression. Same punch line as with testosterone.

CAROL TAVRIS

The Mismeasure of Woman

In the early 1970s, when I was working at *Psychology Today* magazine, we ran an article called "A Person Who Menstruates Is Unfit to Be a Mother." In this spoof of the notion that women's hormones make women crazed, irrational and unreliable, the author said that women could not, therefore, be entrusted with the serious job of mothering. In those heady days of the modern women's movement, we thought we had driven a stake through the heart of the belief that women's hormones make women unfit for certain work.

That, of course, was before the rise of "PMS" as a biomedical abnormality in need of fixing, curing and treatment. To read any of Katherina Dalton's articles on the subject—"Menstruation and Crime," "Menstruation and Acute Psychiatric Illness," "Effect of Menstruation on Schoolgirls' Weekly Work," "The Influence of Mother's Menstruation on Her Child"—is to agree that a person who menstruates is unfit to be a mother, or anything else.

The mismeasure of woman is with us still, and still for the same reasons. In any domain of life in which men set the standard of normalcy, women will be considered abnormal, and society will debate woman's "place" and her "nature." Many women experience tremendous conflict in trying to decide whether to be "like" men or "opposite" from them, and this conflict itself is evidence of the implicit male standard against which they are measuring themselves. This is why it is normal for women to feel abnormal.

When man is the measure of all things, diagnoses of the goose's problem will differ from those of the gander's. Thus:

- Women and men have the same moods and mood swings, but only women get theirs packaged into a syndrome. Women's hormones have never been reliably related to *behavior,* competence or anything to do with work, but male hormones are related to a variety of antisocial behaviors. Yet there is no disorder called HTS, say, for HyperTestosterone Syndrome.
- The *Diagnostic and Statistical Manual of Mental Disorders (DSM)* has concocted a "disorder"—Self-defeating Personality Disorder—that describes the extreme characteristics of the female role (e.g., putting others

From *Feminism and Psychology,* Vol. 3, no. 2 (1993), pp. 149–168. References have been edited.

first, playing the martyr). But when Kaye-Lee Pantony and Paula Caplan (1991) proposed a comparable disorder describing the extreme characteristics of the male role—they named it "Delusional Domineering Personality Disorder"—they were told there is no "clinical tradition" for such a disorder.

- The problems that are more characteristic of men than women, such as drug abuse, narcissism, rape and other forms of violence, are rarely related to an inherent male psychology the way women's behavior is. When men have problems, it is because of their upbringing, personality or environment; when women have problems, it is because of something in their very psyche or hormones. When men have problems, society tends to look outward for explanations; when women have problems, society looks inward.

In western society today, there are three competing versions of the mismeasure of woman.

One is that man is the norm, and woman is opposite, lesser, deficient—"the problem." This is the view that underlies so much research in psychology that is designed to find out why women are not "as something as" men—as moral, as intelligent, as rational, as funny, as whatever. It is also the view underlying the enormous self-help industry; women consume millions of books advising them on how to be more beautiful, more competent, more independent (or dependent). Men, being normal, feel no need to fix themselves in corresponding ways.

A second view is that man is the norm, and woman is opposite, but better: "the solution." This is the perspective of cultural feminists, who retrieved the qualities associated with women that for so many years had been devalued—nurturance, compassion, attachment and so forth—and who now claim them to be the sources of women's moral superiority.

The third view is that there is no problem, because man is the norm, and woman is just like him. In her brilliant analysis of how this assumption pervades the diagnosis of sexual disorders in the *DSM,* Leonore Tiefer (1992) has observed that in this view, "Men and women are the same, and they're all men."

Today, in this social-constructionist age, the study of gender has entered what Mary Crawford and Jeanne Marecek (1989) call the "transformationist" era, in which the idea is to stand back from the fray and assume that we will never know the essences of male and female, for these are endlessly changing, and depend both on the eye of the observer and the conditions of our lives. These approaches transcend the literal and limited question of "Do men and women differ?" and ask instead: Why is everyone so interested in differences? Which differences? And what function does the *belief* in differences serve? We might ask, for instance, what is the result of the belief that women are emotionally and professionally affected by their hormones, but men are not? What are the results of the belief that women are the love experts, and that men are incapable of love and intimacy? This view asks us to consider where our theories come from, who benefits from them and where they lead us.

The study of "difference" is not the problem; of course people differ. The problem occurs when one group is considered the norm with others differing *from* it, thereby failing to "measure up" to the ideal, superior, dominant standard, and when the dominant group uses the language of difference to justify its social position (Scott, 1988). In *The Mismeasure of Man,* Stephen Jay Gould (1981) used the study of race differences in intelligence to illustrate how science has been used and abused to serve a larger cultural agenda: namely, to confirm prejudices that "blacks, women, and poor people occupy their subordinate roles by the harsh dictates of nature" (1981: 74). The mismeasure of woman serves the same function. The antidote, as Gould reminds us, is always to ask: Who is doing the measuring? And for what purpose?

This article will consider these questions, concluding with new perspectives that go beyond differences in examining the complexities of gender.

Let us start with a contemporary version of the "Women as problem" view. Consider this study of the reasons that women and men offer, in a mock job interview, for their success or failure on creativity tests (Olson, 1988). The researcher reports that women attributed their successes less often to their own abilities than to luck, and they reported less overall confidence in their present and future performance. "Why," she asked, "do women make less self-serving attributions than men do? The feminine social goal of appearing modest inhibits women in making self-promoting attributions in an achievement situation which involves face-to-face interaction." The premise of this study—to explain why the women did not behave like men—is apparent if we rephrase the question and its answer: "Why do men make more self-serving attributions than women do? The masculine social goal of appearing self-confident inhibits them from making modest explanations of their abilities or acknowledging the help of others and the role of chance."

Of course the bias of seeing women's behavior as something to be explained in relation to the male norm makes sense in a world that takes the male norm for granted. In this case, the researcher showed that the female habit of modesty does American women a disservice in job interviews, because they appear to be unconcerned with achievement and unwilling to promote themselves. (This is useful information to *both* sexes in cultures that value modesty, such as Japan and Great Britain, if they want to do business in the United States.) However, the research masks the fact that the male norm frames the very questions that investigators ask, and then creates the impression that women have "problems" and "deficiencies" if they differ from the norm. For example, here are some typical findings in psychology:

- women have lower self-esteem than men do;
- women do not value their efforts as much as men do;
- women are less self-confident than men;
- women are more likely to say they are "hurt" than to admit they are "angry";
- women have more difficulty developing a "separate sense of self."

Most people would agree that it is desirable for women to have high self-esteem, value their work, be self-confident, express anger and develop autonomy, so such studies usually conclude with discussions of "the problem" of why women are so insecure and what can be done about it. But had these studies used women as the basis of comparison, the same findings might then lead to a different notion of what the "problems" are:

- men are more conceited than women;
- men overvalue the work they do;
- men are not as realistic as women in assessing their abilities;
- men are more likely to accuse and attack others when unhappy, instead of stating that they feel hurt and inviting sympathy;
- men have more difficulty in forming and maintaining attachments.

Most people will see at once that this way of talking about men is biased and derogatory, but that is the point: Why has it been so difficult to notice the same negative tone in the way we talk about women? The answer is that we are used to seeing women as the problem, and to regarding women's differences from men as deficiencies and weaknesses.

For this reason, many women have responded to the transformation of women's weaknesses into strengths with delight and relief. It was enormously liberating to believe that women were not the problem; men were. Women are not "gullible"; men are "inflexible." Women are not "humorless"; men do not know what is funny. Women are not "emotionally immature" for remaining attached to their parents throughout life; men are "emotionally inhibited" from expressing their continuing needs for family connection.

After centuries of trying to measure up, many women, understandably, feel exhilarated by having female qualities and female experiences revalued and celebrated at last. This exhilaration has fueled the rise of cultural feminism, the idea that there are indeed profound and basic psychological differences between women and men, but women's ways are better. This view is gaining ground in many areas, including psychoanalysis, theology, history, psychology and feminist theory. Cultural feminists (e.g. Gilligan, 1982) celebrate women's allegedly care-based moral reasoning, their emphasis on attachments and kinder values. "Ecofeminists" (e.g. Eisler, 1987) hope to save the planet by celebrating women's alleged proximity to nature, their empathy, cooperation and peacefulness.

This movement represented an important step forward in the study of gender because it corrected two biases: the habit of excluding women from studies and generalizing from men to women (as happened in life-span research, moral reasoning studies and many other topics); and, as previously noted, the devaluing of women's "differences" that did turn up in the research.

But I am concerned about the current fashion for replacing one set of stereotypes with another. The woman-is-better school, like the woman-is-deficient school, assumes an *essential* opposition between the sexes, and there is no more evidence for one view than for the other. Thinking in opposites leads to what philosophers call "the law of the excluded middle," which is where most men and women fall in terms of their psychological qualities, beliefs, abilities, traits and values.

For example, after the initial excitement about Gilligan's (1982) provocative argument that women and men use different (but equally valuable) criteria in making moral decisions, subsequent research has found little evidence to support this hypothesis. Most researchers report no average differences in the kind of reasoning that men and women use in evaluating moral dilemmas, whether it is care-based or justice-based. Gilligan based her argument on her observations of how schoolchildren make moral decisions. She took excerpts from her interviews to argue that in resolving a conflict between desire and duty, for example, boys think in "hierarchical" terms (what goes first), whereas girls think in "network" terms (who is left out, who is hurt). But when Faye Crosby (1991) took the children's comments out of Gilligan's context and asked her students to tell her which were said by boys and which by girls, it turned out not to be so easy. Consider these responses to the question: "What does responsibility mean"

> It means pretty much thinking of others when I do something . . . [not doing something just for yourself], because you have to live with other people and live with your community, and if you do something that hurts them all, a lot of people will end up suffering, and that is sort of the wrong thing to do.

> That other people are counting on you to do something, and you can't just decide, "Well, I'd rather do this or that." [There is also responsibility] to yourself. If something looks really fun but you might hurt yourself doing it because you don't really know how to do it and your friends say, "Well, come on, you can do it, don't worry," if you're really scared to do it, it's your responsibility to yourself [not to do it] . . . because you have to take care of yourself.

Gilligan sees the boy as operating from "a premise of separation but recognizing that you have to live with other people," whereas the girl is operating "contextually." But it is just as plausible to say that the boy *and* the girl recognize that they have a responsibility to themselves *and* to others. (The boy's comment is first.)

Or consider the research on empathy and intuition. Many people think that women have the empathic advantage, so in studies of self-reports, women tend to score higher than men. Yet when studies measure physiological signs of empathy (physical responses to another person's suffering or unhappiness) or behavioral signs of empathy (doing something to help another person in distress), gender differences vanish. Men and women will be helpful in different ways, of course, but the impetus to help is present in both genders. Similarly, in reviews of studies of ability to feel compassion, to behave altruistically or to help in emergencies, few studies find behavioral differences of any magnitude.

Perhaps the most basic male–female dichotomy is that men are the warlike, dominating, planet-destroying sex and women are the peacemaking, non-aggressive, planet-saving sex. Of course, no one disputes the fact that men are far and away more violent than women. Men and women alike fear the violence of men.

But it does not follow from this very real difference in behavior that women are "naturally" more pacifistic or earth-loving. In the family and other intimate relations, women are just as verbally abusive, hostile and vindictive as men. As Campbell (1993) argues, although women's aggression often has different *meanings* and *causes* than men's, and although men often regard women's acts of aggression as "comic, hysterical, or insane," it is a mistake to infer from the sex difference in violence that women are "unaggressive."

Throughout history women have been just as militant in wartime as men, participating as their societies permitted: as combatants, as defenders, as laborers in the work force to produce war materials, as supporters of their warrior husbands and sons, as resistance fighters themselves. We think of war as a male activity and value, but war also gives women a route out of domestic confinement, a public identity and a chance to play a heroic role, usually denied them in their private lives.

Quite apart from what men and women do in wartime, bellicose and genocidal attitudes are by no means a male preserve. The same propaganda and ideology that motivate male members of a society ensnare its female citizens too. Iranian women joined Iranian men in chanting "Death to America"; German women joined German men to support Hitler's dreams of world conquest; American women have joined American men in supporting virtually every one of their wars. Women, for all their reputed empathic skills, have been as willing and able as men to regard the enemy as beasts or demons to be exterminated rather than as fellow human beings. In America, white women have supported the Ku Klux Klan and its bloody outrages every bit as much as their men did.

None of this means that at any given moment in a society, men and women will be precisely alike in their attitudes and values. Much has been made, for instance, of the American "gender gap" in support for militarism. But when Zur and Morrison (1989) examined surveys conducted in the last 40 years, they noticed a bias in the phrasing of questions. For example, one Roper Poll asked respondents, "Would you be willing to fight in case a foreign power tried to seize land in Central America?" Standing tall lest they be mistaken for wimps, men were far more likely than women to say yes. So, on polls like these, men consistently appear to be more militaristic than women. However, when women are asked whether they would endorse a war for reasons that reflect other motives, such as saving the lives of loved ones or promoting group cohesion, women turn out to be more militaristic than men. Women agree more often than men do with statements such as "Any country which violates the rights of innocent children should be invaded." Well, that should keep everyone's armies occupied for a while.

The point is that "gender gaps" widen or narrow with changing times, motives and conditions, and they cannot be accounted for by an *intrinsic* female pacifism; ideology (religious and political) and economics always override gender in the voting booth. We have been dazzled and deceived by the archetypes of Man as Noble Warrior and Woman as Sweet Pacifist. These archetypes compliment both sexes. But they are ultimately belied by a more complex reality that includes ample illustrations of female bellicosity and male pacifism.

An alternative to thinking in archetypal opposites was proposed by a women's group in Nottingham—Women Oppose the Nuclear Threat (WONT)—in the early 1980s. "We don't think that women have a special role in the peace movement because we are naturally more peaceful, more protective, or more vulnerable than men," they wrote, "nor do we look to women as the Earth Mother who will save the planet from male aggression."

> Rather, we believe that it is this very role division that makes the horrors of war possible. The so-called masculine, manly qualities of toughness, dominance, not showing emotion or admitting dependence can be seen as the driving force behind war; but they depend on women playing the opposite (but not equal) role, in which the caring qualities are associated with inferiority and powerlessness. (Quoted in Anderson and Zinsser, 1988, Vol. II: 430)

Ecofeminists are right to worry about the planet. But it is the *philosophy* of domination and exploitation that must be challenged, in whichever sex supports it, as well as the economic circumstances that make such a philosophy expedient.

The opposing qualities associated with masculinity and femininity, like those of "heterosexuality" and "homosexuality," are caricatures; all sets of polar characteristics overlook the complex realities of people's lives. Yet today we are witnessing a resurgence of the maximalist view that male and female *psyches, nature, brains and biology* create unbridgable chasms between the sexes. The idea tends to recur with renewed vigor whenever women begin to enter the public sphere in greater numbers, as happened with entry into higher education (19th century), professional training (the 1920s) and traditional male occupations (the late 1960s to the present). Invariably, we start hearing about the brain, and how women and men have "different" ones.

The belief that men's and women's brains differ in fundamental ways has a long and inglorious history. Typically, as Stephanie Shields (1975) and Anne Harrington (1987) have documented, when scientists did not find the anatomical differences they were seeking, they did not abandon the goal or their belief that such differences exist; they just moved to another part of the brain. Today, just like the 19th-century researchers who kept changing their minds about which *lobe* of the brain accounted for male superiority, researchers keep changing their minds about which *hemisphere* of the brain accounts for male superiority. Originally, the left hemisphere was considered the repository of intellect and reason. The right hemisphere was the sick, bad, crazy side, the side of passion, instincts, criminality and irrationality. Guess which sex was thought to have left-brain intellectual superiority? (Answer: males.) In the 1960s and 1970s, however, the right brain was rediscovered. Scientists began to suspect that it was the source of genius and inspiration, creativity and imagination, mysticism and mathematical brilliance. Guess which sex was now thought to have "right-brain specialization"? (Answer: males.)

Today's researchers are still determined to find sex differences. Two widely accepted hypotheses are that the left and right hemispheres develop differently in boys and girls, and that the corpus callosum, the bundle of fibers connecting the hemispheres, also differs. As a result, males are said to process visual–spatial information predominantly with the right hemisphere, whereas females use both hemispheres more symmetrically. This sex difference is alleged to originate during fetal development, when testosterone in male fetuses selectively attacks the left hemisphere, briefly slowing its development and resulting in right-hemisphere dominance in men, which in turn explains why men excel in art, music and mathematics. This theory has had tremendous scientific and popular appeal;

Science, the magazine of the American Association for the Advancement of Science, published a report on it with the headline "Math Genius May Have Hormonal Basis."

The late neuroscientist Ruth Bleier (1987, 1988) tried valiantly to get her criticisms of this general line of research published in *Science.* She found numerous scholarly problems in the published articles, such as sample selection and interpretation of data, and argued that it was an "unsupported conceptual leap" to generalize from male rat cortices to greater spatial orientation in rats, let alone from rats to humans. *Science* did not publish Bleier's critical paper or even her letter to the Editor, on the grounds, as one reviewer put it, that Bleier "tends to err in the opposite direction from the researchers whose results and conclusions she criticizes" and because she "argues very strongly for the predominant role of environmental influences" (Bleier, 1988). Apparently, said Bleier, one is allowed to err in only one direction if one wishes to be published in *Science.*

Another study achieved fame when it reported first evidence of gender differences in the corpus callosum (de Lacoste Utamsing and Holloway, 1982). The researchers speculated that "the female brain is less well lateralized—that is, manifests less hemispheric specialization—than the male brain for visuospatial functions." (Notice that the female brain is not said to be *more integrated.* Specialization, in the brain as in academia, is the order of the day.) This article, which also achieved acclaim, had a number of major flaws in sample size and selection. Bleier duly wrote to *Science,* delineating these criticisms and also citing four studies that failed to find gender differences in the corpus callosum. *Science* failed to publish this criticism, as it has failed to publish the studies that find no gender differences in the brain.

The irony is that the very characteristics that brain lateralization theories are attempting to account for—gender differences in cognitive abilities—keep changing. In the last 30 years, gender differences in mathematics scores have declined sharply. Hyde and Linn (1988), having done a meta-analysis of 165 studies of verbal ability (i.e. skills in vocabulary, writing, anagrams, reading comprehension and speaking fluency), concluded that there are no gender differences in verbal ability at this time in America. And in a meta-analysis of 100 studies of mathematics performance representing the testing of 3,985,682 students, Hyde et al. (1990) found that gender differences were smallest and favored *females* in samples of the general population, and grew larger, favoring males, only in selected samples of highly precocious individuals.

Is everybody's brain changing? I think not. To explain why gender differences or similarities in cognitive abilities change so rapidly, let alone why women moved as rapidly as they did into the fields of law, insurance and bar-tending, we do better to look at changes in education, motivation and opportunity, not "innate" differences between male and female brains.

My point is not that there are no sex differences in the brain. Some studies have found differences; more may turn up where no one is yet looking. The situation is analogous to the search for brain differences between "homosexuals" and "heterosexuals." There are three points to keep in mind about all such research:

1. The studies are small and inconclusive, and weak data have been used to support unwarranted speculations.
2. The meanings of terms like "verbal" and "spatial" abilities keep changing, depending on who is using them and for what purpose. For example, when some speak of women's "verbal abilities," they mean women's interest and skill in talking about relationships and feelings. But in everyday life, men interrupt women more than vice versa, dominate the conversation, talk more and are more successful at introducing new topics and having their comments remembered in group discussions. What does this mean for the biological origin of "verbal ability"? Likewise, there are many sexualities, which do not divide up neatly into heterosexuality and homosexuality; what does this mean for the biological origin of "sexual orientation"?
3. The far more convincing evidence for sex *similarity* is rarely published. Jeanette McGlone (1980), whose work is often quoted as supporting sex differences in brain hemispheres, actually concluded: "Thus, one must not overlook perhaps the most obvious conclusion, which is that basic patterns of male and female brain asymmetry seem to be more similar than they are different." Everyone of course promptly overlooked it.

To question the belief that men and women differ in profound and basic ways—their brains, capacities and abilities—is not to deny that men and women differ at all. Of course they do. They differ in power and resources, life experiences and reproductive processes. To say that men and women are equally capable of sexual pleasure, for example, does not mean that heterosexual men and women come to bed equally advantaged, that there are no differences between them in, as Leonore Tiefer (1992) says, communication, sensual experience, worries about commitment and attractiveness, sexual knowledge, safety, respect or feelings about their bodies, pregnancy, contraception or aging. Similarly, to say that both sexes are equally capable of advancing in mathematics, politics and science does not mean that society encourages both sexes equally to pursue these paths. That is why another problem in studying gender has been to overlook the real differences in women's and men's lives and generalize from men—a narrow band of white, middle-class men at that—to all humanity.

This error is particularly egregious and dangerous in the realms of medicine and law, two fields based on the normalcy of men and the applicability of male experience and even the male body to women. Until very recently in American medicine, clinical trials of new drugs were typically conducted only on men. (After the tragedy of Thalidomide, the exclusion of all child-bearing-aged women from clinical trials of new drugs became a Federal guideline for subsequent research.) The results are then applied to women, without consideration of the ways in which the menstrual cycle or birth control pills might affect the drug's efficacy. The male norm has also perpetuated the view of the normal female reproductive system as one that is abnormal and in constant need of medical fixing.

American law likewise is based on the standard of the "reasonable man" and on the normalcy of male experience. Modern jurisprudence, like medicine, is "masculine" rather than "human": the values, dangers, fears and other actual experiences of women's lives are not, as Robin West (1988) says, "reflected at any level whatsoever in contracts, torts, constitutional law, or any other field of legal doctrine." The Rule of Law does not value intimacy, for example, but autonomy:

> Nurturant, intimate labor is neither valued by liberal legalism nor compensated by the market economy. It is not compensated in the home and it is not compensated in the workplace—wherever intimacy is, there is no compensation. Similarly, separation of the individual from his or her family, community, or children is not understood to be a harm, and we are not protected against it. (West, 1988)

The law, Robin West argues, does not reflect the female experience: "Women are absent from jurisprudence because women *as human beings* are absent from the law's protection."

There is, however, one domain in which women set the standard of normalcy, and have defined men as the "opposite" and "deficient" sex: the domain of love, intimacy and emotional expression. Most psychologists—who, after all, are good talkers!—define intimacy as being able to talk about feelings. But many men define intimacy in terms of shared activities, doing things together. Similarly, many women and psychotherapists define "love" as an emotional state; many men define love and nurturance as doing things, being there for their loved ones. Thus the way that many men express their deepest feelings is seen as "deficient," or, worse, as a sign that they lack such feelings altogether.

Likewise, traditional ways of measuring distress and grief are based on typically female responses such as crying, sadness and eating disorders. Men tend to express grief by doing things that are stereotypically masculine, that they have a vocabulary for, that they can reveal without conflict or shame—"frantic work," heavy drinking, driving too fast, singing sentimental songs. The result of this real difference between women and men is that many men are excluded from the very languages of love and distress, leading to incorrect inferences that men suffer less than women when relationships are in trouble, or that men are "incapable" of love.

So, of course, women and men "differ." If we look closely at what men and women do, as a result of their roles, statuses and obligations, we find a wealth of differences. For instance, research has found that women have more than the two basic roles of home and work. Women have many jobs. They do the "interaction work" in conversations, making sure feelings are not hurt and keeping the ball rolling (Fishman, 1983). They do the invisible but time-consuming "kin work" of managing extended family relationships, such as organizing celebrations, sending holiday and birthday cards, making phone calls to keep in touch (di Leonardo, 1987). They do the "emotion work" in close relations, monitoring the course of the relationship and participants' feelings, and are more likely to be in occupations that require the display of cheerful emotion (Hochschild, 1983). And they work fully an extra month of 24-hour-days per year in comparison to husbands, doing a "second shift" of childcare and housekeeping (Hochschild, 1989)—some studies suggest even more: Croghan (1991).

Rhoda Unger (1990) has noted that research on sex differences has rarely concerned itself with behaviors in which the rate is "virtually zero for one sex"—such as rape. Traditional studies of sex differences have focused on those that are the least significant and the most variable. But violence against women—in dating relationships, in marriage, by strangers—permeates the lives of women in ways that it does not permeate the lives of men.

New Directions

If women are not worse than men, better than men or the same as men, how shall we think about gender? The first way I will suggest looks *outward at gender in context,* seeking a renewed emphasis on the external factors and contexts that shape our lives. The second looks *inward at gender as narrative,* focusing on the ways that women and men perceive, interpret and respond to events that befall them.

In the context approach, researchers no longer regard men and women as having a set of fixed "masculine" or "feminine" or even "androgynous" traits; the qualities and behaviors expected of women and men vary across settings and interactions. The behavior that we link to "gender" depends more on what an individual is doing than on biological sex.

For example, Barbara Risman (1987) compared the "parenting" skills and personality traits of single fathers, single mothers and married parents. She found that having responsibility for childcare was as strongly related to "feminine" traits, such as nurturance and sympathy, as being female was. The single men who were caring for children were more like mothers than like married fathers. These men were not an atypical group of nurturant men, either; they had custody of their children through circumstances beyond their control—widowhood, the wife's desertion or the wife's lack of interest in shared custody.

Here is another example, from the child development field, of the importance of context. Studies used to report that little girls were "passive" and boys "active." Eleanor Maccoby (1990), re-analyzing these studies, showed that boys and girls do not differ in "passivity" or "activity" in some consistent, trait-like way; *their behavior depends on the gender of the child they are playing with.* Among children as young as three, for example, girls are seldom passive with each other; however, when paired with boys, girls typically stand on the side-lines and let the boys monopolize the toys. This gender segregation, Maccoby found, is "essentially unrelated to the individual attributes of the children who make up all-girl or all-boy groups." When a boy and girl compete for a shared toy, the boy dominates, unless there is an adult in the room. Girls in mixed classrooms stay nearer to the teacher not because they are "dependent" as a personality trait, but because they want a chance at the toys! Girls play just as independently as boys when they are in all-girl groups.

Such research suggests that gender, like culture, organizes for its members different influence strategies, ways of communicating and ways of perceiving the world. The behavior of men and women often depends more on the gender they are interacting with than on anything intrinsic about the gender they are—a process that West and Zimmerman (1987) call "doing gender."

But there is an important qualification to the "two cultures" approach to gender differences, because the two cultures of gender are not equal in power, resources or status. Indeed, a major aspect of the contexts of people's lives turns out to be the power they have, or lack, in influencing others and in determining their own lives. This is why women are more likely to become "bilingual" than men are—better able to "read" men and "speak" male-speak than men are at "reading" women and "speaking" female-speak. Men are often charmed and amused by what they regard as the "mysterious" behavior of women, but they typically feel no need to decipher it; whereas women learn that for their own safety they had better try to understand and predict the behavior of men.

Many behaviors and personality traits thought to be typical of women are instead typical of women—*and men*—who lack power:

- "Women's intuition"—the ability to read non-verbal cues—is a function of powerlessness rather than gender; when men interact with a more powerful woman, they show as much "female intuition" as women do when interacting with a more powerful man (Snodgrass, 1985, 1992).
- The hesitations and uncertainties of so-called "women's speech" (pauses, hedges, questions, "sort ofs," and the like) are a function of powerlessness and social position, not of gender per se (Carli, 1990; O'Barr, 1983).
- A major literature review of studies of gender differences in power found that women, more than men, typified a "psychological cycle of powerlessness," blaming themselves, losing confidence and limiting their ambitions (Ragins and Sundstrom, 1989). But these symptoms proved to be *results* of powerlessness, not causes. "The path to power for women resembles an obstacle course," they concluded, and powerlessness perpetuates powerlessness.

The second promising direction in gender studies has been the examination of the ways women and men perceive and interpret events that befall them—the stories they tell about their lives. Theodore Sarbin (1986) has proposed that the life story is the key metaphor in understanding human behavior: our plans, our memories, our love affairs and hatreds are guided by narrative plots. It is here, in the narrative plots that men and women tell about their lives, that we find great divergence between them.

New approaches to gender lead us to ask: where do narratives come from? What function do they serve for the storyteller? Why do so many women today feel safer telling stories that place their fate in the stars, or in PMS, than stories that place their fate in their own hands—or society's? What are the psychological results of scientific "stories" of menstruation and menopause that are almost uniformly told in a language of loss, pathology and deterioration? If a woman wishes to believe that her problem is PMS rather than an abusive or simply unresponsive husband, how does she benefit? How does she lose?

The feminist rallying cry of the 1970s, "the personal is political," meant that personal experience can be used to illuminate the darker corners of society's closets. Today that slogan has been reversed: the political is personal, and only personal. There is an immense appeal to personal, psychological narratives about social problems; there is a danger, too, as the case of sexual abuse indicates.

In the late 1970s, when incest was first in the news, public horror and outrage focused on the perpetrator, the father or other adult relative. Louise Armstrong (1978/1987), in her sequel to *Kiss Daddy Goodnight*—an account of her own experience of incest—describes the next phase: "the onslaught of experts" announcing that incest was a "disease" and shifting attention from the perpetrator, the man, to the "enabler," the wife. This change in narrative was, in turn, part of the larger cultural shift, in the Reagan–Bush era, away from collective political action to an individualizing mental-health movement. Each battered or raped woman, each molested or raped child, was regarded as an instance of rare and bizarre family pathology. Nancy Matthews (1989), who traced the evolution of the anti-rape movement in Los Angeles, documented the ways in which the "feminist political agenda of relating violence against women to women's oppression was marginalized, ridiculed, and suppressed." Funding agencies began to redefine rape as an individual problem rather than, as Matthews says, "a personal experience with political implications."

Lloyd de Mause (1984), who analyzed the content of themes in political speeches and the media in the 1980s, argues that the public focus on individual horror stories of abusers and survivors deflected attention from the real story: how the massive cutbacks in funding for children's programs, child-abuse programs, prenatal care, job training programs and "dozens of other government activities directly affecting the welfare and lives of children" led to the maltreatment, neglect, abuse or deaths of thousands of children. Along the way, the original feminist analysis of the sexual abuse of children, that it is not merely a problem of a few disturbed individuals, was coopted and defused.

No one wishes to disparage survivor groups and therapies that help abused women to feel better and stronger about themselves. The problem is, as Armstrong (1987) says, that "where you have systematic power abuse, *the exclusive reliance on individual solutions defuses the possibility of a strong collective voice, and of action for change.* Exclusively personal solutions do nothing to defy the ongoing tacit permission for abuse" (emphasis added).

This is why our stories matter. But stories change, and how and why they do is the heart of psychology and of politics.

CONCLUSIONS

"Show me a woman who doesn't feel guilt," says my friend and colleague Rachel Hare-Mustin, "and I'll show you a man." The mismeasure of woman is responsible for the guilt-inducing analyses that leave women feeling that they lack the right stuff and are not doing the right thing. It has made sicknesses and syndromes of women's normal bodily processes. And it has polarized the discourse between men and women, relegating to men's "inherent abilities" the *human* capacities of reason, achievement, art and politics, and to women's "special nature" the *human* qualities of feeling, attachment, connection and care. Future research can, however, begin to erode the familiar concepts of "normal" men and "different" women (or "normal" whites and people of "different" colors and ethnicities, or "normal" heterosexuals and "different" lesbians and gays, or any other human dichotomy):

1. *We can avoid the "snapshot" problem in the study of abilities, traits and qualities.* A study is a snapshot of behavior at that moment in time, but a snapshot is not a blueprint; on the contrary, human behavior is a moving picture. Most gender "differences" are momentary and changeable, suggesting that they are rooted less in biology, personality and intrapsychic dynamics (which appear to be permanent) than in life experiences, contexts, resources and power (which change culturally and historically).

2. *We can avoid polarizing traits into opposites and therefore deficiencies.* Connection and autonomy, dependence and independence, modesty and self-confidence, reason and intuition, qualitative and quantitative methods: all have their place in human life. In the range of human psychological talents and qualities—including our capacity for stupidity, self-delusion and general dorkiness—neither sex has the lead.

   For some women, definition lies in opposition to the male way. Are men political? Then women must be spiritual. Are men overly rational? Then women must be "intuitive." Is modern medicine patriarchal and overly technological? Then women must choose natural healing and cure themselves exclusively with fasting and yoga, health food and herbal teas, a laying on of hands and a channeling of energy. Is society hopelessly male-dominated? Then women must find or invent societies in which women dominate. Forcing choices between such exaggerated extremes, I believe, is fruitless and self-defeating. It creates animosities rather than alliances across gender lines. The short-run benefit—feeling better about womanhood—has long-run disadvantages because it keeps women out of the realms of power where decisions about what kind of society we will have, and what qualities we will value as a society, are made.

3. *We can observe how qualities, skills and behaviors change over the life span, and identify the factors and contexts that produce or retard change.* The exaggerated attitudes and sex-typed rules of children and the sex games of adolescence are not a blueprint for life. People develop, learn, and have adventures and new experiences; gender rules are not frozen at one moment in time, whether the time is said to be infancy, childhood or adolescence.

4. *We can open our perceptions to the stories people tell as well as to the stories we expect them to tell.* By setting aside predetermined categories, we have learned that there is no one right way to have a love relationship, a baby, a career; no one right way to be lesbian, straight or gay; no one right way to *be.*

5. *We can develop a model of equality that is not based on sameness, but on acceptance of differences.* Women do not need to be "the same as" men in order to strive for a world in which both sexes have equal opportunities to develop their abilities, to feel safe, to share power.

For example, pregnancy is an experience unique to women, but not all women. The "woman as problem" view regards pregnancy as a debilitating condition that makes women weaker than men; therefore pregnant women need to be "protected." (Legislation based on this principle has protected women right out of high-paying jobs.) The "woman as solution" view regards pregnancy as a mystical condition linking women to the secrets of life and the universe. This sentimental inversion of protection theory restores the familiar pro-natal pressures on women who cannot or choose not to have children; it makes women who have a difficult time with childbirth feel guilty that they have pain or might be helped by "male" medicine. Finally, the view that "women are the same as men" regards pregnancy as a temporary disability, something comparable to a male experience, such as a hernia.

An alternative to these inadequate analyses of pregnancy is to say: there is nothing universal in how women will react to pregnancy; the experience will vary from woman to woman, culture to culture, historical epoch to historical epoch. For one woman, pregnancy will be wished-for; for another, or for the same woman on another occasion, a disaster. New views would direct us to ask, instead, *who gets to decide* what pregnancy means to a woman—the woman or the state? What are the social and practical *consequences* of pregnancy for a woman? Her experience needn't be the same as a man's in order to create policies in which women *do not pay economically or in status or in security* by becoming pregnant or taking time off to care for children, as they now do in many cultures.

6. *We can keep our eyes on the prize,* that is, creating the social arrangements that enhance the power, safety, pleasure and possibilities of both sexes, all sexual orientations, all races, all ages, all classes. Those in power will try to tell us we have already won. Or that our brains are not suited to winning. Or that we really do not want to win anyway. Or that we should cultivate our own sweet qualities. All of these narratives deflect us from the vision that one day must become reality: the only way for Man to no longer be the center of the defining universe is for Woman to be in the center ring with him.

References

Anderson, B. S. and Zinsser, J. P. (eds) (1988) *A History of Their Own: Women in Europe from Prehistory to the Present, Vols I and II.* New York: Harper and Row.

Armstrong, L. (1978/1987) *Kiss Daddy Goodnight: Ten Years Later.* New York: Pocket Books.

Blee, K. M. (1991) *Women of the Klan: Racism and Gender in the 1920s.* Berkeley, CA: University of California Press.

Bleier, R. (1987) "Sex Differences Research in the Neurosciences," paper presented at the annual meeting of the American Association for the Advancement of Science, Chicago.

Bleier, R. (1988) "Sex Differences Research: Science or Belief?," in R. Bleier (ed.) *Feminist Approaches to Science,* pp. 147–64. New York: Pergamon.

Campbell, A. (1993) *Men, Women, and Aggression.* New York: Basic Books.

Carli, L. L. (1990) "Gender, Language, and Influence," *Journal of Personality and Social Psychology* 59: 941–51.

Crawford, M. and Marecek, J. (1989) "Psychology Reconstructs the Female: 1968–1988," *Psychology of Women Quarterly* 13: 147–65.

Croghan, R. (1991) "First-time Mothers' Accounts of Inequality in the Division of Labour," *Feminism & Psychology* 1(2): 221–46.

Crosby, F. J. (1991) *Juggling*. New York: Free Press.

de Lacoste-Utamsing, C. and Holloway, R. L. (1982) "Sexual Dimorphism in the Human Corpus Callosum," *Science* 216: 1431–2.

de Mause, L. (1984) *Reagan's America*. New York: Creative Roots.

di Leonardo, M. (1987) "The Female World of Cards and Holidays: Women, Families and the Work of Kinship," *Signs* 12: 1–20.

Eisler, R. (1987) *The Chalice and the Blade*. San Francisco: Harper and Row.

Fishman, P. M. (1983) "Interaction: The Work Women Do," in B. Thorne, C. Kramarae and N. Henley (eds.) *Language, Gender and Society*, Rowley, MA: Newbury House.

Gilligan, C. (1982) *In a Different Voice*. Cambridge, MA: Harvard University Press.

Gould, S. J. (1981) *The Mismeasure of Man*. New York: Norton.

Harrington, A. (1987) *Medicine, Mind, and the Double Brain: A Study in 19th-century Thought*. Princeton, NJ: Princeton University Press.

Hochschild, A. R. (1983) *The Managed Heart*. Berkeley: University of California Press.

Hochschild, A. R. (1989) *The Second Shift: Working Parents and the Revolution at Home*. New York: Viking Press.

Hyde, J. S., Fennema, E. and Lamon, S. J. (1990) "Gender Differences in Mathematics Performance: A Meta-analysis," *Psychological Bulletin* 107: 139–55.

Hyde, J. S. and Linn, M. C. (1988) "Gender Differences in Verbal Ability: A Meta-analysis," *Psychological Bulletin* 104: 53–69.

Maccoby, E. E. (1990) "Gender and Relationships: A Developmental Account," *American Psychologist* 45: 513–20.

Matthews, N. (1989) "Stopping Rape or Managing Its Consequences? State Intervention and Feminist Resistance in the Los Angeles Anti-rape Movement, 1972–1987," Doctoral dissertation, University of California at Los Angeles.

McGlone, J. (1980) "Sex Differences in Human Brain Asymmetry: A Critical Survey," *The Behavioral and Brain Sciences* 3: 215–63.

O'Barr W. M. (1983) "The Study of Language in Institutional Contexts," *Journal of Language and Social Psychology* 2: 241–51.

Olson, C. B. (1988) "The Influence of Context on Gender Differences in Performance Attributions: Further Evidence of a 'Feminine Modesty' Effect," paper presented at the meeting of the Western Psychological Association, San Francisco.

Pantony, K. and Caplan, P. J. (1991) "Delusional Domineering Personality Disorder: A Modest Proposal for Identifying Some Consequences of Rigid Masculine Socialization." *Canadian Psychology* 32: 120–33.

Ragins B. R. and Sundstrom, E. (1989) "Gender and Power in Organizations: A Longitudinal Perspective," *Psychological Bulletin* 105: 51–88.

Risman, B. J. (1987) "Intimate Relationships from a Microstructural Perspective: Men Who Mother." *Gender and Society* 1: 6–32.

Sarbin, T. R. (1986) "The Narrative as a Root Metaphor for Psychology," in T. R. Sarbin (ed.) *Narrative Psychology: The Storied Nature of Human Conduct*, pp. 129–51. New York: Praeger.

Scott, J. W. (1988) "Deconstructing Equality-Versus-Difference: Or, the Uses of Poststructuralist Theory for Feminism," *Feminist Studies* 14 (Spring): 33–50.

Shields, S. A. (1975) "Functionalism, Darwinism, and the Psychology of Women: A Study in Social Myth," *American Psychologist* 30: 739–54.

Snodgrass S. E. (1985) "Women's Intuition: The Effect of Subordinate Role on Interpersonal Sensitivity," *Journal of Personality and Social Psychology* 49: 146–55.

Snodgrass, S. E. (1992) "Further Effects of Role Versus Gender on Interpersonal Sensitivity," *Journal of Personality and Social Psychology* 62: 154–8.

Tiefer, Leonore (1992) "Critique of DSM-III-R Nomenclature for Sexual Dysfunctions," *Psychiatric Medicine* 10: 227–45.

Unger, R. K. (1990) "Imperfect Reflections of Reality: Psychology Constructs Gender," in R. T. Hare-Mustin and J. Marecek (eds) *Making a Difference: Psychology and the Construction of Gender*, pp. 102–49. New Haven, CT: Yale University Press.

West, R. (1988) "Jurisprudence and Gender," *The University of Chicago Law Review* 55: 1–72.

West, C. and Zimmerman, D. H. (1987) "Doing Gender," *Gender and Society* 1: 125–51.

Zur, O. and Morrison, A. (1989) "Gender and War: Reexamining Attitudes," *American Journal of Orthopsychiatry* 59: 528–33.

PART 2 CULTURAL CONSTRUCTIONS OF GENDER

Biological evidence helps explain the ubiquity of gender difference and gender inequality, but social scientific evidence modifies both the universality and the inevitability implicit in biological claims. Cross-cultural research suggests that gender and sexuality are far more fluid, far more variable, than biological models would have predicted. If biological sex alone produced observed sex differences, Margaret Mead asked in the 1920s and '30s, why did such *different* definitions of masculinity and femininity develop in different cultures? In her path-breaking study, *Sex and Temperament in Three Primitive Societies,* Mead began an anthropological tradition of exploring and often celebrating the dramatically rich and varied cultural constructions of gender.

Anthropologists are more likely to locate the origins of gender difference and gender inequality in a sex-based division of labor, the near-universality of and the variations in the ways in which societies organize the basic provision and distribution of material goods. They've found that when women and men's spheres are most distinctly divided—where women and men do different things in different places—women's status tends to be lower than when men and women share both work and work places.

Some researchers have explored the function of various cultural rituals and representations in creating the symbolic justification for gender differences and inequality based on this sex-based division of labor. For example, as the selection from John Whiting and his colleagues suggests, the function of male initiation rituals at puberty are to delineate symbolically the severing of the boy's ties to his mother and therefore the acquisition of masculine gender identity. That these rituals tend to be associated with cultures in which male and female are highly differentiated and in which there is a significant level of gender inequality indicates that there is a lot at stake for a boy to demonstrate that separation from the world of women.

Finally, Peggy Reeves Sanday explores the ways in which gender inequality is also a predictor for the likelihood that a culture will have either high or low rape rates. By locating the origins of rape in male domination—dramatic separation of spheres, gender inequality, low levels of male participation in child care—Sanday effectively lays to rest the facile biological argument that rape is the evolutionary sexual strategy of male "failures" in reproductive competition.

MARGARET MEAD

Sex and Temperament in Three Primitive Societies

We have now considered in detail the approved personalities of each sex among three primitive peoples. We found the Arapesh—both men and women—displaying a personality that, out of our historically limited preoccupations, we would call maternal in its parental aspects, and feminine in its sexual aspects. We found men, as well as women, trained to be co-operative, unaggressive, responsive to the needs and demands of others. We found no idea that sex was a powerful driving force either for men or for women. In marked contrast to these attitudes, we found among the Mundugumor that both men and women developed as ruthless, aggressive, positively sexed individuals, with the maternal cherishing aspects of personality at a minimum. Both men and women approximated to a personality type that we in our culture would find only in an undisciplined and very violent male. Neither the Arapesh nor the Mundugumor profit by a contrast between the sexes; the Arapesh ideal is the mild, responsive man married to the mild, responsive woman; the Mundugumor ideal is the violent aggressive man married to the violent aggressive woman. In the third tribe, the Tchambuli, we found a genuine reversal of the sex attitudes of our own culture, with the woman the dominant, impersonal, managing partner, the man the less responsible and the emotionally dependent person. These three situations suggest, then, a very definite conclusion. If those temperamental attitudes which we have traditionally regarded as feminine—such as passivity, responsiveness, and a willingness to cherish children—can so easily be set up as the masculine pattern in one tribe, and in another be outlawed for the majority of women as well as for the majority of men, we no longer have any basis for regarding such aspects of behaviour as sex-linked. And this conclusion becomes even stronger when we consider the actual reversal in Tchambuli of the position of dominance of the two sexes, in spite of the existence of formal patrilineal institutions.

The material suggests that we may say that many, if not all, of the personality traits which we have called masculine or feminine are as lightly linked to sex as are the clothing, the manners, and the form of head-dress that a society at a given period assigns to either sex. When we consider the behaviour of the typical Arapesh man or woman as contrasted with the behaviour of the typical Mundugumor man or woman, the evidence is overwhelmingly in favour of the strength of social conditioning. In no other way can we account for the almost complete uniformity with which Arapesh children develop into contented, passive, secure persons, while Mundugumor children develop as characteristically into violent, aggressive, insecure persons. Only to the impact of the whole of the integrated culture upon the growing child can we lay the formation of the contrasting types. There is no other explanation of race, or diet, or selection that can be adduced to explain them. We are forced to conclude that human nature is almost unbelievably malleable, responding accurately and contrastingly to contrasting cultural conditions. The differences between individuals who are members of different cultures, like the differences between individuals within a culture, are almost entirely to be laid to differences in conditioning, especially during early childhood, and the form of this conditioning is culturally determined. Standardized personality differences between the sexes are of this order, cultural creations to which each generation, male and female, is trained to conform. There remains, however, the problem of the origin of these socially standardized differences.

While the basic importance of social conditioning is still imperfectly recognized—not only in lay thought, but even by the scientist specifically concerned with such matters—to go beyond it and consider the possible influence of variations in hereditary equipment is a hazardous matter. The following pages will read very differently to one who has made a part of his thinking a recognition of the whole amazing mechanism of cultural conditioning—who has really accepted the fact that the same infant could be developed into a full participant in any one of these three cultures—than they will read to one who still believes that the minutiae of cultural behaviour are carried in the individual germ-plasm. If it is said, therefore, that when we have grasped the full significance of the malleability of the human organism and the preponderant importance of cultural conditioning, there are still further problems to solve, it must be remembered that these problems come *after* such a comprehension of the force of conditioning; they cannot precede it. The forces that make children born among the Arapesh grow up into typical Arapesh personalities are entirely social, and any discussion of the variations which do occur must be looked at against this social background.

With this warning firmly in mind, we can ask a further question. Granting the malleability of human nature, whence arise the differences between the standardized personalities that different cultures decree for all of their members, or which one culture decrees for the members of one sex as contrasted with the members of the opposite sex? If such differences are culturally created, as this material would most strongly suggest that they are, if the new-born child can be shaped with equal ease into an unaggressive Arapesh or an aggressive Mundugumor, why do these striking contrasts occur at all? If the clues to the different personalities decreed for men and women in Tchambuli do not lie in the physical constitution of the two sexes—an assumption that we must reject both for the Tchambuli and for our own society—where can we find the clues upon which the Tchambuli, the Arapesh, the Mundugumor, have built? Cultures are man-made, they are built of human materials; they are diverse but comparable structures within which human beings can attain full human stature. Upon what have they built their diversities?

We recognize that a homogeneous culture committed in all of its gravest institutions and slightest usages to a co-operative, unaggressive course can bend every child to that emphasis, some to a perfect accord with it, the majority to an easy acceptance, while only a few deviants fail to receive the cultural imprint. To consider such traits as aggressiveness or passivity to be sex-linked is not possible in the light of the facts. Have such traits, then, as aggressiveness or passivity, pride or humility, objectivity or a preoccupation with personal relationships, an easy response to the needs of the young and the weak or a hostility to the young and the weak, a tendency to initiate sex-relations or merely to respond to the dictates of a situation or another person's advances—have these traits any basis in temperament at all? Are they potentialities of all human temperaments that can be developed by different kinds of social conditioning and which will not appear if the necessary conditioning is absent?

When we ask this question we shift our emphasis. If we ask why an Arapesh man or an Arapesh woman shows the kind of personality that we have considered in the first section of this book, the answer is: Because of the Arapesh culture, because of the intricate, elaborate, and unfailing fashion in which a culture is able to shape each new-born child to the cultural image. And if we ask the same question about a Mundugumor man or woman, or about a Tchambuli man as compared with a Tchambuli woman, the answer is of the same kind. They display the personalities that are peculiar to the cultures in which they were born and educated. Our attention has been on the differences between Arapesh men and women as a group and Mundugumor men and women as a group. It is as if we had represented the Arapesh personality by a soft yellow, the Mundugumor by a deep red, while the Tchambuli female personality was deep orange, and that of the Tchambuli male, pale green. But if we now ask whence came the original direction in each culture, so that one now shows yellow, another red, the third orange and green by sex, then we must peer more closely. And learning closer to the picture, it is as if behind the bright consistent yellow of the Arapesh, and the deep equally consistent red of the Mundugumor, behind the orange and green that are Tchambuli, we found in each case the delicate, just discernible outlines of the whole spectrum, differently overlaid in each case by the monotone which covers it. This spectrum is the range of individual differences which lie back of the so much more conspicuous cultural emphases, and it is to this that we must turn to find the explanation of cultural inspiration, of the source from which each culture has drawn.

There appears to be about the same range of basic temperamental variation among the Arapesh and among the Mundugumor, although the violent man is a misfit in the first society and a leader in the second. If human nature were completely homogeneous raw material, lacking specific drives and characterized by no important constitutional differences between individuals, then individuals who display personality traits so antithetical to the social pressure should not reappear in societies of such differing emphases. If the variations between individuals were to be set down to accidents in the genetic process, the same accidents should not be repeated with similar frequency in strikingly different cultures, with strongly contrasting methods of education.

But because this same relative distribution of individual differences does appear in culture after culture, in spite of the divergence between the cultures, it seems pertinent to offer a hypothesis to explain upon what basis the personalities of men and women have been differently standardized so often in the history of the human race. This hypothesis is an extension of that advanced by Ruth Benedict in her *Patterns of Culture.* Let us assume that there are definite temperamental differences between human beings which if not entirely hereditary at least are established on a hereditary base very soon after birth. (Further than this we cannot at present narrow the matter.) These differences finally embodied in the character structure of adults, then, are the clues from which culture works, selecting one temperament, or a combination of related and congruent types, as desirable, and embodying this choice in every thread of the social fabric—in the care of the young child, the games the children play, the songs the people sing, the structure of political organization, the religious observance, the art and the philosophy.

Some primitive societies have had the time and the robustness to revamp all of their institutions to fit one extreme type, and to develop educational techniques which will ensure that the majority of each generation will show a personality congruent with this extreme emphasis. Other societies have pursued a less definitive course, selecting their models not from the most extreme, most highly differentiated individuals, but from the less marked types. In such societies the approved personality is less pronounced, and the culture often contains the types of inconsistencies that many human beings display also; one institution may be adjusted to the uses of pride, another to a casual humility that is congruent neither with pride nor with inverted pride. Such societies, which have taken the more usual and less sharply defined types as models, often show also a less definitely patterned social structure. The culture of such societies may be likened to a house the decoration of which has been informed by no definite and precise taste, no exclusive emphasis upon dignity or comfort or pretentiousness or beauty, but in which a little of each effect has been included.

Alternatively, a culture may take its clues not from one temperament, but from several temperaments. But instead of mixing together into an inconsistent hotchpotch the choices and emphases of different temperaments, or blending them together into a smooth but not particularly distinguished whole, it may isolate each type by making it the basis for the approved social personality for an age-group, a sex-group, a caste-group, or an occupational group. In this way society becomes not a monotone with a few discrepant patches of an intrusive colour, but a mosaic, with different groups displaying different personality traits. Such specializations as these may be based upon any facet of human endowment—different intellectual abilities, different artistic abilities, different emotional traits. So the Samoans decree that all young people must show the personality trait of unaggressiveness and punish with opprobrium the aggressive child who displays traits regarded as appropriate only in titled middle-aged men. In societies based upon elaborate ideas of rank, members of the aristocracy will be permitted, even compelled, to display a pride, a sensitivity to insult, that would be deprecated as inappropriate in members of the plebeian class. So also in professional groups or in religious sects some temperamental traits are selected and institutionalized, and taught to each new member who enters the profession or sect. Thus the physician learns the bedside manner, which is the natural behaviour of some temperaments and the standard behaviour of the general practitioner in the medical profession; the Quaker learns at least the outward behaviour and the rudiments of meditation, the capacity for which is not necessarily an innate characteristic of many of the members of the Society of Friends.

So it is with the social personalities of the two sexes. The traits that occur in some members of each sex are specially assigned to one sex, and disallowed in the other. The history of the social definition of sex-differences is filled with such arbitrary arrangements in the intellectual and artistic field, but because of the assumed congruence between physiological sex and emotional endowment we have been less able to recognize that a similar arbitrary selection is being made among emotional traits also. We have assumed that because it is convenient for a mother to wish to care for her child, this is a trait with which women have been more generously endowed by a carefully teleological process of evolution. We have assumed that because men have hunted, an activity requiring enterprise, bravery, and initiative, they have been endowed with these useful attitudes as part of their sex-temperament.

Societies have made these assumptions both overtly and implicitly. If a society insists that warfare is the major occupation for the male sex, it is therefore insisting that all male children display bravery and pugnacity. Even if the insistence upon the differential bravery of men and women is not made articulate, the difference in occupation makes this point implicitly. When, however, a society goes further and defines men as brave and women as timorous, when men are forbidden to show fear and women are indulged in the most flagrant display of fear, a more explicit element enters in. Bravery, hatred of any weakness, of flinching before pain or danger—this attitude which is so strong a component of *some human* temperaments has been selected as the key to masculine behaviour. The easy unashamed display of fear or suffering that is congenial to a different temperament has been made the key to feminine behaviour.

Originally two variations of human temperament, a hatred of fear or willingness to display fear, they have been socially translated into inalienable aspects of the personalities of the two sexes. And to that defined sex-personality every child will be educated, if a boy, to suppress fear, if a girl, to show it. If there has been no social selection in regard to this trait, the proud temperament that is repelled by any betrayal of feeling will display itself, regardless of sex, by keeping a stiff upper lip. Without an express prohibition of such behaviour the expressive unashamed man or woman will weep, or comment upon fear or suffering. Such attitudes, strongly marked in certain temperaments, may by social selection be standardized for everyone, or outlawed for everyone, or ignored by society, or made the exclusive and approved behaviour of one sex only.

Neither the Arapesh nor the Mundugumor have made any attitude specific for one sex. All of the energies of the culture have gone towards the creation of a single human type, regardless of class, age, or sex. There is no division into age-classes for which different motives or different moral attitudes are regarded as suitable. There is no class of seers or mediums who stand apart drawing inspiration from psychological sources not available to the majority of the people. The Mundugumor have, it is true, made one arbitrary selection, in that they recognize artistic ability only among individuals born with the cord about their necks, and firmly deny the happy exercise of artistic ability to those less unusually born. The Arapesh boy with a tinea infection has been socially selected to be a disgruntled, antisocial individual, and the society forces upon sunny co-operative children cursed with this affliction a final approximation to the behaviour appropriate to a pariah. With these two exceptions no emotional role is forced upon an individual because of birth or accident. As there is no idea of rank which declares that some are of high estate and some of low, so there is no idea of sex-difference which declares that one sex must feel differently from the other. One possible imaginative social construct, the attribution of different personalities to different members of the community classified into sex-, age-, or caste-groups, is lacking.

When we turn however to the Tchambuli, we find a situation that while bizarre in one respect, seems nevertheless more intelligible in another. The Tchambuli have at least made the point of sex-difference; they have used the obvious fact of sex as an organizing point for the formation of social personality, even though they seem to us to have reversed the normal picture. While there is reason to believe that not every Tchambuli woman is born with a dominating, organizing, administrative temperament, actively sexed and willing to initiate sex-relations, possessive, definite, robust, practical and impersonal in outlook, still most Tchambuli girls grow up to display these traits. And while there is definite evidence to show that all Tchambuli men are not, by native endowment, the delicate responsive actors of a play staged for the women's benefit, still most Tchambuli boys manifest this coquettish play-acting personality most of the time. Because the Tchambuli formulation of sex-attitudes contradicts our usual premises, we can see clearly that Tchambuli culture has arbitrarily permitted certain human traits to women, and allotted others, equally arbitrarily, to men.

JOHN W. M. WHITING, RICHARD KLUCKHOHN, AND ALBERT ANTHONY

The Function of Male Initiation Ceremonies at Puberty

Our society gives little formal recognition of the physiological and social changes a boy undergoes at puberty. He may be teased a little when his voice changes or when he shaves for the first time. Changes in his social status from childhood to adulthood are marked by a number of minor events rather than by any single dramatic ceremonial observance. Graduation from grammar school and subsequently from high school are steps to adulthood, but neither can be considered as a *rite de passage*. Nor may the accomplishment of having obtained a driver's license, which for many boys is the most important indication of having grown up, be classed as one. Legally the twenty-first birthday is the time at which a boy becomes a man; but, except for a somewhat more elaborate birthday party, this occasion is not ceremonially marked and, therefore, cannot be thought of as a *rite de passage*. Neither physiologically, socially, nor legally is there a clear demarcation between boyhood and manhood in our society.

From *Readings in Social Psychology*, edited by Eleanor Maccoby, T. M. Newcomb, and E. L. Hatlet. Reprinted by permission of Harcourt Brace. Notes have been renumbered and edited.

Such a gradual transition from boyhood to manhood is by no means universal. Among the Thonga, a tribe in South Africa, every boy must go through a very elaborate ceremony in order to become a man.[1] When a boy is somewhere between 10 and 16 years of age, he is sent by his parents to a "circumcision school" which is held every four or five years. Here is company with his age-mates he undergoes severe hazing by the adult males of the society. The initiation begins when each boy runs the gauntlet between two rows of men who beat him with clubs. At the end of this experience he is stripped of his clothes and his hair is cut. He is next met by a man covered with lion manes and is seated upon a stone facing this "lion man." Someone then strikes him from behind and when he turns his head to see who has struck him, his foreskin is seized and in two movements cut off by the "lion man." Afterwards he is secluded for three months in the "yards of mysteries," where he can be seen only by the initiated. It is especially taboo for a woman to approach these boys during their seclusion, and if a woman should glance at the leaves with which the circumcised covers his wound and which form his only clothing, she must be killed.

During the course of his initiation, the boy undergoes six major trials: beatings, exposure to cold, thirst, eating of unsavory foods, punishment, and the threat of death. On the slightest pretext he may be severely beaten by one of the newly initiated men who is assigned to the task by the older men of the tribe. He sleeps without covering and suffers bitterly from the winter cold. He is forbidden to drink a drop of water during the whole three months. Meals are often made nauseating by the half-digested grass from the stomach of an antelope which is poured over his food. If he is caught breaking any important rule governing the ceremony, he is severely punished. For example, in one of these punishments, sticks are placed between the fingers of the offender, then a strong man closes his hand around that of the novice practically crushing his fingers. He is frightened into submission by being told that in former times boys who had tried to escape or who revealed the secrets to women or to the uninitiated were hanged and their bodies burnt to ashes.

Although the Thonga are extreme in the severity of this sort of initiation, many other societies have rites which have one or more of the main features of the Thonga ceremony. Of a sample of 55 societies chosen for this study, 18 have one or more of the four salient features of the Thonga ceremony, e.g., painful hazing by adult males, genital operations, seclusion from women, and tests of endurance and manliness; the remaining 37 societies either have no ceremony at all or one which does not have any of the above features.

HYPOTHESES

It is the purpose of this paper to develop a set of hypotheses concerning the function of male initiation rites which accounts for the presence of these rites in some societies and the absence of them in others. The theory that we have chosen to test has been suggested by previous explanations for the rites, particularly those of psychoanalytic origin. These explanations were modified to fit the problem of this research in two respects. First, certain of the concepts and hypotheses were restated or redefined so as to be coherent with the growing general behavioral theory of personality development, and second, they were restated in such a way as to be amenable to cross-cultural test, i.e., cultural indices were specified for each variable.

We assume that boys tend to be initiated at puberty in those societies in which they are particularly hostile toward their fathers and dependent upon their mothers. The hazing of the candidates, as well as the genital operations, suggests that one function of the rites is to prevent open and violent revolt against parental authority at a time when physical maturity would make such revolt dangerous and socially disruptive. Isolation from women and tests of manliness suggest that another function of the rites is to break an excessively strong dependence upon the mother and to ensure identification with adult males and acceptance of the male role.

It is to be noted here that the educational and disciplinary functions of the initiation are not limited in time to the actual period of initiation. The boy knows all during childhood and latency about the initiation which he will face at puberty. While he is overtly not supposed to know any of the secrets of the rite, he actually knows almost everything that will happen to him. He is both afraid of what he knows will happen and also envious of the kudos and added status which his older friends have acquired through having successfully gone through this rite. Thus, through the boy's whole life the initiation ceremony serves as a conditioner of his behavior and his attitudes towards male authority, while at the same time emphasizing the advantages of becoming a member of the male group through initiation.

We assume that a long and exclusive relationship between mother and son provides the conditions which should lead to an exceptionally strong dependence upon the mother. Also, we assume that if the father terminates this relationship and replaces his son, there should be strong envy and hostility engendered in the boy which, although held in check during childhood, many dangerously manifest itself with the onset of puberty, unless measures are taken to prevent it.

As we indicated above, the hypothesis is derived from psychoanalytic theory. However, it should be noted that there are some modifications which may be important. First, no assumption is being made that the envy is exclusively sexual in character. We are making the more general assumption that if the mother for a prolonged period devotes herself to the satisfaction of all the child's need—including hunger, warmth, safety, freedom from pain, as well as sex—he will become strongly dependent upon her. In accordance with this we believe rivalry may be based upon a competition for the fulfillment of any of these needs. Second, we do not propose, as most psychoanalysts do, that Oedipal rivalry is a universal, but rather we claim it is a variable which may be strong or weak depending upon specific relationships between father, mother, and son. Thus, we assume father-son rivalry may range from a value of zero to such high intensities that the whole society may be required to adjust to it.

An illustration of cultural conditions which should intensify the dependency of a boy on his mother and rivalry with his father is found in the following case.

Kwoma Dependency

The Kwoma, a tribe living about 200 miles up the Sepik River in New Guinea, have initiation rites similar to those of the Thonga. Examination of the differences in the relationship of a mother to her infant during the first years of his life reveals some strong contrasts between the Kwoma and our own society. While in our society an infant sleeps in his own crib and the mother shares her bed with the father, the Kwoma infant sleeps cuddled in his mother's arms until he is old enough to be weaned, which is generally when he is two or three years old. The father, in the meantime, sleeps apart on his own bark slab bed. Furthermore during this period, the Kwoma mother abstains from sexual intercourse with her husband in order to avoid having to care for two dependent children at the same time. Since the Kwoma are polygynous and discreet extramarital philandering is permitted, this taboo is not too hard on the husband. In addition, it is possible that the mother obtains some substitute sexual gratification from nursing and caring for her infant. If this be the case, it is not unlikely that she should show more warmth and affection toward her infant that if she were obtained sexual gratification from her husband. Whether or not the custom can be attributed to this sex taboo, the Kwoma mother, while her co-wife does the housework, not only sleeps with her infant all night but holds it in her lap all day without apparent frustration. Such a close relationship between a mother and child in our society would seem not only unbearably difficult to the mother, but also somewhat improper.

When the Kwoma child is weaned, a number of drastic things happen all at once. He is suddenly moved from his mother's bed to one of his own. His father resumes sexual relations with his mother. Although the couple wait until their children are asleep, the intercourse takes place in the same room. Thus, the child may truly become aware of his replacement. He is now told that he can no longer have his mother's milk because some supernatural being needs it. This is vividly communicated to him by his mother when she puts a slug on her breasts and daubs the blood-colored sap of the breadfruit tree over her nipples. Finally he is no longer permitted to sit on his mother's lap. She resumes her work and goes to the garden to weed or to the swamp to gather sago flour leaving him behind for the first time in his life. That these events are traumatic to the child is not surprising. He varies between sadness and anger, weeping and violent temper tantrums.

It is our hypothesis that it is this series of events that makes it necessary, when the boy reaches adolescence, for the society to have an initiation rite of the type we have already described. It is necessary to put a final stop to (1) his wish to return to his mother's arms and lap, (2) to prevent an open revolt against his father who has displaced him from his mother's bed, and (3) to ensure identification with the adult males of the society. In other words, Kwoma infancy so magnifies the conditions which should produce Oedipus rivalry that the special cultural adjustment of ceremonial hazing, isolation from women, and symbolic castration, etc., must be made to resolve it.

If our analysis of the psychodynamics in Kwoma society is correct, societies with initiation rites should have similar child-rearing practices, whereas societies lacking the rite should also lack the exclusive mother-son sleeping arrangements and *post-partum* sexual taboo of the Kwoma.

TESTING THE HYPOTHESIS

To test this hypothesis a sample of 56 societies was selected. First, the ethnographic material on more than 150 societies was checked to determine whether or not there was an adequate description of our variables e.g., sleeping arrangements, *post-partum* sex taboo, and initiation rites at puberty. Only half of the societies reviewed fulfilled these conditions. Although we had initially endeavored to select our cases so as to have maximum distribution throughout the world, we found that some areas were represented by several societies, while others were not represented by any. To correct for any bias that might result from this sample, we made a further search of the ethnographic literature in order to fill in the gaps, and we thereby added several societies from areas previously not represented. Finally, to maximize diversity and to minimize duplication through selection of closely related societies, whenever there were two or more societies from any one culture area which had the same values on all our variables, we chose only one of them. Using these criteria, our final sample consisted of 56 societies representing 45 of the 60 culture areas designated by Murdock.[2]

The societies comprising our final sample range in size and type from small, simple, tribal groups to segments of large, complex civilizations such as the United States or Japan. In the latter case, our information has been drawn from ethnographic reports on a single delineated community.

When this sample had finally been chosen, the material relevant to our variables was first abstracted, and then judgments were made for each society as to the nature of the transition from boyhood to manhood, the sleeping arrangements, and the duration of the *post-partum* sex taboo. To prevent contamination, the judgments on each variable were made at different times and the name of the society disguised by a code. All judgments were made by at least two persons and in every case where there was a disagreement (less than 15 percent of the cases for any given variable), the data were checked by one of the authors, whose judgment was accepted as final. Our findings with respect to initiation rites have been tabulated in Table 1 below.

We discovered that only five societies out of the total number had sleeping arrangements similar to our own, that is, where the father and mother share a bed and the baby sleeps alone. In only three societies did the mother, the father, and the baby each have his or her own bed. In the remaining 48, the baby slept with his mother until he was at least a year old and generally until he was weaned. In 24 of the latter, however, the father also shared the bed, the baby generally sleeping between the mother and father. The remaining 24 societies had sleeping arrangements like the Kwoma in which the mother and child sleep in one bed and the father in another. Often the father's bed was not even in the same house. He either slept in a men's club house or in the hut of one of his other wives leaving mother and infant not only alone in the same bed but alone in the sleeping room.

Similarly, the societies of our sample were split on the rules regulating the resumption of sexual intercourse following parturition. Twenty-nine, like our own, have a brief taboo of a few weeks to permit the mother to recover from her delivery. In the remaining 27, the mother did not resume sexual intercourse

Table 1.
The Relationship Between Exclusive Mother-Son Sleeping Arrangements and a *Post-partum* Sex Taboo* and the Occurrence of Initiation Ceremonies at Puberty

Customs in infancy		Customs at adolescent initiation ceremonies		
Exclusive mother-son sleeping arrangements	*Post-partum* sex taboo	Absent	Present	
Long	Long		Azande	*hgs*[†]
			Canayura	*hs*
			Chagga	*hgs*
			Cheyenne	*ht*
			Chiricahua	*ht*
			Dahomeans	*hgs*
			Fijians	*gs*
			Jivaro	*ht*
		Ganda	Kwoma	*hgs*
		Khalapur (Rajput)	Lesu	*gs*
		Nyakyusa	Nuer	*hs*
		Tepoztlan	Samoans	*g*
		Trobrianders	Thonga	*hgs*
		Yapese	Tiv	*hgs*
	Short	Ashanti		
		Malaita	Cagaba	*ht*
		Siriono		
Short	Long	Araucanians	Kwakiutl	*s*
		Pilaga	Ojibwa	*t*
		Pondo	Ooldea	*hgs*
		Tallensi		
	Short	Atorese	Hopi	*hs*
		Balinese	Timbira	*hst*
		Droz		
		Egyptians (Silwa)		
		Eskimos (Copper)		
		French		
		Igorot (Bontoc)		
		Japanese (Suye Mura)		
		Koryak (Maritime)		
		Lakher		
		Lamba		
		Lapps		
		Lepcha		
		Maori		
		Mixtecans		
		Navaho		
		Ontong Javanese		
		Papago		
		Serbs		
		Tanala (Menabe)		
		Trukese		
		United States (Homestead)		
		Yagua		

*Both of a year or more duration.
[†]The letters following the tribal designations in the right-hand column indicate the nature of the ceremony—*h* = painful hazing, *g* = genital operations, *s* = seclusion from women, and *t* = tests of manliness.

for at least nine months after the birth of her child, and in one instance, the Cheyenne, the ideal period adhered to was reported as ten years. The duration of the taboo generally corresponded to the nursing period and in many cases was reinforced by the belief that sexual intercourse curdles or sours the mother's milk, thus making it harmful for the infant. In other societies, like the Kwoma, the taboo is explicitly for the purpose of ensuring a desired interval between children where adequate means of contraception are lacking. In these societies the taboo is terminated when the infant reaches some maturational stage, e.g., "until the child can crawl," "until the child can walk," or "until he can take care of himself." For the 27 societies that have this taboo, more than a few weeks long, the average duration is slightly more than two years.

RESULTS AT THE CULTURAL LEVEL

Our hypothesis may now be restated in cultural terms as follows: *Societies which have sleeping arrangements in which the mother and baby share the same bed for at least a year to the exclusion of the father and societies which have a taboo restricting the mother's sexual behavior for at least a year after childbirth will be more likely to have a ceremony of transition from boyhood to manhood than those societies where these conditions do not occur (or occur for briefer periods).* For the purposes of this hypothesis, transition ceremonies include only those ceremonies characterized by at least one of the following events: painful hazing of the initiates, isolation from females, tests of manliness, and genital operations.

The test of this hypothesis is presented in Table 1. It will be observed from this table that of the 20 societies where both antecedent variables are present, 14 have initiation ceremonies and only six do not. Where both antecedent variables are absent only two of the 25 societies have the ceremonies. Thus, over 80 percent of the 45 pure cases correspond with the prediction. Though our hypothesis was not designed for predicting the mixed cases, that is, where only one of the antecedent variables is present, it seems that they tended not to have the transition ceremonies.

Although the eight cases which are exceptional to our theory, the six in the upper left-hand column and the two in the lower right-hand column, may be simply misclassified through error of measurement, re-examination uncovers some other unanticipated factor which may account for their placement. This analysis turns out to be enlightening.

Reviewing, first the six cases in the upper left-hand column, that is, the societies which have both exclusive mother-son sleeping arrangements and a *post-partum* sex taboo but no initiation, we found that four of them (Khalapur, Trobrianders, Nyakusa, and Yapese) have an adjustment at adolescence which may serve as a psychological substitute for the initiation ceremony. The boys at this time leave the parental home and move to a men's house or a boys' village where they live until they are married. Malinowski observed this type of adjustment amongst the Trobrianders in 1927. He wrote:

> But the most important change, and the one which interests us most is the partial break-up of the family at the time when the adolescent boys and girls cease to be permanent inmates of the parental home . . . a special institution . . . special houses inhabited by groups of adolescent boys and girls. A boy as he reaches puberty will join such a house. . . . Thus the parent home is drained completely of its adolescent males, though until the boy's marriage he will always come back for food, and will also continue to work for his household to some extent. . . .
>
> At this stage, however, when the adolescent has to learn his duties, to be instructed in traditions and to study his magic, his arts and crafts, his interest in his mother's brother, who is his teacher and tutor, is greatest and their relations are at their best.[3]

This account suggests that this change of residence serves the same functions that we have posited for initiation ceremonies, for example, by establishing male authority, breaking the bond with the mother, and ensuring acceptance of the male role. It is important for our hypothesis, also, that there are only two other societies in our sample where such a change of residence occurs. One of these is the Malaita which has one but not both of our antecedent variables; the other is the Ashanti where the boy may move to the village of his mother's brother at or before puberty, but this is not mandatory and only half the boys do so. Thus, if we were to revise our hypothesis such that a change of residence was considered to be equivalent to initiation, the four societies mentioned should be moved over to the right-hand column and the exceptional cases would be reduced from eight to four.

Some comment should be made on the two remaining cases in the upper left-hand column. The Ganda are reported to have an interesting method of child rearing which may or may not be relevant to our theory. For the first three years of his life, a Ganda child sleeps exclusively with his mother and she is subject to a sexual taboo. At this point the boy is reported to be weaned and transferred to the household of his father's brother by whom he is brought up from then on. It might be assumed that this event would obviate the need for later ceremonial initiation into manhood. Since several other societies that do have initiation also have a change of residence at weaning, however, this simple explanation cannot be accepted and the Ganda must remain an unexplained exception. Finally Lewis[4] reports for the Tepoztlan that there was some disagreement among his informants as to the length of the taboo and exclusive sleeping arrangements. Since again there were other equally equivocal cases, we shall have to accept the verdict of our judges and let this case also remain an exception.

A reconsideration of the two exceptions in the lower right-hand column, the Hopi and the Timbira, which have the type of initiation into manhood required by our theory but have neither exclusive sleeping arrangements nor a prolonged *post partum* sex taboo, also turns out to be fruitful. In neither of these societies does the father have authority over the children. This is vested in the mother's brother who lives in another household. That these societies should have an initiation rite, again, does not seem to contradict our general theory, even though it does contradict our specific hypothesis. From clinical studies in our own society it is clear that even with the lack of exclusive sleeping arrangements and a minimal *post partum* sex taboo, an appreciable degree of dependence upon the mother and rivalry with the father is generated. The cases here suggest that, although these motives are not strong enough to require ceremonial initiation into manhood if the father is present in the household and has authority over the child, this may be required if he lacks such authority.

But what of the cases which have but one of the antecedent variables? Taking into account the societies with exclusive sleeping arrangements but no *post-partum* sex taboo, our theory predicts that these conditions should produce dependency and rivalry. However, since the mother is receiving sexual satisfaction from her husband, she has less need to obtain substitute gratification from nurturing her infant, so that the dependency she produces in her child would be less intense and the need for initiation should be attenuated. Three of the four cases with exclusive sleeping arrangements but no taboo appear to fulfill these conditions. As we have reported above, the Ashanti and the Malaita practice a change of residence which, it could be argued, is somewhat less drastic than initiation. In any case this is permissive and not required for the Ashanti. When the Cagaba boy reaches adolescence, he is given instruction in sexual intercourse by a priest and then sent to practise these instructions with a widow who lives with him temporarily in a specially built small hut. The boy is not allowed to leave this hut until he succeeds in having sexual intercourse with her. This trial is reported to be terrifying to the boy and it is often several days before he does succeed. This type of initiation, however, does not seem to compare with other societies which like the Thonga have a full-fledged ceremony. The Siriono, on the other hand, do not have any ceremonial recognition of the shift from boyhood to manhood and they must be regarded as an exception to our theory.

The final group of cases to consider are those that have a long *post-partum* sex taboo but not exclusive mother-son sleeping arrangements. For these, our theory would also predict an attenuated need for initiation ceremonies. Although the mothers of this group are presumed to gain substitute sexual gratification from being especially nurturant and loving toward their infants, they have less opportunity to do so than with those of societies where there are also exclusive sleeping arrangements.

As in the previous group of societies the ceremonies are, except for the Ooldea which will be discussed below, mild. The Kwakiutl have a ceremony which consists of a potlach given by the father for the son. There the boys undergo no hazing or genital operations but are secluded and expected to perform a dance. For the Ojibwa, the boy is expected to obtain a guardian spirit in a vision before he reaches maturity. Thus, generally when he is 11 or 12 years old, he goes alone into the forest where he stays often for several days without food, water, and generally without sleep until he either has a vision or returns home to recuperate before trying again. Again neither hazing nor genital operations are involved.

The Ooldea, a tribe situated in south-western Australia do, however, have a full-fledged initiation rite with hazing, isolation, and a very painful genital operation. This apparently runs counter to our assumption that the rites should be mild if only one determinant is present.

Radcliffe-Brown, however, reports that in many Australian tribes

> . . . the discipline of very young children is left to the mother and the other women of the horde. A father does not punish and may not even scold his infant children, but if they misbehave he will scold the mother and perhaps give her a blow with a stick. He regards the mother as responsible for misbehavior by very young children. When they are a little older, the father undertakes the education of the boys but leaves the education of the girls to the mother and the women of the horde. But the father behaves affectionately and is very little of a disciplinarian. Discipline for a boy begins when he approaches puberty and is exercised by the men of the horde. The big change comes with the initiation ceremonies when, in some tribes, the father, by a ceremonial (symbolic) action, hands over his son to the men who will carry out the initiation rites. During the initiation period of several years the boy is subjected to rigid and frequently painful discipline by men other than his father.[5]

If the Ooldea be one of those Australian tribes described above, they fall, along with the Trobrianders, Hopi, and Timbira, into the class of societies where the function of initiation is to make up for the lack of discipline exercised by a father over the boy during childhood.

A study of those societies without exclusive sleeping arrangements and with a long *post-partum* sex taboo which do not have the rites is interesting. In the first place both the Pondo and the Araucanians are reported to have had initiation ceremonies in the recent past, indicating that they are perhaps near the threshold of needing them. The Tallensi also are interesting. An observer notes that the Tallensi should have invented the Oedipus-conflict theory since they are quite open and conscious of the strong rivalry and hostility between father and son, a conflict which remains strong and dangerous, guarded only by ritualized forms of etiquette, until the father dies and the son takes his place. Furthermore, family fissions are reported to occur frequently and the oldest son often leaves the family to establish a new lineage of his own.

Thus, the presence of a *post-partum* sex taboo alone seems to produce tension, which these societies commonly seek to resolve through initiation ceremonies. Societies in this group which do not have ceremonies either had them recently or show evidence of unresolved tension.

Summary

The cross-cultural evidence indicates that:

1. A close relationship is established between mother and son during infancy as a consequence of either (a) their sleeping together for at least a year to the exclusion of the father or (b) the mother being prohibited from sexual intercourse for at least a year after the birth of her child or (c) both of these together have measurable consequences which are manifested in cultural adjustments at adolescence.

2. The cultural adjustments to the presence of the above factors are made when the boy approaches or reaches sexual maturity. These adjustments are either (a) a ceremony of initiation into manhood involving at least one and generally several of the following factors; painful *hazing* by the adult males of the society, tests of endurance and manliness, seclusion from women, and genital operations, or (b) a change of residence which involves separation of the boy from his mother and sisters and may also include some formal means for establishing male authority such as receiving instructions from and being required to be respectful to the mother's brother or the members of the men's house.
3. If both the factors specified in (1) are present, the consequences at adolescence tend to be more elaborate and severe than if only one is present.
4. The cultural adjustments specified in (2) also occur in societies where the father does not have the right to discipline his son, whether or not the conditions specified in (1) are present.

The evidence for these statements is summarized in Table 2.

THE SOCIOPSYCHOLOGICAL IMPLICATIONS

So much for the manifest results at the cultural level. But what is the most reasonable sociopsychological interpretation of these relationships? What are the psychodynamics involved? We are not concerned with the bizarre rites of the Thonga or the peculiar life of a Kwoma infant, for their own sakes, but rather in discovering some general truths about human nature. We, therefore, wish to state what we believe to be the underlying processes that are involved. These are processes that we have not directly observed and which must be accepted or rejected on the grounds of their plausibility or, more important, on the basis of further research implied by our theory.

We believe that six sociopsychological assumptions are supported by our findings:

Table 2.
The Relationship of Infancy Factors to Cultural Adjustments at Adolescence

Customs in infancy and childhood			Cultural adjustment of adolescence		
Authority of father over son	Exclusive mother-son sleeping arrangement	Post-partum sex taboo	None	Change of residence	Initiation ceremony
Present	Long	Long	2	3	14
		Short	1	2	1
	Short	Long	4	0	2
		Short	23	0	0
Absent			0	1	3

1. The more exclusive the relationship between a son and his mother during the first years of his life, the greater will be his emotional dependence upon her.
2. The more intensely a mother nurtures (loves) an infant during the early years of his life, the more emotionally dependent he will be upon her.
3. The greater the emotional dependence of a child upon a mother, the more hostile and envious he will be toward anyone whom he perceives as replacing him in her affection.
4. If a child develops a strong emotional dependence upon his mother during infancy, and hostility toward and envy of his father in early childhood at the time of weaning and the onset of independence training, these feelings (although latent during childhood) will manifest themselves when he reaches physiological maturity in (a) open rivalry with his father and (b) incestuous approaches to his mother, unless measures are taken to prevent such manifestations.
5. Painful hazing, enforced isolation from women, trials of endurance or manliness, genital operations, and change of residence are effective means for preventing the dangerous manifestation of rivalry and incest.
6. Even a moderate or weak amount of emotional dependence upon the mother and rivalry with the father will be dangerous at adolescence if the father has no right to (or does not in fact) exercise authority over his son during childhood.

If these sociopsychological hypotheses are true, they have some interesting implications for individual differences in our own society. It has long been known that there is an association between certain types of juvenile delinquency and broken homes. We would predict that the probability of a boy becoming delinquent in such instances would be highest where the separation of the mother and father occurred during the early infancy of the boy and where she remarried when he was two or three years old.

We would further predict that insofar as there has been an increase in juvenile delinquency in our society, it probably has been accompanied by an increase in the exclusiveness of mother-child relationships and/or a decrease in the authority of the father. It is not unreasonable that industrialization and urbanization have done just this, but, of course, this matter should be investigated before such an interpretation is accepted.

Finally, if further research shows that juvenile delinquency in our society is in part a function of the early childhood factors that have been described in this paper, then it can be countered either by decreasing the exclusiveness of the early mother-child relationship, increasing the authority of the father during childhood, or instituting a formal means of coping with adolescent boys functionally equivalent to those described in this paper. Change of residence would seem more compatible with the values of our society than an initiation ceremony. The Civilian Conservation Corps camps of the 1930's were an experiment which should provide useful data in this regard. The present institution of selective service would perhaps serve this purpose were the boys to be drafted at an earlier age and exposed to the authority of responsible adult males.

Notes

1. The following account is taken from Henri A. Junod, *The Life of a South African Tribe* (London: Macmillan & Co., Ltd., 1927), pp. 74–95.
2. G. P. Murdock, "World Ethnographic Sample," *Am. Anthropol.*, 1957, LIX, 664–687.
3. B. Malinowski, *Sex and Repression in Savage Society* (New York: Harcourt, Brace & Co., 1927), p. 67, 69.
4. O. Lewis, *Life in a Mexican Village: Tepoztlan Restudied* (Urbana: University of Illinois Press, 1951).
5. Cited from a letter by A. R. Radcliffe-Brown.

PEGGY REEVES SANDAY

The Socio-cultural Context of Rape: A Cross-cultural Study

In her comprehensive and important analysis of rape, Susan Brownmiller says that "when men discovered that they could rape, they proceeded to do it" and that "from prehistoric times to the present rape has played a critical function" (1975, p. 14–15). The critical function to which Brownmiller refers has been "to keep all women in a constant state of intimidation, forever conscious of the knowledge that the biological tool must be held in awe for it may turn to weapon with sudden swiftness borne of harmful intent" (1975, p. 209).

Brownmiller's attribution of violence to males and victimization to females strums a common theme in Western social commentary on the nature of human nature. Most of the popularizers of this theme present what amounts to a socio-biological view of human behavior which traces war, violence, and now rape to the violent landscape of our primitive ancestors, where, early on, the male tendency in these directions became genetically programmed in the fight for survival of the fittest. Human (viz. male) nature is conceived as an ever present struggle to overcome baser impulses bequeathed by "apish" ancestors.

The research described in the present paper departs from the familiar assumption that male nature is programmed for rape, and begins with another familiar, albeit less popular, assumption that human sexual behavior, though based in a biological need, "is rather a sociological and cultural force than a mere bodily

From *Journal of Social Issues*, Vol. 37, no. 4 (1981), pp. 5–27. Reprinted by permission of Blackwell publishers. References have been edited.

relation of two individuals." With this assumption in mind, what follows is an examination of the socio-cultural context of sexual assault and an attempt to interpret its meaning. By understanding the meaning of rape, we can then make conjectures as to its function. Is it, as Susan Brownmiller suggests, an act that keeps all women in a constant state of intimidation, or is it an act that illuminates a larger social scenario?

This paper examines the incidence, meaning, and function of rape in tribal societies. Two general hypotheses guided the research: first, the incidence of rape varies cross-culturally; second, a high incidence of rape is embedded in a distinguishably different cultural configuration than a low incidence of rape. Using a standard cross-cultural sample of 156 tribal societies, the general objectives of the paper are:

1. to provide a descriptive profile of "rape prone" and "rape free" societies;
2. to present an analysis of the attitudes, motivations, and socio-cultural factors related to the incidence of rape.

DESCRIPTION OF THE EVIDENCE

In most societies for which information on rape was available, rape is an act in which a male or a group of males sexually assaulted a woman. In a few cases, descriptions of women sexually assaulting a male or homosexual rape are reported. This study, however, was oriented exclusively to the analysis of rape committed by males against women.

The standard cross-cultural sample published by Murdock and White (1969) formed the basis for this research. This sample offers to scholars a representative sample of the world's known and well-described societies. The complete sample consists of 186 societies, each "pinpointed" to an identifiable sub-group of the society in question at a specific point in time. The time period for the sample societies ranges from 1750 B.C. (Babylonians) to the late 1960's. The societies included in the standard sample are distributed relatively equally among the following six major regions of the world: Sub-Saharan Africa, Circum-Mediterranean, East Eurasia, Insular Pacific, North America, South and Central America.

This analysis of rape was part of a larger study on the origins of sexual inequality. Due to the amount of missing information on the variables included in this larger study, thirty of the standard sample societies were excluded, reducing the final sample size to 156. Since many of the variables included in the larger study were pertinent to the analysis of the socio-cultural context of rape, the same sample was employed here.

The information for coding the variables came from codes published in the journal *Ethnology;* library materials; and the Human Relations Area Files. The data obtained from the latter two sources were coded by graduate students in anthropology at the University of Pennsylvania using codes developed by me on one-third of the standard sample societies. When the coding was completed, a random sample of societies was selected for checking. The percentage of items on which coders and checkers agreed averaged 88% of the 21 variables checked for each society. Disagreements were resolved either by myself or still another coder after rechecking the material.

There was a significant discrepancy between the number of societies for which information was obtained on rape for this study and that obtained by other authors employing the same sample. Broude and Greene (1976) were able to find information on the frequency of rape in only 34 of the standard sample societies, whereas for this study information was obtained for 95 of these societies. This discrepancy raises questions about the operational definitions of rape employed in the coding.

Although the codes used in the two studies were similar, my definition of "rape prone" included cases in which men rape enemy women, rape is a ceremonial act, and rape may be more a threat used by men to control women in certain ways than an actuality. Broude and Greene appear to have excluded such incidents from their coding and to have focused only on the intra-societal incidence of uncontrolled rape. The differences in these operational definitions are apparent from the information presented in Table 1.

A sub-sample of societies are listed in Table 1 along with the codes used in this study and the code given by Broude and Greene (1976). Broude and Greene report no information in nine societies where information on the incidence of rape was recorded in this study. The two codes agree in seven out of the remaining nine and disagree in two cases. Broude and Greene report that among the Azande rape is a rare occurrence while in this study the Azande were classified as rape prone due to the practice of raiding for wives. Broude and Greene report that rape is absent among the Omaha, whereas I found evidence from several sources that rape is present. The ethnographic descriptions which led to my rape codes for the eighteen societies listed in Table 1 can be found in the following sections profiling "rape prone" and "rape free" societies.

Broude and Greene (1976) find that rape is absent or rare in 59 percent of the 34 societies for which they found information on the frequency of rape (see Table 2). They say that rape is "common, not atypical" in the remaining 41 percent. In this study, forty-seven percent of the societies were classified as "rape free", 35 percent were classified in an intermediate category; and 18 percent were classified as "rape prone" (see Table 2). Thus both studies support the first general hypothesis of this study: sexual assault is not a universal characteristic of tribal societies. The incidence of rape varies cross-culturally.

PROFILES OF "RAPE PRONE" SOCIETIES

In this study a "rape prone" society was defined as one in which the incidence of rape is high, rape is a ceremonial act, or rape is an act by which men punish or threaten women.

An example of a "rape prone" society is offered by Robert LeVine's (1959) description of sexual offenses among the Gusii of southwestern Kenya. In the European legal system which administers justice in the District where the Gusii live, a

Table 1.
Comparison of Two Codes for Rape

Society #[a]	Society name	Sanday Code[b] Rape Code	Sanday Code[b] Type of rape[c]	Broude & Greene Code[b]
11	Kikuyu	3	Ceremonial rape	No information
19	Ashanti	1	Rape is rare or absent	No information
13	Mbuti	1	Rape is rare or absent	Agrees with Sanday Code
14	Mongo	1	Rape is rare or absent	Agrees with Sanday Code
28	Azande	3	Rape of enemy women Rape cases reported	Disagrees (Rape rare)
41	Tuareg	1	Rape is rare or absent	No information
60	Gond	1	Rape is rare or absent	No information
66	Mongols	1	Rape is rare or absent	No information
70	Lakher	1	Rape is rare or absent	Agrees with Sanday Code
91	Arunta	3	Ceremonial rape	No information
108	Marshallese	3	Gang rape is accepted	Agrees with Sanday Code
127	Saulteaux	3	Rape used as threat	No information
143	Omaha	3	Rape used as punishment	Disagrees (Rape absent)
158	Cuna	1	Rape is rare or absent	Agrees with Sanday Code
163	Yanomamo	3	Rape of enemy women	Agrees with Sanday Code
166	Mundurucu	3	Rape used as punishment	Agrees with Sanday Code
169	Jivaro	1	Rape is rare or absent	No information
179	Shavante	3	Rape used as punishment	No information

[a]Refers to standard sample number listed by Murdock and White (1969).
[b]See Table 2 for the two rape codes.
[c]For each of the societies listed, the ethnographic descriptions of the incidence of rape are presented later in this paper.

heterosexual assault is classified as rape when a medical examination indicates that the hymen of the alleged victim was recently penetrated by the use of painful force. When medical evidence is unobtainable, the case is classified as "indecent assault." Most cases are of the latter kind. The Gusii do not distinguish between rape and indecent assault. They use the following expressions to refer to heterosexual assault: "to fight" (a girl or woman); "to stamp on" (a girl or woman); "to spoil" (a girl or woman); "to engage in illicit intercourse." All of these acts are considered illicit by the Gusii. LeVine uses the term rape "to mean the culturally disvalued use of coercion by a male to achieve the submission of a female to sexual intercourse" (1959, p. 965).

Based on court records for 1955 and 1956 LeVine estimates that the annual rate of rape is 47.2 per 100,000 population. LeVine believes that this figure grossly underestimates the Gusii rape rate. During the same period the annual rape rate in urban areas of the United States was 13.85 per 100,000 (13.1 for rural areas). Thus, the rate of Gusii rape is extraordinarily high.

Normal heterosexual intercourse between Gusii males and females is conceived as an act in which a man overcomes the resistance of a woman and causes her pain. When a bride is unable to walk after her wedding night, the groom is

Table 2.
Cross-cultural Incidence of Rape

Sanday Code	No. and % of Societies		Broude & Greene (1976:417) Code	No. and % of Societies	
Incidence of Rape (RA4)—	N	%	Frequency of Rape	N	%
1. *Rape Free.* Rape is reported as rare or absent.	45	47%	1. Absent	8	24%
2. Rape is reported as present, no report of frequency, or suggestion that rape is not atypical.	33	35%	2. Rare: isolated cases	12	35%
3. Rape Prone. Rape is an accepted prac tice used to punish women, as part of a ceremony, or is *clearly* an act of moderate to high frequency carried out against own women or women of other societies.	17	18%	3. Common: not atypical	14	41%
Total	95	100%		34	100%

considered by his friends "a real man" and he is able to boast of his exploits, particularly if he has been able to make her cry. Older women contribute to the groom's desire to hurt his new wife. These women insult the groom, saying:

> "You are not strong, you can't do anything to our daughter. When you slept with her you didn't do it like a man. You have a small penis which can do nothing. You should grab our daughter and she should be hurt and scream—then you're a man" (LeVine, 1959, p. 969).

The groom answers boastfully:

> "I am a man! If you were to see my penis you would run away. When I grabbed her she screamed. I am not a man to be joked with. Didn't she tell you? She cried—ask her!" (LeVine, 1959, p. 969).

Thus, as LeVine says, (1959, p. 971) "legitimate heterosexual encounters among the Gusii are aggressive contests, involving force and pain-inflicting behavior." Under circumstances that are not legitimate, heterosexual encounters are classified as rape when the girl chooses to report the act.

LeVine estimates that the typical Gusii rape is committed by an unmarried young man on an unmarried female of a different clan. He distinguishes between three types of rape: rape resulting from seduction, premeditated sexual assault, and abduction (1959).

Given the hostile nature of Gusii sexuality, seduction classifies as rape when a Gusii female chooses to bring the act to the attention of the public. Premarital sex is forbidden, but this does not stop Gusii boys from trying to entice girls to intercourse. The standard pose of the Gusii girl is reluctance, which means that it is difficult for the boy to interpret her attitude as being either willing or unwilling. Misunderstandings between girl and boy can be due to the eagerness of the boy and his inability to perceive the girl's cues of genuine rejection, or to the girl's failure to make the signs of refusal in unequivocal fashion. The boy may discover the girl's unwillingness only after he has forced himself on her.

Fear of discovery may turn a willing girl into one who cries rape. If a couple engaging in intercourse out of doors is discovered, the girl may decide to save her reputation by crying out that she was being raped. Rape may also occur in cases when a girl has encouraged a young man to present her with gifts, but then denies him sexual intercourse. If the girl happens to be married, she rejects the boy's advances because she is afraid of supernatural sanctions against adultery. Out of frustration, the boy (who may not know that the girl is married) may resort to rape and she reports the deed.

In some cases one or more boys may attack a single girl in premeditated sexual assault. The boys may beat the girl badly and tear her clothing. Sometimes the girl is dragged off to the hut of one of them and forced into coitus. After being held for a couple of days the girl is freed. In these cases rupture of the hymen and other signs of attack are usually present.

The third type of rape occurs in the context of wife abduction. When a Gusii man is unable to present the bridewealth necessary for a normal marriage and cannot persuade a girl to elope, he may abduct a girl from a different clan. The man's friends will be enlisted to carry out the abduction. The young men are frequently rough on the girl, beating her and tearing her clothes. When she arrives at the home of the would-be lover, he attempts to persuade her to remain with him until bridewealth can be raised. Her refusal is ignored and the wedding night sexual contest is performed with the clansmen helping in overcoming her resistance.

Of these three types of rape, the first and third are unlawful versions of legitimate patterns. Seduction is accepted when kept within the bounds of discretion. Abduction is an imitation of traditional wedding procedures. Abduction lacks only the legitimizing bridewealth and the consent of the bride and her parents. In both of these cases LeVine says, "there is a close parallel between the criminal act and the law-abiding culture pattern to which it is related." Seduction and abduction classify as rape when the girl chooses to report the incident.

Data collected from the standard cross-cultural sample allows us to place the hostility characterizing Gusii heterosexual behavior in cross-cultural perspective. Broude and Greene (1976), who published codes for twenty sexual practices, find that male sexual advances are occasionally or typically hostile in one-quarter (26%) of the societies for which information was available. They found that males were typically forward in verbal (not physical) sexual overtures in forty percent of the societies, that females solicited or desired physical aggression in male sexual overtures in eleven percent of the societies, and that males did not make sexual overtures or were diffident or shy in twenty-three percent of the societies.

Examination of a variety of "rape prone" societies shows that the Gusii pattern of rape is found elsewhere but that it is by no means the only pattern which can be observed. For example, in several societies the act of rape occurs to signal readiness for marriage and is a ceremonial act. Since this act signifies male domination of female genitals, its occurrence was treated as a diagnostic criterion for classification as "rape prone."

Among the Kikuyu of East Africa it is reported that in former times, as part of initiation, every boy was expected to perform the act of ceremonial rape called *Kuihaka muunya* (to smear oneself with salt earth) in order to prove his manhood. It was thought that until a boy had performed the act of rape he could not have lawful intercourse with a Kikuyu woman and hence could not marry. During the initiation period boys would wander the countryside in bands of up to 100 in number. The object of each band was to find a woman on whom to commit the rape. The ideal woman was one from an enemy tribe who was married. In practice it appears that the ceremonial rape consisted of nothing more than masturbatory ejaculation on the woman's body or in her presence. Immediately after the act the boy was able to throw away the paraphernalia which marked him with the status of neophite.

Rape marks a girl as marriageable among the Arunta of Australia. At age 14 or 15 the Arunta girl is taken out into the bush by a group of men for the vulva cutting ceremony. A designated man cuts the girl's vulva after which she is gang raped by a group of men which does not include her future husband. When the ceremony is concluded the girl is taken to her husband and from then on no one else has the right of access to her.

In other rape prone societies, rape is explicitly linked to the control of women and to male dominance. Among the Northern Saulteaux the assumption of male dominance is clearly expressed in the expectation that a man's potential sexual rights over the woman he chooses must be respected. A woman who turns a man down too abruptly insults him and invites aggression. There is a Northern Saulteaux tale about a girl who was considered too proud because she refused to marry. Accordingly, a group of medicine men lured her out into the bush where she was raped by each in turn. Such tales provide women with a fairly good idea of how they should behave in relation to men.

The attitude that women are "open" for sexual assault is frequently found in the societies of the Insular Pacific. For example, in the Marshall Islands one finds the belief that "every woman is like a passage." Just as every canoe is permitted to sail from the open sea into the lagoon through the passage, so every man is permitted to have intercourse with every woman (except those who are excluded on account of blood kinship). A trader, well acquainted with the language and customs of one group of Marshall Islanders, reported the following incident. One day while standing at the trading post he saw 20 young men enter the bushes, one after another. Following the same path, he discovered a young girl stretched out on the ground, rigid and unconscious. When he accused the young men of cruel treatment they replied: "It is customary here for every young man to have intercourse with every girl" (Erdland, 1914, p. 98–99).

In tropical forest societies of South America and in Highland New Guinea it is fairly frequent to find the threat of rape used to keep women from the men's houses or from viewing male sacred objects. For example, Shavante women were strictly forbidden to observe male sacred ceremonies. Women caught peeking are threatened with man handling, rape, and disfigurement.

Perhaps the best known example of rape used to keep women away from male ritual objects is found in the description of the Mundurucu, a society well known to anthropologists due to the work of Robert and Yolanda Murphy. The Mundurucu believe that there was a time when women ruled and sex roles were reversed with the exception that women could not hunt. During that time, it is said, women were the sexual aggressors and men were sexually submissive and did women's work. Women controlled the "sacred trumpets" (the symbols of power) and the men's houses. The trumpets are believed to contain the spirits of the ancestors who demand ritual offering of meat. Since women did not hunt and could not make these offerings, men were able to take the trumpets from them, thereby establishing male dominance. The trumpets are secured in special chambers within the men's houses and no woman can see them under penalty of gang rape. Such a threat is necessary because men believe that women will attempt to seize from the men the power they once had. Gang rape is also the means by which men punish sexually "wanton" women (Murphy & Murphy, 1974).

Another expression of male sexual aggressiveness, which is classified as rape in this study, is the practice of sexually assaulting enemy women during warfare. The Yanomamo, described by Napoleon Chagnon and Marvin Harris, are infamous for their brutality toward women. The Yanomamo, according to Harris (1977), "practice an especially brutal form of male supremacy involving polygyny, frequent wife beating, and gang rape of captured enemy women." The Yanomamo, Harris says, "regard fights over women as the primary causes of their wars" (1977, p. 69). Groups raid each other for wives in an area where marriageable women are in short supply due to the practice of female infanticide. The number of marriageable women is also affected by the desire on the part of successful warriors to have several wives to mark their superior status as "fierce men." A shortage of women for wives also motivates Azande (Africa) warfare. Enemy women were taken by Azande soldiers as wives. Evans-Pritchard calls these women "slaves of war" and says that they were "not regarded very differently from ordinary wives, their main disability being that they had no family or close kin to turn to in times of trouble" (1971, p. 251). The absence of close kin, of course, made these women more subservient and dependent on their husbands.

Another source on the Azande discusses how the act of rape when committed against an Azande woman is treated. If the women is not married, this source reports, the act is not treated as seriously. If the woman is married, the rapist can be put to death by the husband. If the rapist is allowed to live, he may be judged guilty of adultery and asked to pay the chief 20 knives (the commonly used currency in marriage exchanges) and deliver a wife to the wronged husband. This source indicates that the rape of a woman is not permitted but the punishments are established, suggesting that rape is a frequent occurrence (Lagae, 1926).

Among some American Indian buffalo hunters, it is not uncommon to read that rape is used as a means to punish adultery. There is a practice among the Cheyenne of the Great Plains known as "to put a woman on the prairie." This means that the outraged husband of an adulterous woman invites all the unmarried members of his military society to a feast on the prairie where they each rape the woman. Among the Omaha, a woman with no immediate kin who commits adultery may be gang raped and abandoned by her husband. Mead reports that the Omaha considered a "bad woman" fair game for any man. No discipline, no set of standards, other than to be cautious of an avenging father or brother and to observe the rule of exogamy, Mead says, kept young men from regarding rape as a great adventure. Young Omaha men, members of the Antler society, would prey upon divorced women or women considered loose (Mead, 1932).

Summarizing, a rape prone society, as defined here, is one in which sexual assault by men of women is either culturally allowable or, largely overlooked. Several themes interlink the above descriptions. In all, men are posed as a social group against women. Entry into the adult male or female group is marked in some cases by rituals that include rape. In other cases, rape preserves the ceremonial integrity of the male group and signifies its status vis-a-vis women. The theme of women as property is suggested when the aggrieved husband is compensated for the rape of his wife by another man, or when an adulterous woman is gang raped by her husband and his unmarried compatriots. In these latter cases, the theme of the dominant male group is joined with a system of economic exchange in which men act as exchange agents and women comprise the medium of exchange. This is not to say that rape exists in all societies in which there is ceremonial induction into manhood, male secret societies, or compensation for adultery. For further illumination of the socio-cultural context of rape we can turn to an examination of rape free societies.

PROFILES OF "RAPE FREE" SOCIETIES

Rape free societies are defined as those where the act of rape is either infrequent or does not occur. Forty-seven percent of the societies for which information on the incidence or presence of rape was available (see Table 2) were classified in the rape free category. Societies were classified in this category on the basis of the following kinds of statements found in the sources used for the sample societies.

Among the Taureg of the Sahara, for example, it is said that "rape does not exist, and when a woman refuses a man, he never insists nor will he show himself jealous of a more successful comrade" (Blanguernon, 1955, p. 134). Among the Pygmies of the Ituri forest in Africa, while a boy may rip off a girl's outer bark cloth, if he can catch her, he may never have intercourse with her without her permission. Turnbull (1965), an anthropologist who lived for some time among the Pygmies and became closely identified with them, reports that he knew of no cases of rape. Among the Jivaro of South America rape is not recognized as such, and informants could recall no case of a woman violently resisting sexual intercourse. They say that a man would never commit such an act if the woman resisted, because she would tell her family and they would punish him. Among the Nkundo Mongo of Africa it is said that rape in the true sense of the word—that is, the abuse of a woman by the use of violence—is most unusual. If a woman does not consent, the angry seducer leaves her, often insulting her to the best of his ability. Rape is also unheard of among the Lakhers, and in several villages the anthropologist was told that there had never been a case of rape.

Other examples of statements leading to the classification of rape free are listed as follows:

> Cuna (South America), "Homosexuality is rare, as is rape. Both . . . are regarded as sins, punishable by God" (Stout, 1947, p. 39).
>
> Khalka Mongols (Outer Mongolia), "I put this question to several well-informed Mongols:—what punishment is here imposed for rape? . . . one well-educated lama said frankly: "We have no crimes of this nature here. Our women never resist." (Maiskii, 1921, p. 98).
>
> Gond (India), "It is considered very wrong to force a girl to act against her will. Such cases of ghotul-rape are not common . . . If then a boy forces a girl against her will, and the others hear of it, he is fined" (Elwin, 1947, p. 656).

The above quotes may obscure the actual incidence of rape. Such quotes, leading to the classification of societies as "rape free," achieve greater validity when placed within the context of other information describing heterosexual interaction.

There is considerable difference in the character of heterosexual interaction in societies classified as "rape prone" when compared with those classified as "rape free." In "rape free" societies women are treated with considerable respect, and prestige is attached to female reproductive and productive roles. Interpersonal violence is minimized, and a people's attitude regarding the natural environment is one of reverence rather than one of exploitation. Turnbull's description of the Mbuti Pygmies, of the Ituri forest in Africa, provides a prototypical profile of a "rape free" society (1965).

Violence between the sexes, or between anybody, is virtually absent among the net hunting Mbuti Pygmies when they are in their forest environment. The Mbuti attitude toward the forest is reflective of their attitude toward each other. The forest is addressed as "father," "mother," "lover," and "friend." The Mbuti say that forest is everything—the provider of food, shelter, warmth, clothing, and affection. Each person and animal is endowed with some spiritual power which "derives from a single source whose physical manifestation is the forest itself." The ease of the Mbuti relationship to their environment is reflected in the relationship between the sexes. There is little division of labor by sex. The hunt is frequently a joint effort. A man is not ashamed to pick mushrooms and nuts if he finds them, or to wash and clean a baby. In general, leadership is minimal and there is no attempt to control, or to dominate, either the geographical or human environment. Decision-making is by common consent; men and women have equal say because hunting and gathering are both important to the economy. The forest is the only recognized authority of last resort. In decision making, diversity of opinion may be expressed, but prolonged disagreement is considered to be "noise" and offensive to the forest. If husband and wife disagree, the whole camp may act to mute their antagonism, lest the disagreement become too disruptive to the social unit (see Turnbull, 1965).

The essential details of Turnbull's idyllic description of the Mbuti are repeated in other "rape free" societies. The one outstanding feature of these societies is the ceremonial importance of women and the respect accorded the contribution women make to social continuity, a respect which places men and women in relatively balanced power spheres. This respect is clearly present among the Mbuti and in more complex "rape free" societies.

In the West African kingdom of Ashanti, for example, it is believed that only women can contribute to future generations. Ashanti women say:

> I am the mother of the man. . . . I alone can transmit the blood to a king. . . . If my sex die in the clan then that very clan becomes extinct, for be there one, or one thousand male members left, not one can transmit the blood, and the life of the clan becomes measured on this earth by the span of a man's life (Rattray, 1923, p. 79).

The importance of the feminine attributes of growth and reproduction are found in Ashanti religion and ritual. Priestesses participate with priests in all major rituals. The Ashanti creation story emphasizes the complementarity and inseparability of male and female. The main female deity, the Earth Goddess, is believed to be the receptacle of past and future generations as well as the source of food and water. (Rattray, 1923, 1927). The sacred linkage of earth-female-blood makes the act of rape incongruous in Ashanti culture. Only one incident of rape is reported by the main ethnographer of the Ashanti. In this case the man involved was condemned to death.

In sum, rape free societies are characterized by sexual equality and the notion that the sexes are complementary. Though the sexes may not perform the same duties or have the same rights or privileges, each is indispensable to the activities of the other. The key to understanding the relative absence of rape in rape free as opposed to rape prone societies is the importance, which in some cases is sacred, attached to the contribution women make to social continuity. As might be expected, and as will be demonstrated below, interpersonal violence is uncommon in rape free societies. It is not that men are necessarily prone to rape; rather, where interpersonal violence is a way of life, violence frequently achieves sexual expression.

APPROACHES TO THE ETIOLOGY OF RAPE

Three general approaches characterize studies of the etiology of rape. One approach focuses on the broader socio cultural milieu, another turns to individual characteristics. The first looks at how rapists act out the broader social script, the second emphasizes variables like the character of parental-child interaction. A third approach, which may focus on either individual or social factors, is distinguishable by the assumption that male sexual repression will inevitably erupt in the form of sexual violence. These approaches, reviewed briefly in this section, guided the empirical analysis of the socio-cultural context of rape in tribal societies.

Based on his study of the Gusii, LeVine (1959) hypothesizes that four factors will be associated with the incidence of rape cross-culturally:

1. severe formal restrictions on the nonmarital sexual relations of females;
2. moderately strong sexual inhibitions on the part of females;
3. economic or other barriers to marriage that prolong the bachelorhood of some males into their late twenties;
4. the absence of physical segregation of the sexes.

The implicit assumption here is that males who are denied sexual access to women, will obtain access by force unless men are separated from women. Such an assumption depicts men as creatures who cannot control their sexual impulses, and women as the unfortunate victims.

LeVine's profile of the Gusii suggests that broader social characteristics are related to the incidence of rape. For example, there is the fact that marriage among the Gusii occurs almost always between feuding clans. The Gusii have a proverb which states "Those whom we marry are those whom we fight" (1959, p. 966). The close correspondence between the Gusii heterosexual relationship and intergroup hostilities suggests the hypothesis that the nature of intergroup relations is correlated with the nature of the heterosexual relationship and the incidence of rape.

The broader approach to the etiology of rape is contained in Susan Brownmiller's contention that rape is the means by which men keep women in a state of fear. This contention is certainly justified in societies where men use rape as a threat to keep women from viewing their sacred objects (the symbol of power) or rape is used to punish women. In societies like the Mundurucu, the ideology of male dominance is upheld by threatening women with rape. Just as the quality of intergroup relations among the Gusii is reflected in heterosexual relations, one could suggest that the quality of interpersonal relations is reflected in the incidence of rape. In societies where males are trained to be dominant and interpersonal relations are marked by outbreaks of violence, one can predict that females may become the victims in the playing out of the male ideology of power and control.

A broader socio-cultural approach is also found in the work of Wolfgang & Ferracuti (1967) and Amir (1971). Wolfgang & Ferracuti present the concept of the subculture of violence which is formed of those from the lower classes and the disenfranchised. The prime value is the use of physical aggression as a demonstration of masculinity and toughness. In his study of rape, Amir placed the rapist "squarely within the subculture of violence." Rape statistics in Philadelphia showed that in 43% of the cases examined, rapists operated in pairs or groups. The rapists tended to be in the 15–19 age bracket, the majority were not married, and 90% belonged to the lower socio-economic class and lived in inner city neighborhoods where there was also a high degree of crime against the person. In addition, 71% of the rapes were planned. In general, the profile presented by Amir is reminiscent of the pattern of rape found among the Kikuyu, where a band of boys belonging to a guild roamed the country side in search of a woman to gang rape as a means of proving their manhood and as a prelude to marriage. Brownmiller summarizes Amir's study with the following observations:

> Like assault, rape is an act of physical damage to another person, and like robbery it is also an act of acquiring property: the intent is to "have" the female body in the acquisitory meaning of the term. A woman is perceived by the rapist both as hated person and desired property. Hostility against her and possession of her may be simultaneous motivations, and the hatred for her is expressed in the same act that is the attempt to "take" her against her will. In one violent crime, rape is an act against person and property.

The importance of the work of Wolfgang and Ferracuti, Amir, and Brownmiller's observations lies in demonstrating that rape is linked with an overall pattern of violence and that part of this pattern includes the concept of woman as property. From the short descriptions of rape in some of the societies presented above, it is clear rape is likely to occur in what I would call, to borrow from Wolfgang, cultures of violence. Rape prone societies, as noted, are likely to include payment to the wronged husband, indicating that the concept of women as property also exists. This concept is not new to anthropology. It has been heavily stressed in the work of Levi-Strauss who perceives tribal women as objects in an elaborate exchange system between men.

The second type of approach to the understanding of rape focuses on the socialization process and psychoanalytic variables. This approach is reflected in the following quote from the conclusions of David Abrahamsen who conducted a Rorschach study on the wives of eight convicted rapists in 1954. Abrahamsen (1960, p. 165) says:

> The conclusions reached were that the wives of the sex offenders on the surface behaved toward men in a submissive and masochistic way but latently denied their femininity and showed an aggressive masculine orientation; they unconsciously invited sexual aggression, only to respond to it with coolness and rejection. They stimulated their husbands into attempts to prove themselves, attempts which necessarily ended in frustration and increased their husbands' own doubts about their masculinity. In doing so, the wives unknowingly continued the type of relationship the offender had had with his mother. There can be no doubt that the sexual frustration which the wives caused is one of the factors motivating rape, which might be tentatively described as a displaced attempt to force a seductive but rejecting mother into submission.

Brownmiller (1975, p. 179) includes this quote in her analysis of policeblotter rapists and her reaction to it is rather interesting. She rejects Abrahamsen's conclusions because they place the burden of guilt not on the rapist but on his mother and wife. The fact of the matter is that dominance cannot exist without passivity, as sadism cannot exist without masochism. What makes men sadistic and women masochistic, or men dominant and women passive, must be studied as part of an overall syndrome. Abrahamsen's conclusions certainly apply to Gusii males and females. With respect to the way in which Gusii wives invite sexual aggression from their husbands consider the following description of various aspects of Gusii nuptials:

> . . . , the groom in his finery returns to the bride's family where he is stopped by a crowd of women who deprecate his physical appearance. Once he is in the house of the bride's mother and a sacrifice has been performed by the marriage priest, the women begin again, accusing the groom of impotence on the wedding night and claiming that his penis is too small to be effective. . . . When the reluctant bride arrives at the groom's house, the matter of first importance is the wedding night sexual performance. . . . The bride is determined to put her new husband's sexual competence to the most severe test possible. She may take magical measures which are believed to result in his failure in intercourse. . . . The bride usually refuses to get onto the bed; if she did not resist the groom's advances she would be thought sexually promiscuous. At this point some of the young men may forcibly disrobe her and put her on the bed. . . . As he proceeds toward sexual intercourse she continues to resist and he must force her into position. Ordinarily she performs the practice known as *ogotega,* allowing him between her thighs but keeping the vaginal muscles so tense that penetration is impossible. . . . Brides are said to take pride in the length of time they can hold off their mates (LeVine, 1959, pp. 967–969).

The relations between parents and children among the Gusii also fit Abrahamsen's conclusions concerning the etiology of rape. The son has a close and dependent relationship with his mother. The father is aloof from all his children, but especially his daughters. The father's main function is to punish which means that for the Gusii girl, her early connection with men is one of avoidance and fear. On the other hand, the relationship of the Gusii boy with his mother is characterized by dependence and seduction.

Studies of the etiology of rape suggest several hypotheses that can be tested cross-culturally. These hypotheses are not opposed; they are stated at different explanatory levels. One set phrases the explanation in socio-cultural terms, the other in psycho-cultural terms. Still another, only touched on above, suggests that male sexuality is inherently explosive unless it achieves heterosexual outlet. This latter assumption, implicit in LeVine's hypotheses mentioned above, also draws on the notion, most recently expressed in the work of Stoller (1979), that sexual excitement is generated by the desire, overt or hidden, to harm another. If the latter were the case, we would be led to believe that rape would exist in all societies. The argument presented here, however, suggests that rape is an enactment not of human nature, but of socio-cultural forces. Thus, the prevalence of rape should be associated with the expressions of these forces. Some of these expressions and their correlation with the incidence of rape are examined in the next section.

SOCIO-CULTURAL CORRELATES OF RAPE

Four general hypotheses are suggested by the work of LeVine, Brownmiller, Abrahamsen, Wolfgang and Amir. These hypotheses are:

1. Sexual repression is related to the incidence of rape;
2. intergroup and interpersonal violence is enacted in male sexual violence;
3. the character of parent-child relations is enacted in male sexual violence;
4. rape is an expression of a social ideology of male dominance.

These hypotheses were tested by collecting data on: variables relating to childrearing; behavior indicating sexual repression; interpersonal and intergroup violence; sexual separation; glorification of the male role and an undervaluation of the female role.

The relevant variables are listed in Table 3 along with the correlation of each with the incidence of rape (see Table 4 for variable codes). The correlations presented in Table 3 support all but the first of the general hypotheses listed above. There is no significant correlation between variables measuring sexual repression and the incidence of rape. Admittedly, however, sexual repression is very difficult to measure. The variables presented in Table 3 may not, in fact, be related to sexual abstinence. These variables are: length of the post-partum sex taboo (a variable

Table 3.
Correlates of Rape

Variables Related to Sexual Repression[a]	Correlation with Incidence of Rape (RA4)[b]
1. Length of the post-partum sex taboo (Inf 10)	NS
2. Attitude toward pre-marital sex (Psex)	NS
3. Age at marriage for males (Agem)	NS
4. No. of taboos reflecting male avoidance of female sexuality (All)	NS
Variables Related to Intergroup and Interpersonal Violence	
5. Raiding other groups for wives (Wie)	r = –.29 (N = 83, p = .004)
6. Degree of Interpersonal violence (Viol)	r = .47 (N = 90, p = .000)
7. Ideology of Male Toughness (Macho)	r = –.42 (N = 73, p = .000)
8. War	r = .21 (N = 86, p = .03)
Variables Related to Childrearing	
9. Character of father-daughter relationships (Fada)	r = –.20 (N = 65, p = .06)
10. Proximity of father in care of infants (Inf 23)	r = –.16 (N = 83, p = .08)
11. Character of mother-son relationships (Moso)	NS
Variables Related to Ideology of Male Dominance	
12. Female power and authority (Stat)	r = –.22 (N = 83, p = .03)
13. Female political decision making (HO5)	r = –.33 (N = 88, p = .001)
14. Attitude toward women as citizens (HO8)	r = –.28 (N = 84, p = .005)
15. Presence of special places for men (Mho)	r = –.26 (N = 71, p = .01)
16. Presence of special places for women (Fho)	r = –.17 (N = 70, p = .08)

[a]Codes for variables are presented in Table 4.
[b]Code presented in Table 2. Correlation coefficient is Pearson r.

Table 4.
Variable Codes for Correlations Listed in Table 3

1. Inf 10: 1 = intercourse after birth → 7 = intercourse after more than 2 yrs.
2. Psex: 1 = premarital sex expected → 6 = strongly disapproved.
3. Agem: 1 = men marry around puberty → 3 = 25 yrs. or older.
4. All: 0 = no taboos reflecting male avoidance of intercourse → 3 = 3 taboos.
5. Wie: 1 = Wives taken from hostile groups → 2 = practice absent.
6. Viol: 1 = interpersonal violence mild or absent → 3 = strong.
7. Macho: 1 = ideology of male toughness present → 2 = absent.
8. War: 1 = war reported or absent or occasional → 2 = frequent or endemic.
9. Fada: 1 = fathers affectionate with daughters → 2 = aloof, cold.
10. Inf 23: 1 = no close proximity between fathers and infants → 5 = regular, close proximity.
11. Moso: 1 = mothers affectionate with sons → 2 = aloof, cold.
12. Stat: 1 = no female political or economic power → 6 = females have political and economic pow-
13. HO5: 0 = females have no influence—public decision making → 1 = females have influence.
14. HO8: 1 = males express contempt for women or citizens → 4 = women are respected as citizens.
15. Mho: places where males congregate alone are present → 2 = absent.
16. Fho: 1 = places where females congregate alone are present → 2 = absent.

*This variable forms a Guttman Scale. See Sanday (1981) for scale properties.

which indicates how long the mother abstains from sexual intercourse after the birth of a child); attitude toward premarital sex (a variable which ranges between the disapproval and approval of premarital sex); age at marriage for males; and the number of taboos reflecting male avoidance of female sexuality.

The correlations presented in Table 3 support the hypothesis that intergroup and interpersonal violence is enacted in sexual violence against females. Raiding other groups for wives is significantly associated with the incidence of rape. The intensity of interpersonal violence in a society is also positively correlated with the incidence of rape, as is the presence of an ideology which encourages men to be tough and aggressive. Finally, when warfare is reported as being frequent or endemic (as opposed to absent or occasional) rape is more likely to be present.

The character of relations between parents and children is not strongly associated with the incidence of rape. When the character of the father-daughter relationship is primarily indifferent, aloof, cold and stern, rape is more likely to be present. The same is true when fathers are distant from the care of infants. However, there is no relationship between the nature of the mother-son tie (as measured in this study) and the incidence of rape.

There is considerable evidence supporting the notion that rape is an expression of a social ideology of male dominance. Female power and authority is lower in rape prone societies. Women do not participate in public decision making in these societies and males express contempt for women as decision makers. In addition, there is greater sexual separation in rape prone societies as indicated by the presence of structures or places where the sexes congregate in single sex groups.

The correlates of rape presented in Table 3 strongly suggest that rape is the playing out of a socio-cultural script in which the expression of personhood for males is directed by, among other things, interpersonal violence and an ideology of toughness. If we see the sexual act as the ultimate emotional expression of the self, then it comes as no surprise that male sexuality is phrased in physically aggressive terms when other expressions of self are phrased in these terms. This explanation does not rule out the importance of the relationship between parents and children, husbands and wives. Raising a violent son requires certain behavior patterns in parents, behaviors that husbands may subsequently act out as adult males. Sexual repression does not explain the correlations presented in Table 3. Rape is not an instinct triggered by celibacy, enforced for whatever reason. Contrary to what some social scientists assume, men are not animals whose sexual behavior is programmed by instinct. Men are human beings whose sexuality is biologically based and culturally encoded.

CONCLUSION

Rape in tribal societies is part of a cultural configuration that includes interpersonal violence, male dominance, and sexual separation. In such societies, as the Murphys (1974, p. 197) say about the Mundurucu: "men . . . use the penis to dominate their women." The question remains as to what motivates the rape prone cultural configuration. Considerable evidence (see Sanday, 1981) suggests that this configuration evolves in societies faced with depleting food resources, migration, or other factors contributing to a dependence on male destructive capacities as opposed to female fertility.

In tribal societies women are often equated with fertility and growth, men with aggression and destruction. More often than not, the characteristics associated with maleness and femaleness are equally valued. When people perceive an imbalance between the food supply and population needs, or when populations are in competition for diminishing resources, the male role is accorded greater prestige. Females are perceived as objects to be controlled as men struggle to retain or to gain control of their environment. Behaviors and attitudes prevail that separate the sexes and force men into a posture of proving their manhood. Sexual violence is one of the ways in which men remind themselves that they are superior. As such, rape is part of a broader struggle for control in the face of difficult circumstances. Where men are in harmony with their environment, rape is usually absent.

The insights garnered from the cross-cultural study of rape in tribal societies bear on the understanding and treatment of rape in our own. Ours is a heterogeneous society in which more men than we like to think feel that they do not have mastery over their destiny and who learn from the script provided by nightly television that violence is a way of achieving the material rewards that all Americans expect. It is important to understand that violence is socially and not biologically programmed. Rape is not an integral part of male nature, but the means by which men programmed for violence express their sexual selves. Men who are conditioned to respect the female virtues of growth and the sacredness of life, do not violate women. It is significant that in societies where nature is held sacred, rape occurs only rarely. The incidence of rape in our society will be reduced to the extent that boys grow to respect women and the qualities so often associated with femaleness in other societies—namely, nurturance, growth, and nature. Women can contribute to the socialization of boys by making these respected qualities in their struggle for equal rights.

References

Abrahamsen, D. *The psychology of crime.* New York: Columbia University Press, 1960.

Amir, M. *Patterns in forcible rape.* Chicago, IL: University of Chicago Press, 1971.

Blanguernon, C. *Le hogger (The Hogger).* Paris: B. Arthaud, 1955 (Translated from the French for the Human Relations Area Files by Thomas Turner).

Broude, G. J. & Greene, S. J. Cross-cultural codes on twenty sexual attitudes and practices. *Ethnology,* 1976, 15(4), 409–430.

Brownmiller, S. *Against our will.* New York: Simon & Schuster, 1975.

Elwin, V. *The muria and their ghotal.* Bombay: Geoffrey Cumberlege, Oxford University Press, 1947.

Erdland, P. A. *Die Marshall-insulaner (The Marshall islanders).* Munster: Anthropos Bibliotek Ethnological Monographs 1914, 2(1). (Translated by Richard Neuse for Human Relations Area Files).

Evans-Pritchard, E. E. *The Azande.* London: Oxford University Press, 1971.

Harris, M. *Cannibals and kings.* New York: Vintage/Random House, 1977.

Lagae, C. R. Les Azande ou Niam Niam. *Biblioteque—Congo* (Vol. 18). Brussels: Vromant & Co., 1926. (Translated for Human Relations Area Files, New Haven, CT: HRAF.)

LeVine R. A. Gusii sex offenses: A study in social control. *American Anthropologist,* 1959, 61, 965–990.

Maiskii, I. *Sovremennaia Mongolia (Contemporary Mongolia).* Irkutsk: Gosudarstvennoe Izdatel'stvo, Irkutskoe Otedelenie, 1921. (Translated from the Russian for Human Relations Area Files by Mrs. Dayton and J. Kunitz).

Maybury-Lewis, D. *Akwe—Shavante society.* Oxford: Clarendon Press, 1967.

Mead, M. *The changing culture of an indian tribe.* New York: Columbia University Press, 1932.

Murdock, G. P. & White, D. R. Standard cross-cultural sample. *Ethnology,* 1969, 8, 329–369.

Murphy Y. & Murphy, R. *Women of the forest.* New York: Columbia University Press, 1974.

Rattray, R. S. *Ashanti.* Oxford: Clarendon Press, 1923.

Rattray, R. S. *Religion and art in Ashanti.* Oxford: Clarendon Press, 1927.

Sanday, P. R. *Female power and male dominance: On the origins of sexual inequality.* New York: Cambridge University Press, 1981.

Stoller, R. J. *Sexual excitement.* New York: Pantheon Books, 1979.

Stout, D. B. *San Blas Cura accultation.* New York: Viking Fund Publications in Anthropology, 1947, *9.*

Turnbull, C. *Wayward servants.* New York: Natural History Press, 1965.

Wolfgang, M. E. & Ferracuti, F. *The subculture of violence.* London: Tavistock, 1967.

PART 3 THE PSYCHOLOGY OF SEX ROLES

Even if biology were destiny, the founder of psychoanalysis Sigmund Freud argued, the process by which biological males and females become gendered men and women happens neither naturally nor inevitably. Gender identity, he argued, is an achievement—the outcome of a struggle for boys to separate from their mothers and identify with their fathers, and of a parallel and complementary struggle for girls to reconcile themselves to their sexual inadequacy and therefore maintain their identification with their mothers.

Subsequent generations of psychologists have attempted to specify the content of that achievement of gender identity, and how it might be measured. In the early 1930s, Lewis Terman, one of the country's most eminent social psychologists, codified gender identity into a set of attitudes, traits, and behaviors that enabled researchers to pinpoint exactly where any young person was on a continuum between masculinity and femininity. If one had successfully acquired the "appropriate" collection of traits and attitudes, one (and one's parents) could rest assured that one would continue to develop "normally." Gender nonconformity—boys who scored high on the femininity side of the continuum, or girls who scored high on the masculine side—was a predictor, Terman argued, for sexual nonconformity. Homosexuality was the sexual behavioral outcome of a gender problem, of men who had not successfully mastered masculinity or women who had not successfully mastered femininity.

Though its origins lie in Freudian understandings of how the child acquires gender identity, this notion, that one can "read" sexuality, that is, know whether someone is heterosexual or homosexual by the way he or she enacts gender, has become a staple in American popular culture. Many contemporary psychologists have been uncomfortable with the ways in which traditional psychoanalytic models of gender identity and sexual orientation reproduced male domination and the "deviantization" of homosexuality as the outcome of gender problems. Kay Deaux and Brenda Major offer a psychodynamic perspective on gender difference that corrects the implicit problematization of female development, and stresses the ways in which gender inequality is part of gender socialization. Daryl Bem offers a more dynamic understanding that explains the origins of sexual orientation not through gender nonconformity, but through a process by which the child comes to eroticize what is different from his or her own sense of self. Far less normative than Terman or Freud—who believed that homosexuality was a problem to be explained by familial psychodynamics—Bem offers no value judgments about the person's eventual sexual orientation, but offers a psychological model of how he or she acquires it.

LEWIS TERMAN AND CATHARINE COX MILES

Sex and Personality: Studies in Masculinity and Femininity

We may now consider two questions to which the present findings give rise: (1) Can we extract from them a single prime principle of sex difference at once not too vague to be ambiguous, and not so particular as to be insignificant? (2) What, so far as our evidence goes, appears to be the relation of the differences we have enumerated to nature and nurture, to endowment and environment? We shall take these questions in succession.

1. *Is there one dominant principle?*

It is obvious that from whatever point we have started, whether from the knowledge shown by the sexes or from their associations or their likes and dislikes for people, vocations, pastimes, books, or objects of travel; or whether we have explored directly or deviously their emotions, tastes, opinions, and inner experiences, we have found ourselves arriving at much the same conclusions—all our ways have led to Rome. But the final scene has two aspects—two sides of the same picture—one showing differences in the direction of interest, the other differences in the direction of emotions and impulses.

From whatever angle we have examined them the males included in the standardization groups evinced a distinctive interest in exploit and adventure, in outdoor and physically strenuous occupations, in machinery and tools, in science, physical phenomena, and inventions; and, from rather occasional evidence, in business and commerce. On the other hand, the females of our groups have evinced a distinctive interest in domestic affairs and in aesthetic objects and occupations; they have distinctively preferred more sedentary and indoor occupations, and occupations more directly ministrative, particularly to the young, the helpless, the distressed. Supporting and supplementing these are the more subjective differences—those in emotional disposition and direction. The males directly or indirectly manifest the greater self-assertion and aggressiveness; they express more hardihood and fearlessness, and more roughness of manners, language, and sentiments. The females express themselves as more compassionate and sympathetic, more timid, more fastidious and aesthetically sensitive, more emotional in general (or at least more expressive of the four emotions considered), severer moralists, yet admit in themselves more weaknesses in emotional control and (less noticeably) in physique.

But we must define some of our terms more precisely, for instance, "aggressiveness" and "self-assertion." The evidence is for initiative, enterprise, vigorous activity, outdoor adventure; "aggressiveness" need not imply selfishness or tyranny or unfair attack. The compassion and sympathy of the female, again, appears from the evidence personal rather than abstract, less a principled humanitarian-

From *Sex and Personality: Studies in Masculinity and Femininity*. Reprinted from Lewis Terman Papers, Stanford University Libraries. Notes have been renumbered and edited.

ism than an active sympathy for palpable misfortune or distress. In disgust, in aesthetic judgment, and in moral censure, the evidence is rather for the influence of fashion and of feeling than of principle or reason. Our evidence need not imply the possession of a "truer" taste or a more discerning conscience.

But in asking how deep these sex distinctions go we reach our second question: *What appears to be the relation of our main sex difference to nature and nurture, to endowment and environment?*

The question is not, let as remind ourselves, whether this or that trait is innate or acquired, for every human act or thought is both, but whether the actual sex differences we are discovering are ascribable to biological (genetic) factors dividing the sexes or to sex differences in their training and environment. So far as the evidence of our experiment goes, we are not justified in ascribing the manifest differences to one alternative exclusively. Certainly we do not have enough evidence to exclude the gross physiological differences between the sexes from any part in determining the distinctive preference of the male for heavy muscular work and of the female for less active occupations, or in determining her greater sympathy for the young and weak or her greater interest in home life, with the relegation of outside interests to the male. To actual or anticipated childbearing and motherhood—differences physiologically determined—we have found no reason to deny a part in determing differences in overt habits and emotional dispositions. And in the present state of our ignorance it would be even more rash to deny the possible influence upon sex temperaments of the manifold differences between the sexes in their endocrine equipment and functioning.

Whatever our view as to the innateness of the distinctive tendencies, at least as to maternal tenderness in the one sex and comparative aggressiveness in the other, our experimental evidence is inconclusive. However, when we examine the more direct manifestations of these and other contrasting tendencies in our exercises, and consider how any particular manifestation comes about, the power and reach of what we have named cultural sex bias, its many plain and subtle effects on the upbringing and environment of the sexes within the groups we are considering, keep coming to one's mind. In so many ways too familiar to realize, each sex gives and receives such different treatment as largely to explain the divergences in expression or in fact revealed by the material we have studied. Singularly powerful in shaping our development are other people's expectations of us, past and present, as shown by their practice and their precept. Whether the boy is innately more aggressive and fearless, more handy with the electric lighting than with the cooking stove, more interested and informed about public affairs and about science, more active and enterprising physically; and whether the girl is by nature more sympathetic, gentle, timid, fastidious, more attracted to pots and pans than to rods and guns, more punctilious in dress, personal appearance, manners, and language; at any rate society in the shape of parents, teachers, and one's own fellows of whichever sex expects these differences between the sexes, and literature reflects them. Irresistibly each sex plays the role assigned, even in spite of its own protests. The consequence is that throughout these several exercises, however statistically consistent the distinctive sex responses may prove, we cannot tell how deep the difference lies—or how the deeper and shallower factors combine.

And here we must be content to leave the problem, for it is clear that the deciding answer can be wrested, not by a more meticulous struggle with this one set of exercises administered to groups comparatively homogeneous, but from: (1) parallel examinations of socially and racially different groups widely different in social tradition and circumstance, and (2) combined psychological and biological case studies of extreme deviants in sex temperaments within a given culture.

THE SIGNIFICANCE OF M-F DIFFERENCES FOR PERSONALITY

Masculinity and femininity are important aspects of human personality. They are not to be thought of as lending to it merely a superficial coloring and flavor; rather they are one of a small number of cores around which the structure of personality gradually takes shape. The masculine-feminine contrast is probably as deeply grounded, whether by nature or by nurture, as any other which human temperament presents. Certainly it is more specifically rooted in a structural dichotomy than the cycloid-schizoid or the extrovertive-introvertive contrasts. Whether it is less or more grounded in general physiological and biochemical factors than these remains to be seen. In how far the lines of cleavage it represents are inevitable is unknown, but the possibility of eliminating it from human nature is at least conceivable. The fact remains that the M-F dichotomy, in various patterns, has existed throughout history and is still firmly established in our mores. In a considerable fraction of the population it is the source of many acute difficulties in the individual's social and sexual adjustment and in a greater fraction it affords a most important impetus to creative work and happiness. The indications are that the present situation, together with the problems it raises for education, psychology, and social legislation, will remain with us for a long time to come.

As long as the child is faced by two relatively distinct patterns of personality, each attracting him by its unique features, and is yet required by social pressures to accept the one and reject the other, a healthy integration of personality may often be difficult to achieve. Cross-parent fixations will continue to foster sexual inversion; the less aggressively inclined males will be driven to absurd compensations to mask their femininity; the more aggressive and independent females will be at a disadvantage in the marriage market; competition between the sexes will be rife in industry, in politics, and in the home as it is today.

Even if it could be shown that the malleability of personality is such as to make the adoption of a single ideal pattern of temperament feasible, no one knows whether the consequences would be more desirable than undesirable. So far only one single-standard society has been described for us, that an extremely primitive one consisting of but a few hundred individuals living in the wilds of New Guinea. Mead's description[1] of this society, challenging as it is, offers no very convincing evidence that a system of unipolarity reduces the difficulties of individual adjustment. Conceivably, in a more complex society it might increase them. It is possible that in an enlightened culture, no longer held in leash by traditions and taboos, dual patterns of sexual temperament are an aid in the development of heterosexuality.

But it is not our purpose to defend the prevailing ideals with respect to sex temperaments. The irrelevance and absurdity of many of their features are evident enough. That in most cultures they have been shaped to the advantage of the physically stronger sex is obvious. It does not necessarily follow that a dichotomy of temperaments is per se an evil to be got rid of. In any case it is not the business of the scientist either to condemn or to praise any given type of human behavior. His task is to understand it. The application of his findings to social betterment he is willing to leave to the social reformer, but with respect to the personality problems with which we are here concerned, he knows that intelligent reform will have to await the establishment of a substantial body of knowledge which does not now exist.

THE NEED FOR MORE ADEQUATE DESCRIPTION OF SEX TEMPERAMENTS

The first step in the investigation of the sex temperaments is to make possible their more adequate description and more exact identification. We have shown that descriptions based upon common observation are often contradictory and that even a subject's intimate friends register little agreement in rating him for degree of masculinity and femininity. This state of affairs betokens the vagueness of current ideas with respect to what constitutes the masculine or feminine temperament and the chaos of opinion with regard to what is valid evidence of its existence. Three sources of confusion may be briefly mentioned.

1. Erroneous ratings may result from the too ready acceptance of overt behavior as the criterion. In this respect the investigator of personality or character is at a disadvantage in comparison with the investigator of intelligence or other abilities. Subjects do not often try to hide their intelligence and they are unable to hide very effectively their stupidities, but character and personality can be rather successfully simulated. Within limits the dishonest can simulate honesty, hatred can be hidden under honeyed words, anger can be disguised, the introvert can force himself to behave as an extrovert, the homosexual may deport himself so normally as to remain undetected in our midst.
2. Errors may be due to lack of a sufficiently large sampling of observational data. The teacher's contacts with her pupils are limited to certain types of situations. The same is true of our contacts with most of the people we know.
3. Among the hardest errors to eliminate are those that arise from traditional biases, such as the notion that the masculine temperament nearly always goes with a particular type of voice, physique, carriage, manner of dress, or occupation. There are doubtless other biases more or less peculiar to the individual or to the class to which he belongs, varying according to whether he is male or female, masculine or feminine, young or old, strongly or weakly sexed, etc.

It is evident that no clear delineation of sexual temperaments is possible on the basis of uncontrolled observation. The M-F test is an attempt to remedy this situation. Its scientific intent is to free the concepts of masculinity and femininity from the irrelevancies and confusions which have become attached to them as the result of superficial consideration of everyday behavior. It is necessary to go back of behavior to the individual's attitudes, interests, information, and thought trends, which constitute the real personality behind the front presented to his fellows.

That the purpose of the test has been accomplished only in part hardly needs to be said. Our sampling of the universe of mental attitudes and interests which differentiate the sexes is far from adequate. The sampling used has not been validated by item counts for sufficiently large populations. Numerous questions remain unanswered with respect to the selection of test items, the best method of weighting responses, and the most meaningful kinds of score to employ. The defects of our technique will be remedied by experiment, the technique itself seems to us inescapable however much it may require supplementation by direct experimental procedures.

NATURE AND NURTURE AS DETERMINERS OF SEX TEMPERAMENT

The nature-nurture problem occupies a central position in any theory of sex temperament. The M-F test rests upon no assumption as to the causes responsible for the individual differences it discloses. The aim has been to devise a test which would measure whatever differences may exist in the hope that this would open the way to an empirical estimation of the relative influence of various determiners. At present no one knows whether the M-F deviant is primarily a problem for the neurologist, biochemist, and endocrimologist or for the parent and educator. The question cannot be answered without thoroughgoing search for the constitutional correlates of M-F deviation. The final answer cannot be obtained until both endocrinology and psychometrics have advanced beyond their present stage, though this is no excuse for delaying the initiation of research on the problem at hand. It should be emphasized, however, that failure to find the sought-for correlates can never be taken as conclusive proof that they do not exist. On the other hand, in so far as any such correlates may be demonstrated the nurture hypothesis is to that extent weakened.

In a recent treatise Mead has presented a mass of descriptive evidence favoring the extreme environmental hypothesis for the causes of sex differences in personality. If her observations and interpretations can be taken at their face value it would not be easy to escape the conclusion that among human beings constitutional factors are distinctly secondary to psychological as determiners of the M and F temperaments. Her book is based upon a study of three primitive tribes in New Guinea. She reports that in one of these, the Arapesh, males and females both exhibit in the main a single temperamental pattern, one that corresponds closely to the feminine pattern of present-day occidental cultures. A similar situation was found with the Mundugumors, except that in this case the single standard is typically masculine. The Tehambuli, on the other hand, present both masculine and feminine patterns, but reversed as between the sexes, males approximating what we should call the feminine in temperament and females approximating the masculine. The author describes in considerable detail the cultural influences which she believes to be responsible for these results.

That Mead's contribution offers impressive evidence of the modifiability of human temperament will be readily conceded, but we are by no means convinced that the case for nurture is as strong as a casual perusal of her book would suggest. Psychologists who have investigated personality by means of observational and rating techniques will inevitably question the accuracy of anyone's estimates of the degree of masculinity or femininity of behavior characterizing either an individual or a group of individuals. It is not to be supposed that the field anthropologist, any more than the psychologist, is immune to error in such estimates; indeed, because the groups under observation by him belong to an alien culture, and because his command of the tribal language is almost invariably limited, the anthropologist who attempts to rate the masculinity or femininity of behavior in a primitive tribal group labors under tremendous disadvantages.

We have shown that when subjects are rated by their teachers or intimate acquaintances either on general masculinity-femininity or on specific aspects of personality related thereto, so little agreement is found that the pooled estimates of several independent judges are necessary to increase the reliability of such ratings to a reasonable figure. Even then we do not rule out the types of constant error that result from a common bias among the raters. When subjective methods are employed, greater or less bias is inevitable, however competent and honest the observer may be; and observers who have had a particular kind of training, whether in anthropology or psychology, are bound to be influenced by the effect of biases common to their group—by the "idols of the den."

Notwithstanding the above criticisms, the book in question is one of the most provocative contributions thus far made to the psychology of sex. Written for the general reader, it naturally does not contain the wealth of specific detail that would be necessary to enable the social scientist to judge the correctness of its conclusions. It does, however, present a number of observations which clearly suggest the operation of a nature as well as a nurture factor. The author admits that the cultural pressures in these tribes have not succeeded in forcing acceptance by all individuals of the personality standards imposed. Concrete examples are given of individuals who have become maladjusted by inability to conform. The author even admits that individual differences within a given sex are about as great as in our own culture, and that the chief result of the pressures has been to shift the location of the distribution of differences on the M-F axis without appreciably diminishing its range.

The literature of anthropology furnishes an abundance of cogent testimony as to the plasticity of temperament and personality. Of the treatises bearing on this question, the above-mentioned book by Mead and another not less notable by Benedict[2] are outstanding examples. Nevertheless, valuable as the anthropological evidence is, it cannot be accepted as a final answer to the nature-nurture problem. Primitive cultures are rapidly becoming more rare; the interpretation of behavior offers many pitfalls to observers unaccustomed to think in quantitative terms; conclusions reached by the anthropologist's field observations are usually not amenable to laboratory checks. For these and other reasons the psychologist, the physiologist, the psychiatrist, and the biochemist need not fear that their contributions to the theory of personality are likely to be rendered superfluous by other approaches.

EVIDENCE OF NURTURE INFLUENCES UPON THE M-F SCORE

Several convergent lines of evidence have been mentioned in preceding chapters which point to the efficacy of nurture factors as at least partial determiners of an individual's M-F score. The latter is definitely, even though not closely, associated with amount of schooling, with age, with occupation, with interests, and with domestic milieu. Perhaps the closest association of all, though its degree is suggested rather than measured, is that between cross-parent fixation and M-F deviation toward the norm of the opposite sex. The data do not define the reasons for these or other deviations. Old men test more feminine than young men, but the casual factor may be either experiential or physiological and endocrinal. Superior culture, in the case of women, tends to be associated with masculinity; in the case of men with femininity; but our data do not tell us whether education causes the change, or whether it merely tends to select the already feminine male and the already masculine female. Similarly for occupational classification, though the selective influence of the occupation is more clearly evidenced than in the case of education. Even in instances of cross-parent fixation it is not easy to rule out all possible selective factors: parents may be more likely to foster such an attachment in that particular opposite-sex child who is already a deviant, or, conversely, the already deviant child may be the only one who is affected by the overcherishing parent. Accordingly, although the evidence in favor of a considerable nurture influence is in our opinion very weighty, it is by no means crucial.

From the point of view of science progress could be made more rapidly if experimental and control groups of infants could be artifically segregated and the effects watched in them of reversing nurture influences. Our method for human study can, however, not parallel the "sacrifical" procedure of the physical sciences. Fortunately advance is not blocked by this condition. Comparison of parent-child resemblance in sex temperament with resemblance between foster parent and foster child can be accomplished, also comparison of resemblance between identical twins on the one hand and between like-sex fraternal twins on the other.

Another approach would be to locate parents who belong to one of two extreme types with respect to the kind of influence they have tried to exert in shaping the sex temperaments of their children: *(a)* parents who accept the usual dichotomy as desirable and have endeavored to inculcate it in their sons and daughters, and *(b)* parents who adhere radically to the opposite theory and have done their best to counteract every influence that would develop in their daughters the distinctively feminine, or in their sons the distinctively masculine, personality. If enough parents of the second type could be found to permit reliable determinations, the parental influence would be measured by the M-F score difference separating their sons and daughters as compared to the difference separating the sons and daughters of the other parental group. In such an investigation one would of course need to bear in mind that parental pressures may be largely nullified by subtle pressures of the larger social milieu, including playmates, the school, the newpaper, the theater, literature, industry, government, and innumerable other factors Even so, we believe that a careful study of parental influences upon the sex temperament of offspring would be worth making.

As to what the outcome of such investigations might be, we prefer not to hazard a guess. On the one hand is a respectable body of evidence pointing to nurture effects; on the other is the spectacular and ever increasing evidence from animal laboratories on the effects of hormone concentration upon patterns of sexual behavior. To assume a partisan position at the present time with respect to the relative influence of nature and nurture upon human personality is hardly warranted.

Notes

1. Mead, Margaret, *Sex and temperament in three primitive societies,* 335 pp. Morrow, 1935.
2. Benedict, Ruth, *Patterns of culture,* p. 291, Houghton Mifflin, 1934.

KAY DEAUX AND BRENDA MAJOR

A Social-Psychological Model of Gender

Psychology's record of considering gender has been, with too few exceptions, a tradition of sex differences. Taking sexual dimorphism as a starting point, investigators have tried to establish, or in some cases refute, the existence of differences between women and men. Whichever conclusion is sought or reached, the debate has its origin in an implicit oppositional model.

This tendency to create oppositions between elements that can be dichotomized is a seductive feature of human thought. In a fascinating study by Barnes[1] parents were asked to describe their children. Parents who had three or more children described each child in separate terms: for example, Jane is intellectual, Bill is sociable, and Pamela is athletic. Parents of two children, in contrast, succumbed to oppositional thinking: If Jane was a leader, Bill was a follower; if Bill was more sociable, Jane was less sociable. This tendency toward bipolar contrasts is probably exaggerated in the case of males and females, where there is consensus as to what the two categories are and where the categories serve as significant markers in most societies. Dualistic assumptions about gender may also preclude other relevant categories—race, class, age—from entering the analysis.

Those who conclude that there are differences between women and men often assume that these differences are stable. This stability is implicit, we would argue, whether nature or nurture is invoked as the cause. The "different voice" that Carol Gilligan[2] describes with reference to moral reasoning, for example, is attributed primarily to differences in socialization experiences. Yet as the historian Joan Scott has suggested in analyzing the dualism expressed in this work, assumptions of differential experience often fall victim to a certain slippage, in which the original premise, namely, "Women are this way because of different experience," becomes "Women are this way because they are women." In Scott's words, "Implied in this line of reasoning is the ahistorical, if not essentialist, notion of women."[3]

As a group, psychologists have a pernicious tendency to develop a concept, devise a way to measure it, and then assume its reality. This reification creates a belief that people are, if their assessment scores so reveal, compulsive people, dependent people, aggressive people, and the like. These descriptions, in turn, connote both generality across situations and stability across time (despite numerous disputes within the discipline as to whether those assumptions are justified). In addition, the hypothesized dimensions often take on causal properties, as they are used to explain and justify actions that may seem consistent with the characterization.

This general tendency to infer causality from stability is particularly evident in analyses of sex differences, for which the explanatory concepts tend to be global. As the prototypical case, the conceptualization of "masculinity" and "femininity" was intended to represent the psychological essence of being male and female. It was not linked directly to biological sex but was capable of predicting those behaviors that tend to be associated with gender. Slightly less broad at first glance, but equally pervasive in their implications, are such concepts as "instrumentality" and "expressiveness," or "justice" versus "caring." Like masculinity and femininity, these characteristics or behavioral styles are seen to reside primarily in one or the other sex and to dictate a wide range of outcomes and life choices.

Such diagnostic categories at most assess potentials and estimate probabilities. They do not dictate outcomes. As Hubbard suggests, human nature as an abstract concept means very little.[4] To give this concept meaning, we need to look at the things people actually do. The viewpoint this represents may be too behaviorist for some. Yet while pure behaviorism is as out of fashion in psychology as in the wider intellectual community, Hubbard's injunction provides a useful antidote to the more global diagnoses some psychological and psychoanalytic models make. The analysis of gender is ill served by a reliance on inflexible and often ephemeral conceptions of the nature of woman and man. Attention to actual behavior, in contrast, demands a model that recognizes variability and similarity—as well as stability and difference.

A SOCIAL-PSYCHOLOGICAL PERSPECTIVE ON GENDER

Our analysis is informed by a social-psychological perspective. In contrast to more traditional psychological analyses of gender that tend toward essentialism, a social-psychological perspective emphasizes the varying forces that influence women and men. Social psychology considers the situational influences on human behavior as a defining characteristic, assigning them a priority over individual traits and personality dispositions. From this perspective we ask quite different questions about sex differences in human behavior.

Our model takes as its point of departure the behavior of women and men in dyadic interaction. Such social interactions can involve many forms of behavior—for example, leadership, social influence, moral choices, cooperation, and competition. Although the basis for our analysis is the empirical literature of psychology, we believe that the implications of the analysis go considerably beyond this domain. The emphasis is not on structural constants that program behavior but on conditions that foster variability and change. In contrast to developmental models of gender that deal with the acquisition of gender-linked behavior, our model is concerned with gender as experienced and enacted in a particular social context. The model is intended to supplement, not supplant, earlier theoretical models that stress the origins of specifiable tendencies and habits.

Fundamental to our perspective is the assumption that gender-related behavior is marked by flexibility, fluidity, and variability. Without denying that there may be some regularities in male and female behavior that are the result of biological propensity or socialization experience, we believe it is essential to recognize evidence of changes over time and circumstance. Acknowledging this variation makes the task of analysis more complex—but it is a complexity we need to confront.

A second assumption that underlies the current perspective is that women and men make choices in their actions. In contrast to the deterministic models offered by both psychoanalysis and behaviorism, our framework presumes a repertoire of possibilities from which individual men and women choose different responses on varying occasions with varying degrees of self-consciousness. In other words, gender-related behaviors are a process of individual and social construction. A number of commentators in other disciplines have argued a similar position. Scott, as one recent example, states that "there is room for a concept of human agency as the attempt (at least partially rational) to construct an identity, a life, a set of relationships, a society with certain sets of limits and with language."[5] The sociologists Gerson and Peiss describe gender as a set of "socially constructed relationships which are produced and reproduced through people's actions."[6] In both of these statements, as in our own model, an active dynamic replaces a passive determinism.

To assume flexibility and choice in an analysis of gender requires an appreciation of context. Choices are not made in a vacuum but are shaped by such transitory factors as the other people involved and the prevailing societal norms. In the present analysis, we reflect our disciplinary bias by emphasizing the immediate interpersonal context. Within such situations, individuals simultaneously react to others and present themselves. Social interaction can be viewed as a process of identity negotiation where individuals pursue particular goals for the interaction.

Our view of gender-related behavior in terms of negotiated social interaction draws heavily on two theoretical perspectives in social psychology. Research on expectancy confirmation—sometimes called self-fulfilling prophecy—focuses on the active role of observers in maintaining or creating social reality through their cognitions or behaviors toward a particular individual. This process involves a sequence in which individuals take actions on the basis of their beliefs, and these actions then influence the behavior of the recipient, leading to a confirmation of the initial belief. In applying this analysis here, we consider how the gender belief system of another can impact upon the individual woman, channeling her behavior in ways that support the stereotypic beliefs.

A second theoretical tradition concerns the factors that motivate an individual to vary how she presents herself to others. On the one hand, concerns with self-verification may lead the person to emphasize those underlying beliefs and characteristics that define a stable self-identity. On the other, external pressures may encourage the choice of self-presentation strategies that increase the likelihood of positive reactions from another. In either case the person shows a freedom of choice to select some facet of self from among a number of possible alternatives.

The model that we are developing attempts to deal both with the variation between people and with the variation in a given individual across situations and time. Clearly people confronted with the same situational pressures vary in their responses. Similarly, a single person may take a different course of action depending on the context in which the choice occurs. Dyadic interaction is our chosen testing ground, although our model has implications for other domains as well. In the model, two individuals bring specific beliefs and identities to an interaction, and their interaction occurs within a specifiable context. We do not assume that gender is always salient in these interactions. One of the objectives of our formulation is to specify and to predict just when gender substantially shapes the course of an interaction and when its influence is more muted. To make these predictions, we look at three influences: first, the individual woman or man; second, other individuals with whom the person interacts; and third, the context or setting in which the interaction takes place.

GENDER IDENTITY AND GENDER-BASED ACTION

Gender identity, as the term is typically used by psychologists, refers to a "fundamental, existential sense of one's maleness or femaleness, an acceptance of one's gender as a social-psychological construction that parallels acceptance of one's biological sex."[7] This sense of maleness or femaleness is acquired early in most people's lives. As Spence has stated, "It is inarguable . . . that gender is one of the earliest and most central components of the self concept and serves as an organizing principle through which many experiences and perceptions of self and other are filtered."[8]

Although the concept of gender identity is universal, substantial individual differences occur in the characteristics of these identities. First, people differ in the degree to which gender is a salient aspect of their identity. Chodorow, for example, has suggested that gender identity is differentially important to women and to men.[9] Data from a recent study of self-definition support this suggestion. When asked what identities were important to them, women were more likely than men either to mention gender spontaneously or to acknowledge gender as a central identity when questioned by the interviewer. (Such findings are consistent with the argument that dominant groups have less need to be self-reflective than do groups who must define themselves vis-à-vis a more powerful other.)

A second way in which gender identities differ among individuals concerns the particular features associated with those identities. People may think of themselves as womanly, feminine, or feminist; within any of these general categories, the beliefs and behaviors associated with the label can differ dramatically. Two individuals who are equally conscious of their identities as women may, by virtue of experience or belief, have markedly different conceptions of what that identity means.

The influence of gender on social interaction depends heavily on the degree to which associations with gender are invoked, either consciously or unconsciously. In cognitive psychologists' terms, we can talk about the *accessibility* of gender identity—the degree to which concepts of gender are actively involved in a particular experience or are part of what has been called the "working self-concept."[10] Accessibility is affected by at least two sets of factors: the strength or centrality of that aspect of the self and features of the immediate situation that make gender salient.

For some people, gender will always be part of the working self-concept, an ever-present filter for experience. Individuals differ in how much gender is a chronically accessible aspect of self, and the prominence of gender identity can differ for the same individual across different situations and stages of life. Gender is more likely to shape a woman's experience, for example, when she has her first child or when she receives a diagnosis of breast cancer than it is on other less gender-linked occasions.

External cues can also evoke gender identity, moving it into the working self-concept. In a laboratory demonstration of gender awareness, for example, college students mentioned gender more often when their sex was a minority in a group situation than when it was a majority. Kanter has vividly described how in other work environments gender becomes salient for the individual who is a token in an organizational setting.[11]

Not always recognized in feminist analyses is the fact that people have identities other than gender. A person may think of herself not only as a woman, but as a Black, a professor, an Easterner, or any of numerous other identities. These various senses of self may exist as independent units having little implication for each other. Or two identities may have different implications for action in the same setting and hence prove contradictory. Which identity is dominant in a situation in which both might be accessible depends both on the individual (the relative prominence of a particular identity in some hierarchy of identities) and on the situation (the degree to which circumstances make a particular identity salient). Gender is most likely to dominate interaction, by this account, when it is an identity of primary importance and when the situation contrives to make gender relevant.

Awareness of gender does not automatically dictate action. Instead people choose how to present themselves to others, with the choices reflecting a variety of motivations. Choices may be based on conscious intentions to present a particular stance or to convey a particular image; individuals may act for the sake of goals that are not clearly recognized in conscious thought. The motives of actions vary. One line of psychological investigation has stressed the degree to which individuals act to verify self-concepts, choosing actions that will be consistent with previous definitions of self. An alternative perspective stresses the degree to which people are sensitive to the social significance of their conduct and strive to present themselves in ways that will ensure social rewards. These two processes are not necessarily contradictory. Rather, concerns with self-verification and self-presentation may be interwoven in any social interaction, as the individual uses both internal and external standards to monitor and shape behavioral choice.

Some empirical investigations have shown how gender concerns can alter the image one presents. In one study, for example, women presented descriptions of themselves to a man who was believed to hold either traditional or liberal views of the appropriate roles for women and men. When the target of their presentation was a man possessing socially desirable characteristics (e.g., not in a steady dating relationship, attractive, wealthy), women modified their presentation to approximate the man's alleged views. In contrast, when the man was described as having traits that would presumably not motivate goals of continued interaction (e.g., currently engaged, unattractive, limited career goals), the women did not alter their presentation from what it had been at an earlier assessment. Such alterations are evident in men confronting women as well. Another empirical study of self-presentational shifts found that women ate fewer available snacks when they were interacting with a desirable male partner as compared to a less desirable one. In extending their analysis, the investigators suggested that such eating disorders as anorexia and bulimia might be linked to self-presentational concerns, as women attempting to appear feminine choose behaviors that they believe are consistent with societal norms of femininity.[12]

THE INFLUENCE OF OTHERS

Social interaction occurs in a context in which certain expectations are conveyed by participants toward each other. Within a given setting, whether the dyadic case emphasized in our model or in a larger arena, the individual is generally aware of what is expected, prescribed, or typical in that setting. These expectations can shape the interaction so as to constitute a self-fulfilling prophecy. People interacting with each other may come to manifest the previously held beliefs of their companions.

We know, from both extensive research and common observation, that gender stereotypes are pervasive. People typically believe that men and women differ in a wide range of personality traits, physical characteristics, role behaviors, and occupational positions. Traits related to instrumentality, dominance, and assertiveness, for example, are believed more characteristic of men, while such traits as warmth, expressiveness, and concern for other people are thought more characteristic of women. These beliefs are not all-or-nothing ascriptions; rather, people make judgments about the relative likelihood that women and men will exhibit various characteristics.

People not only have beliefs about women and men at the most general level. They also have clear images of certain types of women and men, such as businesswomen or blue-collar working men. These types correspond to roles that men and women occupy in society and are often described in terms of physical features as well as personality traits. A macho man, for example, is most frequently characterized as being muscular, having a hairy chest and a moustache. Images of sexy women include references to the woman's hair, figure, clothes, facial appearance, and nail polish. These beliefs, operating at various levels of specificity, serve as a framework or orientation for the individual approaching any particular interaction, and because information about physical appearance is both readily available and prominently coded, stereotypic thinking may be triggered quite early in initial encounters.

Of course individuals differ in the degree to which they endorse these beliefs and in the attributes they associate with gender categories. Some people may, as Bem has argued, be gender schematic, readily imposing stereotypical beliefs and making sharp distinctions between male and female. Aschematic people eschew such distinctions.[13] More generally, one can think of people as varying along a range of stereotypy, showing greater or lesser propensity to endorse the pervasive cultural beliefs. It seems quite unlikely, however, that many people in contemporary society are unencumbered by some gender-linked expectations and beliefs.

As in the case of self, we do not believe that gender is always salient to the observer or that gender-related beliefs are necessarily activated in social interaction. Yet the obviousness of a person's sex in most instances makes it very likely to influence implicit assumptions. Kessler and McKenna argue that gender attribution is universal, taking precedence over many other forms of categorization.[14]

Both parties in an interaction can influence the likelihood of gender schemata's being activated. Specific features of a person's appearance can trigger a subset of gender beliefs in the mind of the observer, for example, shifting the expectancies from those associated with women and men in general to those linked to more particular subtypes. A woman with a briefcase elicits different associations for most people than does a woman in an apron and housedress. A woman with a low-cut blouse, slit skirt, and high-heeled shoes elicits more attributions of sexiness and seductiveness than does her more conservatively dressed counterpart. Predispositions in the observer may lower the threshold for seeing gender relevance or influence the way in which a particular behavior is interpreted. Men, for example, are more likely than women to assume sexual intent in the friendly behavior of a woman. An analysis of these beliefs is important because of their consequences. The expectancy confirmation sequence describes processes linking beliefs to actions. This link manifests itself in a number of ways, including active avoidance or termination of an interaction. A person can avoid individuals who are presumed undesirable, and such avoidance allows the retention of beliefs in the (untested) attributes of the undesirable one. More typically, perhaps, expectancies shape the form of interaction that occurs. To take an example from the employment realm, consider the case of a female manager whose supervisor believes her to be unfit for leadership positions. The supervisor might engage in such actions toward the woman as shunting her into a subordinate role that allows no room for the display of leadership qualities. The woman's subordinate behavior would then confirm the supervisor's initial belief independent of the woman's actual qualities.

SITUATION AND CONTEXT

The context in which an interaction takes place, like the characters of the actors, shapes the outcome. Context can be considered at many levels, from cultural norms and societal structures to the more immediate circumstances of an interaction. Although our analysis emphasizes immediate circumstances, we do not suggest that others are insignificant, for these more general forces shape, modify, and often limit the range of behaviors available to the individual actor.

Certain situations make gender more salient, increasing the likelihood that each of the participants will bring gender scripts to bear. Some environments, such as a nursery school or an automobile repair shop, are closely linked to gender. Other situations make gender salient because of the particular participants, as Kanter's analysis of tokenism illustrates.[15] Established norms can make gender more or less appropriate as an organizing principle.

To predict whether sex differences will be the rule or the exception, one must analyze the total set of influencing factors. The actual behavior of women and men in a situation depends on the relative weight of the three elements: the self-definitions and goals of each participant, the beliefs and expectations of the other, and the context in which the interaction takes place. By this analysis, sex differences, that is, observed differences in the actions of women and men, are one of several possible outcomes. In most cases this outcome could be altered relatively easily if one or more elements were changed.

The most straightforward predictions for observed behavior are possible when all forces press toward the same outcome. Using as an example a pair of entry-level managers in a corporation, we can describe conditions of maximal and minimal likelihood for the appearance of sex differences. Sex differences will be most likely, according to our analysis, when:

1. The man and the woman have different conceptions of themselves as managers and different goals for their corporate experience.
2. The supervisor holds strong stereotypic beliefs about women and men

and is prone to act on those beliefs, creating different experiences for women and men.

3. The situation is one in which men and women have traditionally assumed different roles and in which the organizational structure is based on a premise of different activities for women and men.

In contrast, sex differences should be rare when the opposite influences prevail. If women and men bring similar experiences and self-conceptions to a situation, if they aspire to the same outcomes, and if they are acting in a context within which sex discrimination is minimal, relatively few differences should be observed.

Both of these scenarios represent pure cases, in which the various influences converge toward a single outcome. In reality cases are rarely that simple. Women with identities and aspirations that match men's encounter situations that press for differentiation. Contexts that are seemingly neutral may still provide a venue for display of sharp differences between particular women and men. When two sources of influence produce contradictory pressures—one fostering difference and the other stressing similarity—what form does behavior take?

To deal with the complexity of frequently conflicting messages and pressures, we turn to a microlevel analysis of the social-psychological process involved in interaction. Rather than offering general statements of sex difference or similarity, we suggest that many dynamic factors must be considered. In each general domain—individual self-systems, expectancies of others, and contextual influences—the range of alternatives is great. With reference to the self-system, for example, people vary in the importance they attach to pleasing others versus verifying internal truths. If pleasing others is more important, situational factors should be much more influential. Characteristics of the other's expectancy that can be important include the desirability of the advocated behavior for the individual and the certainty with which that message is sent. *Who* is conveying the expectation also matters a great deal. A person is far more likely to confirm the expectations of those who are powerful, likable, and control rewards and outcomes than of those whose resources are more limited. Confirmation of another person's expectancies is more likely in public situations than in private, and more common in novel situations than in familiar ones.

The enactment of gender is a dynamic, not a static, phenomenon. People choose (although not necessarily at a conscious level) to act out gender-related behaviors and to vary their behavior with circumstances. Their choices reflect the joint contribution of cognitive factors like the accessibility of relevant beliefs and self-definitions, and motivational factors that relate to one's objectives for a particular interaction. Although we use observable behavior as a criterion, we *recognize* the determinants of these behaviors in mental acts. The actions of individual women and men cannot be understood without reference to social context. Changes in context mean changes in outcome, belying the stability of male-female differences so often posited.

The present analysis is more microlevel than some. We are concerned less with human nature than with human actions; with where the repertoires of behavior come from than with how people make choices within those repertoires. Our framework does not deny the usefulness of other formulations, but we believe that the social-psychological perspective is a valuable one. It offers little in the way of ultimatums. What it does, and does in a way lacking in many previous accounts, is to affirm the range of human behavior available to both women and men. By so doing, it moves us away from the oppositional thought that has guided so much previous work.

Notes

1. This study is reported in an unpublished doctoral dissertation from the Harvard Graduate School of Education (W. S. Barnes, "Sibling Influences within Family and School Contexts," 1984) and is described in Deborah Belle, "Ironies in the Contemporary Study of Gender," *Journal of Personality* 53 (June 1985): 400–5.

2. Carol Gilligan, *In a Different Voice* (Cambridge: Harvard University Press, 1982).

3. Joan W. Scott, "Gender: A Useful Category of Historical Analysis," *American Historical Review* 91 (1986): 1053–75, 1065.

4. Ruth Hubbard, "The Political Nature of 'Human Nature,'" in Deborah Rhode, ed., *Theoretical Perspectives on Sexual Difference* (New Haven: Yale University Press, 1990): 63–73.

5. Scott, "Gender," 1067.

6. Judith M. Gerson and Kathy Peiss, "Boundaries, Negotiation, Consciousness: Reconceptualizing Gender Relations," *Social Problems* 32 (April 1985): 327.

7. Janet T. Spence, "Masculinity, Femininity, and Gender-Related Traits: A Conceptual Analysis and Critique of Current Research," *Progress in Experimental Personality Research* 13 (1984): 84. For more traditional discussions of gender identity, see Richard Green, *Sexual Identity Conflict in Children and Adults* (New York: Basic, 1974); John Money and Anke A. Ehrhardt, *Man and Woman, Boy and Girl* (Baltimore: Johns Hopkins University Press, 1972); Robert J. Stoller, *Sex and Gender: On the Development of Masculinity and Femininity* (New York: Science House, 1968).

8. Janet T. Spence, "Gender Identity and Its Implications for Concepts of Masculinity and Femininity," in T. Sondregger, ed., *Nebraska Symposium on Motivation* (Lincoln: University of Nebraska Press, 1985).

9. Nancy Chodorow, "What is the Relation Between Psychoanalytic Feminism and the Psychoanalytic Psychology of Women?" In Deborah Rhode, ed., *Theoretical Perspectives on Sex Differences* (New Haven: Yale University Press, 1990).

10. For more discussion, see E. Tory Higgins and Gillian King, "Accessibility of Social Constructs: Information-Processing Consequences of Individual and Contextual Variability," in Nancy Cantor and John F. Kihlstrom, eds., *Personality, Cognition, and Social Behavior* (Hillsdale, N.J.: Lawrence Erlbaum, 1981), 69–121; also Hazel Markus and Ziva Kunda, "Stability and Malleability of the Self-Concept," *Journal of Personality and Social Psychology* 51 (October 1986): 858–66.

11. Rosabeth Moss Kanter, *Men and Women of the Corporation* (New York: Basic, 1977).

12. DeAnna Mori, Shelly Chaiken, and Patricia Pliner, "'Eating Lightly' and the Self-Pre-

sentation of Femininity," *Journal of Personality and Social Psychology* 53 (October 1987): 693–702.

13. Sandra L. Bem, "Gender Schema Theory: A Cognitive Account of Sex Typing, *Psychological Review* 88 (July 1981): 354–64.

14. Suzanne J. Kessler and Wendy McKenna, *Gender: An Ethnomethodological Approach* (New York: John Wiley, 1978).

15. Kanter, *Men and Women of the Corporation.*

DARYL J. BEM

The Exotic-Becomes-Erotic Theory of Sexual Orientation

The question "What causes homosexuality?" is both politically suspect and scientifically misconceived. Politically suspect because it is so frequently motivated by an agenda of prevention and cure. Scientifically misconceived because it presumes that heterosexuality is so well understood—so obviously the "natural" evolutionary consequence of reproductive advantage—that only deviations from it are theoretically problematic. Accordingly, the theory described in this article addresses the question "What causes sexual orientation?" and proposes the same basic account for both opposite-sex and same-sex desire. In particular, Figure 1 displays the proposed temporal sequence of events that leads to sexual orientation for most men and women in a gender-polarizing culture like ours—a culture that emphasizes the differences between the sexes by pervasively organizing both the perceptions and realities of communal life around the male/female dichotomy. The sequence begins at the top of the figure with biological variables (labeled *A*) and ends at the bottom with erotic/romantic attraction (*F*).

A → *B*: Biological variables such as genes or prenatal hormones do not code for sexual orientation per se, but for childhood temperaments, such as aggression or activity level.

B → *C:* Children's temperaments predispose them to enjoy some activities more than others. One child will enjoy rough-and-tumble play and competitive team sports (male-typical activities); another will prefer to socialize quietly or play jacks or hopscotch (female-typical activities). Children will also prefer to play with peers who share their activity preferences. Children who prefer sex-typical activities and same-sex playmates are referred to as "gender conforming"; children who prefer sex-atypical activities and opposite-sex playmates are referred to as "gender nonconforming."

A revised and shortened version of Daryl Bem, "Exotic Becomes Erotic: A Developmental Theory of Sexual Orientation," in *Psychological Review,* Vol. 103, no. 2 (1996). Notes have been renumbered and edited.

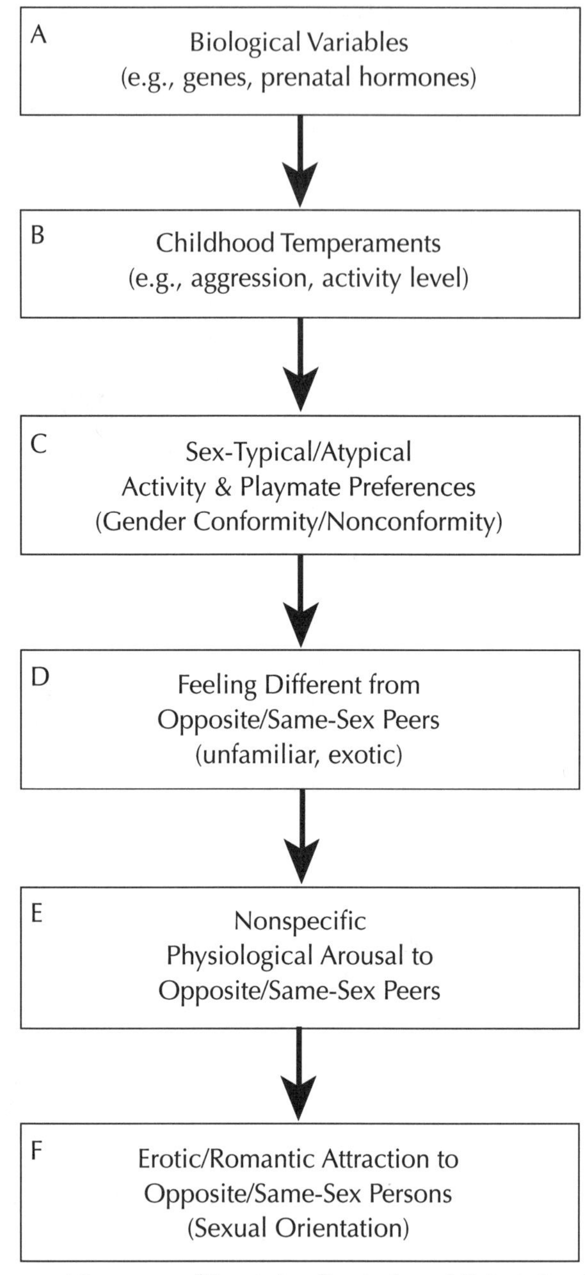

Figure 1. The Temporal Sequence of Events Leading to Sexual Orientation for Most Men and Women in a Gender-Polarizing Culture.

C → *D:* Gender-conforming children will feel different from opposite-sex peers, perceiving them as unfamiliar and exotic. Similarly, gender-nonconforming children will perceive same-sex peers as unfamiliar and exotic.

D → *E:* These feelings of unfamiliarity produce heightened physiological arousal. For the male-typical child, it may be felt as antipathy toward girls; for the female-typical child, it may be felt as timidity or apprehension in the presence of boys. A particularly clear example is provided by the "sissy" boy who is taunted by male peers for his gender nonconformity and, as a result, is likely to experience the strong physiological arousal of fear and anger in their presence. The theory claims, however, that every child, conforming or nonconforming, experiences heightened nonspecific physiological arousal in the presence of peers from whom he or she feels different. In this most common case, the arousal will not necessarily be affectively toned or consciously felt.

E → *F:* This physiological arousal is transformed in later years into erotic/romantic attraction. Steps *D* → *E* and *E* → *F* thus encompass specific psychological mechanisms that transform exotic into erotic (*D* → *F*). For brevity, the entire sequence outlined in Figure 1 will be referred to as the "EBE (exotic becomes erotic)" theory of sexual orientation.

As noted above, Figure 1 does not describe an inevitable, universal path to sexual orientation but, rather, the most common path followed by men and women in a gender-polarizing culture like ours. Individual variations, alternative paths, and cultural influences on sexual orientation are discussed later in the chapter.

EVIDENCE FOR THE THEORY

Evidence for EBE theory is organized into the following narrative sequence: gender conformity or nonconformity in childhood is a causal antecedent of sexual orientation in adulthood (*C* → *F*). This is so because gender conformity or nonconformity causes a child to perceive opposite or same-sex peers as exotic (*C* → *D*), and the exotic class of peers subsequently becomes erotically or romantically attractive to him or her (*D* → *F*). This occurs because exotic peers produce heightened physiological arousal (*D* → *E*) which is subsequently transformed into erotic/romantic attraction (*E* → *F*). This entire sequence of events can be initiated, among other ways by biological factors that influence a child's temperaments (*A* → *B*), which in turn, influence his or her preferences for gender-conforming or gender nonconforming activities and peers (*B* → *C*).

Gender Conformity or Nonconformity in Childhood Is a Causal Antecedent of Sexual Orientation (C → F)

In a study designed to test hypotheses about the development of sexual orientation, researchers conducted intensive interviews with approximately 1,000 gay men and lesbians and with 500 heterosexual men and women in the San Francisco Bay Area. The study (hereinafter, the San Francisco study) found that childhood gender conformity or nonconformity was not only the strongest, but also the only

Table 1.
Percentage of Respondents Reporting Gender-Nonconforming Preferences and Behaviors During Childhood

	Men		Women	
Response	Gay (n = 686)	Heterosexual (n = 337)	Lesbian (n = 293)	Heterosexual (n = 140)
Had not enjoyed sex-typical activities	63	10	63	15
Had enjoyed sex-atypical activities	48	11	81	61
Atypically sex-typed (masculin ity/femininity)	56	8	80	24
Most childhood friends were opposite sex	42	13	60	40

Note: All chi-square comparisons between gay and heterosexual subgroups are significant at $p < .0001$.

significant, childhood predictor of later sexual orientation for both men and women. As Table 1 shows, the effects were large and significant.[1]

For example, gay men were significantly more likely than heterosexual men to report that as children they had not enjoyed boys' activities (e.g., baseball and football), had enjoyed girls' activities (e.g., hopscotch, playing house, and jacks), and had been nonmasculine. These were the three variables that defined gender nonconformity in the study. Additionally, gay men were more likely than heterosexual men to have had girls as childhood friends. The corresponding comparisons between lesbian and heterosexual women were also large and significant.

It is also clear from the table that relatively more women than men had enjoyed sex-atypical activities and had opposite-sex friends during childhood. (In fact, more heterosexual women than gay men had enjoyed boys' activities as children—61 percent versus 37 percent, respectively.)

Many other studies have also shown that gay men and lesbians are more likely than heterosexual men and women to have gender-nonconforming behaviors and interests in childhood, including some studies that began with children and followed them into adulthood. The largest of these reported that approximately 75 percent of gender-nonconforming boys became bisexual or homosexual in adulthood, compared with only 4 percent of gender-conforming boys.[2]

Gender Conformity and Nonconformity Produce Feelings of Being Different from Opposite- and Same-Sex Peers, Respectively (C → D)

EBE theory proposes that gender-nonconforming children will come to feel different from their same-sex peers. In the San Francisco study, 70 percent of gay men and lesbians reported that they had felt different from same-sex peers in childhood, compared with only 38 percent and 51 percent of heterosexual men and women, respectively ($p < .0005$ for both gay/heterosexual comparisons).

They further reported that they had felt this way throughout childhood and adolescence.

When asked in what way they had felt different from same-sex peers, gay men were most likely to say that they did not like sports; lesbians were most likely to say that they were more interested in sports or were more masculine than other girls. In contrast, those heterosexual men and women who had felt different from their same-sex peers typically cited differences unrelated to gender, such as being poorer, more intelligent, or more introverted. Heterosexual women frequently cited differences in physical appearance.

Exotic Becomes Erotic (D → F)

The heart of EBE theory is the proposition that individuals become erotically or romantically attracted to those who were unfamiliar to them in childhood. We have already seen some evidence for this in Table 1: those who played more with girls in childhood, gay men and heterosexual women, preferred men as sexual/romantic partners in later years; those who played more with boys in childhood, lesbian women and heterosexual men, preferred women as sexual/romantic partners in later years. Moreover, it has long been known that childhood familiarity is antithetical to later erotic or romantic attraction. For example, Westermarck observed over a century ago that married couples who had been betrothed in childhood experienced problematic sexual relationships when the girl had been taken in by the future husband's family and treated like one of the siblings.

A contemporary example is provided by children on Israeli kibbutzim, who are raised communally with age-mates in mixed-sex groups and exposed to one another constantly during their entire childhood. Sex play is not discouraged and is quite intensive during early childhood. After childhood, there is no formal or informal pressure or sanction against heterosexual activity within the peer group from educators, parents, or members of the peer group itself. Yet despite all this, there is a virtual absence of erotic attraction between peer group members in adolescence or adulthood. A review of nearly 3,000 marriages contracted by second-generation adults in all Israeli kibbutzim revealed that there was not a single case of an intrapeer group marriage.[3]

The Sambian culture in New Guinea illustrates the phenomenon in a homosexual context. Sambian males believe that boys cannot attain manhood without ingesting semen from older males. At seven years of age, Sambian boys are removed from the family household and initiated into secret male rituals, including ritualized homosexuality. For the next several years, they live in the men's clubhouse and regularly fellate older male adolescents. When they reach sexual maturity, they reverse roles and are fellated by younger initiates. During this entire time, they have no sexual contact with girls or women. And yet, when it comes time to marry and father children in their late teens or early twenties, all but a small minority of Sambian males become exclusively heterosexual. Although Sambian boys enjoy their homosexual activities, the context of close familiarity in which it occurs apparently prevents the development of strongly charged homoerotic feelings.[4]

How Does Exotic Become Erotic? (D → E → F): *The Extrinsic Arousal Effect*

In his first-century Roman handbook, *The Art of Love,* Ovid advised any man who was interested in sexual seduction to take the woman in whom he was interested to a gladiatorial tournament, where she would more easily be aroused to passion. He did not say why this should be so, however, and it was not until 1887 that an elaboration appeared in the literature:

> Love can only be excited by strong and vivid emotion, and it is almost immaterial whether these emotions are agreeable or disagreeable. The Cid wooed the proud heart of Donna Ximene, whose father he had slain, by shooting one after another of her pet pigeons.[5]

A contemporary explanation of this effect is that it is a special case of the two-factor theory of emotion. That theory states that the physiological arousal of our autonomic nervous system provides the cues that we are feeling emotional but that the more subtle judgment of which emotion we are feeling often depends on our cognitive appraisal of the surrounding circumstances. Thus, the experience of passionate love or erotic/romantic attraction results from the conjunction of physiological arousal and the cognitive causal attribution (or misattribution) that the arousal has been elicited by the potential lover.

There is now extensive experimental evidence that an individual who has been physiologically aroused will show heightened sexual responsiveness to an appropriate target stimulus. In one set of studies, male participants were physiologically aroused by running in place, by hearing an audiotape of a comedy routine, or by hearing an audiotape of a grisly killing. They then viewed a taped interview with a physically attractive woman. Finally, they rated the woman's attractiveness, sexiness, and the degree to which they would like to date or kiss her. No matter how the arousal had been elicited, participants were more erotically responsive to the attractive woman than were control participants who had not been aroused.[6]

This extrinsic arousal effect can also be detected physiologically. In a pair of studies, men or women watched a sequence of two videotapes. The first portrayed either an anxiety-inducing or nonanxiety-inducing scene; the second videotape portrayed a nude heterosexual couple engaging in sexual foreplay. Preexposure to the anxiety-inducing scene produced greater penile tumescence in men and greater vaginal blood volume increases in women in response to the erotic scene than did preexposure to the nonanxiety-inducing scene.[7]

In short, physiological arousal, regardless of its source or affective tone, can subsequently be experienced cognitively, emotionally, and physiologically as erotic/romantic attraction. At that point, it is erotic/romantic attraction. The pertinent question, then, is whether this effect can account for the link between the hypothesized "exotic" physiological arousal in childhood and the erotic/romantic attraction later in life. One difficulty is that the effect occurs in the laboratory over brief time intervals, whereas the proposed developmental process spans several years.

The time gap may be more apparent than real, however. As noted earlier, an individual sense of being different from same- or opposite-sex peers is not a one-time event, but a protracted and sustained experience throughout the childhood and adolescent years. This implies that the arousal will also be present throughout that time, ready to be converted into erotic or romantic attraction whenever the maturational, cognitive, and situational factors coalesce to provide the defining moment.

In fact, the laboratory experiments may actually underestimate the strength and reliability of the effect in real life. In the experiments, the arousal is deliberately elicited by a source extrinsic to the intended target, and there is disagreement over whether the effect even occurs when participants are aware of that fact. But in the real-life scenario envisioned by EBE theory, the physiological arousal is genuinely elicited by the class of individuals to which the erotic/romantic attraction develops. The exotic arousal and the erotic arousal are thus likely to be subjectively indistinguishable to the individual.

The Biological Connection: (A → F) *versus* (A → B)

In recent years, researchers, the mass media, and segments of the lesbian/gay/bisexual community have rushed to embrace the thesis that a homosexual orientation is coded in the genes or determined by prenatal hormones and brain neuroanatomy. In contrast, EBE theory proposes that biological factors influence sexual orientation only indirectly, by intervening earlier in the chain of events to determine a child's temperaments and subsequent activity preferences.

One technique used to determine whether a trait is correlated with an individual's genotype (inherited characteristics) is to compare monozygotic (identical) twins, who share all their genes, with dizygotic (fraternal) twins, who, on average, share only 50 percent of their genes. If a trait is more highly correlated across monozygotic pairs of twins than across dizygotic pairs, this provides evidence for a correlation between the trait and the genotype. Using this technique, researchers have recently reported evidence for a correlation between an individual's genotype and his or her sexual orientation. For example, in a sample of gay men who had male twins, 52 percent of monozygotic twin brothers were also gay compared with only 22 percent of dizygotic twin brothers. In a comparable sample of lesbians, 48 percent of monozygotic twin sisters were also lesbian compared with only 16 percent of dizygotic twin sisters. A more systematic study of nearly 5,000 twins who had been drawn from a twin registry confirmed the genetic correlation for men but not for women.[8]

But these same studies provide even stronger evidence for the link proposed by EBE theory between an individual's genotype and his or her childhood gender nonconformity—even when sexual orientation is held constant. For example, in the 1991 twin study of gay men, the correlation on gender nonconformity in which both brothers were gay was .76 for monozygotic twins but only .43 for gay dizygotic twins, implying that gender conformity is significantly correlated with the genotype. Childhood gender nonconformity was also significantly correlated with the genotype for both men and women in the large twin registry study, even though sexual orientation itself was not correlated for the women. These studies are thus consistent with the link specified by EBE theory between the genotype and gender nonconformity ($A \rightarrow C$).

EBE theory further specifies that this link is composed of two parts; a link between the genotype and childhood temperaments ($A \rightarrow B$) and a link between those temperaments and gender nonconformity ($B \rightarrow C$). The temperaments most likely to be involved are aggression—and its benign cousin, rough-and-tumble play—and activity level. There is now substantial evidence that boys' play shows higher levels of rough-and-tumble play and activity than girls' play, that gender-nonconforming children of both sexes are sex-atypical on both traits, and that both traits are significantly correlated with the genotype.

In addition to these empirical findings, there are, I believe, conceptual grounds for preferring the EBE account to the competing hypothesis that there is a direct link between biology and sexual orientation. First, no theoretical rationale for a direct link between the genotype and sexual orientation has been clearly articulated, let alone established. At first glance, the theoretical rationale would appear to be nothing less than the powerful and elegant theory of evolution. The belief that sexual orientation is coded in the genes would appear to be just the general case of the implicit assumption, mentioned in the introduction, that heterosexuality is the obvious "natural" evolutionary consequence of reproductive advantage. But if that is true, then a homosexual orientation is an evolutionary anomaly that requires an explanation of how lesbians and gay men would pass on their "homosexual genes" to successive generations. Although several hypothetical scenarios have been suggested, they have been faulted on both theoretical and empirical grounds.

But the main problem with the direct-link hypothesis is that it fails to spell out any developmental process through which an individual's genotype actually gets transformed into his or her sexual orientation—which is precisely what EBE theory attempts to do. It is not that an argument for a direct link has been made and found wanting; it is that it has not yet been made.

I am certainly willing to concede that heterosexual behavior is reproductively advantageous, but it does not follow that it must therefore be sustained through genetic transmission. In particular, EBE theory suggests that heterosexuality is the most common outcome across time and culture because virtually all human societies polarize the sexes to some extent, setting up a sex-based division of labor and power, emphasizing or exaggerating sex differences, and, in general, superimposing the male/female dichotomy on virtually every aspect of communal life. These gender-polarizing practices ensure that most boys and girls will grow up seeing the other sex as unfamiliar and exotic—and, hence, erotic.

The more general point is that as long as the environment supports or promotes a reproductively successful behavior sufficiently often, it will not necessarily get programmed into the genes. For example, it is presumably reproductively advantageous for ducks to mate with other ducks, but as long as most baby ducklings first meet—and get imprinted on—other ducks, evolution can simply implant the imprinting process itself into the species rather than the specific content of what, reproductively speaking, needs to be imprinted. Analogously, because most cultures ensure that the two sexes will see each other as exotic, it would be sufficient for evolution to implant exotic-becomes-erotic processes into our species rather than heterosexuality per se. In fact, ethological studies of birds show that an exotic-becomes-erotic mechanism is actually a component of sexual imprinting. If ducks, which are genetically free to mate with any moving object, have not perished from the earth, then neither shall we.

In general, any biological factor that correlates with one or more of the intervening processes proposed by EBE theory could also emerge as a correlate of sexual orientation. Even if EBE theory turns out to be wrong, the more general point, that a mediating personality variable could account for observed correlations between biological variables and sexual orientation, still holds.

INDIVIDUAL VARIATIONS AND ALTERNATIVE PATHS

As noted earlier, Figure 1 is not intended to describe an inevitable, universal path to sexual orientation but only the path followed by most men and women in a gender-polarizing culture. Individual variations can arise in several ways. First, different individuals might enter the EBE path at different points in the sequence. For example, a child might come to feel different from same-sex peers not because of a temperamentally induced preference for gender-nonconforming activities, but because of an atypical lack of contact with same-sex peers or a physical disability. In general, EBE theory predicts that the effect of any childhood variable on an individual's sexual orientation depends on whether it prompts him or her to feel more similar to or more different from same-sex or opposite-sex peers.

Individual variations can also arise from differences in how individuals interpret the "exotic" arousal emerging from the childhood years, an interpretation that is inevitably guided by social norms and expectations. For example, girls might be more socially primed to interpret the arousal as romantic attraction, whereas boys might be more primed to interpret it as sexual arousal. Certainly, most individuals in our culture are primed to anticipate, recognize, and interpret opposite-sex arousal as erotic or romantic attraction and to ignore, repress, or differently interpret comparable same-sex arousal. In fact, the heightened visibility of gay men and lesbians in our society is now prompting individuals who experience same-sex arousal to recognize it, label it, and act on it at earlier ages than in previous years.[9]

In some instances, the EBE process itself may be supplemented or even superseded by processes of conditioning or social learning, both positive and negative. Such processes could also produce shifts in an individual's sexual orientation over the life course. For example, the small number of bisexual respondents in the San Francisco study appeared to have added same-sex erotic attraction to an already established heterosexual orientation after adolescence. Similar findings were reported in a more extensive study of bisexual individuals, with some respondents adding heterosexual attraction to a previously established homosexual orientation. This same study also showed that different components of an individual's sexual orientation need not coincide; for example, some of the bisexual respondents were more erotically attracted to one sex but more romantically attracted to the other.

Finally, some women who would otherwise be predicted by the EBE model to have a heterosexual orientation might choose for social or political reasons to center their lives around other women. This could lead them to avoid seeking out men for sexual or romantic relationships, to develop affectional and erotic ties to other women, and to self-identify as lesbians or bisexuals. In general, issues of sexual orientation identity are beyond the formal scope of EBE theory.

DECONSTRUCTING THE CONCEPT OF SEXUAL ORIENTATION

Nearly fifty years ago, Alfred Kinsey took a major step in deconstructing or redefining the concept of sexual orientation by construing it as a bipolar continuum, ranging from exclusive heterosexuality, through bisexuality, to exclusive homosexuality. Because many of the studies cited in this chapter have selected their respondents on the basis of Kinsey-like scales, EBE theory has necessarily been couched in that language: but the theory itself is not constrained by such bipolar dimensions. In fact, Figure 1 actually treats sexual orientation as two separate dimensions—a heteroerotic dimension and a homoerotic dimension—and EBE theory describes the processes that determine an individual's location on each of the two dimensions.

Conceptually, the two paths are independent, thereby allowing for a panoply of individual differences, including several variants of bisexuality (e.g., being erotically attracted to one sex and romantically attracted to the other). Empirically, however, the two dimensions are likely to be negatively correlated in a gender-polarizing culture in which most individuals come to be familiar with one sex while being estranged from the other. EBE theory predicts that this should be especially true for men in American society because, as shown in Table 1, boys are less likely than girls to have childhood friends of both sexes. This prediction is supported in a survey of a national probability sample of Americans. When asked to whom they were sexually attracted, men were likely to report that either they were exclusively heterosexual or exclusively homosexual. In contrast, women were more likely to report that they were bisexual than that they were exclusively homosexual.[10]

Culture influences not only the structure and distribution of sexual orientation in a society, but also how its natives, including its biological and behavioral scientists, conceptualize sexual orientation. Like the natives of any gender-polarizing culture, we have learned to look at the world through the lenses of gender, to impose the male/female dichotomy on virtually every aspect of life, especially sexuality. Which brings us to the most deeply embedded cultural assumption of all: that sexual orientation is necessarily based on sex. As Sandra Bem remarked,

> I am not now and never have been a "heterosexual." But neither have I ever been a "lesbian" or a "bisexual." . . . The sex-of-partner dimension implicit in

> the three categories . . . seems irrelevant to my own particular pattern of erotic attractions and sexual experiences. Although some of the (very few) individuals to whom I have been attracted . . . have been men and some have been women, what those individuals have in common has nothing to do with either their biological sex or mine—from which I conclude, not that I am attracted to both sexes, but that my sexuality is organized around dimensions other than sex.[11]

This statement also suggests the shape that sexual orientation might assume in a nongender-polarizing culture, a culture that did not systematically estrange its children from either opposite-sex or same-sex peers. Such children would not grow up to be asexual; rather, their erotic and romantic preferences would simply crystallize around a more diverse and idiosyncratic variety of attributes. Gentlemen might still prefer blonds, but some of those gentlemen (and some ladies) would prefer blonds of any sex. In the final deconstruction, then, EBE theory reduces to but one "essential" principle: exotic becomes erotic.

A POLITICAL POSTSCRIPT

Biological explanations of homosexuality have become more popular with the public in the 1990s, and many members of the lesbian/gay/bisexual community welcome this trend. For example, *The Advocate,* a national gay and lesbian newsmagazine, reported that 61 percent of its readers believed that "it would mostly help gay and lesbian rights if homosexuality were found to be biologically determined."[12]

Because EBE theory proposes that an individual's sexual orientation is more directly the result of childhood experiences than of biological factors, it has prompted concerns that it could encourage an antigay agenda of prevention and "cure." In particular, the theory appears to suggest that parents could prevent their gender-nonconforming children from becoming gay or lesbian by encouraging sex-typical activities and same-sex friendships and by discouraging sex-atypical activities and opposite-sex friendships.

Of course, our society hardly needed EBE theory to suggest such a strategy. The belief that childhood gender nonconformity leads to later homosexuality is already so widely believed that many parents (especially fathers) already discourage their children (especially sons) from engaging in gender-nonconforming behaviors lest they become homosexual. And, if EBE theory is correct in positing that both homosexuality and heterosexuality derive from the same childhood processes, then it is clear that a gender-polarizing society like ours is already spectacularly effective in producing heterosexuality: 85–95 percent of all men and women in the United States are exclusively heterosexual.

But this same figure suggests that those children who continue to express sex-atypical preferences despite such cultural forces must have their gender nonconformity strongly determined by their basic inborn temperaments—as EBE theory proposes. Forcing such children to engage exclusively in sex-typical activities is unlikely to diminish their feelings of being different from same-sex peers and, hence, is unlikely to diminish their subsequent erotic attraction to those peers.

Empirical support for this hypothesis emerges from the longitudinal study of gender-nonconforming boys, cited earlier. About 27 percent of these boys had been entered by their parents into some kind of therapy, including behavioral therapy specifically designed to prevent a homosexual orientation from developing. Compared with parents of other gender-nonconforming boys, these parents were more worried about their sons' later sexuality, which suggests that they probably tried to discourage their sons' gender nonconformity in many other ways as well. All of this effort was for naught: 75 percent of their sons emerged as homosexual or bisexual, slightly more than the percentage of boys whose more laid-back parents had not entered them into therapy.[13] In the context of our society's current gender-polarizing practices, then, EBE theory does not provide a successful strategy for preventing gender-nonconforming children from becoming homosexual adults.

In general, I suggest that biological explanations of homosexuality are no more likely to promote gay-positive attitudes and practices than experienced-based explanations. For example, whenever new evidence for a "gay gene" is announced in the media, the researchers receive inquiries about techniques for detecting pregay children before they are born—presumably so that such children could be aborted. This chilling prevention strategy should disabuse us of the optimistic notion that biological explanations of homosexuality necessarily promote tolerance. Historically, of course, biological theories of human differences have tended to produce the least tolerant attitudes and the most conservative, even draconian, public policies—as in Nazi Germany.

Even more generally, I do not believe that attitudes toward homosexuality are substantially influenced by beliefs about causality; on the contrary, I believe that an individual's beliefs about causality are influenced by his or her preexisting attitudes toward homosexuality: people tend to find most credible those beliefs that best rationalize their attitudes. In short, EBE theory does not threaten the interests of the lesbian/gay/bisexual community any more than does a biological theory.

Notes

1. Alan P. Bell, Martin S. Weinberg, and Sue Kiefer Hammersmith, *Sexual Preference: Its Development in Men and Women* (Bloomington: Indiana University Press, 1981). The percentages in Table 10.1 have been calculated from the data given in the separately published appendix: Alan P. Bell, Martin S. Weinberg, and Sue Kiefer Hammersmith, *Sexual Preference: Its Development in Men and Women: Statistical Appendix* (Bloomington: Indiana University Press, 1981), 74–75, 77.

2. A summary review of retrospective studies appears in J. Michael Bailey, and Kenneth J. Zucker, "Childhood Sex-Typed Behavior and Sexual Orientation: A Conceptual Analysis and Quantitative Review," *Developmental Psychology*, 31 (1995) 43–55. Seven prospective studies are summarized in Kenneth J. Zucker and Richard Green, "Psychological and Familial Aspects of Gender Identity Disorder," *Child and Adolescent Psychiatric Clinics of North America*, 2(1993): 513–542. The largest of these is fully reported in Richard Green, *The 'Sissy*

Boy Syndrome' and the Development of Homosexuality (New Haven: Yale University Press, 1987).

3. Edward A. Westermarck, *The History of Human Marriage,* (London: Macmillan, 1891). Observations on children of the kibbutzim will be found in Bruno Bettelheim, *The Children of the Dream* (New York: Macmillan, 1969); Albert Israel Rabin, *Growing Up in a Kibbutz* (New York: Springer, 1965); Joseph Shepher, "Mate Selection among Second Generation Kibbutz Adolescents and Adults: Incest Avoidance and Negative Imprinting," *Archives of Sexual Behavior* (1971): 1, 293–307; Melford E. Spiro, *Children of the Kibbutz* (Cambridge, MA: Harvard University Press, 1958); and Y. Talmon, "Mate Selection in Collective Settlements," *American Sociological Review* (1964): 29, 481–508.

4. Gilbert Herdt, *Sambia: Ritual and Gender in New Guinea* (New York: Holt, Rinehart and Winston, 1987).

5. Horwicz, quoted in Henry Theophilus Finck, *Romantic Love and Personal Beauty: Their Development, Causal Relations, Historic and National Peculiarities* (London: Macmillan, 1887).

6. Gregory L. White and Thomas D. Kight, "Misattribution of Arousal and Attraction: Effects of Salience of Explanations for Arousal," *Journal of Experimental Social Psychology,* (1984): 20, 55–64.

7. Peter W. Hoon, John P. Wincze, and Emily Franck Hoon, "A Test of Reciprocal Inhibition: Are Anxiety and Sexual Arousal in Women Mutually Inhibitory?" *Journal of Abnormal Psychology,* 86 (1977): 65–74; Sharlene A. Wolchik, Vicki E. Beggs, John P. Wincze, David K. Sakheim, David H., Barlow, and Matig Mavissakalian, "The Effect of Emotional Arousal on Subsequent Sexual Arousal in Men," *Journal of Abnormal Psychology,* 89 (1980): 595–598.

8. The twin studies are J. Michael Bailey and Richard C. Pillard, "A Genetic Study of Male Sexual Orientation," *Archives of General Psychiatry,* 48 (1991): 1089–1096; J. Michael Bailey, Richard C. Pillard, Michael C. Neale, and Yvonne Agyei, "Heritable Factors Influence Sexual Orientation in Women," *Archives of General Psychiatry,* 50 (1993): 217–223; and J. Michael Bailey and N. G. Martin, "A Twin Registry Study of Sexual Orientation," Paper presented at the annual meeting of the International Academy of Sex Research, Provincetown, MA, September, 1995.

9. Ronald C. Fox, "Bisexual Identities," in Anthony R. D'Augelli and Charlotte J. Petterson, eds., *Lesbian, Gay and Bisexual Identities Over the Lifespan* (New York: Oxford University Press, 1995), 48–86.

10. Edward I. Laumann, John H. Gagnon, Robert T. Michael, and Stuart Michaels, *The Social Organization of Sexuality: Sexual Practices in the United States* (Chicago: University of Chicago Press, 1994).

11. Sandra Lipsitz Bem, "The Lenses of Gender: Transforming the Debate on Sexual Inequality" (New Haven, CT: Yale University Press, 1993), vii.

12. "*Advocate* Poll results." *The Advocate,* February 6, 1996, 8.

13. Green, "Psychological and Familial Aspects," 318.

PART 4 THE SOCIAL CONSTRUCTION OF GENDER RELATIONS

To sociologists, the psychological discussion of sex roles—that collection of attitudes, traits, and behaviors that are normative for either boys or girls—exposes the biological sleight of hand that suggests that what is normative—enforced, socially prescribed—is actually normal. But psychological models themselves do not go far enough; they are unable to fully explain the variations *among* men or women based on class, race, ethnicity, sexuality, and age, or to explain the ways in which one gender consistently enjoys power over the other. And, most importantly to sociologists, psychological models describe how individuals acquire sex role identity, but then assume that these gendered individuals enact their gendered identities in institutions that are gender-neutral.

Sociologists have taken up each of these themes in exploring (1) how the institutions in which we find ourselves are also gendered, (2) the ways in which those psychological prescriptions for gender identity reproduce *both* gender difference and male domination, and (3) the ways in which gender is accomplished and expressed in everyday interaction.

In their essay, Judith Gerson and Kathy Peiss provide a conceptual mapping of the field of gender relations based on asymmetries of power and inequality between women and men. Using the terms *boundaries, negotiation,* and *consciousness,* they renavigate the study of gender toward a model that explains both difference and domination, as well as establishing the foundations for resistance.

Joan Acker explains the ways in which institutions themselves are gendered, and that individuals—regardless of their gender identity—are pressed to act according to certain organizational logics that reproduce gender relations. Taking a very different approach, Candace West and Don Zimmerman make it clear that gender is not a property of the individual, something that one has, but rather is a process that one does in everyday interaction with others.

JOAN ACKER

Hierarchies, Jobs, Bodies: A Theory of Gendered Organizations

Most of us spend most of our days in work organizations that are almost always dominated by men. The most powerful organizational positions are almost entirely occupied by men, with the exception of the occasional biological female who acts as a social man. Power at the national and world level is located in all-male enclaves at the pinnacle of large state and economic organizations. These facts are not news, although sociologists paid no attention to them until feminism came along to point out the problematic nature of the obvious. Writers on organizations and organizational theory now include some consideration of women and gender, but their treatment is usually cursory, and male domination is, on the whole, not analyzed and not explained.

Among feminist social scientists there are some outstanding contributions on women and organizations, such as the work of Kanter (1977), Feldberg and Glenn (1979), MacKinnon (1979), and Ferguson (1984). In addition, there have been theoretical and empirical investigations of particular aspects of organizational structure and process, and women's situations have been studied using traditional organizational ideas. Moreover, the very rich literature, popular and scholarly, on women and work contains much material on work organizations. However, most of this new knowledge has not been brought together in a systematic feminist theory of organizations.

A systematic theory of gender and organizations is needed for a number of reasons. First, the gender segregation of work, including divisions between paid and unpaid work, is partly created through organizational practices. Second, and related to gender segregation, income and status inequality between women and men is also partly created in organizational processes; understanding these processes is necessary for understanding gender inequality. Third, organizations are one arena in which widely disseminated cultural images of gender are invented and reproduced. Knowledge of cultural production is important for understanding gender construction. Fourth, some aspects of individual gender identity, perhaps particularly masculinity, are also products of organizational processes and pressures. Fifth, an important feminist project is to make large-scale organizations more democratic and more supportive of humane goals.

In this article, I begin by speculating about why feminist scholars have not debated organizational theory. I then look briefly at how those feminist scholars who have paid attention to organizations have conceptualized them. In the main part of the article, I examine organizations as gendered processes in which both gender and sexuality have been obscured through a gender-neutral, asexual discourse, and suggest some of the ways that gender, the body, and sexuality are part of the

From *Gender & Society,* Vol. 4, no. 2 (June 1990), pp. 139–158. References have been edited.

processes of control in work organizations. Finally, I point to some directions for feminist theory about this ubiquitous human invention.

WHY SO LITTLE FEMINIST DEBATE ON ORGANIZATIONS?

The early radical feminist critique of sexism denounced bureaucracy and hierarchy as male-created and male-dominated structures of control that oppress women. The easiest answer to the "why so little debate" question is that the link between masculinity and organizational power was so obvious that no debate was needed. However, experiences in the feminist movement suggest that the questions are not exhausted by recognizing male power.

Part of the feminist project was to create nonhierarchical, egalitarian organizations that would demonstrate the possibilities of nonpatriarchal ways of working. Although many feminist organizations survived, few retained this radical-democratic form. Others succumbed to the same sorts of pressures that have undermined other utopian experiments with alternative work forms, yet analyses of feminist efforts to create alternative organizations were not followed by debates about the feasibility of nonpatriarchal, nonhierarchical organization or the relationship of organizations and gender. Perhaps one of the reasons was that the reality was embarrassing; women failing to cooperate with each other, taking power and using it in oppressive ways, creating their own structures of status and reward were at odds with other images of women as nurturing and supportive.

Another reason for feminist theorists' scant attention to conceptualizing organizations probably lies in the nature of the concepts and models at hand. As Dorothy Smith (1979) has argued, the available discourses on organizations, the way that organizational sociology is defined as an area or domain "is grounded in the working worlds and relations of men, whose experience and interests arise in the course of and in relation to participation in the ruling apparatus of this society" (p. 148). Concepts developed to answer managerial questions, such as how to achieve organizational efficiency, were irrelevant to feminist questions, such as why women are always concentrated at the bottom of organizational structures.

Critical perspectives on organizations, with the notable exception of some of the studies of the labor process, although focusing on control, power, exploitation, and how these relations might be changed, have ignored women and have been insensitive to the implications of gender for their own goals. The active debate on work democracy, the area of organizational exploration closest to feminist concerns about oppressive structures, has been almost untouched by feminist insights. For example, Carole Pateman's influential book, *Participation and Democratic Theory* (1970), critical in shaping the discussions on democratic organization in the 1970s, did not consider women or gender. More recently, Pateman (1983a, 1983b, 1988) has examined the fundamental ideas of democracy from a feminist perspective, and other feminist political scientists have criticized theories of democracy, but on the whole, their work is isolated from the main discourse on work organization and democracy.

Empirical research on work democracy has also ignored women and gender.

For example, in the 1980s, many male Swedish researchers saw little relation between questions of democracy and gender equality with a few exceptions. Other examples are studies of Mondragon, a community in the Spanish Basque country, which is probably the most famous attempt at democratic ownership, control, and organization. Until Sally Hacker's feminist study (1987), researchers who went to Mondragon to see this model of work democracy failed to note the situation of women and asked no questions about gender. In sum, the absence of women and gender from theoretical and empirical studies about work democracy provided little material for feminist theorizing.

Another impediment to feminist theorizing is that the available discourses conceptualize organizations as gender neutral. Both traditional and critical approaches to organizations originate in the male, abstract intellectual domain and take as reality the world as seen from that standpoint. As a relational phenomenon, gender is difficult to see when only the masculine is present. Since men in organizations take their behavior and perspectives to represent the human, organizational structures and processes are theorized as gender neutral. When it is acknowledged that women and men are affected differently by organizations, it is argued that gendered attitudes and behavior are brought into (and contaminate) essentially gender-neutral structures. This view of organizations separates structures from the people in them.

Current theories of organization also ignore sexuality. Certainly, a gender-neutral structure is also asexual. If sexuality is a core component of the production of gender identity, gender images, and gender inequality, organizational theory that is blind to sexuality does not immediately offer avenues into the comprehension of gender domination. Catharine MacKinnon's (1982) compelling argument that sexual domination of women is embedded within legal organizations has not to date become part of mainstream discussions. Rather, behaviors such as sexual harassment are viewed as deviations of gendered actors, not, as MacKinnon (1979) might argue, as components of organizational structure.

FEMINIST ANALYSES OF ORGANIZATIONS

The treatment of women and gender most assimilated into the literature on organizations is Rosabeth Moss Kanter's *Men and Women of the Corporation* (1977). Kanter sets out to show that gender differences in organizational behavior are due to structure rather than to characteristics of women and men as individuals (1977, 291–92). She argues that the problems women have in large organizations are consequences of their structural placement, crowded in dead-end jobs at the bottom and exposed as tokens at the top. Gender enters the picture through organizational roles that "carry characteristic images of the kinds of people that should occupy them" (p. 250). Here, Kanter recognizes the presence of gender in early models of organizations:

> A "masculine ethic" of rationality and reason can be identified in the early image of managers. This "masculine ethic" elevates the traits assumed to belong

> to men with educational advantages to necessities for effective organizations: a tough-minded approach to problems; analytic abilities to abstract and plan; a capacity to set aside personal, emotional considerations in the interests of task accomplishment; a cognitive superiority in problem-solving and decision making. (1974, 43)

Identifying the central problem of seeming gender neutrality, Kanter observes: "While organizations were being defined as sex-neutral machines, masculine principles were dominating their authority structures" (1977, 46).

In spite of these insights, organizational structure, not gender, is the focus of Kanter's analysis. In posing the argument as structure *or* gender, Kanter also implicitly posits gender as standing outside of structure, and she fails to follow up her own observations about masculinity and organizations (1977, 22). Kanter's analysis of the effects of organizational position applies as well to men in low-status positions. Her analysis of the effect of numbers, or the situation of the "token" worker, applies also to men as minorities in women-predominant organizations, but fails to account for gender differences in the situation of the token. In contrast to the token woman, white men in women-dominated workplaces are likely to be positively evaluated and to be rapidly promoted to positions of greater authority. The specificity of male dominance is absent in Kanter's argument, even though she presents a great deal of material that illuminates gender and male dominance.

Another approach, using Kanter's insights but building on the theoretical work of Hartmann (1976), is the argument that organizations have a dual structure, bureaucracy and patriarchy (Ressner 1987). Ressner argues that bureaucracy has its own dynamic, and gender enters through patriarchy, a more or less autonomous structure, that exists alongside the bureaucratic structure. The analysis of two hierarchies facilitates and clarifies the discussion of women's experiences of discrimination, exclusion, segregation, and low wages. However, this approach has all the problems of two systems theories of women's oppression: the central theory of bureaucratic or organizational structure is unexamined, and patriarchy is added to allow the theorist to deal with women. Like Kanter, Ressner's approach implicitly accepts the assumption of mainstream organizational theory that organizations are gender-neutral social phenomena.

Ferguson, in *The Feminist Case Against Bureaucracy* (1984), develops a radical feminist critique of bureaucracy as an organization of oppressive male power, arguing that it is both mystified and constructed through an abstract discourse on rationality, rules, and procedures. Thus, in contrast to the implicit arguments of Kanter and Ressner, Ferguson views bureaucracy itself as a construction of male domination. In response to this overwhelming organization of power, bureaucrats, workers, and clients are all "feminized," as they develop ways of managing their powerlessness that at the same time perpetuate their dependence. Ferguson argues further that feminist discourse, rooted in women's experiences of caring and nurturing outside bureaucracy's control, provides a ground for opposition to bureaucracy and for the development of alternative ways of organizing society.

However, there are problems with Ferguson's theoretical formulation. Her argument that feminization is a metaphor for bureaucratization not only uses a stereotype of femininity as oppressed, weak, and passive, but also, by equating the experience of male and female clients, women workers, and male bureaucrats, obscures the specificity of women's experiences and the connections between masculinity and power. Ferguson builds on Foucault's (1979) analysis of power as widely diffused and constituted through discourse, and the problems in her analysis have their origin in Foucault, who also fails to place gender in his analysis of power. What results is a disembodied, and consequently gender-neutral, bureaucracy as the oppressor. That is, of course, not a new vision of bureaucracy, but it is one in which gender enters only as analogy, rather than as a complex component of processes of control and domination.

In sum, some of the best feminist attempts to theorize about gender and organizations have been trapped within the constraints of definitions of the theoretical domain that cast organizations as gender neutral and asexual. These theories take us only part of the way to understanding how deeply embedded gender is in organizations. There is ample empirical evidence: We know now that gender segregation is an amazingly persistent pattern and that the gender identity of jobs and occupations is repeatedly reproduced, often in new forms. The reconstruction of gender segregation is an integral part of the dynamic of technological and organizational change. Individual men and particular groups of men do not always win in these processes, but masculinity always seems to symbolize self-respect for men at the bottom and power for men at the top, while confirming for both their gender's superiority. Theories that posit organization and bureaucracy as gender neutral cannot adequately account for this continual gendered structuring. We need different theoretical strategies that examine organizations as gendered processes in which sexuality also plays a part.

ORGANIZATION AS GENDERED PROCESSES

The idea that social structure and social processes are gendered has slowly emerged in diverse areas of feminist discourse. Feminists have elaborated gender as a concept to mean more than a socially constructed, binary identity and image. This turn to gender as an analytic category is an attempt to find new avenues into the dense and complicated problem of explaining the extraordinary persistence through history and across societies of the subordination of women. Scott, for example, defines gender as follows: "The core of the definition rests on an integral connection between two propositions; gender is a constitutive element of social relationships based on perceived differences between the sexes, and gender is a primary way of signifying relationships of power" (1986, 1067).

New approaches to the study of waged work, particularly studies of the labor process, see organizations as gendered, not as gender neutral and conceptualize organizations as one of the locations of the inextricably intertwined production of both gender and class relations. Examining class and gender, I have argued that class is constructed through gender and that class relations are always gendered.

The structure of the labor market, relations in the workplace, the control of the work process, and the underlying wage relation are always affected by symbols of gender, processes of gender identity, and material inequalities between women and men. These processes are complexly related to and powerfully support the reproduction of the class structure. Here, I will focus on the interface of gender and organizations, assuming the simultaneous presence of class relations.

To say that an organization, or any other analytic unit, is gendered means that advantage and disadvantage, exploitation and control, action and emotion, meaning and identity, are patterned through and in terms of a distinction between male and female, masculine and feminine. Gender is not an addition to ongoing processes, conceived as gender neutral. Rather, it is an integral part of those processes, which cannot be properly understood without an analysis of gender. Gendering occurs in at least five interacting processes that, although analytically distinct, are, in practice, parts of the same reality.

First is the construction of divisions along lines of gender—divisions of labor, of allowed behaviors, of locations in physical space, of power, including the institutionalized means of maintaining the divisions in the structures of labor markets, the family, the state. Such divisions in work organizations are well documented as well as often obvious to casual observers. Although there are great variations in the patterns and extent of gender division, men are almost always in the highest positions of organizational power. Managers' decisions often initiate gender divisions, and organizational practices maintain them—although they also take on new forms with changes in technology and the labor process. For example, Cynthia Cockburn (1983, 1985) has shown how the introduction of new technology in a number of industries was accompanied by a reorganization, but not abolition, of the gendered division of labor that left the technology in men's control and maintained the definition of skilled work as men's work and unskilled work as women's work.

Second is the construction of symbols and images that explain, express, reinforce, or sometimes oppose those divisions. These have many sources or forms in language, ideology, popular and high culture, dress, the press, television. For example, as Kanter (1975), among others, has noted, the image of the top manager or the business leader is an image of successful, forceful masculinity. In Cockburn's studies, men workers' images of masculinity linked their gender with their technical skills; the possibility that women might also obtain such skills represented a threat to that masculinity.

The third set of processes that produce gendered social structures, including organizations, are interactions between women and men, women and women, men and men, including all those patterns that enact dominance and submission. For example, conversation analysis shows how gender differences in interruptions, turn taking, and setting the topic of discussion recreate gender inequality in the flow of ordinary talk. Although much of this research has used experimental groups, qualitative accounts of organizational life record the same phenomena: Men are the actors, women the emotional support.

Fourth, these processes help to produce gendered components of individual identity, which may include consciousness of the existence of the other three aspects of gender, such as, in organizations, choice of appropriate work, language use, clothing, and presentation of self as a gendered member of an organization.

Finally, gender is implicated in the fundamental, ongoing processes of creating and conceptualizing social structures. Gender is obviously a basic constitutive element in family and kinship, but, less obviously, it helps to frame the underlying relations of other structures, including complex organizations. Gender is a constitutive element in organizational logic, or the underlying assumptions and practices that construct most contemporary work organizations. Organizational logic appears to be gender neutral; gender-neutral theories of bureaucracy and organizations employ and give expression to this logic. However, underlying both academic theories and practical guides for managers is a gendered substructure that is reproduced daily in practical work activities and, somewhat less frequently, in the writings of organizational theorists.

Organizational logic has material forms in written work rules, labor contracts, managerial directives, and other documentary tools for running large organizations, including systems of job evaluation widely used in the comparable-worth strategy of feminists. Job evaluation is accomplished through the use and interpretation of documents that describe jobs and how they are to be evaluated. These documents contain symbolic indicators of structure; the ways that they are interpreted and talked about in the process of job evaluation reveals the underlying organizational logic. I base the following theoretical discussion on my observations of organizational logic in action in the job-evaluation component of a comparable-worth project.

Job evaluation is a management tool used in every industrial country, capitalist and socialist, to rationalize the organizational hierarchy and to help in setting equitable wages. Although there are many different systems of job evaluation, the underlying rationales are similar enough so that the observation of one system can provide a window into a common organizational mode of thinking and practice.

In job evaluation, the content of jobs is described and jobs are compared on criteria of knowledge, skill, complexity, effort, and working conditions. The particular system I observed was built incrementally over many years to reflect the assessment of managers about the job components for which they were willing to pay. Thus today this system can be taken as composed of residues of these judgments, which are a set of decision rules that, when followed, reproduce managerial values. But these rules are also the imagery out of which managers construct and reconstruct their organizations. The rules of job evaluation, which help to determine pay differences between jobs, are not simply a compilation of managers' values or sets of beliefs, but are the underlying logic or organization that provides at least part of the blueprint for its structure. Every time that job evaluation is used, that structure is created or reinforced.

Job evaluation evaluates jobs, not their incumbents. The job is the basic unit in a work organization's hierarchy, a description of a set of tasks, competencies, and responsibilities represented as a position on an organizational chart. A job is separate from people. It is an empty slot, a reification that must continually be reconstructed, for positions exist only as scraps of paper until people fill them. The rationale for evaluating jobs as devoid of actual workers reveals further the organizational logic—the intent is to assess the characteristics of the job, not of their incumbents who may vary in skill, industriousness, and commitment. Human beings are to be motivated, managed, and chosen to fit the job. The job exists as a thing apart.

Every job has a place in the hierarchy, another essential element in organizational logic. Hierarchies, like jobs, are devoid of actual workers and based on abstract differentiations. Hierarchy is taken for granted, only its particular form is at issue. Job evaluation is based on the assumption that workers in general see hierarchy as an acceptable principle, and the final test of the evaluation of any particular job is whether its place in the hierarchy looks reasonable. The ranking of jobs within an organization must make sense to managers, but it is also important that most workers accept the ranking as just if the system of evaluation is to contribute to orderly working relationships.

Organizational logic assumes a congruence between responsibility, job complexity, and hierarchical position. For example, a lower-level position, the level of most jobs filled predominantly by women, must have equally low levels of complexity and responsibility. Complexity and responsibility are defined in terms of managerial and professional tasks. The child-care worker's responsibility for other human beings or the complexity facing the secretary who serves six different, temperamental bosses can only be minimally counted if the congruence between position level, responsibility, and complexity is to be preserved. In addition, the logic holds that two jobs at different hierarchical levels cannot be responsible for the same outcome; as a consequence, for example, tasks delegated to a secretary by a manager will not raise her hierarchical level because such tasks are still his responsibility, even though she has the practical responsibility to see that they are done. Levels of skill, complexity, and responsibility, all used in constructing hierarchy, are conceptualized as existing independently of any concrete worker.

In organizational logic, both jobs and hierarchies are abstract categories that have no occupants, no human bodies, no gender. However, an abstract job can exist, can be transformed into a concrete instance, only if there is a worker. In organizational logic, filling the abstract job is a disembodied worker who exists only for the work. Such a hypothetical worker cannot have other imperatives of existence that impinge upon the job. At the very least, outside imperatives cannot be included within the definition of the job. Too many obligations outside the boundaries of the job would make a worker unsuited for the position. The closest the disembodied worker doing the abstract job comes to a real worker is the male worker whose life centers on his full-time, life-long job, while his wife or another woman takes care of his personal needs and his children. While the realities of life in industrial capitalism never allowed all men to live out this ideal, it was the goal for labor unions and the image of the worker in social and economic theory. The woman worker, assumed to have legitimate obligations other than those required by the job, did not fit with the abstract job.

The concept "a job" is thus implicitly a gendered concept, even though organizational logic presents it as gender neutral. "A job" already contains the gender-based division of labor and the separation between the public and the private sphere. The concept of "a job" assumes a particular gendered organization of domestic life and social production. It is an example of what Dorothy Smith has called "the gender subtext of the rational and impersonal" (1988, 4).

Hierarchies are gendered because they also are constructed on these underlying assumptions: Those who are committed to paid employment are "naturally" more suited to responsibility and authority; those who must divide their commitments are in the lower ranks. In addition, principles of hierarchy, as exemplified in most existing job-evaluation systems, have been derived from already existing gendered structures. The best-known systems were developed by management consultants working with managers to build methods of consistently evaluating jobs and rationalizing pay and job classifications. For example, all managers with similar levels of responsibility in the firm should have similar pay. Job-evaluation systems were intended to reflect the values of managers and to produce a believable ranking of jobs based on those values. Such rankings would not deviate substantially from rankings already in place that contain gender typing and gender segregation of jobs and the clustering of women workers in the lowest and the worst-paid jobs. The concrete value judgments that constitute conventional job evaluation are designed to replicate such structures. Replication is achieved in many ways; for example, skills in managing money, more often found in men's than in women's jobs, frequently receive more points than skills in dealing with clients or human relations skills, more often found in women's than in men's jobs.

The gender-neutral status of "a job" and of the organizational theories of which it is a part depend upon the assumption that the worker is abstract, disembodied, although in actuality both the concept of "a job" and real workers are deeply gendered and "bodied." Carole Pateman (1986), in a discussion of women and political theory, similarly points out that the most fundamental abstraction in the concept of liberal individualism is "the abstraction of the 'individual' from the body. In order for the individual to appear in liberal theory as a universal figure, who represents anyone and everyone, the individual must be disembodied" (p. 8). If the individual were not abstracted from bodily attributes, it would be clear that the individual represents one sex and one gender, not a universal being. The political fiction of the universal "individual" or "citizen," fundamental to ideas of democracy and contract, excluded women, judging them lacking in the capacities necessary for participation in civil society. Although women now have the rights of citizens in democratic states, they still stand in an ambiguous relationship to the universal individual who is "constructed from a male body so that his identity is always masculine" (Pateman 1988, 223). The worker with "a job" is the same universal "individual" who in actual social reality is a man. The concept of a universal worker excludes and marginalizes women who cannot, almost by definition, achieve the qualities of a real worker because to do so is to become like a man.

ORGANIZATIONAL CONTROL, GENDER, AND THE BODY

The abstract, bodiless worker, who occupies the abstract, gender-neutral job has no sexuality, no emotions, and does not procreate. The absence of sexuality, emotionality, and procreation in organizational logic and organizational theory is an additional element that both obscures and helps to reproduce the underlying gender relations.

New work on sexuality in organizations, often indebted to Foucault (1979), suggests that this silence on sexuality may have historical roots in the development of large, all-male organizations that are the primary locations of societal power. The history of modern organizations includes, among other processes, the suppression of sexuality in the interests of organization and the conceptual exclusion of the body as a concrete living whole.

In a review of historical evidence on sexuality in early modern organizations, Burrell (1984, 98) suggests that "the suppression of sexuality is one of the first tasks the bureaucracy sets itself." Long before the emergence of the very large factory of the nineteenth century, other large organizations, such as armies and monasteries, which had allowed certain kinds of limited participation of women, were more and more excluding women and attempting to banish sexuality in the interests of control of members and the organization's activities. Active sexuality was the enemy of orderly procedures, and excluding women from certain areas of activity may have been, at least in part, a way to control sexuality. As Burrell (1984) points out, the exclusion of women did not eliminate homosexuality, which has always been an element in the life of large all-male organizations, particularly if members spend all of their time in the organization. Insistence on heterosexuality or celibacy were ways to control homosexuality. But heterosexuality had to be practiced outside the organization, whether it was an army or a capitalist workplace. Thus the attempts to banish sexuality from the workplace were part of the wider process that differentiated the home, the location of legitimate sexual activity, from the place of capitalist production. The concept of the disembodied job symbolizes this separation of work and sexuality.

Similarly, there is no place within the disembodied job or the gender-neutral organization for other "bodied" processes, such as human reproduction or the free expression of emotions. Sexuality, procreation, and emotions all intrude upon and disrupt the ideal functioning of the organization, which tries to control such interferences. However, as argued above, the abstract worker is actually a man, and it is the man's body, its sexuality, minimal responsibility in procreation, and conventional control of emotions that pervades work and organizational processes. Women's bodies—female sexuality, their ability to procreate and their pregnancy, breast-feeding, and child care, menstruation, and mythic "emotionality"—are suspect, stigmatized, and used as grounds for control and exclusion.

The ranking of women's jobs is often justified on the basis of women's identification with childbearing and domestic life. They are devalued because women are assumed to be unable to conform to the demands of the abstract job. Gender segregation at work is also sometimes openly justified by the necessity to control sexuality, and women may be barred from types of work, such as skilled blue-collar work or top management, where most workers are men, on the grounds that potentially disruptive sexual liaisons should be avoided. On the other hand, the gendered definition of some jobs "includes sexualization of the woman worker as a part of the job" (MacKinnon 1979, 18). These are often jobs that serve men, such as secretaries, or a largely male public.

The maintenance of gendered hierarchy is achieved partly through such often-tacit controls based on arguments about women's reproduction, emotionality, and sexuality, helping to legitimate the organizational structures created through abstract, intellectualized techniques. More overt controls, such as sexual harassment, relegating childbearing women to lower-level mobility tracks, and penalizing (or rewarding) their emotion management also conform to and reinforce hierarchy. MacKinnon (1979), on the basis of an extensive analysis of legal cases, argues that the willingness to tolerate sexual harassment is often a condition of the job, both a consequence and a cause of gender hierarchy.

While women's bodies are ruled out of order, or sexualized and objectified, in work organizations, men's bodies are not. Indeed, male sexual imagery pervades organizational metaphors and language, helping to give form to work activities. For example, the military and the male world of sports are considered valuable training for organizational success and provide images for teamwork, campaigns, and tough competition. The symbolic expression of male sexuality may be used as a means of control over male workers, too, allowed or even encouraged within the bounds of the work situation to create cohesion or alleviate stress. Management approval of pornographic pictures in the locker room or support for all-male work and play groups where casual talk is about sexual exploits or sports are examples. These symbolic expressions of male dominance also act as significant controls over women in work organizations because they are per se excluded from the informal bonding men produce with the "body talk" of sex and sports.

Symbolically, a certain kind of male heterosexual sexuality plays an important part in legitimating organizational power. Connell (1987) calls this hegemonic masculinity, emphasizing that it is formed around dominance over women and in opposition to other masculinities, although its exact content changes as historical conditions change. Currently, hegemonic masculinity is typified by the image of the strong, technically competent, authoritative leader who is sexually potent and attractive, has a family, and has his emotions under control. Images of male sexual function and patriarchal paternalism may also be embedded in notions of what the manager does when he leads his organization. Women's bodies cannot be adapted to hegemonic masculinity; to function at the top of male hierarchies requires that women render irrelevant everything that makes them women.

The image of the masculine organizational leader could be expanded, without altering its basic elements, to include other qualities also needed, according to many management experts, in contemporary organizations, such as flexibility and sensitivity to the capacities and needs of subordinates. Such qualities are not necessarily the symbolic monopoly of women. For example, the wise and experienced coach is empathetic and supportive to his individual players and flexibly leads his team against devious opposition tactics to victory.

The connections between organizational power and men's sexuality may be even more deeply embedded in organizational processes. Sally Hacker (1989) argues that eroticism and technology have common roots in human sensual pleasure and that for the engineer or the skilled worker, and probably for many other kinds of workers, there is a powerful erotic element in work processes. The pleasures of technology, Hacker continues, become harnessed to domination, and passion becomes directed toward power over nature, the machine, and other people, particularly women, in the work hierarchy. Hacker believes that men lose a great deal in this transformation of the erotic into domination, but they also win in other ways. For example, many men gain economically from the organizational gender hierarchy. As Crompton and Jones (1984) point out, men's career opportunities in white-collar work depend on the barriers that deny those opportunities to women. If the mass of female clerical workers were able to compete with men in such work, promotion probabilities for men would be drastically reduced.

Class relations as well as gender relations are reproduced in organizations. Critical, but nonfeminist, perspectives on work organizations argue that rational-technical systems for organizing work, such as job classification and evaluation systems and detailed specification of how work is to be done, are parts of pervasive systems of control that help to maintain class relations. The abstract "job," devoid of a human body, is a basic unit in such systems of control. The positing of a job as an abstract category, separate from the worker, is an essential move in creating jobs as mechanisms of compulsion and control over work processes. Rational-technical, ostensibly gender-neutral, control systems are built upon and conceal a gendered substructure (Smith 1988) in which men's bodies fill the abstract jobs. Use of such abstract systems continually reproduces the underlying gender assumptions and the subordinated or excluded place of women. Gender processes, including the manipulation and management of women's and men's sexuality, procreation, and emotion, are part of the control processes of organizations, maintaining not only gender stratification but contributing also to maintaining class and, possibly, race and ethnic relations. Is the abstract worker white as well as male? Are white-male-dominated organizations also built on underlying assumptions about the proper place of people with different skin colors? Are racial differences produced by organizational practices as gender differences are?

CONCLUSION

Feminists wanting to theorize about organizations face a difficult task because of the deeply embedded gendering of both organizational processes and theory. Commonsense notions, such as jobs and positions, which constitute the units managers use in making organizations and some theorists use in making theory, are posited upon the prior exclusion of women. This underlying construction of a way of thinking is not simply an error, but part of processes of organization. This exclusion in turn creates fundamental inadequacies in theorizing about gender-neutral systems of positions to be filled. Creating more adequate theory may come only as organizations are transformed in ways that dissolve the concept of the abstract job and restore the absent female body.

Such a transformation would be radical in practice because it would probably require the end of organizations as they exist today, along with a redefinition of work and work relations. The rhythm and timing of work would be adapted to the rhythms of life outside of work. Caring work would be just as important and well rewarded as any other; having a baby or taking care of a sick mother would be as valued as making an automobile or designing computer software. Hierarchy would be abolished, and workers would run things themselves. Of course, women and men would share equally in different kinds of work. Perhaps there would be some communal or collective form of organization where work and intimate relations are closely related, children learn in places close to working adults, and workmates, lovers, and friends are all part of the same group. Utopian writers and experimenters have left us many possible models (Hacker 1989). But this brief listing begs many questions, perhaps the most important of which is how, given the present organization of economy and technology and the pervasive and powerful, impersonal, textually mediated relations of ruling (Smith 1988), so radical a change could come about.

Feminist research and theorizing, by continuing to puzzle out how gender provides the subtext for arrangements of subordination, can make some contributions to a future in which collective action to do what needs doing—producing goods, caring for people, disposing of the garbage—is organized so that dominance, control, and subordination, particularly the subordination of women, are eradicated, or at least minimized, in our organization life.

References

Burrell, Gibson. 1984. Sex and organizational analysis. *Organization Studies* 5:97–118.

Cockburn, Cynthia. 1983. *Brothers: Male dominance and technological change.* London: Pluto Press.

———. 1985. *Machinery of dominance.* London: Pluto Press.

Connell, R. W. 1987. *Gender and power.* Stanford, CA: Stanford University Press.

Crompton, Rosemary, and Gareth Jones. 1984. *White-collar proletariat: deskilling and gender in clerical work.* Philadelphia: Temple University Press.

Feldberg, Roslyn, and Evelyn Nakano Glenn. 1979. Male and female: Job versus gender models in the sociology of work. *Social Problems* 26:524–38.

Ferguson, Kathy E. 1984. *The feminist case against bureaucracy.* Philadelphia: Temple University Press.

Foucault, Michel. 1979. *The history of sexuality,* Vol. 1. London: Allen Lane.

Hacker, Sally. 1987. Women workers in the Mondragon system of industrial cooperatives. *Gender & Society* 1:358–79.

———. 1989. *Pleasure, power and technology.* Boston: Unwin Hyman.

Hartmann, Heidi. 1976. Capitalism, patriarchy and job segregation by sex. *Signs* 1:137–70.

Kanter, Rosabeth Moss. 1975. Women and the structure of organizations: Explorations in

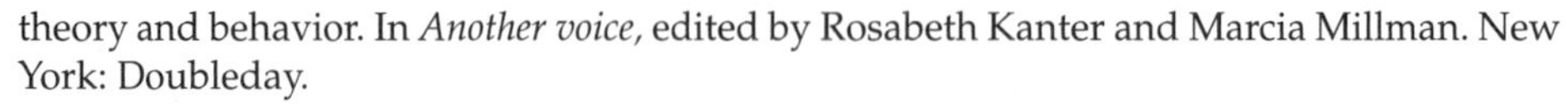

theory and behavior. In *Another voice,* edited by Rosabeth Kanter and Marcia Millman. New York: Doubleday.

———. 1977. *Men and women of the corporation.* New York: Basic Books.

MacKinnon, Catharine A. 1979. *Sexual harassment of working women.* New Haven, CT: Yale University Press.

———. 1982. Feminism, Marxism, method and the state: An agenda for theory. *Signs* 7:515–44.

Pateman, Carole. 1970. *Participation and democratic theory.* Cambridge: Cambridge University Press.

———. 1983a. Feminist critiques of the public private dichotomy. In *Public and private in social life,* edited by S. I. Benn and G. F. Gaus. Beckenham, Kent: Croom Helm.

———. 1983b. Feminism and democracy. In *Democratic theory and practice,* edited by Graeme Duncan. Cambridge: Cambridge University Press.

———. 1986. Introduction: The theoretical subversiveness of feminism. In *Feminist challenges,* edited by Carole Pateman and Elizabeth Gross. Winchester, MA: Allen & Unwin.

———. 1988. *The sexual contract.* Cambridge, MA: Polity.

Ressner, Ulla. 1986. Review of K. Ferguson, *The feminist case against bureaucracy. Economic and Industrial Democracy* 7:130–34.

———. 1987. *The hidden hierarchy.* Aldershot: Gower.

Scott, Joan. 1986. Gender: A useful category of historical analysis. *American Historical Review* 91:1053–75.

Smith, Dorothy E. 1979. A sociology for women. In *The prism of sex: Essays in the sociology of knowledge,* edited by Julia A. Sherman and Evelyn Torten Beck. Madison: University of Wisconsin Press.

———. 1988. *The everyday world as problematic.* Boston: Northeastern University Press.

JUDITH M. GERSON AND KATHY PEISS

Boundaries, Negotiation, Consciousness: Reconceptualizing Gender Relations

Over the last fifteen years research on sex and gender has examined the role of women in the past and present, recovered neglected human experiences, and transformed social analysis. A key contribution of this work—one that directly confronts traditional interpretations of women—is that gender is a primary social category which cannot be subsumed under such analytical categories as class and caste. Conceptualizing gender, however, remains a problem. Questions of how

From *Social Problems,* Vol. 32, no. 4 (April 1985), pp. 317–331. References have been edited.

gender systems operate, their cultural construction, and their relation to individual and social interactions often are implicit in the analysis of women's experience. As a result, calls for greater definitional and theoretical clarity have been issued and scholars in this field increasingly have asserted the need to understand gender as a system of social relations.

This formulation of gender asserts that gender is defined by socially constructed relationships between women and men, among women, and among men in social groups. Gender is not a rigid or reified analytic category imposed on human experience, but a fluid one whose meaning emerges in specific social contexts as it is created and recreated through human actions. Analysis of gender relations necessarily goes beyond comparisons of the status and power of the sexes, involving examination of the dynamic, reciprocal, and interdependent interactions between and among women and men. In these relationships—those, for example, which construct the sexual division of labor and the social organization of sexuality and reproduction—women and men constitute distinct social groups.

While the problems of conceptualization remain significant, scholars have identified and elaborated several major constructs central to an analysis of gender as a system of social relations: (1) separate spheres; (2) domination of women; and (3) sex-related consciousness. The first, separate spheres, has allowed scholars to examine the different material and ideological worlds in which women and men work, live, and think. The literature on domination explains the forms and processes of physical intimidation, economic exploitation, and ideological control to which women are subjected. Lastly, women's consciousness as well as feminist consciousness have been analyzed as rooted in women's distinctive experiences as a social category.

Our aim in this paper is to recast these basic constructs in several ways, by reconsidering gender relations in terms of boundaries, processes of negotiation as well as domination, and gender consciousness as an interactive and multidimensional process. The concept of boundaries describes the complex structures—physical, social, ideological, and psychological—which establish the differences and commonalities between women and men, among women, and among men, shaping and constraining the behavior and attitudes of each gender group. The reciprocal processes of negotiation and domination elucidate the ways in which women and men act to support and challenge the existing system of gender relations. Domination describes the systems of male control and coercion, while negotiation addresses the processes by which men and women bargain for privileges and resources. Each group has some assets which enable it to cooperate with or resist existing social arrangements, although clearly these resources and the consequent power are unequal. Finally, although women's consciousness is grounded conceptually in shared female experiences, it is also an interactive and multidimensional process, developing dialectically in the social relations of the sexes, and involving different forms of awareness among individuals and social groups. We argue that thinking about gender in this way provides a set of more sensitive and complex analytical tools for understanding women's experiences.

BOUNDARIES

The development of the idea of separate spheres in the social science literature has stressed the assignment of women to the domestic realm, men to the public one, the physical separation between both spheres, and the social prestige attached to the public domain. Research on sex and gender has been influenced profoundly by the description of this basic structural division between the sexes, the apparent universality of the concept, and its explanatory power in the analysis of women's experience. Concurrently, the concept of separate spheres has been criticized for its tendency to reify the division of social experience into public/male and private/female worlds, and to overlook the interactions between them.

The use of the "separate spheres" formulation becomes increasingly problematic in the analysis of contemporary society. Unlike 19th century social life with its rigid social, physical, and ideological separation of the sexes, American society today is marked by the blurring of the public and private spheres, as women have entered the workforce in larger numbers, and men seemingly have become more involved in family life. At the same time, considerable social and cultural distance remains. Women's positions in the marketplace are neither secure nor taken for granted, while men's household roles are often marginal and limited. The dichotomy of separate spheres tends to simplify and reduce social life to two discrete physical environments without capturing the complexity of social and cultural divisions. Moreover, the concept has been used in a relatively static way, as a descriptive tool to chronicle and compare women's and men's activities. Only rarely have scholars gone beyond this approach to analyze the interactions between women and men (and among them) as they are influenced by and in turn shape these spheres.

We need a conceptualization that will allow us to express a basic commonality in the division(s) between the sexes and also to encompass definitions of changing patterns of social relations. Refocusing the analysis of gender divisions by using the concept of boundaries has several distinct advantages. First, it overcomes the problem of universality in the "separate spheres" formulation. Boundary is a more generic term which simultaneously allows us to see specific commonalities and discern actual differences in historical and current patterns of gender-based experiences. Second, the concept of boundaries allays the problem of bifurcating gender relations through the assignment of women and men to separate spheres. There are many more boundaries which mark people's lives than the public-private dichotomy suggests. There are boundaries which divide women and men in leisure and work activities, as well as in face-to-face interactions. There are also smaller boundaries within larger ones. In the workplace, for example, gender difference may be maintained by an overall segmentation of the labor force by sex, denoted by the allocation of social space and privileges (e.g., typing pools vs. executive offices, different dining facilities, etc.) and reinforced by limitations on interpersonal behavior (e.g., unidirectional patterns of touch and naming). Finally, the concept of boundaries also suggests permeability, whereas the image of spheres connotes comparatively autonomous environments. Boundaries mark the social territories of gender relations, signalling who ought to be admitted or excluded. There are codes and rules which guide and regulate traffic, with instructions on which boundaries may be transversed under what conditions. As a consequence, boundaries are an important place to observe gender relations; these intersections reveal the normal, acceptable behaviors and attitudes as well as deviant, inappropriate ones. At the same time, boundaries highlight the dynamic quality of the structures of gender relations, as they influence and are shaped by social interactions.

Describing the nature of boundaries and analyzing their congruence or lack of congruence will reveal a complex picture of gender arrangements. This approach should be particularly useful in comparative studies across time and in different cultures. In some periods and places, boundaries are mutually reinforcing or complementary, while in other instances they come into conflict. Within the American middle class in the 19th century, for example, the growing physical boundary between home and workplace was reinforced by a hegemonic ideological boundary, the cult of domesticity, as well as smaller social and cultural distinctions. While some women crossed these boundaries, and entered the public arena of education and voluntary association, most did so within the dynamics of their assignment to the home, rationalizing their activities as an extension of women's mission to protect and uplift the family. A somewhat similar ideological boundary marked the 1950s, in the set of ideas and images Betty Friedan (1963) labelled the "feminine mystique." Unlike the 19th century, however, other boundaries operated at cross-purposes. Physical boundaries between home and workplace become less salient in the mid-20th century as middle-class women entered the labor force in large numbers. Moreover, the ideology of companionate marriage cut across the feminine mystique with its assertion of mutuality, togetherness and male involvement in family life. Examination of the different relationships between boundaries may provide descriptive categories for viewing gender relations over time and in different settings.

The analysis of boundaries—their congruence and contradictions—may be useful in assessing stability and change in a system of gender relations. The above example suggests that mutually reinforcing boundaries will be indicators of relatively stable gender relations, while those that are contradictory may promote or reflect social change. An analysis of such change raises two important questions: How are boundaries reconstituted as existing boundaries are challenged and lose importance? What boundaries become or remain significant in defining gender difference and asymmetry as macro-level divisions become less distinct over time?

The boundaries between home and work provide examples of such changes. How is womens' place redefined when family/work divisions become less rigid and women are no longer anomalies as wage-earners? One consequence is that boundaries *within* the workplace (e.g., occupational segregation) and interactional, micro-level boundaries assume increased significance in defining the subordinate position of women. Occupational segregation sets up divisions within the labor force which reduce women to secondary status; with low-paying, low-status jobs and their continued assignment to the home, women retain their primary definition as housewives. For women entering nontraditional occupations, other boundaries maintain women's marginal and subordinate place. Micro-level phenomena—the persistence of informal group behavior among men (e.g., after-work socializing, the uses of male humor, modes of corporate attire)—act to define insiders and outsiders thus maintaining gender-based distinctions.

A similar definition of boundaries may be seen in the current debate over men's growing role in the household. Men's household labor appears to have increased somewhat in recent years, while ideological support for it (e.g., public discussion of paternity leaves) has grown. At the same time, women and men continue to define male household activity as secondary and marginal, taking the form of "helping out." The bulk of housework, childrearing and caretaking remains women's work.

In both these examples, boundaries shift in small but important ways, indicating a change in gender relations and the ways individual women and men may experience them. At the same time, challenges to the stability of patriarchal social arrangements may be met by concessions which in effect readjust the boundaries, but allow the overall system of male dominance to persist.

Since gender involves the accentuation of human difference into dichotomous categories of femininity and masculinity, the social divisions between women and men constitute the primary boundary of gender relations. On the micro level of analysis, what happens at the boundaries between sexes is frequently evidence of exaggerated gender-specific behavior, as compared with same-sex behavior. Perhaps the most common example of this phenomenon is heterosexual dating behavior, with women and men often playing out traditional stereotypical feminine and masculine roles. On a broader level of analysis, the primacy of the heterosocial boundary is assured by the sexual division of labor and the enforcement of compulsory heterosexuality, both of which assert women's difference from men, their subordinate position, and their dependency.

The concept of boundaries should help delineate the interaction between homosocial and heterosocial relationships, and their role in the construction of gender. Recent research has identified the significance of female friendships, networks, and cultures in providing women with varying degrees of autonomy, support, and influence. Similarly, scholars have documented the same-sex bonding in the realms of business, sports, and the military which supply men with resources, skills, solidarity, and power. Such homosocial relations are influenced by the boundaries between the sexes, and in turn shape these same boundaries. Among 19th century middle-class women, for example, friendships centered on the home, kinship, and ritualistic events; these constituted a separate "female world," which owed its emergence to the rigid structural differentiation between male/public and female/private domains. At the same time, the dynamics of female solidarity led some women into political agitation and reform activities, crossing and subverting this primary boundary. On the other hand, homosocial bonds among men may operate to strengthen the boundaries between the sexes, as they have in the world of sports. Women may pursue individual athletic activities which conflict least with social definitions of femininity, but they do not participate in team sports characterized by masculine rituals. Such rituals not only affirm male dominance through the exclusion of women, but they also promote group bonding, teamwork, and skills at negotiation and conflict resolution, qualities which help build and reinforce men's power in other realms of life.

At the same time, there are boundaries within same-sex groups which influence and in turn are shaped by the division between women and men. For example, the historical barriers between prostitutes and "respectable" married women have reinforced the double standard by strengthening male sexual privilege while dividing women on the basis of sexual morality. In contemporary society, aging is a boundary which separates younger and older women according to standards of physical attractiveness and youth, standards not applied to men. This in turn reinforces competition among women for men thus buttressing the institutional heterosexuality which constructs the primary male-female division and women's subordination.

Boundaries between the sexes and within each sex, in their respective spatial, social, and psychological dimensions, delineate the structure of gender relations at a given time and place. However, to explain how and why boundaries change, we must uncover the ways in which individuals make and reshape their social worlds. Thus, the interpretation of gender relations must involve a theory of social process and consciousness. First we examine the social interactions between individuals and groups which establish, maintain, and potentially subvert boundaries; these are the processes of negotiation and domination.

PROCESSES OF NEGOTIATION AND DOMINATION

A major contribution of scholarship on gender has been the analysis of *domination* in explaining the subordinate position of women. In numerous studies of sex and gender, researchers have documented the ways in which men as a group have power over women as a group. Theorists have raised fundamental questions about the sources of domination and have proposed strategies for changing extant power relations. Analyses of social life in the past and present reveal the extent of male control through physical coercion, reproductive policies, the institution of heterosexuality, economic exploitation, and ideology.

Although this analysis is essential for understanding the dynamics of gender arrangements, it nevertheless has an inherent conceptual shortcoming. Regardless of the theoretical orientation, the assumption is made that women are the passive victims of a system of power or domination. While women are not responsible for their own oppression and exploitation, at the same time they are not fully passive either. We need to explore the various ways women participate in setting up, maintaining, and altering the system of gender relations. This statement does not presume that women somehow ask for the sexism they experience. Rather we are suggesting that there is more than one process going on, perhaps simultaneously. Domination explains the ways women are oppressed and either accommodate or resist, while negotiation describes the ways women and men bargain for privileges and resources. Given the considerable scholarship about domination, we focus our discussion on the process of negotiation, recognizing that the two processes are interdependent and exist concurrently.

The concept of negotiation suggests human agency. Both women and men are active participants, sometimes asking or inviting, sometimes demanding that resources be shared or real located. Implicit in this formulation is the recognition that both women and men have some resources they initially control. In addition, this conceptualization suggests that both parties to a negotiation must somehow agree in order for it to take effect. Not only must there be mutuality in consent, but the process of negotiation is reciprocal. Though men seem to do most of the inviting, women also have done the asking and made demands. Furthermore, the heterosocial negotiations which occur usually involve crossing a boundary, however small. The negotiations which do take place may act to either maintain or change structural boundaries.

The entry of women into the office as clerical workers provides one such example of gender negotiation. Margery Davies (1982) has shown that women were allowed into the office only after the invention of the typewriter and its popular acceptance as a tool for low-paid, unskilled labor. In other words, women were "invited" into the office as clerical workers, crossing a boundary that years earlier they could not have trespassed. Office work for women appeared to be a real asset to them since other opportunities for wage earning were limited. Women may choose to participate because they perceive possibilities for economic gains or status enhancement. While we can speak of individual women being invited into the office by individual male bosses, it is important to remember that the processes of invitation and negotiation operate on the level of social groups.

Women also have the resources to negotiate with men for access to privileges and opportunities. Micaela di Leonardo (1984) has demonstrated that women do the kin work—the labor involved in sustaining and nurturing ties and affiliations among family kin. Her sample, a group of Italian American families living in California, showed a pattern in which women had greater knowledge about kin, had stronger familial ties, and did more of the planning of kin gatherings than did the men. These women derived not only responsibilities and obligations from these duties, but prerogatives and power as well. As a result, women had control over a set of kin-based resources and permitted men access to those resources only if and when the women so desired.

While these examples demonstrate that women and men actively participate in negotiations, they also suggest a fundamental asymmetry in the process of negotiation which is integrally tied to the process of domination. Women's dependency is ensured through domination in many forms, including exploitation in the system of wage labor, structured through occupational segregation. Given their low economic status, most women are in some way ultimately dependent on men's work, a dependency reinforced by the ideology and material conditions of compulsory heterosexuality. Given their relative lack of structural power, women have fewer resources with which to negotiate, experience fewer situations in which they can set up negotiations, and derive fewer advantages from their negotiations.

What then is the effect of these negotiations on the system of gender relations? On the one hand, they may permit the system to continue in "dynamic stasis," with reciprocal negotiations between women and men reifying structural boundaries in daily life. The traditional act of marriage exemplifies this form of negotiation, being a "free" exchange of obligations and responsibilities which reinforce heterosexuality and the sexual division of labor. However, an alternative consequence might be an adjustment in the boundaries either proceeded, accompanied, or followed by an alteration in consciousness. Men inviting women to cross a boundary or vice versa will not necessarily lead to lasting structural change. Indeed, ample evidence suggests that boundaries may be transversed and consciousness reconstructed in such a way that a changed status for women is largely cosmetic or minimal. When women were invited into the office, for example, a change in consciousness occurred (i.e., it was then considered proper for women to be secretaries), but the boundaries merely shifted to incorporate the precise change without seriously disrupting the dominant system of gender relations. One could even argue that the system was strengthened, since the ideological and material conditions of secretarial work reinforced women's role in the family.

A similar pattern emerges for women in traditionally male occupations. Women are now "invited" to enter the corporation, but the consequences of the negotiation are contradictory: by insisting that women be "male" in their job performance (i.e., have managerial ability) while retaining their "femaleness," the rules insure that women will remain outsiders. The popular literature on dress for success and assertiveness training exemplifies forms of negotiation that may lead to a change in some women's behaviors and consciousness, but not to lasting changes in the structure of opportunity, achievement and power for all women.

At the same time, changes in consciousness and shifts in boundaries arising from negotiations, however small, may have real and direct consequences in people's lives, even if they do not result in a major change in women's status or in the system of gender relations. To understand the creation and impact of those changes, it is necessary to explore the realm of consciousness. At the most general of levels, consciousness may be depicted in a reciprocal and dynamic relation to social structure. The structural location of a person or group in a social system (i.e., boundaries) as well as individual or collective acts (i.e., social processes), both shape and are shaped by social consciousness.

CONSCIOUSNESS

Traditionally when researchers have studied gender consciousness, they have focussed their efforts essentially on one of two questions. Either they have investigated the conditions and consequences of feminist consciousness or they have considered the foundations and components of female consciousness. Studies of feminist consciousness have concentrated on the social and historical context which gives rise to an active awareness and visible consequences of that awareness. For example, DuBois (1978) has chronicled the relationship between the anti-slavery movement and the subsequent movement for women's suffrage;

Eisenstein (1983) has traced the growth of feminist consciousness in women's groups. Studies such as these generally situate feminist consciousness in an active social movement, associating consciousness with those people participating in the movement and conversely attributing a lack of feminist consciousness to those outside it. One of the tendencies of this research, therefore, is to understand feminist consciousness as an either/or phenomenon—either you have it or you do not.

Scholars working on the content of female consciousness have proposed a similar formulation. They understand female consciousness as the outcome of women's unique set of experiences. Whether as the primary caretakers of children or more generally because of their social roles which are distinct from men's, women apprehend the world in ways that are unique to them. This female consciousness replicates the same dichotomy apparent in the treatment of feminist consciousness. Women share a common culture, ostensibly autonomous from the male world, from which they derive their consciousness. Comparable to the problem with feminist consciousness, female consciousness is understood as a dichotomous, discrete variable.

One shortcoming of these formulations is that the possible varieties of feminist and female consciousness often remain unexplored. We know very little about the actual forms of nascent consciousness and which factors help explain the means by which that consciousness develops or recedes. Moreover, if gender relations shape women's experience then it is necessary to consider both the interaction of women and men as social groups as well as the dynamics within "women's culture" if we are to apprehend the formation of female and feminist consciousness. We propose that viewing forms of gender consciousness along a continuum produces a more useful conception of consciousness, while examining gender-based interactions allows us to explain how these forms of consciousness develop and change.

Our analysis of consciousness distinguishes among three types—gender awareness, female/male consciousness, feminist/anti-feminist consciousness—that represent three points along a continuum. The first, gender awareness, is basic to the development of the subsequent two forms—female/male and feminist/anti-feminist consciousness. Social scientists studying child development and socialization consistently report that very young children understand that they are either a girl or a boy and that this understanding has actual consequences for what they may or may not do. This form of consciousness which we label gender awareness is the most basic type. In this culture gender awareness is virtually universal past infancy, although it is neither infantile nor restricted to youngsters; it is present in parallel or reciprocal forms among both females and males. Gender awareness permeates most facets of everyday life in either real or symbolic ways. People continue to believe in a dimorphic world, even though the research on sex differences has shown that no quality or trait is associated exclusively with one sex or the other, except primary sex characteristics. Women are still thought of as weak or dependent, although we routinely encounter women who "objectively" are strong and independent. In fact gender attribution is so strong that it frequently distorts the empirical phenomenon.

Gender awareness involves a non-critical description of the existing system of gender relations, whereby people accept the current social definitions of gender as natural and inevitable. Gender awareness, then, means that people may associate or correlate certain phenomena with one gender group or another, but there is no evaluation of the ultimate significance or meaning of these attributions. For example, while a person's awareness of gender might indicate that women, in contrast to men, tend to be more sensitive and nurturant, this awareness would not enable her or him to discern the causes or effects of these traits. This form of gender consciousness ultimately involves a statement about the status quo, a remark concerning the ways things are for males and females. Moreover, as gender awareness is characterized by a basic acceptance of gender arrangements, any lingering or residual dissatisfaction with the status quo is individualized as a personal trouble. Being overly sensitive is seen as a personal female shortcoming; there is no social context for this problem. Similarly, a woman's failure to gain a job in the skilled trades is perceived as a result of her personal shortcomings, not an outcome of sexist hiring practices. Small dissatisfactions with gender arrangements may arise, but they do not result in a questioning of that system or one's place within it.

The second form of gender consciousness female or male consciousness, is based on gender awareness but goes beyond the descriptive attributions to a recognition of the rights and obligations associated with being female or male. These privileges and responsibilities are socially constructed and specific to a particular culture at a given point in time. The gender-linked traits which are descriptive of women and men at the level of gender awareness come to be vested with a sense of reciprocal rights and responsibilities at the level of female or male consciousness.

Kaplan (1982) defines female consciousness as acceptance of a society's gender system. Female consciousness ". . . emerges from the division of labor by sex, which assigns women the responsibility of preserving life. But, accepting this task, women with female consciousness demand the rights that their obligations entail" (Kaplan, 1982:545). While we agree with Kaplan, we want to offer two refinements. First, our understanding of boundaries tells us that the sexual division of labor represents a sum total of several more discrete boundaries. Thus, our model suggests that the source of this form of consciousness is more accurately depicted as a person's specific location in a system of gender arrangements. Second, we want to emphasize a notion implicit in Kaplan's definition. By demanding rights, the conceptualization of female consciousness connotes the idea that this consciousness is dynamic and malleable. Female consciousness is the outcome of processes of negotiation and domination, and their reciprocal interaction, as well as the result of women's structural location. Moreover, female consciousness influences processes of negotiation and domination, and ultimately, the boundaries shaping gender relations.

Recent research suggests the general dimensions of female consciousness: First, women are concerned with immediate material reality. The sexual division of labor situates women in the position of child bearers, responsible for sustaining life as well. As such, women are obligated and feel responsible for meeting survival needs of their families. Women, therefore, behave in accordance with normative expectations and act to further support those expectations. Concerns for the necessities of everyday life take numerous forms. Women concerned about food, shelter, and well-being, for example, have organized and protested when state regulations made it difficult if not impossible for them to feed their families.

At a more general level, responsibility for everyday life has meant that women are more apt to apprehend phenomena concretely rather than abstractly. In part because of their heightened responsibility for others, women act as mediators. Gilligan (1982:147) discusses women's complex negotiation between the ethic of self sacrifice and the sense of moral responsibility: "Thus morality, rather than being opposed to integrity or to an ideal of agreement, is aligned with 'the kind of integrity' that comes from 'making decisions after working through everything you think is involved and important in the situation,' and taking resposibility for choice." Finally, the constraints women experience in their daily lives lead to a consciousness of female inferiority. In comparison with men, women learn intellectual, moral, emotional, and physical inferiority. This generalized sense of inferiority leads women to believe that they are incomplete and inadequate without a man—father, husband, etc. Moreover, because of their perceived inabilities and the existence of real threats, women learn fear and have an ingrained sense of curfew and exclusion.

As Kaplan (1982) clearly documents in her research, female consciousness has both a progressive or revolutionary potential as well as a conservative or reactionary one. When women act to protest or disrupt the existing social order because they cannot satisfactorily fulfill their obligations, they challenge existing powers. The eventual outcome of such protests depends on a larger social context, but at a minimum underscores the value women place on maintaining social life (Kaplan, 1982). We would want to know what the relationship is between clearly demarcated boundaries of gender and the development of female consciousness.

An understanding of female consciousness and more broadly, gender relations, must entail an analysis of male consciousness. Is it identical to or even comparable to female consciousness? Given the differences in structural locations and social processes between women and men, male consciousness appears to be profoundly distinct from female consciousness. Male consciousness is characterized by the value placed on individual autonomy, a sense of entitlement, and a relative superiority to women. Men's moral judgments are guided by abstract principles rather than the concrete dimensions of everyday life. Recently Ehrenreich (1983) has chronicled some of the changes in male consciousness over the last thirty years. Her analysis is instructive but raises additional questions central to our concerns here. For example, what is the effect of relative power, and differences in the type or form of power, on consciousness? In what way is consciousness heightened or diminished by such power? Further research into the relationship between female and male consciousness, and its consequences for the system of gender relations is needed.

Finally, female/male consciousness must be distinguished from consciousness that is explicitly feminist or antifeminist/masculinist. To paraphrase Marx, we need to understand the formation of a gender *for* itself. Feminist and antifeminist consciousness involves a highly articulated challenge to or defense of the system of gender relations in the form of ideology, as well as a shared group identity and a growing politicization resulting in a social movement. Recent research extensively explores this issue, documenting the origins, organizational development, and ideology of the first and second waves of feminism. It also has examined the circumstances in which feminist consciousness reinforced or conflicted with other forms of consciousness based on class, race, ethnicity or sexual preference. In investigating the circumstances in which women define their interests as gender-based, it is necessary to examine the areas of female assertion and power, and the ways women move from female to feminist consciousness. At the same time, the formation of feminist consciousness must be seen in relation to antifeminist ideology and activity. The rise of feminism occurs in a dialectical context, in which the feminist challenge to the existing system of gender arrangements evokes an organized response, which in turn influences the nature of feminist consciousness and practice. This process has become particularly apparent in the New Right's movement against feminist demands for legal equality, economic justice and reproductive rights; it may also be seen in earlier historical periods such as the organized opposition to suffrage in the late 19th century. The dynamics of gender-conscious groups, particularly in the last one hundred years, have forcefully shaped gender relations, contributing to the changing definition of boundaries and rules for negotiation and domination.

CONCLUSIONS

In this paper we have argued that gender relations can be fruitfully understood by recasting our conceptual framework. These redefinitions should focus our attention on several issues which have consequences for future research on sex and gender.

From a definitional perspective, the conception of gender as a set of socially constructed relationships which are produced and reproduced through people's actions is central. Such a view highlights social interaction rather than more unidirectional processes of socialization, adaptation, and/or oppression. This emphasis suggests that we appreciate women as the active creators of their own destines within certain constraints, rather than as passive victims or objects. At the same time, this suggests that feminist scholars must avoid analyzing men as one-dimensional, omnipotent oppressors. Male behavior and consciousness emerge from a complex interaction with women as they at times initiate and control, while at other times, cooperate or resist the action of women. Clearly researchers need to examine men in the context of gender relations more precisely and extensively than they have at the present time.

This conceptualization also urges us to examine stasis and change in a more consistent and comprehensive fashion, thereby avoiding the mistake of studying change as an either/or phenomenon. We want to identify the mechanisms which perpetuate existing gender arrangements and those which tend to elicit change. Changes in gender relations occur along the three dimensions of boundaries, negotiation/domination, and consciousness; change in any one variable elicits change in the other two. For example, there cannot be a boundary shift unless it is preceded, accompanied, or followed by changes in negotiation/domination and consciousness. The sequencing of such changes, both in terms of patterns and timing, needs further study. In addition to these questions we also need to look at the magnitude of change. Large versus small-scale change in gender arrangements must be evaluated in terms of the number and proportion of groups affected, their centrality and susceptibility to change, and the degree and suddenness of change. We are also interested in the durability of change. Which kinds of changes are resistant to counter-vailing forces, and which seem to be more tentative, temporary, or makeshift? How are changes in gender relations challenged or co-opted? With the nature of change specified, we will be able to compare more precisely systems of gender relations across historical time and across cultures.

Grounding our research in these dimensions also will facilitate comparisons of systems of gender relations with other systems of domination. Such comparative work is important as it yields a greater understanding of the dynamics of domination. We can distinguish the forms of oppression that are unique to gender from those that are common to all systems of oppression.

Recently, scholars have pointed to the concepts of gender, gender relations, and sex/gender systems as potentially integrating the wide-ranging empirical research on women. Toward this end, our approach has been to redefine three concrete categories for the analysis of gender. These categories offer both a conceptual framework and a research strategy which recommend greater specificity and comparability in examining gender relations. We hope that this framework will encourage researchers to clarify and extend their analyses of gender relations along both empirical and theoretical dimensions.

References

Bernard, Jessie. 1981. The Female World. New York: Free Press.

Davies, Margery. 1982. Women's Place Is at the Typewriter. Office Work and Office Workers 1870–1930. Philadelphia: Temple University Press.

di Leonardo, Micaela. 1984. The Varieties of Ethnic Experience: Kinship, Class and Gender Among Italian Americans in Northern California. Ithaca: Cornell University Press.

DuBois, Ellen Carol. 1978. Feminism and Suffrage: The Emergence of an Independent Women's Movement in America 1848–1869. Ithaca: Cornell University Press.

Ehrenreich, Barbara. 1983. The Hearts of Men: American Dreams and the Flight from Commitment. Garden City NY: Anchor/Doubleday.

Eisenstein, Hester. 1983. Contemporary Feminist thought. Boston: G. K. Hall & Co.

Friedan, Betty. 1963. The Feminine Mystique. New York: Dell.

Gilligan, Carol. 1982. In a Different Voice: Psychological Theory and Women's Development. Cambridge: Harvard University Press.

Kaplan, Temma. 1982. "Female consciousness and collective action: The case of Barcelona, 1910–1918." Signs 7:545–66.

CANDACE WEST AND DON H. ZIMMERMAN

Doing Gender

In the beginning, there was sex and there was gender. Those of us who taught courses in the area in the late 1960s and early 1970s were careful to distinguish one from the other. Sex, we told students, was what was ascribed by biology: anatomy, hormones, and physiology. Gender, we said, was an achieved status: that which is constructed through psychological, cultural, and social means. To introduce the difference between the two, we drew on singular case studies of hermaphrodites and anthropological investigations of "strange and exotic tribes."

Inevitably (and understandably), in the ensuing weeks of each term, our students became confused. Sex hardly seemed a "given" in the context of research that illustrated the sometimes ambiguous and often conflicting criteria for its ascription. And gender seemed much less an "achievement" in the context of the anthropological, psychological, and social imperatives we studied—the division of labor, the formation of gender identities, and the social subordination of women by men. Moreover, the received doctrine of gender socialization theories conveyed the strong message that while gender may be "achieved," by about age five it was certainly fixed, unvarying, and static—much like sex.

Since about 1975, the confusion has intensified and spread far beyond our individual classrooms. For one thing, we learned that the relationship between biological and cultural processes was far more complex—and reflexive—than we previously had supposed. For another, we discovered that certain structural arrangements, for example, between work and family, actually produce or enable some capacities, such as to mother, that we formerly associated with biology. In the midst of all this, the notion of gender as a recurring achievement somehow fell by the wayside.

Our purpose in this article is to propose an ethnomethodologically informed, and therefore distinctively sociological, understanding of gender as a routine, methodical, and recurring accomplishment. We contend that the "doing" of gender is undertaken by women and men whose competence as members of society is

From *Gender & Society,* Vol. 1, no. 2 (June 1987), pp. 125–151. References have been edited.

hostage to its production. Doing gender involves a complex of socially guided perceptual, interactional, and micropolitical activities that cast particular pursuits as expressions of masculine and feminine "natures."

When we view gender as an accomplishment, an achieved property of situated conduct, our attention shifts from matters internal to the individual and focuses on interactional and, ultimately, institutional arenas. In one sense, of course, it is individuals who "do" gender. But it is a situated doing, carried out in the virtual or real presence of others who are presumed to be oriented to its production. Rather than as a property of individuals, we conceive of gender as an emergent feature of social situations: both as an outcome of and a rationale for various social arrangements and as a means of legitimating one of the most fundamental divisions of society.

To advance our argument, we undertake a critical examination of what sociologists have meant by *gender,* including its treatment as a role enactment in the conventional sense and as a "display" in Goffman's (1976) terminology. Both *gender role* and *gender display* focus on behavioral aspects of being a woman or a man (as opposed, for example, to biological differences between the two). However, we contend that the notion of gender as a role obscures the work that is involved in producing gender in everyday activities, while the notion of gender as a display relegates it to the periphery of interaction. We argue instead that participants in interaction organize their various and manifold activities to reflect or express gender, and they are disposed to perceive the behavior of others in a similar light.

To elaborate our proposal, we suggest at the outset that important but often overlooked distinctions be observed among *sex, sex category,* and *gender. Sex* is a determination made through the application of socially agreed upon biological criteria for classifying persons as females or males. The criteria for classification can be genitalia at birth or chromosomal typing before birth, and they do not necessarily agree with one another. Placement in a *sex category* is achieved through application of the sex criteria, but in everyday life, categorization is established and sustained by the socially required identificatory displays that proclaim one's membership in one or the other category. In this sense, one's sex category presumes one's sex and stands as proxy for it in many situations, but sex and sex category can vary independently; that is, it is possible to claim membership in a sex category even when the sex criteria are lacking. *Gender,* in contrast, is the activity of managing situated conduct in light of normative conceptions of attitudes and activities appropriate for one's sex category. Gender activities emerge from and bolster claims to membership in a sex category.

We contend that recognition of the analytical independence of sex, sex category, and gender is essential for understanding the relationships among these elements and the interactional work involved in "being" a gendered person in society. While our primary aim is theoretical, there will be occasion to discuss fruitful directions for empirical research following from the formulation of gender that we propose.

We begin with an assessment of the received meaning of gender, particularly in relation to the roots of this notion in presumed biological differences between women and men.

PERSPECTIVES ON SEX AND GENDER

In Western societies, the accepted cultural perspective on gender views women and men as naturally and unequivocally defined categories of being with distinctive psychological and behavioral propensities that can be predicted from their reproductive functions. Competent adult members of these societies see differences between the two as fundamental and enduring—differences seemingly supported by the division of labor into women's and men's work and an often elaborate differentiation of feminine and masculine attitudes and behaviors that are prominent features of social organization. Things are the way they are by virtue of the fact that men are men and women are women—a division perceived to be natural and rooted in biology, producing in turn profound psychological, behavioral, and social consequences. The structural arrangements of a society are presumed to be responsive to these differences.

Analyses of sex and gender in the social sciences, though less likely to accept uncritically the naive biological determinism of the view just presented, often retain a conception of sex-linked behaviors and traits as essential properties of individuals. The "sex differences approach" is more commonly attributed to psychologists than to sociologists, but the survey researcher who determines the "gender" of respondents on the basis of the sound of their voices over the telephone is also making trait-oriented assumptions. Reducing gender to a fixed set of psychological traits or to a unitary "variable" precludes serious consideration of the ways it is used to structure distinct domains of social experience.

Taking a different tack, role theory has attended to the social construction of gender categories, called "sex roles" or, more recently, "gender roles" and has analyzed how these are learned and enacted. Beginning with Linton (1936) and continuing through the works of Parsons (Parsons 1951; Parsons and Bales 1955) and Komarovsky (1946, 1950), role theory has emphasized the social and dynamic aspect of role construction and enactment. But at the level of face-to-face interaction, the application of role theory to gender poses problems of its own. Roles are *situated* identities—assumed and relinquished as the situation demands—rather than *master identities,* such as sex category, that cut across situations. Unlike most roles, such as "nurse," "doctor," and "patient" or "professor" and "student," gender has no specific site or organizational context.

Moreover, many roles are already gender marked, so that special qualifiers—such as "female doctor" or "male nurse"—must be added to exceptions to the rule. Thorne (1980) observes that conceptualizing gender as a role makes it difficult to assess its influence on other roles and reduces its explanatory usefulness in discussions of power and inequality. Drawing on Rubin (1975), Thorne calls for a reconceptualization of women and men as distinct social groups, constituted in "concrete, historically changing—and generally unequal—social relationships" (Thorne 1980, p. 11).

We argue that gender is not a set of traits, nor a variable, nor a role, but the product of social doings of some sort. What then is the social doing of gender? It is more than the continuous creation of the meaning of gender through human actions. We claim that gender itself is constituted through interaction. To develop the implications of our claim, we turn to Goffman's (1976) account of "gender display." Our object here is to explore how gender might be exhibited or portrayed through interaction, and thus be seen as "natural," while it is being produced as a socially organized achievement.

GENDER DISPLAY

Goffman contends that when human beings interact with others in their environment, they assume that each possesses an "essential nature"—a nature that can be discerned through the "natural signs given off or expressed by them" (1976, p. 75). Femininity and masculinity are regarded as "prototypes of essential expression—something that can be conveyed fleetingly in any social situation and yet something that strikes at the most basic characterization of the individual" (1976, p. 75). The means through which we provide such expressions are "perfunctory, conventionalized acts" (1976, p. 69), which convey to others our regard for them, indicate our alignment in an encounter, and tentatively establish the terms of contact for that social situation. But they are also regarded as expressive behavior, testimony to our "essential natures."

Goffman (1976, pp. 69–70) sees *displays* as highly conventionalized behaviors structured as two-part exchanges of the statement-reply type, in which the presence or absence of symmetry can establish deference or dominance. These rituals are viewed as distinct from but articulated with more consequential activities, such as performing tasks or engaging in discourse. Hence, we have what he terms the "scheduling" of displays at junctures in activities, such as the beginning or end, to avoid interfering with the activities themselves. Goffman (1976, p. 69) formulates *gender display* as follows:

> If gender be defined as the culturally established correlates of sex (whether in consequence of biology or learning), then gender display refers to conventionalized portrayals of these correlates.

These gendered expressions might reveal clues to the underlying, fundamental dimensions of the female and male, but they are, in Goffman's view, optional performances. Masculine courtesies may or may not be offered and, if offered, may or may not be declined (1976, p. 71). Moreover, human beings "themselves employ the term 'expression,' and conduct themselves to fit their own notions of expressivity" (1976, p. 75). Gender depictions are less a consequence of our "essential sexual natures" than interactional portrayals of what we would like to convey about sexual natures, using conventionalized gestures. Our human nature gives us the ability to learn to produce and recognize masculine and feminine gender displays—"a capacity [we] have by virtue of being persons, not males and females" (1976, p. 76).

Upon first inspection, it would appear that Goffman's formulation offers an engaging sociological corrective to existing formulations of gender. In his view, gender is a socially scripted dramatization of the culture's *idealization* of feminine and masculine natures, played for an audience that is well schooled in the presentational idiom. To continue the metaphor, there are scheduled performances presented in special locations, and like plays, they constitute introductions to or time out from more serious activities.

There are fundamental equivocations in this perspective. By segregating gender display from the serious business of interaction, Goffman obscures the effects of gender on a wide range of human activities. Gender is not merely something that happens in the nooks and crannies of interaction, fitted in here and there and not interfering with the serious business of life. While it is plausible to contend that gender displays—construed as conventionalized expressions—are optional, it does not seem plausible to say that we have the option of being seen by others as female or male.

It is necessary to move beyond the notion of gender display to consider what is involved in doing gender as an ongoing activity embedded in everyday interaction. Toward this end, we return to the distinctions among sex, sex category, and gender introduced earlier.

SEX, SEX CATEGORY, AND GENDER

Garfinkel's (1967, pp. 118–40) case study of Agnes, a transsexual raised as a boy who adopted a female identity at age 17 and underwent a sex reassignment operation several years later, demonstrates how gender is created through interaction and at the same time structures interaction. Agnes, whom Garfinkel characterized as a "practical methodologist," developed a number of procedures for passing as a "normal, natural female" both prior to and after her surgery. She had the practical task of managing the fact that she possessed male genitalia and that she lacked the social resources a girl's biography would presumably provide in everyday interaction. In short, she needed to display herself as a woman, simultaneously learning what it was to be a woman. Of necessity, this full-time pursuit took place at a time when most people's gender would be well-accredited and routinized. Agnes had to consciously contrive what the vast majority of women do without thinking. She was not "faking" what "real" women do naturally. She was obliged to analyze and figure out how to act within socially structured circumstances and conceptions of femininity that women born with appropriate biological credentials come to take for granted early on. As in the case of others who must "pass," such as transvestites, Kabuki actors, or Dustin Hoffman's "Tootsie," Agnes's case makes visible what culture has made invisible—the accomplishment of gender.

Garfinkel's (1967) discussion of Agnes does not explicitly separate three analytically distinct, although empirically overlapping, concepts—sex, sex category, and gender.

Sex

Agnes did not possess the socially agreed upon biological criteria for classification as a member of the female sex. Still, Agnes regarded herself as a female, albeit a female with a penis, which a woman ought not to possess. The penis, she insisted, was a "mistake" in need of remedy (Garfinkel 1967, pp. 126–27, 131–32). Like other competent members of our culture, Agnes honored the notion that there are "essential" biological criteria that unequivocally distinguish females from males. However, if we move away from the commonsense viewpoint, we discover that the reliability of these criteria is not beyond question. Moreover, other cultures have acknowledged the existence of "cross-genders" and the possibility of more than two sexes.

More central to our argument is Kessler and McKenna's (1978, pp. 1–6) point that genitalia are conventionally hidden from public inspection in everyday life; yet we continue through our social rounds to "observe" a world of two naturally, normally sexed persons. It is the *presumption* that essential criteria exist and would or should be there if looked for that provides the basis for sex categorization. Drawing on Garfinkel, Kessler and McKenna argue that "female" and "male" are cultural events—products of what they term the "gender attribution process"—rather than some collection of traits, behaviors, or even physical attributes. Illustratively they cite the child who, viewing a picture of someone clad in a suit and a tie, contends, "It's a man, because he has a pee-pee" (Kessler and McKenna 1978, p. 154). Translation: "He must have a pee-pee [an essential characteristic] because I see the *insignia* of a suit and tie." Neither initial sex assignment (pronouncement at birth as a female or male) nor the actual existence of essential criteria for that assignment (possession of a clitoris and vagina or penis and testicles) has much—if anything—to do with the identification of sex category in everyday life. There, Kessler and McKenna note, we operate with a moral certainty of a world of two sexes. We do not think, "Most persons with penises are men, but some may not be" or "Most persons who dress as men have penises." Rather, we take it for granted that sex and sex category are congruent—that knowing the latter, we can deduce the rest.

Sex Categorization

Agnes's claim to the categorical status of female, which she sustained by appropriate identificatory displays and other characteristics, could be *discredited* before her transsexual operation if her possession of a penis became known and after by her surgically constructed genitalia. In this regard, Agnes had to be continually alert to actual or potential threats to the security of her sex category. Her problem was not so much living up to some prototype of essential femininity but preserving her categorization as female. This task was made easy for her by a very powerful resource, namely, the process of commonsense categorization in everyday life.

The categorization of members of society into indigenous categories such as "girl" or "boy," or "woman" or "man," operates in a distinctively social way. The act of categorization does not involve a positive test, in the sense of a well-defined set of criteria that must be explicitly satisfied prior to making an identification. Rather, the application of membership categories relies on an "if-can" test in everyday interaction. This test stipulates that if people *can be seen* as members of relevant categories, *then categorize them that way.* That is, use the category that seems appropriate, except in the presence of discrepant information or obvious features that would rule out its use. This procedure is quite in keeping with the attitude of everyday life, which has us take appearances at face value unless we have special reason to doubt. It should be added that it is precisely when we have special reason to doubt that the issue of applying rigorous criteria arises, but it is rare, outside legal or bureaucratic contexts, to encounter insistence on positive tests.

Agnes's initial resource was the predisposition of those she encountered to take her appearance (her figure, clothing, hair style, and so on), as the undoubted appearance of a normal female. Her further resource was our cultural perspective on the properties of "natural, normally sexed persons." Garfinkel (1967, pp. 122–28) notes that in everyday life, we live in a world of two—and only two—sexes. This arrangement has a moral status, in that we include ourselves and others in it as "essentially, originally, in the first place, always have been, always will be, once and for all, in the final analysis, either 'male' or 'female'" (Garfinkel 1967, p. 122).

Consider the following case:

> This issue reminds me of a visit I made to a computer store a couple of years ago. The person who answered my questions was truly a *salesperson.* I could not categorize him/her as a woman or a man. What did I look for? (1) Facial hair: She/he was smooth skinned, but some men have little or no facial hair. (This varies by race, Native Americans and Blacks often have none.) (2) Breasts: She/he was wearing a loose shirt that hung from his/her shoulders. And, as many women who suffered through a 1950s' adolescence know to their shame, women are often flat-chested. (3) Shoulders: His/hers were small and round for a man, broad for a woman. (4) Hands: Long and slender fingers, knuckles a bit large for a woman, small for a man. (5) Voice: Middle range, unexpressive for a woman, not at all the exaggerated tones some gay males affect. (6) His/her treatment of me: Gave off no signs that would let me know if I were of the same or different sex as this person. There were not even any signs that he/she knew his/her sex would be difficult to categorize and I wondered about that even as I did my best to hide these questions so I would not embarrass him/her while we talked of computer paper. I left still not knowing the sex of my salesperson, and was disturbed by that unanswered question (child of my culture that I am). (Diane Margolis, personal communication)

What can this case tell us about situations such as Agnes's or the process of sex categorization in general? First, we infer from this description that the computer salesclerk's identificatory display was ambiguous, since she or he was not dressed or adorned in an unequivocally female or male fashion. It is when such a display *fails* to provide grounds for categorization that factors such as facial hair or tone of voice are assessed to determine membership in a sex category. Second, beyond the fact that this incident could be recalled after "a couple of years," the customer was not only "disturbed" by the ambiguity of the salesclerk's category but also assumed that to acknowledge this ambiguity would be embarrassing to the salesclerk. Not only do we want to know the sex category of those around us (to see it at a glance, perhaps), but we presume that others are displaying it for us, in as decisive a fashion as they can.

Gender

Agnes attempted to be "120 percent female" (Garfinkel 1967, p. 129), that is, unquestionably in all ways and at all times feminine. She thought she could protect herself from disclosure before and after surgical intervention by comporting herself in a feminine manner, but she also could have given herself away by overdoing her performance. Sex categorization and the accomplishment of gender are not the same. Agnes's categorization could be secure or suspect, but did not depend on whether or not she lived up to some ideal conception of femininity. Women can be seen as unfeminine, but that does not make them "unfemale." Agnes faced an ongoing task of being a woman—something beyond style of dress (an identificatory display) or allowing men to light her cigarette (a gender display). Her problem was to produce configurations of behavior that would be seen by others as normative gender behavior.

Agnes's strategy of "secret apprenticeship," through which she learned expected feminine decorum by carefully attending to her fiancé's criticisms of other women, was one means of masking incompetencies and simultaneously acquiring the needed skills (Garfinkel 1967, pp. 146–47). It was through her fiancé that Agnes learned that sunbathing on the lawn in front of her apartment was "offensive" (because it put her on display to other men). She also learned from his critiques of other women that she should not insist on having things her way and that she should not offer her opinions or claim equality with men (Garfinkel 1967, pp. 147–48). (Like other women in our society, Agnes learned something about power in the course of her "education.")

Popular culture abounds with books and magazines that compile idealized depictions of relations between women and men. Those focused on the etiquette of dating or prevailing standards of feminine comportment are meant to be of practical help in these matters. However, the use of any such source *as a manual of procedure* requires the assumption that doing gender merely involves making use of discrete, well-defined bundles of behavior that can simply be plugged into interactional situations to produce recognizable enactments of masculinity and femininity. The man "does" being masculine by, for example, taking the woman's arm to guide her across a street, and she "does" being feminine by consenting to be guided and not initiating such behavior with a man.

Agnes could perhaps have used such sources as manuals, but, we contend, doing gender is not so easily regimented. Such sources may list and describe the sorts of behaviors that mark or display gender, but they are necessarily incomplete. And to be successful, marking or displaying gender must be finely fitted to situations and modified or transformed as the occasion demands. Doing gender consists of managing such occasions so that, whatever the particulars, the outcome is seen and seeable in context as gender-appropriate or, as the case may be, gender-*in*appropriate, that is, *accountable.*

GENDER AND ACCOUNTABILITY

As Heritage (1984, pp. 136–37) notes, members of society regularly engage in "descriptive accountings of states of affairs to one another," and such accounts are both serious and consequential. These descriptions name, characterize, formulate, explain, excuse, excoriate, or merely take notice of some circumstance or activity and thus place it within some social framework (locating it relative to other activities, like and unlike).

Such descriptions are themselves accountable, and societal members orient to the fact that their activities are subject to comment. Actions are often designed with an eye to their accountability, that is, how they might look and how they might be characterized. The notion of accountability also encompasses those actions undertaken so that they are specifically unremarkable and thus not worthy of more than a passing remark, because they are seen to be in accord with culturally approved standards.

Heritage (1984, p. 179) observes that the process of rendering something accountable is interactional in character:

> [This] permits actors to design their actions in relation to their circumstances so as to permit others, by methodically taking account of circumstances, to recognize the action for what it is.

The key word here is *circumstances.* One circumstance that attends virtually all actions is the sex category of the actor. As Garfinkel (1967, p. 118) comments:

> [T]he work and socially structured occasions of sexual passing were obstinately unyielding to [Agnes's] attempts to routinize the grounds of daily activities. This obstinacy points to the *omnirelevance* of sexual status to affairs of daily life as an invariant but unnoticed background in the texture of relevances that compose the changing actual scenes of everyday life. (italics added)

If sex category is omnirelevant (or even approaches being so), then a person engaged in virtually any activity may be held accountable for performance of that activity as a *woman* or a *man,* and their incumbency in one or the other sex category can be used to legitimate or discredit their other activities. Accordingly, virtually any activity can be assessed as to its womanly or manly nature. And note, to "do" gender is not always to live up to normative conceptions of femininity or masculinity; it is to engage in behavior *at the risk of gender assessment.* While it is individuals who do gender, the enterprise is fundamentally interactional and institutional in character, for accountability is a feature of social relationships and its idiom is drawn from the institutional arena in which those relationships are enacted. If this be the case, can we ever *not* do gender? Insofar as a society is partitioned by "essential" differences between women and men and placement in a sex category is both relevant and enforced, doing gender is unavoidable.

RESOURCES FOR DOING GENDER

Doing gender means creating differences between girls and boys and women and men, differences that are not natural, essential, or biological. Once the differences have been constructed, they are used to reinforce the "essentialness" of gender. In a delightful account of the "arrangement between the sexes," Goffman (1977) observes the creation of a variety of institutionalized frameworks through which our "natural, normal sexedness" can be enacted. The physical features of social setting provide one obvious resource for the expression of our "essential" differences. For example, the sex segregation of North American public bathrooms distinguishes "ladies" from "gentlemen" in matters held to be fundamentally biological, even though both "are somewhat similar in the question of waste products and their elimination" (Goffman 1977, p. 315). These settings are furnished with dimorphic equipment (such as urinals for men or elaborate grooming facilities for women), even though both sexes may achieve the same ends through the same means (and apparently do so in the privacy of their own homes). To be stressed here is the fact that:

> The *functioning* of sex-differentiated organs is involved, but there is nothing in this functioning that biologically recommends segregation; that arrangement is a totally cultural matter . . . toilet segregation is presented as a natural consequence of the difference between the sex-classes when in fact it is a means of honoring, if not producing, this difference. (Goffman 1977, p. 316)

Standardized social occasions also provide stages for evocations of the "essential female and male natures." Goffman cites organized sports as one such institutionalized framework for the expression of manliness. There, those qualities that ought "properly" to be associated with masculinity, such as endurance, strength, and competitive spirit, are celebrated by all parties concerned—participants, who may be seen to demonstrate such traits, and spectators, who applaud their demonstrations from the safety of the sidelines (1977, p. 322).

Assortative mating practices among heterosexual couples afford still further means to create and maintain differences between women and men. For example, even though size, strength, and age tend to be normally distributed among females and males (with considerable overlap between them), selective pairing ensures couples in which boys and men are visibly bigger, stronger, and older (if not "wiser") than the girls and women with whom they are paired. So, should situations emerge in which greater size, strength, or experience is called for, boys and men will be ever ready to display it and girls and women, to appreciate its display.

Gender may be routinely fashioned in a variety of situations that seem conventionally expressive to begin with, such as those that present "helpless" women next to heavy objects or flat tires. But, as Goffman notes, heavy, messy, and precarious concerns can be constructed from *any* social situation, "even though by standards set in other settings, this may involve something that is light, clean, and safe" (Goffman 1977, p. 324). Given these resources, it is clear that any interactional situation sets the stage for depictions of "essential" sexual natures. In sum, these situations "do not so much allow for the expression of natural differences as for the production of that difference itself" (Goffman 1977, p. 324).

Many situations are not clearly sex categorized to begin with, nor is what transpires within them obviously gender relevant. Yet any social encounter can be pressed into service in the interests of doing gender. Thus, Fishman's (1978) research on casual conversations found an asymmetrical "division of labor" in talk between hetero-sexual intimates. Women had to ask more questions, fill more silences, and use more attention-getting beginnings in order to be heard. Her conclusions are particularly pertinent here:

> Since interactional work is related to what constitutes being a woman, with what a woman is, the idea that it is work is obscured. The work is not seen as what women do, but as part of what they are. (Fishman 1978, p. 405)

We would argue that it is precisely such labor that helps to constitute the essential nature of women as women in interactional contexts.

Individuals have many social identities that may be donned or shed, muted or made more salient, depending on the situation. One may be a friend, spouse, professional, citizen, and many other things to many different people—or, to the same person at different times. But we are always women or men—unless we shift into another sex category. What this means is that our identificatory displays will provide an ever-available resource for doing gender under an infinitely diverse set of circumstances.

Some occasions are organized to routinely display and celebrate behaviors that are conventionally linked to one or the other sex category. On such occasions, everyone knows his or her place in the interactional scheme of things. If an individual identified as a member of one sex category engages in behavior usually associated with the other category, this routinization is challenged. Hughes (1945, p. 356) provides an illustration of such a dilemma:

> [A] young woman . . . became part of that virile profession, engineering. The designer of an airplane is expected to go up on the maiden flight of the first plane built according to the design. He [sic] then gives a dinner to the engineers and workmen who worked on the new plane. The dinner is naturally a stag party. The young woman in question designed a plane. Her co-workers urged her not to take the risk—for which, presumably, men only are fit—of the maiden voyage. They were, in effect, asking her to be a lady instead of an engineer. She chose to be an engineer. She then gave the party and paid for it like a man. After food and the first round of toasts, she left like a lady.

On this occasion, parties reached an accommodation that allowed a woman to engage in presumptively masculine behaviors. However, we note that in the end, this compromise permitted demonstration of her "essential" femininity, through accountably "ladylike" behavior.

Hughes (1945, p. 357) suggests that such contradictions may be countered by managing interactions on a very narrow basis, for example, "keeping the relationship formal and specific." But the heart of the matter is that even—perhaps, especially—if the relationship is a formal one, gender is still something one is accountable for. Thus a woman physician (notice the special qualifier in her case) may be accorded respect for her skill and even addressed by an appropriate title. Nonetheless, she is subject to evaluation in terms of normative conceptions of appropriate attitudes and activities for her sex category and under pressure to prove that she is an "essentially" feminine being, despite appearances to the contrary. Her sex category is used to discredit her participation in important clinical activities, while her involvement in medicine is used to discredit her commitment to her responsibilities as a wife and mother. Simultaneously, her exclusion from the physician colleague community is maintained and her accountability *as a woman* is ensured.

In this context, "role conflict" can be viewed as a dynamic aspect of our current "arrangement between the sexes" (Goffman 1977), an arrangement that provides for occasions on which persons of a particular sex category can "see" quite clearly that they are out of place and that if they were not there, their current troubles would not exist. What is at stake is, from the standpoint of interaction, the management of our "essential" natures, and from the standpoint of the individual, the continuing accomplishment of gender. If, as we have argued, sex category is omnirelevant, then any occasion, conflicted or not, offers the resources for doing gender.

We have sought to show that sex category and gender are managed properties of conduct that are contrived with respect to the fact that others will judge and respond to us in particular ways. We have claimed that a person's gender is not simply an aspect of what one is, but, more fundamentally, it is something that one does, and *does* recurrently, in interaction with others.

What are the consequences of this theoretical formulation? If, for example, individuals strive to achieve gender in encounters with others, how does a culture instill the need to achieve it? What is the relationship between the production of gender at the level of interaction and such institutional arrangements as the division of labor in society? And, perhaps most important, how does doing gender contribute to the subordination of women by men?

RESEARCH AGENDAS

To bring the social production of gender under empirical scrutiny, we might begin at the beginning, with a reconsideration of the process through which societal members acquire the requisite categorical apparatus and other skills to become gendered human beings.

Recruitment to Gender Identities

The conventional approach to the process of becoming girls and boys has been sex-role socialization. In recent years, recurring problems arising from this approach have been linked to inadequacies inherent in role theory *per se*—its emphasis on "consensus, stability and continuity" (Stacey and Thorne 1985, p. 307), its a historical and depoliticizing focus (Thorne 1980, p. 9; Stacey and Thorne 1985, p. 307), and the fact that its "social" dimension relies on "a general assumption that people choose to maintain existing customs" (Connell 1985, p. 263).

In contrast, Cahill (1982, 1986a, 1986b) analyzes the experiences of preschool children using a social model of recruitment into normally gendered identities. Cahill argues that categorization practices are fundamental to learning and displaying feminine and masculine behavior. Initially, he observes, children are primarily concerned with distinguishing between themselves and others on the basis of social competence. Categorically, their concern resolves itself into the opposition of "girl/boy" classification versus "baby" classification (the latter designating children whose social behavior is problematic and who must be closely supervised). It is children's concern with being seen as socially competent that evokes their initial claims to gender identities:

> During the exploratory stage of children's socialization . . . they learn that only two social identities are routinely available to them, the identity of "baby," or, depending on the configuration of their external genitalia, either "big boy" or "big girl." Moreover, others subtly inform them that the identity of "baby" is a discrediting one. When, for example, children engage in disapproved behavior, they are often told "You're a baby" or "Be a big boy." In effect, these typical verbal responses to young children's behavior convey to them that they must behaviorally choose between the discrediting identity of "baby" and their anatomically determined sex identity. (Cahill 1986a, p. 175)

Subsequently, little boys appropriate the gender ideal of "efficaciousness," that is, being able to affect the physical and social environment through the exercise of physical strength or appropriate skills. In contrast, little girls learn to value "appearance," that is, managing themselves as ornamental objects. Both classes of children learn that the recognition and use of sex categorization in interaction are not optional, but mandatory.

Being a "girl" or a "boy" then, is not only being more competent than a "baby," but also being competently female or male, that is, learning to produce behavioral displays of one's "essential" female or male identity. In this respect, the task of four- to five-year-old children is very similar to Agnes's:

> For example, the following interaction occurred on a preschool playground. A 55-month-old boy (D) was attempting to unfasten the clasp of a necklace when a preschool aide walked over to him.
>
> *A:* Do you want to put that on?
>
> *D:* No. It's for girls.

A: You don't have to be a girl to wear things around your neck. Kings wear things around their necks. You could pretend you're a king.

D: I'm not a king. I'm a boy. (Cahill 1986a, p. 176)

As Cahill notes of this example, although D may have been unclear as to the sex status of a king's identity, he was obviously aware that necklaces are used to announce the identity "girl." Having claimed the identity "boy" and having developed a behavioral commitment to it, he was leery of any display that might furnish grounds for questioning his claim.

In this way, new members of society come to be involved in a *self-regulating process* as they begin to monitor their own and others' conduct with regard to its gender implications. The "recruitment" process involves not only the appropriation of gender ideals (by the valuation of those ideals as proper ways of being and behaving) but also *gender identities* that are important to individuals and that they strive to maintain. Thus gender differences, or the sociocultural shaping of "essential female and male natures," achieve the status of objective facts. They are rendered normal, natural features of persons and provide the tacit rationale for differing fates of women and men within the social order.

Additional studies of children's play activities as routine occasions for the expression of gender-appropriate behavior can yield new insights into how our "essential natures" are constructed. In particular, the transition from what Cahill (1986a) terms "apprentice participation" in the sex-segregated worlds that are common among elementary school children to "bona fide participation" in the heterosocial world so frightening to adolescents is likely to be a keystone in our understanding of the recruitment process.

Gender and the Division of Labor

Whenever people face issues of *allocation*—who is to do what, get what, plan or execute action, direct or be directed, incumbency in significant social categories such as "female" and "male" seems to become pointedly relevant. How such issues are resolved conditions the exhibition, dramatization, or celebration of one's "essential nature" as a woman or man.

Berk (1985) offers elegant demonstration of this point in her investigation of the allocation of household labor and the attitudes of married couples toward the division of household tasks. Berk found little variation in either the actual distribution of tasks or perceptions of equity in regard to that distribution. Wives, even when employed outside the home, do the vast majority of household and childcare tasks. Moreover, both wives and husbands tend to perceive this as a "fair" arrangement. Noting the failure of conventional sociological and economic theories to explain this seeming contradiction, Berk contends that something more complex is involved than rational arrangements for the production of household goods and services:

> Hardly a question simply of who has more time, or whose time is worth more,

> who has more skill or more power, it is clear that a complicated relationship between the structure of work imperatives and the structure of normative expectations attached to work as *gendered* determines the ultimate allocation of members' time to work and home. (Berk 1985, pp. 195–96)

She notes, for example, that the most important factor influencing wives' contribution of labor is the total amount of work demanded or expected by the household; such demands had no bearing on husbands' contributions. Wives reported various rationales (their own and their husbands') that justified their level of contribution and, as a general matter, underscored the presumption that wives are essentially responsible for household production.

Berk (1985, p. 201) contends that it is difficult to see how people "could rationally establish the arrangements that they do solely for the production of household goods and services"—much less, how people could consider them "fair." She argues that our current arrangements for the domestic division of labor support *two* production processes: household goods and services (meals, clean children, and so on) and, at the same time, gender. As she puts it:

> Simultaneously, members "do" gender, as they "do" housework and child care, and what [has] been called the division of labor provides for the joint production of household labor and gender; it is the mechanism by which both the material and symbolic products of the household are realized. (1985, p. 201)

It is not simply that household labor is designated as "women's work," but that for a woman to engage in it and a man not to engage in it is to draw on and exhibit the "essential nature" of each. What is produced and reproduced is not merely the activity and artifact of domestic life, but the material embodiment of wifely and husbandly roles, and derivatively, of womanly and manly conduct. What are also frequently produced and reproduced are the dominant and subordinate statuses of the sex categories.

How does gender get done in work settings outside the home, where dominance and subordination are themes of overarching importance? Hochschild's (1983) analysis of the work of flight attendants offers some promising insights. She found that the occupation of flight attendant consisted of something altogether different for women than for men:

> As the company's main shock absorbers against "mishandled" passengers, their own feelings are more frequently subjected to rough treatment. In addition, a day's exposure to people who resist authority in a woman is a different experience than it is for a man. . . . In this respect, it is a disadvantage to be a woman. And in this case, they are not simply women in the biological sense. They are also a highly visible distillation of middle-class American notions of femininity. They symbolize Woman. Insofar as the category "female" is mentally associated with having less status and authority, female flight attendants are more readily classified as "really" females than other females are. (Hochschild 1983, p. 175)

In performing what Hochschild terms the "emotional labor" necessary to maintain airline profits, women flight attendants simultaneously produce enactments of their "essential" femininity.

Sex and Sexuality

What is the relationship between doing gender and a culture's prescription of "obligatory heterosexuality"? As Frye (1983, p. 22) observes, the monitoring of sexual feelings in relation to other appropriately sexed persons requires the ready recognition of such persons "before one can allow one's heart to beat or one's blood to flow in erotic enjoyment of that person." The appearance of heterosexuality is produced through emphatic and unambiguous indicators of one's sex, layered on in ever more conclusive fashion (Frye 1983, p. 24). Thus, lesbians and gay men concerned with passing as heterosexuals can rely on these indicators for camouflage; in contrast, those who would avoid the assumption of heterosexuality may foster ambiguous indicators of their categorical status through their dress, behaviors, and style. But "ambiguous" sex indicators are sex indicators nonetheless. If one wishes to be recognized as a lesbian (or heterosexual woman), one must first establish a categorical status as female. Even as popular images portray lesbians as "females who are not feminine" (Frye 1983, p. 129), the accountability of persons for their "normal, natural sexedness" is preserved.

Nor is accountability threatened by the existence of "sex-change operations"—presumably, the most radical challenge to our cultural perspective on sex and gender. Although no one coerces transsexuals into hormone therapy, electrolysis, or surgery, the alternatives available to them are undeniably constrained:

> When the transsexual experts maintain that they use transsexual procedures only with people who ask for them, and who prove that they can "pass," they obscure the social reality. Given patriarchy's prescription that one must be *either* masculine or feminine, free choice is conditioned. (Raymond 1979, p. 135, italics added)

The physical reconstruction of sex criteria pays ultimate tribute to the "essentialness" of our sexual natures—as women *or* as men.

GENDER, POWER, AND SOCIAL CHANGE

Let us return to the question: Can we avoid doing gender? Earlier, we proposed that insofar as sex category is used as a fundamental criterion for differentiation, doing gender is unavoidable. It is unavoidable because of the social consequences of sex-category membership: the allocation of power and resources not only in the domestic, economic, and political domains but also in the broad arena of interpersonal relations. In virtually any situation, one's sex category can be relevant, and one's performance as an incumbent of that category (i.e., gender) can be subjected to evaluation. Maintaining such pervasive and faithful assignment of lifetime status requires legitimation.

But doing gender also renders the social arrangements based on sex category accountable as normal and natural, that is, legitimate ways of organizing social life. Differences between women and men that are created by this process can then be portrayed as fundamental and enduring dispositions. In this light, the institutional arrangements of a society can be seen as responsive to the differences—the social order being merely an accommodation to the natural order. Thus if, in doing gender, men are also doing dominance and women are doing deference, the resultant social order, which supposedly reflects "natural differences," is a powerful reinforcer and legitimator of hierarchical arrangements. Frye observes:

> For efficient subordination, what's wanted is that the structure not appear to be a cultural artifact kept in place by human decision or custom, but that it appear *natural*—that it appear to be quite a direct consequence of facts about the beast which are beyond the scope of human manipulation. . . . That we are trained to behave so differently as women and men, and to behave so differently toward women and men, itself contributes mightily to the appearance of extreme dimorphism, but also, the *ways* we act as women and men, and the *ways* we act toward women and men, mold our bodies and our minds to the shape of subordination and dominance. We do become what we practice being. (Frye 1983, p. 34)

If we do gender appropriately, we simultaneously sustain, reproduce, and render legitimate the institutional arrangements that are based on sex category. If we fail to do gender appropriately, we as individuals—not the institutional arrangements—may be called to account (for our character, motives, and predispositions).

Social movements such as feminism can provide the ideology and impetus to question existing arrangements, and the social support for individuals to explore alternatives to them. Legislative changes, such as that proposed by the Equal Rights Amendment, can also weaken the accountability of conduct to sex category, thereby affording the possibility of more widespread loosening of accountability in general. To be sure, equality under the law does not guarantee equality in other arenas. As Lorber (1986, p. 577) points out, assurance of "scrupulous equality of categories of people considered essentially different needs constant monitoring." What such proposed changes can do is provide the warrant for asking why, if we wish to treat women and men as equals, there needs to be two sex categories at all.

The sex category/gender relationship links the institutional and interactional levels, a coupling that legitimates social arrangements based on sex category and reproduces their asymmetry in face-to-face interaction. Doing gender furnishes the interactional scaffolding of social structure, along with a built-in mechanism of social control. In appreciating the institutional forces that maintain distinctions between women and men, we must not lose sight of the interactional validation of those distinctions that confers upon them their sense of "naturalness" and "rightness."

Social change, then, must be pursued both at the institutional and cultural level of sex category and at the interactional level of gender. Such a conclusion is hardly novel. Nevertheless, we suggest that it is important to recognize that the analytical distinction between institutional and interactional spheres does not pose an either/or choice when it comes to the question of effecting social change. Reconceptualizing gender not as a simple property of individuals but as an integral dynamic of social orders implies a new perspective on the entire network of gender relations:

> [T]he social subordination of women, and the cultural practices which help sustain it; the politics of sexual object-choice, and particularly the oppression of homosexual people; the sexual division of labor, the formation of character and motive, so far as they are organized as femininity and masculinity; the role of the body in social relations, especially the politics of childbirth; and the nature of strategies of sexual liberation movements. (Connell 1985, p. 261)

Gender is a powerful ideological device, which produces, reproduces, and legitimates the choices and limits that are predicated on sex category. An understanding of how gender is produced in social situations will afford clarification of the interactional scaffolding of social structure and the social control processes that sustain it.

References

Berk, Sarah F. 1985. *The Gender Factory: The Apportionment of Work in American Households.* New York: Plenum.

Cahill, Spencer E. 1982. "Becoming Boys and Girls." Ph.D. dissertation, Department of Sociology, University of California, Santa Barbara.

———. 1986a. "Childhood Socialization as Recruitment Process: Some Lessons from the Study of Gender Development." Pp. 163–86 in *Sociological Studies of Child Development,* edited by P. Adler and P. Adler. Greenwich, CT: JAI Press.

———. 1986b. "Language Practices and Self-Definition: The Case of Gender Identity Acquisition." *The Sociological Quarterly* 27:295–311.

Connell, R.W. 1985. "Theorizing Gender." *Sociology* 19:260–72.

Fishman, Pamela. 1978. "Interaction: The Work Women Do." *Social Problems* 25:397–406.

Frye, Marilyn. 1983. *The Politics of Reality: Essays in Feminist Theory.* Trumansburg, NY: The Crossing Press.

Garfinkel, Harold. 1967. *Studies in Ethnomethodology.* Englewood Cliffs, NJ: Prentice-Hall.

Goffman, Erving. 1976. "Gender Display." *Studies in the Anthropology of Visual Communication* 3:69–77.

———. 1977. "The Arrangement Between the Sexes." *Theory and Society* 4:301–31.

Heritage, John. 1984. *Garfinkel and Ethnomethodology.* Cambridge, England: Polity Press.

Hochschild, Arlie R. 1983. *The Managed Heart. Commercialization of Human Feeling.* Berkeley: University of California Press.

Hughes, Everett C. 1945. "Dilemmas and Contradictions of Status." *American Journal of Sociology* 50:353–59.

Kessler, Suzanne J., and Wendy McKenna. 1978. *Gender: An Ethnomethodological Approach.* New York: Wiley.

Komarovsky, Mirra. 1946. "Cultural Contradictions and Sex Roles." *American Journal of Sociology* 52:184–89.

———. 1950. "Functional Analysis of Sex Roles." *American Sociological Review* 15:508–16.

Linton, Ralph. 1936. *The Study of Man.* New York: Appleton-Century.

Lorber, Judith. 1986. "Dismantling Noah's Ark." *Sex Roles* 14:567–80.

Parsons, Talcott. 1951. *The Social System.* New York: Free Press.

———, and Robert F. Bales. 1955. *Family, Socialization and Interaction Process.* New York: Free Press.

Raymond, Janice G. 1979. *The Transsexual Empire.* Boston: Beacon.

Rossi, Alice. 1984. "Gender and Parenthood." *American Sociological Review* 49:1–19.

Rubin, Gayle. 1975. "The Traffic in Women: Notes on the 'Political Economy' of Sex." Pp. 157–210 in *Toward an Anthropology of Women*, edited by R. Reiter. New York: Monthly Review Press.

Stacey, Judith, and Barrie Thorne. 1985. "The Missing Feminist Revolution in Sociology." *Social Problems* 32:301–16.

Thorne, Barrie. 1980. "Gender . . . How Is It Best Conceptualized?" Unpublished manuscript.

PART 5 THE GENDERED FAMILY

The current debates about the "crisis" of the family—a traditional arrangement that some fear is collapsing under the weight of contemporary trends ranging from relaxed sexual attitudes, increased divorce, and women's entry into the labor force, to rap music and violence in the media—actually underscores how central the family is to the reproduction of social life, and to gender identity. If gender identity were biologically "natural," we probably wouldn't need such strong family structures to make sure that everything turned out all right.

Though the "typical" family of the 1950s television sit-com—breadwinner father, housewife/mother, and 2.5 happy and well-adjusted children—is the empirical reality for less than 10 percent of all households, it remains the cultural ideal against which contemporary family styles are measured. And some, like sociologist David Popenoe, would like to see us "return" as close as possible to that imagined idealized model—perhaps by restricting access to easy divorce, or restricting women's entry into the labor force, or promoting sexual abstinence and delegitimating homosexuality.

Others, though, see the problem differently. Sociologist Scott Coltrane notices a relationship between housework and child care and the status of women in society. The more housework and child care women do, the lower their status. Thus he suggests that sharing housework and child care is not only a way for husbands and wives to enact more egalitarian relationships, but also a way to ensure that the next generation will have more egalitarian attitudes.

Demographers Kathleen Allen and David Demo explore the empirical realities of gay and lesbian families. Instead of these families causing problems with gender role identity in their offspring, the children seem to be developing healthy attitudes about themselves. Allen and Demo suggest that whether intact or divorced, single-parent or dual parent, heterosexual, lesbian, or gay, the content of the family—the love, compassion, and nurturing that go on there—is more important than its form.

DAVID POPENOE

Modern Marriage: Revising the Cultural Script

Of all the parts in the cultural scripts of modern societies, few have become more vague and uncertain than those concerning marriage and marital gender roles. Should we even bother to marry? And if and when we do marry and have children, who should do what—within the home and outside of it? Throughout history the answers to both of these questions have been relatively clear. Marriage is one of the few universal social institutions found in every known culture. And in most historical cultures the scripts for marital gender roles have been unambiguously formulated; indeed, in the world's remaining premodern societies the prescription of marital gender roles is a principal cultural focal point.

In the industrialized nations today, marriage is becoming deinstitutionalized. Growing numbers of people are cohabiting outside of marriage. The assigned roles for husband and wife are endlessly negotiated, especially with regard to the allocation of work and child care responsibilities. You work now, I'll work later—no, let's both work. I'll take care of the kids while you work—no, let's both take care of the kids. One may call it the growth of personal freedom and self-fulfillment, and for many women it has been just that. But such endless negotiation is no way to run a family—or a culture. The whole point of a cultural script, or in sociological terms an institutionalized set of social norms, is to provide people in common situations with social expectations for behavior that are geared to maintaining long-term societal well-being and promoting generational continuity.

Is there not some way out of this predicament? With full realization that I am climbing out on a long limb, I believe that a new set of role expectations for marriage and marital gender roles can be established which is adapted to the new conditions of modern life and which, in a balanced and fair manner, maximizes the life experiences of men, women, and children, helps to maintain social order, and represents a "best fit" with biosocial reality. The purpose of this chapter is to review the sociocultural and biological bases for a new set of marital norms and to put forth for discussion some tenets toward establishing these norms.

AN ASSUMPTION AND SOME ALTERNATIVES

If the family trends of recent decades are extended into the future, the result will be not only growing uncertainty within marriage but the gradual elimination of marriage in favor of casual liaisons oriented to adult expressiveness and self-fulfillment. The problem with this scenario is that children will be harmed, adults

From *Promises to Keep: The Decline and Renewal of Marriage in America*, edited by David Popenoe, Jean Bethke Elshtain, and David Blankenhorn, chapter 11. Notes have been renumbered and edited.

will probably be no happier, and the social order could collapse. For this chapter, therefore, I hold the assumption that marriage is a good and socially necessary institution worthy of being preserved in some form, and that the alternative of "letting things go on as they are" should be rejected.

In considering what marriage path modern societies should take instead, several broad alternatives have been widely discussed. We could try to restore the traditional nuclear family of bread-winning husband and full-time housewife that flourished in the 1950s (a time when marriage rates were at an all-time high). This alternative, I suggest, is neither possible nor desirable. We could encourage married women to shift to the traditional marital role of men, centered on a full-time career and involving a high level of detachment from the home, leaving the children to be raised by someone else. This would mean, however, that large numbers of children would face the highly undesirable prospect of being raised in institutional day care. Or we could encourage married men to shift to the so-called "new man" role in which, based on the ideal of social androgyny, men and women in marriage fully share both outside work and child care on an exactly fifty-fifty basis. There are a variety of problems with this solution, which I will discuss.

In place of these alternatives, what is needed is a marriage pattern and set of marital gender-role expectations that will feel "comfortable" yet be reasonably fair and equitable to both men and women, that stands the best chance of generating an enduring marriage, and that will benefit children. (Of these factors, the generation of a lasting marriage is often overlooked, yet it is wisely said that the very best thing parents can give their children is a strong marriage.) Obviously, this is a tall order, and there are some basically conflicting needs that must be reconciled—those of men, of women, of children, and of society as a whole.

SETTING THE SCENE: TODAY'S CONFUSION OVER MARITAL ROLES

For about 150 years, from the early eighteenth century to the 1960s, what we now call the traditional nuclear family was the prevailing family ideal in American culture. The main distinguishing characteristics of this family form were a legally and culturally dominant breadwinning husband and an economically dependent full-time housewife; both parents were devoted to raising their children, but the wife played the role of primary nurturer and teacher. Marital gender-role expectations were unequivocally clear.

At least in its distribution across the American population, this family form had its apogee in the 1950s. More adults were able to live up to these family expectations in "the '50s" than at any other period of our history. Part of the reason is demographic. For women born between the periods of 1830 to 1920, maternal and child mortality rates steadily declined and marriage rates increased. A high point was reached in America by the mid-twentieth century in the percentage of women who married, bore children who survived, and had husbands who lived jointly with them until at least the age of fifty. This was a time when death rates had dropped sharply, leaving many fewer widows, and divorce rates had not reached their current high levels. Another reason is economic. The 1950s in America was an era of unparalleled affluence and economic growth, enabling many families to live comfortably on the income of a single wage earner.

Then, with the coming of age of the baby boom generation in the 1960s, traditional family expectations began to falter. Associated with this faltering was what many today see as "family decline," not just a shift to some different family form but a manifest weakening of the family as an institution—especially as regards the care of children. Today, even though many Americans would probably still claim the traditional nuclear family as their family ideal, a sizable segment of the younger generation—especially the college educated—has largely rejected it.

Much confusion over family expectations and marital gender roles now exists. To the degree that they think about such things, young people coming into adulthood today are highly uncertain about the kind of marital gender roles they want, although almost everyone plans to marry eventually and nearly 90 percent are likely to do so if current age-specific rates continue. Many men still tend to prefer the traditional family form, yet a growing number would also like their wives to work in order to bring in a second income. At the same time, most men believe that childrearing is fundamentally a woman's responsibility. Many women plan to work after they are married and have children, often believing that they will have to in order to make ends meet. And many college-educated women desire to have full-blown work careers combined with marriage. Among women, both ordinary workers and careerists are uncertain about how they will mesh work goals with family responsibilities and child care.

Some women (and a few men), especially those influenced by left-feminist thinking, hold to a new ideal of coequal and fully-shared breadwinning and parenting, what can be called social androgyny. Believing that primary authority for child care should rest with women, however, this is an arrangement that few men seem prepared to accept. Some women and men intend to rely heavily on day care to raise children, thus lessening the direct child-care responsibilities of both parents (for single parents, of course, this is sometimes a necessity). In general, women expect their husbands to play a larger role than earlier generations of fathers did in the home and with children. And, although resistance among men is seemingly widespread, the evidence points to a growing, albeit still modest, equalization of gender roles in this respect.

Before children arrive, marital gender roles across all segments of society now tend to be relatively similar to one another, or "egalitarian." Typically, both partners work outside the home, and both share in the domestic responsibilities. Cooking, for example, can be done by either sex. Moreover, with ever-increasing median ages at first marriage and at the birth of the first child, such marital role similarity takes up an ever-longer portion of each person's life, especially if one includes the stage of premarital cohabitation that precedes more than half of all formal marriages today. Indeed, males and females living together with similar roles and no children has become a formative period of young adulthood, a far cry from the days when women (especially) lived with their parents until they married, and then had children soon thereafter.

If people today never moved beyond this stage of life, the present chapter would not have to be written. With the coming of children, however, the situation of marital-role similarity suddenly changes. Far from bringing joy to the new parents, an abundance of scholarly studies has shown that the least happy time in the life course of recently married couples is when they have young children. A major reason is that the division of labor within the household abruptly shifts, and gender-role expectations become uncertain; it is no longer clear who should do what. Marital gender-role expectations not only become ambiguous, but they typically revert to their traditional family form—with wife at home taking care of the children and husband becoming the sole breadwinner—to a degree far beyond anything anticipated by either party.

The marital-role stresses that arise from this sudden change can be enormous, especially after the couple have settled in with their new infant. Frequently, the wife becomes resentful and the husband becomes angry. The wife becomes resentful because she has had to leave her job while her husband is still occupationally progressing and because her husband doesn't help out enough. Often, in addition, she herself has had little preparation for the trials and tribulations that come with infant care. Also, she suddenly finds herself economically dependent (and perhaps guilty about not contributing financially), vulnerable, and stuck at home doing a job that has low status in our society. The husband, meanwhile, is angry because of his sudden new responsibilities and loss of freedom and because he has diminished sexual access to his wife and no longer receives as much of her attention. The baby has become the important figure in the home and the new focus of the wife's affections. While having young children (especially sons) slightly retards the chances of divorce, the animosities set up during this period are often long lasting and can lead to eventual breakup. The animosities negatively impact not only the marriage, of course, but also the children.

Probably the most common piece of advice now offered to young people at this stage of life is that "every situation is different," and they will simply have to work things out for themselves—find what is best for them. But this is not "cultural advice"; it is an unthoughtful reaction in an over-optioned society. It does forcefully raise the question, however: If not the marital roles of the traditional nuclear family, then what? The traditional roles were at least clear cut: the wife's job in life was childrearing, and the husband's was to provide economically for the mother-child unit.

THE TRADITIONAL NUCLEAR FAMILY: WHY WE CANNOT RETURN

While some are tempted to think that a return to the era of the traditional nuclear family would provide a solution to this set of problems, there are powerful reasons why this is neither desirable nor possible. To understand these reasons, we must consider why the traditional nuclear family fell into decline in the first place. Although most readers are probably well aware of the causes for this decline, they are worth a moment's reflection.

Social change of the past few centuries has affected women's roles much more than men's. Throughout history, the role of married men has principally been that of provider and protector of the mother-child unit. And, in virtually every known human society, the main role of married women has been that of child nurturer. Unlike today, however, married women almost never undertook the childrearing task all by themselves. Many others were around to help, especially older children, parents, and other close relatives. Most mothers were involved as well in what was the equivalent in preindustrial times of today's paid labor force where "productive work" took place, the typical work being home-generated agricultural production.

It was not until economic conditions permitted, mainly after the industrial revolution, that women left the labor force and became full-time mothers. Although most American women in the last century were in the labor market sometime during their lives, the pattern was typically this: They finished school at fourteen or fifteen and only worked until they got married in their early twenties. They then soon had children, and for the rest of their lives (shorter than today) they played the role of mother of at-home children. At the turn of the twentieth century, less than 10 percent of married women were gainfully employed, and the chances were that a woman would die before her last child left home.

But by the late 1940s, the Bureau of Labor Statistics listed nearly half of all American women as "essentially idle." They did not have children under eighteen, did not work in the labor force, and were not aged or infirm, a combination leading to the proverbial "bored housewife." In what represents a major historical shift, only about one-third of the adult life of the average married women today will be spent as the mother of at-home children. This is because of later ages at first marriage and birth of the first child, average family sizes of less than two children, and a much longer life span. Thus, even if one were to assume that a woman's main purpose in life was to be a mother, that role today clearly would no longer take up more than a fraction of her adult years. Moreover, because of the high divorce rate, a woman may well spend one-half to two-thirds of her adulthood not only without children but also without a husband to care for and to rely on economically, forcing her to rely on her own resources.

With such a steep reduction in the portion of women's lives that is taken up by marriage and childrearing, is it any wonder that women have been looking more to their own careers as separate individuals, and attaching less importance to their domestic roles? Under the new social circumstances, the demographers Kingsley Davis and Pietronella van den Oever have noted, "for best results [women] must choose an occupation early in order to get the necessary training, and they must enter employment while young and remain employed consistently in order to build up experience, seniority, reputation, and whatever other cumulative benefit comes from occupational commitment."[1]

The Downside

"Once under way," Davis and van den Oever continue,

> the system of change exhibits a dynamic of its own. Insofar as demographic trends lead women to downgrade marriage and stress employment, they also

> lead them to reduce not only their dependence on their husbands but also their service to them. Men, in turn, are induced to reconsider the costs and benefits of marriage. They sense that, at older ages, men are increasingly scarce compared with women, that they do not have to marry to enjoy female company, and that if they do marry, their role as father and family head has somehow been eroded. Not surprisingly, the divorce rate rises to unprecedented levels, making marriage less secure and therefore less valuable for both sexes. Marriage undergoes attrition in two ways: it is postponed or not undertaken at all, and when it is undertaken, it is increasingly brittle.[2]

The available evidence suggests that, for durable demographic and economic reasons, this scenario of "family decline" has largely come to pass and it has been accompanied by some devastating personal and social consequences. First, more families have broken up, fatherlessness has rapidly increased, and parents have had less time to spend with their children. Such family instability has undoubtedly been an important factor in the decline of child well-being in recent years, as indicated by numerous statistics. Second, women have not entirely been well served. There is substantial evidence that almost all women deeply want not just a job or a career or financial independence, but also to be a mother and to have a strong and hopefully lasting relationship with a man. And while women's financial independence has improved, their family relationships have deteriorated. Third, and least widely discussed, there have been important negative repercussions for men. Despite the great importance for cultures to direct men into family roles (men gain tremendously in health and happiness from marriage and fatherhood, and single men are a universal social problem), any "new men" have probably been more than offset by men who have largely abandoned family life.

In all, society has suffered. Such trends are surely a major component in the view of most adult Americans today that, in many ways, "things are not as good as they were when I was growing up."

THE NUCLEAR FAMILY: ELEMENTS TO BE MAINTAINED

If the era of the traditional nuclear family must be recognized as a thing of the past, and if we should not continue in the direction we are headed, then what? Rather than the alternatives of institutional day care or androgynous gender roles in marriage, a strong case can be made for the maintenance of relatively traditional marital gender roles—*but only at the stage of marriage when children are young.* This case is based on the requirements of optimal child development, on the biological differences between men and women, and on what is ultimately personally fulfilling for men and women and what they "really want" out of marriage.

Childrearing Requirements

No one has spoken more eloquently about the requirements for optimum child development than Urie Bronfenbrenner. He recently summarized the main findings of the "scientific revolution" that has occurred in the study of human development. Two of his findings bear special attention:[3]

1. In order to develop—intellectually, emotionally, socially, and morally—a child requires participation in progressively more complex reciprocal activity, on a regular basis over an extended period in the child's life, with one or more persons with whom the child develops a strong, mutual, irrational attachment and who is committed to the child's well-being and development, preferably for life.

2. The establishment and maintenance of patterns of progressively more complex interaction and emotional attachment between caregiver and child depend in substantial degree on the availability and involvement of another adult, a third party, who assists, encourages, spells off, gives status to, and expresses admiration and affection for the person caring for and engaging in joint activity with the child.

Here we have not just the "main findings of the scientific revolution," but a statement of a relatively traditional division of labor in marriages between husbands and wives. Note that as they stand the statements are gender neutral, but we shall turn to that issue below.

The key element in proposition number one is the "irrational attachment" of the child with at least one caretaker. Empirical support for this proposition has grown enormously in recent years, mostly stemming from the many psychological studies that have upheld "attachment theory"—the theory that infants have a biosocial necessity to have a strong, enduring socioemotional attachment to a caretaker, especially during the first year of life. This is what pioneering attachment theorist John Bowlby has called starting life with "a secure base."[4] Empirical studies have shown that failure to become attached, to have a secure base, can have devastating consequences for the child, and that patterns of attachment developed in infancy and childhood largely stay with the individual in adulthood, affecting one's relationships and sense of well-being.

The work on attachment theory has been paralleled by research showing some negative effects of placing infants in group care. While still controversial, a widely discussed finding is that extensive (more than twenty hours per week) nonparental care initiated during the first year of life is likely to cause attachment problems (insecurity, aggression, and noncompliance) in children. Some recent evidence suggests that negative consequences may also occur from nonparental care during the second year of life. None of this research is conclusive; social science research seldom is. But it certainly supports what almost every grandmother would have told us from the outset—that there is considerable risk during the first few years of life in the reduction of infant-parent contacts and in nonparental childrearing.

After the child reaches age three, on the other hand, there is little or no evidence that limited, high quality day care has any ill effects on children. Indeed,

American children have long gone to "nursery school" at ages three and four, and group care at these ages is common in most other industrialized nations, including Japan.

Why is close contact with a parent so important in the first few years of life? Because parents are typically motivated, like no one else, to provide warm and supportive care for their children. The task of parenting could be, and occasionally is, successfully accomplished by a nonrelated caretaker, such as a full-time nanny. But attachment is much less likely in group settings where there is normally a high caretaker-child ratio and also a very high turnover of staff members.

But why should the primary parent of young children ordinarily be a mother and not a father? There is now a substantial body of evidence that fathers can do the job "if they are well-trained and strongly motivated." Some scholars have turned this research into the message that "daddies make good mommies, too," holding that the two roles might really be interchangeable. Yet it is much harder to train and motivate men than women for child care. Most dads do not want to be moms, and they do not feel comfortable being moms. And, in my opinion, neither children nor society in general benefits from such androgyny. To understand why the sexes are not interchangeable with one another in child care, it is necessary to review the biological differences between them.

Biological Differences Between the Sexes

No society in the world has ever been known to exist in which men were the primary caretakers of young children, and the reason for this certainly has much to do with the biological nature of males and females. Unfortunately, any discussion of biologically influenced sex differences has in recent years been fraught with peril. As historian Carl Degler has noted, the idea of a biological rootedness to human nature was almost universally accepted at the turn of the twentieth century, only to all but vanish from social thought as the century wore on, mainly due to the vigorous (and reasonably successful) battle against sexism (and racism).[5] Understandably, this knowledge blackout on the discussion of sex differences was associated with the need to challenge centuries-old stereotypes about the capacities of women, and to overcome strong resistances to a more forceful and equal role for women in economic and public life. The result was, however, that about the only sex differences that everyone within the academic community has been willing to accept over the past few decades are that women menstruate and are capable of becoming pregnant, giving birth, and lactating and that men are on average taller and muscularly stronger. But, when they have been discussed at all, the behavioral implications of even these differences are left vague.

Today, the full recognition of biological influences on human behavior is returning, albeit very slowly. Although the idea is still foreign, even inimical, to most social scientists, in probably no other area has the idea of biological roots to human nature become more widely discussed than in the field of sex and gender. A cover story in *Time* on "Sizing Up the Sexes" began, "Scientists are discovering that gender differences have as much to do with the biology of the brain as with the way we are raised."[6]

Having been trained as a sociologist, I have long been partial to sociocultural explanations. But I must say, quite apart from the scientific evidence, that after a lifetime of experiences which consisted, in part, of growing up in a family of four boys and fathering a family of two girls, I would be utterly amazed if someone were to prove that biology is unimportant in gender differences. The "natural and comfortable" way that most males think, feel, and act seems to me fundamentally different from the way most women think, feel, and act, and I have encountered these differences across the world's societies. (I probably need add that I don't believe one way is better than the other; indeed, I find symmetry and complementarity remarkable, even astonishing.)

It is not that biology is "determinant" of human behavior; that is a poorly chosen word. All human behavior represents a combination of biological and sociocultural forces, and it makes little sense, as sociologist Alice Rossi has stressed, to view them "as separate domains contesting for election as primary causes."[7] Also, the case can certainly be made, in the promotion of female equality, for a culture's not accentuating the biological differences that do exist. (Cultures differ radically in this respect; consider the difference in gender roles between Arab cultures and Nordic cultures.) Yet in my judgment a stronger case should be presented at this time, one of declining family stability and personal well-being, for a more frank acknowledgement of the very real differences between men and women. More acknowledgement by both sexes of the differences between them in sexual motives, cognitive styles, and communication patterns, for example, would probably make for stronger marriages, and recognition that the roles of father and mother are not interchangeable would probably make for better parenting.

Differences between men and women have universally been found with respect to four behavioral/psychological traits: aggression and general activity level, cognitive skills, sensory sensitivity, and sexual and reproductive behavior. That differences are universally found does not unequivocally mean they are heavily influenced by biology, but it seems to me that the implication is stronger than for most other scientific findings about human affairs. Moreover, a large body of evidence points to the fact that many universally found differences are rooted in a distinct "wiring" of male and female brains, and in a pronounced hormotial variation between the sexes.

What some call the greatest behavioral difference is in aggression. From birth onward, boys tend to be more aggressive and, in general, to have a higher physical activity level than girls. To a large degree, this accounts for the male dominance that universally has been prevalent in human societies. Differences in male and female cognitive skills are less well known and perhaps not as large as aggressive behavior, but they are now widely confirmed by empirical studies. From early adolescence onward, males tend to have greater visual-spatial and mathematical ability than females, and females tend to have greater verbal ability than males. (Spatial ability refers to being able to mentally picture physical objects in terms of their shape, position, geography, and proportion.) Also, there is a female superiority in being more sensitive to all sensory stimuli. Females typically receive a wider array of sensory information, are able to communicate it better, and place a primacy on personal relationships within which such information is communicated.

In brief, while male strengths rest with "things and theorems," female strengths rest with personal relationships. Even shortly after birth, girls are more interested than boys in people and faces, whereas boys "just seem as happy with an object dangled in front of them."[8] That these differences become accentuated at adolescence strongly suggests the role of hormones, specifically testosterone in men and estrogen in women. The role of hormones gains further support from the fact that the behavioral differences decline at older age levels, when hormonal levels are dropping. It is also worth noting that males are the best and the worst with respect to several of these traits. Males, for example, disproportionately make up math geniuses, but also math dysfunctionals.

Not all of these behavioral differences, however, could be expected to have a direct effect on family behavior. Most important for family behavior are differences that stem from the dissimilar role of males and females in sexual activity and the reproductive process. The differential "sexual strategies" of men and women have long been commented on; in popular terminology, they roughly boil down to the fact that women give sex to get love, and men give love to get sex. The world over, sex is something that women have that men want, rather than vice versa, while relationships and intimacy are the special province of women.

Probably the most compelling explanation for male-female differences in sexuality and sexual strategies comes from the field of evolutionary psychology. It goes something like this: In evolutionary terms, the goal of each individual's life is to perpetuate one's genes through reproduction and maximize the survival of all those with the same genes. In the mammalian world, the primary reproductive function is for males to inseminate and for females to harbor the growing fetus. Since sperm is common and eggs are rare (both being the prime genetic carriers), a different sexual or reproductive strategy is most adaptive for males and females, with males having more incentive to spread their sperm more widely among many females, and females having a strong incentive to bind males to themselves for the long-term care of their offspring.

Thus males universally are the more sexually driven and promiscuous while females are universally the more relationship oriented, setting up a continuing tension between the sexes. One psychologist found, for example, that the strongest predictor of sexual dissatisfaction for American males was "sexual withholding by the wife," and for females was "sexual aggressiveness by the husband."[9] And, according to the plausible explanation of evolutionary psychologists, men tend to be far more upset by their mate's sexual infidelity than vice versa because a man can never be certain that a child borne by his mate is really his, while women tend to be much more upset by the loss of their mate's emotional fidelity, which threatens long-term commitment and support.

Male promiscuity *à la* the tom cat is not characteristic of humankind, however. Wide variation in male sexual strategies can be found, ranging from the relatively promiscuous and low-paternal-investment "cad" approach, in which sperm is widely distributed with the hope that more offspring will survive to reproduce, to the "dad" approach, in which a high paternal investment is made in a limited number of offspring. But in every society the biological fathers of children are identified if possible, and required to hold some responsibility for their children's upbringing. In fact, compared to other species, human beings are noted for a relatively high paternal investment because human children have a long period of dependency and require extensive cultural training to survive, and because the character of human female sexuality (loss of estrus) encourages men to stay around.

Culture, of course, has a major say in which sexual strategies are institutionalized, and in all industrialized societies a very high paternal-investment strategy is the culturally expected one for males. Monogamy is strongly encouraged in these societies (although "serial monogamy" has become the norm in many nations, especially the United States), polygamy is outlawed, and male promiscuity is somewhat contained. Because it promotes high paternal investment, monogamy is well suited to modern social conditions.

Whatever the sexual strategies, our underlying biological nature dictates that every society faces the problem of how to keep men in the reproductive pair-bond. Especially for males, sex is rather ill-designed for lasting marriages. Margaret Mead is once purported to have said that there is no society in the world where men will stay married for very long unless culturally required to do so. This is not to suggest that marriage isn't "good" for men, only that their inherited biological propensities push them in another direction.

Biologically, male attachment to the mother-child pair is said to be largely through the sexual relationship with the mother. Many anthropologists have noted that motherhood is a biological necessity while fatherhood is mainly a cultural invention. Because it is not so biologically based as the mother's, a father's attachment to the children must be culturally fostered. Cross-cultural comparisons have shown that men are most likely to take active care of their children "if they are sure they are the fathers, if they are not needed as warriors and hunters, if mothers contribute to food resources, and if male parenting is encouraged by women."[10] Fortunately, these conditions largely prevail in modern societies. But bear in mind that it is not male care of infants that is at issue here. Universally, men have almost never been highly involved in child care at the early stages of life.

Sex Differences and Modern Family Behavior

What is the relevance for modern marriage and family behavior of all this biological and anthropological information? There is much evidence suggesting that men make a significant contribution to child development, especially in the case of sons, and that the absence of a male presence typically poses a handicap for the child. Indeed, men's assistance to women in childrearing may be more important now than ever before because mothers have become so isolated from their traditional support systems. Even more than in the past, it is crucial to maintain cultural measures that induce men to take an active interest in their families. It should be recognized, however, that the parenting of young infants is not a "natural" activity for males, and to perform well they require much training and experience plus encouragement from their wives.

All this said, there appear to be some dangers in moving too far in the direction of androgynous marital gender roles. Especially in American circumstances one hates to say anything that could possibly be used to feed stereotypes and to deter men from providing more help at home, yet it is important to point out that fully androgynous roles in marriage may not be best for child development, and they may not be the kind of personal relationships that men and women really want.

Regarding child development, a large body of evidence suggests that, while females may not have a "maternal instinct," hormonal changes occur after childbirth that strongly motivate women (but not men) to care for their new-born children. These hormonal changes are linked, in part, to the woman's capacity to breast-feed. Also, a number of the female sex differences noted above are directly related to this stage of the reproductive process. "In caring for a nonverbal, fragile infant," it has been noted, "women have a head start in reading an infant's facial expressions, smoothness of body motions, ease in handling a tiny creature with tactile gentleness, and soothing through a high, soft, rhythmic use of the voice."[11] Such evidence provides a strong case for women, rather than men, being the primary caretakers of infants.

Men seem better able to perform the parental role after children reach the age of 18 months, by which age children are more verbal and men don't have to rely so much on a wide range of senses.[11] Yet even at that age many studies have shown that men interact with children in a different way than women, suggesting that the father's mode of parenting is not interchangeable with that of the mother's; for example, men emphasize "play" more than "caretaking," and their play is more likely to involve a "rough-and-tumble" approach. Moreover, there is evidence to support the value of reasonably sex-typed parenting in which mothers are "responsive" and fathers are "firm"; one research review determined that "children of sex-typed parents are somewhat more competent than children of androgynous parents."[12] As social psychologist Willard W. Hartup has concluded, "The importance of fathers, then, may be in the degree to which their interactions with their children do not duplicate the mother's and in the degree to which they support maternal caregiving rather than replicate it."[13]

Less widely discussed, but probably no less important, is the effect of androgyny on the marriage relationship. The most common idea cited in this connection is that many men, being of a more independent spirit, will simply avoid marrying and having children if they are going to be asked to give up their independence and over-engage in "unnatural" nurturing and caretaking roles. And it is not as if they have few alternatives. Under the old system the marital exchange of sex for love was largely operative: if a man wanted regular sex (other than with prostitutes) he had to marry. Today, with permissive sexual standards and the availability of a huge pool of single and divorced women (to say nothing of married women), men obviously have abundant opportunities for sex outside of permanent attachments, much less those attachments which involve extensive child care responsibilities. Such a sociocultural reality may help to explain men's current delay of marriage, and the growing complaint of women that "men will not commit."

Nevertheless, most men eventually do marry and have children, and when they do they receive enormous personal benefits. My real concern, therefore, is not with men's delay of marriage (it is largely to the good) but rather with what happens to the marriage after it takes place. If it is the case that the best thing parents can do for their children is to stay together and have a good marriage, one serious problem with the "new man" alternative, in which dad tries to become mom, is that there is some evidence that marriages which follow this alternative are not very happy and have a high likelihood of divorce, especially those marriages in which a "role-reversal" has taken place. This is a most significant consequence that is seldom discussed by "new man" proponents.

Why should marriages in which the husband is doing "just what he thought his wife always wanted" have a high breakup rate? The answer concerns the fundamental nature of modern marriages. Marriages today are based on two basic principles: companionship, by which husbands and wives are expected to be each other's close friends, and romantic love based on sexual attraction, by which husbands and wives are expected to be each other's exclusive sexual partners. The joining of these two different principles is not without problems. For a good companion, you want someone who is as much like yourself as possible. But for a sexual partner, people tend to be attracted to the differences in the other. Therein lies a continuing tension that must be resolved if the modern marriages are to endure—the partners must be similar enough to remain best friends, but different enough so that sexual attraction is maintained.

The basis of sexual and emotional attraction between men and women is based not on sameness but on differences. If we closely examine the marital roles of childrearing couples who have been able to stay together and remain interested in each other for a long period of time (an important area for new research), I doubt that we will find such couples relentlessly pursuing the ideal of social androgyny.

SEVEN TENETS FOR ESTABLISHING NEW MARITAL NORMS

What I propose as a remedy for society's confusion over marital gender-role expectations, in conclusion, is a pattern of late marriage followed, in the early childrearing years, by what one could call a "modified traditional nuclear family." The main elements of this pattern can be summarized as follows. (I recognize, of course, that this pattern—being a set of normative expectations—is not something to which everyone can or should conform.)

1. Girls, as well as boys, should be trained according to their abilities for a socially useful paid job or career. It is important for women to be able to achieve the economic, social, and psychic rewards of the workplace that have long been reserved for men. It is important for society that everyone be well educated, and that they make an important work contribution over the course of their lives.

2. Young people should grow up with the expectation that they will marry, only once and for a lifetime, and that they will have children. Reproduction is a fundamental purpose of life, and marriage is instrumental to its success. Today,

close to 90 percent of Americans actually marry and about the same percentage of American women have children; although these figures have been dropping, the social expectation in these respects is currently quite well realized. Lifetime monogamy is not so well realized, however, with the divorce rate now standing at over 50 percent.

3. Young adults should be encouraged to marry later in life than is common now, with an average age at time of marriage in the late twenties or early thirties (the average ages currently are twenty-six for men and twenty-four for women). Even later might be better for men, but at older ages than this for women who want children, the "biological clock" becomes a growing problem.

From society's viewpoint, the most important reasons why people should be encouraged to marry relatively late in life is that they are more mature, they know better what they want in a mate, they are more established in their jobs or careers, and the men have begun to "settle down" sexually (partly due to a biological diminution of their sex drive). Age at marriage has proven to be the single most important predictor of eventual divorce, with the highest divorce rates found among those who marry in their teenage years. But we must also recognize that both women and men want to have time, when they are young, to enjoy the many opportunities for personal expression and fulfillment that modern, affluent societies are able to provide.

We should anticipate that many of these years of young adulthood will be spent in nonmarital cohabitation, an arrangement that often makes more sense than the alternatives to it, especially living alone or continuing to live with one's family of origin. I am not implying, much less advocating, sexual promiscuity here, but rather serious, caring relationships which may involve cohabitation.

4. From the perspective of promoting eventual family life, however, the downside to late age of marriage is that people live for about a decade or more in a nonfamily, "singles" environment which reinforces their personal drive for expressive individualism and conceivably reduces their impulse toward carrying out eventual family obligations, thus making the transition to marriage and childrearing more difficult. To help overcome the anti-family impact of these years, young unmarried adults should be encouraged to save a substantial portion of their income for a "family fund" with an eye toward offsetting the temporary loss of the wife's income after marriage and childbirth.

5. Once children are born, wives should be encouraged to leave the labor market and become substantially full-time mothers for a period of at least a year to eighteen months per child. The reason for this is that mother-reared infants appear to have distinct advantages over those reared apart from their mothers. It is desirable for children to have full-time parenting up to at least age three, but after eighteen months—partly because children by then are more verbal—it is appropriate for fathers to become the primary caretakers, and some men may wish to avail themselves of the opportunity. At age three, there is no evidence

that children in quality group care suffer any disadvantages (in fact, for most children there are significant advantages). Once children reach that age, therefore, the average mother could resume working part-time until the children are at least of school age, and preferably in their early to middle teen years, at which point she could resume work full-time. Alternatively, when the children reach the age of three the father could stay home part-time, and the mother could resume work full-time.

For women, this proposal is essentially the strategy known as "sequencing." The main difficulty with it, as sociologist Phyllis Moen has noted, "is that child-nurturing years are also the career-nurturing years. What is lost in either case cannot be 'made up' at a later time."[14] Yet I would argue that it is possible to "make up" for career loss, but impossible to make up for child-nurturing loss. To make it economically more possible for a family with young children to live on a single income, we should institute (in addition to the "family fund") what virtually every other industrialized society already has in place—parental leave and child allowance programs. And, to help compensate women for any job or career setbacks due to their time out of the labor force, we should consider the development of "veterans benefits" type programs that provide mothers with financial subsidies and job priorities when they return to the paid work force. In general, women must be made to feel that caring for young children is important work, respected by the working community.

6. According to this proposal, the mother and not the father ordinarily would be the primary caretaker of infants. This is because of fundamental biological differences between the sexes that assume great importance in childrearing, as discussed above. The father should be an active supporter of the mother-child bond during this period, however, as well as auxiliary homemaker and care provider. Fathers should expect to spend far more time in domestic pursuits than their own fathers did. Their work should include not only the male's traditional care of the house as a physical structure and of the yard and car, but in many cases cooking, cleaning, and child care, the exact distribution of such activities depending on the individual skills and talents of the partners. And, as noted above, after children reach age eighteen months it may be desirable for the father and not the mother to become the primary caretaker. This means that places of employment must make allowances for substantial flex-time and part-time job absence for fathers as well as for mothers.
7. It should be noted that there is some balancing out of domestic and paid-work roles between men and women over the course of life. Under current socioeconomic conditions husbands, being older, retire sooner than their wives. Also, in later life some role switching occurs, presumably caused in part by hormonal changes, in which women become more work-oriented and men become more domestic. Given current male-female differences in longevity, of course, the average woman can expect to spend an estimated seven years of her later life as a widow.

CONCLUDING REMARKS

Later marriage, together with smaller families, earlier retirement, and a longer life in a society of affluence, provide both men and women in modern societies an historically unprecedented degree of freedom to pursue personal endeavors. Yet what David Gutmann has called the "parental imperative"[15] is also a necessary and important part of life, and during the parental years expressive freedom for adults must be curtailed in the interest of social values, especially the welfare of children.

Male bread winning and female childrearing have been the pattern of social life throughout history, albeit not always in quite so extreme a form as found in modern societies over the past century and a half. Except perhaps for adult pairbonds in which no young children are involved, where much social experimentation is possible, it is foolhardy to think that the nuclear family can or should be entirely scrapped. When children become a part of the equation, fundamental biological and social constraints come into play—such as the importance of mothers to young children—and central elements of the nuclear family are dismissed at society's peril. Rather than strive for androgyny and be continuously frustrated and unsettled by our lack of achievement of it, we would do much better to more readily acknowledge, accommodate, and appreciate the very different needs, sexual interests, values, and goals of each sex. And rather than the unisex pursuit of "freedom with a male bias," we should be doing more to foster a culture in which the traditional female values of relationship and caring are given a higher priority and respect.

In a much modified form, then, traditional marital gender roles are necessary if the good of society—and of individuals—is to be advanced. But the period of time in which these gender roles still apply has become a relatively short phase of life, and not adult life in its entirety as once was the case. This leaves individuals abundant time for the pursuit of self-fulfillment through social roles of their own choosing.

Notes

1. Kingsley Davis and Pietronella van den Oever, "Demographic Foundations of New Sex Roles." *Population and Development Review* 8, no. 3 (1982): 495–511, 508.

2. Ibid.

3. Urie Bronfenbrenner, "Discovering What Families Do," in *Rebuilding the Nest,* ed. David Blankenhorn, Steven Bayme, and Jean Bethke Elshtain (Milwaukee: Family Service America, 1990), 27–38.

4. John Bowlby, *Attachment and Loss,* 3 vols. (New York: Basic Books, 1969–77).

5. Carl N. Degler, In *Search of Human Nature* (New York: Oxford University Press, 1991).

6. *Time,* January 20, 1992: 42.

7. Alice Rossi, "Parenthood in Transition: From Lineage to Child to Self-Orientation." in *Parenting Across the Life Span: Biosocial Dimensions,* ed. Jane B. Lancaster et al. (New York: Aldine de Gruyter, 1987), 31–81, quote from 64.

8. Moir and Jessel, *Brain Sex,* 17.

9. David M. Buss, "Conflict Between the Sexes," *Journal of Personality and Social Psychology* 56 (May 1989), cited in Degler, *In Search of Human Nature,* 305.

10. M. M. West and M. L. Konner, "The Role of the Father: An Anthropological Perspective," in *The Role of the Father in Child Development,* 1st ed., ed. Michael E. Lamb (New York: Wiley-Interscience, 1976), 185–218, cited in Rossi, "Parenthood in Transition," 67–68.

11. Alice S. Rossi, "Parenthood In Transition: From Lineage to child to self-orientation." In *Parenting Across The Life Span: Biosocial Dimensions.* Jane B. Lancaster et al., eds. (New York: Aldine de Gruyter, 1987): 56–61.

12. Diana Baumrind, "Are Androgynous Individuals More Effective Persons and Parents?" *Child Development* 53 (1982): 44–75. In another study of adolescent outcomes, it was found that the most effective parenting was that which was both highly demanding and highly responsive, a difficult task for either a man or a woman to combine. Diana Baumrind, "The Influence of Parenting Style on Adolescent Competence and Substance Use," *Journal of Early Adolescence* 11, no. 1 [1991]: 56–95). See also Frances K. Grossman, William S. Pollack, and Ellen Golding, "Fathers and Children: Predicting the Quality and Quantity of Fathering," *Developmental Psychology* 24, no. 1 (1988): 82–92.

13. Willard W. Hartup, "Social Relationships and Their Developmental Significance," *American Psychologist,* February 1989: 120–26, quote from 122.

14. Phyllis Moen, *Women's Two Roles: A Contemporary Dilemma* (New York: Auburn House, 1992), 133.

15. David Gutmann, "Men, Women, and the Parental Imperative," *Commentary* 56, no. 5 (1973): 59–64.

SCOTT COLTRANE

Household Labor and the Routine Production of Gender

Motherhood is often perceived as the quintessence of womanhood. The everyday tasks of mothering are taken to be "natural" expressions of femininity, and the routine care of home and children is seen to provide opportunities for women to express and reaffirm their gendered relation to men and to the world. The traditional tasks of fatherhood, in contrast, are limited to begetting, protecting, and providing for children. While fathers typically derive a gendered sense of self from these activities, their masculinity is even more dependent on *not* doing the things that mothers do. What happens, then, when fathers share with mothers those tasks that we define as expressing the true nature of womanhood?

This chapter describes how a sample of twenty dual-earner couples talk about sharing housework and child care. Since marriage is one of the least script-

From *Social Problems,* Vol. 36, no. 5 (December 1989), pp. 473–490. References have been edited.

ed or most undefined interaction situations, the marital conversation is particularly important to a couple's shared sense of reality. I investigate these parents' construction of gender by examining their talk about negotiations over who does what around the house; how these divisions of labor influence their perceptions of self and other; how they conceive of gender-appropriate behavior; and how they handle inconsistencies between their own views and those of the people around them. Drawing on the parents' accounts of the planning, allocation, and performance of child care and housework, I illustrate how gender is produced through everyday practices and how adults are socialized by routine activity.

GENDER AS AN ACCOMPLISHMENT

Candace West and Don Zimmerman (1987) suggest that gender is a routine, methodical, and recurring accomplishment. "Doing gender" involves a complex of socially guided perceptual, interactional, and micropolitical activities that cast particular pursuits as expressions of masculine and feminine "natures." Rather than viewing gender as a property of individuals, West and Zimmerman conceive of it as an emergent feature of social situations that results from and legitimates gender inequality. Similarly, Sarah Fenstermaker Berk (1985, 204, emphasis in original) suggests that housework and child care

> can become the occasion for producing commodities (e.g., clean children, clean laundry, and new light switches) and a reaffirmation of one's *gendered* relation to the work and to the world. In short, the "shoulds" of gender ideals are fused with the "musts" of efficient household production. The result may be something resembling a "gendered" household-production function.

If appropriately doing gender serves to sustain and legitimate existing gender relations, would inappropriate gender activity challenge that legitimacy? Or, as West and Zimmerman (1987, 146) suggest, when people fail to do gender appropriately, are their individual characters, motives, and predispositions called into question? If doing gender is unavoidable and people are held accountable for its production, how might people initiate and sustain atypical gender behaviors?

By investigating how couples share child care and housework, I explore (1) the sorts of dyadic and group interactions that facilitate the sharing of household labor; (2) how couples describe the requirements of parenting and how they evaluate men's developing capacities for nurturing; and (3) the impact of sharing domestic labor on conceptions of gender.

THE SAMPLE

To find couples who shared child care, I initially contacted schools and day care centers in several suburban California communities. Using snowball sampling techniques, I selected twenty moderate- to middle-income dual-earner couples with children. To compensate for gaps in the existing literature and to enhance comparisons between sample families, I included couples if they were the biological parents of at least two school-aged children, they were both employed at least half time, and both identified the father as assuming significant responsibility for routine child care. I observed families in their homes and interviewed fathers and mothers separately at least once and as many as five times. I recorded the interviews and transcribed them for coding and constant comparative analysis.

The parents were primarily in their late thirties and had been living together for an average of ten years. All wives and 17 of 20 husbands attended some college and most couples married later and had children later than others in their birth cohort. The median age at marriage for the mothers was 23; for fathers, 26. Median age at first birth for mothers was 27; for fathers, 30. Fifteen of 20 fathers were at least one year older than their wives. Median gross annual income was $40,000, with three families under $25,000 and three over $65,000. Sixteen of the couples had two children and four had three children. Over two-thirds of the families had both sons and daughters, but four families had two sons and no daughters, and two families had two daughters and no sons. The children's ages ranged from four to fourteen, with 80 percent between the ages of five and eleven and with a median age of seven.

Mothers were more likely than fathers to hold professional or technical jobs, although most were employed in female-dominated occupations with relatively limited upward mobility and moderate pay. Over three-quarter held jobs in the "helping" professions: seven mothers were nurses, five were teachers, and four were social workers or counselors. Other occupations for the mothers were administrator, laboratory technician, filmmaker, and bookbinder. Sample fathers held both blue-collar and white collar jobs, with concentrations in construction (3), maintenance (2), sales (3), business (3), teaching (3), delivery (4), and computers (2). Like most dual-earner wives, sample mothers earned, on average, less than half of what their husband's did, and worked an average of eight fewer hours per week. Eleven mothers (55 percent), but only five fathers (25 percent) were employed less than 40 hours per week. In nine of twenty families, mothers were employed at least as many hours as fathers, but in only four families did the mother's earnings approach or exceed those of her husband.

DEVELOPING SHARED PARENTING

Two-thirds of the parents indicated that current divisions of labor were accomplished by making minor practical adjustments to what they perceived as an already fairly equal division of labor. A common sentiment was expressed by one father who commented.

> Since we've both always been working since we've been married, we've typically shared everything as far as all the working—I mean all the housework responsibilities as well as child care responsibilities. So it's a pattern that was set up before the kids were even thought of.

Nevertheless, a full three-quarters of the couples reported that the mother performed much more of the early infant care. All of the mothers and only about half of the fathers reported that they initially reduced their hours of employment after having children. About a third of the fathers said they increased their employment hours to compensate for the loss of income that resulted from their wives taking time off work before or after the births of their children.

In talking about becoming parents, most of the fathers stressed the importance of their involvement in conception decisions, the birth process, and early infant care to later assumption of child care duties. Most couples planned the births of their children jointly and intentionally. Eighty percent reported that they mutually decided to have children, with two couples reporting that the wife desired children more than the husband and two reporting that the husband was more eager than the wife to become a parent. For many families, the husband's commitment to participate fully in childrearing was a precondition of the birth decision. One mother described how she and her husband decided to have children.

> Shared parenting was sort of part of the decision. When we decided to have children, we realized that we were both going to be involved with our work, so it was part of the plan from the very beginning. As a matter of fact, I thought that we only could have the one and he convinced me that we could handle two and promised to really help (laughs), which he really has, but two children is a lot more work than you realize (laughs).

By promising to assume partial responsibility for childrearing, most husbands influenced their wives' initial decision to have children, the subsequent decision to have another child, and the decision of whether and when to return to work. Almost all of the mothers indicated that they had always assumed that they would have children, and most also assumed that they would return to paid employment before the children were in school. Half of the mothers did return to work within six months of the birth of their first child.

All but one of the fathers were present at the births of their children and most talked about the importance of the birth experience, using terms like "incredible," "magical," "moving," "wonderful," and "exciting." While most claimed that they played an important part in the birth process by providing emotional support to their wives or acting as labor coaches, a few considered their involvement to be inconsequential. Comments included, "I felt a little bit necessary and a lot unnecessary," and "I didn't bug her too much and I might have helped a little." Three quarters of the fathers reported that they were "very involved" with their newborns, even though the mother provided most of the daily care for the first few months. Over two-thirds of the mothers breastfed their infants. Half of the fathers reported that they got up in the night to soothe their babies, and many described their early infant care experience in terms that mothers typically use to describe "bonding" with newborns. The intensity of father-infant interaction was discussed by fathers as enabling them to experience a new and different level of intimacy and was depicted as "deep emotional trust," "very interior," "drawing me in," and "making it difficult to deal with the outside world."

About half of the fathers referred to the experience of being involved in the delivery and in early infant care as a necessary part of their assuming responsibility for later child care. Many described a process in which the actual performance of caretaking duties provided them with the self-confidence and skills to feel that they knew what they were doing. They described their time alone with the baby as especially helpful in building their sense of competence as a shared primary caretaker. One man said,

> I felt I needed to start from the beginning. Then I learned how to walk them at night and not be totally p.o'ed at them and not feel that it was an infringement. It was something I *got* to do in some sense, along with changing diapers and all these things. It was certainly not repulsive and in some ways I really liked it a lot. It was not something innate, it was something to be learned. I managed to start at the beginning. If you *don't* start at the beginning then you're sort of left behind.

This father, like almost all of the others, talked about having to learn how to nurture and care for his children. He also stressed how important it was to "start at the beginning." While all fathers intentionally shared routine child care as the children approached school age, only half of the fathers attempted to assume a major share of daily infant care, and only five couples described the father as an equal caregiver for children under one year old. These early caregiving fathers described their involvement in infant care as explicitly planned:

> She nursed both of them completely, for at least five or six months. So, my role was—we agreed on this—my role was the other direct intervention, like changing, and getting them up and walking them, and putting them back to sleep. For instance, she would nurse them but I would bring them to the bed afterward and change them if necessary, and get them back to sleep. . . . I really initiated those other kinds of care aspects so that I could be involved. I continued that on through infant and toddler and preschool classes that we would go to, even though I would usually be the only father there.

This man's wife offered a similar account, commenting that "except for breastfeeding, he always provided the same things that I did—the emotional closeness and the attention."

Another early caregiving father described how he and his wife "very consciously" attempted to equalize the amount of time they spent with their children when they were infants: "In both cases we very consciously made the decision that we wanted it to be a mutual process, so that from the start we shared, and all I didn't do was breastfeed. And I really would say that was the only distinction." His wife also described their infant care arrangements as "equal," and commented that other people did not comprehend the extent of his participation:

> I think that nobody really understood that Jennifer had two mothers. The burden of proof was always on me that he was literally being a mother. He wasn't nursing, but he was getting up in the night to bring her to me, to change her

poop, which is a lot more energy than nursing in the middle of the night. You have to get up and do all that, I mean get awake. So his sleep was interrupted, and yet within a week or two, at his work situation, it was expected that he was back to normal, and he never went back to normal. He was part of the same family that I was.

This was the only couple who talked about instituting, for a limited time, an explicit record-keeping system to ensure that they shared child care equally.

[Father]: We were committed to the principle of sharing and we would have schedules, keep hours, so that we had a pretty good sense that we were even, both in terms of the commitment to the principle as well as we wanted to in fact be equal. We would keep records in a log—one might say in a real compulsive way—so that we knew what had happened when the other person was on.

[Mother]: When the second one came we tried to keep to the log of hours and very quickly we threw it out completely. It was too complex.

PRACTICALITY AND FLEXIBILITY

Both early- and later-sharing families identified practical considerations and flexibility as keys to equitable divisions of household labor. Most did not have explicit records or schedules for child care or housework. For example, one early involved father reported that practical divisions of labor evolved "naturally":

Whoever cooks doesn't have to do the dishes. If for some reason she cooks and I don't do the dishes, she'll say something about it, certainly. Even though we never explicitly agreed that's how we do it, that's how we do it. The person who doesn't cook does the dishes. We don't even know who's going to cook a lot of the time. We just get it that we can do it. We act in good faith.

Couples who did not begin sharing routine child care until after infancy were even more likely to describe their division of labor as practical solutions to shortages of time. For example, one mother described sharing household tasks as "the only logical thing to do," and her husband said, "It's the only practical way we could do it." Other fathers describe practical and flexible arrangements based on the constraints of employment scheduling:

Her work schedule is more demanding and takes up a lot of evening time, so I think I do a lot of the every day routines, and she does a lot of the less frequent things. Like I might do more of the cooking and meal preparation, but she is the one that does the grocery shopping. An awful lot of what gets done gets done because the person is home first. That's been our standing rule for who fixes dinner. Typically, I get home before she does so I fix dinner, but that isn't a fixed rule. She gets home first, then she fixes dinner. Making the beds and doing the laundry just falls on me because I've got more time during the day to do

> it. And the yardwork and cuttin' all the wood, I do that. And so I'm endin' up doin' more around here than her just because I think I've got more time.

While mothers were more likely than fathers to report that talk was an important part of sharing household labor, most couples reported that they spent little time planning or arguing about who was going to do what around the house. Typical procedures for allocating domestic chores were described as "ad hoc," illustrated by one mother's discussion of cooking:

> Things with us have happened pretty easily as far as what gets done by who. It happened without having to have a schedule or deciding—you know—like cooking. We never decided that he would do all the cooking; it just kind of ended up that way. Every once in a while when he doesn't feel like cooking he'll say, "Would you cook tonight?" "Sure, fine." but normally I don't offer to cook. I say, "What are we having for dinner?"

In general, divisions of labor in sample families were described as flexible and changing. One mother talked about how routine adjustments in task allocation were satisfying to her: "Once you're comfortable in your roles and division of tasks for a few months then it seems like the needs change a little bit and you have to change a little bit and you have to regroup. That's what keeps it interesting. I think that's why it's satisfying."

UNDERLYING IDEOLOGY

While ad hoc divisions of labor were described as being practical solutions to time shortages, there were two major ideological underpinnings to the sharing of housework and child care: child-centeredness and equity ideals. While those who attempted to share infant care tended to have more elaborate vocabularies for talking about these issues, later sharing couples also referred to them. For instance, all couples provided accounts that focused on the sanctity of childhood and most stressed the impossibility of mothers "doing it all."

Couples were child-centered in that they placed a high value on their children's well-being, defined parenting as an important and serious undertaking, and organized most of their nonemployed hours around their children. For instance, one father described how his social life revolved around his children:

> Basically if the other people don't have kids and if they aren't involved with the kids, then we aren't involved with them. It's as simple as that. The guys I know at work that are single or don't have children my age don't come over because then we have nothing in common. They're kind of the central driving force in my life.

While about half of the couples (11 of 20) had paid for ongoing out-of-home child care, and three-quarters had regularly used some form of paid child care, most of the parents said that they spent more time with their children than the other dual-earner parents in their neighborhoods. One father commented that he and his wife had structured their lives around personally taking care of their children:

> An awful lot of the way we've structured our lives has been based around our reluctance to have someone else raise our children. We just really didn't want the kids to be raised from 7:30 in the morning 'till 4:30 or 5:00 in the afternoon by somebody else. So we've structured the last ten years around that issue.

Many parents also advocated treating children as inexperienced equals or "little people," rather than as inferior beings in need of authoritarian training. For example, an ex-military father employed in computer research stated, "We don't discipline much. Generally the way it works is kind of like bargaining. They know that there are consequences to whatever actions they take, and we try and make sure they know what the consequences are before they have a chance to take the action." Another father described his moral stance concerning children's rights:

> I'm not assuming—when I'm talking about parent-child stuff—that there's an inequality. Yes, there are a lot of differences in terms of time spent in this world, but our assumption has been, with both children, that we're peers. And so that's how we are with them. So, if they say something and they're holding fast to some position, we do not say, "You do this because we're the parent and you're the child."

About half of the parents talked directly about such equity ideals as applied to children.

Concerning women's rights, 80 percent of fathers and 90 percent of mothers agreed that women were disadvantaged in our society, but only two mothers and one father mentioned equal rights or the women's movement as motivators for sharing household labor. Most did not identify themselves as feminists, and a few offered derogatory comments about "those women's libbers." Nevertheless, almost all parents indicated that no one should be forced to perform a specific task because they were a man or a woman. This implicit equity ideal was evidenced by mothers and fathers using time availability, rather than gender, to assign most household tasks.

DIVISIONS OF HOUSEHOLD LABOR

Contributions to 64 household tasks were assessed by having fathers and mothers each sort cards on a five-point scale to indicate who most often performed them (see Table 1). Frequently performed tasks, such as meal preparation, laundry, sweeping, or putting children to bed, were judged for the two weeks preceding the interviews. Less frequently performed tasks, such as window washing, tax preparation, or car repair, were judged as to who typically performed them.

Some differences occurred between mothers' and fathers' accounts of household task allocation, but there was general agreement on who did what.

Table 1.
Household Tasks by Person Most Often Performing Them

Mother More	Fathers and Mother Equally	Father More
Cleaning		
Mopping	Vacuuming	Taking out trash
Sweeping	Cleaning tub/shower	Cleaning porch
Dusting	Making beds	
Cleaning bathroom sink	Picking up toys	
Cleaning toilet	Tidying living room	
	Hanging up clothes	
	Washing windows	
	Spring cleaning	
Cooking		
Planning menus	Preparing lunch	Preparing breakfast
Grocery shopping	Cooking dinner	
Baking	Making snacks	
	Washing dishes	
	Putting dishes away	
	Wiping kitchen counters	
	Putting food away	
Clothes		
Laundry	Shoe care	
Hand laundry		
Ironing		
Sewing		
Buying clothes		
Household		
	Running errands	Household repairs
	Decorating	Exterior painting
	Interior painting	Car maintenance
	General yardwork	Car repair
	Gardening	Washing car
		Watering lawn
		Mowing lawn
		Cleaning rain gutters
Finance, Social		
Writing or phoning	Deciding major purchases	Investments
Relatives/friends	Paying bills	
	Preparing taxes	
	Handling insurance	
	Planning couple dates	
Children		
Arranging baby-sitters	Waking children	
	Helping children dress	
	Helping children bathe	
	Putting children to bed	
	Supervising children	
	Disciplining children	
	Driving children	
	Taking children to doctor	
	Caring for sick children	
	Playing with children	
	Planning outings	

Note: Tasks were sorted separately by fathers and mothers according to relative frequency of performance: (1) Mother mostly or always, (2) Mother more than father, (3) Father and mother about equal, (4) Father more than mother, (5) Father mostly or always, For each task a mean ranking by couple was computed with 1.00–2.49 = Mother, 2.50–3.50 = Shared, 3.51–5.0 = Father. If over 50 percent of families ranked a task as performed by one spouse more than the other, the task is listed under that spouse, otherwise tasks are listed as shared. N = 20 couples.

Table 1 shows that in the majority of families, most household tasks were seen as shared. Thirty-seven of 64 tasks (58 percent), including all direct child care, most household business, meal preparation, kitchen clean-up, and about half of other housecleaning tasks were reported to be shared about equally by fathers and mothers. Nevertheless, almost a quarter (15) of the tasks were performed principally by the mothers, including most clothes care, meal planning, kin-keeping, and some of the more onerous repetitive housecleaning. Just under one-fifth (12) of the tasks were performed principally by the fathers. These included the majority of the occasional outside chores such as home repair, car maintenance, lawn care, and taking out the trash. As a group, sample couples can thus be characterized as sharing an unusually high proportion of housework and child care, but still partially conforming to a traditional division of household labor. The fathers and mothers in this study are pioneers in that they divided household tasks differently than their parents did, differently from most others in their age cohort, and from most families studied in time-use research.

MANAGING VERSUS HELPING

Household divisions of labor in these families also can be described in terms of who takes responsibility for planning and initiating various tasks. In every family there were at least six frequently performed household chores over which the mother retained almost exclusive managerial control. That is, mothers noticed when the chore needed doing and made sure that someone adequately performed it. In general, mothers were more likely than fathers to act as managers for cooking, cleaning, and child care, but over half of the couples shared responsibility in these areas. In all households the father was responsible for initiating and managing at least a few chores traditionally performed by mothers.

Based on participants' accounts of strategies for allocating household labor, I classified twelve couples as sharing responsibility for household labor and eight couples as reflecting manager-helper dynamics. Helper husbands often waited to be told what to do, when to do it, and how it should be done. While they invariably expressed a desire to perform their "fair share" of housekeeping and childrearing, they were less likely than the other fathers to assume responsibility for anticipating and planning these activities. Manager-helper couples sometimes referred to the fathers' contributions as "helping" the mother.

When asked what they liked most about their husband's housework, about half of the mothers focused on their husband's selfresponsibility: voluntarily doing work without being prodded. They commented, "He does the everyday stuff" and "I don't have to ask him." The other mothers praised their husbands for particular skills with comments such as "I love his spaghetti" or "He's great at cleaning the bathroom." In spite of such praise, three-fourths of the mothers said that what bothered then most about their husband's housework was the need to remind him to perform certain tasks, and some complained of having to "train him" to correctly perform the chores. About a third of the fathers complained that their wives either didn't notice when things should be done or that *their* standards were too low. Although the extent of domestic task sharing varied considerably among couples, 90 percent of both mothers and fathers independently reported that their divisions of labor were "fair."

Some mothers found it difficult to share authority for household management. For instance, one mother said, "There's a certain control you have when you do the shopping and the cooking and I don't know if I'm ready to relinquish that control." Another mother who shares most child care and housework with her husband admitted that "in general, household organization is something that I think I take over." In discussing how they divide housework, she commented on how she notices more than her husband does:

> He does what he sees needs to be done. That would include basic cleaning kinds of things. However, there are some detailed kinds of things that he doesn't see that I feel need to be done, and in those cases I have to ask him to do things. He thinks some of the details are less important and I'm not sure, that might be a difference between men and women.

Like many of the mothers who maintained a managerial position in the household, this mother attributed an observed difference in domestic perceptiveness to an essential difference between women and men. By contrast, mothers who did not act as household managers were unlikely to link housecleaning styles to essential gender differences.

Many mothers talked about adjusting their housecleaning standards over the course of their marriage and trying to feel less responsible for being "the perfect homemaker." By partially relinquishing managerial duties and accepting their husband's housecleaning standards, some mothers reported that they were able to do less daily housework and focus more on occasional thorough cleaning or adding "finishing touches." A mother with two nursing jobs whose husband delivered newspapers commented:

> He'll handle the surface things no problem, and I get down and do the nitty gritty. And I do it when it bugs me or when I have the time. It's not anything that we talk about usually. Sometimes if I feel like things are piling up, he'll say "Well, make me a list," and I will. And he'll do it. There are some things that he just doesn't notice and that's fine: he handles the day-to-day stuff. He'll do things, like for me cleaning off the table—for him it's getting everything off it; for me it's putting the tablecloth on, putting the flowers on, putting the candles on. That's the kind of stuff I do and I like that; it's not that I want him to start.

This list-making mother illustrates that responsibility for managing housework sometimes remained in the mother's domain, even if the father performed more of the actual tasks.

Responsibility for managing child care, on the other hand, was more likely to be shared. Planning and initiating "direct" child care, including supervision, discipline and play, was typically an equal enterprise. Sharing responsibility for "indirect" child care, including clothing, cleaning, and feeding, was less common, but was still shared in over half of the families. When they cooked, cleaned, or tended to the children, fathers in these families did not talk of "helping" the mother; they spoke of fulfilling their responsibilities as equal partners and parents. For example, one father described how he and his wife divided both direct and indirect child care:

> My philosophy is that they are my children and everything is my responsibility, and I think she approaches it the same way too. So when something needs to be done, it's whoever is close does it . . . whoever it is convenient for. And we do keep a sense of what the other's recent efforts are, and try to provide some balance, but without actually counting how many times you've done this and I've done that.

In spite of reported efforts to relinquish total control over managing home and children, mothers were more likely than fathers to report that they would be embarrassed if unexpected company came over and the house was a mess (80 percent vs. 60 percent). When asked to compare themselves directly to their spouse, almost two-thirds of both mothers and fathers reported that the mother would be more embarrassed than the father. Some mothers reported emotional reactions to the house being a mess that were similar to those they experienced when their husbands "dressed the kids funny." The women were more likely to focus on the children "looking nice," particularly when they were going to be seen in public. Mothers' greater embarrassment over the kemptness of home or children might reflect their sense of mothering as part of women's essential nature.

ADULT SOCIALIZATION THROUGH CHILDREARING

Parents shared in creating and sustaining a worldview through the performance and evaluation of childrearing. Most reported that parenting was their primary topic of conversation, exemplified by one father's comment: "That's what we mostly discuss when we're not with our kids—either when we're going to sleep or when we have time alone—is how we feel about how we're taking care of them." Others commented that their spouse helped them to recognize unwanted patterns of interaction by focusing on parenting practices. For instance, one father remarked,

> I'm not sure I could do it as a one-parent family, cause I wouldn't have the person, the other person saying, "Hey, look at that, that's so much like what you do with your own family." In a one-parent family, you don't have that, you don't have the other person putting out that stuff, you have to find it all out on your own and I'm not sure you can.

Usually the father was described as being transformed by the parenting experience and developing increased sensitivity. This was especially true of discourse between parents who were trying to convert a more traditional division of family labor into a more egalitarian one. A self-employed construction worker said his level of concern for child safety was heightened after he rearranged his work to do half of the parenting:

> There's a difference in being at the park with the kids since we went on the schedule. Before it was, like, "Sure, jump off the jungle bars." But when you're totally responsible for them, and you know that if they sprained an ankle or something you have to pick up the slack, it's like you have more investment in the kid and you don't want to see them hurt and you don't want to see them crying. I find myself being a lot more cautious.

Mothers also reported that their husbands began to notice subtle cues from the children as a result of being with them on a regular basis. The wife of the construction worker quoted above commented that she had not anticipated many of the changes that emerged from sharing routine child care.

> I used to worry about the kids a lot more. I would say in the last year it's evened itself out quite a bit. That was an interesting kind of thing in sharing that started to happen that I hadn't anticipated. I suppose when you go into this your expectations about what will happen—that you won't take your kids to day care, that they'll be with their dad, and they'll get certain things from their dad and won't that be nice, and he won't have to worry about his hours—but then it starts creeping into other areas that you didn't have any way of knowing it was going to have an impact. When he began to raise issues about the kids or check in on them at school when they were sick, I thought, "Well, that's my job, what are you talking about that for?" or, "Oh my god. I didn't notice that!" Where did he get the intuitive sense to know what needed to be done? It wasn't there before. A whole lot of visible things happened.

Increased sensitivity on the part of the fathers, and their enhanced competence as parents, was typically evaluated by adopting a vocabulary of motives and feelings similar to the mothers', created and sustained through an ongoing dialogue about the children: a dialogue that grew out of the routine child care practices. Another mother described how her husband had "the right temperament" for parenting, but had to learn how to notice the little things that she felt her daughters needed:

> When it comes to the two of us as parents, I feel that my husband's parenting skills are probably superior to mine, just because of his calm rationale. But maybe that's not what little girls need all the time. He doesn't tend to be the one that tells them how gorgeous they look when they dress up, which they really like, and I see these things, I see when they're putting in a little extra effort. He's getting better as we grow in our relationship, as the kids grow in their relationship with him.

Like many fathers in this study, this one was characterized as developing sensitivity to the children by relying on interactions with his wife. She "see things" which he has to learn to recognize. Thus, while he may have "superior" parenting skills, he must learn something subtle from her. His reliance on her expertise suggests that his "calm rationale" is insufficient to make him "maternal" in the way that she is. Her ability to notice things, and his inattention to them, serves to render them both accountable: parenting remains an essential part of her nature, but is a learned capacity for him. Couples talked about fathers being socialized, as adults, to become nurturing parents. This talking with their wives about child care helped husbands construct and sustain images of themselves as competent fathers.

Greater paternal competence was also reported to enhance marital interaction. Fathers were often characterized as paying increased attention to emotional cues from their wives and engaging in more reciprocal communication. Taking responsibility for routine household labor offered some men the opportunity to better understand their mother's lives as well. For instance, one involved father who did most of the housework suggested that he could sometimes derive pleasure from cleaning the bathroom or picking up a sock if he looked at it as an act of caring for his family:

> It makes it a different job, to place it in a context of being an expression of caring about a collective life together. It's at that moment that I'm maybe closest to understanding what my mother and other women of my mother's generation, and other women now, have felt about being housewives and being at home, being themselves. I think I emotionally understand the satisfaction and the gratification of being a homemaker.

More frequently, however, sharing child care and housework helped fathers understand its drudgery. One father who is employed as a carpenter explained how assuming more responsibility for housework motivated him to encourage his wife to buy whatever she needs to make housework easier.

> It was real interesting when I started doing more housework. Being in construction, when I needed a tool, I bought the tool. And when I vacuum floors, I look at this piece of shit, I mean I can't vacuum the floor with this and feel good about it, it's not doing a good job. So I get a good vacuum system. So I have more appreciation for housecleaning. When I clean the tubs, I want something that is going to clean the tubs; I don't want to work extra hard. You know I have a kind of sponge to use for cleaning the tubs. So I have more of an appreciation for what she had to do. I tell her "If you know of something that's going to make it easier, let's get it."

Most sample fathers reported that performance of child care, in and of itself, increased their commitment to both parenting and housework. All of the fathers had been involved in some housework before the birth of their children, but many indicated that their awareness and performance of housework increased in conjunction with their involvement in parenting. They reported that as they spent more time in the house alone with their children, they assumed more responsibility for cooking and cleaning. Fathers also noted that as they became more involved in the daily aspects of parenting, and in the face of their wives' absence and relinquishment of total responsibility for housekeeping, they became more aware that certain tasks needed doing and they were more likely to perform them.

This was conditioned by the amount of time fathers spent on the job, but more than half reported that they increased their contributions to household labor when their children were under ten years old. This did not always mean that fathers' relative proportion of household tasks increased, because mothers were also doing more in response to an expanding total household workload.

GENDER ATTRIBUTIONS

Approximately half of both mothers and fathers volunteered that men and women brought something unique to child care, and many stressed that they did not consider their own parenting skills to be identical to those of their spouse. One mother whose husband had recently increased the amount of time he spent with their school-aged children commented: "Anybody can slap together a cream cheese and cucumber sandwich and a glass of milk and a few chips and call it lunch, but the ability to see that your child is troubled about something, or to be able to help them work through a conflict with a friend, that is really much different." A list-making mother who provided less child care and did less housework than her husband described herself as "more intimate and gentle," and her husband as "rough and out there." Like many others she emphasized that mothers and fathers provide "a balance" for their children. She described how she had to come to terms with her expectations that her husband would "mother" the way that she did:

> One of the things that I found I was expecting from him when he started doing so much here and I was gone so much, I was expecting him to mother the kids. And you know, I had to get over that one pretty quick and really accept him doing the things the way he did them as his way, and that being just fine with me. He wasn't mothering the kids, he was fathering the kids. It was just that he was the role of the mother as far as the chores and all that stuff.

A mother who managed and performed most of the housework and child care used different reasoning to make similar claims about essential differences between women and men. In contrast to the mothers quoted above, this mother suggested that men could nurture, but not perform daily child care:

> Nurturance is one thing, actual care is another thing. I think if a father had to—like all of a sudden the wife was gone, he could nurture it with the love that it needed. But he might not change the diapers often enough, or he might not give 'em a bath often enough and he might not think of the perfect food to feed. But as far as nurturing, I think he's capable of caring . . . If the situation is the mother is there and he didn't have to, then he would trust the woman to.

This mother concluded, "The woman has it more in her genes to be more equipped for nurturing" Thus many of the manager-helper couples legitimated their divisions of labor and reaffirmed the "naturalness" of essential gender differences.

Parents who equally shared the responsibility for direct and indirect child care, on the other hand, were more likely to see similarities in their relationships with their children. They all reported that their children were emotionally "close" to both parents. When asked who his children went to when they were hurt or upset, one early- and equal-sharing father commented: "They'll go to either of us, that is pretty indistinguishable." Mothers and fathers who equally shared most direct child care reported that their children typically called for the parent with whom they had most recently spent time, and frequently called her mother "daddy" or the father "mommy," using the gendered form to signify "parent." Most often, parents indicated that their children would turn to "whoever's closest" or "whoever they've been with," thus linking physical closeness with emotional closeness. In-home observations of family interactions confirmed such reports.

The central feature of these and other parental accounts is that shared activities formed an emotional connection between parent and child. Shared activities were also instrumental in constructing images of fathers as competent, nurturing care givers. Two-thirds of both mothers and fathers expressed the belief that men could care for children's emotional needs as well as women. When asked whether men, in general, could nurture like women, mothers used their husbands as examples. One said, "I don't necessarily think that that skill comes with a sex type. Some women nurture better than others, some men nurture better than other men. I think that those skills can come when either person is willing to have the confidence and commitment to prioritize them."

However, the parents who were the most successful at sharing child care were the most likely to claim that men could nurture like women. Those who sustained manager-helper dynamics in child care tended to invoke the images of "maternal instincts" and alluded to natural differences between men and women. In contrast, more equal divisions of household labor were typically accompanied by an ideology of gender *similarity* rather than gender difference. The direction of causality is twofold: (1) those who believed that men could nurture like women seriously attempted to share all aspects of child care, and (2) the successful practice of sharing child care facilitated the development of beliefs that men could nurture like women.

NORMALIZING ATYPICAL BEHAVIOR

Mothers and fathers reported that women friends, most of whom were in more traditional marriages or were single, idealized their shared-parenting arrangements. About two-thirds of sample mothers reported that their women friends told them that they were extremely fortunate, and labeled their husbands "wonderful," "fantastic," "incredible," or otherwise out of the ordinary. Some mothers said that women friends were "jealous," "envious," or "amazed," and that they "admired" and "supported" their efforts at sharing domestic chores.

Both mothers and fathers said that the father received more credit for his family involvement than the mother did, because it was expected that she would perform child care and housework. Since parenting is assumed to be "only natural" for women, fathers were frequently praised for performing a task that would go unnoticed if a mother had performed it:

> I think I get less praise because people automatically assume that, you know, the mother's *supposed* to do the child care. And he gets a lot of praise because he's the visible one. Oh, I think that he gets far more praise. I can bust my butt at that school and all he has to do is show up in the parking lot and everybody's all *gah gah* over him. I don't get resentful about that—think it's funny and I think it's sad.

While the fathers admitted that they enjoyed such praise, many indicated that they did not take these direct or implied compliments very seriously.

> I get more credit than she does, because it's so unusual that the father's at home and involved in the family. I realize what it is: it's prejudice. The strokes feel real nice, but I don't take them too seriously. I'm sort of proud of it in a way that I don't really like. It's nothing to be proud of, except that I'm glad to be doing it and I think it's kind of neat because it hasn't been the style traditionally. I kind of like that, but I know that it means nothing.

These comments reveal that fathers appreciated praise, but actively discounted compliments received from those in dissimilar situations. The fathers's everyday parenting experiences led them to view parenthood as drudgery as well as fulfillment. They described their sense of parental responsibility as taken-for-granted and did not consider it to be out of the ordinary or something worthy of special praise. Fathers sometimes reported being puzzled by compliments from their wives' acquaintances and judged them to be inappropriate. When I asked one what kinds of reactions he received when his children were infants, he said,

> They all thought it was really wonderful. They thought she'd really appreciate how wonderful it was and how different that was from her to father. They'd say, "You ought to know how lucky you are, he's doing so much." I just felt like I'm doing what any person should do. Just like shouldn't anybody be this interested in their child? No big deal.

Another father said he resented all the special attention he received when he was out with his infant son:

> Constant going shopping and having women stop me and say "Oh it's so good to see you fathers." I was no longer an individual: I was this generic father who was now a liberated father who could take care of his child. I actually didn't like it. I felt after a while that I wanted the time and the quality of my relationship with my child at that point, what was visible in public, to simply be accepted as what you do. It didn't strike me as worthy of recognition, and it pissed me off a lot that women in particular would show this sort of appreciation, which I think is well-intentioned, but which also tended to put a frame around the whole thing as though somehow this was an experience that could be extracted from one's regular life. It wasn't. It was going shopping with my

> son in a snuggly or on the backpack was what I was doing. It wasn't somehow this event that always had to be called attention to.

Thus fathers discounted and normalized extreme reactions to their divisions of labor and interpreted them in a way that supported the "natural" character of what they were doing.

One mother commented on a pattern that was typically mentioned by both parents: domestic divisions of labor were "normal" to those who were attempting something similar, and "amazing" to those who were not: "All the local friends here think it's amazing. They call him 'Mr. Mom' and tell me how lucky I am. I'm waiting for someone to tell him how lucky *he* is. I have several friends at work who have very similar arrangements and they just feel that it's normal."

Because fathers assumed traditional mothering functions, they often had more social contact with mothers than with other fathers. They talked about being the only fathers at children's lessons, parent classes and meetings, at the laundromat, or in the market. One father said it took mothers there a while before they believed he really shared a range of household tasks.

> At first they ask me, "Is this your day off?" And I say, "If it's the day off for me, why isn't it the day off for you?" 'Well, I work 24 hours a day!' And I say, "Yeah, right. I got my wash done and hung out and the beds made." It takes the mother a couple of times to realize that I really do that stuff.

In general, fathers resisted attempts by other people to compare them to traditional fathers, and often compared themselves directly to their wives, or to other mothers.

Fathers tended to be employed in occupations predominantly composed of men, and in those settings were often discouraged from talking about family or children. Several fathers reported that people at their place of employment could not understand why they did "women's work," and a few mentioned that coworkers would be disappointed when they would repeatedly turn down invitations to go out "with the boys" for a drink. One of three self-employed carpenters in the study said that he would sometimes conceal that he was leaving work to do something with his children because he worried about negative reactions from employers or coworkers:

> I would say reactions that we've got—in business, like if I leave a job somewhere that I'm on and mention that I'm going to coach soccer, my son's soccer game, yeah. I have felt people kind of stiffen, like, I was more shirking my job, you know, such a small thing to leave work for, getting home, racing home for. I got to the point with some people where I didn't necessarily mention what I was leaving for, just because I didn't need for them to think that I was being irresponsible about their work, I mean, I just decided it wasn't their business. If I didn't know them well enough to feel that they were supportive. I would just say, "I have to leave early today"—never lie, if they asked me a question. I'd tell them the answer—but not volunteer it. And, maybe in some cases, I feel like, you know, you really have to be a little careful about being too *groovy* too,

> that what it is that you're doing is just so wonderful. "I'm a father, I'm going to go be with my children." It isn't like that, you know. I don't do it for what people think of me; I do it because I enjoy it.

Some fathers said their talk of spending time with their children was perceived by coworkers as indicating they were not "serious" about their work. They reported receiving indirect messages that *providing* for the family was primary and *being with* the family was secondary. Fathers avoided negative workplace sanctions by selectively revealing the extent of their family involvement.

Many fathers selected their current jobs because the work schedule was flexible, or so they could take time off to care for their children. For instance, even though most fathers worked full-time, two-thirds had some daytime hours off, as exemplified by teachers, mail carriers, and self-employed carpenters. Similarly, most fathers avoided extra, work-related tasks or overtime hours in order to maximize time spent with their children. One computer technician said that he was prepared to accept possible imputations of nonseriousness:

> I kind of tend to choose my jobs. When I go to a job interview, I explain to people that I have a family and the family's very important to me. Some companies expect you to work a lot of overtime or work weekends, and I told them that I don't have to accept that sort of thing. I may not have gotten all the jobs I ever might have had because of it, but it's something that I bring up at the job interview and let them know that my family comes first.

The same father admitted that it is sometimes a "blessing" that his wife works evenings at a local hospital, because it allows him to justify leaving his job on time:

> At five o'clock or five thirty at night, when there are a lot of people that are still going to be at work for an hour or two more. I go "Adios!" [laughs]. I mean, I *can't* stay. I've gotta pick up the kids. And there are times when I feel real guilty about leaving my fellow workers behind when I know they're gonna be there for another hour or so. About a block from work I go "God, this is great!" [laughs].

Over half of the study participants also indicated that their own mothers or fathers reacted negatively to their divisions of labor. Parents were described as "confused," "bemused," and "befuddled," and it was said that they "lack understanding" or "think it's a little strange." One mother reported that her parents and in-laws wouldn't "dare to criticize" their situation because "times have changed," but she sensed their underlying worry and concern:

> I think both sides of the family think it's fine because it's popular now. They don't dare—I mean if we were doing this thirty years ago, they would dare to criticize. In a way, now they don't. I think both sides feel it's a little strange. I thought my mom was totally sympathetic and no problem, but when I was going to go away for a week and my husband was going to take care of the kids, she said something to my sister about how she didn't think I should do it. There's a little underlying tension about it, I think.

Other study participants reported that disagreements with parents were common, particularly if they revolved around trying to change childrearing practices their own parents had used.

Many couples reported that initial negative reactions from parents turned more positive over time as they saw that the children were "turning out all right," that the couple was still together after an average of ten years, and that the men were still employed. This last point, that parents were primarily concerned with their son's or son-in-law's provider responsibilities, highlights how observers typically evaluated the couple's task sharing. A number of study participants mentioned that they thought their parents wanted the wife to quit work and stay home with the children and that the husband should "make up the difference." Most mentioned, however, that parents were more concerned that the husband continue to be the provider than they were that the wife made "extra money" or that the husband "helped out" at home.

> In the beginning there was a real strong sense that I was in the space of my husband's duty. That came from his parents pretty strongly. The only way that they have been able to come to grips with this in any fashion is because he has also been financially successful. If he had decided, you know, "Outside work is not for me, I'm going to stay home with the kids and she's going to work." I think there would have been a whole lot more talk than there was. I think it's because he did both and was successful that it was okay.

Another mother noted that parental acceptance of shared parenting did not necessarily entail acceptance of the woman as provider:

> There is a funny dynamic that happens. It's not really about child care, where I don't think in our families—with our parents—I don't get enough credit for being the breadwinner. Well they're still critical of him for not earning as much money as I do. In a way they've accepted him as being an active parenting father more than they've accepted me being a breadwinner.

Here again, the "essential nature" of men is taken to be that of provider. If the men remain providers, they are still accountable as men, even if they take an active part in child care.

DISCUSSION

This brief exploration into the social construction of shared parenting in twenty dualearner families illustrates how more equal domestic gender relations arise and under what conditions they flourish. All couples described flexible and practical task-allocation procedures that were responses to shortages of time. All families were child-centered in that they placed a high value on their children's well-being, defined parenting as an important and serious undertaking, and organized most of their nonemployed time around their children. Besides being well-educated and delaying childbearing until their late twenties or early thirties, couples who shared most of the responsibility for household labor tended to involve the father in routine child care from the children's early infancy. As Sara Rudduck (1982) has noted, the everyday aspects of child care and housework help share ways of thinking, feeling, and acting that become associated with what it means to be a mother. My findings suggest that when domestic activities are equally shared, "maternal thinking" develops in fathers, too, and the social meaning of gender begins to change. This deemphasizes notions of gender as personality and locates it in social interaction.

To treat gender as the "cause" of household division of labor overlooks its emergent character and fails to acknowledge how it is in fact implicated in precisely such routine practices.

References

Berk, Sarah Fenstermaker. 1985. *The Gender Factory.* New York: Plenum.

Ruddick, Sara. 1982. "Maternal thinking." In *Rethinking the Family,* ed. Barrie Thorne and Marilyn Yalom, 76–94. New York: Longman.

West, Candace, and Don H. Zimmerman. 1987. "Doing gender." *Gender & Society* 1:125–51.

KATHERINE R. ALLEN AND DAVID H. DEMO

The Families of Lesbians and Gay Men: A New Frontier in Family Research

A paradigm shift is occurring in family studies, from viewing the family as a monolithic entity to recognizing family pluralism. Recent works have cited the elaboration of existing family structures and the emergence of new family forms. Recognition of diversity by race, class, and gender are at the heart of this shift. Feminist scholars have made impressive progress in deconstructing assumptions about women's locations in families, but sexual orientation has been virtually ignored. Assessing the state of family theory and research, Doherty, Boss, LaRossa, Schumm, and Steinmetz (1993) cited lesbian and gay family research as one of the "major streams of family scholarship that have not yet influenced mainstream family science" (p. 16).

Families that include lesbian and gay individuals are part of the increasingly diverse family landscape. Lesbians and gay men are involved in family relationships as sons and daughters, as partners, as parents and stepparents, and as ex-

From *Journal of Marriage and the Family,* Vol. 57 (February 1995), pp. 111–127. References have been edited.

tended and chosen kin. In a comprehensive review of research on lesbian and gay families, Laird (1993) observed that only a small core of studies have been conducted on this population, providing brief glimpses of the everyday lives of these families. Three areas comprise the core of our knowledge base to date: (a) same-sex partnerships and romantic relationships; (b) lesbian mothers and, to a lesser degree, gay fathers; and (c) the psychological development and social adjustment of children of lesbian and gay parents. These studies reflect a needed shift in the research literature and public discourse from a deficit stance about "homosexuals as individuals" to a focus on the familial and social contexts in which lesbians and gay men live (Laird, 1993). Although this body of work forms an important base for beginning to conceptualize how sexual orientation impacts family experiences, much more work needs to be done in order to integrate the family relations of lesbians and gay men into mainstream family studies.

Sexist and heterosexist assumptions continue to underlie most of the research on families by focusing analysis on heterosexual partnerships and parenthood. Lesbians and gay men are thought of as individuals, but not as family members. This reflects the society-wide belief that "gayness" and family are mutually exclusive concepts, a belief that prevails because "the same-sex family, more than any other form, challenges fundamental patriarchal notions of family and gender relationships" (Laird, 1993, p. 295). Experience that does not fit the narrow definitions of family and kinship fails to be named or included in research investigations. The inclusion of lesbian and gay family experiences into representative studies of the population has yet to occur. By ignoring the diverse structures, processes, and outcomes of lesbian and gay families in mainstream family research, family scholars have failed to capitalize on opportunities to contribute to new theoretical understandings of families.

Perhaps some of the invisibility and silence surrounding these families is due to the lack of a clear agenda defining what researchers need to do. Given the limited information about family structure and process related to the households of lesbians and gay men, we argue that researchers must move beyond the assumption of gay and lesbian households as a social address. A social address, as Bronfenbrenner and Crouter (1983) explained, is an "environmental label—with no attention to what the environment is like, what people are living there, what they are doing, or how the activities taking place could affect the child" (pp. 361–362). We argue that, in addition to examining family structure, researchers must focus attention on family processes such as attitudes and beliefs about childrearing, decision-making and conflict resolution strategies, and parental support and discipline. A more adequate conceptualization than an exclusive focus on structure examines the person in relation to various family processes and within multiple interdependent and overlapping contexts (e.g., employment and family).

In this article, we will report on our examination of nine journals that publish family research and document the limited attention given to lesbian and gay families. We will describe and define the families of lesbians and gay men to illustrate their diversity and to highlight why the neglect of this population is no longer tenable. Our goal is to direct researchers' attention away from a social address model and toward a social ecologies model that incorporates the dynamics of family relationships (e.g., parent-child, stepparent-stepchild, grandparent-grandchild, aunt/uncle-child, couple, siblings, peers, etc.) and the multiple contexts in which sexual orientation is relevant. We will discuss theoretical implications for family studies from the study of lesbian and gay families. Finally, we will propose a research agenda to stimulate and guide future investigations that integrate lesbian and gay family experience. Our work is informed by three theoretical orientations prominent in family studies: ecological, feminist, and life course.

DEFINING THE FAMILIES OF LESBIANS AND GAY MEN

Diversity

There are millions of lesbians and gay men in the United States and throughout the world about whose family lives we know very little. A preliminary step in the recognition and investigation of such families is attention to issues of identification and definition. There are many types of families that include lesbians and gay men, requiring family researchers to adopt a broad or inclusionary definition, especially in the early stages of inquiry. Yet we must be careful in labeling families. Family researchers have grappled with the limitations imposed by defining families as intact, broken, remarried, dysfunctional, military, or alcoholic. We maintain that it is equally problematic to define families that include lesbians or gay men as heterosexual families, or to define them as lesbian or gay families if some members of the family are heterosexual. In our view, levels of analysis must be distinguished clearly, and it should be explicit that individuals, not families, have sexual orientations. At the same time, in relationships where individuals share a sexual orientation, it is reasonable to define such relationships as lesbian or gay partnerships.

Defining families becomes more complex when family members have different sexual orientations (e.g., family of origin relationships) and when there are dependent children (e.g., parent-child relationships). The proper term for families in which there is at least one lesbian or gay member is a point of controversy. Paradoxically, labels—which are necessary to define a population for study and to provide common ground for accumulating data about a subject matter—can reduce the complexity of the phenomenon to a monolithic entity. Patterson (1994) observed that many issues in families are the same, regardless of sexual orientation, but, in other ways, the issues lesbian and gay members face are quite different. Because of the importance of those differences and the necessity of drawing attention to the unique circumstances they face, such as coming out and prejudice, Patterson (1994) has supported the label "lesbian and gay families" for defining families that include at least one gay or lesbian member. There are advantages and disadvantages of using the terms "lesbian and gay families" and "same-sex families," and Laird (1993) concludes that any attempt to define families is fraught with political and ideological implications. In the strictest sense, families in which members have different sexual orientations require "some new terminology such as 'mixed gay/straight' or 'dual-orientation' families" (Laird, 1993, p. 282). Thus, a gay adult from a heterosexual family of origin lives in a dual-orientation family, but he and his partner maintain a gay household. Further, although the terminology has not been widely used, a gay partnership, with or without the presence of children or stepchildren, constitutes a gay family. Limitations of the term *lesbian and gay families* notwithstanding, families and households containing lesbian and gay individuals have been systematically excluded from family research, requiring us to define the types of families that need to be identified and studied.

Toward this end, and recognizing the tremendous diversity characterizing the families in which lesbians and gay men live, we suggest that lesbian and gay families are defined by the presence of two or more people who share a same-sex orientation (e.g., a couple), or by the presence of at least one lesbian or gay adult rearing a child. Of course, many other families more properly would be termed dual-orientation families, and we argue that all families involving one or more lesbian or gay member(s)—whether child, adolescent, one or more parents, grandparents, or other kin—represent families that are influenced in various ways by issues and dynamics associated with homosexuality. Lesbian, gay, or bisexual individuals need not reside in the household to influence family relationships (parent-child, sibling, couple, or extended kin relations). For many reasons, residential and coresidential status are likely to vary in the case of gay male and lesbian parents, with this variation impacting on family relations, that is, lesbians are far more likely than gay men to have custody or to reside with their children.

To illustrate some of the family issues associated with homosexuality, consider the multiple life course trajectories and complex family dynamics of a common three-member family structure: a child living with her heterosexual mother and having a nonresidential relationship with her gay father. The identification and study of such families requires a sensitivity to, and broad definition of, lesbian and gay families. Until now, family researchers have ignored these populations, assumed their heterosexuality, studied them as single-parent families, and thus neglected a critical element in the formation, composition, and daily interaction of these families. Using the same illustration and viewing the family from the child's point of view, the daughter's family also may comprise her father's live-in male partner (or her gay stepfather) and his kin. Although research on these relationships is sparse, it is clear that many lesbians and gay men who are partnered or were formerly partnered live in stepfamily structures, and it is likely that such families are as diverse in their dynamics as stepfamilies in which all members are heterosexual.

A further advantage of a broad definition is it enables us to better understand the rich diversity characterizing lesbian and gay families. As with heterosexual families, we lack even a rudimentary taxonomy for describing family diversity. Yet countless variations of lesbian and gay families exist, including families that "are formed from lovers, friends, biological and adopted children, blood relatives, stepchildren, and even ex-lovers, families that do not necessarily share a common household" (Laird, 1993, p. 294). Among these are families that are diverse with respect to the number and sexual orientation of adults heading the household. For example, there may be one adult lesbian, one adult gay male, two adults (both gay males), two adults (both lesbians), two adults (one lesbian and one heterosexual or bisexual partner), two adults (one gay male and one heterosexual or bisexual partner), or some combination of more than two lesbian, gay, and/or heterosexual partners. A second dimension of diversity within lesbian and gay families is signified by the presence of lesbian or gay children, adolescents, or adult children in families headed by one or more gay adults—that is, families in which there are at least two members with a lesbian or gay identity. A third dimension is characterized by the presence of a lesbian or gay child, adolescent, or adult child living with one or more heterosexual parents. Fourth, there are lesbian or gay families consisting of stepparent-stepchild and/or stepsibling relations involving at least one lesbian or gay family member, again requiring careful distinctions between families and households and between stepfamilies and step-households. A fifth dimension of family interaction influenced by homosexuality involves relations with a lesbian or gay grandparent, aunt, uncle, or other kin, whether affinal or consanguineal. All of these variations exist in addition to the variation that characterizes other, presumably heterosexual, families, including variation by race, age, income, education, number of children, children's gender, and duration of couple relationship. Unfortunately, what little we know about lesbian and gay families to date is based on small samples of predominantly white, urban, middle-class, highly educated respondents. One final and important consideration regarding diversity is that the intersections of gender and sexual orientation have implications for varying structures and dynamics in the families of lesbians compared with the families of gay men.

Demographics

It is impossible to know precisely how many lesbian and gay individuals live in this country or how many children under the age of 18 have lesbian or gay parents. PFLAG, the Federation of Parents, Families and Friends of Lesbians and Gays, states that one out of every four families has a gay member. However, three problems in identifying accurate demographics are: (a) varying definitions of sexual orientation, (b) the ongoing exclusion of lesbian and gay people from research investigations, and (c) the further exclusion of bisexuality. Harry (1983) concluded that sampling biases will continue until questions on sexual orientation are included in general probability surveys. Further, it is important to note that in the climate of heterosexism and homophobia in the wider society, many people who identify as lesbian or gay do not disclose their orientation because of fear of the reactions of others.

Many researchers cite the estimates provided by Kinsey and associates that approximately 10% of the population in the United States defines itself as predominantly lesbian or gay. Voeller (1990) clarified how the Kinsey Institute data led to the widely cited 10% figure:

> 37% of males had a postpubertal homosexual experience, as had 20% of women. . . . For those who had predominantly homosexual experience (4s, 5s, and 6s on the Kinsey scale), the percentages were about 7% for women and 13% for men (depending on just which data you used). As there are about equal numbers of each gender, an average of 10% of the population could be designated

> as gay, that is, to the homosexual side of the midpoint 3 on the scale, a percentage Gebhard, at the Kinsey Institute, recalculated and confirmed.

However, the Kinsey et al. figures are questionable because: (a) the prevalence of same-sex sexual orientations and experiences may be much different now from when the original data were collected between 1938 and 1948, and/or may be different now from when the follow-up data were collected, ending in 1963, and (b) the Kinsey sample was not a probability sample and has been criticized on methodological grounds. Analyzing national probability survey data collected in 1970 and 1988, Fay et al. (1989) estimated that roughly one-fifth of adult American males have had at least one homosexual experience, and that between 3% and 6% of the adult population is exclusively homosexual. They speculated that many individuals with regular or frequent homosexual activity are currently married or were previously married, indicating bisexual orientations and changes in sexual orientations over time. Although they did not provide comparable data for lesbians, they argued that because of societal intolerance, the observed percentages probably represent lower bounds of the true incidence of same-sex behavior:

> Clearly, there is good reason to suspect that the net bias in self-reports of homosexual experiences is negative. . . . Societal intolerance of same-gender sex may diminish survey respondents' willingness to provide complete and accurate reports of behaviors that are classified as crimes in many states. (Fay et al., 1989, p. 346)

Adopting a broad definition of lesbian and gay families also means that the numbers or percentages pertaining to lesbian or gay adults are probably very conservative estimates of the number of households including lesbians and gay men, not to mention families including lesbians and gay men. Harry (1983) summarized the demographics of seven studies of gay men and found that an average of 20% of gay men have been heterosexually married, with a range of 14% to 25% across the seven investigations. Bell and Weinberg (1978) found that about half (52%) of these former marriages resulted in at least one biological child. Bozett (1987) estimated that between 1 and 3 million gay men are natural fathers. However, this is a conservative estimate of gay fathers because it does not include gay men with adopted, foster, or stepchildren, or those who become fathers through other means such as sperm donation.

Harry's (1983) summary of four studies of lesbians revealed that about one-third have been heterosexually married. About half of these marriages resulted in children. Estimates of lesbian mothers vary. Falk (1989) cited a range of 1.5 to 5 million lesbians who reside with their children. It is unknown how many women become mothers through donor insemination, but clinicians and researchers agree that it is substantial and increasing. In spite of the problems of determining exact estimates of the number of children living with lesbian or gay parents, most researchers accept Schulenberg's (1985) estimate that at least 6 million children under age 18 have gay or lesbian parents. The Editors of the *Harvard Law Review* (1990) reported that "approximately three million gay men and lesbians in the United States are parents, and between eight and ten million children are raised in gay or lesbian households" (p. 119). In short, the sheer demographic prevalence of lesbian and gay individuals provides ample justification for family researchers to acknowledge and investigate the diverse families in which lesbians and gay men live.

EXCLUDING THE FAMILIES OF LESBIANS AND GAY MEN IN FAMILY RESEARCH

Very little research has been published or presented in family studies that identifies or examines gay men, lesbian women, and their family relations. Some theories and research traditions explicitly exclude consideration of lesbian and gay families. For example, pro-marriage and pro-nuclear family biases are evident in family development theory, which defines the family "as a social group regulated by the norms of the institution of marriage and the family" (Rodgers & White, 1993, p. 236). The 1990 *Journal of Marriage and the Family* Decade in Review mentions the term "homosexual couples" in only one article, thus offering even less than the two columns of print in the 1980s review, in which Macklin (1980) included a brief summary of literature on same-sex intimate relationships.

To identify and assess the extant literature on lesbian and gay families, we conducted a systematic review of the three leading journals in family studies: *Journal of Marriage and the Family (JMF), Family Relations (FR), and Journal of Family Issues (JFI).* We selected these journals for several reasons. *JMF* and *FR* are the two journals published by the National Council on Family Relations. *JMF* is widely recognized as the flagship journal in family studies, and *FR* is the leading outlet for applied family research. *JFI,* published by Sage, also is a highly respected journal in the field and is sponsored by the National Council on Family Relations.

We examined the topics of articles published in these journals from 1980 to 1993. First, we searched for the following key words in the subject index of *JMF* and *FR* (*JFI* does not have a subject index) indicating an explicit reference to a same-sex orientation: bisexual, gay, heterosexism, homophobia, homosexual, lesbian, sexual orientation, and sexual preference. We also looked for terms such as AIDS, alternative lifestyles, feminism, heterosexuality, nontraditional families, reproductive technologies, and sexuality. This process yielded few studies, thus requiring a careful examination of the contents of each article.

Next, we examined every article published from 1980 through 1993. We read the titles and abstracts of every article published during this period, and we read the complete articles in cases where any of the above key words were included in the title or abstract. We also skimmed articles with titles and abstracts that did not contain any explicit terms referring to sexual orientation. To obtain the numbers reported in Table 1, we counted all original substantive articles, resource reviews, and invited exchanges, and excluded editor's comments, book and media reviews, and feedback regarding previously published articles. To be counted as "explicit content," the central focus of the article had to be on sexual orientation or preference, the experiences of gay men or lesbians, homosexuality, or bisexuality. If the focus of the article was on something else, but one of these topics regarding

Table 1.
Studies on Lesbian or Gay Families Published in Family Journals, 1980 to 1993

Journal	Total Articles	Explicit Content	Related Content
Family Relations	971	10	40
Journal of Marriage and the Family	1,209	2	23
Journal of Family Issues	418	0	14
Total	2,598	12	77

sexual orientation was mentioned in the article, it was counted as an article with "related content."

Family Relations

For the period from January 1980 through October 1993, a total of 971 articles was published in *Family Relations*, a journal dedicated to applied family studies. Of these articles, 10 (or 1%) involved explicit study of lesbians, gay men, or issues pertaining to sexual orientation (see Table 1). Eight articles in the past 14 years examined issues of family relations (e.g., parent-child relations, childrearing values, couple relations, support, communication, conflict, violence) in the context of lesbian or gay families, or what we call the social ecology of families that include one or more lesbian or gay members. Two articles examined AIDS (acquired immune deficiency syndrome) and gay family members.

An additional 40 articles (or 4%) contained information on sexuality education and other issues that mentioned homosexuality or sexual orientation. Most of these articles, termed "related content" in Table 1, are concerned with homosexuality as an alternative lifestyle, as deviant, as related to AIDS, and as an environment or social address with unique problems. Over the span covering 1980 to 1993, there were some gradual but noticeable shifts in the attention devoted to lesbian and gay families, in the topics studied, and in the language used to describe issues bearing on lesbian and gay families. Through 1987, there were very few articles (16 out of a total of 564, or less than 3%) that even mentioned homosexuality. In the October 1981 special issue on family life education, homosexuality was not among the topics discussed. During these years, the focus was on marriage as a monolithic relationship type. Certain values were reflected in the articles: having two parents, involvement of fathers, and good communication between parents and children. Articles on sexuality education assumed that heterosexuality is normative, exclusive, and permanent. Alternative lifestyles were defined in terms of heterosexual variations, such as cohabitation. Homosexuality was never advocated nor seen as acceptable for youth.

Some shifts occurred in the late 1980s. Although the frequency of articles in *Family Relations* mentioning or focusing on homosexuality increased slightly during this period, the articles continued to be mostly about sexuality education curricula. Issues about homosexuality appeared in more diverse contexts, using more appropriate and gay-affirmative language. The frequency of articles related to AIDS increased sharply beginning in 1988. Of course, AIDS is a disease affecting individuals (and families) of all sexual orientations, but there was not a corresponding increase in research on other issues affecting lesbians and gay men, such as their relationships or parenting styles. Instead, the preoccupation continued with defining lesbians and gay men by their sexual behavior.

Over the most recent period, 1990–1993, lesbians and gay men gained modest visibility in applied family studies, but still with definite limits. Three trends are apparent: There was a marked increase in articles examining sexual orientation during this period, AIDS forced people to talk about sexual behavior of all types, and there was greater recognition of family diversity, including the families of lesbians and gay men. This recognition ranges from a perfunctory mention of "homosexual families" in a list of other diverse family types to illustrations and examples involving lesbians and gay men. The editor's call for papers for a special issue on family diversity (July, 1993) specifically requested articles examining a wide variety of family types. Over the past 2 years, articles on relationship quality and domestic partnerships involving lesbian and gay couples appeared for the first time in *FR.*

In sum, the gradual trend since 1980 has been from mentioning monolithic homosexuality as a topic to be included in a sexuality education program, to discussing gay men in articles about AIDS, to discussing lesbians and gay men in contexts beyond their homosexuality, that is, as family members, parents, and partners. Still, it is clear that lesbian and gay families are commonly ignored, poorly understood, stigmatized, and problematized. Family practitioners view gay parents as holding a master status; their sexual orientation clouds the perception of them as parents, partners, or extended kin. We have yet to reach the point where they are viewed as family members who happen to be lesbian or gay. Only in the past few years have there been discussions in the premier applied family journal—a journal designed for practitioners—of multiple contexts associated with being lesbian or gay.

Journal of Marriage and the Family

Our review of the *Journal of Marriage and the Family,* the flagship journal for basic research on families, uncovered even fewer studies related to lesbian and gay families. For the period from February 1980 to November 1993, a total of 1,209 articles was published in *JMF,* only two of which involved explicit study of sexual orientation or homosexual experience (Table 1). The first of these was Reiss' (1986) Burgess Award Address in which he expanded his theory of sexuality to apply to "both heterosexual and homosexual relationships" and integrated references to homosexuality throughout. In the second article, Williams and Jacoby (1989) compared attitudes about homosexual and heterosexual experiences of college students from the University of North Dakota and Harvard University. They found evidence of a generalized homophobia, whereby students overwhelmingly rejected as potential mates those individuals with any form of same-sex experience. Family and relational issues were not studied.

An additional 23 articles (or less than 2% of articles published in *JMF*) either mentioned homosexuality or addressed only peripherally issues related to sexual orientation. In articles examining a wide range of topics including dating, nuclear and extended family structures, marital adjustment, wives' employment, parenting behavior, and premarital and/or extramarital sexual permissiveness, the status of marriage and heterosexuality are automatically and routinely assumed. Generally, each attempt at new knowledge begins with marriage and heterosexuality as baseline assumptions. There are, of course, exceptions. Reiss (1981) described Americans' intolerance and fear of homosexuality, and D'Antonio (1985) documented that, in American Catholic families, "Homosexuality is presented as an even graver deficiency [than masturbation] since it prevents people from becoming sexually mature, maturation being a function of the heterosexual relationship" (p. 397).

For the most part, lesbians and gay men, as individuals or couples, but rarely as members of families, are mentioned at the beginning or end of an article in a list of examples of diverse experience. Hendrick (1988), for example, recognized gay couples as one type of alternative relationship for which her revision of the Dyadic Adjustment Scale might apply.

Research published in the *Journal of Marriage and the Family* in the past few years seems to indicate that family researchers are beginning to be more sensitive to, or at least more cognizant of, sexual orientation. Thompson (1992), for example, illustrated feminist standpoint theory with a cogent discussion of lesbian identity. Tucker and Taylor (1989), in the only article that mentions Black Americans and sexual orientation, addressed a methodological problem in posing questions about romantic involvement to unmarried individuals. They explained that the question, "Do you have a main romantic involvement at this time?" did not distinguish gender and could have "elicited some gay and lesbian relationships" (p. 658). Fossett and Kiecolt (1991) explicitly recognized the problem presented by "homosexuals" for investigators conducting research on the sex ratio and heterosexual marriage markets. Noting that reliable information about the geographic distribution of gays and lesbians is "virtually nonexistent" (p. 955), they advised that "homosexuals should probably be excluded from the sex ratio in conventional analyses," but as a practical matter, researchers should keep them "in mind when examining outliers and anomalous cases" (p. 944). Despite this growing recognition that lesbian and gay populations challenge conventional ways of thinking about and studying families, family research is derelict in its responsibility to investigate, describe, and explain the life course and social ecology of lesbian and gay families.

Another trend is evident in recent investigations that do not examine or consider sexual orientation but have implications for lesbian and gay parenting. Downey and Powell (1993) conducted a comprehensive analysis of 35 social psychological and educational outcomes for children in different living arrangements to evaluate the evidence for the "same-sex parent argument." This argument, based largely on psychoanalytic and social learning theories, holds that the presence of and identification with the same-sex parent is necessary for the child's healthy emotional adjustment and appropriate gender role development. The argument is frequently used to deny lesbians and gay men custody of their children, and more broadly to challenge the adequacy and competence of lesbian and gay parents. Importantly, Downey and Powell found no evidence to support the same-sex argument. However, the authors were unable to consider the parents' (or children's) sexual orientation because the national data set they used did not collect these data.

Basic family research lags behind applied work intended for practitioners. Much of the research published in *JMF* is based on large data sets that systematically exclude lesbians and gay men. For example, nonmarital cohabitation, consistent with U. S. Bureau of the Census designation, is explicitly defined as "opposite sex partners." The deletion of same-sex unions from new data sets that are supposed to be representative of the population denies lesbian and gay couples and families an opportunity to be counted.

Journal of Family Issues

For the period spanning March 1980 (the first issue of *JFI*) to December 1993, a total of 418 articles was published. There is far less substantive inclusion of lesbians and gay men in *JFI* than in *JMF* or *FR*. No article explicitly examined lesbian or gay families or issues related to sexual orientation; 14 articles (3.3%) contained related content.

For the first 7 years of *JFI* (1980–1986), same-sex relationships were mentioned in only two contexts: in a list of several alternative lifestyles departing from the traditional nuclear family, or as an experience opposed by the extreme religious right. An exception is Walker and Thompson's (1984) suggestion that studying lesbians and gay men provides a way of broadening the literature and gaining a better understanding of family life.

One sign of visibility appeared in the late 1980s, as discussion of homosexuality and homosexual relationships was used as a criterion for evaluating family textbooks. Through the early 1990s, however, there was a consistently narrow interpretation of family issues. One of the distinguishing characteristics of *JFI* is that, each year, two of its four issues are devoted to special topics. A liberating feature of special issues, and of the many invited papers they contain, is the greater latitude researchers have to transcend conventional boundaries, frameworks, and modes of thinking. Yet research published in *JFI* is characterized by a systematic exclusion of lesbians and gay men, an exclusion that is manifested in both subtle and covert ways. At a subtle level, some authors acknowledge that they deliberately excluded lesbians and/or gay men and cite a particular reason for doing so, thus recognizing both the diversity and the relevance of sexual orientation. For example, Martinson and Wu (1992) described how their elaborate coding scheme used to define 20 family types excluded families in which children are raised by same-sex couples. As with other studies using secondary analysis, the authors were unable to examine the influence of parental sexual orientation because these data were not collected. Similarly, Marsiglio (1991) acknowledged that he excluded gay fathers from his analysis of male procreative consciousness and responsibility. At a more covert level, most authors ignore sexual orientation altogether, assume its irrelevance, or assume their sample consists entirely of heterosexuals. Studies of cohabitation, for example, routinely assume this experience is a developmental stage in a natural progression leading to mate selection and marriage. Likewise, research on teenage sexuality rarely acknowledges same-sex scripts, relationships, or attractions. The pervasive, insidious, and multidimensional nature of heterosexist bias in family research also is evidenced by a persisting focus on the sexual behavior of lesbians and gay men, by references to their relationships using the pejorative term "homosexual," and by ignoring broader aspects of their family relations.

Recently, there has been greater recognition of diversity. The March 1993 special issue, "Rethinking the Family as a Social Form," shows some change, containing three articles that mention diversity by sexual orientation. There are indications that researchers are beginning to question the adequacy of their concepts, measures, and theories. White (1992) pointed out some limitations of relying on marital status as a major explanatory variable. Bould (1993) argued that the census definition of the term *familial* obscures many aspects of familial caregiving by failing to recognize "ties that are solely emotional and lacking in any legal or blood relationship" (p. 136). And Scanzoni and Marsiglio (1993) proposed a theoretical framework for incorporating and valuing a variety of family structures, including same-sex couples, a framework intended to replace "the prevailing dichotomy" of benchmark family versus deviant alternative family.

Other Outlets for Family Scholarship

Collectively, the three leading journals dedicated to family research published 2,598 articles between 1980 and 1993, of which 12 articles (less than half of 1%) focused on the families of lesbians and gay men. With so few studies of lesbian and gay families appearing in the major family journals, the question arises as to whether the exclusion and invisibility extend to related fields. Has relevant research been published in journals in psychology, sociology, human development, or close relationships? Or are these fields similarly characterized by the marginalization of issues related to diverse sexual orientations?

To address these questions, we conducted a thorough review of leading journals in related fields. We examined the following: the preeminent developmental journal, *Child Development*, published by the University of Chicago Press for the Society for Research on Child Development; two journals published by the American Psychological Association (APA), *Journal of Family Psychology and Developmental Psychology;* two highly influential and prestigious general sociology journals, one published by the American Sociological Association, *American Sociological Review,* and one published by University of Chicago Press, *American Journal of Sociology;* and a top journal in the field of close relationships, *Journal of Social and Personal Relationships.* We read the titles and abstracts of every article and research note published in these journals between 1980 and 1993, searching for any of the key words described earlier (bisexual, gay, heterosexism, homophobia, homosexual, lesbian, sexual orientation, and sexual preference). We read articles containing these key words in the abstract, as well as articles containing related wording in the abstract (e.g., male couples, female couples).

Space does not permit a detailed discussion of our review of each of these jour-

Table 2.
Studies on Lesbian or Gay Families Published in Journals in Related Fields, 1980 to 1993

Journal	Total Articles	Articles on Topic
Journal of Family Psychology	213	3
Child Development	2,102	1
Developmental Psychology	1,491	2
Journal of Social and Personal Relationships	312	3
American Sociological Review	817	4
American Journal of Sociology	530	2
Total	5,465	15

nals, but we provide below a concise summary of the frequency and general content of articles related to sexual orientation. The numbers reported in Table 2 specify the total number of articles and research notes published in each journal over the 14-year period. We did not include comments, replies, editors' introductions, book reviews, or other reports that did not contain abstracts, with one exception. For the *Journal of Family Psychology,* the first 5 years of the journal contained numerous lengthy comments, replies, and key editorials, and these are reflected in the numbers we report in Table 2. We also report in Table 2 the number of articles each journal published between 1980 and 1993 on the broad topic of sexual orientation.

Collectively, the six related journals published 5,465 articles and research notes over this period, of which only 15 articles (less than one-third of 1%) concerned issues related to sexual orientation. In short, research is sparse on the families of lesbians and gay men, and the exclusion characterizes diverse disciplines, substantive areas, and publication outlets.

The *Journal of Family Psychology (JFP),* which began as a family therapy journal in 1987, has become a mainstream psychology journal since its publication by APA in 1992. Marriage is the cornerstone of the families treated and studied by psychologists publishing in JFP. Only three articles out of 213 (or slightly more than 1%) broached the subject of sexual orientation, reflecting the marginalization of lesbians and gay men in family psychology. The traditional model, legal definitions of family, and "the standard package" prevail, with studies routinely employing samples of husbands and wives, fathers and mothers. Few studies even acknowledge that heterosexual marriage was a requirement for inclusion.

Child Development (CD) published 2,102 articles between 1980 and 1993, the vast majority of which were experimental studies involving infants and young children in laboratory settings. Although many studies linked aspects of the family environment such as mother-child interaction, sibling relationships, and maternal employment to a broad array of children's outcomes, there was not a single empirical study examining parent-child relations in lesbian or gay families, the influences of parents' or others' sexual orientation on children, the diverse environmental and genetic factors affecting children's developing sexual orientations, or the characteristics and experiences of pre-gay, pre-lesbian, gay, or lesbian youth. Our key words did not appear in the titles or abstracts of any article, with one exception. A thorough and provocative review article identified emerging patterns in the study of children reared in lesbian and gay house-holds, documented the overall well-being of such children, and directed attention to the urgent need for more systematic investigation of the diverse living arrangements and life circumstances of children with lesbian or gay parents. In most of the research published in CD, however, it is assumed that normal child development involves two biological parents (one male, one female), same-sex friendships in middle to late childhood, and a transition to heterosexual relationships in adolescence.

Developmental Psychology (DP) published 1,491 articles between 1980 and 1993. The terms gay or lesbian appeared in the title or abstract of only one article and the term *sexual orientation* appeared in the abstract of one other article. None of the other titles or abstracts contained any of the key words we identified. In addition to these two articles that focused on the topic of sexual orientation, we noticed four articles that briefly mentioned in the text one of our key words: two articles listed homosexuality or cohabiting gay and lesbian couples as types of nonnormative lifestyles, one article included heterosexuality in a list of personality traits, and one study mentioned sexual orientation in relation to same-sex friendships. Although the majority of studies published in this journal involved subjects pertaining to young children, many issues contained sections on parenting, parental and family influences on development, family relationships, and family processes. Yet it is clear that issues of social location are still marginalized or sidestepped in developmental psychology. Instead, the focus is on differences, especially differences by age and gender and, to a lesser degree, differences by social class and race. However, a special issue titled "Sexual Orientation and Human Development" was scheduled to appear in DP in January 1995.

The *Journal of Social and Personal Relationships (JSPR)* began in 1984 as a journal devoted to the interdisciplinary study of personal and close relationships. Associate editors are assigned responsibility for submissions in the fields of clinical psychology (which became "clinical and community psychology" in 1986), communications, developmental psychology, and sociology (which became "family studies and sociology" in 1990). Of 312 articles published since its inception, three articles (or less than 1%) examined lesbian and/or gay relationship issues. Three articles by Kurdek (1989, 1991, 1992) analyzed data from a sample of lesbian and gay cohabiting couples to investigate relationship quality, dissolution, and stability, respectively. Consistent with other studies, Kurdek's findings challenged the gender difference model which posits that men are agentic and women are communal, illustrating many similarities in lesbian and gay styles of relating. Three other articles, although they did not contain our key words in the title or abstract, involved closely related subjects and illustrated ways in which sexual orientation diversity can be integrated into family research: Dosser, Balswick, and Halverson (1986) explained how homophobia contributes to male inexpressiveness; Milardo (1992) described some distinctive characteristics of exchange networks among lesbian couples; and Crandall and Coleman (1992) discussed the connection between AIDS-related stigmatization of homosexuals (and other groups) and the disruption of their social relationships. Most studies, however, are unreflexively heterosexist in that they are designed to explore patterns of attraction to and intimacy with opposite sex partners, thus excluding consideration of same-sex partners. In many cases, this occurs because researchers restrict their sample to married couples or to people who are romantically involved with individuals of the opposite sex, but, in a few cases, a homosexual orientation was mentioned as a reason for eliminating respondents from the sample and analysis.

The *American Sociological Review*, the premier general sociology journal published by the American Sociological Association, published 817 articles between 1980 and 1993, of which four articles (half of 1%) concerned aspects of sexual orientation. These numbers corroborate Risman and Schwartz's (1988) conclusion that sociological research on male and female homosexuality "is conspicuously absent from prominent sociological journals" (p. 126). Further, and perhaps equally important, extant sociological work treats homosexuality as deviant, focuses on sexual behavior and attitudes, and ignores the family context and family relations of lesbians and gay men. Stephen and McMullin (1982) identified correlates of tolerance of sexual nonconformity, Bainbridge (1989) discussed the influence of religion in deterring homosexuality and other forms of deviance, and Connell (1992) described the construction of diverse masculine identities among a sample of gay men. One other article commented on some similarities and differences in conversational privileges and duties among female couples, male couples, and opposite-sex couples. In general, however, sociologists have not examined sexual orientation or have assumed that it is irrelevant.

The *American Journal of Sociology* published 530 articles between 1980 and 1993, with only two articles examining topics related to sexual orientation. Davies (1982) associated homosexuality with bestiality and transvestism, and discussed a same-sex orientation as a perverse form of sexual deviance. Greenberg and Bystryn (1982) traced the social history of Christian intolerance of homosexuality. No article published in AJS since 1982 has focused on the social context, correlates, or consequences of sexual orientation.

As a discipline, sociology emphasizes social stratification and inequality by socioeconomic status, race, age, and gender, but sexual orientation has been ignored as an axis of stratification. Sociologists routinely study the social structural influences of "background variables" such as religion, residence, region, and rural/urban background, but they have not seriously addressed sexual orientation. They are concerned with social movements and social change, with the intersection of biography and history, and with understanding socialization and the life course, but have not applied or extended these interests and theoretical frameworks to the study of the gay civil rights movement or the lives of lesbians and gay men. Longstanding concern with prejudice, discrimination, oppression, and social conflict has not been extended to the situation of lesbians and gay men. Where sexuality is studied, teenage and premarital sexual activity are the foci, behaviors which are assumed (falsely) to be uniformly heterosexual. Marriage and parenthood are often studied as indicators of a successful transition to adulthood. For example, Hirschman and Rindfuss (1982), in an article titled, "The Sequence and Timing of Family Formation Events in Asia," stated that "the transition from adolescence to adulthood is marked by a number of role changes, none more central than the beginnings of family formation with marriage and parenthood" (p.

660). By not even mentioning in abstracts or in sample descriptions the words heterosexual or homosexual, gay or lesbian, researchers are assuming either that respondents are heterosexual, or that sexual orientation is irrelevant.

CHALLENGING HETEROSEXISM IN FAMILY RESEARCH

Our review of journals that publish family research leads to two observations: First, there is very little research in which the families of lesbians and gay men are the central focus, and the research that does exist is conducted by a small and sometimes prolific group of scholars. Second, mainstream family research does not include sexual orientation of family members as an integrative component of investigations. Although there is growing recognition of a paradigm shift toward family pluralism, and lesbian and gay families often are listed as an indicator of that shift, researchers have yet to find meaningful ways to incorporate sexual orientation into their studies of family phenomena. We concur with other commentators that heterosexism underlies the limited information accumulated to date about lesbian and gay families and the impact of sexual orientation on family life. Heterosexism is a bias, defined as "conceptualizing human experience in strictly heterosexual terms and consequently ignoring, invalidating, or derogating homosexual behaviors and sexual orientation, and lesbian, gay, and bisexual relationships and lifestyles" (Herek, Kimmel, Amaro, & Melton, 1991, p. 958). Heterosexist bias reflects a widespread cultural ignorance surrounding sexuality and relationships, and the subsequent labeling of sexual orientations other than exclusive heterosexuality as different and therefore deviant. Few social scientists have incorporated Bell and Weinberg's (1978) finding that lesbians and gay men are a heterogeneous group, characterized by diversity in age, race, education, and religion; instead, their diversity "has been pre-empted by a focus—perhaps an obsession—on characteristics thought to distinguish homosexual from heterosexual people" (Savin-Williams, 1990, p. 198).

Heterosexism operates in personal belief systems and in institutional practices. Like racism, sexism, and classism, heterosexism is a form of institutional oppression designed to ridicule, limit, or silence alternative discourses about identity and behavior. Societal institutions reinforce heterosexism by shaping and controlling knowledge. Gatekeepers, including funding agency administrators and proposal reviewers, human subjects review members, reviewers for professional journals, and academic colleagues on promotion and tenure committees, exert considerable power in their evaluations of proposals, manuscript submissions, and published papers that focus on what may be deemed sensitive topics. Such evaluations, in turn, govern what is researched and what is not researched, determine what is published and what is not published, and influence the career advancement of scholars interested in sexual orientation as a topic for study. In addition, there are practical impediments. As suggested by one reviewer, school boards may not allow questions about sexual orientation to be included in surveys that are administered to adolescents in their schools. National funding agencies may want to avoid situations where they have to defend to elected officials why they awarded a grant on a topic as controversial as "lesbian mothers." An untenured assistant professor may be warned by a superior never to disclose his sexual orientation in class lest he jeopardize his chances for promotion and tenure. In these and other ways, institutional and individual heterosexist biases limit the scope of knowledge generated by family research.

IMPLICATIONS FOR FAMILY THEORY AND RESEARCH

Lesbian and Gay Standpoint Theories

A new and affirmative research paradigm is needed that recognizes "the legitimacy of lesbian, gay male, and bisexual orientations, behaviors, relationships, and lifestyles" (Herek et al., 1991, p. 962). The small core of studies that is beginning to accumulate across disciplines suggests that the families of lesbians and gay men are diverse, variable, resilient, and thriving. Because of their diversity and complexity and the limited empirical research describing their lives, they require their own standpoint for investigation to yield what is unique, positive, and valuable about lesbian and gay family life (Brown, 1989). Laird (1993) argued that ethnographic research is the most urgent research direction at the present time, needed to generate "detailed, wholistic accounts of the daily lives of gay and lesbian families" (p. 320). Studies from lesbian and gay standpoints would place their narratives, meanings, and beliefs in the center of analysis, would bracket existing, presumably heterosexist, theories, and would avoid producing "what it is we thought we would see in the first place" (Laird, 1993, p. 320).

Biculturalism—the contradiction of being between two cultures—offers a promising theoretical direction from a lesbian and gay standpoint. For example, lesbian mothers and gay fathers are bicultural in terms of the mainstream heterosexual culture in which they interact as parents of their children, and the lesbian and gay community in which they relate with peers who share a same-sex identity. An aspect of biculturalism is resilience and creative adaptation in the context of minority group oppression and stigma. The concept of biculturality offers a potential link to other oppressed groups in American society. Peters (1988) documented, for example, the dual socialization that many Black parents provide for their children, preparing them for the institutionalized racism they will confront and at the same time helping them "to become self-sufficient, competent adults" (p. 238).

Family Theories

In addition to descriptions of lesbian and gay families from their own standpoints, family theories can illuminate the multiple contexts of lesbian and gay family relations. Like symbolic interactionist theories, family ecology and feminist theories emphasize that researchers must understand these families from the subjective perspectives of individuals living within them. How do they *feel* about their family situations, their time together, their relationships with one another, their sexual orientation, their parenting experiences, practices, values, and involvement? How do children in these families view their family experiences and relationships?

Young children, for example, are not likely to define their parents as "lesbian" or "gay." More consequential for understanding these children and their well-being is whether they feel secure and attached to their parent(s), whether they view parents and others as warm, supportive, and nurturant, and whether their social environment provides control and stability.

The underlying values of family ecology theory—values including justice, freedom, loving and nurturing relationships, a sense of community, tolerance, and trustworthiness—dictate that researchers "must attend to special problems of groups and subcultures who lack power, self-determination, and access to resources and who experience discrimination and prejudice" (Bubolz & Sontag, 1993, p. 427). As we gain understanding of the social ecologies of lesbian and gay families, including the societal and institutional constraints on their well-being, the "knowledge can be used to transform oppressive social structures in order to bring about greater justice and freedom for all family members and for a diversity of families" (Bubolz & Sontag, 1993, p. 428).

Feminist perspectives contribute to our understanding of the interaction of gender and other social locations, such as sexual orientation. Consider the example of lesbianism and motherhood, formerly viewed as two mutually exclusive and opposing life domains, and now recognized as simultaneous and interdependent experiences. The lesbian and gay civil rights movement, the feminist movement, and women's disenchantment with traditional marriage and parenting arrangements have allowed mothers who are lesbians to be more open about their sexual orientation. Lesbians have always raised children, but until recently, they were likely to be restricted and closeted due to fears of harassment and of losing custody of their children. In a male-dominated society, women's responsibilities for childrearing and childbearing are assumed to be natural, and mothering is assumed to be essential for the adequate development of the child. A feminist perspective reveals that mothering in the context of legal marriage is the standard against which all other forms of mothering (and parenting) are judged. Within this cultural context for appropriate motherhood, lesbian mothers are devalued relative to heterosexually married mothers, yet motherhood pulls lesbians, "however ambiguously, into a central position in the gender system" (Lewin, 1993, p. 184).

A life course perspective underscores the need to recognize the multiple pathways and transitions involved in the formation and development of lesbian and gay families, the short-term changes and long-term trajectories of individual development and family life, and the socially created and organized meanings of these life events. In addition to illuminating the rich diversity of lesbian and gay families, a life course framework highlights the interplay of historical, demographic, and social structural influences in shaping family experiences, as well as the dynamics of intergenerational relations. A life course perspective also provides a conceptual framework for guiding inclusion of lesbians and gay men and their families in samples representative of the general population. Taken together, the ecological, feminist, and life course perspectives offer the promise to enrich our understanding of the internal dynamics, social ecologies, transitions, and turning points of lesbian and gay families.

Research Directions

We have described some of the costs and problems of excluding a significant minority population, lesbian and gay families, from investigations of families. Lesbians, gay men, and their families are not a demographic anomaly. By ignoring them, family research misrepresents how diverse all families are. This distortion, like the distortion in research on African American families, is not harmless or value-free. Our silence as family researchers on this issue contributes to a general climate of intolerance and to maintenance of the status quo. Lesbian and gay partnerships and some parent-child relationships do not have the same civil rights or legal status that heterosexual marriage and legal parenthood confer on non-gay people.

The neglect of lesbian and gay families in family research can be corrected. First, sexual orientation is relevant to most aspects of family life; thus including questions about sexual orientation in large-scale data sets would contribute knowledge that is more representative of all families. We found in our review of research published in nine leading journals that a substantial proportion of family research relies on secondary data analysis. The a priori exclusion of lesbians and gay men from these samples precludes examination and comparison of particular kinds of questions and subjects. Recognition and appreciation of lesbian and gay families can be and should be incorporated into the research and peer review processes at all levels. Investigators should acknowledge these families in conceptualizing and designing their projects, in defining research questions and devising measures, and in testing, revising, and constructing theories. Colleagues, journal reviewers, and editors can challenge sample descriptions in which sexual orientation is not mentioned or heterosexuality is assumed. In this regard, it is important to recognize that marital status is not always an appropriate proxy measure for sexual orientation.

Relevant questions to be included in general population research would address the multiple contexts in which sexual orientation is expressed and experienced in families. It would use language that affirms the complexity of lesbian and gay experience but does not reduce gay people to their sexual orientation (e.g., "homosexuals"). Research on cohabitation, romantic relationship development and dissolution, sexual behavior and attitudes, and intergenerational relations are among the many content areas in which heterosexist bias should be challenged and replaced with knowledge of diversity. Guidelines for avoiding heterosexist bias in psychological research can be adapted to inform research designs in family studies. In formulating the research question, for example, Herek et al. (1991) suggested that investigators consider whether the research question devalues or stigmatizes lesbians, gay men, and bisexual people, and whether the research question implicitly assumes that observed characteristics are caused by the subjects' sexual orientation. Regarding research design and procedures, Herek et al. (1991) recommended considering, among other issues, whether sexual orientation is assessed appropriately, if all participants are assumed to be heterosexual, and in what ways researchers' personal attitudes and feelings might influence participants' responses.

Second, in addition to integrating questions about sexual orientation and family relations into general family research, detailed investigations of lesbian and gay families will help family researchers shed new light on such little-understood phenomena as the intersections of sexual orientation and gender in families and the ability of families to cope with stigma while forging permanent, enduring bonds without societal support. Lesbian and gay family kin relations offer new conceptual inroads into older concepts in the family literature, such as the static dichotomies of voluntary versus obligatory ties or family of origin versus family of procreation. While knowledge accumulates about lesbian and gay intimate relationships and parenting, new investigations of intergenerational and extended family relations beyond the procreative family life cycle will become a priority. Holistic, ethnographic studies of lesbian and gay families from their own standpoints will correct the deficit character of much of the existing research and balance the existing record with positive aspects.

The investigation of lesbian and gay family relations is a new frontier in family studies. Integrating these families into our knowledge base will require uprooting timeworn assumptions about the primacy of heterosexual identity, coupling, parenting, and kin relations. Yet, the challenge is offset by the promise of new ways of thinking about families, broad enough to include family forms and processes still on the margins of how we conceptualize family diversity.

References

Bainbridge, W. S. (1989). The religious ecology of deviance. *American Sociological Review, 54,* 288–295.

Bell, A. P., & Weinberg, M. S. (1978). *Homosexualities: A study of diversity among men and women.* New York: Simon & Schuster.

Bould, S. (1993). Familial caretaking: A middle range definition of family in the context of social policy. *Journal of Family Issues, 14,* 133–151.

Bozett, F. W. (1980). Gay fathers: How and why they disclose their homosexuality to their children. *Family Relations,* 29, 173–179.

Bozett, F. W. (1987) Children of gay fathers. In F. W. Bozett (Ed.), *Gay and lesbian parents* (pp. 39–57). New York: Praeger.

Bronfenbrenner, U., & Crouter, A. C. (1983). The evolution of environmental models in developmental research. In P. H. Mussen (Ed.), *Handbook of child psychology* (4th ed., pp. 357–414). New York: John Wiley.

Brown, L. S. (1989). New voices, new visions: Toward a lesbian/gay paradigm for psychology. *Psychology of Women Quarterly, 13,* 445–458.

Bubolz, M. M., & Sontag, M. S. (1993). Human ecology theory. In P. G. Boss, W. J. Doherty, R. LaRossa, W. R. Schumm, & S. K. Steinmetz (Eds.), *Sourcebook of family theories and methods* (pp. 419–448). New York: Plenum.

Connell, R. W. (1992). A very straight gay: Masculinity, homosexual experience, and the dynamics of gender. *American Sociological Review, 57,* 735–751.

Crandall, C. S., & Coleman, R. (1992). AIDS-related stigmatization and the disruption of social relationships. *Journal of Social and Personal Relationships, 9,* 163–177.

D'Antonio, W. V. (1985). The American Catholic family: Signs of cohesion and polarization. *Journal of Marriage and the Family, 47,* 395–405.

Davies, C. (1982). Sexual taboos and social boundaries. *American Journal of Sociology, 87,* 1032–1063.

Doherty, W. J., Boss, P. G., LaRossa, R., Schumm, W. R., & Steinmetz, S. K. (1993). Family theories and methods: A contextual approach. In P. G. Boss, W. J. Doherty, R. LaRossa, W. R. Schumm, & S. K. Steinmetz (Eds.), *Sourcebook of family theories and methods* (pp. 3–30). New York: Plenum.

Dosser, D. A., Balswick, J. O., & Halverson, C. F. (1986). Male inexpressiveness and relationships. *Journal of Social and Personal Relationships, 3,* 241–258.

Downey, D. B., & Powell, B. (1993). Do children in single-parent households fare better living with same-sex parents? *Journal of Marriage and the Family, 55,* 55–71.

Editors of the *Harvard Law Review.* (1990). *Sexual orientation and the law.* Cambridge: Harvard University Press.

Falk, P. J. (1989). Lesbian mothers: Psychosocial assumptions in family law. *American Psychologist, 44,* 941–947.

Fay, R. E., Turner, C. F., Klassen, A. D., & Gagnon, J. H. (1989). Prevalence and patterns of same-gender sexual contact among men. *Science, 243,* 338–348.

Fossett, M. A., & Kiecolt, K. J. (1991). A methodological review of the sex ratio: Alternatives for comparative research. *Journal of Marriage and the Family, 53,* 941–957.

Greenberg, D. F., & Bystryn, M. H. (1982). Christian intolerance of homosexuality. *American Journal of Sociology, 88,* 515–548.

Harry, J. (1983). Gay male and lesbian relationships. In E. D. Macklin & R. H. Rubin (Eds.), *Contemporary families and alternative life styles* (pp. 216–234). Beverly Hills, CA: Sage.

Hendrick, S. S. (1988). A generic measure of relationship satisfaction. *Journal of Marriage and the Family, 50,* 93–98.

Herek, G. M., Kimmel, D. C., Amaro, H., & Melton. G. B. (1991). Avoiding heterosexist bias in psychological research. *American Psychologist, 46,* 957–963.

Hirschman, C., & Rindfuss, R. (1982). The sequence and timing of family formation events in Asia. *American Sociological Review, 47,* 660–680.

Kurdek, L. A. (1989). Relationship quality in gay and lesbian cohabiting couples: A 1-year follow study. *Journal of Social and Personal Relationships, 6,* 39–59.

Kurdek, L. A. (1991). The dissolution of gay and lesbian couples. *Journal of Social and Personal Relationships, 8,* 265–278.

Kurdek, L. A. (1992). Relationship stability and relationship satisfaction in cohabiting gay and lesbian couples: A prospective longitudinal test of the contextual and interdependence models. *Journal of Social and Personal Relationships, 9,* 125–142.

Laird, J. (1993). Lesbian and gay families. In F. Walsh (Ed.), *Normal family processes* (2nd ed., pp. 282–328). New York: Guilford.

Lewin, E. (1993). *Lesbian mothers: Accounts of gender in American culture.* Ithaca, NY: Cornell University Press.

Macklin, E. D. (1980). Nontraditional family forms: A decade of research. *Journal of Marriage and the Family, 42,* 905–922.

Macklin, E. D. (1988). AIDS: Implications for families. *Family Relations, 37,* 141–149.

Marsiglio, W. (1991). Male procreative consciousness and responsibility: A conceptual analysis and research agenda: *Journal of Family Issues, 12,* 268–290.

Martinson, B. C., & Wu, L. L. (1992). Parent histories: Patterns of change in early life. *Journal of Family Issues, 13,* 351–377.

Milardo, R. M. (1992). Comparative methods for delineating social networks. *Journal of Social and Personal Relationships, 9,* 447–461.

Patterson, C. J. (1994). Lesbian and gay families. *Current Directions in Psychological Science, 3*(2), 62–64.

Peters, M. F. (1988). Parenting in Black families with young children: A historical perspective. In H. P. McAdoo (Ed.), *Black families* (2nd ed., pp. 228–241). Newbury Park, CA: Sage.

Reiss, I. L. (1981). Some observations on ideology and sexuality in America. *Journal of Marriage and the Family, 43,* 271–283.

Reiss, I. L. (1986). A sociological journey into sexuality. *Journal of Marriage and the Family, 48,* 233–242.

Risman, B., & Schwartz, P. (1988). Sociological research on male and female homosexuality. *Annual Review of Sociology, 14,* 125–147.

Rodgers, R. H., & White, J. M. (1993). Family development theory. In P. G. Boss, W. J. Doherty, R. LaRossa, W. R. Schumm, & S. K. Steinmetz (Eds.), *Sourcebook of family theories and methods* (pp. 225–254). New York: Plenum.

Savin-Williams, R. C. (1990). Gay and lesbian adolescents. In F. W. Bozett & M. B. Sussman (Eds.), *Homosexuality and family relations* (pp. 197–216). New York: Harrington Park.

Savin-Williams, R. C. (1993). Personal reflections on coming out, prejudice, and homophobia in the academic workplace. In L. Diamant (Ed.), *Homosexual issues in the workplace* (pp. 225–241). Washington, DC: Taylor & Francis.

Scanzoni, J., & Marsiglio, W. (1993). New action theory and contemporary families. *Journal of Family Issues, 14,* 105–132.

Schulenberg, J. (1985). *Gay parenting,* New York: Doubleday.

Stephen, G. E., & McMullin, D. R. (1982). Tolerance of sexual nonconformity: City size as a situational and early learning determinant. *American Sociological Review, 47,* 411–415.

Thompson, L. (1992). Feminist methodology for family studies. *Journal of Marriage and the Family, 54,* 3–18.

Tucker, M. B., & Taylor, R. J. (1989). Demographic correlates of relationship status among Black Americans. *Journal of Marriage and the Family, 51,* 655–665.

Voeller, B. (1990). Some uses and abuses of the Kinsey Scale. In D. P. McWhirter, S. A. Sanders, & J. M. Reinisch (Eds.), *Homosexuality/heterosexuality* (pp. 32–38). New York: Oxford University.

Walker, A. J., & Thompson, L. (1984). Feminism and family studies. *Journal of Family Issues, 5,* 545–570.

White, J. M. (1992). Marital status and well-being in Canada. *Journal of Family Issues, 13,* 390–409.

Williams, J. D., & Jacoby, A. P. (1989). The effects of premarital heterosexual and homosexual experience on dating and marriage desirability. *Journal of Marriage and the Family, 51,* 489–497.

PART 6 THE GENDERED CLASSROOM

Along with the family, educational institutions—from primary schools to secondary schools, colleges, universities and professional schools—are central arenas in which gender is reproduced. Students learn more than the formal curriculum—they learn what the society considers appropriate behavior for men and women. And for adults, educational institutions are gendered work places, where the inequalities found in other institutions are also found.

From the earliest grades, students' experiences in the classroom differ by gender. Boys are more likely to interrupt, to be called upon by teachers, and to have any misbehavior overlooked. Girls are more likely to remain obedient and quiet and to be steered away from math and science. As Myra Sadker, David Sadker, Lynn Fox, and Melinda Salata show in their summary of the findings of the Sadkers' path-breaking book, *Failing at Fairness,* every arena of elementary and secondary education reproduces both gender difference and gender inequality. Katherine Canada and Richard Pringle demonstrate that this process doesn't end when we graduate from high school, but it continues into our collegiate classrooms as well.

And it's not just what happens in the classroom or in the content of our textbooks. As Nan Stein argues in this summary of her research on bullying behavior, it is in both the classroom and on the playground that gender boundaries are most rigidly enforced.

MYRA SADKER, DAVID SADKER, LYNN FOX, AND MELINDA SALATA

Gender Equity in the Classroom: The Unfinished Agenda

"In my science class the teacher never calls on me, and I feel like I don't exist. The other night I had a dream that I vanished."[1]

Our interviews with female students have taught us that it is not just in science class that girls report the "disappearing syndrome" referred to above. Female voices are also less likely to be heard in history and math classes, girls' names are less likely to be seen on lists of national merit finalists, and women's contributions infrequently appear in school textbooks. Twenty years after the passage of Title IX, the law prohibiting gender discrimination in U.S. schools, it is clear that most girls continue to receive a second-class education.

The very notion that women should be educated at all is a relatively recent development in U.S. history. It was not until late in the last century that the concept of educating girls beyond elementary school took hold. Even as women were gradually allowed to enter high school and college, the guiding principle in education was separate and unequal. Well into the twentieth century, boys and girls were assigned to sex-segregated classes and prepared for very different roles in life.

In 1833 Oberlin became the first college in the United States to admit women; but these early female college students were offered less rigorous courses and required to wait on male students and wash their clothes. Over the next several decades, only a few colleges followed suit in opening their doors to women. During the nineteenth century, a number of forward-thinking philanthropists and educators founded postsecondary schools for women—Mount Holyoke, Vassar, and the other seven-sister colleges. It was only in the aftermath of the Civil War that coeducation became more prevalent on campuses across the country, but even here economics and not equity was the driving force. Since the casualties of war meant the loss of male students and their tuition dollars, many universities turned to women to fill classrooms and replace lost revenues. In 1870 two-thirds of all universities still barred women. By 1900 more than two-thirds admitted them. But the spread of coeducation did not occur without a struggle. Consider that as late as the 1970s the all-male Ivy League colleges did not admit women, and even now state-supported Virginia Military Institute fights to maintain both its all-male status and its state funding.

CYCLE OF LOSS

Today, most female and male students attend the same schools, sit in the same classrooms, and read the same books; but the legacy of inequity continues beneath the veneer of equal access. Although the school door is finally open and girls are inside the building, they remain second-class citizens.

In the early elementary school years, girls are ahead of boys academically, achieving higher standardized test scores in every area but science. By middle school, however, the test scores of female students begin a downward spiral that continues through high school, college, and even graduate school. Women consistently score lower than men on the Graduate Record Exams as well as on entrance tests for law; business, and medical schools. As a group, women are the only students who actually lose ground the longer they stay in school.

Ironically, falling female performance on tests is not mirrored by lower grades. Some have argued that women's grade-point averages are inflated because they tend not to take the allegedly more rigorous courses, such as advanced mathematics and physics. Another hypothesis suggests that female students get better grades in secondary school and college as a reward for effort and better behavior rather than a mastery of the material. Another possibility is that the standardized tests do not adequately measure that female students know and what they are really able to do. Whatever the reason, course grades and test grades paint very different academic pictures.

Lower test scores handicap girls in the competition for places at elite colleges. On average, girls score 50 to 60 points less than boys on the Scholastic Aptitude Test (SAT), recently renamed the Scholastic Assessment Test, which is required for admission to most colleges. Test scores also unlock scholarship money at 85 percent of private colleges and 90 percent of the public ones. For example, in 1991, boys scored so much higher on the Preliminary SAT/National Merit Scholarship Qualifying Test (PSAT/NMSQT) that they were nominated for two-thirds of the Merit Scholarships—18 thousand boys compared to 8 thousand girls in 1991.

The drop in test scores begins around the same time that another deeply troubling loss occurs in the lives of girls: self-esteem. There is a precipitous decline from elementary school to high school. Entering middle school, girls begin what is often the most turbulent period in their young lives. According to a national survey sponsored by the American Association of University Women, 60 percent of elementary school girls agreed with the statement "I'm happy the way I am," while only 37 percent still agreed in middle school. By high school, the level had dropped an astonishing 31 points to 29 percent, with fewer than three out of every 10 girls feeling good about themselves. According to the survey, the decline is far less dramatic for boys: 67 percent report being happy with themselves in elementary school, and this drops to 46 percent in high school.

Recent research points to the relationship between academic achievement and self-esteem. Students who do well in school feel better about themselves; and in turn, they then feel more capable. For most female students, this connection has a negative twist and a cycle of loss is put into motion. As girls feel less good about themselves, their academic performance declines, and this poor performance further erodes their confidence. This pattern is particularly powerful in math and science classes, with only 18 percent of middle school girls describing themselves as good in these subjects, down from 31 percent in elementary school. It is not surprising that the testing gap between boys and girls is particularly wide in math and science.

INEQUITY IN INSTRUCTION

During the past decade, Myra and David Sadker have investigated verbal interaction patterns in elementary, secondary, and college classrooms in a variety of settings and subject areas. In addition, they have interviewed students and teachers across the country. In their new book, *Failing at Fairness: How America's Schools Cheat Girls,* they expose the microinequities that occur daily in classrooms across the United States—and they show how this imbalance in attention results in the lowering of girls' achievement and self-esteem. Consider the following:

- From grade school to graduate school, girls receive less teacher attention and less useful teacher feedback.
- Girls talk significantly less than boys do in class. In elementary and secondary school, they are eight times less likely to call out comments. When they do, they are often reminded to raise their hands while similar behavior by boys is accepted.
- Girls rarely see mention of the contributions of women in the curricula; most textbooks continue to report male worlds.
- Too frequently female students become targets of unwanted sexual attention from male peers and sometimes even from administrators and teachers.

From omission in textbooks to inappropriate sexual comments to bias in teacher behavior, girls experience a powerful and often disabling education climate. A high school student from an affluent Northeastern high school describes her own painful experience:

> My English teacher asks the class, "What is the purpose of the visit to Johannesburg?" . . . I know the answer, but I contemplate whether I should answer the question. The boys in the back are going to tease me like they harass all the other girls in our class . . . I want to tell them to shut up. But I stand alone. All of the other girls don't even let themselves be bold. Perhaps they are all content to be molded into society's image of what a girl should be like—submissive, sweet, feminine . . . In my ninth period class, I am actually afraid—of what [the boys] might say . . . As my frustration builds, I promise myself that I will yell back at them. I say that everyday . . . and I never do it.[2]

Teachers not only call on male students more frequently than on females; they also allow boys to call out more often. This imbalance in instructional attention is greatest at the college level. Our research shows that approximately one-half of the students in college classrooms are silent, having no interaction whatsoever with the professor. Two-thirds of these silent students are women. This verbal domination is further heightened by the gender segregation of many of today's classes. Sometimes teachers seat girls and boys in different sections of the room, but more often students segregate themselves. Approximately one-half of the elementary and high school classrooms and one-third of the coeducational college classrooms that the Sadkers visited are sex-segregated. As male students talk and call out more, teachers are drawn to the noisier male sections of the class, a development that further silences girls.

Not only do male students interact more with the teacher but at all levels of schooling they receive a higher quality of interaction. Using four categories of teacher responses to student participation—praise, acceptance, remediation, and criticism—the Sadkers' studies found that more than 50 percent of all teacher responses are mere acceptances, such as "O.K." and "uh huh." These nonspecific reactions offer little instructional feedback. Teachers use remediation more than 30 percent of the time, helping students correct or improve answers by asking probing questions or by phrases such as "Try again." Only 10 percent of the time do teachers actually praise students, and they criticize them even less. Although praise, remediation, and criticism provide more useful information to students than the neutral acknowledgment of an "O.K." these clearer, more precise teacher comments are more often directed to boys.

Who gets taught—and how—has profound consequences. Student participation in the classroom enhances learning and self-esteem. Thus, boys gain an educational advantage over girls by claiming a greater share of the teacher's time and attention. This is particularly noteworthy in science classes, where, according to the AAUW report, *How Schools Shortchange Girls,* boys perform 79 percent of all student-assisted demonstrations. When girls talk less and do less, it is little wonder that they learn less. Even when directing their attention to girls, teachers sometimes short-circuit the learning process. For example, teachers frequently explain how to focus a microscope to boys but simply adjust the microscope for the girls. Boys learn the skill; girls learn to ask for assistance.

When female students do speak in class, they often preface their statements with self-deprecating remarks such as, "I'm not sure this is right," or "This probably isn't what you're looking for." Even when offering excellent responses, female students may begin with this self-criticism. Such tentative forms of speech project a sense of academic uncertainty and self-doubt—almost a tacit admission of lesser status in the classroom.

Women are not only quiet in classrooms; they are also missing from the pages of textbooks. For example, history textbooks currently in use at middle and high schools offer little more than 2 percent of their space to women. Studies of music textbooks have found that 70 percent of the figures shown are male. A recent content analysis of five secondary school science textbooks revealed that more than two-thirds of all drawings were of male figures and that not a single female scientist was depicted. Furthermore, all five books used the male body as the model for the human body, a practice that continues even in medical school texts. At the college level, too, women rarely see themselves reflected in what they study. For example, the two-volume *Norton Anthology of English Literature* devotes less than 15 percent of its pages to the works of women. Interestingly, there was greater representation of women in the first edition of the anthology in 1962 than in the fifth edition published in 1986.

PRESENCE AND POWER

Not only are women hidden in the curriculum and quiet in the classroom, they are also less visible in other school locations. Even as early as the elementary grades, considered by some to be a distinctly feminine environment, boys tend to take over the territory. At recess time on playgrounds across the country, boys grab bats and balls as they fan out over the school yard for their games. Girls are likely to be left on the sideline—watching. In secondary school, male students become an even more powerful presence. In *Failing at Fairness,* high school teachers and students tell these stories:

> A rural school district in Wisconsin still has the practice of having the cheerleaders (all girls, of course) clean the mats for the wrestling team before each meet. They are called the "Mat Maidens."

> In our local high school, boys' sports teams received much more support from the school system and the community. The boys' team got shoes, jackets, and played on the best-maintained grounds. The girls' softball team received no clothes and nobody took care of our fields. Cheerleaders did not cheer for us. When we played, the bleachers were mostly empty.

Sports are not the only fields where women lose ground. In many secondary schools, mathematics, science, and computer technology remain male domains. In the past, girls were actively discouraged or even prohibited from taking the advanced courses in these fields. One woman, now a college professor, recalls her high school physics class:

> I was the only girl in the class. The teacher often told off-color jokes and when he did he would tell me to the leave the room. My great regret today is that I actually did it.

Today, we hope such explicitly offensive behavior is rare, yet counselors and teachers continue to harbor lower expectations for girls and are less likely to encourage them to take advanced classes in math and science. It is only later in life that women realize the price they paid for avoiding these courses as they are screened out of lucrative careers in science and technology.

By the time they reach college, male students' control of the environment is visible. Male students are more likely to hold positions of student leadership on campus and to play in heavily funded sports programs. College presidents and deans are usually men, as are most tenured professors. In a sense, a "glass wall" divides today's college campus. On one side of the glass wall are men, comprising 70 percent of all students majoring in chemistry, physics, and computer science. The percentage is even higher in engineering. While the "hard sciences" flourish on the men's side of the campus, the women's side of the glass wall is where education, psychology, and foreign languages are taught. These gender walls not only separate programs, they also indicate social standing. Departments with higher male enrollment carry greater campus prestige and their faculty are often paid higher salaries.

These gender differences can be seen outside academic programs, in peer relationships both at college and in high school. In 1993 a national survey sponsored by the AAUW and reported in *Hostile Hallways* found that 76 percent of male students and 85 percent of female students in the typical high school had experienced sexual harassment. What differed dramatically for girls and boys was not the occurrence of unwanted touching or profane remarks but their reaction to them. Only 28 percent of the boys, compared to 70 percent of the girls, said they were upset by these experiences. For 33 percent of the girls, the encounters were so troubling that they did not want to talk in class or even go to school. On college campuses problems range from sexist comments and sexual propositions to physical assault. Consider the following incidents:

- A UCLA fraternity manual found its way into a campus magazine. Along with the history and bylaws were songs the pledges were supposed to memorize. The lyrics described sexual scenes that were bizarre, graphic, and sadistic.
- One fraternity on a New England campus hosted "pig parties" where the man bringing the female date voted the ugliest wins.
- A toga party on the campus of another elite liberal arts college used for decoration the torso of a female mannequin hung from the balcony and splattered with paint to look like blood. A sign below suggested the female body was available for sex.

When one gender is consistently treated as less important and less valuable, the seeds of contempt take root and violence can be the result.

STRATEGIES FOR CHANGE

One of the ironies of gender bias in schools is that so much of its goes unnoticed by educators. While personally committed to fairness, many are unable to see the microinequities that surround them. The research on student-teacher interactions led the Sadkers to develop training programs to enable teachers and administrators to detect this bias and create equitable teaching methods. Program evaluations indicate that biased teaching patterns can be changed, and teachers can achieve equity in verbal interactions with their students. Research shows that for elementary and secondary school teachers, as well as college professors, this training leads not only to more equitable teaching but to more effective teaching as well.

During the 1970s, content analysis research showed women missing from schoolbooks. Publishers issued guidelines for equity and vowed to reform. But recent studies show that not all publishing companies have lived up to the promise of their guidelines. The curriculum continues to present a predominately male model of the world. Once again publishers and authors must be urged to incorporate women into school texts. Teachers and students need to become aware of the vast amount of excellent children's literature, including biographies that feature resourceful girls and strong women. *Failing at Fairness* includes an extensive list of these resources for both elementary and secondary schools.

In postsecondary education, faculty members typically select instructional materials on the basis of individual preference. Many instructors would benefit from programs that alert them to well-written, gender-fair books in their academic fields. And individual professors can enhance their own lectures and discussions by including works by and about women.

Education institutions at every level have a responsibility for students in and beyond the classroom. Harassing and intimidating behaviors that formerly might have been excused with the comment "boys will be boys" are now often seen as less excusable and less acceptable. Many schools offer workshops for students and faculty to help eliminate sexual harassment. While controversy surrounds the exact definition of sexual harassment, the education community must take this issue seriously and devise strategies to keep the learning environment open to all.

After centuries of struggle, women have finally made their way into our colleges and graduate schools, only to discover that access does not guarantee equity. Walls of subtle bias continue to create different education environments, channeling women and men toward separate and unequal futures. To complete the agenda for equity, we must transform our education institutions and empower female students for full participation in society.

Notes

1. M. Sadker and D. Sadker, *Failing at Fairness: How America's Schools Cheat Girls* (New York: Charles Scribner's Sons, 1994). The research for this article as well as the anecdotes are drawn from this book.
2. L. Kim, "Boys Will Be Boys . . . Right?" *The Lance*, Livingston High School (June 1993), 32:5.

NAN STEIN

Sexual Harassment in K–12 Schools

No doubt many of us can still conjure up the image of Jonathan Prevette, that cute little blond 6-year-old boy with thick glasses from Lexington, North Carolina, who said he kissed, at her request, a little 6-year-old girl classmate and was then accused of sexual harassment by his school district in late September 1996. While he,

Adaptation of "Bullying as Sexual Harassment in Elementary Schools." Reprinted by permission of Teachers College Press, from *Classrooms and Courtrooms: Facing Sexual Harassment in K–12 Schools.*

his parents, and the spokesperson for the school district could be found for several weeks on the evening news and talk shows, nothing was ever heard from the little girl and her parents. However, through a secondary source (Craig Koontz, chair of the school board), two journalists (Goodman, 1996; and D. Nathan, personal communication, 1996) reported that the kiss was not mutual; that the little girl had not asked for it, that it was she who revealed the kiss to the school's administrators, and that she had subsequently blamed herself for all the fuss. However, as long as the parents of the little girl maintain their silence, the public will never know, and the little boy's version of the events will dominate.

According to the sociologist Laura O'Toole (1997) who did an analysis of 25 articles appearing in the national and regional press during a 2-week period at that time, one of the major motifs of the events as constructed by Jonathan's parents was the one of Alfalfa of "The Little Rascals" fame. That metaphor may well indeed linger in the public's consciousness about this event, subsuming all rational discussion and analysis of the events, the context, and the actors.

A critical question that lies at the heart of this and any discussion of sexual harassment is the one of mutuality. Had the kiss been mutually desired, requested, and/or performed, whether the children were 6 or 16, kissing might have been against school rules but it would not be sexual harassment: that is, behavior that is unwanted and unwelcomed. Yet, the fact that the school chose to cast this event as sexual harassment is revealing. On the one hand, it demonstrates their vigilance to the existence of inappropriate, unwanted, and unwelcomed behaviors of a sexual nature in schools. By leaping to call it sexual harassment, maybe they hoped to ward off litigation by the girl's family; fear of lawsuits with their negative publicity and monetary damage awards are a major concern for many school administrators and school board attorneys. On the other hand, the administrators' panic attack followed by their retraction that "we never called it sexual harassment," and the feeding frenzy of the press, did nothing to illuminate the larger problem of bullying in schools or to acknowledge that sexual harassment could and does exist in elementary schools.

The interviews with the boy's family and the school officials reinforced for me the absurdity of attempting to have conversations with young children about sexual harassment. Common sense should lead us to use language and concepts that are already in young children's vocabulary to talk about interactions with their peers that are unwanted and wanted, whether those interactions are verbal, touching, or playing. I have found that the word and concept of "bullying" is one that young children understand and use, and may capture the coercive, invasive, unwanted and/or intrusive nature of both bullying and sexual harassment. Unfortunately, never once did the national press during the Jonathan Prevette episode touch on this larger problem of bullying that is indeed omnipresent in children's lives.

BULLYING: DEFINITIONS AND RESEARCH

The antecedents of peer-to-peer sexual harassment in schools may be found in "bullying," behaviors children learn, practice, and/or experience beginning at a very young age. All boys know what a bully is, and many boys as well as girls have been victims of bullying. Much of the bullying which takes place at this age is between members of the same sex. Teachers and parents know about bullying, and many accept it as an unfortunate stage that some children go through on their way to adolescence and adulthood. Left unchecked and unchallenged, bullying may in fact serve as fertile practice ground for sexual harassment (Stein, 1993, 1995).

Like its older cousin, sexual harassment, bullying deprives children of their rightful entitlement to be educated and secure in the knowledge that they will be safe and free from harm. While laws in 38 states outlaw the practice of "hazing" in educational institutions (defined as the organized practice of induction, usually into a fraternity or sports team, through degrading behaviors and/or physical assault), bullying floats free from legal restraint and adult intervention, and is often not discussed as a deliberate part of the school curriculum (Stein, 1995).

World-wide Research on Bullying

Bullying among children has been studied for several decades in Western Europe, including the countries of Scandinavia and the United Kingdom. However, before we try to import the findings from that research to children and schools in the United States, there are two major differences that need to be articulated. First of all, with the exception of Britain, the countries where the research has been undertaken are largely homogenous countries, without much diversity in race, ethnicity, language, or religion—factors that often serve as triggers for bullying. Secondly, all European countries have a standardized, nationalized curriculum, allowing for more comparisons to be made across the country and classroom. Many of the recommendations coming from the research are predicated upon national regulation of the whole school environment, including classroom content, pedagogy, informal and formal activities, guidance and counseling, and activities to stimulate parental involvement.

The preeminent researcher in the world in the field of childhood bullying research is Dan Olweus (1993, 1994), professor of psychology at the University of Bergen, Norway, who has conducted over 20 years of research on bullying. Olweus defines bullying as when someone is "exposed, repeatedly and over time, to negative actions on the part of one or more other students" (Olweus, 1993, p. 9; 1994). "Negative actions" to Olweus are intentional infliction or attempts at such, including threatening, taunting, teasing, name calling, hitting, pushing, kicking, pinching, and restraining. He also acknowledges that it is possible to carry out negative actions "without the use of words or physical contact, such as by making faces or dirty gestures, intentionally excluding someone from a group, or refusing to comply with another person's wishes" (1993, p. 9). Bullying implies an imbalance of strength and can include single incident of serious nature yet not all acts of meanness, pestering, or picking on someone constitute bullying. Olweus emphasizes that the salient feature of his definition of bullying is that the negative actions are repeated and carried out over time. Almost to a word, Olweus' definitions of bullying seem interchangeable with definitions of sexual harassment in the United States.

Olweus' major findings on bullying have indicated:

- 15% of all children are involved in bully/victim problems at some point in elementary and junior high. He estimates that approximately 7% of children have been bullies and 9% have been victimized; 3% have been bullied "about once a week or more frequently," and somewhat less than 2% bullied others at that rate (1993, p. 14).
- Boys tend to engage in more direct physical bullying than girls, but the most common forms of bullying among boys were with words and gestures.
- Boys were more often victims and in particular perpetrators of direct bullying.
- Girls engaged in more indirect bullying such as slandering, spreading rumors, and manipulation of friendships.
- Boys carried out much of the bullying that girls were subjected to: 60% of the bullied girls in grades 5–7 reported being bullied mainly by boys; an additional 15–20% said they were bullied by both sexes while 80% of boys said that they were bullied chiefly by boys.
- In secondary/junior high school, more than four times as many boys as girls reported having bullied other students.
- Bullying peaks in elementary school, and then decreases; there is a steady decline as children get older, meaning there is less of it at high school; however, a considerable part of the bullying that exists is carried out by older students, particularly in the earlier elementary grades.
- Most bullying happens in school rather than on the way to or from school, especially in those places where students tend to be less closely supervised by adults (playground, lunch, hallways); those students who were bullied on their way to and from school tended to be bullied at school, too.
- Parents and teachers are relatively unaware of the extent and intensity of bullying that exists. Children tend to under-report it to their parents and teachers due to embarrassment and fear of retaliation if the adult were to become involved.

In addition, Olweus' research has disclosed important information about the victims and bullies. He pointed out that there is not one universal type of bully or victim, so therefore a variety of interventions need to be designed for different kinds of bullies and different kinds of victims. Moreover, he refined the types of bullying into direct and indirect bullying (Ross, 1996). Moreover, the victims have no aberrant trait for the most part, though bullies may focus on or look for such a characteristic. It is important to note that according to Olweus (1993), having an aberrant trait is not at the root cause of the bullying. Bullies are popular and have friends, whereas a victim is often a loner; popularity is likely to decrease a boy's risk of being bullied, and popularity is very tied to physical strength. Interestingly, Olweus points out that for girls, it is not clear whether any factor serves a similar protection function against bullying.

Olweus' research also laid to rest some myths that bullying is a big city problem or that the size of the school and/or class was a salient feature. His research as well as that of another researcher in Finland (Lagerspetz et. al. 1982, p. 24) gave no support at all to these hypotheses. He states conclusively that size of the class or school appears to be of negligible importance for the relative frequency or level of bully/victim problems in the class or the school. What does matter and have major significance in terms of the extent of bullying is the responses and attitudes of the adults in the school community.

United Kingdom

In the United Kingdom, initially the research was focused on single-sex boarding schools (Keise, 1992; Tattum and Lane, 1988; Tattum, 1993), but since the late 1980s, the research has expanded to include coed schools and racial bullying (Tattum and Lane, 1988; Tattum, 1993). A valuable contribution from the British researchers has been to document and acknowledge more indirect bullying and exclusion that is more typical of the repertoire of girls when they bully. Ahmad and Smith (1994) found in their research studies that while boys engaged in verbal and physical abuse, girls were mainly involved in verbal abuse. Moreover, girls seemed to be more involved in perpetrating indirect bullying, which include name-calling, gossip, rumors, secret telling, refusing to be friends, refusing to allow someone to play, shunning, and playing tricks on someone.

In particular, two British studies illuminate the gendered nature of bullying. Whitney and Smith (1993) in their 1990 study of 6,700 students, ranging in age from 8 to 16 years old, in 24 schools in Sheffield found that the sex difference for being bullied is slight, but that girls tended to be bullied less than boys. In addition, boys admitted to bullying other boys considerably more than girls. They found that most bullying was carried out mainly by one boy; next came bullying by several boys; then mixed sex bullying; followed by bullying by several girls; and least of all bullying by one girl. They found this pattern to be consistent in both junior/middle schools and secondary schools. Moreover, their research also confirmed previous findings on gender differences: girls are equally likely to be bullied (slightly less so in secondary schools), but are only about half as likely to be involved in bullying others; and boys are bullied almost entirely by other boys, whereas girls are bullied by both sexes. Furthermore, boys are more involved in physical forms of bullying while girls specialize in more verbal and indirect forms. In other words, boys bully both sexes, often in physical ways while girls only bully other girls, often in indirect ways. It remains, however, that the most common form of bullying is "being called nasty names" (p. 22), and the playground the most common location for bullying.

Smith, along with researcher Yvette Ahmad (1994), reviewed sex differences in bullying. They state unequivocally that "sex differences in all forms of aggression have been repeatedly found, and bullying is no exception" (p. 70). In their own study they modified Olweus' (1993) definitions and accordingly the questionnaires to include forms of indirect bullying, which were not explicit in Olweus' original definitions in order to be able to capture those forms of bullying in which girls typically engage. They surveyed over 1,400 students in five schools (two middle and three secondary) with a mixture of racial groups. Their results confirmed that boys are more involved than girls in bullying others, whether one is looking at indirect or direct bullying. Boys in both middle school and secondary (high) school are usually bullied by other boys and rarely by girls. For girls, however, the picture is different: at the middle school level, they are most likely bullied by boys, but at the secondary (high) level, they are most likely to be bullied by other girls (1994). Moreover, for girls and boys in middle school, the playground is the most common location for bullying, but by secondary school, the most common location for girls becomes the classroom, then the corridors, while for boys, the playground remains the most common location.

Their results were similar to Whitney and Smith's 1993 study: bullying decreased with age; boys were more likely than girls to report being bullied by one or several boys while girls were more likely than boys to report being bullied by one or several girls, or by both boys and girls; it was unusual for boys to report being bullied by one or several girls. Furthermore, boys were more likely to be physically hit and threatened than girls, while girls were more likely to experience verbal forms of bullying (being called nasty names) and indirect bullying (like no one talking to them). These sex differences were found in both middle and secondary schools. By secondary school, physical bullying had largely decreased for girls, but there was an escalation of their involvement in indirect bullying, especially spreading rumors about someone else (p. 81, 1994). Ahmad and Smith conclude that there is both qualitative and quantitative research findings that confirm the existence of male and female forms of bullying, but assert that this finding does not mean that these forms are exclusive to each sex.

Canada

Recent studies in Canada (1991–1995), summarized in a paper by O'Connell and colleagues (1997) include for the first time a study of 588 children in grades 1–3, the first study of bullying and victimization problems among such young children.

Results from this younger sample included the following developmental differences: peers intervened (at 24% of the incidents) in bullying episodes for grades 1–3 as opposed to interventions in grades 4–6 (at 11% of the time) or grades 7 and 8 (at 7% of the time). Other developmental differences emerged when the students were asked, "Could you join in bullying?" In grades 1–3, 12% of the children answered yes, while 31% in grades 4–6 said yes, compared to 49% in grades 7 and 8. The final striking developmental difference was in the realm of willingness to help the victim. In short it declined with age: 57% of the students in grades 1–3 were willing, but only 39% in grades 4–6, and 27% in grades 7 and 8. Indeed, the cumulative results of this study provide a sad portrait of aging, compassion, and empathy.

Moreover, these Canadian studies showed a decline in adult involvement in bullying episodes. Children in the younger grades (1–3) reported higher (37%) adult interventions as opposed to 26% in grades 4–6, and only 30% in grades 7 and

8. In summary, the Canadian researchers found that with age children were more willing to join in the bullying, less willingness to help a victim, and there was a decrease in reports of peers helping victims. This final finding is consistent with the finding of decreased concern for victims in Rigby, Slee and Conolly (1991) Australian study.

United States

In the United States, on the other hand, most of the initial research on bullying was designed from psychological/psycho-pathological point of view. There seems to have been a tendency to pathologize the problem, with a focus on bullies and/or on treatment programs to rid them of their bullying tendencies or to develop guideposts by which to judge potential bullies. Largely this research has consisted of interviews with criminals, including jailed molesters or pedophiles who traced back their conduct and behavior. While this methodology may illuminate their trajectories, it is not a particularly good measure for making generalizations about normative behavior for the majority of boys and men.

Several recent studies have focused on school-aged children in the United States. In a study conducted by Oliver, Hazler and Hoover (1994) looked at children in grades 7–12, and found that girls, significantly more than boys, felt that bullies had higher social status than did their victims. This study also found that even in small-town, allegedly safe environments, 81% of the males and 72% of the females reported being bullied by their peers, with ridicule, verbal and social harassment as the most common forms.

A second study from the Center for Adolescent Studies at Indiana University of 558 middle-school boys and girls found that bullies, compared to other children, face more forceful parental discipline at home, spent less time with adults and had fewer positive adult role models or positive peer influences (Seppa, 1996). Gender was not teased out in this study.

The work of two U.S. researchers have bearing on the issue of gender-based teasing and bullying. Barrie Thorne's book *Gender Play: Girls and Boys in School* (1993) while not explicitly about bullying, certainly raises questions about the nature of gendered play and interactions, and offers many insights into the development of gender relations in elementary school. She found that boys use sexual insults against girls, and that they regard girls as a group as a source of contamination. Boys and girls who don't conform to this prototype, and especially those that desire to be friends with one another, are at risk of teasing or ostracization. One girl, speaking of her friendship with a boy—at church and in their neighborhood—poignantly offers the reason why they don't speak to each other at school: "we pretend not to know each other so we won't get teased" (p. 50). The threat of heterosexual teasing may act as a deterrent to cross-gender friendships or may drive those friendships underground.

In addition, Donna Eder and colleagues at Indiana University in their book *School Talk: Gender and Adolescent Culture* (1995), and in a more recent book chapter (Eder, 1997), studies sexual aggression within the culture of middle school students. She and her colleagues have studied language and informal talk in middle school, including gossip, teasing, insulting, and story-telling. As with the European studies, Eder found that boys and girls alike used sexual put-downs towards girls, and that girls' use of words like "sluts" or "whores" helped to maintain a hierarchy with male-oriented, tough, and sexually aggressive boys at the top. Girls also tormented boys who were friendly towards them by casting doubt on their heterosexuality. Eder points out these and other ways in which girls contribute indirectly towards sexual aggression.

Finally, my own research into sexual harassment through the Seventeen magazine survey (September 1992) garnered responses from girls as young as 9 and 10 years old. Out of 4,300 surveys returned by the time of the deadline, we randomly selected 2,000 of them to be analyzed (Stein, Marshall and Tropp, 1993); of those 2,000 surveys, one came from a 9-year-old; seven from 10-year-olds, 38 from 11-year-olds, and 226 from 12-year-olds. There was no doubt from their responses that girls even at this young age, knew about sexual harassment—either from their own experiences or from observing it happening in their schools.

PILOT STUDIES ON BULLYING

Beginning in 1993, I have been engaged in research on gender-based teasing and bullying in grades K–5. Beginning in 1993 as a small research study involving seven teachers in three schools in Boston and Brookline, Massachusetts, my three years in their classrooms resulted in the development of a teaching guide for fourth and fifth grade students, *Bullyproof: A Teacher's Guide on Teasing and Bullying for use with Fourth and Fifth Grade Students* (Sjostrom and Stein, 1996). In 1995, further research was funded by the U.S. Department of Education (Women's Educational Equity Act Project, and Safe and Drug-free Schools Act) to look at gender-based teasing and bullying in grades K–3. With research partners in New York City (Educational Equity Concepts), our research was conducted at one elementary school on the upper west side of New York City and in three schools in Framingham, Massachusetts. This research resulted in the creation of another teaching guide, *Quit It: A Teacher's Guide on Teasing and Bullying for Use with Students in Grades K–3* (Froschl, Sprung and Mullin-Rindler, 1998).

In the three Massachusetts schools, we found that the responses and attitudes of the adults had major significance on the extent of bullying that occurred. In fact, we could identify distinct trends in the three different schools, with the principal's leadership style and responses playing a central role that also had a bearing upon the teachers' responses to children's teasing and bullying. In addition, the tone and climate that the teachers set in the classroom had an impact on the incidence of teasing and bullying that we observed. Our observations at two of the schools with the greatest difficulties, and later confirmed by comments from the teacher focus groups, pointed towards a lack of respect by the teachers towards their students and their families. Teachers tended to use authoritarian measures, such as yelling at students; saying comments that embarrassed them or demeaned them.

Findings from the Children

The interviews with the children confirmed and corroborated both our observations and the information provided by the teachers in the focus groups. Notwithstanding, the parents and teachers doubted the veracity of what the children would reveal to us; the adults assumed that the children would invent events or distort reality. However, the students we interviewed told it like we saw it.

In the Massachusetts sites, we observed little overt gender-based teasing and bullying except for teasing about body parts, and incidents of exclusion by gender. However, teachers and parents reported gender-based incidents largely occurring on the buses or in bathrooms. According to the parents and teachers, these incidents involved same sex initiators and recipients. On the other hand, we observed numerous incidents of class and racially-based bullying; for example students were singled out because they were Hispanic or poor; new immigrants were targeted; students were excluded from informal-time playing on the basis of their appearance and/or ethnicity. Interestingly, we observed several students with obvious disabilities, but they were not targeted for their disabilities (one wonders if teasing about disabilities was "off limits").

There were some incidents of gender-based exclusion or teasing that we couldn't adequately document because those events were not overt and/or we were unable to hear comments or talk among the children. These gender-based incidents included two salient interactions. The first revealing incident that was typical and repeated occurred at both indoor and outdoor play times, when groups of girls or boys were able to effectively exclude (or systematically eliminate) opposite-sex peers by setting rules or tasks that the opposite sex peers either couldn't or wouldn't follow. Among those that opposite sex peers would not do were giving them undesirable roles in a game (roles which were eliminated once the offending peer, usually a boy, left); or creating new rules such as hitting hard slams during ball games which no one did once the peer (usually girls) left. At no point did we overhear gendered exclusion spoken about; in other words, we never heard "no boys allowed" or "girls can't play with us." However, whatever code was operating was unspoken and subtle, yet fully operative.

The second salient event occurred during recess at one school, where the boys typically played with balls and the girls typically played with jump ropes. Often these items were brought from home because the school didn't have any to offer to the children (particularly jump ropes); without these items, there was virtually nothing for the children to do other than run around the playground. In previous weeks, the boys had been teasing the girls by making a game of stealing their ropes. The teachers had become so annoyed at the fussing that resulted (girls complaining to the teachers about the boys' behavior) that the teachers responded by prohibiting jump ropes from the playground, thereby effectively taking away the girl's play. The boys seemed to recognize this development as a gendered triumph.

Our interviews with children about their experiences in schools produced similar findings to those reported in other research studies (Olweus, 1993, 1994; Ahmad and Smith, 1994). Those results include:

- Transition time, lunch, and recess were times when teasing and bullying were most likely to occur.
- Teasing and bullying were most prevalent when adults were not present, not paying attention, or not physically available. In the Massachusetts schools where we observed, transition times, recess, lunch, arrival, and departure times were supervised by untrained parent volunteers or other low-paid employees, individuals whom the children viewed as people without much authority. Moreover, at these times, adult-to-child ratios were very high.
- When students go to adults, or when adults witness incidents of teasing and bullying, the students feel they are not listened to or taken seriously; they are often admonished to work it out on their own. Ironically, the students felt that they were doing just what the adults told them to do, which was to try to work out their problems with other students, and if that didn't work, then they should tell an adult. But when they did approach an adult, students got a conflicting message because the adults were typically annoyed and impatient and seemed to brushed them off by telling the child to go back and deal with it on their own. The adults typically didn't give students helpful guidance about how to do this, nor did they give support to them for attempting to do it.
- Students felt that perpetrators are not punished; many children felt that the consequences (like going to the principal's office) are fun, and do not carry a negative connotation. The victims were then often subjected to more teasing either because they told (other words for this behavior include: ratted, dimed, squealed) or because the teasers felt that they could get away with it, because the adult hadn't intervene. So the cycle continued and often escalated.
- Students surmised that children resort to bullying for fun or because they're bored.

As one might expect, when the adults were asked about this cycle, they put an entirely different spin on the events. Both parents and teachers felt that students came to them with very trivial concerns, and couldn't understand why the children couldn't work out these problems on their own. Nonetheless, teachers also frequently complained that principals trivialized their concerns with teasing and bullying, claiming that they had more important and/or difficult issues to manage, usually problems that involved the older students in the school. Teachers complained and hypothesized that if the little problems in grades K–3 were appropriately handled with discipline, then there wouldn't be as many big issues in the upper grades.

Based on our observations and interviews with the children, it seemed that the students were asking for better and/or more effective skills (what to say; models of conduct) to manage their problems on their own, and secondly for support, authority, and belief in their attempts to deal with the offending peer. What we found particularly disturbing about this cycle was that it echoed exactly what my research has found with older students about their experiences of sexual harassment—that it happens in public, that adults were often watching, and when students reported the sexual harassment to the adults, the adults either did not believe the students, trivialized it, or dismissed the events entirely.

Results from Focus Groups with Parents and Teachers

Two sets of separate focus groups were held, one set with parents and a separate set with teachers. The results revealed that both parents and teachers felt that teasing and bullying were problems that existed both at school and at home with siblings, and that the problem seemed to be getting worse, in both the amount and degree of teasing and bullying. The following is a long list of the behaviors that the adults noticed about teasing and bullying behaviors in children:

- "Teases du jour": cooties; being fat (directed at girls more than boys).
- Talk about "dating" or "love" (even among second- and third-graders); threatening to kiss or hug another child, a threat particularly used by girls towards boys.
- "Meanness" which usually meant exclusion; refusing to be friends; name-calling; focusing on a feature of a child's appearance, typically clothing, which seemed to be a stand-in for a socio-economic class commentary.
- Put-downs that involved one's mother ("your mother . . .").
- Physical behaviors that usually involved boys on boys; giving another child a wedgie (that is, picking up a child by his underwear), pantsing (which means pulling down a child's pants or underwear).
- Body-part talk (especially boys teasing other boys about the size or shape of their penis).
- Using the F word ("f—— you") towards other adults as well as other kids.
- Taking the possessions of other children.
- Telling a child that he or she is a member of the opposite sex: "you kick/throw/etc. like a girl" and "you look like a boy/girl."
- Using derogatory words about sexual preference (gay, fag, lezzie) or race or ethnic background (nigger, spic).
- Proclaiming "I don't like so-and-so because s/he's a —— (racial epithet)"; calling girls "bitches."

Both parents and teachers indicated that they thought the children really did not understand the meaning of the words that they used, but knew that the words were bad. They also noted that verbal teasing quickly escalated to physical acts between students.

Teachers focused on:

- Students showed no qualms about swearing at or threatening teachers (e.g., "You can't touch me!").
- Lack of support from principals (e.g., being sent to the principal's office was considered fun for students, and principals were afraid to take stands against teasing and bullying).
- Lack of support from administrators (guidance counselors designated to deal with serious or long-standing behavioral difficulties were ineffective).

- Principals not taking a stand with teachers who exhibited disrespectful or bullying behaviors.
- Principals more concerned with older students and trivialized difficulties with the younger students.
- Too much leeway was given to children from so-called troubled backgrounds (e.g., "Don't do it again, OK?").
- Schools lacked consistent, effective policies for teasing and bullying that held consequences (something beyond detentions, or telling the offending students, even those in kindergarten, to "write until their hands fall off" as a punishment for most infractions).
- Frequency of problems such as stealing, fighting, and problems on the bus.

Is Bullying Sexual Harassment?

The simple answer is yes, but if it is a boy-to-girl interaction, then it is more likely to be labeled as sexual harassment than if the interactions occurred between same sex members or if it was behaviors that came from girls directed towards boys; rarely are same sex behaviors deemed as sexual harassment. However, if all the protagonists are in elementary school, then sexual harassment will rarely be acknowledged. Words like pestering, annoying, bothering, hassling, or bugging will more than likely creep into descriptions of the events; the law will rarely be seen as operative or having application. Yet, since sexual harassment is against the law, and bullying is not, more students, their families, and lawyers will try to frame the events as sexual harassment, rather than as bullying, regardless of the ways that school administrators try to characterize the incidents. Irrespective of the ways in which school officials frame or dismiss the incidents, parents may file self-standing criminal complaints against the individuals involved, as opposed to being limited to filing civil court actions against the school district and personnel. There have been lawsuits and complaints that involved children in elementary schools (e.g., fifth-grader in Macon, Georgia whose law suit was heard in the U.S. Supreme Court in January 1999; third-grader Jonathan Harms and first-grader Cheltzie Hentz in Minnesota under Minnesota state law; and the U.S. Department of Education's Office for Civil Rights complaints in Modesto and Newark, California, that both involved elementary school students).

Although much of Olweus' research findings about children's behaviors might qualify as sexual harassment under U.S. law (Title IX), with liability falling on the school system, he never discusses sexual harassment. Nonetheless, his definition of bullying has many parallels to sexual harassment, particularly the feature of repeated and long-term nature of the behaviors targeted against an individual. Severity is not the salient feature for his definition of bullying; similarly with sexual harassment, severity is not the ruling feature: repeated and/or pervasive behavior carry as much weight.

Our research in grades K–3 point towards the existence of conduct that could be labeled and possibly litigated as sexual harassment. Our research also indicates the usefulness of conducting classroom discussions and a whole school approach towards bullying; it is developmentally appropriate and seems to engage the students as relevant and helpful.

If educators and advocates pose and present the problem as "bullying" to young children, rather than labeling it immediately as "sexual harassment," we can engage children and universalize the phenomena as one that boys as well as girls will understand and accept as problematic. Hopefully, such an approach will go a long way towards developing compassion and empathy in the students. Moreover, we can simultaneously avoid demonizing all little boys as potential "harassers" by initially presenting these hurtful and offensive behaviors as bullying, a behavior found in the repertoire of both boys and girls. Activities that ask the children to distinguish between "teasing" and "bullying" can help them focus on the boundaries between appropriate and inappropriate, hurtful behaviors.

References

Ahmad, Y. and Smith, P. K. (1994). Bullying in schools and the issue of sex differences. In J. Archer (Ed.), *Male Violence* (pp. 70–83). New York: Routledge.

Eder, D. (1997). Sexual aggression within the school culture. In Bank and P. Hall (Ed.), *Gender, Equity, and Schooling: Policy and practice* (93–112). New York: Garland.

Eder, D. (with Evans, C. C. and Parker, S.). (1995). *School talk: Gender and adolescent culture.* New Brunswick, NJ: Rutgers University Press.

Froschl, M., Sprung, B., and Mullin-Rindler, N. (with Stein, N. and Gropper, N.). (1998). *Quit it: A teacher's guide on teasing and bullying for use with students in grades K-3.* New York: Educational Equity Concepts, Inc.

Goodman, E. (1996, October 13). The truth behind "the kiss." *The Boston Globe,* pp. F1, F8.

Keise, C. (1992). *Sugar and spice? Bullying in single-sex schools.* Staffordshire, UK: Trentham Books.

Lagerspetz, K. M., Bjorqkvist, K., Berts, M., and King, E. (1982). Group aggression among school children in three schools. *Scandinavian Journal of Psychology,* 23, 45–52.

O'Connell, P., Sedighdeilami, F., Pepler, D. J., Craig, W., Connolly, J., Atlas, R., Smith, C., and Charach, A. (1997, April). *Prevalence of bullying and victimization among Canadian elementary and middle school children.* Poster session presented at the Society for Research on Child Development, Washington, DC.

O'Toole, L. and Schiffman, J. (1997). Conceptualizing Gender Violence. In L. O'Toole and J. Schiffman, *Gender Violence: Interdisciplinary perspectives* (pp. xi–xiv). New York: New York University Press.

Oliver, R., Hazler, R., and Hoover, J. (1994). The perceived role of bullying in small-town midwestern schools. *Journal of Counseling and Development,* 72(4), 416–420.

Olweus, D. (1993). *Bullying at school: What we know and what we can do.* Oxford: Blackwell.

Olweus, D. (1994). Annotation: Bullying at school: Basic facts and effects of a school based intervention program. *Journal of Child Psychology and Psychiatry,* 35, 1171–1190.

Rigby, K., Slee, P., and Conolly, C. (1991). Victims and bullies in school communities. *Journal of the Australian Society of Victimology, 1*, 25–31.

Ross, D. M. (1996). *Childhood bullying and teasing: What school personnel, other professional, and parents can do.* Alexandria, VA: American Counseling Association.

Seppa, N. (1996, October). Bullies spend less time with adults. *APA Monitor*, p. 41.

Sjostrom, L. and Stein, N. (1996). *Bullyproof: A teacher's guide on teaching and bullying for use with fourth and fifth grade students.* Wellesley, MA: Wellesley College Center for Research on Women.

Stein, N. (1993). No laughing matter: sexual harassment in K–12 schools. In E. Buchwald, P. R. Fletcher, & M. Roth, *Transforming a rape culture* (311–331). Minneapolis, MN: Milkweed Editions.

Stein, N. (1995, summer). Sexual harassment in K–12 schools: The public performance of gendered violence. *Harvard Educational Review, Special issue: Violence and youth, 65*(2), 145–162.

Stein, N., Marshall, N., and Tropp, L. (1993). Secrets in public: *Sexual harassment in our schools. A report on the results of a* Seventeen *magazine survey.* Wellesley, MA: Wellesley College Center for Research on Women.

Tattum, D. P. (Ed.). (1993). *Understanding and managing bullying.* Oxford: Heinemann.

Tattum, D. P., and Lane, D. A. (Eds.). (1988). *Bullying in schools.* Stoke-on-Trent, England: Trentham Books.

Thorne, B. (1993). *Gender play: Girls and boys in school.* New Brunswick, NJ: Rutgers University Press.

Whitney, I., and Smith, P. K. (1993). A survey of the nature and extent of bullying in junior/middle and secondary schools. *Educational Research, 31*(1), 3–25.

KATHERINE CANADA AND RICHARD PRINGLE

The Role of Gender in College Classroom Interactions: A Social Context Approach

Increasingly, it seems, the promise of coeducation is regarded suspiciously. Whether comparing the educational outcomes of all-female and mixed-gender schools and colleges, assessing gender equity within mixed-sex educational settings, investigating the social construction of gender differences, or unveiling the social consignment of male privilege and dominance, researchers have found that mixed-sex education, at least as it is typically configured, may pose notable disadvantages for girls and women.

From *Sociology of Education*, Vol. 68 (July 1995), pp. 161–186. Reprinted by permission of the American Sociological Association. References have been edited.

REVIEW OF RESEARCH

Single-Sex Versus Mixed-Sex Education

It has been reported that in comparison to women who attend mixed-sex colleges, women who attend women's colleges have greater self-esteem at graduation, have less gender-stereotypic career aspirations, are more engaged in college activities, are more likely to enter certain traditionally male professions, are more likely to earn higher salaries, and are more likely to reach high levels of achievement in their careers. Also, the career advantage bestowed by an all-female institution may increase with the time one spends in it. Unfortunately, as others have noted, it is impossible to determine, on the basis of the nonequivalent groups design used in these studies, the degree to which the unusual success of women's college graduates is attributable to single-sex education per se: to environmental factors favored by, but not necessarily exclusive to, single-sex education; or to self-selection factors, such as the socioeconomic level, intelligence, and motivation of entering students.

In addition to studies at the postsecondary level, a number of studies have examined the relative outcome advantages of single-sex and mixed-sex schooling at the secondary level. Like its postsecondary counterpart, this research has been plagued by problems inherent in nonequivalent groups design. Although most studies have favored the all-female model on many of the same dimensions just mentioned in the context of postsecondary schools, some studies that have attempted to control statistically for preexisting differences have reported mixed results.

Some may argue that sufficient countervailing evidence exists, and others would almost certainly remain skeptical about particular aspects of the alleged advantage. However, we interpret the evidence, especially at the postsecondary level, as leaning strongly to the advantage of single-sex education for women. In their careful review of this research, Moore et al. (1993:35) stated:

> Considering the general direction of the research and giving more weight to those studies with carefully drawn samples, a reasoned choice of background controls, adequate efforts to compare similar entities, and overall statistical rigor, we conclude that there is empirical support for the view that single-sex schools may accrue positive outcomes, particularly for young women.

Nevertheless, we are skeptical of efforts to assess, once and for all, which is better: single-sex or mixed-sex education. Such comparisons invariably rely on central tendencies and are therefore inclined to disregard each category's potential for change, which may be better represented by variability or even theory. Instead, we regard the evidence that all-female education holds advantages for girls and women as an indication that so-called coeducation, *as it is typically configured,* is "failing at equity," that sound educational production aimed at what Lee, Marks, and Byrd (1994:98) referred to as "positive engenderment," or the "conscious effort to provide equitable education for both sexes, including attempts to counter sexism and its residual effect," lags far behind where it should be.

One reason for this delay, beyond widespread indifference, is that in spite of many educational programs designed to promote positive engenderment, such as the National Women's History Project, the National SEED Project, and Project Kaleidoscope, there is a lack of practical knowledge of how all-female educational environments confer advantages, so, in turn, little is known about the transferability of these advantages to mixed-gender settings. Certainly, some of the outcome studies have attempted to isolate the operative factors. For example, Tidball (1989) argued that women's colleges bestow their advantages indirectly through the critical mass of female role models, the special valuation of women, and the unparalleled opportunities for leadership and engagement with academics that such environments afford. In addition to these advantages, Riordan (1994:491) proposed others: mitigation of the values of the youth culture, fewer gender-based disparities in curricular opportunities, less gender bias in interactions between teacher and student, less gender stereotyping in peer interactions, a "proacademic parent/student choice," special programs for women, and receptivity to women's learning styles. But, for the most part, emphases on outcome do not lend themselves easily to investigations of the mechanisms whereby advantages accrue. In principle, studies of gender equity in the classroom do.

Gender Equity in the Classroom

The role of gender in the dynamic of the mixed-sex college classroom is a potential source of insight into the success of the all-female educational model. Consistent with several of the factors listed earlier, gender inequity in mixed-sex classrooms, compared to its relative absence in all-female classrooms, could be a major, but potentially correctable, weakness in the mixed-gender approach. It was in this spirit, or so it seems to us, that in the title of their provocative article, Hall and Sandler (1982) raised the pivotal question: "The classroom climate: a chilly one for women?" and then went on to suggest, on the basis of their review of a wealth of both quantitative and qualitative evidence, that gender influences interactions in educational environments and that the effects are particularly detrimental to the education of women. The report challenged educators to consider the consequences of prior socialization and gender expectations on students' experiences in coeducational environments and called for heightened awareness that teachers' behaviors can communicate differential expectations for male and female students.

Although Hall and Sandler addressed a wide range of possible negative gender influences on female students in academe, their claim that faculty members are responsible for, or at least inadvertently contribute to, the educational disadvantages for women stimulated the most research. Although these studies generally found little, if any, evidence that faculty themselves impose the chilly climate, they and related studies have consistently shown that male and female students *do* behave differently in mixed-sex classrooms. For example, most reported disproportional numbers of classroom interactions involving male students.

However, rather than explore the educational implications of the observed differences and call for educational programs and environments that would minimize the differences or their negative consequences for women, many of the authors downplayed the gender differences for a variety of reasons. Some of the reasons they gave were that the differences were smaller than the observed differences associated with factors other than gender; were not "pervasive or robust"; were not due to discrimination by the faculty; were stylistic; and, by implication, were immutable and therefore natural.

Similar differences between boys and girls have been observed in primary and secondary classrooms, and like the research on postsecondary classrooms, the focus of these studies was on exonerating teachers at the expense of probing the differences observed. It is the differences between the behaviors of male and female students and, for that matter, between the male and female professors, and the circumstances in which those differences occur, not "who is to blame," that interests us, for there is reason to believe that such differences are socially constructed—and are constructed most readily in mixed-sex groups—and that the differences are symptomatic of a gender politic that pervades the educational and societal landscape. The relative success, on average, of women's colleges may be due to the relative ease with which gender politics can be held at bay in those settings while the educational process is allowed to proceed.

If, as this review suggests, all-female and mixed-sex schools differ, on average, along certain dimensions that are key to positive engenderment, Lee et al. (1994) suggested that mixed-sex institutions themselves vary along some of the same continua. These researchers examined the relative incidence of six kinds of sexism in the classrooms of 21 independent secondary schools of three different gender compositions: all boys, all girls, or mixed. Although each type of school had its share of sexist or negatively engendering events in the classrooms, considerable variations in the volume and kinds of sexism were evinced between and within the types of schools. So, although "the major form of classroom sexism treated in the literature—gender domination (either boys dominating discussions or teachers recognizing boys more often than girls)—was by far the most prevalent form of sexism in the coeducational schools" (p. 104), "explicitly sexual incidents" were observed only in the boys' schools, whereas "gender reinforcement" and "embedded discrimination" were more common in single-sex than in mixed-sex schools.

It is interesting that events that Lee et al. (1994) categorized as "equitable" or as promoting positive engenderment occurred with the greatest frequency in the girls' schools. But what was notable was that the degree of sexism observed in each type of school, including the mixed-gender schools, varied considerably. Two of the mixed-sex schools were essentially nonsexist and, indeed, could be classified as promoting positive engenderment. Lee et al. concluded that circumstances, including an institution's gender mix, but more important, an institution's policy stance with regard to engenderment, have notable effects on the incidence and kinds of sexism that students experience.

Social Construction of Gender Differences

Studies on sex differences and gender roles in group interactions, if generalizable to the classroom, lead us to expect differences between the dynamics in classes with only female students and those in mixed-gender classes. Regarding this expansive research literature, we make the following two general comments.

First, in many contexts, most boys and girls, left to themselves, associate and play with children of the same sex. One important consequence is that within their same-sex groups, boys and girls learn and develop interaction styles that tend to be "restrictive" and "enabling," respectively. In mixed-gender groups, these styles clash in ways that usually favor boys' dominance of group interactions. These patterns continue through adulthood. Within their same-sex groups, however, both males and females are often highly interactive, and dominance and leadership are commonplace. In mixed-gender groups, however, the enabling interactive strategy adopted more often by females, in the face of the restrictive strategy adopted more often by males, favors male leadership of the group; males generally dominate interactions and monopolize desirable items shared by the group, including toys, computers, information, or access to an instructor.

Second, the social roles, or the gender-stereotypic beliefs of the dominant culture, hold that males are more *agentic,* meaning that they tend to be more assertive and controlling, and females are more *communal,* meaning that they tend to be more concerned with the welfare of others. Attributes in common with being agentic include "aggressive, ambitious, dominant, forceful, acts as leader." Attributes in common with being communal include "affectionate, able to devote self completely to others, eager to smooth hurt feelings, helpful, kind, sympathetic, loves children, . . . awareness of feelings of others . . . gentle, soft-spoken" (Eagly 1987:16).

To the extent that people incorporate these gender beliefs into internalized rules that govern their own behavior and into expectations concerning the behavior of others, males and females ought to act differently, especially in situations that, based on norms, carry clear gender prescriptions. An important corollary is that, especially in mixed-gender groups, for a female to be highly interactive or dominant or otherwise to show leadership traits requires her to cross her gender-prescribed role, an act that, at the least, would be more difficult than behaving in accordance with her prescribed role, but at worst would be expected to invoke social penalties.

These findings, like those of Lee et al. (1994), demonstrate the power of the social context, particularly gender composition, in the governance of gender differences. Without alternative mechanisms or policies to hold gender politics at bay, we would expect gender differences within mixed-sex classrooms to parallel those found in other mixed-gender settings. That is, in mixed-sex classrooms, female students, educated and expected to enable, would be inclined to relegate themselves to the role of audience to the more restrictive interaction style of male students. And male students, educated to restrict, would be inclined to assume positions of leadership and dominance.

The results from the research on interaction patterns in mixed-sex college classrooms and on single-sex and mixed-sex educational outcomes largely support this conclusion. However, the fact that the studies revealed varying degrees of adherence to the pattern raises the intriguing hypothesis that the inconsistency across studies reflects classroom and institutional attributes that either contribute to or mitigate students' and professors' tendencies to behave in gender-stereotypic ways. Although whether the classroom does or does not include men is certainly a powerful social context variable insofar as the social construction of gender differences is concerned, many additional factors can be expected to operate, so that some mixed-gender classrooms and schools would be more gender stereotypic than would others. Giele (1987), for example, demonstrated that, on many outcome variables, female graduates of Oberlin College, the nation's first coeducational college, compare favorably with those of two of the seven sister colleges. Oberlin's long-standing commitment to the education of women may be a significant factor. Furthermore, Eccles (1989) showed that mixed-sex, seventh-grade mathematics classrooms vary in their "girl-friendliness," which has a direct impact on girls' interest in and commitment to the subject matter. She characterized girl-friendly classes as having relatively low levels of competition and public drill and high levels of contact between individual students and the teacher.

Understanding how institutional and classroom cultures may enhance positive engenderment is a priority. It is not enough to determine which educational model, all female or mixed sex, serves women better. That approach presumes that the central tendencies capture the essential feature of the categories. Rather, the goal is to understand better the conditions and processes that bring about the differences.

Consignment of Male Privilege

When we think of the social context within which classroom interactions occur, we think of an ever-widening series of concentric circles that define the ever-broadening historical, geographic, social-cultural, and circumstantial perspectives one can bring to bear on the particular classrooms that are observed. It is sheer folly to think that single-sex and mixed-sex educational practices can exist apart from these factors, that in comparing one with the other, one can somehow capture and evaluate their essences. Classrooms exist in context. Many are on campuses in which academic considerations play second fiddle to a youth culture predominated by athletics, parties, and romance. Holland and Eisenhardt (1990) described a campus "culture of romance" in which, unlike men who have a variety of pathways to status, women have one primary pathway to status: attractiveness to men. Sanday (1990) described a campus culture that colludes to privilege men and to allow rapes, even gang rapes, to occur.

That women are treated as second-class citizens of many college and university communities is a central theme in the vast and growing feminist scholarship on education and is the background of Title IX and other efforts to enlighten educators to the perils of sexual harassment and the chilly climate. The consequences for women of attending "unfriendly" schools and classrooms certainly include the sobering ones that their confidence that they will be taken seriously will be repeatedly undercut and that their career aspirations and achievements will be systematically derailed. However, schools and classrooms choose, implicitly at least, either to resist or to conform to these patterns. After examining the relationship of institutional policies and characteristics, on the one hand, and the incidence and severity of sexism within independent secondary schools, on the other hand, Lee et al. (1994:115) concluded:

> Our results suggest that strong policies on the equitable treatment of male and female students make a difference. Such policies, if carefully enforced and periodically monitored by observations in classrooms, are translated into gender-equitable behaviors of teachers and students in classrooms and can profoundly affect students' experiences.

A COLLEGE IN TRANSITION TO COEDUCATION

When a small liberal arts, women's college announced its intention to become coeducational in 1987, we began a longitudinal study of its transition. This report focuses on our quantitative analyses of the changing classroom dynamic accompanying the first five years following the announcement. Our approach was to compare female students' behaviors in single- and mixed-sex classrooms and to compare both with the classroom behaviors of the entering male students. Our principal goal was to describe female students' interaction patterns in different settings, thereby highlighting and clarifying the relationship between gender and social context in college classroom environments.

Although we kept an eye on the broader concentric rings that define this college's culture, the particular social context variables we investigated were institutional- and classroom-level variables, which included the type of institution, the gender mix of students, the gender of the professors, the class size, and the class level. Our question was, What roles do gender and these social context variables play in the initiation, establishment, and continuation of classroom interactions between students and professors? In contrast to past research (see, for example, Cornelius et al. 1990), in which the emphasis was on describing social context variables as overriding the role of gender in influencing classroom dynamics, we focused on investigating gendered classroom behaviors as socially constructed variables that are influenced by social contexts. This approach is congruent with theoretical perspectives and research traditions that conceptualize gender as a variable variable, rather than as an immutable, inevitable trait that defines and directs behaviors.

METHOD

The Sample

The School. The college began admitting men in the fall of 1987, and we collected classroom data during the spring semesters of 1987, 1988, 1990, and 1991. As was true throughout its history, students at the college during this period were overwhelmingly white and middle and upper-middle class. Approximately 5 percent were African American; 10–15 percent were students of color.

The Classrooms. During the spring semesters of 1987 and 1988, we collected data in 46 all-female student classrooms: 24 introductory-level classes in 1987 and 22 upper-level classes in 1988. During the spring semesters of 1990 and 1991, we collected data in 57 mixed-sex classrooms: 33 introductory-level classes in 1990 and 24 upper-level classes in 1991. In all, we made requests to visit 130 classrooms and were denied permission in only 5 instances—a participation rate of 96 percent.

Excluded from the sample because their classroom interactions were less public or too difficult to code were foreign language, speech, dance, and studio classes. Although we initially tried to observe laboratory sessions, we eventually excluded them for similar reasons. Classes taught by either of the authors and classes with fewer than five students enrolled were also excluded. Classes that met these constraints and were subsequently observed were nevertheless excluded from the analyses if during our classroom visit, an appreciable portion of the period was "team taught" or was devoted to students delivering formal, oral presentations or the professor divided the students into small-group discussions for most of the period. Five of the 115 classes that we actually observed were excluded for these reasons, and an additional seven were excluded because they were laboratory sessions, leaving a total of 103. For the analyses reported here, that is, for analyses that focused on the impact of the transition to mixed-sex education, we excluded an additional 10 classes because there was one male student or male visitor in a classroom that otherwise belonged to the single-sex classroom cohort (4 cases, 1988–89) or because there were no male students in a classroom that otherwise belonged to the mixed-sex classroom cohort (6 cases, 1990–91).

In 1987 and 1988, the observational sample was selected randomly from the pool of all eligible classes. The only stipulation on the random process was that each discipline (such as history, biology, or sociology) should be included in the sample at least once. In 1990 and 1991, our aim was to repeat observations in as many as possible of the classrooms that had been observed during the 1987 and 1988 codings. Our attempts were hindered by the fact that some courses were not offered every year or were replaced by new ones; these issues were particularly evident at the 200 and 300 levels. Nevertheless, in 1990, 20 observations were conducted in classes that had been included in the 1987 sample; in 1991, 10 observations were in classes that had been included in 1988. The remaining classrooms observed in 1990 and 1991 were randomly selected from the pool of eligible courses. No attempt was made to balance artificially the gender of professors and the size of classes across class levels (introductory versus upper level) and/or the type of school (single sex versus mixed sex). Similarly, no attempt was made to balance the proportion of male students across the various types of mixed-sex classes.

Table 1 presents basic descriptive information for the classrooms included in this report, broken down by year, type of school, class level, and gender of professors. As indicated, the observed class sizes were small, ranging from 3 to 42 students present (median = 13) and varied with the gender of the professors, class level, and type of school. Also, the proportion of male students present within the

Table 1.
Class Size and Proportion of Males, by Type of School and Professor's Sex[a]

	Single-Sex School		Mixed-Sex School			
	Female Professor	Male Professor	Female Professor		Male Professor	
	Class size	Class Size	Class Size	P(Male)	Class Size	P(Male)
Mean	9.1	13.5	16.3	.22	15.2	.28
Median	9.0	11.0	14.0	.20	16.6	.26
Range	3–17	3–28	3–42	.05–.64	4–29	.10–.60
SD	4.1	8.6	9.6	.14	7.4	.14
N	21	21	27	—	24	—
$N_{I/U}$	7/14	13/8	15/12	—	17/7	—

[a]*N*, $N_{I/U}$ and P(male) are the number of classes, the number of introductory- and upper-level classes, and the proportion of male students, respectively.

mixed-sex classrooms was small, ranging from 5 to 64 percent (median = 22 percent).

The Students. In all, 1,282 students were observed and included in this analysis. Although classes were visited only once, some students and faculty were observed more than once in different courses; therefore, the number of students and professors observed represents totals, rather than the number of unique participants.

Procedure

We used a modified version of INTERSECT to observe classroom interactions. To provide ample opportunity for the establishment of a classroom interaction pattern, classrooms were observed during a three-to-five-week span in the middle of the semester of observation. Each classroom was observed once. We conducted the observations in 83 (89 percent) of the classrooms included in the following analyses; the remaining 10 (11 percent) were conducted by two research assistants.

On a day prearranged with the professor, the observer arrived early to choose a peripheral seat with a clear view of both the professor and the students. Although the duration of the classes varied, observations were conducted for 30 minutes of the scheduled class time. During the first 10 minutes of a class, the observer diagrammed the classroom, specifying the locations of the professor and each student. Each student was identified by a seating-chart number and by gender. Systematic observations of the classroom interactions began 10 minutes into the class and continued for 30 minutes, or until the class was otherwise over.

RESULTS

Preliminary Considerations

Some of the apparent inconsistencies in the classroom interaction literature may actually reflect the lack of explicitness about what constitutes a classroom interaction and which aspects of classroom interactions are being investigated. We took a more formal and deliberate approach by developing a model of classroom interactions, fundamental aspects of which were borrowed directly from our interpretation of INTERSECT, the classroom observation system we used to collect data. We will detail the development and evaluation of the model in separate reports and present only an overview here. The model, summarized in Figure 1, has four key assumptions.

1. In traditional college classrooms the entire classroom dynamic occurs within an asymmetrical power structure in which the professor has higher status and exerts greater control than the students.
2. The asymmetrical power structure shapes the local classroom context, which, along with other contextual factors, affects the incidence and types of classroom interactions.
3. Each interaction link or exchange is composed of three parts or levels: dialing, responding, and evaluating.
4. Exchanges have the potential of being linked together, chainlike, forming classroom interactions of various lengths and complexity that can sometimes take on the appearance of a conversation between a student and professor or, in principle, between students.

An exchange begins when the professor attempts, within the first level, to engage verbally, or "dial," his or her students, either implicitly, by simply helping to create conditions that favor student-initiated interactions, or explicitly, by raising a question or otherwise requiring some sort of response from the students. A student's response establishes a connection, which defines the second level. In the third level the professor implicitly or explicitly evaluates the student's message. An interaction can terminate at this point, a one-link interaction (one exchange), or it can continue through the cycle any number of times. An extended interaction is represented in the model by a series of successive and connected loops through the interaction sequence by the professor and a single student.

We used this model to create a taxonomy of classroom interactions. The portions of the taxonomy that are most concerned with establishing or failing to establish interactions are detailed in Figure 1. The taxonomy distinguishes between interactions initiated explicitly by the professor and those that are not (referred to as student-initiated interactions). Initiations by professors are of two types: an invitation to interact, usually in the form of a question directed to the class as a whole, and a requirement to interact, whereby the professor calls on a student directly. A professor's invitations can be accepted by one or more students, but often are not. Students' initiations can be directed either to the professor or to other students. Once an interaction is established and then cycles through the student's

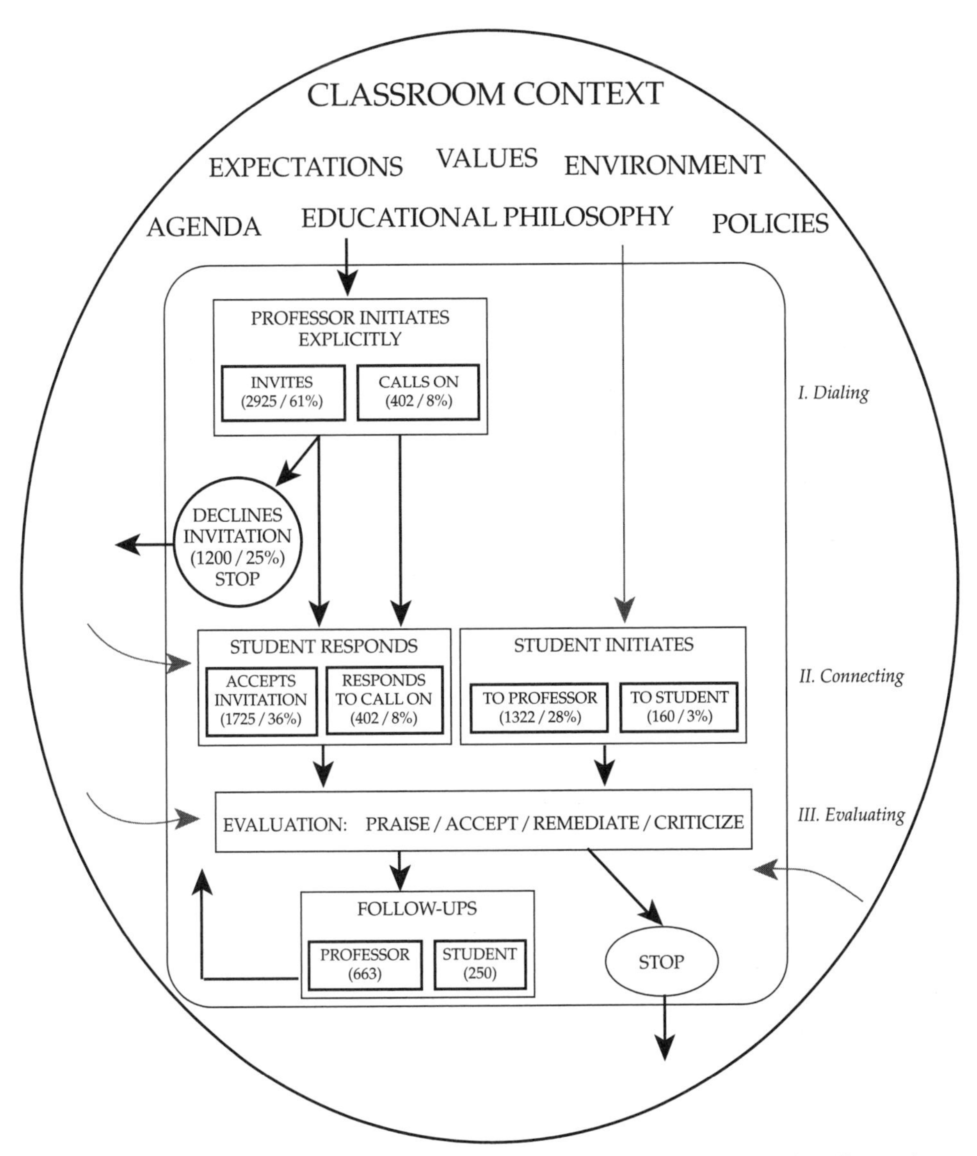

Figure 1. A Model of Classroom Interactions as Configured in Traditional College Classrooms. *Note:* Lighter arrows represent contextual influences that are assumed to operate at every level, darker boxes or ellipses = the dependent variables, and the total observed frequencies and unconditional probabilities are in parentheses

comment and the professor's evaluation, either the student or the professor can choose to keep it going by initiating a follow-up exchange.

Design and Analytic Strategy

Our aim was to assess the role of the gender composition of the group and other contextual factors in constructing gender differences within the classroom. We focused on aspects of the classroom dynamic that the literature on classroom and group interactions indicates are often highly gendered, namely, those that deal directly with the initiation, establishment, and continuation (or the failure therein) of classroom interactions. Our independent or predictor variables (the "social context" variables), included type of school (single sex versus mixed sex), sex of the professor, sex of the student, class size (number of students), class level (introductory versus upper level), and the proportion of males in the class. We selected five dependent or criterion variables that represent behaviors occurring within Levels 1 and 2 of the model (dialing and connecting). These variables were classroom totals for professors' invitations to interact (including separately those invitations that were accepted and those that were not), professors' call-ons, professors' follow-ups, students' initiations with the professor, and students' follow-ups. Students sometimes initiated interactions with other students, but because such interactions were so uncommon, they were not included in these analyses.

Because we used an unbalanced design and because of intercorrelations among independent variables, we used a hierarchical, general linear model approach to analyzing the effects of the independent variables and their interactions. The professor's sex, type of school, class level, and student's sex were all "effect" coded, with female, single-sex, and introductory courses coded as –1 and male, mixed-sex, and upper-level courses coded as +1. For each dependent variable, we examined three classes of models: (I) the overall school-type effects, that is, the "effects" of professor's sex, class level, class size, and school type on the class totals, ignoring the student's sex; (II) the school-type effects for female students only, that is, the effects of professor's sex, class level, class size, and school type on the adjusted female student totals; and (III) student's gender effects, that is, the effects of professor's sex, class level, class size, student's sex, and proportion of male students on the adjusted cohort totals for the mixed-sex classes.

Data were transformed as follows: For each classroom or classroom cohort the observed frequency of each type of interaction was tallied. Because some classrooms were not observed for exactly 30 minutes, either because of the brevity of the class (8 cases) or because of the observer's error of coding too long (4 cases), each class total was normalized to a 30-minute observation period. Also, to avoid spurious effects involving class size, we chose not to base our analyses of cohort activity levels on the activity level per cohort member. Instead, we normalized the 30-minute cohort totals to reflect the interaction volume expected had the cohort in question been as large as the class itself. These adjusted totals provided a common response metric across analyses. Finally, because the dependent variables

Table 2.
Determinants of Overall Patterns of Classroom Interaction, Irrespective of Students' Sex[a]

	Professor Invitation			Student	
Predictor	(Total)	Decline	Accepted	Initiation	Follow-up
School type (S)				.10* (6.6)	
Class size (N)	–.35* (4.2)	–.22 (2.7)	–.30* (3.9)	–.16** (18.5)	–.08** (5.3)
Class level (L)	–.78** (18.3)	–.67** (20.7)	–4.2** (7.2)		
Professor's sex (P)		–.97 (3.8)	–.23 (2.5)		
P × S	–.36* (4.3)	–.33** (5.5)	–.26 (3.2)	–.29* (4.8)	
P × N		.26 (3.8)			
S × L					–.07* (4.1)
P × S × N				–.10** (7.5)	
Constant	6.2** (97.0)	3.8** (56.1)	4.9** (77.8)	1.6** (133.3)	.70** (27.9)
R	.46	.51	.39	.46	.40

*$p \leq .05$, **$p \leq .01$.
[a]Table entries are unstandardized coefficients (*F*-ratios in parentheses). Models are based on a hierarchical, GLM approach. Model parameters reflect skew-correction transformations: square root for N, invitations extended, invitations declined, and invitations accepted: logarithmic for student initiations with the professor and student-initiated follow-ups. School type (S), class level (L), and professor's sex (P) were "effect" coded, so that single-sex schools, introductory classes, and females = –1, and mixed-sex schools, upper-level classes, and males = +1. Only significant factors and those approaching significance are shown here.

and class size were positively skewed, we applied square root or logarithmic transformations, depending solely on which resulted in minimal skew, to class size and to each of the dependent variables.

Separate hierarchical analyses were performed for each of the dependent variables for each of the analytic conditions (I-III). The resulting statistical models summarized in Tables 2–4, respectively, were based on data transformed to correct for skew.

Single-Sex Versus Mixed-Sex Effects

Invitations. The total number of invitations to interact extended by professors during an observation period is equal to the number of invitations accepted by students plus the number of invitations declined. As indicated in Table 2, there were significant negative effects of class size and class level on the number of invitations. Also, as is illustrated in Figure 2, there was a significant interaction involving the sex of the professor and the type of school in that the number of invitations extended by female professors increased with the transition to mixed-sex

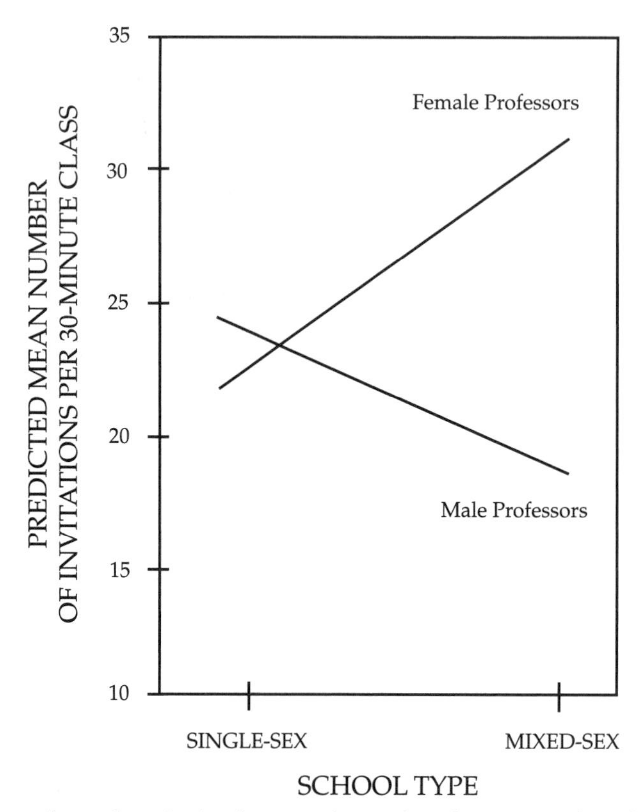

Figure 2. The Relationship of School Type to the Predicted Mean Number of Invitations to Interact Delivered by Male and Female Professors over a 30-Minute Class Period

education, whereas the number of invitations extended by male professors decreased. Male-and female-led all-female classes had statistically equivalent and intermediate numbers of invitations. This pattern of results was almost exactly replicated for invitations accepted and for invitations declined. To see if students were more inclined or less inclined to accept invitations in the mixed-sex classrooms, we performed additional analyses on the ratio of invitations accepted to invitations extended. In general, accepted invitations were more common than declined invitations (a ratio of 1.5 to 1), and this ratio was unaffected by type of school. Apparently, the observed changes in the totals of accepted and unaccepted invitations represent changes in the total number of invitations extended by the professors, rather than fundamental shifts in the willingness of students to respond.

Professor Call-ons. Professors seldom began an interaction by calling on students directly. Only 8 percent of all interactions were of this type, or about 2.5 per 30 minutes of class. There were no significant effects for the call-on interactions, so those results are not included in Table 2.

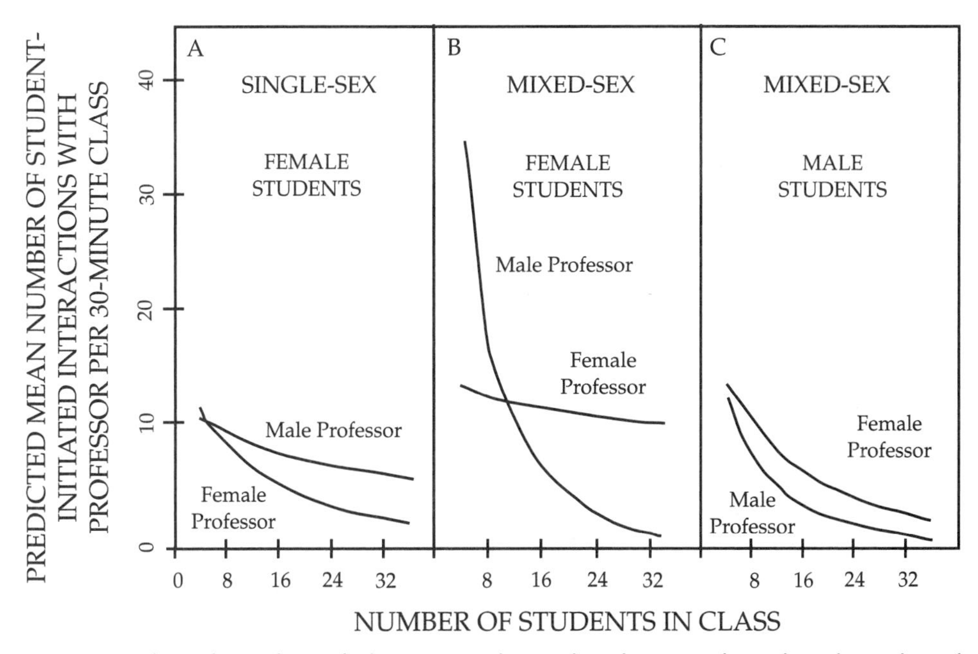

Figure 3. The Relationships of Class Size to the Predicted Mean Adjusted Total Number of Student Initiations to the Professor per 30-Minute Class Period, per Each Student Cohort

Student Initiations. The analyses revealed a negative effect of class size and a positive effect of school type on the student-initiation totals. Also, school type interacted with professor's sex and together, they interacted with class size (see Table 2). These various effects were due primarily to a much higher number of student-initiated interactions in small and middle-size, male-led, mixed-sex classes than in others. Although this particular interaction is not shown here, it is nearly identical to the one illustrated in Figure 3A-B, which presents comparable information for the Type II analytic condition or, in other words, for the female students considered separately.

Although they are complex and interact with one another and with class size, two aspects of these findings are of special interest here. First, the number of student-initiated interactions was greater in the mixed-sex than in the all-female student classrooms. Second, for single-sex classes, the student-initiated interaction patterns in male- versus female-led classrooms were nearly equivalent (see Figure 3A), but for the mixed-sex classes, the patterns within male- versus female-led classrooms were different (see Figure 3B). So here, as with professors' invitations, the mixed-sex classroom made the professor's sex an important determinant of the interactive dynamics.

Professor Follow-ups. Analyses of the numbers of professor-initiated follow-up exchanges revealed no main effects and no interactions. Hence, that model is not reported in Table 2. Taking into consideration a weak and nonsignificant effect of class size, the mean number of professor follow-ups per class was estimated at 4.2 for the median class size of 13 students.

Student Follow-ups. There was a negative effect of class size. In addition, school type interacted with class level, so that the introductory, single-sex class-rooms had approximately half as many student follow-ups as there were in each of the other three types of classrooms. The transition to mixed-sex education was therefore accompanied by an increased willingness by introductory-level students to follow up an initial exchange with another and/or by an increased tolerance or encouragement by the professors for such exchanges. When the college was all female, that relatively higher rate of student follow-ups was not evident until students entered upper-level classes.

Gender Cohort Totals

The foregoing analyses ignored students' gender and focused on how mixed-sex education and other factors (professor's sex, class size, and class level) affected the prominent features of the classroom dynamic. The results reported next consider the additional issue of students' gender. First, we consider how the transition and the other contextual factors influenced interactions involving the female students. Then we consider how students' gender and the other contextual factors influenced the adjusted cohort totals in the mixed-sex classrooms.

Female Students. When only the female students' interactions were considered, so that the hierarchical analyses were performed on the adjusted total frequencies for the female student cohorts, the results, summarized in Table 3, closely duplicated those described earlier and will not be restated here. That these results for the female student cohorts so closely duplicated those obtained for the classroom totals indicates that the shifts in the overall pattern of classroom interactions that accompanied the transition from single-sex to mixed-sex education also held for the classroom interaction patterns of the female students themselves. This finding is not surprising, given that female students still far outnumbered male students during the period of observation. Even so, it is important to emphasize that the overall changes wrought by mixed-sex education were not simply due to the inclusion of male students who behaved differently from female students; rather, female students and both male and female professors behaved differently than they did in the single-sex classrooms. We turn now to the mixed-sex classrooms themselves.

Students in Mixed-Sex Classrooms

The analyses of the mixed-sex classrooms included a somewhat different set of variables. In addition to examining again, now in the mixed-sex context, effects of professor's sex, class size, and class level, we also examined how the behavior of the male student cohort compared with that of the female student cohort and whether or not participation patterns were related to the proportion of male students in the class. The results are summarized in Table 4.

Table 3.
Determinants of Patterns of Classroom Interaction, Female Students Only[a]

	Professor		Student	
Predictor	Invitation Accepted	Follow-up	Initiation	Follow-up
School type (S)			.09* (5.5)	
Class size (N)	−.31* (4.6)		−.16** (16.3)	
Class level (L)	−.46** (9.6)			−.07* (4.0)
Professor's sex (P)	−.23 (2.7)	.37** (7.1)		
P × S	−.26 (3.4)		.35* (6.3)	
P × N		−.08* (5.1)		
S × L				.09* (6.4)
P × S × N			−.11** (9.2)	
Constant	4.7** (78.6)	.73** (353.7)	1.6** (116.5)	.36** (98.2)
R	.40	.29	.45	.31

*$p \leq .05$, **$p \leq .01$.
[a]Table entries are unstandardized coefficients (F-ratios in parentheses). Models are based on a hierarchical, GLM approach. Model parameters reflect skew-correction transformations: square root for N, and invitations accepted; logarithmic for student initiations with the professor and for professor- and student-initiated follow-ups. School type (S), class level (L), and professor's sex (P) were "effect" coded, so that single-sex schools, introductory classes, and females = −1, and mixed-sex schools, upper-level classes, and males = +1. Only significant factors and those approaching significance are shown here.

Professor Invitations Accepted. Consistent with the earlier findings, there was a positive effect of professor's sex in that the adjusted total number of invitations accepted was greater for mixed-sex classes led by female professors than for mixed-sex classes led by male professors. This effect of professor's sex was not related to student's sex. In the results reported in the previous sections, we stated that the female professors extended a greater number of invitations in mixed-sex classrooms than did the male professors. In the analyses we report here, we learned that the male and female students were equally likely to accept those invitations. What was interesting, however, was that there was an overall effect of the proportion of male students—classes with higher proportions of male students were associated with fewer adjusted total numbers of invitations accepted, irrespective of class size and the sex of students or professors.

On the basis of the regression in Table 4, the magnitude of the effect was such that the mean number of predicted invitations accepted dropped from 27 when the proportion of males in the class was set at zero to 3 when the proportion of males was set at 1.0.

Table 4.
Gender Differences in Classroom Interaction Patterns in Mixed-Sex Classrooms[a]

	Professor		Student	
Predictor	Invitation Accepted	Follow-up[b]	Initiation	Follow-up
Student's sex (S)		–.13** (7.4)	–.11* (4.6)	–.19* (5.3)
Class size (N)		–.11* (5.9)	–.19** (10.8)	–.06 (2.7)
Class level (L)			.32** (7.8)	
Professor's sex (P)	–1.6* (5.1)			
Proportion males (M)	–3.6* (4.2)		–.98* (3.8)	
P × S				–.37* (6.5)
P × N	.42* (5.1)			
P × L	.49* (5.5)			
M × S				.69* (5.7)
M × L	–2.6 (2.5)		–1.16* (6.3)	
P × S × N				.09* (6.2)
Constant	5.2** (26.4)	1.00** (33.0)	1.86** (40.7)	.56** (14.9)
R	.43	.34	.45	.38

$*p \leq .05$, $**p \leq .01$.

[a]Table entries are unstandardized coefficients (*F*-ratios in parentheses). Models are based on a hierarchical, GLM approach. Model parameters reflect skew-correction transformations: square root for N, and invitations accepted; logarithmic for student initiations with the professor and for professor- and student-initiated follow-ups. Class level (L), professor's sex (P), and student's sex (S) were "effect" coded, so that introductory classes and females = –1 and upper-level classes and males = +1. Only significant factors and those approaching significance are shown here.

[b]The PLNM interaction was marginally significant; however, when included in the model, the overall model was not significant. Here the four-way interaction was folded back into error variance. These effects should be interpreted cautiously.

In addition to these first-order effects, there were two interactions. First, the effect of professor's sex interacted with class level. In these mixed-sex classes, female professors extended more interactions and therefore had more of them accepted than the male professors did. However, the higher number for female professors was greater for introductory-than for upper-level classes. Second, the effect of professor's sex also depended on class size; the greater number of invitations extended by the female professors (and accepted) diminished with the larger classes because for the female-led classes, but not for the male-led classes, there was a negative effect of class size.

Professor Call-ons. As in the previous analyses of professor call-ons, none of the predictor variables nor their interactions was significant and, consequently, no model is reported in Table 4. In mixed-sex classes, male and female students were apparently equally, albeit rarely, called on.

Student Initiations to Professor. The joint effects of class size and professor's sex are shown separately for male and female students in mixed-sex classes in Figure 3B–C. Within mixed-sex classes, the adjusted total number of student initiations was greater for female than for male students (see Table 4). Indeed, the totals for initiations by male students were comparable to those for female students in the single-sex classrooms. In other words, the earlier finding that the number of student initiations per class increased with mixed-sex education was apparently exclusive to female students. In addition, there was a positive effect of class level and negative effects of class size and the proportion of male students. The latter finding was especially interesting; as the proportion of males in a class increased, both the male and the female students initiated fewer and fewer interactions.

Professor Follow-ups. The hierarchical analysis of the professor follow-ups in mixed-sex classes revealed a four-way interaction involving professor's sex, class level, class size, and proportion of male students (see Table 4, footnote b). Four-way interactions are extremely difficult to interpret under the best circumstances, and the complexities surrounding unbalanced designs and hierarchical analyses only compound the problem. So, we can offer no coherent description, let alone an interpretation, of this particular finding.

Student Follow-ups. For mixed-sex classes, the adjusted total number of student follow-ups was greater for female than for male students, but that effect was, in turn, dependent on the proportion of male students in the class (see Table 4). Indeed, the greater number of follow-ups by female students is a *y*-intercept difference and therefore assumes that the proportion of male students is zero. As shown in Figure 4, as the proportion of male students increased, the adjusted total number of female student follow-ups decreased and the adjusted total number of male student follow-ups increased. Recall that the totals are "adjusted" to reflect the male and female student follow-up rates. In other words, the differences reflect "per student" differences.

In addition, the effect of student's sex interacted with professor's sex, which, in turn, depended on class size. This interaction, illustrated in Figure 5, is an interesting cross-sex effect: The total number of student follow-ups in which the student's gender matched the professor's gender was unaffected by class size and was relatively low. In contrast, the total number of student follow-ups by students of the opposite sex from the professor was relatively high in the smaller classes, but decreased with class size.

In sum, the data show that the males' and females' behaviors differed in many ways. However, in every instance, the nature of the differences, even their very existence, depended on circumstance.

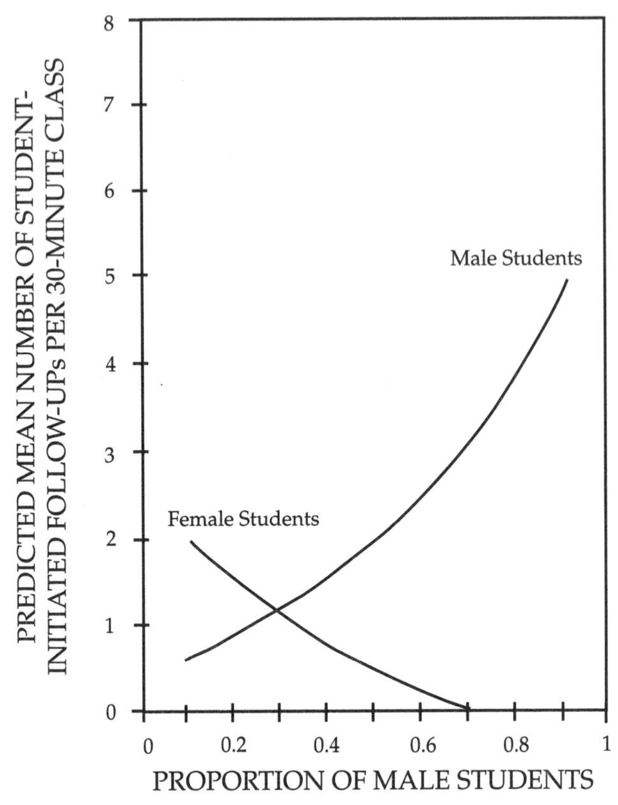

Figure 4. The Relationships of the Proportion of Males in the Class to the Predicted Mean Adjusted Total Number of Male and Female Student-Initiated Follow-ups over a 30-Minute Class Period

Male Versus Female Professors

Within the mixed-sex classes, female professors initiated 63 percent more interactions than did male professors (see Figure 2). The opposite was true for the student-initiated interactions: Mixed-sex classes led by male professors, when they were small to intermediate in size, were associated with many more student-initiated interactions than were comparable-size classes led by female professors (see Figure 3). In effect, female-led, mixed-sex classes were more professor driven and were less student driven than were male-led, mixed-sex classes. These findings would lead one to believe, on the basis of the mixed-sex classes considered in isolation, that male and female professors differ stylistically in how they govern their classrooms. But contrary to what this narrow view would indicate, male and female professors initiated intermediate and statistically equivalent numbers of interactions within the all-female student classes (see Figure 2). Similarly, these male- and female-led classes did not differ in their numbers of student-initiated interactions. Clearly, the "stylistic" difference that seems to have existed between male and female professors when they led mixed-sex classes was not at all evi-

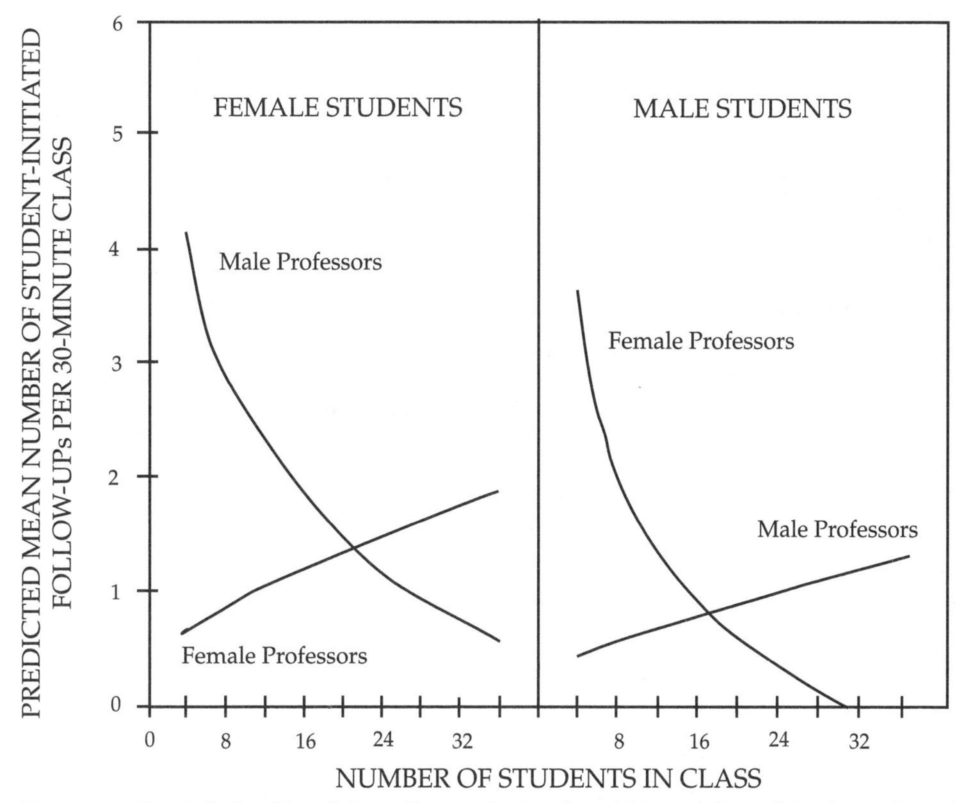

Figure 5. The Relationship of Class Size to the Predicted Mean Adjusted Total Number of Male and Female Student-initiated Follow-ups to Male and Female Professors over a 30-Minute Class Period

dent when they led all-female classes. The difference in style was socially constructed.

These various professor-sex findings both corroborate and extend Statham et al.'s (1991) finding that female and male professors negotiate their authority in different ways. Statham et al. conducted their research at a mixed-sex institution, and the classrooms they studied were mixed sex. Like Statham et al., we found that female and male professors tend to behave differently in mixed-sex classrooms. We also found, however, that in single-sex classrooms, female and male professors tend to behave in similar ways.

For faculty, this finding indicates that with regard to the specific classroom behaviors we observed and analyzed, the single-sex classrooms provided an environment within which female and male professors behaved similarly, which suggests that within that circumscribed domain, gender did not matter. For female students, this finding of gender differences in professors' styles and behaviors in mixed-sex classrooms is particularly interesting and potentially disturbing when it is considered in light of Tidball's (1989) assertion that the high number of female faculty who serve as role models for women students is one of the main reasons women from single-sex colleges outpace women from mixed-sex institutions in their entry into traditional male fields and career accomplishments.

It is not the case that the number of female faculty at the college under study declined since the move to mixed-sex education; the percentage of female professors remained high (over 50 percent) during the course of the research. However, our findings suggest a qualifier to Tidball's assertion: Not only are female students at women's colleges exposed to *more* female faculty members than are their counterparts at mixed-sex colleges, but they are also privy to a different type of female role modeling in the classroom. Specifically, female students at women's colleges reap the benefits of classrooms in which female and male professors model similar behaviors; in relation to their mixed-sex counterparts, the female professors behave more male-like, and the male professors behave more femalelike. Our findings suggest that male students in mixed-sex classes are similarly deprived of the opportunity to interact with female and male professors who are behaving in similar ways; therefore, their opportunities to observe and interact with females in environments in which gender does not matter are reduced.

Male Versus Female Students

There were several differences in the manner in which male and female students interacted in the mixed-sex classrooms, and in every case, the difference depended on the social context. First, although the effect depended somewhat on class size and professor's sex, female students in the mixed-sex classes initiated more interactions than did male students (see Figure 3). One might suppose, on the basis of this finding, considered in isolation, that female students are more inclined than are male students to participate in the classroom dynamic. However, female students in the single-sex classrooms initiated interactions in a manner and level almost exactly equivalent to that of the male students in mixed-sex classrooms.

Second, male and female students in mixed-sex classrooms differed in their numbers (rates) of student follow-ups: Female students started with a higher rate than did male students, but as the proportion of male students in a class increased, the female student follow-up rate decreased and the male student follow-up rate increased. The functions crossed, and hence the student follow-up rates were equal when the proportion of male students was .27 (see Figure 4). Had one examined the difference between male and female students' rates of engagement in conversation-style interactions and examined classrooms that had roughly equal proportions of male and female students, as did Boersma et al. (1981), then one would likely conclude, as they did, that male and female students have a different interaction style, with males being more likely than females to engage in conversationlike interactions with the professor. Here, too, the gender difference depends on the social context, in this case, on the proportion of male students in the class.

Third, in the mixed-sex classes, female students were more likely to engage in student follow-ups when the professor was male than when the professor was female (see Figure 5), suggesting a cross-gender affiliation between female students and male professors. However, there was no such effect among the single-sex classes: The student follow-up rates were unrelated to the professor's sex, which suggests that this so-called cross-gender affiliation was socially constructed in the mixed-sex classrooms.

DISCUSSION

There are countless ways in which gender differences could arise within mixed-sex college classrooms. Our observational techniques, combined with the particular sampling and statistical procedures we used, like casting a net into a single region of the sea, permitted us to examine some small subset of these possibilities. We did not, for example, even attempt to collect data on the content of interactions. We focused instead on classroom and cohort tallies of certain well-defined behaviors that served to initiate, establish, and maintain verbal exchanges or interactions between students and professors. Nor were we able to follow individual students in detail, an approach that would have undoubtedly revealed many individual exceptions to the general trends emphasized here.

But with regard to those trends, within this domain alone we documented a variety of ways in which gender matters. The behaviors of female students and of both male and female professors were strongly related to whether or not male students were present in the classroom, and the behaviors of both female and male students in mixed-sex classes were related to the proportion of male students. The gender of the professor was also important, and these variables sometimes interacted in complex ways. Simply, the shift from all-female to mixed-sex classrooms was accompanied by profound changes in the nature of the dynamic of classroom interaction. That these data indicate that gender mattered in the mixed-sex classrooms in ways that it did not in the all-female classrooms is not surprising. They are consistent with several independent literatures that have documented ways in which gender matters in a variety of educational and group-interaction contexts.

These student-centered gender differences arising with mixed-sex education are consistent with Maccoby's (1990) claims that the verbal and interactive behaviors of females are often strongly affected by the presence of males. The behaviors of women and girls, particularly those of European descent, are greatly affected by the gender composition of the group such that gender differences seem most pronounced in mixed-gender settings. The gender differences observed in our study of classroom interactions can be viewed similarly. We propose that they are a product of a kind of mixed-sex education that takes a laissez-faire approach to engenderment, which is to say, one that largely acquiesces to the broader culture's construction of gender.

Theorizing Gender in Classrooms

From the perspectives of the gender dynamics that ordinarily pervade mixed-sex classrooms and mixed-sex community youth culture, reviewed earlier, it is not hard to imagine events in the mixed-sex classroom that would trigger the kinds of changes we observed during the early phases of the college's transition. For example, one would expect the restrictive interaction styles of the entering male students to have been off-putting to the upperclasswomen who had gotten used to and learned to appreciate its absence. Similarly, some professors might have recognized in the restrictive style of the male students the kind of locution and verbal aggressiveness that they themselves had been taught to value. Others, more sensitive to gender issues or perhaps more vulnerable to the aggressive style because they were women or otherwise favored a more egalitarian and noncompetitive pedagogy, might have felt disconcerted and challenged for leadership within their own classrooms. Mix into this classroom cauldron a tendency by male students to evaluate female students and professors in terms of their attractiveness, as opposed to their intellectual capabilities and contributions, and related tendencies by male students to expect and to exert male privilege, and you have a gender politics in the classroom that was nearly absent in the single-sex environment.

The nature and volatility of the mixture just mentioned may be sufficient to induce the noted bifurcation between the ways in which male and female professors negotiate their classroom interactions. If a female professor believes that her classroom agenda is being challenged in some way, perhaps by body language (we frequently observed males sitting together in the back row, with their feet propped up, seemingly indifferent to the classroom dynamic), perhaps by silence (often the same male students did not participate in class), perhaps by the content of an interaction (we occasionally observed male students making agenda-challenging comments, such as "I resent your bringing that up!"), what recourse does she have? She can openly challenge the student or students, but that may be difficult to do and may, particularly if she does not have tenure, be professionally risky, especially at an institution that measures the success of its transition to coeducation by the number of its fulltime male students. She may, instead, try to keep the agenda alive by asking more questions of the class.

Why did the female students initiate more interactions than the male students? We simply do not know. This behavior may have reflected their reaction to implicit and/or explicit comments by the male students. Or it may have been an attempt to "enable" the professor's agenda. Another possibility is that during these first five years of the transition to mixed-sex education, female students were inclined to contest male privilege and domination in the classroom, perhaps because of the residual effects of the all-female environment, such as pedagogical habits and expectations and the high proportion of female role models. Knowing the content of these interactions may help clarify their role in the classroom dynamic. Therefore, this issue awaits further study.

Interpreting the findings on the male and female students' follow-ups seems more clear cut. For whatever reason, when the proportion of male students was high, women in the new mixed-sex classrooms were not as likely as they were in the single-sex classrooms to enter deliberately into a sustained conversation with the professor. Male students, on the other hand, became increasingly willing to enter into such conversations as the proportion of male students increased. The issue can be understood in terms of intimidation. Note that the neutral point in Figure 4, the point where the two functions cross or, in other words, the female-to-male split that resulted in equal rates of student follow-ups for the two cohorts, is at .7/.3, *not* .5/5. That is, female students were more intimidated by male students than vice versa.

What, on the surface, appears to be an alternative explanation is that by ranking classes in accordance with the proportion of males in them, we may, in fact, have ranked them in accordance with the greater interest they evoked in males than females. For example, the classes with the higher proportions of males may have been those that are supposedly, or so the stereotype would have it, of greater interest to males, such as mathematics, computer science, and the natural sciences. By this alternative account, the relative lack of participation of the females in the student-initiated follow-ups would have been due to their lack of interest or skill in the subject—an intimidation by the subject matter, rather than an intimidation by the presence of male students. From our point of view, however, silencing is silencing. Also, we place little stock in this "essentialist" approach because the point is that these very classes were, when the college was single sex, populated by conversant female students. Now they are not.

The Challenge of Coeducation

We interpret our findings as evidence of the need for increased attention to issues of gender and gender equity in higher education. Though we acknowledge a need for educational reforms to address these issues, we are not ready to conclude, at this time, that the gendered outcomes reported in this article are themselves the things that need to be "corrected." Instead, we believe that these outcomes are the footprints of a gender politic or dynamic that now exists both in the college's classrooms and throughout the college campus that did not exist when the institution was single sex. What we measured, the changing volume of various types of interactions, signaled the entry of some changed circumstance, like a cloud chamber registers the passing of some otherwise invisible and unnoticed subatomic intruder. Given the total circumstance, the differences we observed may be more a reflection of the professors' and female students' survival tactics in response to the altered environment than a direct view of the altered environment itself. Given the reality of the gender politic, raising the number of invitations, for example, may be the best possible negotiation available to the female professors as they search for alternative pedagogies to achieve their educational goals in mixed-sex classes.

The wholesale entry of the gender politic itself occurred within a context. This study is a partial case history of an institution trying to find its way through difficult economic and demographic circumstances. As an all-female institution facing a less-than-critical mass of students for the foreseeable future, it looked to mixed-sex education as a means of increasing its recruitment pool. During the internal discussions of what it would mean to become coeducational, members of the community, and indeed the official proclamations of the institution itself, repeatedly stated the claim that mixing men with women would make little or no educational difference.

That gender does not matter in the domain of education is an institutional stance that Laird (1989) referred to as the "negative claim." That the institution under study maintained its negative claim throughout the period of study is clear: During its first five years, the success of the transition to coeducation was measured internally by the number of male students who were recruited. Furthermore, by the time our project ended, the institution had not established a single communitywide workshop, venue of discussion, database, or policy pertaining to the new role of gender in the business and mission of the college. Toward the end of our project, when we met with the person who was, at that time, president of the college to summarize our findings and concerns, she, too, expressed concern but informed us that "gender equity is not the guiding principle of this college." We would take her statement one step further and say that at least during the period of our research, the college's concern for survival overrode other concerns and values it might otherwise have held, including gender equity.

Naturally, a college that makes the negative claim would not be easily alarmed. The tolerance for the gender politic, the tolerance for quiet students and dominant students in the classroom, and the tolerance for letting things sort themselves out as they will seem to us to guarantee the status quo as our society as a whole defines it, and that, as the literature amply documents, is far too frequently at the expense of female students. We end with this challenge: Making the negative claim is itself a social context. No one yet knows what is possible of a mixed-sex educational environment that soundly rejects the negative claim and aims instead for gender equity.

References

Boersma, P. Dee., Debora Gay, Ruth A. Jones, Lynn Morrison, and Helen Remick. 1981. "Sex Differences in College Student-Teacher Interactions: Fact or Fantasy?" *Sex Roles* 7:775–84.

Cornelius, Randolph R., Janet Gray, and Anne P. Constantinople. 1990. "Student-Faculty Interaction in the College Classroom." *Journal of Research and Development in Education* 23:189–97.

Eagly, Alice H. 1987. *Sex Differences in Social Behavior: A Social-Role Interpretation.* Hillsdale, NJ: Lawrence Erlbaum Associates.

Eccles, Jacquelynne S. 1989. "Bringing Young Women to Math and Science." Pp. 36–58 in *Gender and Thought: Psychological Perspectives,* edited by Mary Crawford and Margaret Gentry. New York: Springer-Verlag.

Giele, Janet Zollinger. 1987. "Coeducation or Women's Education? A Comparison of Alumnae from Two Colleges: 1934–79." Pp. 91–109 in *Educating Men and Women Together,* edited by Carol Lasser. Urbana: University of Illinois Press.

Hall, Roberta M. and Bernice R. Sandler. 1982. *The Classroom Climate: A Chilly One for Women?* Washington, DC: Project on the Status and Education of Women, Association of American Colleges.

Holland, Dorothy C. and Margaret A. Eisenhardt. 1990. Educated in Romance: *Women, Achievement, and College Culture.* Chicago: University of Chicago Press.

Laird, Susan. 1989, March. "Co-education: A Philosophical Anomaly?" In Susan Laird (Chair), *Needed: Research on Co-Education.* Symposium conducted at the annual meeting of the American Educational Research Association, San Francisco.

Lee, Valerie E., Helen M. Marks, and Tina Byrd. 1994. "Sexism in Single-Sex and Coeducational Independent Secondary School Classrooms." *Sociology of Education* 67:92–120.

Maccoby, Eleanor. 1990. "Gender Relationships: A Developmental Account of *American Psychologist* 45:513–20.

Moore, Mary, Valerie Piper, and Elizabeth Schaefer. 1993, December. "Single-Sex Schooling and Educational Effectiveness: A Research Overview." Pp. 7–68 in *Single-Sex Schooling: Perspectives from Practice and Research* (special report from the Office of Educational Research and Improvement, U.S. Department of Education, Vol. 1), edited by Debra K. Hollinger and Rebecca Adamson. Washington, DC: U.S. Department of Education.

Riordan, Cornelius. 1994. "The Value of Attending a Women's College: Education, Occupation, and Income Benefits." *Journal of Higher Education* 65:486–510.

Sanday, Peggy Reeves. 1990. *Fraternity Gang Rape: Sex, Brotherhood, and Privilege on Campus.* New York: New York University Press.

Statham, Anne, Laurel Richardson, and Judith A. Cook. 1991. *Gender and University Teaching: A Negotiated Difference.* Albany: State University of New York Press.

Tidball, M. Elizabeth. 1989. "Women's Colleges: Exceptional Conditions, Not Exceptional Talent, Produce High Achievers." Pp. 157–72 in *Educating the Majority: Women Challenge Tradition in Higher Education,* edited by Carol S. Pearson, Donna L. Shavlik, and Judith G. Touchton. New York: Macmillan.

PART 7 THE GENDERED WORKPLACE

Perhaps the most dramatic social change in industrial countries in the twentieth century has been the entry of women into the workplace. The nineteenth-century ideology of "separate spheres"—the breadwinner husband and the homemaker wife—has slowly and steadily evaporated. While only 20 percent of women and 4 percent of married women worked outside the home in 1900, more than three-fourths did so by 1995, including 60 percent of married women. In the first decade of the next century, 80 percent of the new entrants into the labor force will be women, minorities, and immigrants.

Despite the collapse of the doctrine of separate spheres—work and home—the work place remains a dramatically divided world, where women and men rarely do the same jobs in the same place for the same pay. Occupational sex segregation, persistent sex discrimination, wage disparities—all these are problems faced by working women. As the article by Barbara Reskin demonstrates, workplace inequality is among the most persistent and pernicious forms of gender discrimination.

Even women who are seeking to get ahead by entering formerly all-male fields frequently bump into the "glass ceiling"—a limit on how high they can rise in any organization. On the other hand, as Christine Williams argues, men who do "women's work"—taking occupations such as nurse, nursery school teacher, librarian—not only avoid the glass ceiling but actually glide up a "glass escalator"—finding greater opportunities at the higher, better paying levels of their professions than women.

And, as Judith Lorber points out, even when women are protected by a variety of laws that promise comparable worth for equal work, wage and salary parity, and no occupational sex segregation, they still face myriad psychological and interpersonal struggles, such as sexual harassment, the creation of a "hostile environment," that keeps them in their place.

BARBARA F. RESKIN

Bringing the Men Back In: Sex Differentiation and the Devaluation of Women's Work

One of the most enduring manifestations of sex inequality in industrial and postindustrial societies is the wage gap. In 1986, as in 1957, among full-time workers in the United States, men earned 50 percent more per hour than did women. This disparity translated to $8,000 a year in median earnings, an all-time high bonus for being male. Most sociologists agree that the major cause of the wage gap is the segregation of women and men into different kinds of work. Whether or not women freely choose the occupations in which they are concentrated, the outcome is the same: the more proportionately female an occupation, the lower its average wages. The high level of job segregation means that the 1963 law stipulating equal pay for equal work did little to reduce the wage gap.

This "causal model"—that the segregation of women and men into different occupations causes the wage gap—implies two possible remedies. One is to equalize men and women on the causal variable—occupation—by ensuring women's access to traditionally male occupations. The other is to replace occupation with a causal variable on which women and men differ less, by instituting comparable-worth pay policies that compensate workers for the "worth" of their job regardless of its sex composition.

I contend, however, that the preceding explanation of the wage gap is incorrect because it omits variables responsible for the difference between women and men in their distribution across occupations. If a causal model is incorrect, the remedies it implies may be ineffective. Lieberson's (1985, p. 185) critique of causal analysis as it is commonly practiced explicates the problem by distinguishing between *superficial* (or surface) causes that *appear* to give rise to a particular outcome and *basic* causes that *actually* produce the outcome. For example, he cites the belief that the black-white income gap is due to educational differences and thus can be reduced by reducing the educational disparity. As Lieberson pointed out, this analysis misses the fact that "the dominant group . . . uses its dominance to advance its own position" (p. 166), so that eliminating race differences in education is unlikely to reduce racial inequality in income because whites will find another way to maintain their income advantage. In other words, what appear in this example to be both the outcome variable (the black-white income gap) and the imputed causal variable (the black-white educational disparity) may stem from the same basic cause (whites' attempt to maintain their economic advantage). If so, then if the disparity in education were eliminated, some other factor would arise to produce the same economic consequence.

From *Gender & Society*, Vol. 2, no. 1 (March 1988), pp. 58–81. References have been edited.

Dominant groups remain privileged because they write the rules, and the rules they write "enable them *to continue to write the rules*" (Lieberson 1985, p. 167; emphasis added). As a result, they can change the rules to thwart challenges to their position. Consider the following example. Because Asian American students tend to outscore occidentals on standard admissions tests, they are increasingly overrepresented in some university programs. Some universities have allegedly responded by imposing quotas for Asian students or weighing more heavily admissions criteria on which they believe Asian Americans do less well.

How can one tell whether a variable is a superficial or a basic cause of some outcome? Lieberson offered a straightforward test: Does a change in that variable lead to a change in the outcome? Applying this rule to the prevailing causal theory of the wage gap, we find that between 1970 and 1980 the index of occupational sex segregation declined by 10 percent, but the wage gap for full-time workers declined by just under 2 percent. Although its meaning may be equivocal, this finding is consistent with other evidence that attributing the wage gap to job segregation misses its basic cause: men's propensity to maintain their privileges. This claim is neither novel nor specific to men. Marxist and conflict theory have long recognized that dominant groups act to preserve their position. Like other dominant groups, men are reluctant to give up their advantages (Goode 1982). To avoid having to do so, they construct "rules" for distributing rewards that guarantee them the lion's share (see also Epstein 1985, p. 30). In the past, men cited their need as household heads for a "family wage" and designated women as secondary earners. Today, when millions of women who head households would benefit from such a rule, occupation has supplanted it as the principle for assigning wages.

Neoclassical economic theory holds that the market is the mechanism through which wages are set, but markets are merely systems of rules that dominant groups establish for their own purposes. When other groups, such as labor unions, amassed enough power, they modified the "market" principle. Steinberg (1987) observed that when consulted in making comparable-worth adjustments, male-dominated unions tended to support management over changes that would raise women's salaries.

In sum, the basic cause of the income gap is not sex segregation but men's desire to preserve their advantaged position and their ability to do so by establishing rules to distribute valued resources in their favor. Figure 1 represents this more complete causal model. Note that currently segregation is a superficial cause of the income gap, in part through "crowding," but that some other distributional system such as comparable-worth pay could replace it with the same effect.

With respect to income, this model implies that men will resist efforts to close the wage gap. Resistance will include opposing equalizing women's access to jobs because integration would equalize women and men on the current superficial cause of the wage gap—occupation. Men may also try to preserve job segregation because it is a central mechanism through which they retain their dominance in other spheres, and because many people learn to prefer the company of others like them. My theory also implies that men will resist efforts to replace occupation

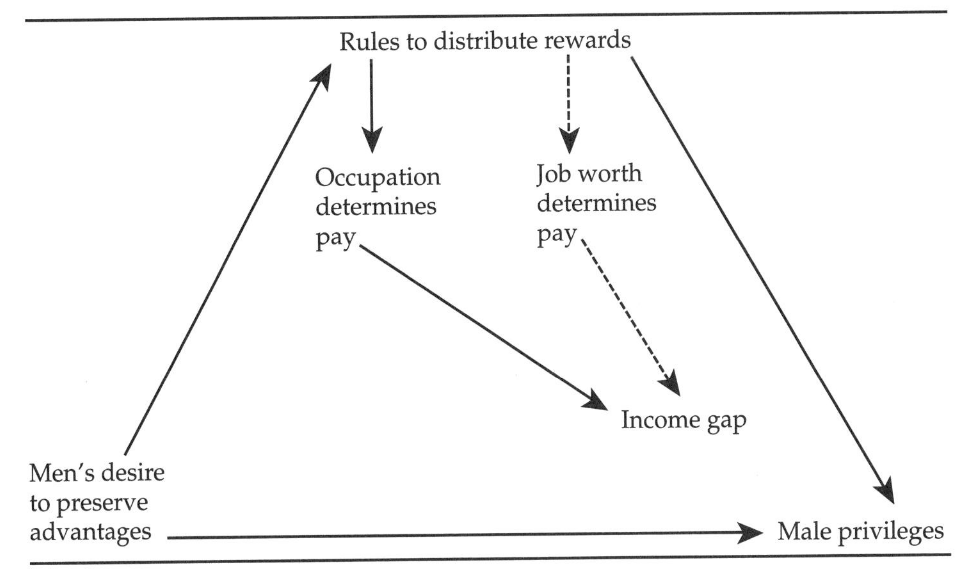

Figure 1. Heuristic Model of the Wage Gap

with alternative principles for assigning pay that would mitigate segregation's effect on women's wages (as pay equity purports to do).

Before I offer evidence for these claims, let us examine how dominant groups in general and men in particular maintain their privileged position. I formulate my analysis with reference to dominant groups to emphasize that the processes I discuss are not specific to sex classes. It also follows that, were women the dominant sex, the claims I make about men's behavior should hold for women.

DIFFERENTIATION, DEVALUATION, AND HIERARCHY

Differentiation—the practice of distinguishing categories based on some attribute—is the fundamental process in hierarchical systems, a logical necessity for differential evaluation and differential rewards. But differentiation involves much more than merely acting on a preexisting difference. In a hierarchical context, differentiation assumes, amplifies, and even creates psychological and behavioral differences in order to ensure that the subordinate group differs from the dominant group, "because the systematically differential delivery of benefits and deprivations require[s] making no mistake about who was who" (MacKinnon 1987, p. 40) and because "differences are inequality's post hoc excuse" (MacKinnon 1987, p. 8).

Differentiated status characteristics influence evaluations of people's behavior and their overall worth. In hierarchical systems in which differentiation takes the form of an Aristotelian dichotomy, individuals are classified as either A ("the subject") or Not-A ("the other"). But these two classes are not construed as natural opposites that both have positive qualities; instead, A's characteristics are valued as normal or good and Not-A's as without value or negative.

The official response to the influx of south- and central-eastern European immigrants to the United States early in this century, when people assumed that each European country represented a distinct biological race, illustrates differentiation's central role in dominance systems. A congressionally mandated immigration commission concluded that "innate, ineradicable race distinctions separated groups of men from one another" and agreed on the

> necessity of classifying these races to know which were most worthy of survival. The immediate problem was to ascertain "whether there may not be certain races that are inferior to other races . . . to discover some test to show whether some may be better fitted for American citizenship than others." (Lieberson 1980, pp. 2–26)

Thus differentiation in all its forms supports dominance systems by demonstrating that superordinate and subordinate groups differ in essential ways and that such differences are natural and even desirable.

"Sex Differentiation" versus "Gender Differentiation": A Note on Terminology. Scholars speak of both "sex" and "gender" differentiation: the former when biological sex or the "sex category" into which people are placed at birth is the *basis for* classification and differential treatment; the latter to refer to the *result* of that differential treatment. In order to emphasize that the initial biological difference (mediated through sex category) is the basis for differential treatment, I use the terms *sex differentiation* and *sex segregation.* This usage should not obscure the fact that the process of converting sex category into gender is a social one or that most differences that are assumed to distinguish the sexes are socially created. I agree with Kessler and McKenna (1978) that the "gender attribution process" assumes dimorphism and seeks evidence of it to justify classifying people as male and female and treating them unequally. This article examines how and why those differences are produced.

Sex Differentiation and Devaluation. Probably no system of social differentiation is as extensive as that based on sex category. Its prevalence led anthropologist Gayle Rubin to claim that there is "a taboo against the sameness of men and women, a taboo dividing the sexes into two mutually exclusive categories, a taboo which exacerbates the biological differences between the sexes and thereby *creates* gender" (1975, p. 178). Moreover, although femaleness is not always devalued, its deviation from maleness in a culture that reserves virtues for men has meant the devaluation of women. Bleier's research on biological scientists' study of sex differences illustrates this point: the "search for the truth about differences, [implies] that difference means *different from the white male norm and, therefore, inferior*" (1987, p. 2; emphasis added). In consequence, men's activities are typically valued above women's, regardless of their content or importance for group survival, and both sexes come to devalue women's efforts. Thus it should be no surprise that women's occupations pay less at least partly *because* women do them.

In short, differentiation is the sine qua non of dominance systems. Because of its importance, it is achieved through myriad ways:

> To go for a walk with one's eyes open is enough to demonstrate that humanity is divided into two classes of individuals whose clothes, faces, bodies, smiles, gaits, interests and occupations are manifestly different. (de Beauvoir 1953, p. xiv)

We differentiate groups in their location, appearance, and behavior, and in the tasks they do. Now let us turn to how these mechanisms operate to differentiate women and men.

PHYSICAL SEGREGATION

Dominant groups differentiate subordinate groups by physically isolating them—in ghettos, nurseries, segregated living quarters, and so on. Physical segregation fosters unequal treatment, because physically separate people can be treated differently and because it spares members of the dominant group the knowledge of the disparity and hides it from the subordinate group. Although women and men are integrated in some spheres, physical separation continues to differentiate them.

Cohn's (1985) vivid account of women's physical segregation in the British Foreign Office in the nineteenth century illustrates the extent to which organizations have gone to separate the sexes. The Foreign Office hid its first female typists in an attic, but it failed to rescind the requirement that workers collect their pay on the ground floor. When payday came, managers evacuated the corridors, shut all the doors, and then sent the women running down the attic stairs to get their checks and back up again. Only after they were out of sight were the corridors reopened to men.

This account raises the question of *why* managers segregate working men and women. What licentiousness did the Foreign Office fear would occur in integrated hallways? Contemporary answers are markedly similar to turn-of-the-century fears. Compare the scenario expressed in a 1923 editorial in the *Journal of Accountancy* ("any attempt at heterogeneous personnel [in after-hours auditing of banks] would hamper progress and lead to infinite embarrassment" [p. 151]) with recent reactions to the prospect of women integrating police patrol cars, coal mines, and merchant marine vessels (e.g., Martin 1980). At or just below the surface lies the specter of sexual liaisons. For years, McDonald's founder Ray Kroc forbade franchisees to hire women counter workers because they would attract "the wrong type" of customers. The U.S. Army ended sex-integrated basic training to "facilitate toughening goals," and the Air Force reevaluated whether women could serve on two-person Minuteman missile-silo teams because "it could lead to stress."

My thesis offers a more parsimonious alternative to these ad hoc explanations—men resist allowing women and men to work together *as equals* because doing so undermines differentiation and hence male dominance.

BEHAVIORAL DIFFERENTIATION

People's behavior is differentiated on their status-group membership in far too many ways for me to review the differences adequately here. I concentrate in this section on differentiation of behaviors that occur in the workplace: task differentiation and social differentiation.

Task differentiation assigns work according to group membership. It was expressed in the extreme in traditional Hindu society in which caste virtually determined life work. Task assignment based on sex category—the sexual division of labor—both prescribes and proscribes assorted tasks to each sex, and modern societies still assign men and women different roles in domestic work, labor-market work, and emotional and interpersonal work. Task differentiation generally assigns to lower-status groups the least desirable, most poorly rewarded work: menial, tedious, and degraded tasks, such as cleaning, disposing of waste, and caring for the dying. This practice symbolizes and legitimates the subordinate group's low status, while making it appear to have an affinity for these undesirable tasks. As an added benefit, members of the dominant group don't have to do them! Important to discussions of the wage gap, because modern law and custom permit unequal pay for different work, task differentiation justifies paying the subordinate group lower wages, thereby ensuring their economic inferiority. Women's assignment to child care, viewed as unskilled work in our society, illustrates these patterns. Women are said to have a "natural talent" for it and similar work; men are relieved from doing it; society obtains free or cheap child care; and women are handicapped in competing with men. As researchers have shown, sex-based task differentiation of both nonmarket and market work legitimates women's lower pay, hinders women's ability to succeed in traditionally male enterprises, and, in general, reinforces men's hegemony.

Social differentiation is achieved through norms that set dominant and subordinate groups apart in their appearance (sumptuary rules) or behavior. When applied to sex, Goffman's (1976) concept of "gender display" encompasses both. Sumptuary rules require certain modes of dress, diet, or life-style of members of subordinate groups as emblems of their inferior status, and reserve other modes to distinguish the dominant group. For example, Rollins (1985) discovered that white female employers preferred black domestic employees to dress shabbily to exaggerate their economic inferiority. Sex-specific sumptuary rules are epitomized in norms that dictate divergent dress styles that often exaggerate physical sex differences and sometimes even incapacitate women. An extreme example is the *burqua* fundamentalist Muslim women wear as a symbol of their status and as a portable system of segregation.

Etiquette rules support differentiation by requiring subordinate group members to display ritualized deference toward dominants Relations between enlistees and officers or female domestic workers and their employers illustrate their role. Although typically it is the subordinate group that must defer, gender etiquette that requires middle- and upper-class men to display deference to women of the same classes preserves differentiation by highlighting women's differentness. Women who do not express gratitude or who refuse to accept the deference are faced with hostility, shattering the fiction that women hold the preferred position.

Physical segregation, behavioral differentiation, social separation, and even hierarchy are functional alternatives for satisfying the need for differentiation in domination systems. For example, when their physical integration with the dominant group means that a subordinate group's status differences might otherwise be invisible, special dress is usually required of them, as servants are required to wear uniforms. Physical separation can even compensate for the absence of hierarchy, a point acknowledged in the black folk saying that southern whites don't care how close blacks get if they don't get too high, and northern whites don't care how high blacks get if they don't get too close.

This substitutability explains why men will tolerate women in predominantly male work settings if they work in "women's" jobs and accept women doing "men's" jobs in traditionally female settings, but resist women doing traditionally male jobs in male work settings. Physical proximity per se is not threatening as long as another form of differentiation sets women apart. But the absence of *any* form of differentiation precludes devaluation and unequal rewards and hence threatens the sex-gender hierarchy. Because of the centrality of differentiation in domination systems, dominant groups have a considerable stake in maintaining it.

DOMINANTS' RESPONSE TO CHALLENGES

Dominants respond to subordinates' challenges by citing the group differences that supposedly warrant differential treatment. Serious challenges often give rise to attempts to demonstrate biological differences scientifically.

The nineteenth-century antislavery and women's rights movements led reputable scientists to try to prove that women's and blacks' brains were underdeveloped. The Great Migration to the United States in the first two decades of this century fueled a eugenics movement that purported to establish scientifically the inferiority of south- and central-eastern Europeans. The civil rights movement of the 1960s stimulated renewed efforts to establish racial differences in intelligence. And we are once again witnessing a spate of allegedly scientific research seeking a biological basis for presumed sex differences in cognitive ability and, specifically, for boys' higher average scores on math questions in some standardized tests. As Bleier pointed out, "The implication if not purposes of [such] research is to demonstrate that the structure of society faithfully reflects the natural order of things." According to Bleier, reputable journals have published studies that violate accepted standards of proof, and the scientific press has given dubious findings considerable attention (as in the news story in *Science* that asked, "Is There a Male Math Gene?"). Although subsequently these studies have been discredited, the debate serves its purpose by focusing attention on how groups differ.

MEN'S RESPONSE TO OCCUPATIONAL INTEGRATION

An influx of women into male spheres threatens the differentiation of men and women, and men resist. One response is to bar women's entry. Women have had to turn to the courts to win entry into Little League sports, college dining clubs, private professional clubs, and the Rotary. Recently, University of North Carolina trustees decried the fact that women are now a majority of UNC students, and some proposed changing the weights for certain admission criteria to restore the male majority. Twice since a shortage of male recruits forced the army to lift its quota on women, it has reduced the number of jobs open to women.

Numerous studies have documented men's resistance to women entering "their" jobs. Sometimes the resistance is simply exclusion; at other times it is subtle barriers that block women's advancement or open harassment. Now that more women hold managerial jobs, one hears of "a glass ceiling" that bars middle-management women from top-level positions, and Kanter (1987) claimed that organizations are changing the rules of what one must do to reach the top in order to make it more difficult for women to succeed.

My thesis implies that men will respond to women's challenge in the workplace by emphasizing how they differ from men. Especially common are reminders of women's "natural" roles as wife, mother, or sexual partner. Witness the recent—and subsequently disputed—claims that women who postponed marriage and childbearing to establish their careers had a negligible chance of finding husbands and were running the risk that their "biological clocks" would prevent pregnancy, and accounts of women dropping out of middle management to spend more time with their children.

Men who cannot bar women from "male" jobs can still preserve differentiation in other spheres. Their attempts to do so may explain why so few husbands of wage-working women share housework, as well as elucidating Wharton and Baron's (1987) finding that among men working in sex-integrated jobs, those whose wives were employed were more dissatisfied than unmarried men or men married to homemakers.

Another response to women's challenge is to weaken the mechanisms that have helped women advance in the workplace. Since 1980, the Reagan administration has sought to undermine equal-opportunity programs and affirmative-action regulations, and the campaign has partly succeeded. Efforts to dilute or eliminate Equal Employment Opportunity (EEO) programs are advanced by claims that sex inequality has disappeared (or that men now experience "reverse discrimination"). For example, the *New York Times* recently described the Department of Commerce announcement that women now compose the majority in professional occupations as a "historic milestone," adding that "the barriers have fallen."

THE ILLUSION OF OCCUPATIONAL INTEGRATION

If male resistance is so pervasive, how can we explain the drop in the index of occupational sex segregation in the 1970s and women's disproportionate gains in a modest number of male-dominated occupations? In order to answer this question, Patricia Roos and I embarked on a study of the changing sex composition of occupations. The results of our case studies of a dozen traditionally male occupations in which women made disproportionate statistical gains during the 1970s cast doubt on whether many women can advance economically through job integration.

The case studies revealed two general patterns. First, within many occupations nominally being integrated, men and women remain highly segregated, with men concentrated in the highest-status and best-paying jobs. For example, although women's representation in baking grew from 25 percent in 1970 to 41 percent in 1980, men continue to dominate production baking. The increase in women bakers is due almost wholly to their concentration in proliferating "in-store" bakeries. Although women now make up the majority of residential real estate salespersons, men still monopolize commercial sales.

The second pattern shows that women often gained access to these occupations after changes in work content and declines in autonomy or rewards made the work less attractive to men. In some occupations, the growth of functions already socially labeled as "women's work" (e.g., clerical, communications, or emotional work) spurred the change. For example, computerization and the ensuing clericalization prompted women's entry into typesetting and composing and insurance adjusting and examining. An increasing emphasis on communicating and interpersonal or emotional work contributed to women's gains in insurance sales, insurance adjusting and examining, systems analysis, public relations, and bank and financial management.

Brief summaries of our findings for two occupations illustrate these processes. First, women's disproportionate gains in pharmacy have been largely confined to the retail sector (male pharmacists work disproportionately in research and management) and occurred after retail pharmacists lost professional status and entrepreneurial opportunities. After drug manufacturers took over the compounding of drugs, pharmacists increasingly resembled retail sales clerks; their primary duties became dispensing and record keeping. As chain and discount-store pharmacies supplanted independently owned pharmacies, retail pharmacy no longer offered a chance to own one's own business, reducing another traditional attraction for men. The resulting shortages of male pharmacy graduates eased women's access to training programs and retail jobs.

Second, book editing illustrates how declining autonomy and occupational prestige contributed to feminization of an occupation. For most of this century, the cultural image of publishing attracted bright young men and women despite very low wages. But during the 1970s, multinational conglomerates entered book publishing, with profound results. Their emphasis on the bottom line robbed publishing of its cultural aura, and the search for blockbusters brought a greater role for marketing people in acquisition decisions, thereby eroding editorial autonomy. As a result, editing could no longer compete effectively for talented men who could choose from better opportunities. Because women's occupational choices are more limited than men's, editing still attracted them, and the occupation's sex composition shifted accordingly.

In sum, although sex integration appears to have occurred in the 1970s among census-designated detailed occupations, our findings indicate that within these occupations, women are segregated into certain specialties or work settings and that they gained entry because various changes made the occupations less attractive to men. The nominal integration that occurred in the 1970s often masks within-occupation segregation or presages resegregation of traditionally male occupations as women's work. In short, the workplace is still overwhelmingly differentiated by sex. Moreover, our preliminary results suggest that real incomes in the occupations we are studying declined during the 1970s; so reducing segregation at the occupational level appears to have been relatively ineffective in reducing the wage gap—and certainly not the remedy many experts predicted. This brings us to the other possible remedy for the wage gap—comparable worth.

IMPLICATIONS FOR COMPARABLE WORTH

The comparable-worth movement calls for equal pay for work of equal worth. Worth is usually determined by job-evaluation studies that measure the skill, effort, and responsibility required, but in practice, assessing worth often turns on how to conceptualize and measure skill.

Although some objective criteria exist for assessing skill (e.g., how long it takes a worker to learn the job, typically the designation of work as skilled is socially negotiated. Workers are most likely to win it when they control social resources that permit them to press their claims, such as a monopoly over a labor supply or authority based on their personal characteristics such as education, training, or sex. As a result, the evaluation of "skill" is shaped by and confounded with workers' sex.

Groups use the same power that enabled them to define their work as skilled to restrict competition by excluding women (among others) from training for and practicing their trade or profession, as Millicent Fawcett recognized almost a hundred years ago when she declared, "Equal pay for equal work is a fraud for women." Because men use their power to keep women "from obtaining equal skills, their work [cannot be] equal" (Hartmann 1976, p. 157). Roos's (1986) case history of the effect of technological change on women's employment in typesetting illustrates these points. When a Linotype machine was developed that "female typists could operate," the International Typographical Union (ITU) used its labor monopoly to force employers to agree to hire as operators only skilled printers who knew *all* aspects of the trade. By denying women access to apprenticeships or other channels to become fully skilled and limiting the job of operating the Linotype to highly skilled printers, the ITU effectively barred women from the new Linotype jobs. In short, the ITU used its monopoly power both to restrict women's access to skills and credentials and to define its members as "uniquely skilled" to operate the Linotype.

Excluded from occupations male workers define as skilled, women are often unable, for several reasons, to press the claim that work in traditionally female occupations is skilled. First, as I have shown, the devaluation of women's work leads whatever work women do to be seen as unskilled. Second, women's powerlessness prevents their successfully defining their work—caring for children, entering data, assembling microelectronic circuits—as skilled. Third, because many female-dominated occupations require workers to acquire skills before employment, skill acquisition is less visible and hence unlikely to be socially credited. Fourth, the scarcity of apprenticeship programs for women's jobs and women's exclusion from other programs denies women a credential society recognizes as denoting skill. Finally, "much of women's work involves recognizing and responding to subtle cues" (Feldberg 1984, p. 321), but the notion of "women's intuition" permits men to define such skills as inborn and hence not meriting compensation. Thus women are both kept from acquiring socially valued skills and not credited for those they do acquire. As a result, the sex of the majority of workers in an occupation influences whether or not their work is classified as skilled.

In view of these patterns, how effective can comparable worth be in reducing the wage gap? As with the Equal Pay Act, implementing it has symbolic value. Moreover, it would bar employers from underpaying women relative to their job-evaluation scores, the practice alleged in *AFSCME v. Washington State* (1985). But setting salaries according to an occupation's worth will reduce the wage gap only to the extent that (1) women have access to tasks that society values, (2) evaluators do not take workers' sex into account in determining a job's worth, and (3) implementers do not sacrifice equity to other political agendas.

Neither of the first two conditions holds. As I have shown, men already dominate jobs society deems skilled. Moreover, the tendency to devalue women's work is embedded in job-evaluation techniques that define job worth; so such techniques may yield biased evaluations of traditionally female jobs and lower their job-evaluation scores. Beyond these difficulties is the problem of good-faith implementation. Acker (1987), Brenner (1987), and Steinberg (1987) have documented the problems in implementing comparable-worth pay adjustments. According to Steinberg (p. 8), New York State's proposed compensation model *negatively* values working with difficult clients, work performed in historically female and minority jobs (in other words, workers lose pay for doing it!), and Massachusetts plans to establish separate comparable-worth plans across sex-segregated bargaining units. For these reasons, the magnitude of comparable-worth adjustments have been about half of what experts expected—only 5 percent to 15 percent of salaries (Steinberg 1987).

Moreover, to the extent that equity adjustments significantly raise salaries in women's jobs, men can use their power to monopolize them. It is no accident that the men who integrated the female semiprofessions moved rapidly to the top. The recent experience of athletic directors provides an additional illustration. Title IX required college athletic programs to eliminate disparities in resources between women's and men's programs including salaries. Within ten years the proportion of coaches for women's programs who were male grew from 10 percent to 50 percent. Finally, men as the primary implementers of job evaluation have a second line of defense—they can and do subvert the process of job evaluation.

CONCLUSION

Integrating men's jobs and implementing comparable-worth programs have helped some women economically and, more fully implemented, would help others. But neither strategy can be broadly effective because both are premised on a flawed causal model of the pay gap that assigns primary responsibility to job segregation. A theory that purports to explain unequal outcomes without examining the dominant group's stake in maintaining them is incomplete. Like other dominant groups, men make rules that preserve their privileges. With respect to earnings, the current rule—that one's job or occupation determines one's pay—has maintained white men's economic advantage because men and women and whites and nonwhites are differently distributed across jobs.

Changing the allocation principle from occupation to job worth would help nonwhites and women if occupation were the pay gap's basic cause. But it is not. As long as a dominant group wants to subordinate others' interests to its own and is able to do so, the outcome—distributing more income to men than women—is, in a sense, its own cause, and tinkering with superficial causes will not substantially alter the outcome. Either the rule that one's occupation determines one's wages exists *because* men and women hold different occupations, or men and women hold different occupations because we allocate wages according to one's occupation. Obviously the dominant group will resist attempts to change the rules. In *Lemon v. City and County of Denver* (1980), the court called comparable worth "pregnant with the possibility of disrupting the entire economic system" (Steinberg 1987). "Disrupting the entire white-male dominance system" would have been closer to the mark.

If men's desire to preserve their privileges is the basic cause of the wage gap, then how can we bring about change? The beneficiaries of hierarchical reward systems yield their privileges only when failing to yield is more costly than yielding. Increasing the costs men pay to maintain the status quo or rewarding men for dividing resources more equitably may reduce their resistance.

As individuals, many men will gain economically if their partners earn higher wages. Of course, these men stand to lose whatever advantages come from outearning one's partner. But more important than individual adjustments are those achieved through organizations that have the power to impose rewards and penalties. Firms that recognize their economic stake in treating women equitably (or can be pressed by women employees or EEO agencies to act as if they do) can be an important source of pressure on male employees. Employers have effectively used various incentives to overcome resistance to affirmative action (e.g., rewarding supervisors for treating women fairly [Shaeffer and Lynton 1979; Walshok 1981]). Employers are most likely to use such mechanisms if they believe that regulatory agencies are enforcing equal-opportunity rules. We can attack men's resistance through political pressure on employers, the regulatory agencies that monitor them, and branches of government that establish and fund such agencies.

Analyses of sex inequality in the 1980s implicitly advance a no-fault concept of institutionalized discrimination rather than fixing any responsibility on men. But men *are* the dominant group, the makers and the beneficiaries of the rules. Of course, most men do not consciously oppose equality for women or try to thwart women's progress. When men and women work together, both can gain, as occurred when the largely male blue-collar union supported the striking Yale clerical and technical workers. But as a rule, this silent majority avoids the fray, leaving the field to those who do resist to act on behalf of all men. It is time to bring men back into our theories of economic inequality. To do so does not imply that women are passive agents. The gains we have made in the last two decades in the struggle for economic equality—redefining the kinds of work women can do, reshaping young people's aspirations, and amassing popular support for pay equity despite opponents' attempt to write it off as a "loony tune" idea—stand as testimony to the contrary. Just as the causal model I propose views the dominant group's self-interest as the source of unequal outcomes, so too does it see subordinate groups as the agents of change.

References

Acker, Joan. 1987. "Sex Bias in Job Evaluation: A Comparable-Worth Issue." Pp. 183–96 in *Ingredients for Women's Employment Policy,* edited by Christine Bose and Glenna Spitze. Albany: SUNY University Press.

AFSCME v. *State of Washington.* 1985. 770 F.2d 1401. 9th Circuit.

Bleier, Ruth. 1987. "Gender Ideology: The Medical and Scientific Construction of Women." Lecture presented at the University of Illinois, Urbana.

Brenner, Johanna. 1987. "Feminist Political Discourses: Radical vs. Liberal Approaches to the Feminization of Poverty and Comparable Worth." *Gender & Society* 1:447–65.

Cohn, Samuel. 1985. *The Process of Occupational Sex Typing.* Philadelphia: Temple University Press.

de Beauvoir, Simone. 1953. *The Second Sex.* New York: Knopf.

Epstein, Cynthia F. 1985. "Ideal Roles and Real Roles or the Fallacy of Misplaced Dichotomy." *Research on Social Stratification and Mobility* 4:29–51.

Feldberg, Roslyn L. 1984. "Comparable Worth: Toward Theory and Practice in the U.S." *Signs: Journal of Women in Culture and Society* 10:311–28.

Goffman, Erving. 1976. "Gender Display." *Studies in the Anthropology of Visual Communication* 3:69–77.

Goode, William C. 1964. *The Family.* Englewood Cliffs, NJ: Prentice Hall.

Hartmann, Heidi. 1976. "Capitalism, Patriarchy, and Job Segregation by Sex." *Signs: Journal of Women in Culture and Society* 1 (Part 2):137–69.

Kanter, Rosabeth Moss. 1987. "Men and Women of the Change Master Corporation (1977–1987 and Beyond): Dilemmas and Consequences of Innovations of Organizational Structure." Paper presented at Annual Meetings, Academy of Management, New Orleans.

Kessler, Suzanne and Wendy McKenna. 1978. *Gender: An Ethnomethodological Approach.* New York: John Wiley.

Lieberson, Stanley. 1980. *A Piece of the Pie.* Berkeley: University of California Press.

———. 1985. *Making It Count.* Berkeley: University of California Press.

MacKinnon, Catharine. 1987. *Feminism Unmodified.* Cambridge, MA: Harvard University Press.

Martin, Susan E. 1980. *Breaking and Entering.* Berkeley: University of California Press.

Rollins, Judith. 1985. *Between Women.* Philadelphia: Temple University Press.

Roos, Patricia A. 1986. "Women in the Composing Room: Technology and Organization as the Determinants of Social Change." Paper presented at Annual Meetings, American Sociological Association, New York.

Rubin, Gayle. 1975. "The Traffic in Women: Notes on the 'Political Economy' of Sex." Pp. 157–210 in *Toward an Anthropology of Women,* edited by Rayna R. Reiter. New York: Monthly Review Press.

Shaeffer, Ruth Gilbert and Edith F. Lynton. 1979. *Corporate Experience in Improving Women's Job Opportunities.* Report no. 755. New York: The Conference Board.

Steiger, Thomas. 1987. "Female Employment Gains and Sex Segregation: The Case of Bakers." Paper presented at Annual Meetings, American Sociological Association, Chicago.

Steinberg, Ronnie J. 1987. "Radical Challenges in a Liberal World: The Mixed Successes of Comparable Worth." *Gender & Society* 1:466–75.

Walshok, Mary Lindenstein. 1981. "Some Innovations in Industrial Apprenticeship at General Motors." Pp. 173–82 in *Apprenticeship Research: Emerging Findings and Future Trends* edited by Vernon M. Briggs, Jr., and Felician Foltman. Ithaca: New York State School of Industrial Relations.

Wharton, Amy and James Baron. 1987. "The Impact of Gender Segregation on Men at Work." *American Sociological Review* 52:574–87.

JUDITH LORBER

Guarding the Gates: The Micropolitics of Gender

You're proposing your interpretation of the universe, and for that you need to have the recognition of your colleagues. You must assert that this is a good idea, the right interpretation, and that you thought of it, because all three of those things have to be accepted by your colleagues. It doesn't do your career any good to have the theory accepted, without anyone giving you the credit.

—Harriet Zuckerman, Jonathan R. Cole,
and John T. Bruer (1991, 103)

Twenty-five years ago, Muriel F. Siebert bought a seat on the New York Stock Exchange, the first woman to be permitted to do so. In 1992, receiving an award for her accomplishments, she said bluntly that despite the numbers of women coming into high finance, the professions, and government, the arenas of power are still overwhelmingly dominated by men. The numbers bear her out.

In 1980 in the United States, only two women were chief executive officers of the largest corporations, the Fortune 500. They were Katherine Graham, chief executive of the Washington Post Company, and Marion O. Sandler, co-chief executive of Golden West Financial Corporation, in Oakland, California. In 1985, there were three: Graham, Sandler, and Elisabeth Claiborne of the Liz Claiborne clothing company. In 1990, there were also three: Graham, Sandler, and Linda Wachner of the Warnaco Group, Inc., New York. In 1992, Charlotte Beers became chief executive of Ogilvie & Mather Worldwide, the fifth largest international advertising agency, with billings of $5.4 billion, making her the world's highest ranking woman executive in that field. Linda Wachner (earning $3.1 million in 1991) was the first woman in *Fortune*'s "roster of exorbitantly paid executives." Thus, in the past decade, in the United States, where women composed between 42.4 and 45.4 percent of the work force, and numbered between 42.1 and 53.5 million, a total of five women were heads of the largest corporations. When *Fortune* culled the lists of the highest paid officers and directors of 799 U.S. industrial and service companies, out of 4,012 it found 19 women, or less than one-half of 1 percent.

The belief that upward mobility and leadership positions would automatically follow if women increased their numbers in the workplace greatly underestimated the social processes that get some people onto the fast track and systematically derail others. These processes are used by those at the top to ensure that those coming up will be as similar as possible to themselves so that their values and ideas about how things should be done will be perpetuated. The markers of homogeneity are gender, race, religion, ethnicity, education, and social background. The few heterogeneous "tokens" who make it past the gatekeepers first must prove their similarity to the elite in outlook and behavior. The numbers at the bottom in any field have little relation to the numbers at the top, where power politics is played and social policies are shaped.

The gender segregation so evident in the modern work world is exacerbated at the top echelons of business, the professions, and politics by gendered concepts of authority and leadership potential. Women are seen as legitimate leaders only in areas considered of direct concern to women, usually health, education, and welfare. Women's accomplishments in men's fields tend to be invisible or denigrated by the men in the field, and so women rarely achieve the stature to be considered leaders in science or space, for example. The U.S. National Aeronautics and Space Administration put twenty-five women pilots through rigorous physical and psychological testing from 1959 to 1961. Thirteen demonstrated "exceptional suitability" for space flight, but neither they nor seventeen women with advanced science degrees were chosen to be astronauts or space scientists, even though the Russians had sent Valentina Tereshkova into space in 1963. As Gloria Steinem said, recalling these invisible women almost twenty years later, women's demonstrating they have the "right stuff" turns into the "wrong stuff" without the approval of the men in charge (1992).

When a leader is chosen among colleagues, women are often overlooked by the men of the group, and there are usually too few women to support one another. Even where women are the majority of workers, men tend to be favored for positions of authority because women and men will accept men leaders as representing their general interests but will see women as representing only women's interests. As a result, men in occupations where most of the workers are women, such as nursing and social work, tend to be over represented in high-level administrative positions, and women in occupations where most of the workers are men rarely reach the top ranks.

When men choose a woman for a position of power and prestige, she is often considered "on probation." For example, an Israeli woman physician who was made head of a prestigious department of obstetrics and gynecology where she was the only woman told me that a year later, the men colleagues who had chosen her told her that they were now enormously relieved. She had not made any serious mistakes, so their decision to choose her as head of the department was validated. She was furious that they had felt she had to prove herself; she had been their colleague and friend for seventeen years, and they surely should have known her worth and her leadership capabilities. At that point, she said, she realized that her men colleagues had never really considered her "one of them."

THE GLASS CEILING

The pervasive phenomenon of women going just so far and no further in their occupations and professions has come to be known as the *glass ceiling*. This concept assumes that women have the motivation, ambition, and capacity for positions of power and prestige, but invisible barriers keep them from reaching the top. They can see their goal, but they bump their heads on a ceiling that is both hidden and impenetrable. The U.S. Department of Labor defines the glass ceiling as "those artificial barriers based on attitudinal or organizational bias that prevent qualified individuals from advancing upward in their organization into management level positions" (L. Martin 1991, 1).

A recent study of the pipelines to power in large-scale corporations conducted by the U.S. Department of Labor found that the glass ceiling was lower than previously thought—in middle management. Members of disadvantaged groups were even less likely than white women to be promoted to top positions, and the upper rungs were "nearly impenetrable" for women of color (L. Martin 1991). A random sample of ninety-four reviews of personnel in corporate headquarters found that of 147,179 employees, 37.2 percent were women and 15.5 percent were minorities. Of these employees, 31,184 were in all levels of management, from clerical supervisor to chief executive officer; 16.9 percent were women and 6 percent were minorities. Of 4,491 managers at the level of assistant vice president and higher, 6.6 percent were women and 2.6 percent were minorities. Thus, in this survey, the higher the corporate position, the smaller the proportion of women; if the numbers of women in the top ranks had been proportional with the number of women in the lower ranks, over a third of the vice presidents, presidents, and executive officers would have been women. There was no separate breakdown of these figures for women of color, but another report cited by the Labor Department indicated that they make up 3.3 percent of the women corporate officers, who make up only 1 to 2 percent of all corporate officers.

Karen Fulbright's (1987) interviews with twenty-five African-American women managers found fifteen who had reached the level of vice president, department head, or division director in oil, automobile manufacturing, telecommunications, and banking, or had moved rapidly up the hierarchy. The factors in their upward mobility were long tenure, a rapidly growing company, or a Black-owned or operated company. The others had experienced blocked mobility, despite positioning themselves on career tracks that were known to be the routes to the top.

Similar attrition in the numbers of women at the top has been found in public-sector jobs in the United States. As of 1990, 43.5 percent of the employees in lower-level jobs were women, but they were only 31.3 percent of the department heads, division chiefs, deputies, and examiners in state and local government agencies. African-American women were 9.8 percent of the workers at lower levels, 5.1 percent at the top levels.

The ways that most people move up in their careers are through *networking* (finding out about job opportunities through word-of-mouth and being recommended by someone already there), *mentoring* (being coached through the informal norms of the workplace), and *sponsorship* (being helped to advance by a senior colleague). In civil service bureaucracies, where promotion depends on passing a test or getting an additional credential, those who receive encouragement and advice from senior members of the organization tend to take the qualifying tests or obtain the requisite training. In the sciences, research productivity depends to a significant degree on where you work, whom you work with, and what resources are available to you. All these processes of advancement depend on the support of colleagues and superiors, which means that in a workplace where men outnumber women and whites outnumber any other racial ethnic group, white women and women and men of disadvantaged racial ethnic groups have to be helped by white men if they are to be helped at all.

An in-depth study of nine Fortune 500 companies with a broad range of products and services located in different parts of the country found that despite differences in organizational structure, corporate culture, and personnel policies, the same practices results in a glass ceiling for women, especially women of color. These practices were recruitment policies for upper-management levels that depended on word-of-mouth networking and employee referrals. When "head hunters" were used, they were not instructed to look for women and men of social groups underrepresented at managerial levels. The few white women and women and men of color who were already hired were not given the opportunity to build up their credentials or enhance their careers by assignment to corporate committees, task forces, and special projects. These are traditional avenues of advancement, since they bring junior members into contact with senior members of the organization and give them visibility and the chance to show what they can do. There was not monitoring of evaluation or compensation systems that determine salaries, bonuses, incentives, or perks to make sure that white women and women and men of color were getting their fair share. In general, "monitoring for equal access and opportunity, especially as managers move up the corporate ladder to senior management levels where important decisions are made, was almost never considered a corporate responsibility or part of the planning for developmental programs and policies" (L. Martin 1991, 4). In short, none of the white men in senior management saw it as their responsibility to sponsor white women or women and men of color to be their replacements when they retired.

Men in traditional women's occupations report the opposite phenomenon. Their minority status turns out to be a career advantage. Christine Williams's study of seventy-six men and twenty-three women in nursing, teaching, librarianship, and social work in the United States, whom she interviewed from 1985 to 1991, found that the men were tracked into the more prestigious, better-paying specialties within the occupation, and urged by their mentors, mostly other men, to move into positions of authority. Most of these men were white, so they were the most advantaged workers. For them not to move up to supervisory and administrative positions was considered inappropriate. As a result, they were on a "glass escalator," Williams says: "Often, despite their intentions, they face invisible pressures to move up in their professions. As if on a moving escalator, they must work to stay in place" (1992, 256). But they sometimes faced a glass ceiling at higher levels. The affirmative action policies of many institutions make the women deans and heads of departments in the women's areas too visible for them to be replaced by men (257).

Although these processes may seem benign, the imbalance of lower-level workers with disadvantaged social characteristics compared to upper-level workers with advantaged social characteristics implies a deliberate, though unstated, policy of hostility and resistance that deepens with each additional mark of disadvantage. Kimberlé Crenshaw presents a graphic analysis of who can make it through the glass ceiling:

> Imagine a basement which contains all people who are disadvantaged on the basis of race, sex, class, sexual preference, age and/or physical ability. These people are stacked—feet standing on shoulders—with those on the bottom being disadvantaged by the full array of factors, up to the very top, where the heads of all those disadvantaged by a single factor brush up against the ceiling. . . . A hatch is developed through which those placed immediately below can crawl. Yet this hatch is generally available only to those who—due to the singularity of their burden and their otherwise privileged position relative to those below—are in the position to crawl through. Those who are multiply-burdened are generally left below. (1991, 65)

Bands of Brothers

Parallel to the formal organization of a large, modern workplace, which is structured as a task-related, bureaucratic hierarchy, is the informal organization, which is based on trust, loyalty, and reciprocal favors. Because the unspoken rules are often as significant to the way business is conducted as the written rules, colleagues want to work with people who know what goes without saying: "In order that men [sic] may communicate freely and confidentially, they must be able to take a good deal of each other's sentiments for granted. They must feel easy about their silences as well as about their utterances. These factors conspire to make colleagues, with a large body of unspoken understandings, uncomfortable in the presence of what they consider odd kinds of fellows" (Hughes 1971, 146).

Personal discretion and reliability are particularly necessary for those in positions of authority because of the uncertainties they face. According to Dianne Feinstein, former mayor of San Francisco who was elected to the U.S. Senate in 1992, women have to bend over backward to prove not only their competence but their trustworthiness:

> Women have to prove themselves effective and credible time and time again. Experience has taught me that the keys to a woman's effectiveness in public office are to be "trustable": to give directions clearly and to follow up, to verify every statement for accuracy, to guard her integrity carefully, and to observe the public's trust one hundred percent. Most important, she must be a team player and build relationships with her colleagues that are based on integrity and respect. (Cantor and Bernay 1992, xv)

Almost twenty years ago, Margaret Hennig and Ann Jardim predicted that conscientious and hard-working women would find it difficult to get out of middle management because their performance was geared to formal training and bureaucratic responsibilities. They felt that if women knew that senior management relies on informal networking, gathering extensive sources of knowledge from areas other than one's own, planning, policy-making, and delegating responsibility to reliable subordinates, they would be able to move up corporate career ladders (1976, 55, 68). Career mobility, however, does not depend only on competent performance and other efforts by the ambitious individual. To move up, a young person's worth has to be recognized and encouraged by those in the upper echelons. Promising young men of the right social characteristics are groomed for senior management by "godfathers" or "rabbis"—sponsors who take them under their wing and see to it that they learn the informal organizational rules for getting ahead. Promising young women are left to fend for themselves.

Brotherly trust among men who are business associates goes back to the nineteenth century. Before the creation of the impersonal corporation, each partner in an enterprise was personally responsible for raising capital and making a profit. Credit depended on personal trustworthiness; bankruptcy was a personal tragedy. In these transactions, the active players were all men. Women were passive partners; their money was used by kinsmen and men friends who acted as trustees. In order to cement the brotherly bonds among men who were in business together, women were encouraged to marry cousins or their brothers' partners; two sisters often married two brothers, or a brother and sister married a sister and brother: "Free choice marriage controlled in this way provided a form of security in binding together members of the middle class in local, regional and national networks, a guarantee of congenial views as well as trustworthiness in economic and financial affairs" (Davidoff and Hall 1987, 221).

In twentieth-century business, professions, and politics, trust and loyalty are built not through kin ties (which is considered nepotism) but through *homosociali-*

ty—the bonding of men of the same race, religion, and social-class background (Lipman-Blumen 1976). These men have the economic, political, professional, and social resources to do each other favors. Women with the same social characteristics may be included in men's circles when they have equivalent wealth, power, and social position. Most men and women, however, relate to each other socially only in familial or sexual roles.

Homosociality starts early. In childhood play, boys separate themselves from girls and become contemptuous of girls' activities in their efforts to keep themselves apart. This segregation, attributed to boys' needs to establish their masculinity, makes friendship between girls and boys difficult because it is discouraged by same-gender peers. Gender grouping is not perfect in mixed-gender schools but is broached by social class and racial ethnic cross-currents and sometimes by the organizing activities of teachers. In adulthood, whenever men and women come together as equals, in coed schools and workplaces that are not gender-segregated, cross-gender friendships are undermined by intimations of sexual attraction. One study of white middle-class young adults found that the women preferred same-gender friendships more than the men did because the men were more interested in them sexually than as companions. The men invested more time and attention in their friendships with men than they did in their friendships with women, while the women gave as much emotional support to their men friends as they did to their women friends. Letty Cottin Pogrebin (1987, 311–40) feels that the main reason that women and men are rarely intimate friends is that they are rarely true equals.

Many working women are expected as part of their job to smile be cordial, sympathetic, agreeable, and a bit sexy. Men workers are supposed to display masculine emotions—coolness under fire, rationality, and objectivity, which are part of the performance of power. The qualities men want in women in the workplace as well as in the home—sympathy, looking out for the other person, understanding the nuances and cues of behavior, caretaking, flattering them sexually—keep women out of the top ranks of business, government, and the professions. Such qualities are gender-marked as "womanly"; they are also subordinating.

Much of men's workplace small talk is about sports or sex. Replaying the weekend's games gives men the chance to compete and win vicariously. Sexist jokes establish the boundaries of exclusion, and if the men are of the same race or religion, so do racist and anti-Semitic or anti-Catholic jokes. Sexist joking also keeps men from revealing their emotional bonds with each other and deflects their anger from their bosses onto women. Women who can talk and joke like men may be allowed entry into the men's brotherhood, as honorary men, but then they cannot protest against sexism and sexual harassment, even if they themselves are the victims.

Although men or women may be "odd fellows" in their workplace or job, the pressures of being a woman in a man's job and a man in a woman's job are quite different. Men nurses can talk cars and sports with men physicians. In doing so, they affiliate with a higher status group, affirm their masculinity, and gain a benefit from these informal contacts in more favorable evaluations of their work. Men physicians' status is too high to be compromised by chatting with men nurses (or flirting with women nurses). Men who are openly homosexual, however, may face discrimination from men supervisors. Women physicians socialize with women medical students, interns, and residents, but not with women nurses. Women physicians' status is more tenuous, and they end up in a bind. They need to get along with the women nurses so that their work proceeds efficiently, yet they lose status if they bond with a lower-status group as women. Women physicians need to build colleague relationships with the men physicians who are their peers, but these men may not treat them as equals. They also need to seek sponsors among senior men who can help them advance their careers, but these men may not want them as protégées.

Because men know the power of homosocial bonding, they are discomfited when women do the same thing and often accuse such women of lesbianism, particularly because women's attentions are turned to each other and not to them. As Carol Barkalow said of the military:

> They often appear to possess an irrational fear of women's groups, believing that, in their midst, men will be plotted against, or perhaps worst of all, rendered somehow unnecessary. If women soldiers do try to develop a professional support network among themselves, they are faced with the dilemma that something as simple as two women officers having lunch together more than once might spark rumors of lesbianism—a potentially lethal charge, since even rumored homosexuality can damage an officer's career. (1990, 167–68)

Women officers who want to bond without innuendoes of homosexuality often turn to sports, which is as legitimate a place to build trust and loyalty among women as it is among men.

For the most part, as colleagues, friends, and wives, women are relegated to acting as audience or sex objects for men. According to Kathryn Ann Farr (1988), who studied a group of upper-class white men whose bonding preserved their race and class as well as their gender privileges, wives and girlfriends were needed to serve as foils for the men's exclusive sociability. The women listened as the men talked about their exploits. When the men went off on an escapade, their women warned them against getting into too much trouble, prepared food for them, and stayed behind. The men defined the boundaries of their homosocial world by excluding women, just as they maintained its racial and class exclusivity by keeping out the "wrong" kind of men. The irony is that they built their superior status in a direct and immediate way by denying their own wives and girlfriends the privileges of their race and class. In this way, the domination of men over women in their own social group is sustained, and the women collude in the process:

> These men do not view themselves as sexist, and they do not appear to be viewed by the women *with whom they interact* as sexist. In their choice of wives and girlfriends, the majority of these men seem to value independent and intelligent women. Yet their socialization into a male-dominated environment and a culture in which male sociability is highly valued causes them to think

> and act in ways that conflict with their intellectual assessments of the worth of and the value of social relationships with women. (Farr 1988, 269)

By excluding women who share their social characteristics from their social space, these men never have to treat women as equals or as serious competitors for positions of power.

THE "MOMMY TRACK"

If they could not exclude women completely or relegate them to subordinate positions, men have reduced competition and encouraged turnover by refusing to hire married women or mothers and by encouraging women employees who get married or have children to quit. Marriage bars were used against women schoolteachers, stewardesses, and other occupations in the United States well into the twentieth century and are still used today in other countries. When the marriage bar fell out of use in the United States in the late 1950s, partly because there was a dearth of young single women workers, it was replaced by what Claudia Goldin calls "the pregnancy bar" (1990, 176). The ideology that children need full-time mothering produced turnover not at marriage but at first pregnancy.

Discriminating against women workers and job applicants who are married, pregnant, or mothers is now illegal in the United States; informally, however, these practices have been replaced by a tacit or openly acknowledged "mommy track." Ostensibly intended to make it easier for married women with children to continue managerial and professional jobs, the "mommy track" offers flexible working hours and generous maternity leave to women but not men in dual-career marriages to ameliorate the pressures of family and work. But women are penalized for taking advantage of these policies, because once they do, their commitment to achieving top-level positions is called into question. The secondary result and, I would argue, latent function of these "mommy tracks" is to derail women who were on fast tracks to the top. As Alice Kessler-Harris says: "To induce women to take jobs while simultaneously restraining their ambition to rise in them required a series of socially accepted constraints on work roles. Unspoken social prescription—a tacit understanding about the primacy of home roles—remained the most forceful influence. This is most apparent in professional jobs where the potential for ambition was greatest" (1982, 231).

Until quite recently in many Westernized countries, the more prestigious professions, such as medicine, law, and the sciences, and the upper-level managerial sector of business were thoroughly dominated by men. Men were easily able to keep women out because they were gatekeepers in several ways: They determined admissions to professional and managerial training schools; they controlled recruitment to and from such schools; and they determined promotion policies. With the advent of affirmative action in the United States, many women have become doctors, lawyers, scientists, and administrators, and they have become formidable competition for men. The "mommy track" keeps women professionals and managers in lower-paid, lower-prestige ranks. This exclusion from top-level positions is considered legitimate because they are mothers. The assumption is that women could not possibly handle the responsibility of leadership and the responsibility for their children's welfare at the same time, but they are never given the chance to try. It is also taken for granted that mothers, never fathers, will supervise their children's day-to-day care. "Mommy tracks" thus reinforce and legitimate the structural glass ceiling, the processes of exclusion, and the justifying stereotypes.

Paradoxically, "mommy tracks" are not the way most married women professionals and executives with children organize their careers. Such women order their lives so they can be productive. Jonathan Cole and Harriet Zuckerman's interviews with seventy-three women and forty-seven men scientists, eminent and rank and file, who received their doctorates between 1920 and 1979 found little difference in the rates and patterns of publication of the men and women, the married and single women, and the childless women and those with children (1991). A woman with an endowed chair in a major department of behavioral science was married four times, divorced three times, and had four children by three different husbands, but the largest dip in her publication rate came in a year when there were no changes in her personal life (167). The rate of publication for all these scientists depended on stage of career, extent of collaboration, and the completion of projects. The women they interviewed were successful scientists as well as wives and mothers not because of a "mommy track" but because they carefully timed both marriage and childbearing, had child care and household help, and cut out leisure-time activities that had no professional payoff.

When women put their families before their careers, they are often responding to a generalized cultural mandate that is mediated through direct pressures from their husbands at home and other women's husbands in the workplace. These men, according to Mirra Komarovsky, have inconsistent ideas about their women peers:

> Some of the revealed inconsistencies are: . . . the right of an able woman to a career of her choice; the admiration for women who measure up in terms of the dominant values of our society; the lure but also the threat that such women present; the low status attached to housewifery but the conviction that there is no substitute for the mother's care of young children; the deeply internalized norm of male occupational superiority pitted against the principle of equal opportunity irrespective of sex. (1976, 37)

These inconsistencies are resolved by rewarding men's efforts to move up in their careers but not rewarding women's efforts, and both rewarding and punishing women for taking care of their families—rewarding them as women and punishing them as professionals, managers, and politicians. Should any woman not make the appropriate "choice" to put her family before her career, both she and her husband often face subtle and not-so-subtle harassment from their men colleagues. African-American women and men may have more egalitarian norms and expectations about women's ambitions, but these women face discrimination from white men on two counts and may be competing with African-American men for the same few "minority" positions (Fulbright 1987). Women may feel it is their choice to stay home with their small children and to limit their career commitments, but their choices are constrained by real and direct social pressures.

THE SALIERI PHENOMENON AND THE MATTHEW EFFECT

What happens when women can't be excluded from the workplace and don't choose to put family before career, but instead become men's competitors? The unspoken practices of the informal organization of work make women particularly vulnerable to the covert undercutting I have called the *Salieri phenomenon,* after the highly placed composer who allegedly sabotaged Mozart's career. In Peter Shaffer's play *Amadeus,* Salieri never openly criticized Mozart to the emperor who employs both of them; he simply fails to recommend him enthusiastically. Salieri also suggests that Mozart be paid much less than the musician he is replacing. Mozart later thanks Salieri for his help in getting a position; he blames the emperor for the low salary. Salieri's damning with faint praise is one way women are undermined by their men colleagues and bosses, often without being aware of it.

Nijole Benokraitis and Joe Feagin (1986) describe other ways men subtly undercut women: *condescending chivalry,* where a boss protects a woman employee from what could be useful criticism; *supportive discouragement,* where a woman is not encouraged to compete for a challenging position because she might not make it; *friendly harassment,* such as being joshed in public when visibly pregnant or dressed for a social occasion; *subjective objectification,* or being grouped with "all women"; *radiant devaluation,* when a woman is given extravagant praise for doing what is considered routine when men do it—the "dancing dog" effect; *liberated sexism,* such as inviting a woman for an after-work drink but not letting her pay for a round; *benevolent exploitation,* where a woman is given all the detail work so she can learn the job, but a man takes credit for the final product; *considerate domination,* such as deciding what responsibilities a married woman can and cannot handle, instead of letting her determine how she wants to organize her time; and *collegial exclusion,* thoughtlessly scheduling networking meetings for times women are likely to have family responsibilities. These practices undermine a woman's reputation for competence in the eyes of others and her abilities in her own eyes, making it less likely that she will be visible to gatekeepers or considered a legitimate competitor for a position of power.

Once out of the fast track for advancement, it is very difficult to accrue the necessary resources to perform valued professional activities. Those who have access to personnel, work space, and money have the opportunity to do the kind of work that increases their reputation, brings the approval of superiors, and garners additional rewards and promotions. The circular proliferation of prestige, resources, and power is the *Matthew effect.* As attributed to Christ in the Gospel according to Matthew, those who have faith become more and more favored and those who do not sink lower and lower: "For whosoever hath, to him shall be given, and he shall have more abundance: but whosoever hath not, from him shall be taken away even that he hath." (Bible, King James version, 25:29).

The Matthew effect in science was first described by Robert Merton (1968) and Harriet Zuckerman (1977) to explain the "halo" that winning the Nobel Prize confers. The process of accumulating advantages in science, however, starts with the scientist's working at a prestigious university or laboratory that encourages the kind of research and productivity that wins Nobel Prizes. Women scientists are disadvantaged by positions that give them fewer resources and less encouragement to do high-quality work and by a lesser payoff for their achievements in recognition, rewards, and additional resources. Citations of published papers by others in a field are a form of visibility that adds to the researcher's or scholar's reputation. According to Marianne Ferber (1986, 1988), women tend to cite other women more than men cite women, and the fewer women in a field, the greater the citations gap. As a result of the accumulation of disadvantages, women often have stop-and-go careers that may start out well, but then founder.

Two brilliant twentieth-century women scientists who were loners had totally different fates that had little to do with the value of their scientific work. One of them, Rosalind Franklin, was a well-born Jewish woman scientist who launched a productive career in England in the 1950s. Her crucial contribution to the discovery of the double-helix structure of DNA was minimally acknowledged in the initial announcement by James Watson and Francis Crick in 1953. She herself was denigrated by Watson in his widely read book, *The Double Helix* (1968). His description of her and her work is a classic example of the Salieri phenomenon: "Rosy . . . spoke to an audience of about fifteen in a quick, nervous style. . . . There was not a trace of warmth or frivolity in her words. And yet I could not regard her as totally uninteresting. Momentarily I wondered how she would look if she took off her glasses and did something novel with her hair. Then, however, my main concern was her description of the crystalline X-ray diffraction pattern" (68–69). What Franklin was describing was nothing less than a clear X-ray picture of the DNA molecule that actually showed its helical structure! Watson paid little attention to what she had reported for over a year. Working alone, Franklin tried to envisage the three-dimensional structure her photographs of DNA suggested; she alternately played with and rejected a helical model. Watson subsequently was shown her best picture without her knowledge by the man who ran the laboratory she worked in, Maurice Wilkins; to Watson, "the pattern shouted helix" (Judson 1979, 135).

Wilkins could have been the collaborator Franklin needed to help her make an inductive leap, but according to Franklin's biographer, they "hated one another at sight. . . . Only too evidently the antipathy was instant and mutual" (Sayre 1975, 95). Horace Freeland Judson calls the conflict between Wilkins and Franklin "one of the great personal quarrels in the history of science" (1979, 101), noting but underplaying the gendered overtones. Wilkins insisted he hired Franklin to do the X-ray diffractions on DNA; Franklin's friends insisted that she thought she had been given control of the project and "was profoundly angered" by being treated as an assistant rather than a colleague by Wilkins (148). At thirty-one, she was eight years older than Watson and a little younger but "much further along professionally than Crick" (148). Yet Wilkins, Watson, and Crick regularly corresponded, conversed, and ate together (159); Franklin's only associate was a graduate student, and as a woman, "she was denied the fellowship of the luncheon club organized by the senior common room" at King's College, London, where her laboratory was located (148).

Franklin died of cancer in 1958, at the age of thirty-seven; Watson, Crick, and Wilkins were awarded the Nobel Prize in physiology or medicine in 1962. Only in a contrite epilogue to his book, published in 1968, did Watson pay tribute to Franklin:

> The X-ray work she did at King's is increasingly regarded as superb. . . . We both came to appreciate greatly her personal honesty and generosity, realizing years too late the struggles that the intelligent woman faces to be accepted by a scientific world which often regards women as mere diversions from serious thinking. Rosalind's exemplary courage and integrity were apparent to all when, knowing she was mortally ill, she did not complain but continued working on a high level until a few weeks before her death. (225–26)

Another woman scientist, also a loner but luckier because she lived to see her work rewarded with science's highest honor, was Barbara McClintock. She published a landmark paper in 1931 that established the chromosomal basis of genetics and, in 1945, was elected president of the Genetics Society. In the 1950s, the field became dominated by the Watson-Crick model of genetics, in which DNA produces RNA, and RNA produces protein. The research that McClintock published in that decade, which showed that the process was not so straightforward and that genes could "jump," or transpose, was ignored: "In spite of the fact that she had long since established her reputation as an impeccable investigator, few listened, and fewer understood. She was described as 'obscure,' even 'mad'" (Keller 1983, 10).

In 1960, McClintock described the parallels between her own work and that of other scientists, but these scientists did not reciprocate and cite her work. Except for two other women scientists, she was ignored at Cold Spring Harbor Laboratory where she had worked since 1941 (Watson became director in 1968), but she had nowhere else to go. McClintock lived long enough to see "starting new developments in biology that echo many of the findings she described as long as thirty years ago" (Keller 1983, x), and she was awarded the Nobel Prize in medicine in 1983, when she was eighty-one years old. She died on September 2, 1992, at the age of ninety, her work "widely celebrated as prescient" (Kolata 1992b).

The Salieri phenomenon and the Matthew effect are two sides of the same coin. Those who benefit from the Matthew effect receive acknowledgments from their colleagues for good work, which builds their reputation and brings them financial and professional rewards. The work of those subjected to the Salieri phenomenon is not recognized; they do not get credit for good performance, and their careers are stymied. But reputations must be constantly maintained; even those who have built up social credit can lose it, and reversals of fortune are not uncommon. Because women do not have a protective "status shield," they are easy targets for jealous, threatened, or hostile Salieris. Certainly, not all women are future Mozarts, but even those who are may never be heard.

INNER CIRCLES, FRIENDLY COLLEAGUES, AND TOKENS

The discriminatory aspects of the sorting and tracking that occur in every occupation and profession with long career ladders are obscured because colleagues who are not considered for the top jobs are not fired. They simply fail to make it into the inner circle. Colleagues are organized, informally, into three concentric circles—*inner circles, friendly colleagues, and isolated loners.* Power is concentrated and policy is made in inner circles, which are usually homogeneous on gender, race, religion, ethnicity, social class, and education or training. Friendly colleagues usually have some, but not all, of the social characteristics members of the inner circle have. Although they are not totally excluded from the informal colleague network, they are rarely groomed to be part of the inner circle. Women with excellent credentials and work performance in occupations and professions dominated by men tend to end up friendly colleagues if they are of the same race and social class as the men of the inner circle and do similar kinds of work; otherwise, they become loners. Women professionals have formed their own separate colleague groups or professional networks, but many ambitious women do not want to be professionally segregated. They often try to fit in with the men or work on their own and hope that their worth will eventually be recognized by the gatekeepers of their profession or occupation.

Although inner circles tend to be homogeneous on gender, religion, race, ethnicity, education, and class background, a few people with different social characteristics may be accepted if they have a respected sponsor and demonstrate that in all other ways, they are just like the others. They are the true "tokens." They are actively discouraged from bringing more of their kind into the inner circle or from competing for the very top positions in the organization. Tokens usually are eager to fit in and not embarrass their sponsor, so they do not challenge these restrictions or the views, values, or work practices of the inner circle. Indeed, they may outdo the others in upholding the prevailing perspectives and exclusionary practices. That is why token women tend to be "one of the boys."

In order to get support from senior men, a senior woman may end up in the paradoxical position of making a stand for women by proving she is just like a man. A woman physician I interviewed was passed over by one set of gatekeepers in favor of her younger brother for the top position in a hospital department. She went over their heads to more powerful men, who vouched for her "manliness." She said:

> I do give a hoot about titles and I'm enough of a feminist not to let them promote my brother over me. I have put in many years more of service, and I'm a far better dermatologist than my brother. They tried to do this to me because I'm a woman. Those, excuse the French, assholes, said to me, "Do you mind us promoting your brother over you? He needs the honor." And I said, "For the sake of the women who follow after me, I mind." . . . And they said, "Well, if you come to our meetings, we can't tell dirty jokes, and we can't take off our shoes." I said, "Bull to that one. I know just as many dirty jokes as you do, and

> I always take off my shoes." All the board of trustees laughed like hell when they heard about it. They all said, "For God's sake, promote her." Most of them were patients of mine anyway. It's a stupid thing to say to a woman doctor. I don't care for me, but I want to make sure that the next generation gets a fair shake and doesn't get it in the eye. (Lorber 1984, 61–62)

Unfortunately, token junior women cannot afford to be so outspoken.

In 1977, Rosabeth Moss Kanter predicted that as the number of workgroup peers with different characteristics significantly increased, they would lose their token status and characteristics and be better integrated into the group. They would be able to express individual differences and sponsor others with similar social characteristics for leadership positions. When they became almost half of the group, they could become a recognized subgroup, with alternative views and work practices and their own inner circles. Subsequent research on what came to be called the "Kanter hypothesis" showed that as the numbers of women approach 15 percent, paradoxically, they are *more* not less isolated, as she had predicted. They are cut off from organizational information flows, are not able to acquire the loyal subordinates that leaders depend on, and are not central in the organizational structure. Because they lack the protection of a sponsor that tokens have, they may be subject to open and covert harassment. When the occupation is symbolically masculine, such as police work or the military, additional numbers of women rarely break down the interactional barriers, and they continue to be loners. Being few in number, therefore, may result in a more favorable position than a more balanced gender mix, since an increase may be seen as a threat to those in the majority.

Why are men professionals and managers reluctant to allow substantial numbers of women into elite inner circles or to support the ambitions of more than a select few for leadership positions? Competition is one reason. Yet other men are competitors, too. Catholic and Jewish men physicians, once also subject to discriminatory quotas in American medical schools, are more successfully integrated than women into the prestigious ranks of the medical profession. It could be that men feel their profession will "tip" and become feminized if too many women are in high-paid, high-prestige, and high-power positions. Just as one group seems to fear the neighborhood will go down-hill when too many of a devalued group move in, men professionals may be afraid that if too many women become leaders, their profession will become women's work, and the men in it will lose prestige, income, and their control over resources.

People from subordinate social groups do not become half of the work group unless the occupation, profession, or job specialty loses its prestige and power. The leaders, however, tend to stay on and continue to choose successors to the top positions who are like themselves, not like the new people who outnumber them. The men in colleague groups of mostly women and the whites in groups of mostly people of color (at least in the United States) tend to remain the supervisors and administrators. As administrators, dominant white men need to keep productivity high and costs low. If the members of formerly excluded groups can be relegated to the necessary lower-paid and less prestigious jobs (such as primary care in medicine), administrators can keep costs down and use the increasing numbers of white women and women and men of color who are highly trained professionals and managers without disturbing the status quo.

GENDER AND AUTHORITY

Are men so much more acceptable in positions of authority because women "do power" differently? There tend to be two models of women's leadership styles: women are exactly like men, and women are different, but equally competent. How women or men act does not give the whole picture; women's and men's leadership styles are socially constructed in interaction and heavily influenced by the situational context and how others perceive them. If women in positions of authority tend to be more accessible, to grant more autonomy, but also to be more demanding of subordinates to perform well, the reason may be that they are in weaker positions in the organization and have fewer resources. They need subordinates' help but may be unable to reward them with raises or other perks. As a result, they ask more of subordinates but are also more likely to give concessions to those who are loyal to them, which may be perceived as contradictory behavior.

Authority in a woman is granted in a woman-dominated situation, such as nursing, but questioned where authority is defined as a masculine trait, such as in police work or the military. In 1986, 10.4 percent of all uniformed U.S. Army personnel were women, but they have been underrepresented in the higher ranks. In 1988, there were nine women who were one-star generals in the U.S. military, 1.2 percent of the total, and none of higher rank. Women constituted 2 percent of the colonels, 3.5 percent of the lieutenant colonels, and 7.1 percent of other officer ranks. In 1991, a woman, Midshipman Juliane Gallina, was chosen the U.S. Naval Academy's brigade commander, student leader of 4,300 midshipmen. Ironically, her appointment came six months after a survey found that a "considerable segment" of students, faculty, and staff believed women had no place in the Naval Academy.

A woman leader is expected to be empathic, considerate of other's feelings, and attuned to the personal. If she is not, she is likely to be called "abrasive." As the editor of the prestigious *Harvard Business Review,* Rosabeth Moss Kanter has been publicly faulted for her confrontational management style by her associates, even though her predecessor, a man, had similar problems in his first year. Her high status as a Harvard Business School professor, corporate consultant, and author of internationally known books on management did not protect her from open criticism by her colleagues.

On the other hand, a more conciliatory style may be criticized by men and women colleagues as insufficiently authoritative. Despite the increase in women managers in the past twenty years, men and women at all career stages, including undergraduate and graduate business students, stereotype the good manager as "masculine." Nonetheless, there are situations where a nonconfrontational approach is highly appropriate. In medicine and police work, quintessential masculine professions in American society, being able to listen and take the role of the other person may be more productive than a distancing, authoritative stance in eliciting information or deflecting conflict. Conciliation and using the other person's views can be threatening to men in police work who have learned to rely on physical force and to men doctors for whom medical expertise is the ultimate authority.

If the goal for women in men-dominated situations is to be treated as if they were men, they are in a double bind, and so are the men. If the women act like men, they challenge men's "natural" right to positions of power. If the women act like women, they don't belong in a situation where they have to take charge (that is, act like a man). As Susan Ehrlich Martin says of policewomen on patrol: "The more a female partner acts like a police officer, the less she behaves like a woman. On the other hand, the more she behaves like a woman, the less protection she provides, the less adequate she is as a partner—although such behavior preserves the man's sense of masculinity. The way out of the bind is simple: keep women out of patrol work" (1980, 93–94).

PRODUCING "FACE"

All these processes of legitimation and validation that build the reputations of stature and ability needed by a competitor for a position of power and prestige take place in face-to-face interaction. In everyday encounters, people present themselves the way they would like to be responded to—as powerful leaders, cooperative colleagues, deferential underlings, more or less intimate friends, possible sexual partners. The ways people dress, gesture, talk, act, and even show emotion produce social identities, consciously or unconsciously crafted for different arenas and a variety of occasions. Ritual behavior, such as bows and handshakes, and the rules of protocol—who goes through a door first, who sits where, who calls whom by their first name—reproduce status hierarchy or create status equality. Ordinary conversations become covert battle-grounds: Who talks more, who interrupts, whose interests are discussed, who gets sustained attention or short shrift, all indicate who has the social upper hand. Whom one walks with or stands with—or puts space between—demonstrates affiliation, hostility, or respect, as does eye contact, touching, and other forms of "body politics." These "face" productions are such delicate balances of power and deference that they can easily be disrupted by rudeness or embarrassment. Secret stigmas, such as deviant behavior in the past or present, or even by members of one's family or by intimate friends, can contaminate a seemingly upright identity if revealed. In face-to-face interaction, accidental attributes, such as beauty or height, may add to social status, and obvious physical deformities often detract from it.

These presentations of self take place in social contexts, and the responses of others validate, neutralize, deny, or subvert them. Status signals, whether they are verbal or nonverbal, practical or symbolic, can be understood only in the social context and only by people who have learned their meaning. You need to know the symbolic language of everyday social interaction to be able to tell who is the boss and who is the employee, who are friends and who are enemies. Signals can be manipulated to shore up or subvert the status quo, or they can be used deliberately in open resistance or rebellion.

These status productions are part of "doing gender" (or of doing race, ethnicity, religion, or social class). In doing gender, as West and Zimmerman point out, "men are also doing dominance and women are doing deference" (1987, 146). That is, in face-to-face interaction, what is being produced, reinforced, or resisted is the society's whole system of social stratification. This system endows women and men, people of different racial ethnic groups and religions, and those with greater or lesser economic resources with different social worth. Everyday interaction reenacts these power and prestige differences because people with different status characteristics are seen as legitimately superior or inferior by the others in the situation. When people are evaluated highly, the others take what they have to say seriously, follow their suggestions, and defer to their judgment. Those who have low status in the eyes of the others are not listened to, their advice is ignored, and their bids for leadership are simply not acknowledged. Status superiors are granted the benefit of the doubt if they make a mistake; status inferiors have to prove their competence over and over again.

The pattern of structured power and prestige in face-to-face interaction replicates the ranking of social characteristics in the larger society because people are seen not as individuals but as representatives of their race, religion, gender, education, occupation, and so on. If everyone in a group has the same social characteristics, then natural leaders and followers emerge; in a group of friends, there is usually one person who is the ringleader. But when the social characteristics of people in a group differ, the social characteristics have more salience than personal characteristics—the woman who leads other women follows when men are present. The solo man does not dominate in a group of women, but he is listened to more than the solo woman is in a group of men. The size of the group, its status mix, endurance, and purpose determine its structure of power and prestige, but the patterns are constant: Status superiors lead because others feel they have the right to lead; they don't have superior status because they lead. Most of the time, the building up and tearing down of "face" goes unnoticed, but conflicts and confrontations reveal that the vital subtext is the social production of prestige and power.

PRODUCING POWER

The week I started to write this chapter was the week of the U.S. Senate Judiciary Committee hearings on Professor Anita Hill's allegations of sexual harassment by Judge Clarence Thomas, nominee to the Supreme Court. These encounters dramatized status production and destruction, and the interplay of race, class, and gender with evaluations of performance and social worth. They laid bare the social processes of upward mobility, and how these differ for women and men of the same race. "The scalding contest was not only about race and sex, and women and men. It was about power, and who knows how to use it more effectively" (Dowd 1991).

Both Clarence Thomas and Anita Hill are African Americans who were born into poverty and segregation, and both received their law degrees from Yale University, one of the most prestigious law schools in the United States, during a time of nationally approved and implemented affirmative action. They met when they worked together in the administration of President Ronald Reagan. Judge Thomas, then thirty-three years old, was at the Department of Education and then head of the Equal Employment Opportunities Commission (EEOC), the body set up to implement the civil rights laws against discrimination. Professor Hill, then twenty-five years old, worked for Judge Thomas in both organizations for several years.

Professor Hill contended that on and off during this time, at both workplaces, she had been subject to Judge Thomas's repeated requests for dates, as well as descriptions of the sexual acts in pornographic movies he had seen, the size of the breasts and penises of the actors in those movies, the size of his own penis, and his own sexual prowess. She had told few people of the incidents—two women friends, a man she was dating who lived in another city, and the dean at a school considering her for an appointment six or seven years later. They testified before the Judiciary Committee that she had been very upset and uncomfortable talking about it, although she had offered none of the graphic details that she was asked to make public at the reconvened hearings.

Judge Thomas denied the allegations categorically and made his own charges that he was the victim of a particularly ugly brand of racism, the stereotyping of African-American men as nothing more than sexual animals. He called it "high-tech lynching," but it was Anita Hill who was verbally lynched by the senators who supported Judge Thomas. The judge's supporters on the Judiciary Committee accused Professor Hill of being a vindictive scorned woman, the tool of anti-Thomas political interests, a fantasizer, and a schizophrenic. The members of the Judiciary Committee who were against confirming Judge Thomas were circumspect when they questioned him, and rambling and disjointed with his witnesses. They did not ask him anything about what was rumored to be his well-known interest in pornography. They called no experts to testify on sexual harassment, its effects, or common responses, but listened respectfully to the rambling, self-serving account of a man who had met Anita Hill at a large party.

Professor Hill's accusation of sexual harassment by Judge Thomas was called into question because she had followed him from the Department of Education to the EEOC and had kept in touch with him professionally after she left the EEOC for a teaching position, once asking him for a needed reference, once to come to her campus as a speaker, and at other times requesting help for others or materials for seminars and grants. She had telephoned him about ten to fifteen times in the decade after she left Washington, D.C. When he came to speak at the school where she had her first teaching job, she participated in the social events around his visit and drove him to the airport. A witness to their interaction said it was very friendly and relaxed.

Judge Thomas's supporters on the Judiciary Committee said over and over that they could not understand why Anita Hill had followed him from one organization to another after he had harassed her. She said that for several months before he took the new position, he had not engaged in lewd talk or pressured her for dates, and he had started seeing someone seriously. After they both moved to EEOC, she said he harassed her again. His relationship had not worked out, and he was also going through a divorce. Pro-Thomas members of the committee also said they could not understand why she had maintained a cordial professional relationship with him in the ensuing years. One of Professor Hill's witnesses tried to explain why by talking about her own experience, which included "touching," and said that as a Black woman you learn to "grit your teeth and bear it" so that you can get to a position where you do not need the support of your harasser any longer.

Professor Hill said she had followed Thomas to EEOC because she was afraid she could not otherwise find employment commensurate with her credentials and abilities. She had been a corporate lawyer and did not want to return to that sector of law. Although this motivation for continuing a relationship with someone she said had subjected her to disgusting talk was challenged by witnesses for Judge Thomas, the evidence of her career path bears out her restricted opportunities. At the time of the alleged incidents, Professor Hill was an African-American woman professional in her twenties, a graduate of a highly prestigious law school, just beginning her career. The position she went to after she left EEOC was with Oral Roberts University, a small low-status school (now defunct). Judge Thomas was an African-American man in his thirties, appointed by the president to direct a large federal agency. He was being groomed for further appointments in Republican circles and was described by one witness as "a rising star." Professor Hill's continued reliance on Judge Thomas for reference letters, speaking engagements, positions for others, and materials on civil rights enhanced her career and standing at her workplace and in the profession. Despite a high level of professional activities, such as research and attendance at conventions of the American Bar Association, she could not afford to alienate an important professional contact.

The women who testified for Judge Thomas lauded him for his respect for women and the help he gave them; except for one, none was a professional. They called Anita Hill "stridently aggressive," "arrogant," "opinionated," "hard," "tough," "ambitious," and "aloof." They suggested that her motivation was that she resented not being his main assistant at EEOC, as she had been at the Department of Education, or that she "had a crush on him" and was scorned.

As a professional woman, Professor Hill realized too late that Clarence Thomas was more interested in her sexually than professionally and was not going to be helpful in advancing her career at EEOC. She said that he had said when she left EEOC that if she ever talked about what he had done, it would ruin *his* career. She did not talk about it publicly, and in turn, he filled any request from her. She had nothing to gain by going public when she finally did so, and she said she would not have done so had she not been approached by staff of the Judiciary Committee, who had been told of rumors that Judge Thomas had been involved in sexual harassment at EEOC.

The Judiciary Committee was made up of fourteen upper-middle-class white men. The Senate, which had to vote to confirm the nomination, consisted of ninety-eight men, almost all white, and two white women. More of the senators (including the Republican woman) and, according to polls, more of the American people, believed him than her. After a weekend of testimony by Professor Hill and Judge Thomas and witnesses for and against her and for him, and a day of debate in the full Senate, on October 16, 1991, he was confirmed, 52–48, to a lifetime term on the Supreme Court. Professor Hill went back to her teaching job, with applause from her colleagues and students and later awards from professional women's groups.

SEXUAL HARASSMENT AS DISCRIMINATION

Barbara Gutek (1985) found that 67.2 percent of 393 men would be flattered if asked to have sex by a woman coworker, but 62.8 percent of 814 women would be insulted by a sexual invitation from a male colleague (table 1, p. 96). Demands for sexual relations by superiors as the cost of keeping a job or advancing in it is quid pro quo, a long-standing ugly phenomenon of work life for heterosexual and lesbian women of all classes and races, and also for many women college and graduate students. Most people understand the unfairness when someone who needs a job or a grade is subject to unwanted sexual advances, verbal or physical. But sexual talk, gestures, and other behavior inappropriate to a work environment or to a professional or student-teacher relationship also constitute discrimination against the targets. This concept of sexual harassment as discrimination, first advanced by Catharine MacKinnon (1979), was promulgated in EEOC guidelines in 1980 but was not upheld in the courts in this or other countries until the late 1980s.

The concept of harassment as discrimination emerged in the United States when white women and women and men of color were hired in workplaces and accepted in training institutions from which they had been excluded. Women in blue-collar jobs tend to come up against sexual harassment and other forms of interpersonal resistance when they successfully break into white men's work worlds, especially when they are women of color and have low-status jobs. The intent of such harassment is to make work life so unpleasant that the woman will quit. Women who enter formerly all-men managerial or professional schools or workplaces are likely to be subject to sexual innuendoes or remarks about their physical appearance, which are aimed at undercutting their poise and work performance. The aim is to induce them to shrink from visibility and assertiveness, the hallmarks of the person who becomes a leader in a field.

Only recently, and only in a very few instances, have formal complaints or grievances been filed and lawsuits instituted over persistent episodes of sexual harassment of women or of homosexual men. The reason for not making the incidents public is that the accuser is often not supported by colleagues or bosses, and in many cases, the harasser is the boss. When the incidents, such as embarrassing sexual remarks or jokes at meetings, are between peers, they are frequently condoned or at least not halted or criticized by those present. Neither senior men nor women are likely to put a stop to such incidents while they are happening or to chastise the harasser and offer support to the person harassed in private afterward. Those "microinequities" are not considered serious enough for a lawsuit, but "in the daily lives of working women, it is precisely these small, taken-for-granted comments, jokes, and physical acts, each individually unlikely to force a woman to initiate administrative action, that may accumulate in the long-term feeling and experience of harassment" (Schneider 1985, 104).

Recently, feminists have begun to speak of a continuum that runs from *gender harassment,* which is inappropriately calling attention to women's or men's bodies, sexuality, and marital status, to *sexual harassment,* which is turning a professional, work or student-teacher relationship into a sexual relationship *that is not wanted by one of the people involved and that is coercive because the initiator has some power over the other person.* The defining criterion for gender harassment is that the person's gender or sexual persuasion is used to comment on the individual's capabilities or career commitment. The defining criterion for sexual harassment is that the behavior is *inappropriate* for the situation; what should be a gender-neutral situation is turned into an *unwanted* sexual situation, and the initiator or instigator has *power,* which makes it difficult for those subject to the harassment to protest, leave, complain to others, or take action without jeopardy to their own status. The immediate reaction to gender and sexual harassment is likely to be discomfort, anger, feelings of powerlessness, inability to work, or feeling demeaned. These feelings may be suppressed if the person feels he or she has no choice but to continue in the situation or relationship.

Even senior women have faced such continued harassment. Several months before Anita Hill's allegations, a woman neurosurgeon, Dr. Frances K. Conley, a fifty-year-old full professor at Stanford Medical School and head of the Faculty Senate, resigned after sixteen years on the faculty. She said she had been subject to continuous verbal sabotage of her professional status, such as comments on her breasts at meetings and being called "honey" in front of patients. Dr. Conley was the only woman faculty member in neurosurgery and one of two full professors in the department. The other, the acting head of neurosurgery, was going to be made chair of the department. He was the man she said was constantly insulting to her and to other women. Her women colleagues and the women medical students reported the long-standing practice of men physicians' use of pictures of naked women in lectures. If women complained or argued, they were labeled "premenstrual." Women medical students have always been subject to sexist practices, but women now constitute almost 40 percent of the classes in the United States. Rather than abating, gender and sexual harassment as a means of curbing the ambitions of women has persisted as the number of women in medicine has increased.

"Speak-out" sessions reveal many incidents of gender and sexual harassment and how situations are differently perceived by women and by men. Neither type of harassment is likely to diminish using only formal methods of complaint and censure because both are so pervasive at every level in every workplace where women and men work together. The best remedy is clear indication from senior men, in a public setting, that *all* women employees, trainees, and students are to be treated *neutrally*—which does not mean coldly and distantly, but in a cordial, friendly, but not sexual manner. Most people do know the difference; they make such distinctions all the time in relating to their friends' spouses, for instance.

It takes a very well-established woman to stand up for her professional status successfully, and she needs the support of senior men. Dr. Conley finally agreed to return to the Stanford Medical School faculty because the administration appointed a task force on discrimination and also set up committees to review claims of sexual harassment. A follow-up interview showed that her actions paid off. Mary Roth Walsh (1992) reported that Conley has become the Anita Hill of American medicine, giving speeches all over the country and garnering awards from feminist organizations. Dr. Gerald Silverberg, the chair who had harassed Conley and many other women who were prepared to testify against him, resigned, made a formal apology, and was attending gender sensitivity classes and counseling sessions!

Women who live on the economic margins and women at the beginning of their careers cannot be expected to counter the constant sexist commentary that men use to guard the boundaries of what they feel is their turf. Nor can sympathetic men in similar positions. Not much support can be expected from senior men, who often engage in gender and sexual harassment themselves. So it is up to senior women to use whatever power they have for social change. They can no longer remain silent: "Woman must put herself into the text—as into the world and into history—by her own movement" (Cixous 1976, 875).

References

Barkalow, Carol, with Andrea Raab. 1990. *In the men's house.* New York: Poseidon Press.

Benokraitis, Nijole V., and Joe R. Feagin. 1986. *Modern sexism: Blatant, subtle, and covert discrimination.* Englewood Cliffs, N.J.: Prentice-Hall.

Cantor, Dorothy W., and Toni Bernay with Jean Stoess. 1992. *Women in power: The secrets of leadership.* Boston: Houghton Mifflin.

Cixous, Hélène. 1976. The laugh of the Medusa, translated by Keith Cohen and Paula Cohen. *Signs* 1:875–93.

Cole, Jonathan R., and Harriet Zuckerman. 1991. Marriage, motherhood, and re-research performance in science. In *The outer circle: Women in the scientific community,* edited by Harriet Zuckerman, Jonathan R. Cole, and John T. Bruer. New York: Norton.

Crenshaw, Kimberlé. 1991. Demarginalizing the intersection of race and sex: A Black feminist critique of antidiscrimination doctrine, feminist theory, and antiracist politics. In *Feminist legal theory: Readings in law and gender,* edited by Katharine T. Bartlett and Rosanne Kennedy. Boulder, Colo: Westview Press.

Davidoff, Leonore, and Catherine Hall. 1987. *Family fortunes: Men and women of the English middle class,* 1780–1850. Chicago: University of Chicago Press.

Dowd, Maureen. 1991. Image more than reality became issue, losers say. *New York Times,* 16 October.

Farr, Kathryn Ann. 1988. Dominance bonding through the good old boys sociability group. *Sex Roles* 18:259–77.

Ferber, Marianne A. 1986. Citations: Are they an objective measure of scholarly merit? *Signs* 11:381–89.

———. 1988. Citations and networking. *Gender & Society* 2:82–89.

Fulbright, Karen. 1987. The myth of the double-advantage: Black female managers. *In Slipping through the cracks: The status of Black women,* edited by Margaret C. Simms and Julianne Malveaux. New Brunswick, N.J.: Transaction Books.

Goldin, Claudia. 1990. *Understanding the gender gap: An economic history of American women.* New York: Oxford University Press.

Gutek, Barbara A. 1985. *Sex and the workplace: The impact of sexual behavior and harassment on women, men, and organizations.* San Francisco: Jossey-Bass.

Hennig, Margaret, and Anne Jardin. 1976. *The managerial woman.* New York: Pocket Books.

Hughes, Everett C. 1971. *The sociological eye.* Chicago: Aldine-Atherton.

Judson, Horace Freeland. 1979. *The eighth day of creation: The makers of the revolution in biology.* New York: Simon & Schuster.

Kanter, Rosabeth Moss. 1977. *Men and women of the corporation.* New York: Basic Books.

Keller, Evelyn Fox. *A feeling for the organism: The life and work of Barbara McClintock.* New York: W. H. Freeman.

Kessler-Harris, Alice. 1982. *Out to work: A history of wage-earning women in the United States.* New York: Oxford University Press.

Kolata, Gina. 1992. Dr. Barbara McClintock, 90, gene research pioneer, dies. *New York Times,* 4 September.

Komarovsky, Mirra. 1976. *Dilemmas of masculinity: A study of college youth.* New York: Norton.

Lipman-Blumen, Jean. 1976. Toward a homosocial theory of sex roles: An explanation of sex segregation in social institutions. *Signs* 1 (Spring, pt. 2): 15–31.

Lorber, Judith. 1984. *Women physicians: Careers, status, and power.* London and New York: Tavistock.

MacKinnon, Catharine A. 1979. *Sexual harassment of working women.* New Haven: Yale University Press.

Martin, Lynn. 1991. *A report on the glass ceiling initiative.* Washington, D.C.: U.S. Department of Labor.

Martin, Susan Ehrlich. 1980. *Breaking and entering: Police women on patrol. Berkeley:* University of California Press.

Merton, Robert K. 1968. The Matthew effect in science. *Science* 159:56–63.

Pogrebin, Letty Cottin. 1987. *Among friends: Who we like, why we like them and what we do with them.* New York: McGraw-Hill.

Sayre, Anne. 1975. *Rosalind Franklin and DNA.* New York: Norton.

Schneider, Beth E. 1985. Approaches, assaults, attractions, affairs: Policy implications of the sexualization of the workplace. *Population Research and Policy Review* 4:93–113.

Steinem, Gloria. 1992. Seeking out the invisible woman. *New York Times,* Arts and Leisure Section, 13 March.

Walsh, Mary Roth. 1992. Before and after Frances Conley. *Journal of the American Medical Women's Association* 48:119–21.

Watson, James D. 1968. *The double helix: A personal account of the discovery of the structure of DNA.* New York: Atheneum.

West, Candace, and Don Zimmerman. 1987. Doing gender. *Gender & Society* 1:125–51.

Williams, Christine L. 1992. The glass escalator: Hidden advantages for men in the "female" professions. *Social Problems* 39:253–67.

Zuckerman, Harriet. 1977. *Scientific elite: Nobel laureates in the United States.* New York: Free Press.

CHRISTINE L. WILLIAMS

The Glass Escalator: Hidden Advantages for Men in the "Female" Professions

The sex segregation of the U.S. labor force is one of the most perplexing and tenacious problems in our society. Even though the proportion of men and women in the labor force is approaching parity (particularly for younger cohorts of workers), men and women are still generally confined to predominantly single-sex occupations. Forty percent of men or women would have to change major occupational categories to achieve equal representation of men and women in all jobs, but even this figure underestimates the true degree of sex segregation. It is extremely rare to find specific jobs where equal numbers of men and women are engaged in the same activities in the same industries.

Most studies of sex segregation in the work force have focused on women's experiences in male-dominated occupations. Both researchers and advocates for social change have focused on the barriers faced by women who try to integrate predominantly male fields. Few have looked at the "flip-side" of occupational sex segregation: the exclusion of men from predominantly female occupations. But the fact is that men are less likely to enter female sex-typed occupations than women are to enter male-dominated jobs. Reskin and Roos, for example, were able to identify 33 occupations in which female representation increased by more than nine percentage points between 1970 and 1980, but only three occupations in which the proportion of men increased as radically (1990).

In this paper, I examine men's underrepresentation in four predominantly female occupations—nursing, librarianship, elementary school teaching, and social work. Throughout the twentieth century, these occupations have been identified with "women's work"—even though prior to the Civil War, men were more likely to be employed in these areas. These four occupations, often called the female "semi-professions," today range from 5.5 percent male (in nursing) to 32 percent male (in social work). (See Table 1.) These percentages have not changed substantially in decades. In fact, as Table 1 indicates, two of these professions—librarianship and social work—have experienced declines in the proportions of men since 1975. Nursing is the only one of the four experiencing noticeable changes in sex

From *Social Problems*, Vol. 39, no. 3 (August 1992), pp. 253–267. References have been edited.

Table 1.
Percent Male in Selected Occupations, Selected Years

Profession	1990	1980	1975
Nurses	5.5	3.5	3.0
Elementary teachers	14.8	16.3	14.6
Librarians	16.7	14.8	18.9
Social workers	31.8	35.0	39.2

Source: U.S. Department of Labor. Bureau of Labor Statistics. *Employment and Earnings* 38:1 (January 1991), Table 22 (Employed civilians by detailed occupation), 185; 28:1 (January 1981), Table 23 (Employed persons by detailed occupation), 180; 22:7 (January 1976), Table 2 (Employed persons by detailed occupation), 11.

composition, with the proportion of men increasing 80 percent between 1975 and 1990. Even so, men continue to be a tiny minority of all nurses.

Although there are many possible reasons for the continuing preponderance of women in these fields, the focus of this paper is discrimination. Researchers examining the integration of women into "male fields" have identified discrimination as a major barrier to women. This discrimination has taken the form of laws or institutionalized rules prohibiting the hiring or promotion of women into certain job specialties. Discrimination can also be "informal," as when women encounter sexual harassment, sabotage, or other forms of hostility from their male co-workers resulting in a poisoned work environment. Women in nontraditional occupations also report feeling stigmatized by clients when their work puts them in contact with the public. In particular, women in engineering and blue-collar occupations encounter gender-based stereotypes about their competence which undermine their work performance. Each of these forms of discrimination—legal, informal, and cultural—contributes to women's underrepresentation in predominantly male occupations.

The assumption in much of this literature is that any member of a token group in a work setting will probably experience similar discriminatory treatment. Kanter (1977), who is best known for articulating this perspective in her theory of tokenism, argues that when any group represents less than 15 percent of an organization, its members will be subject to predictable forms of discrimination. Likewise, Jacobs argues that "in some ways, men in female-dominated occupations experience the same difficulties that women in male-dominated occupations face" (1989:167), and Reskin contends that any dominant group in an occupation will use their power to maintain a privileged position (1988:62).

However, the few studies that have considered men's experience in gender atypical occupations suggest that men may not face discrimination or prejudice when they integrate predominantly female occupations. Zimmer (1988) and Martin (1988) both contend that the effects of sexism can outweigh the effects of tokenism when men enter nontraditional occupations. This study is the first to systematically explore this question using data from four occupations. I examine the barriers to men's entry into these professions; the support men receive from their supervisors, colleagues and clients; and the reactions they encounter from the public (those outside their professions).

METHODS

I conducted in-depth interviews with 76 men and 23 women in four occupations from 1985–1991. Interviews were conducted in four metropolitan areas: San Francisco/Oakland, California; Austin, Texas; Boston, Massachusetts; and Phoenix, Arizona. These four areas were selected because they show considerable variation in the proportions of men in the four professions. For example, Austin has one of the highest percentages of men in nursing (7.7 percent), whereas Phoenix's percentage is one of the lowest (2.7 percent). The sample was generated using "snowballing" techniques. Women were included in the sample to gauge their feelings and responses to men who enter "their" professions.

Like the people employed in these professions generally, those in my sample were predominantly white (90 percent). Their ages ranged from 20 to 66 and the average age was 38. The interview questionnaire consisted of several open-ended questions on four broad topics: motivation to enter the profession; experiences in training; career progression; and general views about men's status and prospects within these occupations. I conducted all the interviews, which generally lasted between one and two hours. Interviews took place in restaurants, my home or office, or the respondent's home or office. Interviews were tape-recorded and transcribed for the analysis.

Data analysis followed the coding techniques described by Strauss (1987). Each transcript was read several times and analyzed into emergent conceptual categories. Likewise, Strauss' principle of theoretical sampling was used. Individual respondents were purposively selected to capture the array of men's experiences in these occupations. Thus, I interviewed practitioners in every specialty, oversampling those employed in the *most* gender atypical areas (e.g., male kindergarten teachers). I also selected respondents from throughout their occupational hierarchies—from students to administrators to retirees. Although the data do not permit within-group comparisons, I am reasonably certain that the sample does capture a wide range of experiences common to men in these female-dominated professions. However, like all findings based on qualitative data, it is uncertain whether the findings generalize to the larger population of men in nontraditional occupations.

In this paper, I review individuals' responses to questions about discrimination in hiring practices, on-the-job rapport with supervisors and co-workers, and prejudice from clients and others outside their profession.

DISCRIMINATION IN HIRING

Contrary to the experience of many women in the male-dominated professions, many of the men and women I spoke to indicated that there is a *preference* for hiring men in these four occupations. A Texas librarian at a junior high school said that his school district "would hire a male over a female."

> *I:* Why do you think that is?
>
> *R:* Because there are so few, and the . . . ones that they do have, the library directors seem to really . . . think they're doing great jobs. I don't know, maybe they just feel they're being progressive or something, [but] I have had a real sense that they really appreciate having a male, particularly at the junior high. . . . As I said, when seven of us lost our jobs from the high schools and were redistributed, there were only four positions at junior high, and I got one of them. Three of the librarians, some who had been here longer than I had with the school district, were put down in elementary school as librarians. And I definitely think that being male made a difference in my being moved to the junior high rather than an elementary school.

Many of the men perceived their token status as males in predominantly female occupations as an *advantage* in hiring and promotions. I asked an Arizona teacher whether his specialty (elementary special education) was an unusual area for men compared to other areas within education. He said,

> Much more so. I am extremely marketable in special education. That's not why I got into the field. But I am extremely marketable because I am a man.

In several cases, the more female-dominated the specialty, the greater the apparent preference for men. For example, when asked if he encountered any problem getting a job in pediatrics, a Massachusetts nurse said,

> No, no, none. . . . I've heard this from managers and supervisory-type people with men in pediatrics: "It's nice to have a man because it's such a female-dominated profession."

However, there were some exceptions to this preference for men in the most female-dominated specialties. In some cases, formal policies actually barred men from certain jobs. This was the case in some rural Texas school districts, which refused to hire men in the youngest grades (K–3). Some nurses also reported being excluded from positions in obstetrics and gynecology wards, a policy encountered more frequently in private Catholic hospitals.

But often the pressures keeping men out of certain specialties were more subtle than this. Some men described being "tracked" into practice areas within their professions which were considered more legitimate for men. For example, one Texas man described how he was pushed into administration and planning in social work, even though "I'm not interested in writing policy; I'm much more interested in research and clinical stuff." A nurse who is interested in pursuing graduate study in family and child health in Boston said he was dissuaded from entering the program specialty in favor of a concentration in "adult nursing." A kindergarten teacher described the difficulty of finding a job in his specialty after graduation: "I was recruited immediately to start getting into a track to become an administrator. And it was men who recruited me. It was men that ran the system at that time, especially in Los Angeles."

This tracking may bar men from the most female-identified specialties within these professions. But men are effectively being "kicked upstairs" in the process. Those specialties considered more legitimate practice areas for men also tend to be the most prestigious, better paying ones. A distinguished kindergarten teacher, who had been voted city-wide "Teacher of the Year," told me that even though people were pleased to see him in the classroom, "there's been some encouragement to think about administration, and there's been some encouragement to think about teaching at the university level or something like that, or supervisory-type position." That is, despite his aptitude and interest in staying in the classroom, he felt pushed in the direction of administration.

The effect of this "tracking" is the opposite of that experienced by women in male-dominated occupations. Researchers have reported that many women encounter a "glass ceiling" in their efforts to scale organizational and professional hierarchies. That is, they are constrained by invisible barriers to promotion in their careers, caused mainly by sexist attitudes of men in the highest positions (Freeman 1990). In contrast to the "glass ceiling," many of the men I interviewed seem to encounter a "glass escalator." Often, despite their intentions, they face invisible pressures to move up in their professions. As if on a moving escalator, they must work to stay in place.

A public librarian specializing in children's collections (a heavily female-dominated concentration) described an encounter with this "escalator" in his very first job out of library school. In his first six-months' evaluation, his supervisors commended him for his good work in storytelling and related activities, but they criticized him for "not shooting high enough."

> Seriously. That's literally what they were telling me. They assumed that because I was a male—and they told me this—and that I was being hired right out of graduate school, that somehow I wasn't doing the kind of management-oriented work that they thought I should be doing. And as a result, really they had a lot of bad marks, as it were, against me on my evaluation. And I said I couldn't believe this!

Throughout his ten-year career, he has had to struggle to remain in children's collections.

The glass escalator does not operate at all levels. In particular, men in academia reported some gender-based discrimination in the highest positions due to their universities' commitment to affirmative action. Two nursing professors reported that they felt their own chances of promotion to deanships were nil because their universities viewed the position of nursing dean as a guaranteed female appointment in an otherwise heavily male-dominated administration. One California social work professor reported his university canceled its search for a dean because no minority male or female candidates had been placed on their short list. It was rumored that other schools on campus were permitted to go forward with their searches—even though they also failed to put forward names of minority candidates—because the higher administration perceived it to be "easier" to fulfill affirmative action goals in the social work school. The interviews provide greater evidence of the "glass escalator" at work in the lower levels of these professions.

Of course, men's motivations also play a role in their advancement to higher professional positions. I do not mean to suggest that the men I talked to all resented the informal tracking they experienced. For many men, leaving the most female-identified areas of their professions helped them resolve internal conflicts involving their masculinity. One man left his job as a school social worker to work in a methadone drug treatment program not because he was encouraged to leave by his colleagues, but because "I think there was some macho shit there, to tell you the truth, because I remember feeling a little uncomfortable there . . .; it didn't feel right to me." Another social worker, employed in the mental health services department of a large urban area in California, reflected on his move into administration:

> The more I think about it, through our discussion, I'm sure that's a large part of why I wound up in administration. It's okay for a man to do the administration. In fact, I don't know if I fully answered a question that you asked a little while ago about how did being male contribute to my advancing in the field. I was saying it wasn't because I got any special favoritism as a man, but . . . I think . . . because I'm a man, I felt a need to get into this kind of position. I may have worked harder toward it, may have competed harder for it, than most women would do, even women who think about doing administrative work.

Elsewhere I have speculated on the origins of men's tendency to define masculinity through single-sex work environments. Clearly, personal ambition does play a role in accounting for men's movement into more "male-defined" arenas within these professions. But these occupations also structure opportunities for males independent of their individual desires or motives.

The interviews suggest that men's under-representation in these professions cannot be attributed to discrimination in hiring or promotions. Many of the men indicated that they received preferential treatment because they were men. Although men mentioned gender discrimination in the hiring process, for the most part they were channelled into the more "masculine" specialties within these professions, which ironically meant being "tracked" into better paying and more prestigious specialties.

SUPERVISORS AND COLLEAGUES: THE WORKING ENVIRONMENT

Researchers claim that subtle forms of work place discrimination push women out of male-dominated occupations. In particular, women report feeling excluded from informal leadership and decision-making networks, and they sense hostility from their male co-workers, which makes them feel uncomfortable and unwanted. Respondents in this study were asked about their relationships with supervisors and female colleagues to ascertain whether men also experienced "poisoned" work environments when entering gender atypical occupations.

A major difference in the experience of men and women in nontraditional occupations is that men in these situations are far more likely to be supervised by a member of their own sex. In each of the four professions I studied, men are overrepresented in administrative and managerial capacities, or, as in the case of nursing, their positions in the organizational hierarchy are governed by men. Thus, unlike women who enter "male fields," the men in these professions often work under the direct supervision of other men.

Many of the men interviewed reported that they had good rapport with their male supervisors. Even in professional school, some men reported extremely close relationships with their male professors. For example, a Texas librarian described an unusually intimate association with two male professors in graduate school:

> I can remember a lot of times in the classroom there would be discussions about a particular topic or issue, and the conversation would spill over into their office hours, after the class was over. And even though there were . . . a couple of the other women that had been in on the discussion, they weren't there. And I don't know if that was preferential or not . . . it certainly carried over into personal life as well. Not just at the school and that sort of thing. I mean, we would get together for dinner . . .

These professors explicitly encouraged him because he was male:

> *I:* Did they ever offer you explicit words of encouragement about being in the profession by virtue of the fact that you were male? . . .
>
> *R:* Definitely. On several occasions. Yeah. Both of these guys, for sure, including the Dean who was male also. And it's an interesting point that you bring up because it was, oftentimes, kind of in a sign, you know. It wasn't in the classroom, and it wasn't in front of the group, or if we were in the student lounge or something like that. It was . . . if it was just myself or maybe another one of the guys, you know, and just talking in the office. It's like . . . you know, kind of an opening-up and saying, "You know, you are really lucky that you're in the profession because you'll really go to the top real quick, and you'll be able to make real definite improvements and changes. And you'll have a real influence," and all this sort of thing. I mean, really, I can remember several times.

Other men reported similar closeness with their professors. A Texas psychotherapist recalled his relationships with his male professors in social work school:

> I made it a point to make a golfing buddy with one of the guys that was in administration. He and I played golf a lot. He was the guy who kind of ran the research training, the research part of the master's program. Then there was a sociologist who ran the other part of the research program. He and I developed a good friendship.

This close mentoring by male professors contrasts with the reported experience of women in nontraditional occupations. Others have noted a lack of solidarity among women in nontraditional occupations. Writing about military academies, for example, Yoder describes the failure of token women to mentor succeeding generations of female cadets. She argues that women attempt to play down their gender difference from men because it is the source of scorn and derision.

> Because women felt unaccepted by their male colleagues, one of the last things they wanted to do was to emphasize their gender. Some women thought that, if they kept company with other women, this would highlight their gender and would further isolate them from male cadets. These women desperately wanted to be accepted as cadets, not as *women* cadets. Therefore, they did everything from not wearing skirts as an option with their uniforms to avoiding being a part of a group of women. (Yoder 1989:532)

Men in nontraditional occupations face a different scenario—their gender is construed as a *positive* difference. Therefore, they have an incentive to bond together and emphasize their distinctiveness from the female majority.

Close, personal ties with male supervisors were also described by men once they were established in their professional careers. It was not uncommon in education, for example, for the male principal to informally socialize with the male staff, as a Texas special education teacher describes:

> Occasionally I've had a principal who would regard me as "the other man on the campus" and "it's us against them," you know? I mean, nothing really that extreme, except that some male principals feel like there's nobody there to talk to except the other man. So I've been in that position.

These personal ties can have important consequences for men's careers. For example, one California nurse, whose performance was judged marginal by his nursing supervisors, was transferred to the emergency room staff (a prestigious promotion) due to his personal friendship with the physician in charge. A Massachusetts teacher acknowledged that his principal's personal interest in him landed him his current job.

> *I:* You had mentioned that your principal had sort of spotted you at your previous job and had wanted to bring you here [to this

school]. Do you think that has anything to do with the fact that you're a man, aside from your skills as a teacher?

R: Yes, I would say in that particular case, that was part of it. . . . We have certain things in common, certain interests that really lined up.

I: Vis-à-vis teaching?

R: Well, more extraneous things—running specifically, and music. And we just seemed to get along real well right off the bat. It is just kind of a guy thing; we just liked each other . . .

Interviewees did not report many instances of male supervisors discriminating against them, or refusing to accept them because they were male. Indeed, these men were much more likely to report that their male bosses discriminated against the *females* in their professions. When asked if he thought physicians treated male and female nurses differently, a Texas nurse said:

> I think yeah, some of them do. I think the women seem like they have a lot more trouble with the physicians treating them in a derogatory manner. Or, if not derogatory, then in a very paternalistic way than the men [are treated]. Usually if a physician is mad at a male nurse, he just kind of yells at him. Kind of like an employee. And if they're mad at a female nurse, rather than treat them on an equal basis, in terms of just letting their anger out at them as an employee, they're more paternalistic or there's some sexual harassment component to it.

A Texas teacher perceived a similar situation where he worked:

> I've never felt unjustly treated by a principal because I'm a male. The principals that I've seen that I felt are doing things that are kind of arbitrary or not well thought out are doing it to everybody. In fact, they're probably doing it to the females worse than they are to me.

Openly gay men may encounter less favorable treatment at the hands of their supervisors. For example, a nurse in Texas stated that one of the physicians he worked with preferred to staff the operating room with male nurses exclusively—as long as they weren't gay. Stigma associated with homosexuality leads some men to enhance, or even exaggerate their "masculine" qualities, and may be another factor pushing men into more "acceptable" specialties for men.

Not all men who work in these occupations are supervised by men. Many of the men interviewed who had female bosses also reported high levels of acceptance—although levels of intimacy with women seemed lower than with other men. In some cases, however, men reported feeling shut-out from decision making when the higher administration was constituted entirely by women. I asked an Arizona librarian whether men in the library profession were discriminated against in hiring because of their sex:

> Professionally speaking, people go to considerable lengths to keep that kind of thing out of their [hiring] deliberations. Personally, is another matter. It's pretty common around here to talk about the "old girl network." This is one of the few libraries that I've had any intimate knowledge of which is actually controlled by women. . . . Most of the department heads and upper level administrators are women. And there's an "old girl network" that works just like the "old boy network," except that the important conferences take place in the women's room rather than on the golf course. But the political mechanism is the same, the exclusion of the other sex from decision making is the same. The reasons are the same. It's somewhat discouraging. . . .

Although I did not interview many supervisors, I did include 23 women in my sample to ascertain their perspectives about the presence of men in their professions. All of the women I interviewed claimed to be supportive of their male colleagues, but some conveyed ambivalence. For example, a social work professor said she would like to see more men enter the social work profession, particularly in the clinical specialty (where they are underrepresented). Indeed, she favored affirmative action hiring guidelines for men in the profession. Yet, she resented the fact that her department hired "another white male" during a recent search. I questioned her about this ambivalence:

> *I:* I find it very interesting that, on the one hand, you sort of perceive this preference and perhaps even sexism with regard to how men are evaluated and how they achieve higher positions within the profession, yet, on the other hand, you would be encouraging of more men to enter the field. Is that contradictory to you, or . . .?
>
> *R:* Yeah, it's contradictory.

It appears that women are generally eager to see men enter "their" occupations. Indeed, several men noted that their female colleagues had facilitated their careers in various ways (including mentorship in college). However, at the same time, women often resent the apparent ease with which men advance within these professions, sensing that men at the higher levels receive preferential treatment which closes off advancement opportunities for women.

But this ambivalence does not seem to translate into the "poisoned" work environment described by many women who work in male-dominated occupations. Among the male interviewees, there were no accounts of sexual harassment. However, women do treat their male colleagues differently on occasion. It is not uncommon in nursing, for example, for men to be called upon to help catheterize male patients, or to lift especially heavy patients. Some librarians also said that women asked them to lift and move heavy boxes of books because they were men.

Teachers sometimes confront differential treatment as well, as described by this Texas teacher:

> As a man, you're teaching with all women, and that can be hard sometimes. Just because of the stereotypes, you know. I'm real into computers . . . and all the time people are calling me to fix their computer. Or if somebody gets a flat tire, they come and get me. I mean, there are just a lot of stereotypes. Not that I mind doing any of those things, but it's . . . you know, it just kind of bugs me that it is a stereotype, "A man should do that." Or if their kids have a lot of discipline problems, that kiddo's in your room. Or if there are kids that don't have a father in their home, that kid's in your room. Hell, nowadays that'd be half the school in my room (laughs). But you know, all the time I hear from the principal or from other teachers, "Well, this child really needs a man . . . a male role model" (laughs). So there are a lot of stereotypes that . . . men kind of get stuck with.

This special treatment bothered some respondents. Getting assigned all the "discipline problems" can make for difficult working conditions, for example. But many men claimed this differential treatment did not cause distress. In fact, several said they liked being appreciated for the special traits and abilities (such as strength) they could contribute to their professions.

Furthermore, women's special treatment sometimes enhanced—rather than poisoned—the men's work environments. One Texas librarian said he felt "more comfortable working with women than men" because "I think it has something to do with control. Maybe it's that women will let me take control more than men will." Several men reported that their female colleagues often cast them into leadership roles. Although not all savored this distinction, it did enhance their authority and control in the work place. In subtle (and not-too-subtle) ways, then, differential treatment contributes to the "glass escalator" men experience in nontraditional professions.

Even outside work, most of the men interviewed said they felt fully accepted by their female colleagues. They were usually included in informal socializing occasions with the women—even though this frequently meant attending baby showers or Tupperware parties. Many said that they declined offers to attend these events because they were not interested in "women's things," although several others claimed to attend everything: The minority men I interviewed seemed to feel the least comfortable in these informal contexts. One social worker in Arizona was asked about socializing with his female colleagues:

> *I:* So in general, for example, if all the employees were going to get together to have a party, or celebrate a bridal shower or whatever, would you be invited along with the rest of the group?
>
> *R:* They would invite me, I would say, somewhat reluctantly. Being a black male, working with all white females, it did cause some outside problems. So I didn't go to a lot of functions with them . . .

I: You felt that there was some tension there on the level of your acceptance . . .?

R: Yeah. It was OK working, but on the outside, personally, there was some tension there. It never came out, that they said, "Because of who you are we can't invite you" (laughs), and I wouldn't have done anything anyway. I would have probably respected them more for saying what was on their minds. But I never felt completely in with the group.

Some single men also said they felt uncomfortable socializing with married female colleagues because it gave the "wrong impression." But in general, the men said that they felt very comfortable around their colleagues and described their work places as very congenial for men. It appears unlikely, therefore, that men's under-representation in these professions is due to hostility towards men on the part of supervisors or women workers.

DISCRIMINATION FROM "OUTSIDERS"

The most compelling evidence of discrimination against men in these professions is related to their dealings with the public. Men often encounter negative stereotypes when they come into contact with clients or "outsiders"—people they meet outside of work. For instance, it is popularly assumed that male nurses are gay. Librarians encounter images of themselves as "wimpy" and asexual. Male social workers describe being typecast as "feminine" and "passive." Elementary school teachers are often confronted by suspicions that they are pedophiles. One kindergarten teacher described an experience that occurred early in his career which was related to him years afterwards by his principal:

> He indicated to me that parents had come to him and indicated to him that they had a problem with the fact that I was a male. . . . I recall almost exactly what he said. There were three specific concerns that the parents had: One parent said, "How can he love my child; he's a man." The second thing that I recall, he said the parent said, "He has a beard." And the third thing was, "Aren't you concerned about homosexuality?"

Such suspicions often cause men in all four professions to alter their work behavior to guard against sexual abuse charges, particularly in those specialties requiring intimate contact with women and children.

Men are very distressed by these negative stereotypes, which tend to undermine their self-esteem and to cause them to second-guess their motivations for entering these fields. A California teacher said,

> If I tell men that I don't know, that I'm meeting for the first time, that that's what I do, . . . sometimes there's a look on their faces that, you know, "Oh, couldn't get a real job?"

When asked if his wife, who is also an elementary school teacher, encounters the same kind of prejudice, he said,

> No, it's accepted because she's a woman. . . . I think people would see that as a . . . step up, you know. "Oh, you're not a housewife, you've got a career. That's great . . . that you're out there working. And you have a daughter, but you're still out there working. You decided not to stay home, and you went out there and got a job." Whereas for me, it's more like I'm supposed to be out working anyway, even though I'd rather be home with [my daughter].

Unlike women who enter traditionally male professions, men's movement into these jobs is perceived by the "outside world" as a step down in status. This particular form of discrimination may be most significant in explaining why men are underrepresented in these professions. Men who otherwise might show interest in and aptitudes for such careers are probably discouraged from pursuing them because of the negative popular stereotypes associated with the men who work in them. This is a crucial difference from the experience of women in nontraditional professions: "My daughter, the physician," resonates far more favorably in most people's ears than "My son, the nurse."

Many of the men in my sample identified the stigma of working in a female-identified occupation as the major barrier to more men entering their professions. However, for the most part, they claimed that these negative stereotypes were not a factor in their own decisions to join these occupations. Most respondents didn't consider entering these fields until well into adulthood, after working in some related occupation. Several social workers and librarians even claimed they were not aware that men were a minority in their chosen professions. Either they had no well-defined image or stereotype, or their contacts and mentors were predominantly men. For example, prior to entering library school, many librarians held part-time jobs in university libraries, where there are proportionally more men than in the profession generally. Nurses and elementary school teachers were more aware that mostly women worked in these jobs, and this was often a matter of some concern to them. However, their choices were ultimately legitimized by mentors, or by encouraging friends or family members who implicitly reassured them that entering these occupations would not type-cast them as feminine. In some cases, men were told by recruiters there were special advancement opportunities for men in these fields, and they entered them expecting rapid promotion to administrative positions.

> *I:* Did it ever concern you when you were making the decision to enter nursing school, the fact that it is a female-dominated profession?
>
> *R:* Not really. I never saw myself working on the floor. I saw myself pretty much going into administration, just getting the background and then getting a job someplace as a supervisor and then working, getting up into administration.

Because of the unique circumstances of their recruitment, many of the respondents did not view their occupational choices as inconsistent with a male gender role, and they generally avoided the negative stereotypes directed against men in these fields.

Indeed, many of the men I interviewed claimed that they did not encounter negative professional stereotypes until they had worked in these fields for several years. Popular prejudices can be damaging to self-esteem and probably push some men out of these professions altogether. Yet, ironically, they sometimes contribute to the "glass escalator" effect I have been describing. Men seem to encounter the most vituperative criticism from the public when they are in the most female-identified specialties. Public concerns sometimes result in their being shunted into more "legitimate" positions for men. A librarian formerly in charge of a branch library's children's collection, who now works in the reference department of the city's main library, describes his experience:

R: Some of the people [who frequented the branch library] complained that they didn't want to have a man doing the storytelling scenario. And I got transferred here to the central library in an equivalent job . . . I thought that I did a good job. And I had been told by my supervisor that I was doing a good job.

I: Have you ever considered filing some sort of lawsuit to get that other job back?

R: Well, actually, the job I've gotten now . . . well, it's a reference librarian; it's what I wanted in the first place. I've got a whole lot more authority here. I'm also in charge of the circulation desk. And I've recently been promoted because of my new stature, so . . . no, I'm not considering trying to get that other job back.

The negative stereotypes about men who do "women's work" can push men out of specific jobs. However, to the extent that they channel men into more "legitimate" practice areas, their effects can actually be positive. Instead of being a source of discrimination, these prejudices can add to the "glass escalator effect" by pressuring men to move *out* of the most female-identified areas, and *up* to those regarded more legitimate and prestigious for men.

CONCLUSION: DISCRIMINATION AGAINST MEN

Both men and women who work in nontraditional occupations encounter discrimination, but the forms and consequences of this discrimination are very different. The interviews suggest that unlike "nontraditional" women workers, most of the discrimination and prejudice facing men in the "female professions" emanates from outside those professions. The men and women interviewed for the most part believed that men are given fair—if not preferential—treatment in hiring and promotion decisions, are accepted by supervisors and colleagues, and are well-integrated into the work place subculture. Indeed, subtle mechanisms seem to enhance men's position in these professions—a phenomenon I refer to as the "glass escalator effect."

The data lend strong support for Zimmer's (1988) critique of "gender neutral theory" (such as Kanter's [1977] theory of tokenism) in the study of occupational segregation. Zimmer argues that women's occupational inequality is more a consequence of sexist beliefs and practices embedded in the labor force than the effect of numerical underrepresentation per se. This study suggests that token status itself does not diminish men's occupational success. Men take their gender privilege with them when they enter predominantly female occupations: this translates into an advantage in spite of their numerical rarity.

This study indicates that the experience of tokenism is very different for men and women. Future research should examine how the experience of tokenism varies for members of different races and classes as well. For example, it is likely that informal work place mechanisms similar to the ones identified here promote the careers of token whites in predominantly black occupations. The crucial factor is the social status of the token's group—not their numerical rarity—that determines whether the token encounters a "glass ceiling" or a "glass escalator."

However, this study also found that many men encounter negative stereotypes from persons not directly involved in their professions. Men who enter these professions are often considered "failures," or sexual deviants. These stereotypes may be a major impediment to men who otherwise might consider careers in these occupations. Indeed, they are likely to be important factors whenever a member of a relatively high status group crosses over into a lower status occupation. However, to the extent that these stereotypes contribute to the "glass escalator effect" by channeling men into more "legitimate" (and higher paying) occupations, they are not discriminatory.

Women entering traditionally "male" professions also face negative stereotypes suggesting they are not "real women." However, these stereotypes do not seem to deter women to the same degree that they deter men from pursuing nontraditional professions. There is ample historical evidence that women flock to male-identified occupations once opportunities are available. Not so with men. Examples of occupations changing from predominantly female to predominantly male are very rare in our history. The few existing cases—such as medicine—suggest that redefinition of the occupations as appropriately "masculine" is necessary before men will consider joining them.

Because different mechanisms maintain segregation in male- and female-dominated occupations, different approaches are needed to promote their integration. Policies intended to alter the sex composition of male-dominated occupations—such as affirmative action—make little sense when applied to the "female professions." For men, the major barriers to integration have little to do with their treatment once they decide to enter these fields. Rather, we need to address the social and cultural sanctions applied to men who do "women's work" which keep men from even considering these occupations.

One area where these cultural barriers are clearly evident is in the media's representation of men's occupations. Women working in traditionally male professions have achieved an unprecedented acceptance on popular television shows. Women are portrayed as doctors ("St. Elsewhere"), lawyers ("The Cosby Show," "L.A. Law"), architects ("Family Ties"), and police officers ("Cagney and Lacey"). But where are the male nurses, teachers and secretaries? Television rarely portrays men in nontraditional work roles, and when it does, that anomaly is made the central focus—and joke—of the program. A comedy series (1991–92) about a male elementary school teacher ("Drexell's Class") stars a lead character who *hates children!* Yet even this negative portrayal is exceptional. When a prime time hospital drama series ("St. Elsewhere") depicted a male orderly striving for upward mobility, the show's writers made him a "physician's assistant," not a nurse or nurse practitioner—the much more likely "real life" possibilities.

Presenting positive images of men in nontraditional careers can produce limited effects. A few social workers, for example, were first inspired to pursue their careers by George C. Scott, who played a social worker in the television drama series, "Eastside/Westside." But as a policy strategy to break down occupational segregation, changing media images of men is no panacea. The stereotypes that differentiate masculinity and femininity, and degrade that which is defined as feminine, are deeply entrenched in culture, social structure, and personality. Nothing short of a revolution in cultural definitions of masculinity will effect the broad scale social transformation needed to achieve the complete occupational integration of men and women.

Of course, there are additional factors besides societal prejudice contributing to men's underrepresentation in female-dominated professions. Most notably, those men I interviewed mentioned as a deterrent the fact that these professions are all underpaid relative to comparable "male" occupations, and several suggested that instituting a "comparable worth" policy might attract more men. However, I am not convinced that improved salaries will substantially alter the sex composition of these professions unless the cultural stigma faced by men in these occupations diminishes. Occupational sex segregation is remarkably resilient, even in the face of devastating economic hardship. During the Great Depression of the 1930s, for example, "women's jobs" failed to attract sizable numbers of men. In her study of American Telephone and Telegraph (AT&T) workers, Epstein (1989) found that some men would rather suffer unemployment than accept relatively high paying "women's jobs" because of the damage to their identities this would cause. She quotes one unemployed man who refused to apply for a female-identified telephone operator job:

> I think if they offered me $1000 a week tax free, I wouldn't take that job. When I . . . see those guys sitting in there [in the telephone operating room], I wonder what's wrong with them. Are they pansies or what? (Epstein 1989:577)

This is not to say that raising salaries would not affect the sex composition of these jobs. Rather, I am suggesting that wages are not the only—or perhaps even the major—impediment to men's entry into these jobs. Further research is needed to explore the ideological significance of the "woman's wage" for maintaining occupational stratification.

At any rate, integrating men and women in the labor force requires more than dismantling barriers to women in male-dominated fields. Sex segregation is a two-way street. We must also confront and dismantle the barriers men face in predominantly female occupations. Men's experiences in these nontraditional occupations reveal just how culturally embedded the barriers are, and how far we have to travel before men and women attain true occupational and economic equality.

References

Epstein, Cynthia Fuchs. 1989. "Workplace boundaries: Conceptions and creations." *Social Research* 56: 571–590.

Freeman, Sue J. M. 1990. *Managing Lives: Corporate Women and Social Change.* Amherst, Mass.: University of Massachusetts Press.

Jacobs, Jerry. 1989. *Revolving Doors: Sex Segregation and Women's Careers.* Stanford, Calif.: Stanford University Press.

Kanter, Rosabeth Moss. 1977. *Men and Women of the Corporation.* New York: Basic Books.

Martin, Susan E. 1980. *Breaking and Entering: Police Women on Patrol.* Berkeley, Calif.: University of California Press.

———. 1988. "Think like a man, work like a dog, and act like a lady: Occupational dilemmas of police-women." In *The Worth of Women's Work: A Qualitative Synthesis,* ed. Anne Statham, Eleanor M. Miller, and Hans O. Mauksch, 205–223. Albany, N.Y.: State University of New York Press.

Reskin, Barbara. 1988. "Bringing the men back in: Sex differentation and the devaluation of women's work." *Gender & Society* 2: 58–81.

Reskin, Barbara, and Patricia Roos. 1990. *Job Queues, Gender Queues: Explaining Women's Inroads into Male Occupations.* Philadelphia: Temple University Press.

Strauss, Anselm L. 1987. *Qualitative Analysis for Social Scientists.* Cambridge, England: Cambridge University Press.

Yoder, Janice D. 1989. "Women at West Point: Lessons for token women in male-dominated occupations." In *Women: A Feminist Perspective,* ed. Jo Freeman, 523–537. Mountain View, Calif.: Mayfield Publishing Company.

Zimmer, Lynn. 1988. "Tokenism and women in the workplace." *Social Problems* 35: 64–77.

PART 8 GENDERED INTIMACIES

"Man's love is of man's life a thing apart," wrote the British Romantic poet, Lord Byron. "'Tis woman's whole existence." Nowhere are the differences between women and men more pronounced than in our intimate lives, our experiences of love, friendship, and sexuality. It is in our intimate relationships that so often men and women seem truly to be from different planets.

The very definitions of emotional intimacy bear the mark of gender. As Francesca Cancian argues, the ideal of love has been "feminized" since the nineteenth century. No longer is love the arduous pining or the sober shouldering of familial responsibility; today, love is expressed as the ability to sustain emotional commitment and connection—a "feminine" definition of love. And in our intimate relationships, men and women perform a dance of "approach-avoidance," argues Lillian Rubin—in which each gender tries to connect despite dramatic differences in psychological makeup.

One issue that underlies these experiences is that gender is the central organizing principle of emotional and sexual life. Men and women are taught to experience these events differently—regardless of sexual orientation. As a result, as the essay by Martin Levine makes clear, gay male friendship patterns and sexual behaviors more closely resemble heterosexual men's friendships and sexual behaviors than they resemble that of women. In their sociosexual activities gay men demonstrate their successful acquisition of male gender identity. Gay men are "real men," all right—at the cost, often, of emotional intimacy and relationship commitment. Equally, lesbians and heterosexual women have more similarities in their friendship patterns and sexual behaviors than either do with men. It is here that we see that sexual orientation is deeply gendered activity.

But there are signs of change, and gender convergence. Women, it appears, find themselves more interested in pursuing explicitly sexual pleasures, despite their "Venutian" temperament that invariably links love and lust. And men's friendships are not nearly as different from women's friendships as we previously thought, suggests Scott Swain. As women and men work together outside the home, and share housework and child care inside the home, many of those intractable, inevitable, and cosmic differences between men and women will begin to evaporate into the egalitarian air of planet Earth.

FRANCESCA M. CANCIAN

The Feminization of Love

A feminized and incomplete perspective on love predominates in the United States. We identify love with emotional expression and talking about feelings, aspects of love that women prefer and in which women tend to be more skilled than men. At the same time we often ignore the instrumental and physical aspects of love that men prefer, such as providing help, sharing activities, and sex. This feminized perspective leads us to believe that women are much more capable of love than men and that the way to make relationships more loving is for men to become more like women. This paper proposes an alternative, androgynous perspective on love, one based on the premise that love is both instrumental and expressive. From this perspective, the way to make relationships more loving is for women and men to reject polarized gender roles and integrate "masculine" and "feminine" styles of love.

THE TWO PERSPECTIVES

"Love is active, doing something for your good even if it bothers me" says a fundamentalist Christian. "Love is sharing, the real sharing of feelings" says a divorced secretary who is in love again. In ancient Greece, the ideal love was the adoration of a man for a beautiful young boy who was his lover. In the thirteenth century, the exemplar of love was the chaste devotion of a knight for another man's wife. In Puritan New England, love between husband and wife was the ideal, and in Victorian times, the asexual devotion of a mother for her child seemed the essence of love. My purpose is to focus on one kind of love: long-term heterosexual love in the contemporary United States.

What is a useful definition of enduring love between a woman and a man? One guideline for a definition comes from the prototypes of enduring love—the relations between committed lovers, husband and wife, parent and child. These relationships combine care and assistance with physical and emotional closeness. Studies of attachment between infants and their mothers emphasize the importance of being protected and fed as well as touched and held. In marriage, according to most family sociologists, both practical help and affection are part of enduring love, or "the affection we feel for those with whom our lives are deeply intertwined."[1] Our own informal observations often point in the same direction: if we consider the relationships that are the prototypes of enduring love, it seems that what we really mean by love is some combination of instrumental and expressive qualities.

Historical studies provide a second guideline for defining enduring love, specifically between a woman and a man. In precapitalist America, such love was

From *Signs,* Vol. 11, no. 4 (Summer 1986), pp. 692–709. Notes have been renumbered and edited.

a complex whole that included work and feelings. Then it was split into feminine and masculine fragments by the separation of home and workplace. This historical analysis implies that affection, material help, and routine cooperation all are parts of enduring love.

Consistent with these guidelines, my working definition of enduring love between adults is a relationship wherein a small number of people are affectionate and emotionally committed to each other, define their collective well-being as a major goal, and feel obliged to provide care and practical assistance for each other. People who love each other also usually share physical contact; they communicate with each other frequently and cooperate in some routine tasks of daily life. My discussion is of enduring heterosexual love only; I will for the sake of simplicity refer to it as "love."

In contrast to this broad definition of love, the narrower, feminized definition dominates both contemporary scholarship and public opinion. Most scholars who study love, intimacy, or close friendship focus on qualities that are stereotypically feminine, such as talking about feelings. For example, Abraham Maslow defines love as "a feeling of tenderness and affection with great enjoyment, happiness, satisfaction, elation and even ecstasy." Among healthy individuals, he says, "there is a growing intimacy and honesty and self-expression."[2] Zick Rubin's "Love Scale," designed to measure the degree of passionate love as opposed to liking, includes questions about confiding in each other, longing to be together, and sexual attraction as well as caring for each other. Studies of friendship usually distinguish close friends from acquaintances on the basis of how much personal information is disclosed, and many recent studies of married couples and lovers emphasize communication and self-disclosure. A recent book on marital love by Lillian Rubin focuses on intimacy, which she defines as "reciprocal expression of feeling and thought, not out of fear or dependent need, but out of a wish to know another's inner life and to be able to share one's own."[3] She argues that intimacy is distinct from nurturance or caretaking and that men are usually unable to be intimate.

Among the general public, love is also defined primarily as expressing feelings and verbal disclosure, not as instrumental help. This is especially true among the more affluent; poorer people are more likely than they to see practical help and financial assistance as a sign of love. In a study conducted in 1980, 130 adults from a wide range of social classes and ethnic backgrounds were interviewed about the qualities that make a good love relationship. The most frequent response referred to honest and open communication. Being caring and supportive and being tolerant and understanding were the other qualities most often mentioned. Similar results were reported from Ann Swidler's study of an affluent suburb: the dominant conception of love stressed communicating feelings, working on the relationship, and self-development. Finally, a contemporary dictionary defines love as "strong affection for another arising out of kinship or personal ties" and as attraction based on sexual desire, affection, and tenderness.

These contemporary definitions of love clearly focus on qualities that are seen as feminine in our culture. A study of gender roles in 1968 found that warmth, expressiveness, and talkativeness were seen as appropriate for women and not for men. In 1978 the core features of gender stereotypes were unchanged although fewer qualities were seen as appropriate for only one sex. Expressing tender feelings, being gentle, and being aware of the feelings of others were still ideal qualities for women and not for men. The desirable qualities for men and not for women included being independent, unemotional, and interested in sex. The only component perceived as masculine in popular definitions of love is interest in sex.

The two approaches to defining love—one broad, encompassing instrumental and affective qualities, one narrow, including only the affective qualities—inform the two different perspectives on love. According to the androgynous perspective, both gender roles contain elements of love. The feminine role does not include all of the major ways of loving; some aspects of love come from the masculine role, such as sex and providing material help, and some, such as cooperating in daily tasks, are associated with neither gender role. In contrast, the feminized perspective on love implies that all of the elements of love are included in the feminine role. The capacity to love is divided by gender. Women can love and men cannot.

SOME FEMINIST INTERPRETATIONS

Feminist scholars are divided on the question of love and gender. Supporters of the feminized perspective seem most influential at present. Nancy Chodorow's psychoanalytic theory has been especially influential in promoting a feminized perspective on love among social scientists studying close relationships. Chodorow's argument—in greatly simplified form—is that as infants, both boys and girls have strong identification and intimate attachments with their mothers. Since boys grow up to be men, they must repress this early identification, and in the process they repress their capacity for intimacy. Girls retain their early identification since they will grow up to be women, and throughout their lives females see themselves as connected to others. As a result of this process, Chodorow argues, "girls come to define and experience themselves as continuous with others; . . . boys come to define themselves as more separate and distinct."[4] This theory implies that love is feminine—women are more open to love than men—and that this gender difference will remain as long as women are the primary caretakers of infants.

Scholars have used Chodorow's theory to develop the idea that love and attachment are fundamental parts of women's personalities but not of men's. Carol Gilligan's influential book on female personality development asserts that women define their identity "by a standard of responsibility and care." The predominant female image is "a network of connection, a web of relationships that is sustained by a process of communication." In contrast, males favor a "hierarchical ordering, with its imagery of winning and losing and the potential for violence which it contains." "Although the world of the self that men describe at times includes 'people' and 'deep attachments,' no particular person or relationship is mentioned. . . . Thus the male 'I' is defined in separation."[5]

A feminized conception of love can be supported by other theories as well. In past decades, for example, such a conception developed from Talcott Parsons's theory of the benefits to the nuclear family of women's specializing in expressive action and men's specializing in instrumental action. Among contemporary social scientists, the strongest support for the feminized perspective comes from such psychological theories as Chodorow's.

On the other hand, feminist historians have developed an incisive critique of the feminized perspective on love. Mary Ryan and other social historians have analyzed how the separation of home and workplace in the nineteenth century polarized gender roles and feminized love. Their argument, in simplified form, begins with the observation that in the colonial era the family household was the arena for economic production, affection, and social welfare. The integration of activities in the family produced a certain integration of expressive and instrumental traits in the personalities of men and women. Both women and men were expected to be hard working, modest, and loving toward their spouses and children, and the concept of love included instrumental cooperation as well as expression of feelings. In Ryan's words, "When early Americans spoke of love they were not withdrawing into a female byway of human experience. Domestic affection, like sex and economics, was not segregated into male and female spheres." There was a "reciprocal ideal of conjugal love" that "grew out of the day-to-day cooperation, sharing, and closeness of the diversified home economy."[6]

Economic production gradually moved out of the home and became separated from personal relationships as capitalism expanded. Husbands increasingly worked for wages in factories and shops while wives stayed at home to care for the family. This division of labor gave women more experience with close relationships and intensified women's economic dependence on men. As the daily activities of men and women grew further apart, a new worldview emerged that exaggerated the differences between the personal, loving, feminine sphere of the home and the impersonal, powerful, masculine sphere of the workplace. Work became identified with what men do for money while love became identified with women's activities at home. As a result, the conception of love shifted toward emphasizing tenderness, powerlessness, and the expression of emotion.

This partial and feminized conception of love persisted into the twentieth century as the division of labor remained stable: the workplace remained impersonal and separated from the home, and married women continued to be excluded from paid employment. According to this historical explanation, one might expect a change in the conception of love since the 1940s, as growing numbers of wives took jobs. However, women's persistent responsibility for child care and housework, and their lower wages, might explain a continued feminized conception of love.

Like the historical critiques, some psychological studies of gender also imply that our current conception of love is distorted and needs to be integrated with qualities associated with the masculine role. For example, Jean Baker Miller argues that women's ways of loving—their need to be attached to a man and to serve others—result from women's powerlessness, and that a better way of loving would integrate power with women's style of love.[7] The importance of combining activities and personality traits that have been split apart by gender is also a frequent theme in the human potential movement. These historical and psychological works emphasize the flexibility of gender roles and the inadequacy of a concept of love that includes only the feminine half of human qualities. In contrast, theories like Chodorow's emphasize the rigidity of gender differences after childhood and define love in terms of feminine qualities. The two theoretical approaches are not as inconsistent as my simplified sketches may suggest, and many scholars combine them; however, the two approaches have different implications for empirical research.

EVIDENCE ON WOMEN'S "SUPERIORITY" IN LOVE

A large number of studies show that women are more interested and more skilled in love than men. However, most of these studies use biased measures based on feminine styles of loving, such as verbal self-disclosure, emotional expression, and willingness to report that one has close relationships. When less biased measures are used, the differences between women and men are often small.

Women have a greater number of close relationships than men. At all stages of the life cycle, women see their relatives more often. Men and women report closer relations with their mothers than with their fathers and are generally closer to female kin. Thus an average Yale man in the 1970s talked about himself more with his mother than with his father and was more satisfied with his relationship with his mother. His most frequent grievance against his father was that his father gave too little of himself and was cold and uninvolved; his grievance against his mother was that she gave too much of herself and was alternately overprotective and punitive.

Throughout their lives, women are more likely to have a confidant—a person to whom one discloses personal experiences and feelings. Girls prefer to be with one friend or a small group, while boys usually play competitive games in large groups. Men usually get together with friends to play sports or do some other activity, while women get together explicitly to talk and to be together.

Men seem isolated given their weak ties with their families and friends. Among blue-collar couples interviewed in 1950, 64 percent of the husbands had no confidants other than their spouses, compared to 24 percent of the wives. The predominantly upper-middle-class men interviewed by Daniel Levinson in the 1970s were no less isolated. Levinson concludes that "close friendship with a man or a woman is rarely experienced by American men."[8] Apparently, most men have no loving relationships besides those with wife or lover; and given the estrangement that often occurs in marriages, many men may have no loving relationship at all.

Several psychologists have suggested that there is a natural reversal of these roles in middle age, as men become more concerned with relationships and women turn toward independence and achievement; but there seems to be no evidence showing that men's relationships become more numerous or more intimate after middle age, and some evidence to the contrary.

Women are also more skilled than men in talking about relationships. Whether working class or middle class, women value talking about feelings and relationships and disclose more than men about personal experiences. Men who deviate and talk a lot about their personal experiences are commonly defined as feminine and maladjusted. Working-class wives prefer to talk about themselves, their close relationships with family and friends, and their homes, while their husbands prefer to talk about cars, sports, work, and politics. The same gender-specific preferences are expressed by college students.

Men do talk more about one area of personal experience: their victories and achievements; but talking about success is associated with power, not intimacy. Women say more about their fears and disappointments, and it is disclosure of such weaknesses that usually is interpreted as a sign of intimacy. Women are also more accepting of the expression of intense feelings, including love, sadness, and fear, and they are more skilled in interpreting other people's emotions.

Finally, in their leisure time women are drawn to topics of love and human entanglements while men are drawn to competition among men. Women's preferences in television viewing run to daytime soap operas, or if they are more educated, the high-brow soap operas on educational channels, while most men like to watch competitive and often aggressive sports. Reading-tastes show the same pattern. Women read novels and magazine articles about love, while men's magazines feature stories about men's adventures and encounters with death.

However, this evidence on women's greater involvement and skill in love is not as strong as it appears. Part of the reason that men seem so much less loving than women is that their behavior is measured with a feminine ruler. Much of this research considers only the kinds of loving behavior that are associated with the feminine role and rarely compares women and men in terms of qualities associated with the masculine role. When less biased measures are used, the behavior of men and women is often quite similar. For example, in a careful study of kinship relations among young adults in a southern city, Bert Adams found that women were much more likely than men to say that their parents and relatives were very important to their lives (58 percent of women and 37 percent of men). In measures of actual contact with relatives, though, there were much smaller differences: 88 percent of women and 81 percent of men whose parents lived in the same city saw their parents weekly. Adams concluded that "differences between males and females in relations with parents are discernible primarily in the subjective sphere; contact frequencies are quite similar."[9]

The differences between the sexes can be small even when biased measures are used. For example, Marjorie Lowenthal and Clayton Haven reported the finding, later widely quoted, that elderly women were more likely than elderly men to have a friend with whom they could talk about their personal troubles—clearly a measure of a traditionally feminine behavior. The figures revealed that 81 percent of the married women and 74 percent of the married men had confidants—not a sizable difference.[10] On the other hand, whatever the measure, virtually all such studies find that women are more involved in close relationships than men, even if the difference is small.

In sum, women are only moderately superior to men in love: they have more close relationships and care more about them, and they seem to be more skilled at love, especially those aspects of love that involve expressing feelings and being vulnerable. This does not mean that men are separate and unconcerned with close relationships, however. When national surveys ask people what is most important in their lives, women tend to put family bonds first while men put family bonds first or second, along with work. For both sexes, love is clearly very important.

EVIDENCE ON THE MASCULINE STYLE OF LOVE

Men tend to have a distinctive style of love that focuses on practical help, shared physical activities, spending time together, and sex. The major elements of the masculine style of love emerged in Margaret Reedy's study of 102 married couples in the late 1970s. She showed individuals statements describing aspects of love and asked them to rate how well the statements described their marriages. On the whole, husband and wife had similar views of their marriage, but several sex differences emerged. Practical help and spending time together were more important to men. The men were more likely to give high ratings to such statements as: "When she needs help I help her," and "She would rather spend her time with me than with anyone else." Men also described themselves more often as sexually attracted and endorsed such statements as: "I get physically excited and aroused just thinking about her." In addition, emotional security was less important to men than to women, and men were less likely to describe the relationship as secure, safe, and comforting.[11] Another study in the late 1970s showed a similar pattern among young, highly educated couples. The husbands gave greater emphasis to feeling responsible for the partner's well-being and putting the spouse's needs first, as well as to spending time together. The wives gave greater importance to emotional involvement and verbal self-disclosure but also were more concerned than the men about maintaining their separate activities and their independence.

The difference between men and women in their views of the significance of practical help was demonstrated in a study in which seven couples recorded their interactions for several days. They noted how pleasant their relations were and counted how often the spouse did a helpful chore, such as cooking a good meal or repairing a faucet, and how often the spouse expressed acceptance or affection. The social scientists doing the study used a feminized definition of love. They labeled practical help as "instrumental behavior" and expressions of acceptance or affection as "affectionate behavior," thereby denying the affectionate aspect of practical help. The wives seemed to be using the same scheme; they thought their marital relations were pleasant that day if their husbands had directed a lot of affectionate behavior to them, regardless of their husbands' positive instrumental behavior. The husbands' enjoyment of their marital relations, on the other hand, depended on their wives' instrumental actions, not on their expressions of affection. The men actually saw instrumental actions as affection. One husband who was told by the researchers to increase his affectionate behavior toward his wife decided to wash her car and was surprised when neither his wife nor the researchers accepted that as an "affectionate" act.

The masculine view of instrumental help as loving behavior is clearly expressed by a husband discussing his wife's complaints about his lack of communication: "What does she want? Proof? She's got it, hasn't she? Would I be knocking myself out to get things for her—like to keep up this house—if I didn't love her? Why does a man do things like that if not because he loves his wife and kids? I swear, I can't figure what she wants. His wife, who has a feminine orientation to love, says something very different: "It is not enough that he supports us and takes care of us. I appreciate that, but I want him to share things with me. I need for him to tell me his feelings."[12] Many working-class women agree with men that a man's job is something he does out of love for his family,[13] but middle-class women and social scientists rarely recognize men's practical help as a form of love. (Indeed, among upper-middle-class men whose jobs offer a great deal of intrinsic gratification, their belief that they are "doing it for the family" may seem somewhat self-serving.)

Other differences between men's and women's styles of love involve sex. Men seem to separate sex and love while women connect them, but paradoxically, sexual intercourse seems to be the most meaningful way of giving and receiving love for many men. A twenty-nine-year-old carpenter who had been married for three years said that, after sex, "I feel so close to her and the kids. We feel like a real family then. I don't talk to her very often, I guess, but somehow I feel we have really communicated after we have made love."[14]

Because sexual intimacy is the only recognized "masculine" way of expressing love, the recent trend toward viewing sex as a way for men and women to express mutual intimacy is an important challenge to the feminization of love. However, the connection between sexuality and love is undermined both by the "sexual revolution" definition of sex as a form of casual recreation and by the view of male sexuality as a weapon—as in rape—with which men dominate and punish women.

Another paradoxical feature of men's style of love is that men have a more romantic attitude toward their partners than do women. In Reedy's study, men were more likely to select statements like "we are perfect for each other." In a survey of college students, 65 percent of the men but only 24 percent of the women said that, even if a relationship had all of the other qualities they desired, they would not marry unless they were in love. The common view of this phenomenon focuses on women. The view is that women marry for money and status and so see marriage as instrumentally, rather than emotionally, desirable. This of course is at odds with women's greater concern with self-disclosure and emotional intimacy and lesser concern with instrumental help. A better way to explain men's greater romanticism might be to focus on men. One such possible explanation is that men do not feel responsible for "working on" the emotional aspects of a relationship, and therefore see love as magically and perfectly present or absent. This is consistent with men's relative lack of concern with affective interaction and greater concern with instrumental help.

In sum, there is a masculine style of love. Except for romanticism, men's style fits the popularly conceived masculine role of being the powerful provider. From the androgynous perspective, the practical help and physical activities included in this role are as much a part of love as the expression of feelings. The feminized perspective cannot account for this masculine style of love; nor can it explain why women and men are so close in the degrees to which they are loving.

NEGATIVE CONSEQUENCES OF THE FEMINIZATION OF LOVE

The division of gender roles in our society that contributes to the two separate styles of love is reinforced by the feminized perspective and leads to political and moral problems that would be mitigated with a more androgynous approach to love. The feminized perspective works against some of the key values and goals of feminists and humanists by contributing to the devaluation and exploitation of women.

It is especially striking how the differences between men's and women's styles of love reinforce men's power over women. Men's style involves giving women important resources, such as money and protection that men control and women believe they need, and ignoring the resources that women control and men need. Thus men's dependency on women remains covert and repressed, while women's dependency on men is overt and exaggerated; and it is overt dependency that creates power, according to social exchange theory. The feminized perspective on love reinforces this power differential by leading to the belief that women need love more than do men, which is implied in the association of love with the feminine role. The effect of this belief is to intensify the asymmetrical dependency of women on men. In fact, however, evidence on the high death rates of unmarried men suggests that men need love at least as much as do women.

Sexual relations also can reinforce male dominance insofar as the man takes the initiative and intercourse is defined either as his "taking" pleasure or as his being skilled at "giving" pleasure, either way giving him control. The man's power advantage is further strengthened if the couple assumes that the man's sexual needs can be filled by any attractive woman while the woman's sexual needs can be filled only by the man she loves.

On the other hand, women's preferred ways of loving seem incompatible with control. They involve admitting dependency and sharing or losing control, and being emotionally intense. Further, the intimate talk about personal troubles that appeals to women requires of a couple a mutual vulnerability, a willingness to see oneself as weak and in need of support. It is true that a woman, like a man, can gain some power by providing her partner with services, such as understanding, sex, or cooking; but this power is largely unrecognized because the man's dependency on such services is not overt. The couple may even see these services as her duty or as her response to his requests (or demands).

The identification of love with expressing feelings also contributes to the lack of recognition of women's power by obscuring the instrumental, active component of women's love just as it obscures the loving aspect of men's work. In a culture that glorifies instrumental achievement, this identification devalues both women and love. In reality, a major way by which women are loving is in the clearly instrumental activities associated with caring for others, such as preparing meals, washing clothes, and providing care during illness; but because of our focus on the expressive side of love, this caring work of women is either ignored or redefined as expressing feelings. Thus, from the feminized perspective on love, child care is a subtle communication of attitudes, not work. A wife washing her husband's shirt is seen as expressing love, even though a husband washing his wife's car is seen as doing a job.

Gilligan, in her critique of theories of human development, shows the way in which devaluing love is linked to devaluing women. Basic to most psychological theories of development is the idea that a healthy person develops from a dependent child to an autonomous, independent adult. As Gilligan comments, "Development itself comes to be identified with separation, and attachments appear to be developmental impediments."[15] Thus women, who emphasize attachment, are judged to be developmentally retarded or insufficiently individuated.

The pervasiveness of this image was documented in a well-known study of mental health professionals who were asked to describe mental health, femininity, and masculinity. They associated both mental health and masculinity with independence, rationality, and dominance. Qualities concerning attachment, such as being tactful, gentle, or aware of the feelings of others, they associated with femininity but not with mental health.[16]

Another negative consequence of a feminized perspective on love is that it legitimates impersonal, exploitive relations in the workplace and the community. The ideology of separate spheres that developed in the nineteenth century contrasted the harsh, immoral marketplace with the warm and loving home and implied that this contrast is acceptable. Defining love as expressive, feminine, and divorced from productive activity maintains this ideology. If personal relationships and love are reserved for women and the home, then it is acceptable for a manager to underpay workers or for a community to ignore a needy family. Such behavior is not unloving; it is businesslike or shows a respect for privacy. The ideology of separate spheres also implies that men are properly judged by their instrumental and economic achievements and that poor or unsuccessful men are failures who may deserve a hard life. Levinson presents a conception of masculine development itself as centering on achieving an occupational dream.[17]

Finally, the feminization of love intensifies the conflicts over intimacy between women and men in close relationships. One of the most common conflicts is that the woman wants more closeness and verbal contact while the man withdraws and wants less pressure. Her need for more closeness is partly the result of the feminization of love, which encourages her to be more emotionally dependent on him. Because love is feminine, he in turn may feel controlled during intimate contact. Intimacy is her "turf," an area where she sets the rules and expectations. Talking about the relationship, as she wants, may well feel to him like taking a test that she made up and that he will fail. He is likely to react by withdrawing, causing her to intensify her efforts to get closer. The feminization of love thus can lead to a vicious cycle of conflict where neither partner feels in control or gets what she or he wants.

CONCLUSION

The values of improving the status of women and humanizing the public sphere are shared by many of the scholars who support a feminized conception of love; and they, too, explain the conflicts in close relationships in terms of polarized gender roles. Nancy Chodorow, Lillian Rubin, and Carol Gilligan have addressed these issues in detail and with great insight. However, by arguing that women's identity is based on attachment while men's identity is based on separation, they reinforce the distinction between feminine expressiveness and masculine instrumentality, revive the ideology of separate spheres, and legitimate the popular idea that only women know the right way to love. They also suggest that there is no way to overcome the rigidity of gender roles other than by pursuing the goal of men and women becoming equally involved in infant care. In contrast, an androgynous perspective on love challenges the identification of women and love with being expressive, powerless, and nonproductive and the identification of men with being instrumental, powerful, and productive. It rejects the ideology of separate spheres and validates masculine as well as feminine styles of love. This viewpoint suggests that progress could be made by means of a variety of social changes, including men doing child care, relations at work becoming more personal and nurturant, and cultural conceptions of love and gender becoming more androgynous. Changes that equalize power within close relationships by equalizing the economic and emotional dependency between men and women may be especially important in moving toward androgynous love.

The validity of an androgynous definition of love cannot be "proven"; the view that informs the androgynous perspective is that both the feminine style of love (characterized by emotional closeness and verbal self-disclosure) and the masculine style of love (characterized by instrumental help and sex) represent necessary parts of a good love relationship. Who is more loving: a couple who confide most of their experiences to each other but rarely cooperate or give each other practical help, or a couple who help each other through many crises and cooperate in running a household but rarely discuss their personal experiences? Both relationships are limited. Most people would probably choose a combination: a relationship that integrates feminine and masculine styles of loving, an androgynous love.

Notes

1. See John Bowlby, *Attachment and Loss* (New York: Basic Books, 1969), on mother-infant attachment. The quotation is from Elaine Walster and G. William Walster, *A New Look at*

Love (Reading, Mass.: Addison-Wesley Publishing Co., 1978), 9. Conceptions of love and adjustment used by family sociologists are reviewed in Robert Lewis and Graham Spanier, "Theorizing about the Quality and Stability of Marriage." in *Contemporary Theories about the Family,* ed. W. Burr, R. Hill, F. Nye, and I. Reiss (New York: Free Press, 1979), 268–94.

2. Abraham Maslow, *Motivation and Personality,* 2d ed. (New York: Harper & Row, 1970), 182–83.

3. Zick Rubin's scale is described in his article "Measurement of Romantic Love." *Journal of Personality and Social Psychology* 16, no. 2 (1970): 265–73; Lillian Rubin's book on marriage is *Intimate Strangers* (New York: Harper & Row, 1983), quote on 90.

4. Nancy Chodorow, *The Reproduction of Mothering* (Berkeley: University of California Press, 1978), 169. Dorothy Dinnerstein presents a similar theory in *The Mermaid and the Minotaur: Sexual Arrangements and Human Malaise* (New York: Harper & Row, 1976). Freudian and biological dispositional theories about women's nurturance are surveyed in Jean Stockard and Miriam Johnson, *Sex Roles* (Englewood Cliffs, N.J.: Prentice-Hall, Inc., 1980).

5. Carol Gilligan, *In a Different Voice* (Cambridge, Mass.: Harvard University Press, 1982), 32, 159–61; see also L. Rubin, *Intimate Strangers.*

6. I have drawn most heavily on Mary Ryan, *Womanhood in America,* 2d ed. (New York: New Viewpoints, 1978), and *The Cradle of the Middle Class: The Family in Oneida County, N.Y., 1790–1865* (New York: Cambridge University Press, 1981); Barbara Ehrenreich and Deidre English, *For Her Own Good: 150 Years of Experts Advice to Women* (New York: Anchor Books, 1978); Barbara Welter, "The Cult of True Womanhood: 1820–1860," *American Quaterly* 18, no. 2 (1966): 151–174.

7. Jean Baker Miller, *Toward a New Psychology of Women* (Boston: Beacon Press, 1976). There are, of course, many exceptions to Miller's generalization, e.g., women who need to be independent or who need an attachment with a woman.

8. Daniel Levinson, *The Seasons of a Man's Life* (New York: Alfred A. Knopf, 1978), 335.

9. Bert Adams, *Kinship in an Urban Setting* (Chicago: Markham Publishing Co., 1968), 169.

10. Marjorie Lowenthal and Clayton Haven, "Interaction and Adaptation: Intimacy as a Critical Variable." *American Sociological Review* 22, no. 4 (1968): 20–30.

11. Margaret Reedy, "Age and Sex Differences in Personal Needs and the Nature of Love." (Ph.D. diss. University of Southern California, 1977). Unlike most studies, Reedy did not find that women emphasized communication more than men. Her subjects were upper-middle-class couples who seemed to be very much in love.

12. Lillian Rubin, *Worlds of Pain* (New York: Basic Books, 1976), 147.

13. See L. Rubin, *Worlds of Pain;* also see Richard Sennett and Jonathan Cobb, *Hidden Injuries of Class* (New York: Vintage, 1973).

14. Interview by Cynthia Garlich, "Interviews of Married Couples" (University of California, Irvine, School of Social Sciences, 1982).

15. Gilligan (n. 5 above), 12–13.

16. Inge Broverman, Frank Clarkson, Paul Rosenkrantz, and Susan Vogel, "Sex-Role Stereotypes and Clinical Judgments of Mental Health," *Journal of Consulting Psychology* 34, no. 1 (1970): 1–7.

17. Levinson (n. 8 above).

LILLIAN B. RUBIN

The Approach-Avoidance Dance: Men, Women, and Intimacy

For one human being to love another, that is perhaps the most difficult of all our tasks, the ultimate, the last test and proof, the work for which all other work is but preparation.

Rainer Maria Rilke

Intimacy. We hunger for it, but we also fear it. We come close to a loved one, then we back off. A teacher I had once described this as the "go away a little closer" message. I call it the approach-avoidance dance.

The conventional wisdom says that women want intimacy, men resist it. And I have plenty of material that would *seem* to support that view. Whether in my research interviews, in my clinical hours, or in the ordinary course of my life, I hear the same story told repeatedly. "He doesn't talk to me," says a woman. "I don't know what she wants me to talk about," says a man. "I want to know what he's feeling," she tells me. "I'm not feeling anything," he insists. "Who can feel nothing?" she cries. "I can," he shouts. As the heat rises, so does the wall between them. Defensive and angry, they retreat—stalemated by their inability to understand each other.

Women complain to each other all the time about not being able to talk to their men about the things that matter most to them—about what they themselves are thinking and feeling, about what goes on in the hearts and minds of the men they're relating to. And men, less able to expose themselves and their conflicts—those within themselves or those with the women in their lives—either turn silent or take cover by holding women up to derision. It's one of the norms of male camaraderie to poke fun at women, to complain laughingly about the mystery of their minds, wonderingly about their ways. Even Freud did it when, in exasperation, he asked mockingly, "What do women want? Dear God, what do they want?"

But it's not a joke—not for the women, not for the men who like to pretend it is.

> The whole goddamn business of what you're calling intimacy bugs the hell out of me. I never know what you women mean when you talk about it. Karen complains that I don't talk to her, but it's not talk she wants, it's some other damn thing, only I don't know what the hell it is. Feelings, she keeps asking for. So what am I supposed to do if I don't have any to give her or to talk about just

> because she decides it's time to talk about feelings? Tell me, will you; maybe we can get some peace around here.

The expression of such conflicts would seem to validate the common understandings that suggest that women want and need intimacy more than men do—that the issue belongs to women alone; that, if left to themselves, men would not suffer it. But things are not always what they seem. And I wonder: "If men would renounce intimacy, what is their stake in relationships with women?"

Some would say that men need women to tend to their daily needs—to prepare their meals, clean their houses, wash their clothes, rear their children—so that they can be free to attend to life's larger problems. And, given the traditional structure of roles in the family, it has certainly worked that way most of the time. But, if that were all men seek, why is it that, even when they're not relating to women, so much of their lives is spent in search of a relationship with another, so much agony experienced when it's not available?

These are difficult issues to talk about—even to think about—because the subject of intimacy isn't just complicated, it's slippery as well. Ask yourself: What is intimacy? What words come to mind, what thoughts?

It's an idea that excites our imagination, a word that seems larger than life to most of us. It lures us, beckoning us with a power we're unable to resist. And, just because it's so seductive, it frightens us as well—seeming sometimes to be some mysterious force from outside ourselves that, if we let it, could sweep us away.

But what is it we fear?

Asked what intimacy is, most of us—men and women—struggle to say something sensible, something that we can connect with the real experience of our lives. "Intimacy is knowing there's someone who cares about the children as much as you do." "Intimacy is a history of shared experience." "It's sitting there having a cup of coffee together and watching the eleven-o'clock news." "It's knowing you care about the same things." "It's knowing she'll always understand." "It's him sitting in the hospital for hours at a time when I was sick." "It's knowing he cares when I'm hurting." "It's standing by me when I was out of work." "It's seeing each other at our worst." "It's sitting across the breakfast table." "It's talking when you're in the bathroom." "It's knowing we'll begin and end each day together."

These seem the obvious things—the things we expect when we commit our lives to one another in a marriage, when we decide to have children together. And they're not to be dismissed as inconsequential. They make up the daily experience of our lives together, setting the tone for a relationship in important and powerful ways. It's sharing such commonplace, everyday events that determines the temper and the texture of life, that keeps us living together even when other aspects of the relationship seem less than perfect. Knowing someone is there, is constant, and can be counted on in just the ways these thoughts express provides the background of emotional security and stability we look for when we enter a marriage. Certainly a marriage and the people in it will be tested and judged quite differently in an unusual situation or in a crisis. But how often does life present us with circumstances and events that are so out of the range of ordinary experience?

These ways in which a relationship feels intimate on a daily basis are only one part of what we mean by intimacy, however—the part that's most obvious, the part that doesn't awaken our fears. At a lecture where I spoke of these issues recently, one man commented also, "Intimacy is putting aside the masks we wear in the rest of our lives." A murmur of assent ran through the audience of a hundred or so. Intuitively we say "yes." Yet this is the very issue that also complicates our intimate relationships.

On the one hand, it's reassuring to be able to put away the public persona—to believe we can be loved for who we *really* are, that we can show our shadow side without fear, that our vulnerabilities will not be counted against us. "The most important thing is to feel I'm accepted just the way I am," people will say.

But there's another side. For, when we show ourselves thus without the masks, we also become anxious and fearful. "Is it possible that someone could love the *real* me?" we're likely to ask. Not the most promising question for the further development of intimacy, since it suggests that, whatever else another might do or feel, it's we who have trouble loving ourselves. Unfortunately, such misgivings are not usually experienced consciously. We're aware only that our discomfort has risen, that we feel a need to get away. For the person who has seen the "real me" is also the one who reflects back to us an image that's usually not wholly to our liking. We get angry at that, first at ourselves for not living up to our own expectations, then at the other, who becomes for us the mirror of our self-doubts—a displacement of hostility that serves intimacy poorly.

There's yet another level—one that's further below the surface of consciousness, therefore, one that's much more difficult for us to grasp, let alone to talk about. I'm referring to the differences in the ways in which women and men deal with their inner emotional lives—differences that create barriers between us that can be high indeed. It's here that we see how those early childhood experiences of separation and individuation—the psychological tasks that were required of us in order to separate from mother, to distinguish ourselves as autonomous persons, to internalize a firm sense of gender identity—take their toll on our intimate relationships.

Stop a woman in mid-sentence with the question, "What are you feeling right now?" and you might have to wait a bit while she reruns the mental tape to capture the moment just passed. But, more than likely, she'll be able to do it successfully. More than likely, she'll think for a while and come up with an answer.

The same is not true of a man. For him, a similar question usually will bring a sense of wonderment that one would even ask it, followed quickly by an uncomprehending and puzzled response. "What do you mean?" he'll ask. "I was just talking," he'll say.

I've seen it most clearly in the clinical setting where the task is to get to the feeling level—or, as one of my male patients said when he came into therapy, to "hook up the head and the gut." Repeatedly when therapy begins, I find myself having to teach a man how to monitor his internal states—how to attend to his thoughts and feelings, how to bring them into consciousness. In the early stages of our work, it's a common experience to say to a man, "How does that feel?", and to see a blank look come over his face. Over and over, I find myself listening as a man speaks with calm reason about a situation which I know must be fraught with pain. "How do you feel about that?" I'll ask. "I've just been telling you," he's likely to reply. "No," I'll say, "you've told me what happened, not how you *feel* about it." Frustrated, he might well respond, "You sound just like my wife."

It would be easy to write off such dialogues as the problems of men in therapy, of those who happen to be having some particular emotional difficulties. But it's not so, as any woman who has lived with a man will attest. Time and again women complain: "I can't get him to verbalize his feelings." "He talks, but it's always intellectualizing." "He's so closed off from what he's feeling, I don't know how he lives that way." "If there's one thing that will eventually ruin this marriage, it's the fact that he can't talk about what's going on inside him." "I have to work like hell to get anything out of him that resembles a feeling that's something besides anger. That I get plenty of—me and the kids, we all get his anger. Anything else is damn hard to come by with him." One woman talked eloquently about her husband's anguish over his inability to get problems in his work life resolved. When I asked how she knew about his pain, she answered:

> I pull for it, I pull hard, and sometimes I can get something from him. But it'll be late at night in the dark—you know, when we're in bed and I can't look at him while he's talking and he doesn't have to look at me. Otherwise, he's just defensive and puts on what I call his bear act, where he makes his warning, go-away faces, and he can't be reached or penetrated at all.

To a woman, the world men live in seems a lonely one—a world in which their fears of exposing their sadness and pain, their anxiety about allowing their vulnerability to show, even to a woman they love, is so deeply rooted inside them that, most often, they can only allow it to happen "late at night in the dark."

Yet, if we listen to what men say, we will hear their insistence that they *do* speak of what's inside them, *do* share their thoughts and feelings with the women they love. "I tell her, but she's never satisfied," they complain. "No matter how much I say, it's never enough," they grumble.

From both sides, the complaints have merit. The problem lies not in what men don't say, however, but in what's not there—in what, quite simply, happens so far out of consciousness that it's not within their reach. For men have integrated all too well the lessons of their childhood—the experiences that taught them to repress and deny their inner thoughts, wishes, needs, and fears; indeed, not even to notice them. It's real, therefore, that the kind of inner thoughts and feelings that are readily accessible to a woman generally are unavailable to a man. When he says, "I don't know what I'm feeling," he isn't necessarily being intransigent and withholding. More than likely, he speaks the truth.

Partly that's a result of the ways in which boys are trained to camouflage their feelings under cover of an exterior of calm, strength, and rationality. Fears are not manly. Fantasies are not rational. Emotions, above all, are not for the strong, the sane, the adult. Women suffer them, not men—women, who are more like children with what seems like their never-ending preoccupation with their emotional life. But the training takes so well because of their early childhood experience when, as very young boys, they had to shift their identification from mother to father and sever themselves from their earliest emotional connection. Put the two together and it does seem like suffering to men to have to experience that emotional side of themselves, to have to give it voice.

This is the single most dispiriting dilemma of relations between women and men. He complains, "She's so emotional, there's no point in talking to her." She protests, "It's him you can't talk to, he's always so darned rational." He says, "Even when I tell her nothing's the matter, she won't quit." She says, "How can I believe him when I can see with my own eyes that something's wrong?" He says, "Okay, so something's wrong! What good will it do to tell her?" She cries, "What are we married for? What do you need me for, just to wash your socks?"

These differences in the psychology of women and men are born of a complex interaction between society and the individual. At the broadest social level is the rending of thought and feeling that is such a fundamental part of Western thought. Thought, defined as the ultimate good, has been assigned to men; feeling, considered at best a problem, has fallen to women.

So firmly fixed have these ideas been that, until recently, few thought to question them. For they were built into the structure of psychological thought as if they spoke to an eternal, natural, and scientific truth. Thus, even such a great and innovative thinker as Carl Jung wrote, "The woman is increasingly aware that love alone can give her her full stature, just as the man begins to discern that spirit alone can endow his life with its highest meaning. Fundamentally, therefore, both seek a psychic relation one to the other, because love needs the spirit, and the spirit love, for their fulfillment."

For a woman, "love"; for a man, "spirit"—each expected to complete the other by bringing to the relationship the missing half. In German, the word that is translated here as spirit is *Geist*. But *The New Cassell's German Dictionary* shows that another primary meaning of *Geist* is "mind, intellect, intelligence, wit, imagination, sense of reason." And, given the context of these words, it seems reasonable that *Geist* for Jung referred to a man's highest essence—his mind. There's no ambiguity about a woman's calling, however. It's love.

Intuitively, women try to heal the split that these definitions of male and female have foisted upon us.

> I can't stand that he's so damned unemotional and expects me to be the same. He lives in his head all the time, and he acts like anything that's emotional isn't worth dealing with.

Cognitively, even women often share the belief that the rational side, which seems to come so naturally to men, is the more mature, the more desirable.

> I know I'm too emotional, and it causes problems between us. He can't stand it when I get emotional like that. It turns him right off.

Her husband agrees that she's "too emotional" and complains:

> Sometimes she's like a child who's out to test her parents. I have to be careful

> when she's like that not to let her rile me up because otherwise all hell would break loose. You just can't reason with her when she gets like that.

It's the rational-man–hysterical-woman script, played out again and again by two people whose emotional repertoire is so limited that they have few real options. As the interaction between them continues, she reaches for the strongest tools she has, the mode she's most comfortable and familiar with: She becomes progressively more emotional and expressive. He falls back on his best weapons: He becomes more rational, more determinedly reasonable. She cries for him to attend to her feelings, whatever they may be. He tells her coolly, with a kind of clenched-teeth reasonableness, that it's silly for her to feel that way, that she's just being emotional. And of course she is. But that dismissive word "just" is the last straw. She gets so upset that she does, in fact, seem hysterical. He gets so bewildered by the whole interaction that his only recourse is to build the wall of reason even higher. All of which makes things measurably worse for both of them.

> The more I try to be cool and calm her the worse it gets. I swear, I can't figure her out. I'll keep trying to tell her not to get so excited, but there's nothing I can do. Anything I say just makes it worse. So then I try to keep quiet, but . . . wow, the explosion is like crazy, just nuts.

And by then it *is* a wild exchange that any outsider would agree was "just nuts." But it's not just her response that's off, it's his as well—their conflict resting in the fact that we equate the emotional with the nonrational.

This notion, shared by both women and men, is a product of the fact that they were born and reared in this culture. But there's also a difference between them in their capacity to apprehend the *logic* of emotions—a difference born in their early childhood experiences in the family, when boys had to repress so much of their emotional side and girls could permit theirs to flower.

. . . It should be understood: Commitment itself is not a problem for a man; he's good at that. He can spend a lifetime living in the same family, working at the same job—even one he hates. And he's not without an inner emotional life. But when a relationship requires the sustained verbal expression of that inner life and the full range of feelings that accompany it, then it becomes burdensome for him. He can act out anger and frustration inside the family, it's true. But ask him to express his sadness, his fear, his dependency—all those feelings that would expose his vulnerability to himself or to another—and he's likely to close down as if under some compulsion to protect himself.

All requests for such intimacy are difficult for a man, but they become especially complex and troublesome in relations with women. It's another of those paradoxes. For, to the degree that it's possible for him to be emotionally open with anyone, it is with a woman—a tribute to the power of the childhood experience with mother. Yet it's that same early experience and his need to repress it that raises his ambivalence and generates his resistance.

He moves close, wanting to share some part of himself with her, trying to do so, perhaps even yearning to experience again the bliss of the infant's connection with a woman. She responds, woman style—wanting to touch him just a little more deeply, to know what he's thinking, feeling, fearing, wanting. And the fear closes in—the fear of finding himself again in the grip of a powerful woman, of allowing her admittance only to be betrayed and abandoned once again, of being overwhelmed by denied desires.

So he withdraws.

It's not in consciousness that all this goes on. He knows, of course, that he's distinctly uncomfortable when pressed by a woman for more intimacy in the relationship, but he doesn't know why. And, very often, his behavior doesn't please him any more than it pleases her. But he can't seem to help it.

SCOTT SWAIN

Covert Intimacy: Closeness in Men's Friendships

This study is an analysis of college men's intimate behavior in same-sex friendships and their standards for assessing intimacy. It documents the development, causes, and manifestation of a covert style of intimate behavior in men's friendships. Covert intimacy is a private, often nonverbal, context-specific form of communication. The concept of covert intimacy is rooted in the behaviors that men reported as indicative of closeness and intimacy in their friendships with other men.

First, I trace differences in the development of men's and women's adolescent friendships that shape and promote differing styles of intimacy. Next, such contexts are linked to the emergence of the separate worlds of men and women and how such separate worlds and microstructural contexts continue into adulthood. I analyze these separate worlds for the specific behaviors and values that shape intimacy among same-sex friends, and then clarify the distinctive cues and nuances of men's intimate behavior by comparing them to behaviors in male-female platonic friendships and friendships among women. I conclude the study with an assessment of the strengths and limitations of men's covert style of intimacy with men friends and its relationship to the inexpressive male.

THE INEXPRESSIVE MALE, OR SEX-SPECIFIC STYLES OF INTIMACY

Sex-role theorists have characterized men as instrumental, agentive, and task-oriented. Women have been characterized as expressive, communal, and empathic. Consistent with these theoretical formulations, researchers on the male role have interpreted men's interpersonal behavior as nonintimate and have stressed the restraints and limitations that cultural conceptions of masculinity impose on intimate expression. Examples of this *deficit approach* to men's intimate capabilities are Jack Balswick's "The Inexpressive Male" (1976) and Mirra Komarovsky's concept of men's "trained incapacity to share" (1964).

In recent years many of these generalizations, which were based on slight yet significant sex differences, have been reexamined. The majority of studies that measure interpersonal skills and relationship characteristics report nonsignificant sex differences. When studies report significant sex differences, the results have been mixed and sometimes conflicting. In support of the male deficit model, men are reported to be less likely than women to disclose sadness and fears, less affective and spontaneous with friends than women, and less adept than women at nonverbal decoding skills. Men are also reported to be more homophobic than women, which may inhibit the use of certain interpersonal skills in men's friendships.

However, the majority of self-disclosure studies reveal nonsignificant sex differences; and related analyses report that men score higher than women on nonverbal decoding skills, rate their friendships as more trusting and spontaneous than do women, and value intimacy in friendship as much as do women. In view of such findings and the conflicting results of other related studies, sex differences in interpersonal behavior appear to be minor or not adequately measured. However, notions of the "inexpressive male" continue to persist and guide research on men's interpersonal behavior.

Perhaps the most consistently reported difference in men's and women's friendships is men's preference for joint activities and women's preference for talking. Men's emphasis on instrumental action has been interpreted by past researchers as a less personal and less intimate form of interaction than verbal self-disclosure. This interpretation may be influenced by researchers' reliance on measuring feminine-typed styles of behavior to assess topics involving love and interpersonal behavior. This bias has been critiqued by Cancian as the "feminization of love" (1986). Researchers concerned with intimacy have assumed that verbal self-disclosure is the definitive referent for intimacy, and have thus interpreted alternative styles that involve instrumental action as a less intimate, or nonintimate, behavior. [Previous definitions of intimacy relied primarily on verbal self-disclosure as an indicator of intimacy. But, the relationship between intimacy and self-disclosure is usually only implied and not specifically defined.]

Caldwell and Peplau (1982) suggest that men and women may place the same value on intimacy in friendships, yet have different ways of assessing intimacy. Men are reported to express a wider range of intimate behaviors, including self-disclosure, while participating in gender-validating activities. Men may develop sex-specific contexts, cues, and meanings, which connote feelings and appraisals of intimacy similar to those connoted by self-disclosure for women.

Intimacy is defined in the present study as *behavior in the context of a friendship that connotes a positive and mutual sense of meaning and importance to the participants.* This definition allows respondents to determine what behaviors are meaningful and intimate, and assumes that there may be several avenues that may result in the experience of intimacy.

The results presented here are based on indepth interviews with fifteen men and five women. The college sample was young and white with a mean age of 22.5 years. This small sample was used to further explore sex-specific friendship behaviors, which have been significantly documented using larger samples of similar populations (Swain, 1984; Caldwell and Peplau, 1982).

The interview protocol was based on two empirical studies; the first was a pilot study (*N* = 232) that measured the relative value of activities in men's and women's same-sex friendships, and the second (*N* = 140) measured the relative importance and meaning that men and women attributed to those activities.

Interviews lasted an average of an hour and a half, with a female interviewer working with female subjects and a male interviewer (myself) working with the male subjects. For analysis, we then transcribed and organized the interviews by question and content. A disadvantage of such a focused sample is that the results may not generalize across age groups, or even represent this particular subgroup. However, we selected a private and personal interview setting to collect more detailed data about sensitive information concerning intimacy in friendships than would otherwise be possible when using larger samples and less personal data-collection techniques. Because of the college setting, we expected the sample to have more friends and contact with same-sex friends than men and women from the general population. The advantages of this sample of young adults are their temporal closeness to the development of adolescent friendships and their frequent interaction with friends because of the college environment. This should promote clarity in their recollections of the development of adolescent friendship behaviors and give them a sharpened and more sensitive vantage point from which to describe their current friendships with men and women.

THE DEVELOPMENT OF SEX-SPECIFIC STYLES OF INTIMACY: THE SEPARATE WORLDS OF BOYS AND GIRLS

Men and women grow up in overlapping, yet distinctively different worlds. Sex segregation begins at an early age when boys and girls are differently rewarded for various play activities. Boys are encouraged to actively participate in the outside environment by parental acceptance of the risks of physical injury and parents' flexible attitude toward personal hygiene and appearance. Torn clothes, skinned knees, and dirty hands are signs of the normal growth of healthy boys. If girls choose these same activities, they may be tolerated; however, they may be sanctioned differently. For example, the term "tomboy" is used to distinguish a girl with "boyish" behaviors, and to designate a stage of development that deviates from normative expectations of the female child. Several men attributed the distinctive friendship behaviors of men to this early segregation while growing up. Jim said:

> Well, you do different things. Little boys, they'll play in the dirt and things, whereas a guy and a girl they might play in the house on something. The guys like . . . they don't mind getting dirty. I don't want to stereotype or anything, but it's just the way I see it. The guys are more rugged and things.

Pete responded to the question, "How do you act just around the guys?"

> You'd talk about anything, do anything. You aren't as polite. You don't care as much how you look, how you dress, what you wear, things of that nature. Even if we're just platonic friends, for some reason when you're around girls you're different. In the United States men and women don't share bathrooms together in the public restrooms. That's a good example, right there—obviously men and women are segregated then. That segregation exists in friendships, too.

Separate restrooms are a concrete manifestation of the different realms experienced by boys and girls as they grow up and of the restrictions on crossing over into the other sex's domain. The curiosity that boys and girls experience about what the bathrooms are actually like for the other sex is evidence of this separateness. A boy who is teased and pushed into the girl's bathrooms called a "girl" as he hastily exits. Thus, children internalize sex-segregated boundaries and enforce these restrictions. Evidence of the longterm influence of this segregation is the humiliation and embarrassment an adult feels when accidentally entering the "wrong" bathroom. The association between gender and specific contexts is also suggested by men referring to a woman who is included in a men's poker game as being "just like one of the guys." The separate contexts of men and women continue throughout the life cycle to shape the ways they express intimacy.

The male world is the outside environment of physical activity. Boys share and learn activities with male friends that involve an engagement with this outside world. Social encouragement is evident in such organizations as the Boy Scouts, sports and recreation programs, and a division of labor that often has boys doing home chores that are outdoors, such as mowing lawns. These outside activities have a shaping influence on their interests and values. Jack recalled his adolescence:

> I can remember only one friend that I had from years past. My friend Jim. Just kind of all the fun we had, boyhood fun. We built a fort, lit firecrackers, and all that stuff.

He refers to "boyhood" rather than "childhood" fun, implying that these experiences tended to be shared with other males. Another man recalled:

> The activities shared were a lot of outdoor-type things—fishing, hunting, Tom Sawyer type things. It's a commonality that we both shared that helped bring us together.

Men mentioned activities that ranged from dissecting lizards, riding bikes, and childhood sports to four-wheeling, lifting weights, playing practical jokes on friends, problem solving, and talking about relationships as they reached adulthood. By the time high school graduation arrives, most males have had more experiences and time with men friends than with women friends. Several men commented on this early division in their friendships. For instance, Rick replied:

> Up to the sixth or seventh grade girls are "stay away from the girls!" So during that whole time you only associate with the guys, and you have all these guy friends. And after that you kind of, you know, the first time you go out, you're kind of shy with the girls, and you don't get to know them too well. . . . I really didn't get over being shy with girls until my senior year.

His first contact with girls is in the dating context of "going out," which implies a heterosexual coupling dimension to the relationship in addition to friendship. The segregated contexts of men and women continue into adulthood, and shape the opportunities for expressing intimacy and the expectations of how that intimacy is to be expressed. As a result, men are more familiar with their men friends, and women are more familiar with their women friends.

CONSEQUENCES OF THE SEPARATE WORLDS OF MEN AND WOMEN

Self-Disclosure: Profanity, Sameness, and Group Lingo

As boys move through adolescence surrounded and immersed in friendships with other boys, behavioral differences emerge that distinguish men's and women's friendships. Men develop language patterns that often rely on blunt, crude, and explicitly sexual terms. Bluntness, crudity, and profanity legitimize masculinity by tending to toughen the tone of any statement that a man may make. Swearing serves as a developmental credential in an adolescent boy's maturation process, much as do smoking, drinking, and getting one's drivers license. The "rugged" and "dirty" environment that boys share is translated into a coarser language during adolescence, which is also labeled as "dirty." Men felt that this language was more appropriate around other men, and they often related this sex-specific language to all-male contexts such as military service and sports. Greg responded:

> Well (laugh), not that I cuss a lot, but when I, you know, get around the baseball field and stuff like that. . . . They [women] don't like that. I try to stay away from the crude or harsh humor as much as I can (laugh).

Greg's laughing suggested a tense recognition that men's use of language in "harsh humor" does not easily translate in the company of women.

Men's harsh language and sexual explicitness in joking behavior are censored and muted when interacting with women friends. The censoring of humor to avoid offending women friends testifies to the different meaning and value men and women attribute to the same behaviors. Mike related:

> Around girls you act more of a gentleman. You don't cuss. You watch what you say. Because you don't want to say anything that will offend them.

Men felt more at ease with close men friends, partially from a perception of "sameness." Men assume that male friends will be more empathetic concerning sexual matters since they have similar bodies. Jack related:

> I find it much easier to talk about sexual things with guys, which makes sense.

A majority of the men said it was easier to talk to men about sexual matters than to women. Another man responded to the question, "What are some of the things that would be easier to talk over with a guy?"

> Anything from financial problems to problems with relationships. That's a big thing I really don't like talking to girls about. For some reason I just . . . I don't know . . . I get . . . usually because what I'm saying is from a male's point of view. And I know this is all sounding really sexist. But you know, there are certain things that I view that girls don't necessarily view the same way. And it's just easier talking to guys about that. Well, lately sex is one of those. I mean you can talk about certain sexual things; there are certain things I had a conversation the other day, and he was talking to me about a sexual act that his girlfriend, his new girlfriend, wanted to do. And he really doesn't care to do it. There's no way I could talk to a girl about what he's talking about.

The men appeared to generalize a common world view to other men that fostered a feeling of comfort. Frank commented:

> I'm more relaxed around guys. You don't have to watch what you say. Around friends like that [men] I wouldn't . . . what could you say? I wouldn't be careful I shouldn't say something like this, or I shouldn't do this. That's because with the guys, they're just like you.

Men friends used the degree of comfort and relaxation experienced with men friends as an indicator of closeness. Matt described this feeling when asked about the meaningful times he has shared with men friends.

> Last week some really good friends of mine in my suite . . . one guy plays the guitar. And so he was just sitting around playing the guitar and we were making up tunes. We were making up songs to this, and that was really a lot of fun. The fun things come to mind. We rented a VCR and some movies and watched those, and just all the laughing together comes to mind as most memorable. As to the most meaningful, those also come pretty close to being the most meaningful, because there was just total relaxation, there. That I felt no need to worry. There's no need to worry about anyone making conversation. The conversation will come. And we can laugh at each other, and you can laugh at yourself, which is handy.

Men were asked to compare their friendships with men to their platonic friendships with women. Generally, men felt more at ease and relaxed when with close men friends than with women friends. John answered the question, "Are there any differences between your friendships with men and your friendships with women?"

> You don't have to worry about the situation you're in. If you have to go to the bathroom, you just run up and go. You don't have to worry about "please excuse me" or anything. And it's a lot more relaxed. A lot more. Like in Jack's house we just go into the kitchen and make ourselves something to eat, you know, part of the family.

The "situation" is comfortable because the men's shared assumptions, cues, and meanings of behavior allow them "not to have to worry" whether they are acting appropriately. The formality associated with women friends is suggestive of Irving Goffman's concept of "frontstage" behavior, which is more rule-bound and distanced, while the "backstage" behavior with men friends is more intimate because of the lack of censoring and the feeling of informality associated with being "part of the family." The shared history, activities, and perception that other men are "just like you" gave a predictable familiarity to men's interactions. Women also felt that their similarity to each other produced an empathy unique between women friends. A woman responded to a question about the differences between her men and women friends:

> There are some things about a woman's feelings that I don't think a man, having never been in a woman's mind, could ever really understand. Because I think most women are a little more sensitive than men.

Men also developed unique terms with their close friends that expressed their history and connectedness. These terms acknowledged the particular experiences shared between friends and underlined their special relationship. When asked about his most meaningful experiences with his men friends, Tim related:

> The best thing, well the thing is, Rick, Mike, and me kind of have our own lingo. I haven't seen other people use them, like "Bonzo" is one of them. Like "go for Bonzo," and anybody else would just go "Well, whatever."

The "lingo" was derived from activities experienced by the group. The private meaning of the language served as a boundary separating friends from people outside the group.

Doing Versus Talking: The Intimacy of Shared Action

The men were asked, "What was the most meaningful occasion spent with a same-sex friend, and why was it meaningful?" The men mentioned a total of 26 meaningful occasions with men friends, and several men mentioned more than one meaningful experience. We analyzed the responses to clarify the link between sharing an activity and feeling close to a friend. Of those occasions, 20 meaningful times were spent in an activity other than talking. Men related a wide variety of meaningful experiences from "flirting with disaster" in an out-of-control car and winning a court case to being with a close friend the night that the friend found out his sister had committed suicide. Activities such as fishing, playing guitars, diving, backpacking, drinking, and weightlifting were central to men's meaningful experiences.

Nine meaningful experiences directly referenced the sharing of skills and accomplishments. These meaningful times involved the shared enjoyment of learning and mastering skills and accomplishing goals ranging from a sexual experience with a woman to staying up all night on a weeknight. The essential ingredients in these experiences seemed to be comfort with a competitive challenge and a sense of shared accomplishment. A man responded to the question of what was the most meaningful experience he had shared with a male friend, and later a group of male friends:

> I've always been extremely shy with women, and one of my friends in between, after high school . . . women were always chasing after him like crazy—and I'm defensive and stuff with women when one time we went to the river. And a couple of girls picked us up and we got laid and everything. And it was kind of, this is going to sound like the standard male thing, but we all kind of went, after, we went and had a few beers and compared notes. You know, and I felt totally accepted because I had just as many good things to say as they did, and I could relate. I knew what they were talking about, because most of my life I've never known what these guys were talking about sexually.

Although this quote might imply sexual exploitation, several aspects should be considered. First, this man admits he is shy with women, and furthermore he indicates that the women initiated the interaction. He was able to discuss with his men friends a new experience that had been alien to him until this occasion. The argument here is not that the sexual experience was exploitive or intimate; it appears to have been a purely physical encounter between strangers. However, the commonality gained from a shared life experience did provide meaningful interaction among the men.

We further examined the influence of men's active emphasis and women's verbal emphasis on intimate friendship behavior by asking men to compare their friendships with men to their friendships with women. Tim responded to the questions, "What part of you do you share with your men friends and what part of you do you share with your women friends? How would you characterize those two different parts of you?"

> I think that the men characteristics would be the whole thing, would be just the whole thing about being a man. You know, you go out and play sports with your brothers, and have a good time with them. You just . . . you're doing that. And there are some things that you can experience, as far as emotional, [with] your best friends that are men . . . you experience both. And that's what makes it so good is that. With most of the girls you're not going to go out and drink beer and have fun with them. Well, you can, but it's different. I mean it's like a different kind of emotion. It's like with the guys you can have all of it. . . .

Tim says that you can have "the whole thing" with men, suggesting that he can do things and talk about things with his close men friends. With women friends doing things is "different." Tim refers to a "different kind of emotion" and speaks of a "good time" when he is with his men friends. This good feeling may result from the ease and comfort of interacting with close friends who have developed a familiar style of communication from sharing activities.

The value of doing things is apparent in Matt's response, which described his most meaningful times with men friends:

> It was like we were doing a lot of things together. It just seemed like we just grew on each other. Can't think of just one thing that stood out in my mind. It was more like a push-pull type thing. Like I'd pull him through things and he'd pull me through things. It wasn't like there was just one thing I can just think of right now, just a lot of things he did, whatever. Just the things we like to do, we just did them together, and just had a good time.

The closeness is in the "doing"—the sharing of interests and activities. When Matt was asked about his meaningful times with his women friends, he responded:

> It's like the things that you'd talk—it's really just like "talk" with them. It's not so much like you'd go out and do something with them, or go out and maybe be with them.

Several men said that with women friends it's "just talking" and referred to interaction with women as "the lighter side of things." For men, it appears that actions speak louder than words and carry greater interpersonal value.

Women were also aware of a difference in men's style of expressing caring. A women commented on the differences in how her men and women friends let her know that they like her:

> Women talk more about feelings than men do. A man might let me know that he likes me because when he was in New York, he saw a book I'd been looking for and he brought it to me. And so I know that he likes me because he did that. Where a woman might say, twelve days in a row, "I've been looking all over for that book, but I can't find it."

Her male friend expressed his caring through a direct action, while her female friend expressed her caring verbally.

The emphasis on activities in men's friendship shapes their communication of closeness and caring. The significance of the doing/talking emphases in men's and women's styles of intimacy is apparent in the following response of a man to the question, "Why do you think they'd [women friends] be more verbal than your guy friends [in showing that they like you]?"

> I don't know why. I think there's just more ways to . . . I think there's more ways for the males to show me their appreciation that's nonverbal. I don't know why. I just think that if, in the way that they respond to things we do together and stuff like that. There's more ways to show it. Like if we're, I make a good shot in a game or something, just give me a high-five or something like that. You don't have to say anything with the guys. That's just an example, it doesn't have to be just sports. But the same type of things, off the field or whatever, just a thumbs-up type thing from a guy or whatever. There's just more

> ways to show being around [each other]. Where with the girls, you know, what can they do? You know, run up and just give you a kiss or something, I know girls who would do that in high school. So it—I think their options are just less—so they opt for the verbal type of thing.

He views talking as one option or style of expressing caring. From his activity-oriented perspective, he actually views women as restricted by a lack of alternatives to verbal expressiveness. These expressive alternatives are available to men through cues developed by sharing and understanding common activities. Nonverbal cues, expressed in active settings, contribute to private, covert, and in general, sex-specific styles of intimacy. This suggests that each sex tends to overlook, devalue, and not fully comprehend the other sex's style of expressing care.

Men and women have different styles of intimacy that reflect the often-separate realms in which they express it. The activities and contexts that men share provide a common general experience from which emerge certain values, gestures, and ways of talking about things that show intimacy. Both men and women are restricted in crossing over into each other's realm by early sex segregation, which results in a lack of experience with the meanings and contexts of the other sex. Researchers often underestimate this segregation because of an emphasis on the loosening of sex-related boundaries in the past several decades. Despite such changes, sex segregation still influences men and women, especially during the development of friendships in adolescence.

Covert Intimacy in Sports and Competition

Sports are the primary format for rewarding the attainment and demonstration of physical and emotional skills among adolescent boys. A man stated:

> I would have rather taken my basketball out than I would a girl . . . you know how young men are in the seventh, eighth, and ninth grade . . . if I had the choice I'd play basketball with the guys instead of going out that night.

Researchers have documented detrimental interpersonal consequences that may result from sports participation. However, the productive aspects of the sports context have received less attention from researchers. For men, the giving and receiving of help and assistance in a challenge context demonstrates trust and caring in a friendship. Engaging in the risk and drama of performing in a competitive activity provides the glue that secures the men in an intimate process of accomplishing shared goals. Jim responded to the question, "What situations or activities would you choose or would you feel most comfortable in with your close men friends?"

> I'm very comfortable, like playing racquetball. A lot of one-on-one things where you're actually doing something. Playing backgammon. Now being competitive makes it a little easier, because it's like a small battle going on. Not that you're out to show who's best, but it gives you something more that you two have in common in the situation.

The competition provides a structured context where friends can use their skills to create "something more" than they previously had in common. Each friend brings his own experiences and talents to join the other friend in the common arena of a competitive activity. The competition provides an overt and practical meaning; the covert goal, however, is not to "show who's best" but to give "something more that you two have in common."

The sports context provides a common experience whereby men can implicitly demonstrate closeness without directly verbalizing the relationship. Nonverbal communication skills, which are essential for achieving goals in the fast-moving sports context, also provide avenues for communicating intimacy. Greg responded to the question, "What were the most meaningful times that you spent with your men friends?"

> In athletics, the majority of these friends that are close to me were on teams of mine. We played together. We were on the same team, me playing first and him catcher, or at times he played third. You know, first and third looking across the infield at each other. Knowing that we were close friends, and winning the CIF championship. I could just see that it meant a lot to me in terms of friendship too. As soon as that last pitch was made, we just clinched the title, to see the first person that he looked for to give, you know, to hug or congratulate, or whatever, was me. And the same for me to him. That was a big, another emotional thing for the two of us. Because I could just . . . it's just . . . you could just see how close your friends really are, or something like that. When there's twenty-five guys on the team and they're all going crazy, you're just trying to rejoice together, or whatever, for the victory. And the first, the main thing you wanted to do was run across the diamond and get to each other, and just congratulate each other first. And that meant a lot to me emotionally as well as far as friendship is concerned. It was only a split second, because after it was just a mob.

The two friends had grown up playing baseball together. Sharing the accomplishment of winning the championship provided a context where a close friendship could be affirmed and acknowledged nonverbally in "only a split second." Other members of the team, and perhaps even family members, may not have been aware of the intimacy that took place. The nonverbal nature of the glance and the context of excitement in the team's rejoicing after the victory allowed the intimacy to be expressed privately in a covert fashion. Both the intimate style and the context in which the intimacy was expressed contributed to an environment that was relatively safe from ridicule.

How Do I Know You Like Me: Intimacy and Affection in Men's Friendships

When asked, "How do you know that your men friends like you?" only one man responded that his friend tells him directly that he likes him. If men do not tend to self-disclose to each other the closeness of their friendship, how do they evaluate closeness and intimacy with a man friend? In men's friendships with other men, doing something together and choosing a friend and asking him if he wants to participate in an activity demonstrate that they like one another and enjoy being together. These acts have a meaning similar to a boy who asks a girl to a dance; it's assumed that he likes her by the nature of the action. Mike responded to the question, "How do you know or get the idea that they [men friends] like you?"

> When I suggest that we do something I can tell in their voice or the way their actions are that they want to do it. Like hey! they really want to do it. Like, "Anyone want to go to the baseball game?" "Yeah, great! That's exactly what I want to do." That's a good feeling to know that you can make some sort of a suggestion that fits. Laughter, the joking, the noise. Knowing that they like to do the things that I like to do and that I like to do the things that they like to do. And it's the same in reverse, and basically I want to do it as well, me agreeing with them. As far as that goes, you'd say, I like it when they show me by asking me, if they want to do it with me.

Men mentioned physical gestures, laughing at jokes, doing one another favors, keeping in touch, "doing stuff," teasing, and just being around friends as ways they know that men friends like each other. The most common responses to the question of how their men friends let them know that they liked them were "doing things together" and "initiating contact." John responded:

> I think it's just something you can sense, that you feel by . . . obviously if you continue to go out and do things with them.

Mike responded:

> Well, they'll call me up and ask me to do stuff, if they have nothing to do, or if they do have something to do and they want me to be a part of it.

Men feel liked by other men as a result of being asked to spend time in activities of common interest. Within such active contexts, reciprocated assistance, physical gestures, language patterns, and joking behaviors all had distinctive meanings that indicated intimacy between male friends.

Reciprocity of Assistance. Men mentioned doing favors, which included mailing a letter, fixing a car, loaning money, and talking about problems relating to heterosexual relationships. The men emphasized a reciprocity of assistance and a goal-orientation to both problem solving and situations that involved self-disclosure. This reciprocity demonstrated mutual interest and also was a means to achieve a balanced dependency. Pete responded to the question, "How do your friends let you know that they like you?"

> We help each other out, just like doing favors for someone. Like right now, me and my roommate were going to class, and he was asking me questions because he slept in and didn't study. So I go "what's this—ok, here, just have my notes." Even though I'm going to need them for my thing at three. You know, just little stuff like that.

Matt referred to the assistance given between his closest male friend and himself as a "barter" arrangement.

> Jack and I had a good relationship about this. He's a very good mechanic, and I would ask him. And I would develop something that I do that was rewarding for him. Like I could pull strings and get free boat trips and stuff like that when I was an [diving] instructor. And he would work on my car and I would turn him on to the Islands and dives and stuff. It was sort of a barter situation.

The sharing of their skills and access to opportunities fostered interdependency, yet also maintained their independence through a mutual give-and-take.

Physical Gestures. Men also reported physically demonstrating affection to each other. However, the physical gestures had a distinctively masculine style that protected them from the fear of an interpretation of a homosexual preference. Men mentioned handshakes, bear hugs, slaps on the back, and an arm on the shoulder as ways that friends demonstrated affection.

Handshakes were the most frequently mentioned. Handshakes offer controlled physical contact between men and are often considered an indicator of strength and manliness. A strong, crisp, and forthright grip is a sign of "respectable" masculinity while a limp and less robust handshake may be associated with femininity and a homosexual orientation. A bear hug also offers a demonstration of strength, often with one friend lifting another off the ground. Gary described an occasion in his response to the question, "How do your men friends let you know that they like you?"

> I came back from a swim meet in Arkansas last week, and I hadn't seen Mike for two weeks. When I came back he came right at me and gave me a big old bear hug, you know, stuff like that. And my mom and dad were in the room, and they're going, "Hey, put my son down!" and we were all laughing.

Men give the affectionate hug a "rugged," nonfeminine veneer by feigning playful aggression through the demonstration of physical strength. The garb and trappings of roughness allow a man to express affection while reducing the risks of making his friend uncomfortable or having his sexual identity ridiculed. A slap on the back is much less risky for a man than a caress on the cheek, although they may have a similar message in the communication of closeness.

Joking Behavior. Men developed joking behaviors that communicate closeness and similar ways of viewing the world. Ken responded to the question, "How do you get the idea that they [men friends] are close friends?"

> Laughter is one of them. I'll admit, when I'm around anybody really, not just them, I try to be the world's best comic. Like I said, humor is just important and I love it. I'd rather . . . I just like to laugh. And when they laugh, and they get along with me, and we joke with each other, and not get personal, they don't take it too harshly.

Although Ken says he attempts to be a comic "when I'm around anybody," he goes on to elaborate about the differences in joking when around men or around women:

> For the girls, not so much the laughter because you can't, with the comedian atmosphere, or whatever, you can't tell with the women. . . . Because, you know, if you get together with some girl or someone that likes you a little bit, or whatever—you can tell them that your dog just died, and they'll laugh. You know what I mean, you know how it goes. It's just, they'll laugh at anything, just to . . . I don't know why it is. But you get together with certain girls and they'll just laugh no matter what you say. So it's kind of hard to base it on that. Because the guys, you know, you can judge that with the guys. Because they'll say it's a crappy joke or something like that, or say that was a terrible thing.

Women friends did not respond to his humor in as straightforward and rigorous a manner as did his men friends. This appears to be a result of a covert sexual agenda between the cross-sex friends and a misunderstanding of the cues and nuances of male joking behavior by his women friends. Joking behaviors often are rooted in the contexts of men's shared experience, an experience that women may have little access to. Joking relationships are used by men to show caring and to establish trust in the midst of competitive activities. The following response to the question, "What are the most meaningful occasions that you spent with a male friend?" demonstrated a context where joking behavior expressed intimacy in the midst of competitive action. First, Greg describes the context in which the joking took place.

> The first time I'd been waterskiing was last summer. And among these guys I was really athletic, maybe more so than them even. And he knew how to waterski and I didn't. And we got there, and I tried maybe six or eight times, and couldn't do it, just couldn't do it. I don't know what the deal was because I'm really an athletic person and I figure it wouldn't be that tough, and it was tough. As far as the friendship goes, for Mark, for him to sit there and have the patience to teach me what to do, what was going on, it must have taken an hour or so or more of just intense teaching. Like he was the coach and I was the player, and we got done with that and I did it. And the next time we went I was on one ski, thanks to him. It was that much of an improvement. And to know that we could communicate that well around something that I love, sports, and to know that we could communicate that well in something that we both like a lot, athletics, that meant a lot to our friendship.

Mark provided assistance that altered a potential traumatic experience into a positive success. Specifically, Mark used a joking relationship to reduce the pressure on Greg and allowed him to perform while in a vulnerable position. Mark did not exploit his superior capabilities, but shared them and empowered his friends. Greg explains:

> We were just able to make jokes about it, and we laughed at each other all day. And it finally worked out. I mean it was great for me to be that frustrated and

> that up-tight about it and know the only thing he was going to do was laugh at me. That may seem bad to some people. They'd have gotten more upset. But for me that was good. . . . It really put things in perspective.

The joking cues expressed acceptance and communicated to Greg that it was okay to fail, and that failing would not jeopardize continuing the lesson. Mark's acceptance of a friend's failures reduced the performance pressure on Greg, and thus released him to concentrate on learning to water-ski.

Joking behavior is important to men because it offers a style of communication that consists of implicit meanings not readily accessible to people outside the group. "In" jokes between friends demand attentiveness to an individual's thinking, emotional states and reactions, and nuances of behavior. They provide a format where a man can be meticulously attentive to the feelings and tastes of another man. An elaborate reciprocation of jokes can be a proxy for more overt forms of caring. Yet, because joking behavior is often used as a distancing gesture and hostile act, joking behavior is not interpreted as an expression of attachment. This adds to the covert nature of the act and further protects men from possible ridicule. The tenuous line between aggression and affection is demonstrated by Tim's response to the question, "Can you think of any other qualities that would be important to a close friendship?"

> Basically that they'll understand you. Like if you do something wrong and they go, "Oh, what a jerk." I mean they can say it, but they'll say it in a different way than some guy who shoots his mouth off, "What a jerk, you fell off your bicycle."

Tim was questioned further, "How would it be different—I know what you mean—but can you describe it?"

> You know, they'll poke fun at you but they'll say it in a friendly way. Where someone else will just laugh, "What an idiot," and they'll mean it. Where your friend will say . . . you know, just make fun of you and stuff. I don't know if I explained it too well.

The same words used by two different men are interpreted and reacted to in very different ways. The tone of voice and social distance between the two men are essential factors in the determination of an understanding friend as opposed to an aggressive enemy. Tim's reactions to both cues reveal the different meanings. The question was asked, "Okay, maybe if I ask another question to get at it, say you fell off your bike, how would you feel when your friend joked about you as opposed to . . .?"

> I would just start laughing, you know. I mean he'd start laughing at me and I'd just look and he'd go, "You jerk," and I'll start laughing. We know each other and stuff. Some guy off the street—I'll just cuss at him and flip him off, you know. So it's a little different.

Such discriminations are difficult for men to explain and describe. This would suggest that the discriminating task may be even more difficult for women, who have not had the experience in the contexts from which men's friendships have developed. Matt explained how he lets his closest male friend know that he likes him.

> I'll have a tendency to say, "Well, why don't you write?" in a teasing way, and "Okay, when are we going to get together? . . . and this bullshit of you being up there in Stockton."

Coarse language is injected into the teasing to legitimize the implicit meaning that he misses his friend and wishes that they were together. Joking relationships provide men with an implicit form of expressing affection, which is an alternative to explicit forms such as hugging and telling people that they care about them. Joking also may be more personal, since it often relies on a knowledge and sensitivity to a friend's attitudes and tastes, thus recognizing and affirming a unique part of him. The following portion of an interview demonstrates this masculine style. Jim responds to the question, "Why do you think [women are more likely than men to come out and tell you that they like you] that is?"

> Oh, it's just the way you were raised. It's society. You might hug a girl and say, "See you later and good luck on your test tomorrow." Whereas you'll joke around with a guy about it.

"Why would you joke around with a guy?"

> It's just a . . . it's just a different relationship, you know. I think society would accept two girls hugging each other and a guy hugging a girl, but it's a little different when you're two guys. I don't know if you saw the movie *Grease* where there, like Danny and that other guy who's driving the car, they do it, well like they hug each other right? After they pull the car out of the shop, it's kind of like that, they stop, they realize what they did. You might even want to, you might wanna say, "Hey, thanks a lot." You do stuff like that. But you don't act silly. You might shake their hand.

Jim was asked if he hugged his closest male friend, to which he responded, "No, I don't do that." He was then asked, "How would it feel if you went up to hug Fred [closest male friend]? How do you think he would react?"

> Well, I can remember a couple of times that we had . . . after a football game when you're real excited and things. It all depends on the situation. If I just did it, you know, out of the clear blue sky, he'd probably look at me and, you know. I could do it jokingly. It might even be pretty funny. I might try that. But I don't think he'd like it. He'd probably think it was a little strange.

Jim was able to hug his friend after a football game, when emotions ran high, and the men's masculinity had just been validated by participating in, and presumably winning, the game. The football context insulated the hugging from being interpreted as unmanly or gay. Jim says, "It depends on the situation." At one point when Jim was asked what it would be like to hug his friend, he interpreted it as a challenge or a dare. "I could do that." However, he translates the act into a joking behavior, "I could do it jokingly," in an effort to stylize the hug as masculine. Men's styles of intimacy attempt to minimize the risks taken when overtly expressing affection. These risks are summed up best by Jim when asked why he would feel strange if he hugged his best male friend. Jim said:

> The guys are more rugged and things, and it wouldn't be rugged to hug another man. That's not a masculine act, where it could be, you know, there's nothing unmasculine about it. But somebody might not see it as masculine and you don't want somebody else to think that you're not, you know—masculine or . . . but you still don't want to be outcast. Nobody I think wants to be outcast.

Thus Jim could not hug his friend "out of the clear blue sky," overtly and without a gender-validating context. The styles of male intimacy attempt to limit these risks. Joking behavior camouflages the hidden agenda of closeness by combining elements of a private awareness of a friend's history and personal nuances with a public tone of aggression and humiliation. A man describes his most meaningful times with men friends.

> The conversation will come and we can kind of laugh at each other. And you can laugh at yourself, which is really handy.

Much as the slap on the back covers an affectionate greeting with an aggressive movement, joking behavior provides a covert avenue in which to express caring and intimacy.

CONCLUSIONS

These findings suggest that microstructural variables, particularly interactional expectations, are powerful explanations for male intimacy styles. Intimacy between men is influenced by their awareness of the restrictive sanctions that are often imposed on men who express certain emotions, such as sadness or fear. Men's intimate verbal style is partially shaped by the fear of sanctions that may be imposed on emotional behaviors deemed culturally unacceptable. Homophobia and the difficulty men have disclosing weaknesses testify to the limitations they experience when attempting to explore certain aspects of their selves. These limitations of male intimacy may distance men from all but their closest men friends, and may also create a premium on privacy and trust in close friendships. Such limitations may be more detrimental later in life where structural settings are less conducive and supportive to maintaining active friendships. A college environment fosters casual access to friendships and friendships may also be integral and functional for the successful completion of a degree. Thus, the sample in the present study may be experiencing an intimacy that is more difficult for men to maintain in job and career settings.

The interview data show that although constraints in the masculine role limit men in certain situations and in verbal intimacy, men do develop intimate friendship behavior that is based on shared action. Men's intimacy often depends on nonverbal cues that are developed in contexts of active engagement. Men expressed intimacy with close friends by exchanging favors, engaging in competitive action, joking, touching, sharing accomplishments, and including one another in activities. The strengths of men's active style of intimacy involve sharing and empowering each other with the skills necessary for problem solving, and gaining a sense of engagement and control of their lives by sharing resources and accomplishments. Nonverbal cues offered an intimacy based on a private affirmation and exchange of the special history that two men share. This unique form of intimacy cannot be replicated solely by self-disclosure.

In addition to the men's active style of intimacy, they also reported self-disclosure to friends. Contrary to previous research, most men reported that they were more comfortable expressing themselves to a close male friend than to female friends. These men assumed that close male friends would be more understanding because of their shared experiences. Men said that self-disclosure and hugging "depended on the situation," and were more likely to self-disclose in a gender-validating context. Thus, men overcome cultural prohibitions against intimacy with this gender-validating strategy.

There are advantages and disadvantages to both feminine and masculine styles of intimacy. Feminine intimacy is productive for acknowledging fears and weaknesses that comprise a person's vulnerability. Admitting and expressing an emotional problem are enhanced by verbal self-disclosure skills. Masculine styles of intimacy are productive for confronting a fear or weakness with alternative strategies that empower them to creatively deal with a difficulty. Both styles appear necessary for a balanced approach to self-realization and the challenge of integrating that realization into a healthy and productive life.

Although this study focused on generalized sex differences to document a previously unrecognized active style of intimacy, women also demonstrated active styles of intimacy, and men demonstrated verbal styles of intimacy. Thus, although the results are based on generalized tendencies, the data also support the flexibility of gender-based behavior and the ability of men and women to cross over and use both active and verbal styles of intimacy.

The documentation of active styles of intimacy sharpens the understanding of intimate male behavior, and it provides a more accurate and useful interpretation of the "inexpressive male." The deficit model of male expressiveness does not recognize men's active style of intimacy, and stresses men's need to be taught feminine-typed skills to foster intimacy in their relationships. This negation or denial of men's active style of intimacy may alienate and threaten men who then assume that intimacy is a challenge they will fail. An awareness of the strengths in men's covert style of intimacy provides a substantive basis from which to address and augment changes in restrictive and debilitating aspects of masculinity. The finding that gender-validating activities foster male self-disclosure suggests that strategies for developing more intimate capabilities in men would be most successful when accompanied by a gender-validating setting that acknowledges, enhances, and expands the use of the intimate skills that men have previously acquired.

The data suggest the influence that sex-segregated worlds exert on the ways women and men choose, and are most comfortable in expressing, intimacy. The separate adult social worlds that women and men often experience shape the opportunities and forms of intimacy shared between friends. These structural opportunities and the styles of intimacy that become integral to specific opportunities become familiar, expected, and assumed between friends of the same sex, and often are bewildering, inaccessible, and misinterpreted by cross-sex friends or partners.

The implications are clear: men and women will have to be integrated in similar microstructural realms in the private and public spheres if we are to expect men and women to develop fluency in what are now termed "male" and "female" styles of intimacy. If such integration does indeed take place, the reduction of misunderstanding, frustration, and abuse in cross-sex relationships could be profound.

References

Balswick, J. "The Inexpressive Male: A Tragedy of American Society." In D. David and R. Brannon (eds.), *The Forty-Nine Percent Majority.* Reading, MA: Addison-Wesley, 1976:55–67.

Caldwell, R., and Peplau, L. "Sex Differences in Same-Sex Friendship." *Sex Roles* 8 (1982):721–732.

Cancian, F. M. "The Feminization of Love." *Signs* 11 (1986):629–709.

Goffman, Irving. *Presentation of Self.* Garden City, NY: Doubleday, 1959.

Komarovsky, M. *Blue-Collar Marriage.* New York: Vintage, 1964.

Swain, S. "Male Intimacy in Same-Sex Friendships: The Influence of Gender-Validating Activities." Conference paper presented at the American Sociological Association Annual Meetings, San Antonio, 1984.

MARTIN P. LEVINE

The Life and Death of Gay Clones

The aims, then, of a sociological approach to homosexuality are to begin to define the factors—both individual and situational—that predispose a homosexual to follow one path as against others; to spell out the contingencies that will shape the career that has been embarked upon; and to trace out the patterns of living in both their pedestrian and their seemingly exotic aspects. Only then will we begin to understand the homosexual. This pursuit must inevitably bring us—though from a particular angle—to those complex matrices wherein most human behavior is fashioned.

—William Simon and John H. Gagnon
"Homosexuality: The Formulation of a Sociological Perspective"

More than two decades ago, William Simon and John Gagnon formulated the first constructionist explanation for the sociocultural organization of gay life. Taking a cue from symbolic interactionist theory, they contextualized the formation of gay life, arguing that "the patterns of adult homosexuality are consequent upon the social structure and values that surround the homosexual after he becomes or conceives of himself as homosexual."[1] In this way, they traced the origin of gay life to the elements of surrounding cultures and social structures.

In other works, Simon and Gagnon stress the role of socialization in the evolution of gay sociocultural patterns. Like most sociologists and anthropologists, they argue that people acquire the cultural values, beliefs, norms, and roles that organize and direct their behavior through socialization into the prevailing sociocultural order. In addition, they feel that patterned regularities in social life occur as a result of individuals shaping their behavior around these sociocultural directives.

According to Simon and Gagnon, gay patterns emerge similarly in societies lacking a separate socialization process for adult homosexuality. They claim that in these cultures men who eventually become gay undergo essentially the same socialization process as other males. That is, they learn the same cultural values, beliefs, norms, and roles as other men. Moreover, they contend that regularities in gay life emerge as gay men shape their behavior within, between, and in reaction to these sociocultural prescriptions.

Subsequent constructionist explanations for gay life narrow the scope of Simon and Gagnon's rather broad formulation. Typically, these accounts appear in sociological studies of homosexuality framed from either a social labeling or a role perspective. In social labeling studies, stigmatization accounts "for the forms homosexuality" takes, "whether in behavior, identity, or community":

> The single most important factor about homosexuality as it exists in this culture is the perceived hostility of the societal reactions that surround it. From this one critical factor flow many of the features that are distinctive about homosexuality. It renders the business of becoming a homosexual a process that is characterized by problems of access, problems of guilt, and problems of identity. It leads to the emergence of a subculture of homosexuality. It leads to a series of interaction problems involved with concealing the discreditable stigma. And it inhibits the development of stable relationships to a considerable degree.[2]

According to role theory, homosexual roles shape the patterns of gay life. That is, regularities in gay life arise as gay men behaviorally enact the cultural expectations embedded in the homosexual role.

This chapter examines the validity of these three constructionist explanations of gay life for the forms of life associated with the gay clone, a social type that first appeared in the mid-1970s in the "gay ghettos" of America's largest cities. Social scientists use the term "social type" to describe an informal role that is based on collective images of a particular kind of person. The clone role reflected the gay world's image of this kind of gay man, a doped-up, sexed-out, Marlboro man.

Although the gay world derisively named this social type the clone, largely because of its uniform look and life-style, clones were the leading social type within gay ghettos until the advent of AIDS. At this time, gay media, arts, and pornography promoted clones as the first post-Stonewall form of homosexual life. Clones came to symbolize the liberated gay man.

The material presented here comes from a longitudinal field study conducted from 1977 to 1984 of a clone social world in New York's West Village. The fieldwork included observation and participant observation in such central meeting places within this world as bars, discos, and bathhouses. In addition, extensive participant observation was conducted among three distinct friendship cliques. Furthermore, unidentified interviews were conducted with both key informants and other participants. All three of these techniques have been used to collect follow-up data since the formal fieldwork ceased in 1984.

In what follows, I will show how Simon and Gagnon's constructionist explanation offers the best account for the patterns of clone life in the West Village. To support my argument, I will discuss the social context of the clone social world, the sociocultural organization of the gay social world, and the sociocultural organization of the clone social world. All undocumented words, phrases, and indented quotations in the third section come from my field notes. The words and phrases constitute gay argot are set off in the text by quotation marks.

THE SOCIAL CONTEXT OF THE CLONE SOCIAL WORLD

America underwent profound social changes over the course of the last three decades. During the 1960s and early 1970s, various student, gender, racial, and ethnic liberation movements struggled against the Vietnam War and social oppression. In particular, these movements removed many of the discriminatory sanctions applied against women and racial, ethnic, and sexual minorities and successfully altered the stigmatized cultural roles and identities assigned to these groups. For example, the black movement effectively ended legalized discrimination in housing, employment, and public accommodations and taught African-Americans to be proud of their racial and cultural heritage, which profoundly reduced black people's internalized self-hatred and low self-esteem.

There were also momentous shifts in culturally hegemonic values during the course of these decades. At the end of the 1960s, the burgeoning counterculture spread a libertarian ethos among millions of young, urban, college-educated, and middle-class Americans, which seriously undermined the cultural dominance of the Protestant ethic. In particular, the libertarian ethos deeply undercut the normative influence of the Protestant ethic's values sanctioning sacrifice and self-denial.

By the mid-1970s, the normative decline of the Protestant ethos permitted the rise of another set of values, known as the self-fulfillment ethic, which idealized gratification of all inner needs and desires. The self-fulfillment ethic transformed the counterculture's libertarian ethos into a value set sanctioning unbridled hedonism, materialism, and expressiveness, which subsequently sparked massive consumerism and experimentation with sex and drugs among followers of this ethic.

The altered social climate of the 1980s sharply curtailed the spread of the self-fulfillment ethic. A contraction in disposable income among the middle class and an epidemic of incurable sexually transmitted diseases eroded the economic and physical basis for unrestrained self-gratification. That is, unchecked consumerism and erotic hedonism became impractical in an era of economic deterioration, genital herpes, hepatitis B, and AIDS. In addition, widespread aspirations for stable relationships further weakened belief in self-fulfillment. More precisely, emergent desires for more permanent relationships and social networks fostered widespread dissatisfaction with the "me-firstism" implicit in the pursuit of unbounded self-gratification.

The waning of the self-fulfillment ethic during the 1980s promoted the growth of alternative value sets that merged values from both the Protestant and the self-fulfillment ethics. Yankelovitch labeled these value sets the ethics of constraint and commitment.[3]

The constraint ethic held that biopsychosocial contingencies sharply restrict gratification of inner needs and desires. It contended that materialistic and hedonistic pursuits had to be weighed against economic, social, and physical limitations. As a result, it sanctioned a form of restrained hedonism in which sensual indulgence was tied to physical well-being and a form of expressive materialism in which materialistic pursuits were linked to autonomy and creativity. In this way, it idealized self-discipline in the quest for restrained hedonism and expressive materialism.

The commitment ethic perceived connectedness as a cultural ideal. Accordingly, it valued attachment to people, avocations, institutions, and communities and approved of self-sacrifice in the service of deeper and more meaningful relationships and sacred or expressive activities.

The ethics of constraint and commitment fostered ready acceptance of sobriety, health maintenance and erotic limitations among those who endorsed these values. Restrained hedonism prompted millions of urban, educated, middle-class Americans to forsake smoking, alcohol, drugs, and recreational sex for strict regimens of abstinence, exercise, nutritional diets, and relational sex. This in turn provoked wide-spread participation in twelve-step recovery programs for substance abuse, eating disorders, and "sexual addiction." In addition, expressive materialism created enormous demands among this population for imaginative and self-reliant jobs. Finally, connectedness engendered tremendous commitment within this group to expressive hobbies, historic preservation, and community service. In the sexual realm, it fostered adherence to relational scripts, which sanctioned obligation, fidelity, and romance between sexual partners.

THE SOCIOCULTURAL ORGANIZATION OF THE GAY SOCIAL WORLD

The social changes of the past three decades profoundly affected the forms of gay life. At the opening of the 1960s, American culture stigmatized homosexuality as a type of gender deviance that required strict social control. That is, gay men were regarded as "failed men," as men who deviated from masculine norms because they were either mentally or morally disordered. In this way, gay men were relegated to cultural roles of "nelly queens," "hopeless neurotics," and "moral degenerates."

The stigmatization of homosexuality fostered harsh social sanctions designed to isolate, treat, correct, or punish gay men. For example, most states criminalized homosexual contact, which exposed gay men to police harassment, imprisonment, and blackmail. Moreover, psychiatry regarded homosexuality as a treatable form of mental illness, which left gay men open to mandatory psychotherapy or psychiatric hospitalization. Finally, family and friends frequently taunted, ostracized, and even violently attacked gay men.

Stigmatization meant that the gay world of the sixties functioned as a deviant subculture. This symbolic world constituted a relatively "impoverished cultural unit." That is, the threat of sanction effectively limited structural and cultural elaboration within this world to covert sets of socially isolated, self-hating social networks and gathering places, which were primarily designed to facilitate social and sexual contacts and the management of stigma.

Three techniques for neutralizing stigma largely shaped the patterns of life within this world: passing, minstrelization, and capitulation. Passing accounted for the secrecy that characterized this world and included a set of behaviors that was designed to hide a gay identity and world under a heterosexual facade. Minstrelization explained the patterns of cross-gendering associated with "camp," a behavioral style entailing the adoption of feminine dress, speech, and demeanor. Finally, capitulation accounted for the feelings of guilt, shame, and self-hatred associated with the damaged sense of self that resulted from believing that homosexuality was a form of gender deviance.

Stigma management also engendered significant impediments to erotic expression during this period. The lack of anticipatory socialization for male homosexuality in our culture signified that men who eventually became gay experienced essentially the same erotic socialization as men who grew up to be straight. Socialization agents taught both prehomosexual and preheterosexual youths the dictates of the male sexual script. Consequently, gay men acquired a recreational erotic code that held that sex was objectified, privatized, and phallocentric and an arena for demonstrating manly prowess.

Passing and capitulation prevented many gay men from engaging in the recreational sex associated with the male sexual script. The threat that recognition and police raids or entrapment posed to heterosexual passing forced some gay men to shun the opportunities for recreational contacts present in the sexual marketplace of bars, bathhouses, and public restrooms. In addition, the belief that same-sex desires constituted gender deviance blocked others from engaging in recreational sexual contacts.

The gay liberation movement of the sixties fundamentally altered forms of gay life. Many early gay rights activists had participated in either countercultural, antiwar, or civil rights movements and were therefore prepared to advocate libertarian values and the destigmatization of homosexuality. For example, they championed an ethic sanctioning self-expression, especially in regard to experimentation with drugs and sex. In addition, they promoted a construction of same-sex love that stripped homosexuality of its discrediting association with gender deviance. That is, they held that same-sex love was a moral, natural, and healthy form of erotic expression among men who typically conformed to cultural expectations for manly demeanor and appearance. Finally, they actively campaigned to reduce the level of criminal, psychiatric, and social sanction and succeeded in forcing some localities either to repeal sodomy statutes or to cease police harassment of gay men, in compelling the mental health professions to remove same-sex love from the official list of psychological disorders, and in provoking a growing acceptance of gay men in the family, media, and workplace.

The lessening of stigmatization reorganized the patterns of life within gay social worlds located in major urban centers. For example, the reduction of legal and social sanctions removed most constraints against structural and cultural elaboration within these worlds. Accordingly, the range of gay services, traditions, gathering places, and cultural subgroupings widened and deepened: "The dozen largest urban areas of North America now have readily identifiable gay neighborhoods with heavy populations of same-sex couples. Each of these districts features not only openly gay bars and restaurants, but clothiers, bookstores, laundromats, a variety of shops, doctors, lawyers, dentists, and realtors that cater to a gay clientele.[4] In addition, these neighborhoods contained an array of gay sexual, recreational, cultural, religious, political, and professional scenes or subcultures. In these areas, gay men could cruise for anonymous sex, join gay baseball teams, sing in gay choruses, attend gay studies groups, worship in gay churches or synagogues, work for gay Democratic or Republican clubs, see exhibitions of gay art, theater, and cinema, and participate in gay bankers, doctors, or lawyers organizations.

The weakening of sanction and the destigmatized definition of homosexuality also modified the forms of life associated with stigma neutralization. For example, the decline in sanction removed the grounds for heterosexual passing, which provoked many gay men to become openly gay. Moreover, the redefinition of homosexuality as a normal, healthy, masculine form of male sexuality erased the basis for the cross-dressing connected with minstrelization, prompting a wholesale abandonment of camp attire, demeanor, and activities. In addition, this definition of same-sex love eliminated the reason for perceiving homosexuality as gender deviance and fostered a new pride and sense of validity in being both gay and a man. Finally, along with the libertarian ethos, the decrease in sanction and heightened self-esteem eradicated many of the impediments to recreational sexual contacts, which provoked an increase in anonymous erotic activity.

The social changes of the 1970s and 1980s further strengthened these emergent urban gay patterns. During the 1970s, the self-fulfillment ethic sanctioned gratification of inner needs and desires, and many urban gay men became openly gay, materialistic, and hedonistic. Consequently, the forms of urban gay life came to include consumerism, erotic exploration, recreational drug use, and disclosure of sexual orientation.

However, these patterns were forsaken during the early eighties. By then, AIDS, a decline in discretionary income, and yearnings for stable relationships caused unbridled self-gratification to be regarded as unsound behavior. That is, a fatal venereal disease, mounting medical and caregiving expenses, and desires for permanent relationships made recreational sex, consumerism, and drug use appear untenable.

By the mid-1980s, the ethics of constraint and commitment became hegemonic within urban gay worlds. At this time, AIDS, economic deterioration, and longings for secure relationships made urban gay men embrace restrained hedonism, expressive materialism, and connectedness as cultural ideals. For example, the medical dangers associated with sex and poor health maintenance, coupled with a decrease in disposable income, prompted these men to accept values linking gratification of hedonistic and material desires with self-discipline for the purpose of either physical and financial well-being or autonomy and creativity. In addition, health concerns and longings for steady relationships led them to endorse values sanctioning commitment, monogamy, coupling, and celibacy.

The ethics of constraint and commitment provoked new forms of life in urban gay worlds. The ideal of restrained hedonism fostered ready acceptance of temperance, erotic restrictions, and health maintenance among urban gay men. These men increasingly gave up liquor, cigarettes, drugs, and risky sex for rigid regimens of exercise, sleep, diet, and safer sex. Many even entered twelve-step programs to "recover" from substance abuse and "sexual addiction." In addition, expressive materialism drove other gay men to work in fields demanding both creativity and autonomy. Finally, connectedness forced some men to become either caregivers for sick or dying friends and lovers or unpaid volunteers for community-based political or health organizations.

THE SOCIOCULTURAL ORGANIZATION OF THE CLONE SOCIAL WORLD

A unique set of sociocultural patterns distinguished the clone social world in the West Village from other gay cultural entities in New York City. The changes in the forms of life within this world between the 1970s and the 1980s paralleled the outbreak of the AIDS epidemic.

The Pre-AIDS Patterns of the 1970s

Prior to AIDS, the clone social world was structured around a group of socially isolated social networks and gathering places, networks and places segregated from the broader gay as well as the heterosexual world. That is, the participants in these networks and places were mainly clones.

The social networks included "cliques" and "crowds." Cliques functioned as friendship circles and met the men's basic social, emotional, and material needs. In this sense, they were surrogate families. A crowd consisted of a group of cliques that frequented the same meeting spot. For example, the Saint crowd involved the set of cliques that routinely gathered at The Saint disco. In addition, the members of a crowd usually either recognized or knew each other.

The crowds mixed in a round of meeting spots that was known as the "Circuit." The gathering places in the Circuit were mainly locales for social, recreational, or sexual activities. For example, the men dined in Circuit restaurants, worked out in Circuit gyms, cruised in Circuit bars, and had sex in Circuit bathhouses. In addition, the men attended Circuit meeting spots according to a fixed schedule called "Circuit hours." A retail clerk in his mid-twenties explained, "After work, we go to the gym, either the Y or the Bodycenter; then we stop by One Potato or Trilogy for dinner. On Friday nights, we cruise the Eagle and Spike. On Saturday nights, we go dancing at the Saint, and on Sunday nights, we go to the baths."

Three distinctive social patterns characterized the clone social world during this period. First, presentational strategies within this world were typically "butch." For example, these men usually fashioned themselves after such archetypically masculine icons as body builders and blue-collar workers, and commonly wore work boots, flannel shirts, and button-up Levis and had gym bodies, short haircuts, and mustaches or beards.

Moreover, clones dressed in such a way as to highlight male erotic features and availability. For example, these men frequently wore form-fitting T-shirts and levis that outlined their musculature, genitals, and buttocks. To highlight the penis even further, they often wore no underwear. In addition, they usually wore keys and handkerchiefs that signaled preference for sexual acts and positions: "White vividly describes the effect of eroticized butchness: a strongly marked mouth and swimming soulful eyes (the effect of the mustache); a V shaped torso by metonymy from the open V of the half unbuttoned shirt above the sweaty chest; rounded buttocks squeezed in jeans, swelling out from the cinched-in waist, further emphasized by the charged erotic insignia of colored handkerchiefs and keys; a crotch instantly accessible through the buttons (bottom one already undone) and enlarged by being pressed, along with the scrotum, to one side."

Furthermore, expressive strategies in Circuit gathering places evinced similar themes. For example, the decor and names of many Circuit meeting spots used western, leather, or high-tech motifs. One popular bar conveyed cowboy imagery through such furnishings as wagon wheels, corral posts, and western paintings, and staff uniforms consisted of cowboy hats, shirts, and boots. Other bars expressed this imagery through such names as Badlands or The Eagle.

The spatial design and names of some gathering places also articulated butchness. For example many bars set aside specific areas for "cruising" and "tricking." Some even showed pornographic films in backrooms. Other places manifested butchness in such names as The Cockring or The International Stud.

Second, erotic patterns within this world included cruising and tricking. Typically, clones cruised Circuit gathering places such as bars, bathhouses, and sex clubs for men who were their "type," that is, their erotic ideal, usually either good looking or "hung," "built," and butch. Generally, clones cruised these men by situating themselves in a position to signal sexual interest and negotiate a time and place for tricking. In most cases, they tricked almost immediately after meeting.

A rough, uninhibited, phallocentric form of sexuality characterized tricking among clones. Tricking frequently involved "deep throating," "hard fucking," and "heavy tit work." For example, fellatio often included vigorously jamming the penis completely down the throat (deep throating), which frequently caused gagging or choking. Anal intercourse usually entailed strenuously ramming the penis entirely up the anus while painfully slapping the buttocks (hard fucking). Nipple stimulation commonly involved robustly sucking, pinching, or biting the nipples to the point of pain (heavy tit work).

Clones often used drugs to overcome pain during rough sex and heighten erotic responsiveness. "Pot," "poppers," and Quaaludes were particularly popular. A thirty-something health professional reported, "I love to do poppers during sex because they cause the muscles in my ass and throat to relax, which allows me to suck dick and get fucked without gagging or feeling any pain."

Most tricks consisted of a single erotic encounter. That is, the men had sex once and never again. For example, a waiter in his twenties in a Circuit restaurant remarked, "I don't know why I give tricks my phone number. No one ever calls. Most of the time you trick with them and they don't even say hello to you the next time you see them."

Third, "partying" constituted the main recreational pattern among clones. These men regularly danced the night away in Circuit discos while "high" on such drugs as MDA, poppers, or cocaine. Typically, the men took drugs at informal clique get-togethers prior to going to the club, usually for the purpose of sensual stimulation for partying. A financial analyst in his early thirties stated, "MDA gives me the energy to dance all night. When I am stoned on MDA I can really get into the music and lights. My legs feel rubbery, like they can move to every beat."

Partying largely occurred on weekend nights in Circuit clubs. On party nights, hundreds of drugged, bare-chested clones jammed the dance floor, where they danced feverishly to throbbing rhythms and dazzling lights while snorting poppers and throwing their arms and clenched fists into the air. The following account incisively depicts partying at the legendary Flamingo:

> As we entered the club at one in the morning (the doors had opened at midnight) I saw a room full of husky men, many of them shirtless, sipping beer or Coke. . . . Everyone in the audience could have been put on professional display, since the crowd was extraordinarily muscular. . . . In the inner room people were dancing. . . . The light show was adequate but not obtrusive. . . . the blending of the records . . . the choice of music were superb. . . . Along one wall enthusiasts from the floor had leaped up onto a ledge and were grinding in dervish solitude. The mirror panels were frosted over with condensed sweat. One after another all the remaining shirts were peeled off. A stranger, face impassive, nosed up to us and soon was lending us his hanky soaked in ethyl chloride—a quick transit to the icy heart of a minor moon drifting around Saturn. Just as casually he stumbled off.[5]

The Post-AIDS Patterns of the 1980s

The distinctive sociocultural patterns of the clone social world largely dissolved during the 1980s. The men's previous erotic patterns meant that many clones were infected with HIV. That is, cruising and tricking had spread HIV infection widely among the men.

Many clones either became sick or died from AIDS. In fact, some of the earliest AIDS fatalities in New York City occurred among these men, and more than half the sample of three intensely studied cliques died. The rest were in varying stages of infection and illness. Only a handful tested negative for the HIV antibody.

AIDS-related diseases and fatalities caused clone structural entities either to collapse or to vanish. In most cases, the deaths of members broke cliques. For example, one clique lost six of its eight participants in three years. One survivor, a corporate executive in his late forties, commented, "Almost all the guys from my group have died. The lovers Tom and Jim went first in '82. Then Bob, Chad, and Ted in '83 and '84. Frank died a year later. Only Steve and I are left, but Steve has KS, and my lymph glands are swollen."[6]

In some cases, the burden of continuous sickness, caregiving, and dying split cliques. That is, emotional strains and pressures caused men to abandon the group. A free-lance writer in his thirties explained: "My clique fell apart after Seth, Bill, and Ed died. Al and Brian were afraid that one of us would get sick, so they moved to California. They just could not go through it again. After Seth died, Ben stopped returning our calls. I think he was pissed because he thought Bill, Ed, and I were not there enough for Seth." Moreover, the disintegration of cliques destroyed crowds. That is, the absence of familiar faces and acquaintances dissolved the social ties within crowds. A fashion designer in his late thirties remarked, "When I came here on Sunday evenings in the past, I would know at least half the bar. I could stand here and talk to different friends all night. Now I hardly know any one, and I don't recognize most of these faces. Most of the old crowd has either died or left town."

Furthermore, the demise of crowds plus official sanctions demolished the Circuit. For example, many clubs, gyms, and restaurants closed for lack of crowd patronage. In this regard, many men believed that lack of crowd clientele shut The Saint. A photographer in his thirties explained: "The Saint's shutdown came as no big surprise. The crowd that went there was dying off. AIDS killed it. I mean how could they keep it open with everyone dying. Each time I went, it was increasingly empty." In addition, local health officials closed bathhouses and sex clubs for being public health hazards.

The remains of the clone social structure blended into the broader gay world. That is, the surviving structural entities were integrated into other gay social worlds. For example, some clone cliques reconstituted themselves as friendship groups in the HIV social world. For example, two surviving members of one clone clique formed a new friendship circle with men from an HIV-positive support group. In addition, a few Circuit bars remained open because they successfully attracted younger gay crowds.

AIDS also altered the meaning of clone erotic, recreational, and presentational patterns. The relation between drug use, inadequate rest, and recreational sex with immunological damage and AIDS caused cruising, tricking, and partying to be perceived as unhealthy and self-destructive, and a widespread decline in these practices resulted. In addition, fear of AIDS erased the reason for eroticized butch imagery.

Several social patterns replaced the previous forms of clone life. First, butch presentational strategies were largely deeroticized. For example, clones still wore manly attire but in such a way as to camouflage musculature, genitals, and buttocks. That is, they wore underwear and looser T-shirts and levis. In addition, clones developed more natural physiques. In this regard, love handles became accepted as indicating health. Furthermore, most gathering places either ceased showing pornographic films or forbade sexual contact in backrooms.

Second, clone erotic patterns switched to safer and relational sex. Typically, clones defined safer sex as protected anal intercourse. In this vein, an actor in his twenties quipped, "The AIDIES [1980s] is the era of latex love." Indeed, the men routinely shared information about safe and comfortable use of condoms.

However, there was considerable ambiguity about the risk involved in other erotic acts. Almost all the men scoffed at official safer-sex guidelines for kissing and fellatio. Most felt that deep kissing was safe because of the low concentrations of HIV in saliva. They felt similarly about oral sex with no ejaculation or preseminal fluids because there was no exchange of body fluids. Hence, they regularly practiced these behaviors.

In addition, relational sex became normative among clones. That is, sex for most men occurred in the context of sociosexual relationships; they had sex mainly with dates, boyfriends, or lovers. In fact, some attended classes on how to date men at an AIDS service organization.

The relational ethos fostered new erotic attitudes. Most men now perceived coupling, monogamy, and celibacy as healthy and socially acceptable. An art dealer who was in his forties stated, "Ten years ago it was déclassé not to have sex. People thought you were weird if you did not trick. Now celibacy is in; people think you are healthy." Conversely, most men devalued routine recreational sex as dated and unhealthy. An educator in his mid-thirties commented while in a bar, "You see the guy over by the wall, the one groping the other guy. He is a real whore. I mean he still cruises the bar for tricks. I've seen him go home with three different people in the last week. You'd think he would know better, with AIDS and all that."

Third, health maintenance and community service became the chief recreational patterns among clones. Typically, the men hoped to boost their immune system through health maintenance. In this way, they felt that strict regimens of rest, diet, and exercise would keep them healthy. Hence, they regularly slept, took vitamins, ate health food, and exercised at health clubs. In addition, many practiced stress reduction and alternative forms of healing, including visualizations, homeopathy, and macrobiotic diets.

Community service chiefly involved caregiving and activism. The men cared for friends with AIDS, who were typically members of their clique. They made them dinner, paid their bills, cleaned their homes, and took them to doctors and hospitals. Moreover, they provided emotional support during the illness, offering love, acceptance, and companionship. At times, they even had power of attorney, with responsibility for making treatment decisions and implementing funeral arrangements. Clones also became unpaid volunteers in political action groups or AIDS service organizations. In particular, many became some of the earliest volunteers at Gay Men's Health Crisis. Others volunteered in more militant direct action groups such as Act-Up.

AIDS made volunteering socially acceptable among clones. Typically, the men devalued volunteering before the epidemic. Many even openly denigrated gay activists as boring. Others saw no need for activism since they did not believe that gay men were oppressed. AIDS forced them to question these assumptions. The government's inadequate response to the AIDS crisis painfully proved that gay men were indeed oppressed. Consequently, many became politicized, and they began to see the importance of volunteering for social and political change.

CONCLUSION

The material presented in this chapter shows that the best constructionist explanation for the sociocultural organization of clone life in the West Village is Simon and Gagnon's model. According to this model, elements of the surrounding culture and social structure largely shape the forms of life within the gay world. The model incorporates the explanatory factors associated with the other constructionist explanations for clone sociocultural patterns. That is, this model views homosexual stigma and roles as some of the sociocultural forces molding clone life.

Following Simon and Gagnon, the social context shaped the forms of clone life. That is, AIDS, gay liberation, male gender roles, and the ethics of self-fulfillment, constraint, and commitment molded and remolded sociocultural patterns within the clone social world. For example, gay liberation and the advent of AIDS significantly affected clone social structure. At first, gay liberation's success in lessening legal and social penalization of homosexuality in New York City engendered the formation of socially isolated cliques, crowds, and gathering places. Later, AIDS-related diseases and deaths either dissolved or socially integrated these structural forms into the broader gay world.

In addition, gay liberation, male gender roles, and self-fulfillment values shaped clone social patterns during the 1970s. Gay liberation's redefinition of same-sex love as a manly form of erotic expression provoked masculine identification among clones, which was conveyed through both butch presentational strategies and cruising, tricking, and partying. In particular, butch attire, muscles, and masculine environments vividly articulated the sense that clones were *men.* In a similar vein, the roughness, objectification, anonymity, and phallocentrism associated with cruising and tricking expressed such macho dictates as toughness and recreational sex. Finally, the endurance, impersonality, and risk taking connected with partying conveyed macho ruggedness and activity-centered forms of social interaction. The cultural ideal of self-gratification further encouraged these patterns, sanctioning the sexual and recreational hedonism inherent in cruising, tricking, and partying.

AIDS and the constraint and commitment ethics reformulated these forms in the 1980s. Health concerns encouraged acceptance of values associated with restrained hedonism, which provoked safer sex and health maintenance. These concerns also prompted endorsement of the ideal of connectedness, which fostered community service and relational sex.

Notes

1. William Simon and John H. Gagnon, "Homosexuality: The Formulation of a Sociological Perspective," *Journal of Health and Social Behavior* 8 (1967):179.

2. Carol A. B. Warren, "Homosexuality and Stigma," in *Homosexual Behavior: A Modern Reappraisal,* ed. Judd Marmor (New York: Basic, 1980), p. 139.

3. Daniel Yankeloviteh, "American Values: Changes and Stability," *Public Opinion* 6 (1984): 2-9.

4. Laud Humphreys, "Exodus and Identity: The Emerging Gay Culture," in Martin P. Levine, ed., *Gay Men: The Sociology of Male Homosexuality* (New York: Harper & Row, 1979), pp. 134–47.

5. Edmund White, *States of Desire* (New York: Dutton, 1980), pp. 278–79.

PART 9 THE GENDER OF VIOLENCE

As a nation, we fret about "teen violence," complain about "inner city crime" or fear "urban gangs." We express shock at the violence in our nation's public schools, where metal detectors crowd the doorways and knives and guns compete with pencils and erasers in students' backpacks. These tragic and terrible public school shootings leave us speechless and sick at heart. Yet when we think about violent events, do we ever consider that, whether white or black, inner city or suburban, troubled teenagers or bands of marauding "youths" are virtually all males?

Men constitute 99 percent of all persons arrested for rape; 88 percent of those arrested for murder; 92 percent of those arrested for robbery; 87 percent arrested for aggravated assault; 85 percent arrested for other assaults; 83 percent arrested for all family violence; 82 percent arrested for disorderly conduct. Men are overwhelmingly more violent than women. Nearly 90 percent of all murder victims are murdered by other men, according to the U.S. Department of Justice (Uniform Crime Reports, 1991, p. 17).

From early childhood to old age, violence is perhaps the most obdurate, intractable gender difference we have observed. The National Academy of Sciences puts the case starkly: "The most consistent pattern with respect to gender is the extent to which male criminal participation in serious crimes at any age greatly exceeds that of females, regardless of source of data, crime type, level of involvement, or measure of participation," a statement that leads criminologists Michael Gottfredson and Travis Hirschi to state that men "are always and everywhere more likely than women to commit criminal acts" (1990, p. 145). Yet how do we understand this obvious association between masculinity and violence? Is it a biological fact of nature, caused by something inherent in male anatomy? Is it culturally universal? And in the United States, what has been the association between gender and violence? Has that association become stronger or weaker over time? What can we, as a culture, do to prevent or at least ameliorate the problem of male violence?

My concern throughout this book has been to observe the construction of gender difference and gender inequality at both the individual level of identity and the institutional level. The readings here reflect these concerns. Carol Cohn's insightful essay penetrates the gendered language of masculine "war talk," in which the human tragedy of nuclear war preparation is masked behind discussions of kill ratios, body counts, and megaton delivery.

And Russell and R. Emerson Dobash and their colleagues use a gendered power analysis to explain why it is that men batter women they say they love in far greater numbers than women hit men. They bring a sensible sobriety to current discussions that suggest that women are just as likely to commit acts of violence against their husbands as men are against their wives.

Of course, to argue that men are more prone to violence than women are does not resolve the political question of what to do about it. It would be foolish to resignedly throw up our hands in despair that "boys will be boys." Whether you believe this gender difference in violence derives from different biological predispositions (which I regard as dubious because these biological impulses do not seem to be culturally universal) or because male violence is socially sanctioned and legitimated as an expression of masculine control and domination (a far more convincing explanation), the policy question remains open. Do we organize society so as to maximize this male propensity toward violence, or do we organize society so as to minimize and constrain it? The answers to this question, like the answers to the questions about alleviating gender inequality in the family, in our educational institutions and in the work place are more likely to come from the voting booth than from the laboratories of scientists. As a society, we decide how much weight to give what few gender differences there are, and how best to address the enormous problem of gendered violence and alleviate the pain of those who are the victims of gendered violence.

References

Gottfredson, Michael, and Travis Hirschi. *A General Theory of Crime.* Stanford: Stanford University Press, 1990.

U.S. Department of Justice, Bureau of Justice Statistics. *Uniform Crime Reports.* Washington, D.C.: U.S. Government Printing Office, 1991.

CAROL COHN

Wars, Wimps, and Women: Talking Gender and Thinking War

I start with a true story, told to me by a white male physicist:

> Several colleagues and I were working on modeling counterforce attacks, trying to get realistic estimates of the number of immediate fatalities that would result from different deployments. At one point, we remodeled a particular attack, using slightly different assumptions, and found that instead of there being thirty-six million immediate fatalities, there would only be thirty million. And everybody was sitting around nodding, saying, "Oh yeah, that's great, only thirty million," when all of a sudden, I heard what we were saying. And I

> blurted out, "Wait, I've just heard how we're talking—Only thirty million! Only thirty million human beings killed instantly?" Silence fell upon the room. Nobody said a word. They didn't even look at me. It was awful. I felt like a woman.

The physicist added that henceforth he was careful to never blurt out anything like that again.

During the early years of the Reagan presidency, in the era of the Evil Empire, the cold war, and loose talk in Washington about the possibility of fighting and "prevailing" in a nuclear war, I went off to do participant observation in a community of North American nuclear defense intellectuals and security affairs analysts—a community virtually entirely composed of white men. They work in universities, think tanks, and as advisers to government. They theorize about nuclear deterrence and arms control, and nuclear and conventional war fighting, about how to best translate military might into political power; in short, they create the discourse that underwrites American national security policy. The exact relation of their theories to American political and military practice is a complex and thorny one; the argument can be made, for example, that their ideas do not so much shape policy decisions as legitimate them after the fact. But one thing that is clear is that the body of language and thinking they have generated filters out to the military, politicians, and the public, and increasingly shapes how we talk and think about war. This was amply evident during the Gulf War: Gulf War "news," as generated by the military briefers, reported by newscasters, and analyzed by the television networks' resident security experts, was marked by its use of the professional language of defense analysis, nearly to the exclusion of other ways of speaking.

My goal has been to understand something about how defense intellectuals think, and why they think that way. Despite the parsimonious appeal of ascribing the nuclear arms race to "missile envy," I felt certain that masculinity was not a sufficient explanation of why men think about war in the ways that they do. Indeed, I found many ways to understand what these men were doing that had little or nothing to do with gender. But ultimately, the physicist's story and others like it made confronting the role of gender unavoidable. Thus, in this paper I will explore gender discourse, and its role in shaping nuclear and national security discourse.

I want to stress, this is not a paper about men and women, and what they are or are not like. I will not be claiming that men are aggressive and women peace loving. I will not even address the question of how men's and women's relations to war may differ, nor of the different propensities they may have to committing acts of violence. Neither will I pay more than passing attention to the question which so often crops up in discussions of war and gender, that is, would it be a more peaceful world if our national leaders were women? These questions are valid and important, and recent feminist discussion of them has been complex, interesting, and contentious. But my focus is elsewhere. I wish to direct attention away from gendered individuals and toward gendered discourses. My question is about the way that civilian defense analysts think about war, and the ways in which that thinking is shaped not by their maleness (or, in extremely rare instances, femaleness), but by the ways in which gender discourse intertwines with and permeates that thinking.

Let me be more specific about my terms. I use the term *gender* to refer to the constellation of meanings that a given culture assigns to biological sex differences. But more than that, I use gender to refer to a symbolic system, a central organizing discourse of culture, one that not only shapes how we experience and understand ourselves as men and women, but that also interweaves with other discourses and shapes *them*—and therefore shapes other aspects of our world—such as how nuclear weapons are thought about and deployed.

So when I talk about "gender discourse," I am talking not only about words or language but about a system of meanings, of ways of thinking, images and words that first shape how we experience, understand, and represent ourselves as men and women, but that also do more than that; they shape many other aspects of our lives and culture. In this symbolic system, human characteristics are dichotomized, divided into pairs of polar opposites that are supposedly mutually exclusive: mind is opposed to body; culture to nature; thought to feeling; logic to intuition; objectivity to subjectivity; aggression to passivity; confrontation to accommodation; abstraction to particularity; public to private; political to personal, ad nauseam. In each case, the first term of the "opposites" is associated with male, the second with female. And in each case, our society values the first over the second.

I break it into steps like this—analytically separating the *existence* of these groupings of binary oppositions, from the association of each group with a gender, from the valuing of one over the other, the so-called male over the so-called female, for two reasons: first, to try to make visible the fact that this system of dichotomies is encoding many meanings that may be quite unrelated to male and female bodies. Yet once that first step is made—the association of each side of those lists with a gender—gender now becomes tied to many other kinds of cultural representations. If a human activity, such as engineering, fits some of the characteristics, it becomes gendered.

My second reason for breaking it into those steps is to try to help make it clear that the meanings can flow in different directions; that is, in gender discourse, men and women are supposed to exemplify the characteristics on the lists. It also works in reverse, however; to evidence any of these characteristics—to be abstract, logical or dispassionate, for example—is not simply to be those things, but also to be manly. And to be manly is not simply to be manly, but also to be in the more highly valued position in the discourse. In other words, to exhibit a trait on that list is not neutral—it is not simply displaying some basic human characteristic. It also positions you in a discourse of gender. It associates you with a particular gender, and also with a higher or lower valuation.

In stressing that this is a *symbolic* system, I want first to emphasize that while real women and men do not really fit these gender "ideals," the existence of this system of meaning affects all of us, nonetheless. Whether we want to or not, we see ourselves and others against its templates, we interpret our own and others' actions against it. A man who cries easily cannot avoid in some way confronting that he is likely to be seen as less than fully manly. A woman who is very aggressive and incisive may enjoy that quality in herself, but the fact of her aggressiveness does not exist by itself; she cannot avoid having her own and others' perceptions of that quality of hers, the meaning it has for people, being in some way mediated by the discourse of gender. Or, a different kind of example: Why does it mean one thing when George Bush gets teary-eyed in public, and something entirely different when Patricia Shroeder does? The same act is viewed through the lens of gender and is seen to mean two very different things.

Second, as gender discourse assigns gender to human characteristics, we can think of the discourse as something we are positioned *by*. If I say, for example, that a corporation should stop dumping toxic waste because it is damaging the creations of mother earth, (i.e., articulating a valuing and sentimental vision of nature), I am speaking in a manner associated with women, and our cultural discourse of gender positions me as female. As such I am then associated with the whole constellation of traits—irrational, emotional, subjective, and so forth—and I am in the devalued position. If, on the other hand, I say the corporation should stop dumping toxic wastes because I have calculated that it is causing $8.215 billion of damage to eight nonrenewable resources, which should be seen as equivalent to lowering the GDP by 0.15 percent per annum, (i.e., using a rational, calculative mode of thought), the discourse positions me as masculine—rational, objective, logical, and so forth—the dominant, valued position.

But if we are positioned *by* discourses, we can also take different positions *within* them. Although I am female, and this would "naturally" fall into the devalued term, I can choose to "speak like a man"—to be hard-nosed, realistic, unsentimental, dispassionate. Jeanne Kirkpatrick is a formidable example. While we can choose a position in a discourse, however, it means something different for a woman to "speak like a man" than for a man to do so. It is heard differently.

One other note about my use of the term *gender discourse:* I am using it in the general sense to refer to the phenomenon of symbolically organizing the world in these gender-associated opposites. I do not mean to suggest that there is a single discourse defining a single set of gender ideals. In fact, there are many specific discourses of gender, which vary by race, class, ethnicity, locale, sexuality, nationality, and other factors. The masculinity idealized in the gender discourse of new Haitian immigrants is in some ways different from that of sixth-generation white Anglo-Saxon Protestant business executives, and both differ somewhat from that of white-male defense intellectuals and security analysts. One version of masculinity is mobilized and enforced in the armed forces in order to enable men to fight wars, while a somewhat different version of masculinity is drawn upon and expressed by abstract theoreticians of war.

Let us now return to the physicist who felt like a woman: what happened when he "blurted out" his sudden awareness of the "only thirty million" dead people? First, he was transgressing a code of professional conduct. In the civilian defense intellectuals' world, when you are in professional settings you do not discuss the bloody reality behind the calculations. It is not required that you be completely unaware of them in your outside life, or that you have no feelings about them, but it is required that you do not bring them to the foreground in the context of professional activities. There is a general awareness that you *could not* do your work if you did; in addition, most defense intellectuals believe that emotion and description of human reality distort the process required to think well about nuclear weapons and warfare.

So the physicist violated a behavioral norm, in and of itself a difficult thing to do because it threatens your relationships to and your standing with your colleagues.

But even worse than that, he demonstrated some of the characteristics on the "female" side of the dichotomies—in his "blurting" he was impulsive, uncontrolled, emotional, concrete, and attentive to human bodies, at the very least. Thus, he marked himself not only as unprofessional but as feminine, and this, in turn, was doubly threatening. It was not only a threat to his own sense of self as masculine, his gender identity, it also identified him with a devalued status—of a woman—or put him in the devalued or subordinate position in the discourse.

Thus, both his statement, "I felt like a woman," and his subsequent silence in that and other settings are completely understandable. To have the strength of character and courage to transgress the strictures of both professional and gender codes *and* to associate yourself with a lower status is very difficult.

This story is not simply about one individual, his feelings and actions; it is about the role of gender discourse. The impact of gender discourse in that room (and countless others like it) is that some things get left out. Certain ideas, concerns, interests, information, feelings, and meanings are marked in national security discourse as feminine, and are devalued. They are therefore, first, very difficult to *speak,* as exemplified by the physicist who felt like a woman. And second, they are very difficult to *hear,* to take in and work with seriously, even if they *are* said. For the others in the room, the way in which the physicist's comments were marked as female and devalued served to delegitimate them. It is almost as though they had become an accidental excrescence in the middle of the room. Embarrassed politeness demanded that they be ignored.

I must stress that this is not simply the product of the idiosyncratic personal composition of that particular room. In other professional settings, I have experienced the feeling that something terribly important is being left out and must be spoken; and yet, it has felt almost physically impossible to utter the words, almost as though they could not be pushed out into the smooth, cool, opaque air of the room.

What is it that cannot be spoken? First, any words that express an emotional awareness of the desperate human reality behind the sanitized abstractions of death and destruction—as in the physicist's sudden vision of thirty million rotting corpses. Similarly, weapons' effects may be spoken of only in the most clinical and abstract terms, leaving no room to imagine a seven-year-old boy with his flesh melting away from his bones or a toddler with her skin hanging down in strips. Voicing concern about the number of casualties in the enemy's armed forces, imagining the suffering of the killed and wounded young men, is out of bounds. (Within the military itself, it is permissible, even desirable, to attempt to minimize immediate civilian casualties if it is possible to do so without compromising military objectives, but as we learned in the Persian Gulf War, this is only an extremely limited enterprise; the planning and precision of military targeting does not admit of consideration of the cost in human lives of such actions as destroying power systems, or water and sewer systems, or highways and food distribution systems.) Psychological effects—on the soldiers fighting the war or on the citizens injured, or fearing for their own safety, or living through tremendous deprivation, or helplessly watching their babies die from diarrhea due to the lack of clean water—all of these are not to be talked about.

But it is not only particular subjects that are out of bounds. It is also tone of voice that counts. A speaking style that is identified as cool, dispassionate, and distanced is required. One that vibrates with the intensity of emotion almost always disqualifies the speaker, who is heard to sound like "a hysterical housewife."

What gets left out, then, is the emotional, the concrete, the particular, the human bodies and their vulnerability, human lives and their subjectivity—all of which are marked as feminine in the binary dichotomies of gender discourse. In other words, gender discourse informs and shapes nuclear and national security discourse, and in so doing creates silences and absences. It keeps things out of the room, unsaid, and keeps them ignored if they manage to get in. As such, it degrades our ability to think *well* and *fully* about nuclear weapons and national security, and shapes and limits the possible outcomes of our deliberations.

What becomes clear, then, is that defense intellectuals' standards of what constitutes "good thinking" about weapons and security have not simply evolved out of trial and error; it is not that the history of nuclear discourse has been filled with exploration of other ideas, concerns, interests, information, questions, feelings, meanings and stances which were then found to create distorted or poor thought. It is that these options have been *preempted* by gender discourse, and by the feelings evoked by living up to or transgressing gender codes.

To borrow a term from defense intellectuals, you might say that gender discourse becomes a "preemptive deterrent" to certain kinds of thought.

Let me give you another example of what I mean—another story, this one my own experience:

One Saturday morning I, two other women, and about fifty-five men gathered to play a war game designed by the RAND Corporation. Our "controllers" (the people running the game) first divided us up into three sets of teams; there would be three simultaneous games being played, each pitting a Red Team against a Blue Team (I leave the reader to figure out which color represents which country). All three women were put onto the same team, a Red Team.

The teams were then placed in different rooms so that we had no way of communicating with each other, except through our military actions (or lack of them) or by sending demands and responses to those demands via the controllers. There was no way to negotiate or to take actions other than military ones. (This was supposed to simulate reality.) The controllers then presented us with maps and pages covered with numbers representing each side's forces. We were also given a "scenario," a situation of escalating tensions and military conflicts, starting in the Middle East and spreading to Central Europe. We were to decide what to do, the controllers would go back and forth between the two teams to relate the other team's actions, and periodically the controllers themselves would add something that would ratchet up the conflict—an announcement of an "intercepted intelligence report" from the other side, the authenticity of which we had no way of judging.

Our Red Team was heavily into strategizing, attacking ground forces, and generally playing war. We also, at one point, decided that we were going to pull our troops out of Afghanistan, reasoning it was bad for us to have them there and that the Afghanis had the right to self-determination. At another point we removed some troops from Eastern Europe. I must add that later on my team was accused of being wildly "unrealistic," that this group of experts found the idea that the Soviet Union might voluntarily choose to pull troops out of Afghanistan and Eastern Europe so utterly absurd. (It was about six months before Gorbachev actually did the same thing.)

Gradually our game escalated to nuclear war. The Blue Team used tactical nuclear weapons against our troops, but our Red Team decided, initially at least, against nuclear retaliation. When the game ended (at the end of the allotted time) our Red Team had "lost the war" (meaning that we had political control over less territory than we had started with, although our homeland had remained completely unviolated and our civilian population safe).

In the debriefing afterwards, all six teams returned to one room and reported on their games. Since we had had absolutely no way to know why the other team had taken any of its actions, we now had the opportunity to find out what they had been thinking. A member of the team that had played against us said, "Well, when he took his troops out of Afghanistan, I knew he was weak and I could push him around. And then, when we nuked him and he didn't nuke us back, I knew he was just such a wimp, I could take him for everything he's got and I nuked him again. He just wimped out."

There are many different possible comments to make at this point. I will restrict myself to a couple. First, when the man from the Blue Team called me a wimp (which is what it felt like for each of us on the Red Team—a personal accusation), I felt silenced. My reality, the careful reasoning that had gone into my strategic and tactical choices, the intelligence, the politics, the morality—all of it just disappeared, completely invalidated. I could not explain the reasons for my actions, could not protest, "Wait, you idiot, I didn't do it because I was weak, I did it because it made sense to do it that way, given my understandings of strategy and tactics, history and politics, my goals and my values." The protestation would be met with knowing sneers. In this discourse, the coding of an act as wimpish is hegemonic. Its emotional heat and resonance is like a bath of sulfuric acid: it erases everything else.

"Acting like a wimp" is an *interpretation* of a person's acts (or, in national security discourse, a country's acts, an important distinction I will return to later). As with any other interpretation, it is a selection of one among many possible different ways to understand something—once the selection is made, the other possibilities recede into invisibility. In national security discourse, "acting like a wimp," being insufficiently masculine, is one of the most readily available interpretive codes. (You do not need to do participant observation in a community of defense intellectuals to know this—just look at the "geopolitical analyses" in the media and on Capitol Hill of the way in which George Bush's military intervention in Panama and the Persian Gulf War finally allowed him to beat the "wimp factor.") You learn that someone is being a wimp if he perceives an international crisis as very dangerous and urges caution; if he thinks it might not be important to have just as many weapons that are just as big as the other guy's; if he suggests that an attack should not necessarily be answered by an even more destructive counterattack; or, until recently, if he suggested that making unilateral arms reductions might be useful for our own security. All of these are "wimping out."

The prevalence of this particular interpretive code is another example of how gender discourse affects the quality of thinking within the national security community, first, because, as in the case of the physicist who "felt like a woman," it is internalized to become a self-censor; there are things professionals simply will not *say* in groups, options they simply will not argue nor write about, because they know that to do so is to brand themselves as wimps. Thus, a whole range of inputs is left out, a whole series of options is foreclosed from their deliberations.

Equally, if not more damagingly, is the way in which this interpretive coding not only limits what is *said*, but even limits what is *thought*. "He's a wimp" is a phrase that *stops* thought. When we were playing the game, once my opponent on the Blue Team "recognized the fact that I was a wimp," that is, once he interpreted my team's actions through the lens of this common interpretive code in national security discourse, he *stopped thinking*; he stopped looking for ways to understand what we were doing. He did not ask, "Why on earth would the Red Team do that? What does it tell me about them, about their motives and purposes and goals and capabilities? What does it tell me about their possible understandings of *my* actions, or of the situation they're in?" or any other of the many questions that might have enabled him to revise his own conception of the situation or perhaps achieve his goals at a far lower level of violence and destruction. Here, again, gender discourse acts as a preemptive deterrent to thought.

"Wimp" is, of course, not the only gendered pejorative used in the national security community; "pussy" is another popular epithet, conjoining the imagery of harmless domesticated (read demasculinized) pets with contemptuous reference to women's genitals. In an informal setting, an analyst worrying about the other side's casualties, for example, might be asked, "What kind of pussy are you, anyway?" It need not happen more than once or twice before everyone gets the message; they quickly learn not to raise the issue in their discussions. Attention to and care for the living, suffering, and dying of human beings (in this case, soldiers and their families and friends) is again banished from the discourse through the expedient means of gender-bashing.

Other words are also used to impugn someone's masculinity and, in the process, to delegitimate his position and avoid thinking seriously about it. "Those Krauts are a bunch of limp-dicked wimps" was the way one U.S. defense intellectual dismissed the West German politicians who were concerned about popular opposition to Euromissile deployments. I have heard our NATO allies referred to as "the Euro-fags" when they disagreed with American policy on such issues as the Contra War or the bombing of Libya. Labeling them "fags" is an effective strategy; it immediately dismisses and trivializes their opposition to U.S. policy by coding it as due to inadequate masculinity. In other words, the American analyst need not seriously confront the Europeans' arguments, since the Europeans' doubts about U.S. policy obviously stem not from their reasoning but from the "fact" that they "just don't have the stones for war." Here, again, gender discourse deters thought.

"Fag" imagery is not, of course, confined to the professional community of security analysts; it also appears in popular "political" discourse. The Gulf War was replete with examples. American derision of Saddam Hussein included bumper stickers that read "Saddam, Bend Over." American soldiers reported that the "U.S.A." stenciled on their uniforms stood for "Up Saddam's Ass." A widely reprinted cartoon, surely one of the most multiply offensive that came out of the war, depicted Saddam bowing down in the Islamic posture of prayer, with a huge U.S. missile, approximately five times the size of the prostrate figure, about to penetrate his upraised bottom. Over and over, defeat for the Iraqis was portrayed as humiliating anal penetration by the more powerful and manly United States.

Within the defense community discourse, manliness is equated not only with the ability to win a war (or to "prevail," as some like to say when talking about nuclear war); it is also equated with the willingness (which they would call courage) to threaten and use force. During the Carter administration, for example, a well-known academic security affairs specialist was quoted as saying that "under Jimmy Carter the United States is spreading its legs for the Soviet Union." Once this image is evoked, how does rational discourse about the value of U.S. policy proceed?

In 1989 and 1990, as Gorbachev presided over the withdrawal of Soviet forces from Eastern Europe, I heard some defense analysts sneeringly say things like, "They're a bunch of pussies for pulling out of Eastern Europe." This is extraordinary. Here they were, men who for years railed against Soviet domination of Eastern Europe. You would assume that if they were politically and ideologically consistent, if they were rational, they would be applauding the Soviet actions. Yet in their informal conversations, it was not their rational analyses that dominated their response, but the fact that for them, the decision for war, the willingness to use force, is cast as a question of masculinity—not prudence, thoughtfulness, efficacy, "rational" cost-benefit calculation, or morality, but masculinity.

In the face of this equation, genuine political discourse disappears. One more example: After Iraq invaded Kuwait and President Bush hastily sent U.S. forces to Saudi Arabia, there was a period in which the Bush administration struggled to find a convincing political justification for U.S. military involvement and the security affairs community debated the political merit of U.S. intervention. Then Bush set the deadline, January 16, high noon at the OK Corral, and as the day approached conversations changed. More of these centered on the question compellingly articulated by one defense intellectual as "Does George Bush have the stones for war?" This, too, is utterly extraordinary. This was a time when crucial political questions abounded: Can the sanctions work if given more time? Just what vital interests does the United States actually have at stake? What would be the goals of military intervention? Could they be accomplished by other means? Is the difference between what sanctions might accomplish and what military violence might accomplish worth the greater cost in human suffering, human lives, even dollars? What will the long-term effects on the people of the region be? On the ecology? Given the apparent successes of Gorbachev's last-minute diplomacy and Hussein's series of nearly daily small concessions, can and should Bush put off the deadline? Does he have the strength to let another leader play a major role in solving the problem? Does he have the political flexibility to not fight, or is he hellbent on war at all costs? And so on, ad infinitum. All of these disappear in the sulfuric acid test of the size of Mr. Bush's private parts.

I want to return to the RAND war simulation story to make one other observation. First, it requires a true confession: *I was stung by being called a wimp.* Yes, I thought the remark was deeply inane, and it infuriated me. But even so, I was also stung. Let me hasten to add, this was not because my identity is very wrapped up with not being wimpish—it actually is not a term that normally figures very heavily in my self-image one way or the other. But it was impossible to be in that room, hear his comment and the snickering laughter with which it was met, and not to feel stung, and humiliated.

Why? There I was, a woman and a feminist, not only contemptuous of the mentality that measures human beings by their degree of so-called wimpishness, but also someone for whom the term *wimp* does not have a deeply resonant personal meaning. How could it have affected me so much?

The answer lies in the role of the context within which I was experiencing myself—the discursive framework. For in that room I was not "simply me," but I was a participant in a discourse, a shared set of words, concepts, symbols that constituted not only the linguistic possibilities available to us but also constituted *me* in that situation. This is not entirely true, of course. How I experienced myself was at least partly shaped by other experiences and other discursive frameworks—certainly those of feminist politics and antimilitarist politics; in fact, I would say my reactions were predominantly shaped by those frameworks. But that is quite different from saying "I am a feminist, and that individual, psychological self simply moves encapsulated through the world being itself"—and therefore assuming that I am unaffected. No matter who else I was at that moment, I was unavoidably a participant in a discourse in which being a wimp has a meaning, and a deeply pejorative one at that. By calling me a wimp, my accuser on the Blue Team *positioned* me in that discourse, and I could not but feel the sting.

In other words, I am suggesting that national security discourse can be seen as having different positions within it—ones that are starkly gender coded; indeed, the enormous strength of their evocative power comes from gender. Thus, when you participate in conversation in that community, you do not simply choose what to say and how to say it; you advertently or inadvertently choose a position in the discourse. As a woman, I can choose the "masculine" (thoughtful, rational, logical) position. If I do, I am seen as legitimate, but I limit what I can say. Or, I can say things that place me in the "feminine" position—in which case no one will listen to me.

Finally, I would like to briefly explore a phenomenon I call the "unitary masculine actor problem" in national security discourse. During the Persian Gulf War, many feminists probably noticed that both the military briefers and George Bush himself frequently used the singular masculine pronoun "he" when referring to Iraq and Iraq's army. Someone not listening carefully could simply assume that "he" referred to Saddam Hussein. Sometimes it did; much of the time it simply reflected the defense community's characteristic habit of calling opponents "he" or "the other guy." A battalion commander, for example, was quoted as saying "Saddam knows where we are and we know where he is. We will move a lot now to keep him off guard."[1] In these sentences, "he" and "him" appear to refer to Saddam Hussein. But, of course, the American forces had *no idea* where Saddam Hussein himself was; the singular masculine pronouns are actually being used to refer to the Iraqi military.

This linguistic move, frequently heard in discussions within the security affairs and defense communities, turns a complex state and set of forces into a singular male opponents. In fact, discussions that purport to be serious explorations of the strategy and tactics of war can have a tone which sounds more like the story of a sporting match, a fistfight, or a personal vendetta.

> I would want to suck him out into the desert as far as I could, and then pound him to death.[2]

> Once we had taken out his eyes, we did what could be best described as the "Hail Mary play" in football.[3]

> [I]f the adversary decides to embark on a very high roll, because he's frightened that something even worse is in the works, does grabbing him by the scruff of the neck and slapping him up the side of the head, does that make him behave better or is it plausible that it makes him behave even worse?[4]

Most defense intellectuals would claim that using "he" is just a convenient shorthand, without significant import or effects. I believe, however, that the effects of this usage are many and the implications far-reaching. Here I will sketch just a few, starting first with the usage throughout defense discourse generally, and then coming back to the Gulf War in particular.

The use of "he" distorts the analyst's understanding of the opposing state and the conflict in which they are engaged. When the analyst refers to the opposing state as "he" or "the other guy," the image evoked is that of a person, a unitary actor; yet states are not people. Nor are they unitary and unified. They comprise complex, multifaceted governmental and military apparatuses, each with opposing forces within it, each, in turn, with its own internal institutional dynamics, its own varied needs in relation to domestic politics, and so on. In other words, if the state is referred to and pictured as a unitary actor, what becomes unavailable to the analyst and policy-maker is a series of much more complex truths that might enable him to imagine many more policy options, many more ways to interact with that state.

If one kind of distortion of the state results from the image of the state as a person, a unitary actor, another can be seen to stem from the image of the state as a specifically *male* actor. Although states are almost uniformly run by men, states are not men; they are complex social institutions, and they act and react as such. Yet, when "he" and "the other guy" are used to refer to states, the words do not simply function as shorthand codes; instead, they have their own entailments, including assumptions about how men act, which just might be different from how states act, but which invisibly become assumed to be isomorphic with how states act.

It also entails emotional responses on the part of the speaker. The reference to the opposing state as "he" evokes male competitive identity issues, as in, "I'm not going to let him push me around," or, "I'm not going to let him get the best of me." While these responses may or may not be adaptive for a barroom brawl, it is probably safe to say that they are less functional when trying to determine the best way for one state to respond to another state. Defense analysts and foreign policy experts can usually agree upon the supreme desirability of dispassionate, logical analysis and its ensuing rationally calculated action. Yet the emotions evoked by the portrayal of global conflict in the personalized terms of male competition must, at the very least, exert a strong pull in exactly the opposite direction.

A third problem is that even while the use of "he" acts to personalize the conflict, it simultaneously abstracts both the opponent and the war itself. That is, the use of "he" functions in very much the same way that discussions about "Red" and "Blue" do. It facilitates treating war within a kind of game-playing model, A against B, Red against Blue, he against me. For even while "he" is evocative of male identity issues, it is also just an abstract piece to moved around on a game board, or, more appropriately, a computer screen.

That tension between personalization and abstraction was striking in Gulf War discourse. In the Gulf War, not only was "he" frequently used to refer to the Iraqi military, but so was "Saddam," as in "Saddam really took a pounding today," or "Our goal remains the same: to liberate Kuwait by forcing Saddam Hussein out."[5] The personalization is obvious: in this locution, the U.S. armed forces are not destroying a nation, killing people; instead, they (or George) are giving Saddam a good pounding, or bodily removing him from where he does not belong. Our emotional response is to get fired up about a bully getting his comeuppance.

Yet this personalization, this conflation of Iraq and Iraqi forces with Saddam himself, also abstracts: it functions to substitute in the mind's eye the abstraction of an implacably, impeccably evil enemy for the particular human beings, the men, women, and children being pounded, burned, torn, and eviscerated. A cartoon image of Saddam being ejected from Kuwait preempts the image of the blackened, charred, decomposing bodies of nineteen-year-old boys tossed in ditches by the side of the road, and the other concrete images of the acts of violence that constitute "forcing Hussein [*sic*] out of Kuwait."[6] Paradoxical as it may seem, in personalizing the Iraqi army as Saddam, the individual human beings in Iraq were abstracted out of existence.

In summary, I have been exploring the way in which defense intellectuals talk to each other—the comments they make to each other, the particular usages that appear in their informal conversations or their lectures. In addition, I have occasionally left the professional community to draw upon public talk about the Gulf War. My analysis does *not* lead me to conclude that "national security thinking is masculine"—that is, a separate, and different, discussion. Instead, I have tried to show that national security discourse is gendered, and that it matters. Gender discourse is interwoven through national security discourse. It sets fixed boundaries, and in so doing, it skews what is discussed and how it is thought about. It shapes expectations of other nations' actions, and in so doing it affects both our interpretations of international events and conceptions of how the United States should respond.

In a world where professionals pride themselves on their ability to engage in cool, rational, objective calculation while others around them are letting their thinking be sullied by emotion, the unacknowledged interweaving of gender discourse in security discourse allows men to not acknowledge that their pristine rational thought is in fact riddled with emotional response. In an "objective" "universal" discourse that valorizes the "masculine" and deauthorizes the "feminine," it is only the "feminine" emotions that are noticed and labeled as emotions, and thus in need of banning from the analytic process. "Masculine" emotions—such as feelings of aggression, competition, macho pride and swagger, or the sense of identity resting on carefully defended borders—are not so easily noticed and identified as emotions, and are instead invisibly folded into "self-evident," so-called realist paradigms and analyses. It is both the interweaving of gender discourse in national security thinking *and* the blindness to its presence and impact that have deleterious effects. Finally, the impact is to distort, degrade, and deter roundly rational, fully complex thought within the community of defense intellectuals and national security elites and, by extension, to cripple democratic deliberation about crucial matters of war and peace.

Notes

1. Chris Hedges, "War Is Vivid in the Gun Sights of the Sniper," *New York Times,* February 3, 1991, A1.

2. General Norman Schwarzkopf, National Public Radio broadcast, February 8, 1991.

3. General Norman Schwarzkopf, CENTCOM News Briefing, Riyadh, Saudi Arabia, February 27, 1991, p. 2.

4. Transcript of a strategic studies specialist's lecture on NATO and the Warsaw Pact (summer institute on Regional Conflict and Global Security: The Nuclear Dimension, Madison, Wisconsin, June 29, 1987).

5. Defense Secretary Dick Cheney, "Excerpts from Briefing at Pentagon by Cheney and Powell," *New York Times,* January 24, 1991, A 11.

6. Scarry explains that when an army is described as a single "embodied combatant," injury, (as in Saddam's "pounding"), may be referred to but is "no longer recognizable or interpretable." It is not only that Americans might be happy to imagine Saddam being pounded; we also on some level know that it is not really happening, and thus need not feel the pain of the wounded. We "respond to the injury . . . as an imaginary wound to an imaginary body, despite the fact that that imaginary body is itself made up of thousands of real human bodies" (Elaine Scarry, *Body in Pain: The Making and Unmaking of the World* [New York: Oxford, 1984], p. 72).

RUSSELL P. DOBASH, R. EMERSON DOBASH, MARGO WILSON, AND MARTIN DALY

The Myth of Sexual Symmetry in Marital Violence

Long denied, legitimized, and made light of, wife-beating is at last the object of widespread public concern and condemnation. Extensive survey research and intensive interpretive investigations tell a common story. Violence against wives (by which term we encompass *de facto* as well as registered unions) is often persistent and severe, occurs in the context of continuous intimidation and coercion, and is inextricably linked to attempts to domininate and control women. Historical and contemporary investigations further reveal that this violence has been explicitly decriminalized, ignored, or treated in an ineffectual manner by criminal justice systems, by medical and social service institutions, and by communities. Increased attention to these failures has inspired increased efforts to redress them, and in many places legislative amendments have mandated arrest and made assault a crime whether the offender is married to the victim or not.

A number of researchers and commentators have suggested that assaults upon men by their wives constitute a social problem comparable in nature and magnitude to that of wife-beating. Two main bodies of evidence have been offered in support of these authors' claims that husbands and wives are similarly victimized: (1) self-reports of violent acts perpetrated and suffered by survey respondents, especially those in two U.S. national probability samples; and (2) U.S. homicide data. Unlike the case of violence against wives, however, the victimization of husbands allegedly continues to be denied and trivialized. "Violence by wives has not been an object of public concern," note Straus and Gelles (1986:472). "There has been no publicity, and no funds have been invested in ameliorating this problem because it has not been defined as a problem."

We shall argue that claims of sexual symmetry in marital violence are exaggerated, and that wives' and husbands' uses of violence differ greatly, both quantitatively and qualitatively. We shall further argue that there is no reason to expect the sexes to be alike in this domain, and that efforts to avoid sexism by lumping male and female data and by the use of gender-neutral terms such as "spouse-beating" are misguided. If violence is gendered, as it assuredly is, explicit characterization of gender's relevance to violence is essential. The alleged similarity of women and men in their use of violence in intimate relationships stands in marked contrast to men's virtual monopoly on the use of violence in other social contexts, and we challenge the proponents of the sexual symmetry thesis to develop coherent theoretical models that would account for a sexual monomorphism of violence in one social context and not in others.

From *Social Problems*, Vol. 39, no. 1 (February 1992), pp. 71–91. References have been edited.

A final thesis of this paper is that resolution of controversies about the "facts" of family violence requires critical examination of theories, methods, and data, with explicit attention to the development of coherent conceptual frameworks, valid and meaningful forms of measurement, and appropriate inferential procedures. Such problems are not peculiar to this research domain, but analysis of the claims regarding violence against husbands provides an excellent example of how a particular approach to construct formation and measurement has led to misrepresentation of the phenomena under investigation.

THE CLAIM OF SEXUALLY SYMMETRICAL MARITAL VIOLENCE

Authoritative claims about the prevalence and sexual symmetry of spousal violence in America began with a 1975 U.S. national survey in which 2,143 married or cohabiting persons were interviewed in person about their actions in the preceding year. Straus (1977/78) announced that the survey results showed that the "marriage license is a hitting license," and moreover that the rates of perpetrating spousal violence, including severe violence, were higher for wives than for husbands. He concluded:

> Violence between husband and wife is far from a one way street. The old cartoons of the wife chasing the husband with a rolling pin or throwing pots and pans are closer to reality than most (and especially those with feminist sympathies) realize (Straus 1977/78:447–448).

In 1985, the survey was repeated by telephone with a new national probability sample including 3,520 husband-wife households, and with similar results. In each survey, the researchers interviewed either the wife or the husband (but not both) in each contacted household about how the couple settled their differences when they had a disagreement. The individual who was interviewed was presented with a list of eighteen "acts" ranging from "discussed an issue calmly" and "cried" to "threw something at him/her/you" and "beat him/her/you up," with the addition of "choked him/her/you" in 1985 (Straus 1990a:33). These acts constituted the Conflict Tactics Scales (CTS) and were intended to measure three constructs: "Reasoning," "Verbal Aggression," and "Physical Aggression" or "Violence," which was further subdivided into "Minor Violence" and "Severe Violence" according to a presumed potential for injury (Straus 1979, Straus and Gelles 1990a). Respondents were asked how frequently they had perpetrated each act in the course of "conflicts or disagreements" with their spouses (and with one randomly selected child) within the past year, and how frequently they had been on the receiving end. Each respondent's self-reports of victimization and perpetration contributed to estimates of rates of violence by both husbands and wives.

According to both surveys, rates of violence by husbands and wives were strikingly similar. The authors estimated that in the year prior to the 1975 survey 11.6 percent of U.S. husbands were victims of physical violence perpetrated by their wives, while 12.1 percent of wives were victims of their husbands' violence. In 1985, these percentages had scarcely changed, but husbands seemed more vulnerable: 12.1 percent of husbands and 11.3 percent of wives were victims. In both surveys, husbands were more likely to be victims of acts of "severe violence": in 1975, 4.6 percent of husbands were such victims versus 3.8 percent of wives, and in 1985, 4.4 percent of husbands versus 3.0 percent of wives were victims. In reporting their results, the surveys' authors stressed the surprising assaultiveness of wives:

> The repeated finding that the rate of assault by women is similar to the rate by their male partners is an important and distressing aspect of violence in American families. It contrasts markedly to the behavior of women outside the family. It shows that within the family or in dating and cohabiting relationships, women are about as violent as men (Straus and Gelles 1990b:104).

Others have endorsed and publicized these conclusions. For example, a recent review of marital violence concludes, with heavy reliance on Straus and Gelles's survey results, that "(a) women are more prone than men to engage in severely violent acts; (b) each year more men than women are victimized by their intimates" (McNeely and Mann 1990:130). One of Straus and Gelles's collaborators in the 1975 survey, Steinmetz (1977/78), used the same survey evidence to proclaim the existence of "battered husbands" and a "battered husband syndrome." She has remained one of the leading defenders of the claim that violence between men and women in the family is symmetrical. Steinmetz and her collaborators maintain that the problem is not wife-beating perpetrated by violent men, but "violent couples" and "violent people". Men may be stronger on average, argues Steinmetz, but weaponry equalizes matters, as is allegedly shown by the nearly equivalent numbers of U.S. husbands and wives who are killed by their partners. The reason why battered husbands are inconspicuous and seemingly rare is supposedly that shame prevents them from seeking help.

Straus and his collaborators have sometimes qualified their claims that their surveys demonstrate sexual symmetry in marital violence, noting, for example, that men are usually larger and stronger than women and thus able to inflict more damage and that women are more likely to use violence in self-defense or retaliation. However, the survey results indicate a symmetry not just in the perpetration of violence but in its initiation as well, and from this further symmetry, Stets and Straus (1990:154–155) conclude that the equal assaultiveness of husbands and wives cannot be attributed to the wives acting in self-defense, after all.

Other surveys using the CTS in the United States and in other countries have replicated the finding that wives are about as violent as husbands. The CTS has also been used to study violence in dating relationships, with the same sexually symmetrical results.

Some authors maintain not only that wives initiate violence at rates comparable to husbands, but that they rival them in the damage they inflict as well. McNeely and Robinson-Simpson (1987), for example, argue that research shows that the "truth about domestic violence" is that "women are as violent, if not more violent than men," in their inclinations, in their actions, and in the damage they inflict. The most dramatic evidence invoked in this context is again the fact that wives kill: spousal homicides—for which detection should be minimally or not at all biased because homicides are nearly always discovered and recorded—produce much more nearly equivalent numbers of male and female victims in the United States than do sublethal assault data, which are subject to sampling biases when obtained from police, shelters and hospitals. According to McNeely and Mann (1990:130), "the average man's size and strength are neutralized by guns and knives, boiling water, bricks, fireplace pokers, and baseball bats."

A corollary of the notion that the sexes are alike in their use of violence is that satisfactory causal accounts of violence will be gender-blind. Discussion thus focuses, for example, on the role of one's prior experiences with violence as a child, social stresses, frustration, inability to control anger, impoverished social skills, and so forth, without reference to gender. This presumption that the sexes are alike not merely in action but in the reasons for that action is occasionally explicit, such as when Shupe et al. (1987:56) write: "Everything we have found points to parallel processes that lead women and men to become violent. . . . Women may be more likely than men to use kitchen utensils or sewing scissors when they commit assault, but their frustrations, motives and lack of control over these feelings predictably resemble men's."

In sum, the existence of an invisibles legion of assaulted husbands is an inference which strikes many family violence researchers as reasonable. Two lines of evidence—homicide data and the CTS survey results—suggest to those supporting the sexual-symmetry-of-violence thesis that large numbers of men are trapped in violent relationships. These men are allegedly being denied medical, social welfare, and criminal justice services because of an unwillingness to accept the evidence from homicide statistics and the CTS surveys.

VIOLENCE AGAINST WIVES

Any argument that marital violence is sexually symmetrical must either dismiss or ignore a large body of contradictory evidence indicating that wives greatly outnumber husbands as victims. While CTS researchers were discovering and publicizing the mutual violence of wives and husbands, other researchers—using evidence from courts, police, and women's shelters—were finding that wives were much more likely than husbands to be victims. After an extensive review of extant research, Lystad (1975) expressed the consensus: "The occurrence of adult violence in the home usually involves males as aggressors towards females." This conclusion was subsequently supported by numerous further studies of divorce records, emergency room patients treated for non-accidential injuries, police assault records, and spouses seeking assistance and refuge. Analyses of police and court records in North America and Europe have persistently indicated that women constitute ninety to ninety-five percent of the victims of those assaults in the home reported to the criminal justice system.

Defenders of the sexual-symmetry-of-violence thesis do not deny these results, but they question their representativeness: these studies could be biased because samples of victims were self-selected. However, criminal victimization surveys using national probability samples similarly indicate that wives are much more often victimized than husbands. Such surveys in the United States, Canada and Great Britain have been replicated in various years, with essentially the same results. Beginning in 1972 and using a panel survey method involving up to seven consecutive interviews at six-month intervals, the U.S. National Crime Survey has generated nearly a million interviews. Gaquin's (1977/78) analysis of U.S. National Crime Survey data for 1973–1975 led her to conclude that men "have almost no risk of being assaulted by their wives" (634–635); only 3 percent of the violence reported from these surveys involved attacks on men by their female partners. Another analysis of the National Crime Survey data from 1973 to 1980 found that 6 percent of spousal assault incidents were directed at men (McLeod 1984). Schwartz (1987) re-analyzed the same victimization surveys with the addition of the 1981 and 1982 data, and found 102 men who claimed to have been victims of assaults by their wives (4 percent of domestic assault incidents) in contrast to 1,641 women who said they were assaulted by husbands. The 1981 Canadian Urban Victimization Survey and the 1987 General Social Survey produced analogous findings, from which Johnson (1989) concluded that "women account for 80–90 percent of victims in assaults or sexual assaults between spouses or former spouses. In fact, the number of domestic assaults involving males was too low in both surveys to provide reliable estimates" (1–2). The 1982 and 1984 British Crime Surveys found that women accounted for all the victims of marital assaults. Self-reports of criminal victimization based on national probability surveys, while not without methodological weaknesses, are not subject to the same reporting biases as divorce, police and hospital records.

The national crime surveys also indicate that women are much more likely than men to suffer injury as a result of assaults in the home. After analyzing the results of the U.S. National Crime Surveys, Schwartz (1987:67) concludes, "there are still more than 13 times as many women seeking medical care from a private physician for injuries received in a spousal assault." This result again replicates the typical findings of studies of police or hospital records. For example, women constituted 94 percent of the injury victims in an analysis of the spousal assault cases among 262 domestic disturbance calls to police in Santa Barbara County, California; moreover, the women's injuries were more serious than the men's. Berk et al. (1983:207) conclude that "when injuries are used as the outcome of interest, a marriage license is a hitting license but for men only." Brush (1990) reports that a U.S. national probability sample survey of over 13,000 respondents in 1987–1988 replicated the evident symmetry of marital violence when CTS-like questions about acts were posed, but also revealed that women were much more often injured than men (and that men down-played women's injuries).

In response, defenders of the sexual-symmetry-of-violence thesis contend that data from police, courts, hospitals, and social service agencies are suspect because men are reluctant to report physical violence by their wives. For example, Steinmetz (1977/78) asserts that husband-beating is a camouflaged social problem because men must overcome extraordinary stigma in order to report that their wives have beaten them. Similarly, Shupe et al. (1987) maintain that men are unwilling to report their wives because "it would be unmanly or unchivalrous to go to the police for protection from a woman" (52). However, the limited available evidence does not support these authors' presumption that men are less likely to report assaults by their spouses than are women. Schwartz's (1987) analysis of the 1973–1982 U.S. National Crime Survey data found that 67.2 percent of men and 56.8 percent of women called the police after being assaulted by their spouses. One may protest that these high percentages imply that only a tiny proportion of the most severe spousal assaults were acknowledged as assaults by respondents to these crime surveys, but the results are nonetheless contrary to the notion that assaulted men are especially reticent. Moreover, Rouse et al. (1988), using "act" definitions of assaults which inspired much higher proportions to acknowledge victimization, similarly report that men were likelier than women to call the police after assaults by intimate partners, both among married couples and among those dating. In addition, a sample of 337 cases of domestic violence drawn from family court cases in Ontario showed that men were more likely than women to press charges against their spouses: there were 17 times as many female victims as male victims, but only 22 percent of women laid charges in contrast to 40 percent of the men, and men were less likely to drop the charges, too. What those who argue that men are reluctant or ashamed to report their wives' assaults over look is that women have their own reasons to be reticent, fearing both the loss of a jailed or alienated husband's economic support and his vengeance. Whereas the claim that husbands underreport because of shame or chivalry is largely speculative, there is considerable evidence that women report very little of the violence perpetrated by their male partners.

The CTS survey data indicating equivalent violence by wives and husbands thus stand in contradiction to injury data, to police incident reports, to help-seeking statistics, and even to other, larger, national probability sample surveys of self-reported victimization. The CTS researchers insist that their results alone are accurate because husbands' victimizations are unlikely to be detected or reported by any other method. It is therefore important to consider in detail the CTS and the data it generates.

DO CTS DATA REFLECT THE REALITY OF MARITAL VIOLENCE?

The CTS instrument has been much used and much criticized. Critics have complained that its exclusive focus on "acts" ignores the actors' interpretations, motivations, and intentions; that physical violence is arbitrarily delimited, excluding, for example, sexual assault and rape; that retrospective reports of the past year's events are unlikely to be accurate; that researchers' attributions of "violence" (with resultant claims about its statistical prevalence) are based on respondents' admitting to acts described in such an impoverished manner as to conflate severe assaults with trivial gestures; that the formulaic distinction between "minor" and "severe violence" (whereby, for example, "tried to hit with something" is definitionally "severe" and "slapped" is definitionally "minor") constitutes a poor operationalization of severity; that the responses of aggressors and victims have been given identical evidentiary status in deriving incidence estimates, while their inconsistencies have been ignored; that the CTS omits the contexts of violence, the events precipitating it, and the sequences of events by which it progresses; and that it fails to connect outcomes, especially injury, with the acts producing them.

Straus (1990b) has defended the CTS against its critics, maintaining that the CTS addresses context with its "verbal aggression" scale (although the assessment of "verbal aggression" is not incident-linked with the assessment of "violence"); that the minor-severe categorization "is roughly parallel to the legal distinction between 'simple assault' and 'aggravated assault'" (58); that other measurement instruments have problems, too; and that you cannot measure everything. Above all, the defense rests on the widespread use of the instrument, on its reliability, and on its validity. That the CTS is widely used cannot be gainsaid, but whether it is reliable or valid is questionable.

Problems with the Reliability and Validity of CTS Responses

Straus (1990b:64) claims that six studies have assessed "the internal consistency reliability" of the CTS. One of the six (Barling and Rosenbaum 1986) contains no such assessment, a second is unreferenced, and a third unpublished. However, a moderate degree of "internal consistency reliability" of the CTS can probably be conceded. For example, those who admit to having "beat up" their spouses are also likely to admit to having "hit" them.

The crucial matter of interobserver reliability is much more problematic. The degree of concordance in couples' responses is an assay of "interspousal reliability" (Jouriles and O'Leary 1985), and such reliability must be high if CTS scores are to be taken at face value. For example, incidence estimates of husband-to-wife and wife-to-husband violence have been generated from national surveys in which the CTS was administered to only one adult per family, with claims of victimization and perpetration by male and female respondents all granted equal evidentiary status and summated. The validity of these widely cited incidence estimates is predicated upon interspousal reliability.

Straus (1990b:66) considers the assessment of spousal concordance to constitute an assay of "concurrent validity" rather than "interspousal reliability," in effect treating each partner's report as the violence criterion that validates the other. But spousal concordance is analogous to interobserver reliability: it is a necessary but by no means sufficient condition for concluding that the self-reports accurately reflect reality. If couples generally produce consistent reports—Mr. and Mrs. Jones both indicate that he struck her, while Mr. and Mrs. Smith both indicate that neither has struck the other—then it is possible though by no means certain that their CTS self-reports constitute valid (veridical) information about the blows actually struck. However, if couples routinely provide discrepant CTS responses, data derived from the CTS simply cannot be valid.

In this light, studies of husband/wife concordance in CTS responses should be devastating to those who imagine that the CTS provides a valid account of the respondents' acts. In what Straus correctly calls "the most detailed and thorough analysis of agreement between spouses in response to the CTS," Szinovacz (1983) found that 103 couples' accounts of the violence in their interactions matched to a degree little greater than chance. On several CTS items, mainly the most severe ones, agreement was actually below chance. On the item "beat up," concordance was nil: although there were respondents of both sexes who claimed to have administered beatings and respondents of both sexes who claimed to have been on the receiving end, there was not a single couple in which one party claimed to have administered and the other to have received such a beating. In a similar study, Jouriles and O'Leary (1985) administered the CTS to 65 couples attending a marital therapy clinic, and 37 control couples from the local community. For many of the acts, the frequency and percentage data reported are impossible to reconcile; for others, Jouriles and O'Leary reported a concordance statistic (Cohen's Kappa) as equalling zero when the correct values were negative. Straus (1990b) cites this study as conferring validity on the CTS, but in fact, its results replicated Szinovacz's (1983): husband/wife agreement scarcely exceeded chance expectation and actually fell below chance on some items.

Straus (1990b) acknowledges that these and the other studies he reviews "found large discrepancies between the reports of violence given by husbands and by wives" (69). He concludes, however, that "validity measures of agreement between family members are within the range of validity coefficients typically reported" (71), and that "the weakest aspect of the CTS are [sic] the scales that have received the least criticism: Reasoning and Verbal aggression" (71), by which he implies that the assessment of violence is relatively strong.

Ultimately, Straus's defense of the CTS is that the proof of the pudding is in the eating: "The strongest evidence concerns the construct validity of the CTS. It has been used in a large number of studies producing findings that tend to be consistent with previous research (when available), consistent regardless of gender of respondent, and theoretically meaningful." And indeed, with respect to marital violence, the CTS is capable of making certain gross discriminations. Various studies have found CTS responses to vary as a function of age, race, poverty, duration of relationship, and registered versus de facto marital unions, and these effects have generally been directionally similar to those found with less problematic measures of violence such as homicides. However, the CTS has also failed to detect certain massive differences, and we do not refer only to sex differences.

Consider the case of child abuse by stepparents versus birth parents. In various countries, including the United States, a stepparent is more likely to fatally assault a small child than is a birth parent, by a factor on the order of 100-fold; sublethal violence also exhibits huge differences in the same direction. Using the CTS, however, Gelles and Harrop (1991) were unable to detect any difference in self-reports of violence by step- versus birth parents. Users of the CTS have sometimes conceded that the results of their self-report surveys cannot provide an accurate picture of the prevalence of violence, but they have made this concession only to infer that the estimates must be gross underestimates of the true prevalence. However, the CTS's failure to differentiate the behavior of step- versus birth parents indicates that CTS-based estimates are not just underestimates but may misrepresent between-group differences in systematically biased ways. One must be concerned, then, whether this sort of bias also arises in CTS-based comparisons between husbands and wives.

Problems with the Interpretation of CTS Responses

With the specific intention of circumventing imprecision and subjectivity in asking about such abstractions as "violence," the CTS is confined to questions about "acts": Respondents are asked whether they have "pushed" their partners, have "slapped" them, and so forth, rather than whether they have "assaulted" them or behaved "violently." This focus on "acts" is intended to reduce problems of self-serving and biased definitional criteria on the part of the respondents. However, any gain in objectivity has been undermined by the way that CTS survey data have then been analyzed and interpreted. Any respondent who acknowledges a single instance of having "pushed," "grabbed," "shoved," "slapped" or "hit or tried to hit" another person is deemed a perpetrator of "violence" by the researchers, regardless of the act's context, consequences, or meaning to the parties involved. Similarly, a single instance of having "kicked," "bit," "hit or tried to hit with an object," "beat up," "choked," "threatened with a knife or gun," or "used a knife or fired a gun" makes one a perpetrator of "severe violence."

Affirmation of any one of the "violence" items provides the basis for estimates such as Straus and Gelles's (1990b:97) claim that 6.8 million U.S. husbands and 6.25 million U.S. wives were spousal assault victims in 1985. Similarly, estimates of large numbers of "beaten" or "battered" wives and husbands have been based on affirmation of any one of the "severe violence" items. For example, Steinmetz (1986:734) and Straus and Gelles (1987:638) claim on this basis that 1.8 million U.S. women are "beaten" by their husbands annually. But note that any man who once threw an "object" at his wife, regardless of its nature and regardless of whether the throw missed, qualifies as having "beaten" her; some unknown proportion of the women and men who are alleged to have been "beaten," on the basis of their survey responses, never claimed to have been struck at all. Thus, the "objective" scoring of the CTS not only fails to explore the meanings and intentions associated with the acts but has in practice entailed interpretive transformations that guarantee exaggeration, misinterpretation, and ultimately trivialization of the genuine problems of violence.

Consider a "slap." The word encompasses anything from a slap on the hand chastizing a dinner companion for reaching for a bite of one's dessert to a tooth-loosening assault intended to punish, humiliate, and terrorize. These are not trivial distinctions; indeed, they constitute the essence of definitional issues concerning violence. Almost all definitions of violence and violent acts refer to intentions. Malevolent intent is crucial, for example, to legal definitions of "assault" (to which supporters of the CTS have often mistakenly claimed that their "acts" correspond; e.g., Straus 1990b:58). However, no one has systematically investigated how respondents vary in their subjective definitions of the "acts" listed on the CTS. If, for example, some respondents interpret phrases such as "tried to hit with an object" literally, then a good deal of relatively harmless behavior surely taints the estimates of "severe violence." Although this problem has not been investigated systematically, one author has shown that it is potentially serious. In a study of 103 couples, Margolin (1987) found that wives surpassed husbands in their use of "severe violence" according to the CTS, but unlike others who have obtained this result, Margolin troubled to check its meaningfulness with more intensive interviews. She concluded:

> While CTS items appear behaviorally specific, their meanings still are open to interpretation. In one couple who endorsed the item "kicking," for example, we discovered that the kicking took place in bed in a more kidding, than serious, fashion. Although this behavior meets the criterion for severe abuse on the CTS, neither spouse viewed it as aggressive, let alone violent. In another couple, the wife scored on severe physical aggression while the husband scored on low-level aggression only. The inquiry revealed that, after years of passively accepting the husband's repeated abuse, this wife finally decided, on one occasion, to retaliate by hitting him over the head with a wine decanter (1987:82).

By the criteria of Steinmetz (1977/78:501), this incident would qualify as a "battered husband" case. But however dangerous this retaliatory blow may have been and however reprehensible or justified one may consider it, it is not "battering," whose most basic definitional criterion is its repetitiveness. A failure to consider intentions, interpretations, and the history of the individuals' relationship is a significant shortcoming of CTS research. Only through a consideration of behaviors, intentions and intersubjective understandings associated with specific violent events will we come to a fuller understanding of violence between men and women. Studies employing more intensive interviews and detailed case reports addressing the contexts and motivations of marital violence help unravel the assertions of those who claim the widespread existence of beaten and battered husbands. Research focusing on specific violent events shows that women almost always employ violence in defense of self and children in response to cues of imminent assault in the past and in retaliation for previous physical abuse. Proponents of the sexual-symmetry-of-violence thesis have made much of the fact that CTS surveys indicate that women "initiate" the violence about as often as men, but a case in which a woman struck the first blow is unlikely to be the mirror image of one in which her husband "initiated." A noteworthy feature of the literature proclaiming the existence of battered husbands and battering wives is how little the meager case descriptions resemble those of battered wives and battering husbands. Especially lacking in the alleged male victim cases is any indication of the sort of chronic intimidation characteristic of prototypical woman battering cases.

Any self-report method must constitute an imperfect reflection of behavior, and the CTS is no exception. That in itself is hardly a fatal flaw. But for such an instrument to retain utility for the investigation of a particular domain such as family violence, an essential point is that its inaccuracies and misrepresentations must not be systematically related to the distinctions under investigation. The CTS's inability to detect the immense differences in violence between stepparents and birth parents, as noted above, provides strong reason to suspect that the test's shortcomings produce not just noise but systematic bias. In the case of marital violence, the other sorts of evidence reviewed in this paper indicate that there are massive differences in the use of confrontational violence against spouses by husbands versus wives, and yet the CTS has consistently failed to detect them. CTS users have taken this failure as evidence for the null hypothesis, apparently assuming that their questionnaire data have a validity that battered women's injuries and deaths lack.

HOMICIDES

The second line of evidence that has been invoked in support of the claim that marital violence is more or less sexually symmetrical is the number of lethal outcomes:

> Data on homicide between spouses suggest that an almost equal number of wives kill their husbands as husbands kill their wives (Wolfgang 1958). Thus it appears that men and women might have equal potential for violent marital interaction; initiate similar acts of violence; and when differences of physical strength are equalized by weapons, commit similar amounts of spousal homicide (Steinmetz and Lucca 1988:241).

McNeely and Robinson-Simpson (1987:485) elevated the latter hypothesis about the relevance of weapons to the status of a fact: "Steinmetz observed that when weapons neutralize differences in physical strength, about as many men as women are victims of homicide."

Steinmetz and Lucca's citation of Wolfgang refers to his finding that 53 Philadelphia men killed their wives between 1948 and 1952, while, 47 women killed their husbands. This is a slender basis for such generalization, but fuller information does indeed bear Steinmetz out as regards the near equivalence of body counts in the United States: Maxfield (1989) reported that there were 10,529 wives and 7,888 husbands killed by their mates in the entire country between 1976 and 1985, a 1.3:1 ratio of female to male victims.

Husbands are indeed almost as often slain as are wives in the United States, then. However, there remain several problems with Steinmetz and Lucca's (as well as McNeely and Robinson-Simpson's) interpretation of this fact. Studies of actual cases lend no support to the facile claim that homicidal husbands and wives "initiate similar acts of violence." Men often kill wives after lengthy periods of prolonged physical violence accompanied by other forms of abuse and coercion; the roles in such cases are seldom if ever reversed. Men perpetrate familicidal massacres, killing spouse and children together; women do not. Men commonly hunt down and kill wives who have left them; women hardly ever behave similarly. Men kill wives as part of planned murder-suicides; analogous acts by women are almost unheard of. Men kill in response to revelations of wifely infidelity; women almost never respond similarly, though their mates are more often adulterous. The evidence is overwhelming that a large proportion of the spouse-killings perpetrated by wives, but almost none of those perpetrated by husbands, are acts of self-defense. Unlike men, women kill male partners after years of suffering physical violence, after they have exhausted all available sources of assistance, when they feel trapped, and because they fear for their own lives.

A further problem with the invocation of spousal homicide data as evidence against sex differences in marital violence is that this numerical equivalence is peculiar to the United States. Whereas the ratio of wives to husbands as homicide victims in the United States was 1.3:1, corresponding ratios from other countries are much higher: 3.3:1 for a 10-year period in Canada, for example, 4.3:1 for Great Britain, and 6:1 for Denmark. The reason why this is problematic is that U.S. homicide data and CTS data from several countries have been invoked as complementary pieces of evidence for women's and men's equivalent uses of violence. One cannot have it both ways. If the lack of sex differences in CTS results is considered proof of sexually symmetrical violence, then homicide data must somehow be dismissed as irrelevant, since homicides generally fail to exhibit this supposedly more basic symmetry. Conversely, if U.S. homicide counts constitute relevant evidence, the large sex differences found elsewhere surely indicate that violence is peculiarly symmetrical only in the United States, and the fact that the CTS fails to detect sex differences in other countries must then be taken to mean that the CTS is insensitive to genuine differences.

A possible way out of this dilemma is hinted at in Steinmetz and Lucca's (1988) allusion to the effect of weapons: perhaps it is the availability of guns that has neutralized men's advantage in lethal marital conflict in the United States. Gun use is indeed relatively prevalent in the U.S., accounting for 51 percent of a sample of 1706 spousal homicides in Chicago, for example, as compared to 40 percent of 1060 Canadian cases, 42 percent of 395 Australian cases, and just 8 percent of 1204 cases in England and Wales (Wilson and Daly forthcoming). Nevertheless, the plausible hypothesis that gun use can account for the different sex ratios among victims fails. When shootings and other spousal homicides are analyzed separately, national differences in the sex ratios of spousal homicide remain dramatic. For example, the ratio of wives to husbands as gunshot homicide victims in Chicago was 1.2:1, compared to 4:1 in Canada and 3.5:1 in Britain; the ratio of wives to husbands as victims of non-gun homicides was 0.8:1 in Chicago, compared to 2.9:1 in Canada and 4.5:1 in Britain (Wilson and Daly forthcoming). Moreover, the near equivalence of husband and wife victims in the U.S. antedates the contemporary prevalence of gun killings. In Wolfgang's (1958) classic study, only 34 of the 100 spousal homicide victims were shot (15 husbands and 19 wives), while 30 husbands were stabbed and 31 wives were beaten or stabbed. Whatever may explain the exceptionally similar death rates of U.S. husbands and wives, it is not simply that guns "equalize."

Nor is the unusual U.S. pattern to be explained in terms of a peculiar convergence in the United States of the sexes in their violent inclinations or capabilities across all domains and relationships. Although U.S. data depart radically from other industrialized countries in the sex ratio of spousal homicide victimization, they do not depart similarly in the sex ratios of other sorts of homicides (Wilson and Daly forthcoming). For example, in the United States as elsewhere men kill unrelated men about 40 times as often as women kill unrelated women.

Even among lethal acts, it is essential to discriminate among different victim-killer relationships, because motives, risk factors, and conflict typologies are relationship-specific. Steinmetz (1977/78, Steinmetz and Lucca 1998) has invoked the occurrence of maternally perpetrated infanticides as evidence of women's violence, imagining that the fact that some women commit infanticide somehow bolsters the claim that they batter their husbands, too. But maternal infanticides are more often motivated by desperation than by hostile aggression and are often effected by acts of neglect or abandonment rather than by assault. To conflate such acts with aggressive attacks is to misunderstand their utterly distinct motives, forms, and perpetrator profiles, and the distinct social and material circumstances in which they occur.

HOW TO GAIN A VALID ACCOUNT OF MARITAL VIOLENCE?

How ought researchers to conceive of "violence"? People differ in their views about whether a particular act was a violent one and about who was responsible. Assessments of intention and justifiability are no less relevant to the labelling of an event as "violent" than are more directly observable considerations like the force exerted or the damage inflicted. Presumably, it is this problem of subjectivity that has inspired efforts to objectify the study of family violence by the counting of "acts," as in the Conflict Tactics Scales.

Unfortunately, the presumed gain in objectivity achieved by asking research subjects to report only "acts," while refraining from elaborating upon their meanings and consequences, is illusory. As noted above, couples exhibit little agreement in reporting the occurrence of acts in which both were allegedly involved, and self-reported acts sometimes fail to differentiate the behavior of groups known to exhibit huge differences in the perpetration of violence. The implication must be that concerns about the validity of self-report data cannot be allayed merely by confining self-reports to a checklist of named acts. We have no more reason to suppose that people will consensually and objectively label events as instances of someone having "grabbed" or "hit or tried to hit" or "used a knife" (items from the CTS) than to suppose that people will consensually and objectively label events as instances of "violence."

If these "acts" were scored by trained observers examining the entire event, there might be grounds for such behavioristic austerity in measurement: whatever the virtues and limitations of behavioristic methodology, a case can at least be made that observational data are more objective than the actors' accounts. However, when researchers have access only to self-reports, the cognitions of the actors are neither more nor less accessible to research than their actions. Failures of candor and memory threaten the validity of both sorts of self-report data, and researchers' chances of detecting such failures can only be improved by the collection of richer detail about the violent event. The behavioristic rigor of observational research cannot be simulated by leaving data collection to the subjects, nor by active inattention to "subjective" matters like people's perceptions of their own and others' intentions, attributions of loss of control, perceived provocations and justifications, intimidatory consequences, and so forth. Moreover, even a purely behavioristic account could be enriched by attending to sequences of events and subsequent behavior rather than merely counting acts.

Enormous differences in meaning and consequence exist between a woman pummelling her laughing husband in an attempt to convey strong feelings and a man pummelling his weeping wife in an attempt to punish her for coming home late. It is not enough to acknowledge such contrasts (as CTS researchers have sometimes done), if such acknowledgments neither inform further research nor alter such conclusions as "within the family or in dating and cohabiting relationships, women are about as violent as men" (Straus and Gelles 1990b:104). What is needed are forms of analysis that will lead to a comprehensive description of the violence itself as well as an explanation of it. In order to do this, it is, at the very least, necessary to analyze the violent event in a holistic manner, with attention to the entire sequences of distinct acts as well as associated motives, intentions, and consequences, all of which must in turn be situated within the wider context of the relationship.

THE NEED FOR THEORY

If the arguments and evidence that we have presented are correct, then currently fashionable claims about the symmetry of marital violence are unfounded. How is it that so many experts have been persuaded of a notion that is at once counterintuitive and counterfactual? Part of the answer, we believe, is that researchers too often operate without sound (or indeed any) theoretical visions of marital relationships, of interpersonal conflicts, or of violence.

Straus (1990a:30), for example, introduces the task of investigating family violence by characterizing families as instances of "social groups" and by noting that conflicts of interest are endemic to groups of individuals, "each seeking to live out their lives in accordance with personal agendas that inevitably differ." This is a good start, but the analysis proceeds no further. The characteristic features of families as distinct from other groups are not explored, and the particular domains within which the "agendas" of wives and husbands conflict are not elucidated. Instead, Straus illustrates family conflicts with the hypothetical example of "Which TV show will be watched at eight?" and discusses negotiated and coerced resolutions in terms that would be equally applicable to a conflict among male acquaintances in a bar. Such analysis obscures all that is distinctive about violence against wives which occurs in a particular context of perceived entitlement and institutionalized power asymmetry. Moreover, marital violence occurs around recurring themes, especially male sexual jealousy and proprietariness, expectations of obedience and domestic service, and women's attempts to leave the marital relationship. In the self-consciously gender-blind literature on "violent couples," these themes are invisible.

Those who claim that wives and husbands are equally violent have offered no conceptual framework for understanding why women and men should think and act alike. Indeed, the claim that violence is gender-neutral cannot easily be reconciled with other coincident claims. For example, many family violence researchers who propose sexual symmetry in violence attribute the inculcation and legitimation of violence to socializing processes and cultural institutions, but then overlook the fact that these processes and institutions define and treat females and males differently. If sexually differentiated socialization and entitlements play a causal role in violence, how can we understand the alleged equivalence of women's and men's violent inclinations and actions?

Another theoretical problem confronting anyone who claims that violent inclinations are sexually monomorphic concerns the oft-noted fact that men are larger than women and likelier to inflict damage by similar acts. Human passions have their own "rationality," and it would be curious if women and men were identically motivated to initiate assaults in contexts where the expectable results were far more damaging for women. Insofar as both parties to a potentially violent transaction are aware of such differences, it is inappropriate to treat a slap (or other "act") by one party as equivalent to a slap by the other, not only because there is an asymmetry in the damage the two slaps might inflict, but because the parties differ in the responses available to them and hence in their control over the dénouement. Women's motives may be expected to differ systematically from those of men wherever the predictable consequences of their actions differ systematically. Those who contend that women and men are equally inclined to violence need to articulate why this should be so, given the sex differences in physical traits, such as size and muscularity, affecting the probable consequences of violence.

In fact, there is a great deal of evidence that men's and women's psychologies are not at all alike in this domain. Men's violent reactions to challenges to their authority, honor, and self-esteem are well-known; comparable behavior by a woman is a curiosity. A variety of convergent evidence supports the conclusion that men (especially young men) are more specialized for and more motivated to engage in dangerous risk-taking, confrontational competition, and interpersonal violence than are women. When comparisons are confined to interactions with members of one's own sex so that size and power asymmetries are largely irrelevant, the differences between men and women in these behavioral domains are universally large.

We cannot hope to understand violence in marital, cohabiting, and dating relationships without explicit attention to the qualities that make them different from other relationships. It is a cross-culturally and historically ubiquitous aspect of human affairs that women and men form individualized unions, recognized by themselves and by others as conferring certain obligations and entitlements, such that the partners' productive and reproductive careers become intertwined. Family violence research might usefully begin by examining the consonant and discordant desires, expectations, grievances, perceived entitlements, and preoccupations of husbands and wives, and by investigating theoretically derived hypotheses about circumstantial, ecological, contextual, and demographic correlates of such conflict. Having described the conflict of interest that characterize marital relationships with explicit reference to the distinct agendas of women and men, violence researchers must proceed to an analysis that acknowledges and accounts for those gender differences. It is crucial to establish differences in the patterns of male and female violence, to thoroughly describe and explain the overall process of violent events within their immediate and wider contexts, and to analyze the reasons why conflict results in differentially violent action by women and men.

References

Barling, Julian, and Alan Rosenbaum. 1986. "Work stressors and wife abuse." Journal of Applied Psychology 71:346–348.

Berk, Richard A., Sarah F. Berk, Donileen R. Loseke, and D. Rauma. 1983. "Mutual combat and other family violence myths." In The Dark Side of Families, ed. David Finkelhor, Richard J. Gelles, Gerald T. Hotaling, and Murray A. Straus, 197–212. Beverly Hills, Calif.: Sage.

Brush, Lisa D. 1990. "Violent acts and injurious outcomes in married couples: Methodological issues in the National Survey of Families and Households." Gender and Society 4:56–67.

Gaquin, Deirdre A. 1977/78. "Spouse abuse: Data from the National Crime Survey." Victimology 2:632–643.

Gelles, Richard J., and John W. Harrop. 1991. "The risk of abusive violence among children with nongenetic caretakers." Family Relations 40:78–83.

Johnson, Holly. 1989. "Wife assault in Canada." Paper presented at the Annual Meeting of the American Society of Criminology, November, Reno, Nevada.

Jouriles, Ernest N., and K. Daniel O'Leary. 1985. "Interspousal reliability of reports of marital violence." Journal of Consulting and Clinical Psychology 53:419–421.

Lystad, Mary H. 1975. "Violence at home: A review of literature." American Journal of Orthopsychiatry 45:328–345.

Margolin, Gayla. 1987. "The multiple forms of aggressiveness between marital partners: How do we identify them?" Journal of Marital and Family Therapy 13:77–84.

Maxfield, Michael G. 1989. "Circumstances in Supplementary Homicide Reports: Variety and validity." Criminology 27:671–695.

McLeod, Maureen. 1984. "Women against men: An examination of domestic violence based on an analysis of official data and national victimization data." Justice Quarterly 1:171–193.

McNeely, R.L., and CoraMae Richey Mann. 1990. "Domestic violence is a human issue." Journal of Interpersonal Violence 5:129–132.

McNeely, R.L., and Gloria Robinson-Simpson. 1987. "The truth about domestic violence: A falsely framed issue." Social Work 32:485–490.

Rouse, Linda P., Richard Ereen, and Marilyn Howell. 1988. "Abuse in intimate relationships. A comparison of married and dating college students." Journal of Interpersonal Violence 3:414–429.

Schwartz, Martin D. 1987. "Gender and injury in spousal assault." Sociological Focus 20:61–75.

Shupe, Anson, William A. Stacey, and Lonnie R. Hazelwood. 1987. Violent Men, Violent Couples: The Dynamics of Domestic Violence. Lexington Mass.: Lexington Books.

Steinmetz, Suzanne K. 1977/78. "The battered husband syndrome." Victimology 2:499–509.

———. 1986. "Family violence. Past, present, and future." In Handbook of Marriage and the Family, ed. Marvin B. Sussman and Suzanne K. Steinmetz, 725–765. New York: Plenum.

Steinmetz, Suzanne K., and Joseph S. Lucca. 1988. "Husband battering." In Handbook of Family Violence ed. Vincent B. Van Hasselt, R.L. Morrison, A.S. Bellack and M. Hersen, 233–246. New York: Plenum Press.

Stets, Jan E., and Murray A. Straus 1990. "Gender differences in reporting marital violence and its medical and psychological consequences." In Physical Violence in American Families, ed. Murray A. Straus and Richard J. Gelles, 151–165. New Brunswick, N.J.: Transaction Publishers.

Straus, Murray A. 1977/78. "Wife-beating: How common, and why?" Victimology 2:443–458.

———. 1990a. "Measuring intrafamily conflict and violence: The Conflict Tactics (CT) Scales." In Physical Violence in American Families, ed. Murray A. Straus and Richard J. Gelles, 29–47. New Brunswick, N.J.: Transaction Publishers.

———. 1990b. "The Conflict Tactics Scales and its critics: An evaluation and new data on validity and reliability." In Physical Violence in American Families, ed. Murray A. Straus and Richard J. Gelles, 49–73. New Brunswick, N.J.: Transaction Publishers.

Straus, Murray A., and Richard J. Gelles, eds. 1990a. Physical Violence in American Families. New Brunswick, N.J.: Transaction Publishers.

Straus, Murray A., and Richard J. Gelles. 1986. "Societal change and change in family violence from 1975 to 1985 as revealed by two national surveys." Journal of Marriage and the Family 48:465–480.

1987. "The costs of family violence." Public Health Reports 102:638–641.

———. 1990b "How violent are American families? Estimates from the National Family Violence Resurvey and other studies." In Physical Violence in American Families ed. Murray A. Straus and Richard J. Gelles, 95–112. New Brunswick, N.J.: Transaction Publishers.

Szinovacz, Maximiliane E. 1983. "Using couple data as a methodological tool: The case of marital violence." Journal of Marriage and the Family 45:633–644.

Wilson, Margo, and Martin Daly. Forthcoming. "Who kills whom in spouse-killings? On the exceptional sex ratio of spousal homicides in the United States." Criminology.

Wolfgang, Marvin E. 1958. Patterns in Criminal Homicide. Philadelphia: University of Pennsylvania Press.